PEOPLES AND CULTURES
OF THE PACIFIC

AN ANTHROPOLOGICAL READER

EDITED AND WITH AN INTRODUCTION BY
ANDREW P. VAYDA

PUBLISHED FOR
THE AMERICAN MUSEUM OF NATURAL HISTORY
THE NATURAL HISTORY PRESS
1968 GARDEN CITY, NEW YORK

The illustrations for this book
were prepared by the Graphic Arts Division of
The American Museum of Natural History

Contents

Introductory Essay

Although the Pacific Ocean covers a third of the earth's surface, its share of the earth's land and people is small. The island of New Guinea has an estimated area of 312,000 square miles and a population in excess of two million, but all the rest of the many thousands of tropical islands strewn over the three Pacific regions of Melanesia, Micronesia, and Polynesia add up to a land area of less than 50,000 square miles with a total population that, at present, numbers fewer than two million.

Yet this small segment of the human species in its island world has long been—and indeed continues to be—of special interest and significance in the study of man. To a large extent, this is precisely because the Polynesians, Micronesians, and Melanesians are people of an island world. Insularity facilitates anthropological observation and analysis because, to a considerable extent, it obviates one of the most serious problems confronting anthropologists on continental land masses: the problem of demarcating human communities or social systems for study. In Oceania, in other words, the sea itself often sets meaningful boundaries. Insularity has, moreover, had the result that cultural traits and social institutions hardly to be found in other parts of the world have developed and survived in the Pacific Islands. Thus, as locales for anthropological observation, the islands are, to an unusual degree, both convenient and interesting. This may be illustrated by reference to some specific studies.

1. The Boundedness of Island Societies

Numerous published articles and monographs illustrate the successful anthropological treatment of island societies as microcosms, little universes, or sea-girt isolates. Good examples are Raymond Firth's works on Tikopia, H. Ian Hogbin's study of Ontong Java Atoll, and the series of Bernice P. Bishop Museum bulletins on Polynesian ethnography, published mainly during the 1920s and 1930s. In the present volume, an example is Mead's article on the Samoans, described as living in "a closed universe."

The boundaries set by the sea have facilitated not only the holistic study of particular human societies but also the comparison of such societies. Specifying the units to be compared has been less of a problem in Oceania than in continental areas. There already have been studies comparing different island societies with respect to both their overall cultural inventories (e.g., Burrows 1938 and in this volume) and to such more specific features as their descent-group organization (e.g., Murdock 1948; Sahlins 1957; and Firth's first article and Goodenough's first article in this volume), their systems of social stratification (e.g., Goldman 1955; Sahlins 1958; and Mason's second article in this volume), their legal institutions (e.g., Hogbin 1934, part 3; Williamson 1924, vol. 3), their warfare (e.g., Williamson 1939: chapter 1), their religious systems (e.g., Williamson 1933, 1937), their folktales (e.g., Fischer 1958 and in this volume), their languages (e.g., Grace and Murdock in this volume), their blood group genes (e.g., Simmons in this volume), and their adaptations to European commercialism (e.g., Finney 1965; Vayda 1959). In some of these comparative studies, the objectives have been, first, to show that certain traits—for example, suprafamilial authority and surplus food production (Mason in this volume) or individualism and the birth rate (Fischer 1958)—covary from one island society to another, and then, to use this covariation as evidence for some kind of functional association between the traits. Other of these comparative studies have had other objectives, one of the more prominent being that of reconstruction either of whole cultures or of the ancestral forms of particular traits. This is well illustrated by Goodenough's essay in this volume, with its objective of reconstructing the common ancestral forms of Malayo-Polynesian landowning groups.

A reason given by some scholars for turning to the islands of the Pacific as laboratories is not simply that the ocean has set convenient boundaries but rather that it has made for situations in which particular cultures have been "unaffected by external contacts" (Goodenough 1957:154). However, the extent to which island societies have been protected from contacts and the effects of diffusion must not be exaggerated. Even in Polynesia, the Pacific region with islands furthest removed from continental land masses and most isolated from one another, significant diffusions appear to have taken place. The articles by Ferdon and by Vayda in this volume present some discussion of this. In Micronesia, canoe voyages enabled people of different islands, in some cases hundreds of miles apart, to have continuing and deliberate contacts with one another. Indeed, in the western Carolines, there was an extensive network of inter-island political, economic, and religious ties whereby numerous low coral islands and atolls were linked to one another and to the high volcanic island of Yap. This is the Yapese "empire" referred to by Lessa and Mason in this volume and described in some detail elsewhere by Lessa (1950, 1956) and by Alkire (1965). Networks of inter-island ties, or what Schwartz (1963) has described as "systems of areal integration," have developed to a notable extent also in Melanesia. Thanks to Malinowski's now classic descriptions (1922 and in this volume), the *kula* ring of the Massim area of Melanesia is the most famous of such networks.

Indeed, there is some evidence for the view that some groups living on the few large land masses of Oceania actually had less extensive contacts with other people than did many of the small island populations of the Pacific. Neolithic villages in continental areas may be isolated and confined to limited land also—for example, if they are surrounded by hostile neighbors (cf. Vayda and Rappaport 1963). Some New Guinea groups seem to provide apt illustrations of this. The considerable linguistic and cultural diversity of the large "continental" island of New Guinea can be understood as partly a result of the fact that many local nuclei of population there had but limited contacts with one another (cf. Vayda 1966).

But the fact that there are insular populations with extensive contacts and continental populations without them does not mean that anything can happen anywhere and that the sea does not set meaningful boundaries after all. While we may agree with Schneider (1963:143) that the problem of isolation in island areas needs far more detailed specification than it has so far received, it may still be suggested that the nature and significance of contacts among island peoples tend to be distinctive. The sea may not be a completely impassable barrier, but it is a barrier nevertheless. Contacts have been perhaps the most distinctive in the case of the people of those Polynesian islands and island groups which, as documented by Sharp (1964), were too far away for voyagers from other islands to reach by any reliable methods of navigation. Under these circumstances, people's contacts with the outside world were mainly a result of accidental landfalls made on their islands by voyagers lost at sea. Some diffusion of cultural and genetic traits no doubt took place as a result of such landfalls (see the articles by Ferdon, Vayda, and Simmons in this volume), but this constituted a mode of diffusion very different from that characteristic process in continental areas whereby influences are received from adjacent regions at a more or less constant rate and a fairly continuous geographical distribution of traits results (cf. Edmonson 1961; Murdock 1963:144).

The effect of the sea upon contacts may be seen in cases of less extreme isolation too. The Micronesian inter-island system discussed by Alkire (1965) provides a good illustration. While regarding the populations of the three western Carolinian atolls of Lamotrek, Elato, and Satawal to be so dependent upon one another as to constitute a single system, Alkire also indicates that the interdependence is paradoxically a result of insularity. The smallness of each island and the infertility of its coralline soils mean that the resources even normally available on any one island are meager. When these resources are further reduced by one of the tropical storms or typhoons to which low coral islands are particularly vulnerable (see Lessa in this volume), starvation and death for the people of the island might ensue if they did not seek help by voyaging to other islands. Under these circumstances, the inter-island voyages may be regarded as constituting emergency survival mechanisms, and it is noteworthy that the emergencies to which they relate are peculiar to island life.

2. THE CONTENT OF ISLAND CULTURES

Our discussion so far has been focused mainly on such characteristics of island societies and cultures as their boundedness. However, at the beginning of this essay, another theme also was announced: the fact that cultural traits and social institutions hardly to be found in other parts of the world have developed and survived in the Pacific Islands. Something must now be said about these traits and institutions.

Some of them may have been, among other things, adjustments to the territorial and resource limitations characteristic of insular conditions. Inter-island voyaging in the western Carolines has already been given as an example. Other examples, as noted by Vayda and Rappaport (1963:137–39), are, on the one hand, various technological and social devices that may have served to improve the utilization of the resources available within limited territories, and on the other hand, such population-limiting devices as the interestingly institutionalized Yapese practice of abortion described by Schneider in this volume. The *arioi* institution of the Society Islands, so shocking to many of the early European voyagers and missionaries because of its erotic aspects, may also be regarded as serving, at least to some extent, to limit population, for the members of the *arioi* society, a formally constituted group of itinerant entertainers who gave secular and religious performances throughout the Society Islands, were committed to the practice of infanticide (Beaglehole 1955:clxxxviii–cxc; Danielsson 1956: chapter 8; Williamson 1939: chapter 4).

Certain other traits and institutions may be related to insular conditions only insofar as the traits are rather singular ones which may have become established through processes like genetic drift. As Bates (1963:110) has noted, when a population is small and limited in its contacts with other populations, the drift processes operate more readily, and accordingly, non-adaptive cultural and biological traits might become established to a noteworthy degree in insular situations. A possible cultural example

cited by Bates are the immense statues of Easter Island, rough
and angular heads and busts of stone, ten, twenty, or thirty feet
high and with their precise significance unknown to the present-
day Easter Islanders (Métraux 1957: chapter 9). Bates regards
the statues as comparable to the towers of Sardinia in being a
"bizarre special cultural development" in an insular situation.

Many of the more bizarre-seeming developments of the islands,
whether the products of drift processes or of systematic adaptations to island conditions, are gone now. In the Society Islands,
the *arioi* dances ended a long time ago. In Easter Island, there
remain stone statues, but no traditional knowledge about their
significance. Massive changes have taken place in many of the
islands since their European discovery and have left intact but
little of the old cultures. These changes have been described in
various special studies and also in such general works as those
by Furnas (1947), Keesing (1941), and Oliver (1961). For many
of the islands, the assertion made earlier is only half true: cultural
traits and social institutions hardly to be found in other parts of
the world have indeed developed there, but they have not conspicuously survived, at least not to the present day.

The island that offers the most notable exceptions to this last
generalization is New Guinea, significantly the least insular component of the tropical island world of Melanesia, Micronesia, and
Polynesia. Here we can still find functioning such traits and institutions as digging-stick cultivation (Barrau 1958), warfare with
spears and bows and arrows (Matthiessen 1962), head-hunting
(Zegwaard in this volume), massive ceremonial pig feasts (see
the references in Vayda, Leeds, and Smith 1961), residential
separation of the sexes (Meggitt 1964), and the big-man complex
rather than more formal patterns of authority or leadership
(Sahlins in this volume). Certainly there have been some major
cultural changes in New Guinea too (see Salisbury's article and
Brown's second article in this volume), and parts of the island
belong very much to the modern world. At the same time, however, there are other parts that continue to offer such opportunities for the observation of primitive culture as are to be no longer
found anywhere else in Oceania (or perhaps anywhere else in
the world). This surely is at least partly a result of the great size
of New Guinea in comparison with other Pacific islands. In the
smaller islands, once the Europeans or other foreigners have

landed, it becomes virtually impossible to escape their influence or to avoid contact either with them or with native agents of acculturation. However, in New Guinea, which was first discovered by Europeans early in the fifteenth century and had been visited by Malay and Chinese traders for hundreds of years before then, small, previously uncontacted populations using stone tools were still being discovered in the 1950s and 1960s. Even the vast and extraordinarily densely peopled Wahgi valley region of New Guinea's central highlands was not discovered until 1933, a circumstance that has lent itself well to concurrent anthropological study of both the indigenous cultures and the early stages in their modification under acculturative influences (see the articles by Brown and Salisbury in this volume).

3. A NOTE ON THE SELECTION OF ARTICLES FOR THIS VOLUME

The selection of articles was made with a number of objectives in mind. One of them was to show something of the distinctiveness of Oceania or parts of Oceania, whether in cultural processes (Vayda's article on inter-island diffusion), environmental influences (Lessa's article on the typhoon), social institutions (the articles on the big-man pattern, *kula* ring, head-hunting, cargo cult movements, etc.), religious concepts (Firth's article on *mana*), or cultural values (Fischer's article on folktales and Schneider's on abortion, love affairs, etc.). Another objective was to illustrate some of the main research interests of scholars working in Oceania. Accordingly, there are articles representative of the research interests noted earlier in this essay: historical reconstruction (Swindler, Simmons, Murdock, Ferdon, Goodenough, and Burrows), the covariation of traits from island to island as evidence of functional association among the traits (Mason's second article), and the holistic study of small societies (Mead). A final objective was to provide information of a more general sort that could serve as an introduction to more specialized studies, and a number of articles were selected at least partly in accordance with this objective (e.g., Thomas' on geography, Swindler's and Simmons' on physical anthropology, Grace's on linguistic classification, Barrau's on ecology, Sahlins' on sociopolitical organization, Burrows' on Polynesian cultural traits, and Mason's on Micronesian ethnology). The reader with no previous familiarity with the anthropology of Oceania may want to consult these more general works first. In addition, he would be well advised to consult some general book such as Douglas Oliver's *The Pacific Islands*. By its very nature, a one-volume anthology such as the present one cannot be comprehensive, and the reader will have to turn to other works to fill in the gaps.

Two articles—Grace's on linguistic classification and Mason's on Micronesian ethnology—were written especially for this volume. All previously published articles are reprinted here in their entirety. The order in which the articles appear is one that I have found convenient in teaching courses on the anthropology of the Pacific, but is not meant to be regarded as an unalterable sequence.

PART I. GENERAL

A. GEOGRAPHY

WILLIAM L. THOMAS, JR.

1. The Pacific Basin: An Introduction

The ocean comprising the Pacific Basin is the largest single earth feature. It occupies one third of the earth's surface, an area greater than all the land above sea level on the face of the globe. In no other ocean has it been as difficult for a piece of the earth's crust to raise its head above the great volume of overlying water to become an island. Yet the Pacific Ocean contains about 25,-000 islands, more than in all the rest of the world's oceans combined (Bryan 1953:1; 1963:37), and totaling more than 1,000,000 square miles of land area. The wonder is not that most islands are small and scattered, but that there are so many of them.

More amazing still, almost all the islands and the continental shores of the Pacific Ocean were discovered and settled in prehistoric time. The European explorers were preceded by Australoids in Australia and Tasmania; by Negroids in southeast Asia, Indonesia, New Guinea, and adjacent islands; by southern Mongoloids in southeast Asia and almost all of the Pacific islands; and by northern Mongoloids in China, Japan, Korea, Siberia, including Aleuts and Eskimos in western and northern Alaska, and Amerindians from Alaska to Tierra del Fuego, the whole length of the Pacific coast of the Americas (Sharp 1956; 1957).

The story of scientific geographical exploration in the Pacific Basin is essentially a record of investigations by the late-comers, the Caucasoids from Europe and North America, after economic

SOURCE: Chapter I of *The Pacific Basin; A History of Its Geographical Exploration*, Herman R. Friis, ed. New York: American Geographical Society of New York, 1967. Reprinted by permission of the author and publisher.

and religious interests had stimulated the age of European discovery in the Pacific Ocean (Lloyd 1946; Sharp 1960). Science was most fully developed in Europe; organized, cumulative, and continually corrected knowledge had and continues to have great economic and strategic value (Morrell 1960). The uniqueness of the Pacific Basin still remains a challenge to man's understanding of the planet he calls home. But in terms of the total human story one should remember that the "Age of European Discovery" came late, and that it was mostly a *re*-discovery, albeit using advanced techniques for analysis and recording most information so that it has now become part of public knowledge (Stephens and Bolton 1917).

The sheer magnitude of the Pacific Basin, the extreme ranges of latitudes of its continental margins, and the widespread distribution of its islands are among the factors contributing to the great variety of physical-biotic environments and human habitats (Thomas 1963). The purpose of this chapter is to introduce the Pacific Basin as we know it today, by surveying the physical differences in location, size, origin, composition, and shapes of the major landform features; by portraying the distribution of climatic types, vegetation associations, and life zones; and by outlining in broad terms the regional patterns of habitats suitable for occupance by man.

There is no shortage of general works describing the Pacific Basin. Some writings focus on the vast ocean, its physical and biotic qualities and/or problems in navigation (Andrade 1954; Plischke 1959; Riesenberg 1940; Schott 1935; Sverdrup et al. 1942; Sverdrup 1941). Others consider the island world (Barrett 1950; Davis 1957), or enlarge Oceania to include Australia and New Zealand (Cumberland 1956; Laborde 1952; Robinson 1960). Still others are concerned with peoples and customs and politics. The best over-all synthesis on the Pacific and its human occupance and utilization is Freeman (1951).

ARRANGEMENT OF LAND

THE PACIFIC RIM

Any consideration of the Pacific Basin must begin with its immensity and great distances. It is 9200 statute miles from Bering

Strait on the north to the Antarctic Circle. The Pacific is 10,400 statute miles wide at the equator from Ecuador to Indonesia, and it is 12,300 miles, almost half the distance around the earth, from Singapore to Panama.

The Pacific Basin is ringed by mountain barriers thrown up along one of the earth's great zones of crustal instability and marked by more than four hundred active volcanoes (Gutenberg and Richter 1954; Internat'l. Volcanological Assoc. 1951–63). On the east the Andes and Rocky Mountains, comprised of thickly folded sediments and abundant volcanic material all strongly faulted, parallel a coastline that is generally regular, except for the fiord coasts of southern Chile and of North America from Seattle northward, with their numerous near-coastal islands and sheltered inlets (Cotton 1958:224). The arc of the Aleutian Islands is the northernmost of a series of island chains that convexly face the western Pacific along the Asian continent. The Aleutians extend nearly to the peninsula of Kamchatka. Southward follow the arcuate structures of the Kurils, Japan, the Ryukyus, the Philippines, Indonesia (the zone of intersection with the Asian arcs from the Himalayas through mainland Southeast Asia), and New Guinea, north of Australia. Between these curving festoons of islands and their adjacent mainlands and comprising the several arms of the western Pacific, are a series of marginal seas: Bering, East China, South China (the Asian equivalent of the Mediterranean), Coral, and Tasman seas, Sea of Okhotsk, Sea of Japan, and eight smaller seas among the Philippines and Indonesia. Vening Meinesz (1960) considers the earth's mantle to be drifting westward, away from the island arcs off Asia, and toward the great oceanic trenches which, over long distances, are situated at the foot of the western continental slope of the Americas.

THE EMPTY AREAS

The most characteristic feature of the Pacific Basin is its emptiness of land. The greatest of the empty areas has the shape of a huge horseshoe open to the west. One arm extends across the North Pacific from Japan to North America, swings south through the eastern Pacific, and thence westward from southern South America to New Zealand north of Antarctica.

Another way to visualize the emptiness of the Pacific is to draw on a map the great circle or shortest distance route diagonally from Tokyo, Japan (about latitude 36° N.) to central Chile (about latitude 30° S.). Only the Galapagos Islands and a few small islands near the American coast lie northeast of such a line. Further, in the South Pacific, between latitude 30° S. and Antarctica, there is a great void of islands across 90 degrees of longitude between New Zealand and Chilean territories.

THE ISLANDS: ARCS, CLUSTERS, AND ISOLATES

All of the larger island masses are situated in the western or southern Pacific, usually as parts of island chains relatively close to the Asian or Australian continents and generally forming arcs curved convexly toward the open Pacific. Deep-sea furrows are situated along their outer, or convex, sides. The island arcs may be single arcs (such as the Bonins or the Marianas), pseudo-single (such as the Aleutians and Kurils, which have double parallel arcs for short distances), or double arcs (such as the Ryukyus or in Indonesia, where the inner arc is always volcanic). Japan and the Philippines are exceptional insofar as several arcs meet to form an intricate pattern (Umbgrove 1945).

Though the many islands in the huge ocean represent a tremendous fragmentation, their arrangement is not just a random scatter. Almost all of the islands of the Pacific lie between latitudes 30° N. and 30° S., extending east-southeastward from mainland southeast Asia in the form of an elongated v, which tapers to a point at Easter Island (latitude 27° S.). Most islands are close enough to others that man tends to group them into island clusters or archipelagos and give them names which distinguish one group from another. From west to east across the Pacific are such island groups as the Philippines, Indonesia, New Guinea (and adjacent islands), Palau Islands, Yap Islands, Volcano Islands, Bonin Islands, Mariana Islands, Caroline Islands, Bismarck Archipelago, Solomon Islands, Santa Cruz Islands, New Caledonia and the Loyalty Islands, New Hebrides, Marshall Islands, Gilbert Islands, New Zealand, Fiji Islands, Ellice Islands, Tonga Islands, Samoa Islands, Phoenix Islands, Tokelau Islands, Hawaiian Islands, Line Islands, Cook Islands, Îles Tubuai (or Austral Islands), Society Islands, Tuamotu Archipelago, Marquesas Islands, and the Galapagos Islands. Wholly isolated islands, more than 400 statute miles from any other, are much fewer. Outstanding examples are, from east to west, Clipperton Island, Easter Island, and Isla Sala y Gomez, Johnston Island, Norfolk Island, Marcus Island, and Parece Vela.

ISLAND ORIGINS AND SIZES

The "Andesite Line"

The most significant regional distinction in the Pacific Basin is that established by the so-called "Andesite Line" which separates the deeper Pacific from the partially submerged continental areas on its margins. The andesite line follows the eastern edge of New Zealand, Tonga, Fiji, the Solomons, Bismarck Archipelago, New Guinea, Yap, Mariana Islands, Japan, the Kurils, and Kamchatka (Andrews 1940; Fisher and Revelle 1955; Hess 1948; Officer 1955; Raitt et al. 1955). Similarly, the andesite line passes south of the Aleutian arc and across the Gulf of Alaska, thence westward of the islands off the California coast and along the western edge of the Albatross Cordillera, a sickle-shaped curve extending 8000 miles from the coast of Mexico nearly to New Zealand (Menard 1961).

Within the closed loop of the andesite line lies the real Pacific Basin with its deep troughs, submerged volcanic mountains, and oceanic volcanic islands predominantly composed of heavy dark basalt, which also comprises the platforms capped by reef corals and atolls. Outside the line, including all of New Zealand, New Guinea, Indonesia, the Philippines, and Japan (which represent the far eastward extension of the continental blocks of Australia and Asia), the islands are composed of mixed rock types characteristic of continental masses and markedly deformed by folding and faulting. They contain such ancient metamorphic rocks as slate, gneiss, and schist; such sediments as coal and clay; and such intrusive and volcanic rocks as andesite, high in silica and alumina.

Volcanoes and Earthquakes

The distinction between basaltic and andesitic lavas is chemically small, but the types of volcanic activity associated with them are very different (Cotton 1958). Floods of quietly flowing basaltic lavas have poured out of rifts to build up huge domical volcanic mountains, whose eroded summits comprise such island chains or clusters as the Samoa, Hawaiian, Society, and Marquesas islands. The vast bulk of these mountain masses are below sea level; for example, Mauna Kea (13,784 feet altitude) and Mauna Loa (13,680 feet) on the island of Hawaii rise from ocean depths of 18,000 feet. Volcanism along the rim outside of the andesite line is largely explosive. The more viscid siliceous lava explodes under gas pressure, and the considerable fragmentary debris builds steep-sided ash cones. Examples of the violence of explosive volcanoes are the famed eruptions of Tamboro (Gunung Tambora), on Sumbawa Island east of Java, and Krakatau (Pulau Rakata) in the Sunda Strait between Sumatra and Java. When Tamboro erupted in 1815 it blew between 28 and 50 cubic miles of lava, ash, and dust into the air. When Krakatau exploded in 1883, the noise was heard in Australia, 1500 miles away, and its dust, thrust into the upper atmosphere, extended around the world.

The andesite line is defined on the basis of underlying magmas and their volcanic products, but the distinction is fundamental. Within the line is the largest homogeneous unit of strong individuality on the earth's surface, a region which is so peacefully at rest that no tectonic earthquakes originate within it, save for the moderate activity associated with the rift structures of the Hawaiian Islands. In direct contrast to this passivity, the Pacific rim outside of the line is not only the world's greatest belt of explosive volcanic activity, but also the most prevalent zone of seismic disturbance. This circum-Pacific zone includes about 80 percent of the shallow shocks, 90 percent of the intermediate shocks, and all of the deep shocks ever recorded. The annual number of true earthquakes around the Pacific is about one million; the annual average includes two great shallow shocks and seventeen other major earthquakes, of which about five are intermediate and one is deep (Gutenberg and Richter 1954:103).

Neither volcanic nor seismic activity is evenly distributed, nor are the areas of these activities everywhere the same. Shallow seismicity is highest in Japan, western Mexico, Melanesia, and the Philippines; South America has an exceptionally high proportion of great shocks. The island arcs of the western Pacific and the mountainous fringe of the American continents are the results of Tertiary to Recent crustal upheavals; earthquakes and much volcanic activity are secondary features which accompany active folding and faulting (Byerly 1953). Pacific earthquakes have caused even more damage than volcanic eruptions. Probably the most devastating earthquake was that in Japan in 1703, which killed about 200,000 people. The Tokyo earthquake of 1923 killed half this number. Submarine earthquakes are the cause of tsunamis, or seismic waves in the ocean. A series of these waves, perhaps as much as 100 feet high, followed the Krakatau explosion in 1883 and swept over the shores of nearby Java and Sumatra, destroying villages and drowning more than 30,000 people. The tsunami of April 1, 1946, which struck the north and east coasts of the Hawaiian Islands, killed more than 150 persons and resulted in $25,000,000 in property damage.

THE OCEAN FLOOR

The last great frontier of the earth's physical geography is the vast, almost unknown floor of the oceans, about which we know much less than we do about the face of the moon. Fifteen elongated trenches in the Pacific mark the seaward extent of the island arcs and the centers of most intensive earthquake activity. The deepest trenches all have about the same maximum depth, as the foundering sea floor being dragged down into the earth stabilizes at about 35,000 feet below sea level. The Albatross Cordillera is another gigantic feature whose crest lies an average of two miles above the floor of the Pacific, yet remains 1.5 miles beneath the ocean's surface, except where volcanic islands such as Easter Island, Isla Sala y Gomez, and the Galapagos Islands thrust upward atop the bulge of the rise (Dietz 1952; Fisher and Revelle 1955:38).

Nearly 200 flat-topped submarine peaks, termed tablemounts or guyots, have been discovered beneath the North Pacific (Betz and Hess 1942; Hess 1947; Hamilton 1956). These were chains of basaltic islands in Cretaceous time whose tops were wave-eroded to relatively flat banks on which reef fauna found lodgement. The tops of these truncated volcanoes now lie at depths of 700 to 900 fathoms as a result of large-scale subsidence of the sea bottom. Due to submergence these fossil landforms are preserved as the oldest uneroded mountains on earth, disturbed only by gentle currents and the slow rain of shallow water debris from above (Hamilton 1956).

CALCAREOUS REEFS

The most distinctive feature of the tropical Pacific is the presence of numerous calcareous reefs, built by coral and calcareous algae which require warm, relatively shallow, clear saline water. The principal development of coral reefs in the world is in the Pacific Ocean and its connecting Asian seas. Reef formations are more numerous in the central and western parts of oceans because of the movements of warm ocean currents, and weakly developed in the eastern parts of oceans because of lower water temperatures due to the equatorward movement of cool ocean currents and the upwelling of colder water from oceanic depths. This is the reason why the volcanic Galapagos Islands are not fringed by coral reefs.

Coral is the skeleton of a fleshy polyp, a marine animal which secretes lime from sea water. Most such polyps live in large colonies with their skeletons connected to one another and overlying the calcareous remains of their predecessors. But corals are not the only reef-building organisms. Mixed among them are calcareous algae, principally of the genera *Porolithon* and *Halimeda,* which encrust and fill up the pores and crevices of the coral, converting the whole mass into more solid limestone. Vigorous reef-forming corals may endure surface water temperatures as low as 18.2° C. (64.7° F.), but generally a temperature of 22.8° C. (73° F.) or above is considered necessary. Most corals thrive at depths of less than 15 fathoms (90 feet), while maximum depths of living reef corals are generally between 20 and 25 fathoms (120 to 150 feet), since sunlight penetration and temperatures decrease with depth. Corals cannot gain a foothold on a muddy sea floor because either the sediments smother the coral polyps or the turbidity cuts down the amount of light necessary for photosynthesis of the symbiotic algae. Corals also require a salinity at least 80 percent that of sea water; hence, reefs are also absent near river mouths where the sea is diluted by fresh water.

During 1951, two deep holes were drilled through the calcareous reef of Eniwetok to the incredible depths of 4222 and 4610 feet before encountering volcanic bedrock. This scoriaceous olivine basalt, associated with tuff and volcanic glass, was the first proof that volcanoes form the bases of the oceanic islands of the Pacific within the andesite line. The hundreds of calcareous reefs were formed in Tertiary time, not upon wave-eroded platforms (which became submerged tablemounts) but atop volcanic mountains, whose higher elevations delayed their subsidence beneath the sea and allowed more time for the calcareous reef organisms to gain a foothold and grow upward as rapidly as the rate of subsidence of the volcanic basement. The upper seaward slopes of calcareous reef islands are generally steeper than the repose angle of loose sediments. This is a consequence of upward growth by the reef-building organisms from a subsiding base now too deep for such growth to take place. Thus, the present existence of calcareous reef islands depends primarily, for their volcanic platforms, upon pre-Pleistocene geologic history and the character of the ocean floor, and secondarily, for their surface form, upon late Pleistocene to Recent geologic history and the existence of reef-building organisms (Emery et al. 1954).

THE PLEISTOCENE HERITAGE

The distribution and extent of land in an ocean area depends in great part upon the "accident" of sea level. The height of the sea with respect to that of rock masses comprising islands is related not solely to localized tectonic activity but also to the fluctuations of continental glaciers which "lock up" water elsewhere on the earth. Thus, the numbers, sizes, and distribution of islands have varied with the successive falls and rises of the sea during Pleistocene glacial and interglacial stages (Flint 1957). At low sea stands during glacial periods, New Guinea was reunited with Australia; Java, Sumatra, and Borneo again became part of the Asian mainland; and Bering Strait became an isthmus. Concurrently, there were many more oceanic islands—hilly, reef-fringed, or barrier-encircled. Sub-aerial erosion, principally chemical solution by sea water, lowered the exposed calcareous reefs down to or near to the Pleistocene sea surface. Then the last great rise of sea level permitted the upbuilding of calcareous reef rims around enclosed central lagoons (Shepard and Seuss 1956; Wiens 1962b).

ISLAND TYPES

Islands in the Pacific range in size from New Guinea and
Borneo (the world's second and third largest, respectively, after
Greenland) to the smallest of rocks visible above the high-tide
line. In the whole of the North Pacific, between the Hawaiian
Islands and the island arcs from Japan to Indonesia, there are
only three islands larger than 100 square miles: Guam (215
square miles); Babelthuap in the Palaus (153 square miles),
and Ponape in the eastern Carolines (127 square miles). By contrast, the 1156 islets of the Marshall Islands have a combined
land area of less than 70 square miles, or 38 acres each on the
average. South of the equator and east of New Guinea and Australia, the largest islands are North Island and South Island of
New Zealand. There are, in addition, a number of islands more
than 3000 square miles in extent, among them New Britain, New
Ireland, Bougainville, New Caledonia, and Viti Levu, all outside
of the andesite line. Again, by contrast, the oceanic Tuamotu
Archipelago, farther east, consists of some 75 main groups of
islets; but the total land area adds up to only 330 square miles.

Throughout the Pacific are four distinct types of islands, each
with some variations that give rise to minor types:

> *Low islands of carbonate rock:* These islands are gen-
> erally very small in land area, but are the most distinctive,
> numerous, and widespread in the tropical Pacific. Examples
> are found in the Tuamotu Archipelago and Society, Cook,
> Line, Tokelau, Phoenix, Ellice, Gilbert, Marshall, and Caro-
> line islands.

> *Islands of elevated reef rock:* These are usually only
> slightly larger than the low islands. Examples are found in
> the Fijis, Loyalty Islands, central and northern Palaus, Fais,
> Ocean Island, Nauru, Niue, and Makatea in the Tuamotus.

> *Volcanic islands:* These are generally small to intermedi-
> ate size, such as Galapagos Islands, Hawaii, Samoa Islands,
> the Marquesas, Kusaie, Ponape, and the northern Mariana
> Islands.

> *Islands containing ancient "continental" rocks:* These in-
> clude the largest of the Pacific islands, all outside of the
> andesite line, from Fiji to Japan, including Babelthuap and
> Yap islands in the western Carolines.

ISLAND LANDFORMS

The landforms of the Pacific islands outside of the andesite line are as varied as those of any other great expanse of the earth's surface. Some are low-lying plains; others are plateaus or cuestas; still others are mountains, flat-topped, serrate, pene-plained, or conical. Some present, on a small scale, the complex structures of great mountain ranges. Likewise, in degree and manner of erosion, the islands range from newly made masses through remnants in all stages of dissection to submarine banks from which all land has been stripped away and on which corals have established themselves. The classic distinction among Pacific islands landforms is between "high" islands of continental or volcanic type and "low" islands of carbonate rock. On the former almost any type of landform may somewhere be found: deep canyons, broadly sloping valleys, and flat floodplains. The sea is bordered by extensive coastal plains or narrow shelves or it meets the land in cliffs of impressive height (Gregory 1928).

"HIGH" ISLANDS: "CONTINENTAL" AND VOLCANIC

New Guinea comprises the best example of a large continental island (Essai 1961). It has an area of about 312,000 square miles and is approximately 1300 miles long by nearly 500 miles wide at its central portion. The most distinctive major landform feature is the towering snow-capped cordillera that dominates almost the whole length of the island's interior, together with the dissected high central plateaus. To the north and south are vast, swampy lowlands covered with dense swamp forests. The coastal pattern is that of alternating small coastal plains, low river terraces, high marine benches, coastal hills, and steep mountain slopes plunging into the sea.

Viti Levu, the largest of the Fiji Islands, is another example of a continental island (Derrick 1957). Its area of 4053 square miles is smaller than New Caledonia (Le Borgne 1957) or New Zealand (McKenzie 1958), yet it forms more than half of the surface area of the Fiji group and is one of the larger islands in the Pacific. Viti Levu has four types of landforms: the high central plateau, the mountain ranges, large areas of hilly uplands, and coastal areas of low-lying plains and river deltas.

All of the large islands of the Pacific lie west of, and outside, the andesite line and are continental in type. The islands between New Zealand and the Philippines thus include a far greater range of landforms, climates, soils, and natural minerals than do the clusters of small oceanic "low" islands of the central Pacific. This major difference in geologic structure is important, for it explains why the islands of the western Pacific have much greater natural resources than those of the east.

Of the volcanic islands, the Hawaiian chain is probably the best known, but there are many more scattered through the southern and western Pacific. On these high islands, precipitous cliffs rise from exposed windward shores where wave erosion has cut into lava slopes which once descended gradually to the sea. Among the remarkable landform features are the large deep valleys with amphitheater heads that rise steeply from a nearly flat floor. Cliffs of such valleys on Tahiti and Molokai tower above 3000 feet. Occasionally, amphitheaters may coalesce to form low passes. Other examples of volcanic high islands are five island groups in the Carolines: from east to west, Kusaie, Ponape, Truk, Yap, and Palau. Each consists of more than a single island, but with varying degrees of complexity. The western two (Yap and Palau) are composed of old volcanic lavas and ancient metamorphic rock that testify to their continental nature; the others are composed chiefly of basaltic lava in keeping with their location inside of the andesite line. Most volcanic islands in the Pacific realm are ringed by coral reefs, either as fringing reefs adjacent to the shore, or, less frequently, as barrier reefs lying offshore.

"Low" Islands: Elevated and Sea-Level Reefs

Tayama (1952) has provided the most thorough morphological classification of coral reefs, which comprise the low islands of the Pacific. He distinguishes among eight forms (Fig. 1) which intergrade from one to the other:

> *Apron reef:* The initial stage of a fringing reef, attached to part of an island but occupying discontinuous small areas.

Fringing or shore reef: A coral reef in contact with a coast, continuous or almost continuous, and covering a substantial area.

Almost barrier reef: A coral reef separated from the island it surrounds by a shallow, narrow lagoon, generally 15 to 60 feet deep, which forms the so-called "boat channel."

Barrier reef: A coral reef surrounding an island or islands like a breakwater, and including a lagoon between the island and the reef.

Almost atoll: A barrier reef around a central island or islands that occupy a much smaller area than the lagoon.

Atoll: A coral reef rim embracing a lagoon but lacking any central island; instead, volcanic material forms the foundation of the reef.

Almost table reef: Like the atoll, it encircles a lagoon, but the ratio of surface area of lagoon to reef-flat is smaller than in an atoll, and the lagoon is shallower.

Table reef: A small coral reef with neither central island nor lagoon.

The distinction between high islands as volcanic and low islands as coral reef forms is too simple, for there are many combinations of the two, as described above. Moreover, these combinations are further varied by being elevated above the sea as raised reefs. Thus there are partly raised and fully raised barrier reefs, almost atolls, atolls, and table reefs, as well as tilted forms with one side elevated and the other sunk beneath the sea.

THE ATOLL ENVIRONMENT

Atolls comprise the most numerous and distinctive form of calcareous reef. Bryan (1953) listed 309 in the Pacific, more than three times the number in all the rest of the world's oceans combined.

Atolls are reefs of organic limestone that are partly, intermittently, or completely covered by water, and on which there are discontinuous, low sandy islets resulting from the accumulation of limestone debris, loose or consolidated, and occasional remnants of former high reef surfaces. These islets are usually not more than 5 to 10 feet above high-tide level, except for storm-built rubble ridges and wind-deposited dunes which rise but a few feet higher. The atoll is thus a limestone cap perched on the top of an underlying volcanic mountain or cluster of cones. This cap is commonly bowl-shaped at the surface with a ringlike ridge or reef enclosing a shallow body of water or lagoon, and in turn surrounded by the open sea (Fosberg 1953, 1961).

The primary distinctions to be noted on an atoll (Fig. 2) are

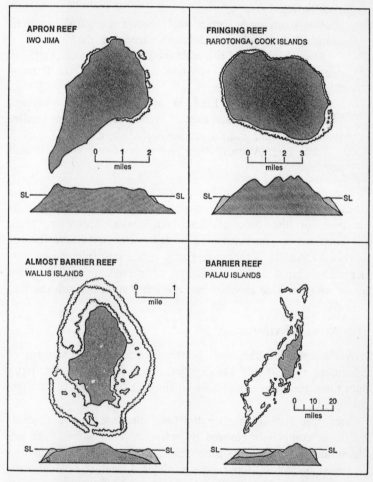

FIGURE 1 (*Above and on facing page*). Types of low islands. After Risaburo Tayama 1952 and Kenneth B. Cumberland 1956.

the outer slope, reef front, seaward reef margin, reef flat, beach, islets, lagoon reef margin, lagoon slope, and lagoon floor (Tracey et al. 1955). Islets are most frequent on the eastern or windward sectors of the reef rim. Almost three-quarters of all atolls have islets on less than one-half of their circumference. The largest and widest islets coincide with wide portions of the reef where sharp outward bends occur. Reef widths tend to be greater in the general direction of prevailing winds, currents, and waves—the areas of greatest reef growth. Conversely, deep passes through reef rims, navigable to ocean-going vessels, occur most frequently

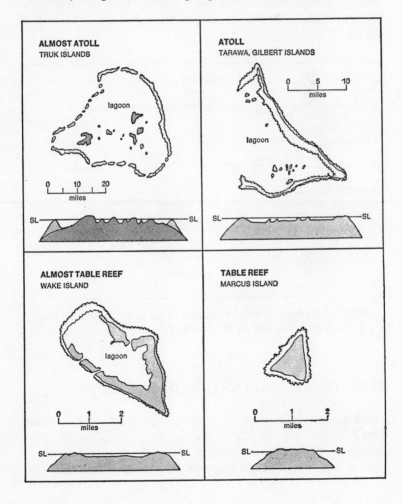

ALMOST ATOLL
TRUK ISLANDS

lagoon

ATOLL
TARAWA, GILBERT ISLANDS

lagoon

ALMOST TABLE REEF
WAKE ISLAND

lagoon

TABLE REEF
MARCUS ISLAND

on the leeward sides of atolls where reef growth is less vigorous
or is inhibited (Wiens 1962a:32–35).

Waves commonly break on the seaward reef margin and water
flows from the sea to the lagoon and back to the sea over the
reef flat or through gaps in it. The flow may be in or out with the
tides, or in over the windward and out over the leeward sides.
The only natural source of fresh water on any atoll islet is the rain
that falls there. If not caught on and evaporated from the plants
or ground surface, it seeps quickly into the porous sediments.
Larger islets are highly permeable and may contain at shallow
depth a lens of fresh ground water floating upon the underlying
salt water and retarded by friction from free diffusion with it
(Stone 1953).

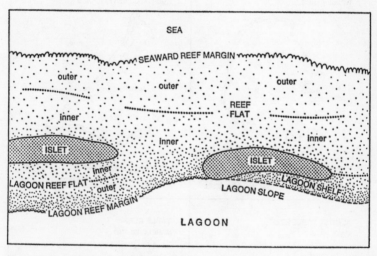

FIGURE 2. Prominent landform features of an atoll. After J. I. Tracey,
Jr., P. E. Cloud, Jr., and K. O. Emery 1955.

CLIMATIC REGIONALIZATION IN THE PACIFIC

All kinds of climate, from tropical warmth to polar cold, are
found in the Pacific. There are the foggy, wind-swept outer
Aleutians, the contrasting seasonality of Japan between snowy
winters and warm humid summers, the constant steaminess of

the lowland interiors of Borneo or New Guinea, and the mild and salubrious climate of Hawaii and other mid-ocean islands. At or near the equator, temperatures remain nearly the same throughout the year, but everywhere else there are definite seasons. These differing climatic patterns are superimposed like a mantle over all islands of whatever origin, location, size, shape, and composition.

CIRCULATION REGIONS

There are five different kinds of atmospheric circulation regions (Fig. 3), within each of which are certain unique climatic features: (1) the "middle latitude" westerlies, (2) the trades, (3) the monsoons, (4) the doldrums (intertropical trough), and (5) the typhoons, which partly overlaps the others (Blumenstock 1958).

1. In the middle-latitude realm occur the extra-tropical cyclones with their distinct frontal systems and the variety of weather patterns that they subsume: cold waves, general rains from occluded systems and from warm fronts, sharp cold-front storms, and the like.

2. The trade winds areas are those in which winds from the northeast quadrant in the Northern Hemisphere and from the southeast quadrant in the Southern Hemisphere occur at least 70 percent of the time in every month of the year, and more than 85 percent during the summer months. On high islands within these regions, windward and leeward become directions of climatic importance, the windward coasts being cloudy and wet and the leeward coasts relatively cloudless and dry. The general climatic regime for the trade-wind regions is one of rather constant prevailing winds with scattered light or moderate showers and occasional rainless periods of a few to many days, interrupted periodically by rainy spells that are sometimes very pronounced and last for three to five days.

3. The monsoon region is in the far western Pacific between northern Australia and southern Japan (Chang 1962). The outstanding climatic characteristics are the seasonal reversal of winds and the marked seasonality of cloudiness and rainfall. Because the monsoon air masses contain waves and eddies, the rainy season is an alternation of spells of heavy and prolonged

rains, moderate interrupted rains, and rainless weather sometimes with virtually clear skies. However, the heavy rains are far
more prolonged and intense than in any other part of the tropics
except for rain spells yielded by typhoons.

4. The doldrums regions are more poorly defined than the others. They are regions within which horizontal temperature gradients are insignificantly small and within which the rainfall is well
distributed throughout the year. They are also regions of high
humidity, considerable cloudiness, and low wind speeds.

5. The fifth circulation region is where typhoons occur. The
tremendous winds and torrential rains generated by these storms
are a serious land-use hazard (Blumenstock 1961; Kidd and
Reed 1946). Whereas the rainfall contribution may form a considerable part of the total annual precipitation, it may be of little
value where run-off is high.

The five core regions outlined on Figure 3 are not mutually
exclusive; neither do they cover all of the tropical Pacific. The
intervening areas are transition zones, wherein characteristics
fluctuate seasonally from those of one to another of the core
regions (U. S. Weather Bureau 1956).

OCEAN CURRENTS

The currents in the surface layer of the ocean (Fig. 3) are
characterized by vast closed anticyclonic eddies in the subtropical
and tropical latitudes, and by smaller cyclonic eddies in the north
temperate latitudes and the high southerly latitudes (Muromçev
1959). The wind-driven circulation of the surface waters involves
a layer about 500 feet deep over almost the whole expanse of
ocean. In the region of the westerlies, where strong west winds,
stable in direction, prevail throughout almost the whole year, the
circulation penetrates to 650 feet or more. But in the countercurrent region of the doldrums, where light and unstable winds
prevail, the wind-driven circulation is limited to depths of 150
to 250 feet.

At greater depths, the circulation is set up mainly by differences
in ocean water density. The general circulatory pattern of the
Pacific Ocean waters begins with the import of water from the
Indian Ocean in the high southerly latitudes. By way of deep
currents and bottom currents such water reaches the northern

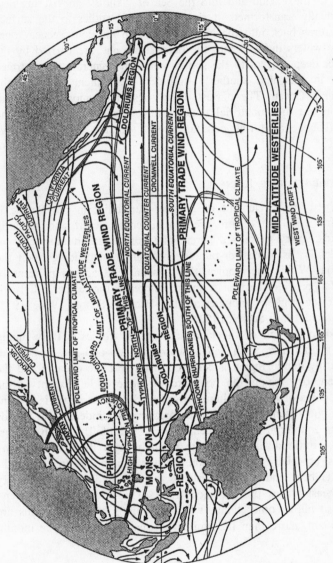

FIGURE 3. Distribution of atmospheric circulation regions and ocean current circulations of the Pacific. After David I. Blumenstock 1958 and John A. Knauss 1961.

part of the Pacific and into the Sea of Okhotsk and Bering Sea. Gradually transformed, it rises in cyclonic eddies to the surface and turns back into the North Pacific. In the convergence zones these waters descend into the deep strata and are carried by the upper deep current to the south, where the general eastern transport in the high southerly latitudes takes them out into the Atlantic Ocean. The newest discoveries in oceanographic exploration are the equatorial undercurrent (Cromwell Current) and the south equatorial countercurrent (Knauss 1961; Tsuchiya 1961).

DISTRIBUTION OF RAINFALL

The climatic element of greatest variability in the Pacific is rainfall (Fig. 4). There are a number of desert and semiarid islands; many more are perennially very wet; on others, water availability is a feast-or-famine proposition, depending upon the season. Within the tropics, the seasonal and annual patterns of rainfall provide the best frame of reference for further differentiating the regional climates of the Pacific (Schott 1934, 1935; Sekiguchi 1952; Seelye 1952).

Not quite half of the land area of the tropics is truly humid and a little more than half is seasonally wet-and-dry. In general, the truly humid region is centered at or near the equator and the wet-and-dry regions lie poleward on either side. Except at the very cores of the truly humid tropics, periodic drought is a common phenomenon; some islands are very dry indeed. The islands of the equatorial eastern Pacific have low rainfall: Canton, Enderbury, Howland, and Baker are virtually desert islands. On many atolls, especially those just south of the equator, as are the southern Gilbert and Phoenix islands, when conditions of the dry southeast trades prevail, more than a year will elapse with no rain at all; at other times, when conditions of the doldrums are dominant, more than the annual average may fall in one month.

CLIMATIC PATTERNS

Climatologically, the western part of the Pacific is basically different from its eastern sector (Fig. 4). The eastern portion, located at the root region of the subtropical anticyclone, is char-

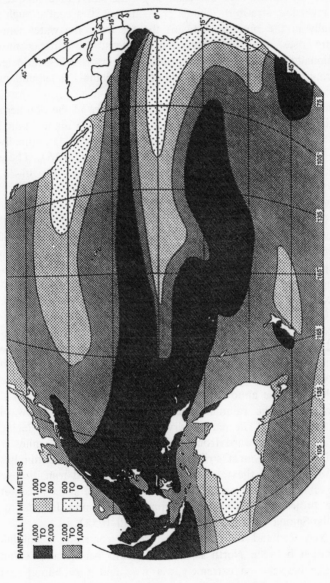

FIGURE 4. Distribution of average annual rainfall in the Pacific. After Gerhard Schott 1934 and Takeshi Sekiguchi 1952.

acterized by cold ocean currents, upper-air subsidence, marked trade inversion, stratiform clouds at night, and persistent drought, especially in the summer. Toward the far west, the water temperature rises, the trade inversion weakens, the air becomes conditionally or convectively unstable, cumulus clouds dominate, and rainfall, usually with a summer maximum, is abundant (Chang 1962).

The overwhelming dominance of ocean surface in the Southern Hemisphere makes possible a strong and relatively uninterrupted zonal circulation. The climatic pattern is far more latitudinally regular than in the Northern Hemisphere (Schott 1936). There are, however, certain anomalies (Trewartha 1961:13–33, 86–88, 174–79).

Because of the more vigorous westerly circulation in the Southern Hemisphere, stemming from the powerful Antarctic cold source and reduced continental friction, the longitudinal axis of the subtropical high in the eastern South Pacific lies closer to the equator than does its counterpart in the North Pacific. Accordingly, over the ocean the equatorial pressure trough is asymmetrically located to the north of the equator at all times of the year. One consequence is that all of the tropical climates of Pacific coastal South America are displaced northward of their expected latitudinal positions. Intense drought conditions are characteristic almost to the equator, then give way abruptly, on the north, to a zone of excessive wetness along the Pacific side of Colombia. The abnormal feature of the dry eastern equatorial Pacific is that the rainfall deficiency extends so far westward along the equator. The narrow dry zone in the equatorial Pacific which reaches westward from Ecuador for some 7000 miles is one of the earth's most striking climatic anomalies. Gentilli has called attention to the remarkably abrupt westward transition to wetter climates in the central Pacific and to the conspicuous wet tongue projecting east-southeast from the Solomon Islands toward the Samoa Islands and Tahiti (Gentilli 1952).

In New Zealand there are conspicuous contrasts in rainfall distribution between North Island and South Island, and within the latter between an extremely wet west and a subhumid east (Garnier 1958). The climatic arrangement in Australia is almost perfect in its simplicity: dry climates occupy all but the northern, eastern, and parts of the southern margins of the continent. The greatest anomaly is the absence of a cool ocean current, fog, and extreme aridity along the west coast.

In Indonesia, one of the climatic peculiarities is the small amount of annual rainfall in the area from eastern Java to southernmost New Guinea. Annual rainfalls of less than 40 inches occur, coupled with dry seasons of seven to eight months. The long dry season coincides with the prevalence of southeast trades, while westerly flow prevails during the wet months. Along the eastern coasts of Asia, extreme winter continentality is the rule. Japan has spring and winter temperatures 4° to 8° F. cooler than for corresponding latitudes of coastal southeastern United States. Summer temperatures in Hokkaido and northern Honshu are abnormally low because of the cool Oyashio (current).

HABITATS FOR MAN

THE RESOURCE BASE

Earth materials, soil, altitude, landforms, location, and climate all combine to create the varied physical environments found among the Pacific islands. Many gradations occur between the luxuriant wet continental-type island and the barren desert sandy islet. In each of the four main types of islands there is a definite relationship among earth materials, landforms, water supply, soil, and mineral resources, with a resulting limitation to their biotic resources and utilization by man.

The *continental* islands have the greatest commercial value and the most varied and abundant natural resources; fertile soil covers much of their mature landforms. Geologically recent *volcanic islands* lack minerals of commercial value; land use is limited by conditions of landforms and rainfall. Most of these islands lie in the trade-wind belt, where moisture-laden winds strike their windward slopes making them wetter than the drier leeward slopes. Islands of *raised reef* also lack mineral resources except deposits of phosphate rock, and ground water is meager or lacking; unless rainfall is abundant, irrigation and water supply become problems. *Sea-level coral reefs* with their low sandy islets provide the most limited range of resources for human existence and are the most tenuous habitats for man in the Pacific. They lack mineral resources, except small deposits of guano from the droppings of sea birds. The soil of reef islets is relatively infertile, lacking humus, and fresh ground water is very limited, or may be brackish, or entirely lacking. Even where rainfall is abundant an atoll can support only meager land vegetation and animal life. On the other hand, marine life is quite highly developed, both on the reefs and in the protected lagoon. Thus people and birds on an atoll obtain much of their sustenance from the sea.

MAN, SPACE, AND TIME

Man is an ancient occupant of the western Pacific margin, evolving from *Homo erectus* to *Homo sapiens* in the area from Java to north China. Man is new to oceanic islands (Smith 1960). In general, the farther away an island is from a continent, the less diverse are its land plants and animals. The populations of islands must pass through the sieves of difficulty of overseas transport, reach the islands, and surmount the mostly overwhelming hazards of survival and colonization. For example, there are about 550 kinds of land birds in New Guinea, but only four on Henderson Island isolated far to the east beyond Pitcairn Island. Age, area, and elevation are of fundamental importance to biotic development and distinctiveness (Haden-Guest 1956:611–30). A high island can develop a diversified biota, an atoll cannot (Marshall 1954). Man has imported to the oceanic islands every important source of food (Keesing 1959). Many of the plants and animals he has introduced purposely or accidentally have greatly altered, largely replaced, or exterminated delicately balanced naturally established organisms (Barrau 1960; Clark 1949; Oliver 1954). He has changed the island environments rapidly and drastically for his own benefit (Johnston 1957, 1959; McKenzie 1958). Man has had a profound and increasing impact as the dominant agent in discovering, investigating, and changing the face of the Pacific world (Price 1963).

B. PHYSICAL ANTHROPOLOGY

DARIS R. SWINDLER

2. Problems of Melanesian Racial History

INTRODUCTION

Since 1556, when the Spanish explorer Ortiz de Retus coined the name Nueva Guinea because the natives bore such a striking resemblance to the Negroes of Africa's Guinea Coast, scholars have propounded numerous theories to explain the origin of Melanesia's people. But to this day their origin remains unknown. Indeed, the problem of the racial history of Melanesia continues to be one of the most productive of theories and issues in Pacific anthropology. There are almost as many opinions concerning Melanesian racial origins as there are authors writing on the subject. There is, to be sure, considerable similarity in all these theories regarding the nature of the presumed original racial components of the present population. There is much disagreement, however, over terminology, temporal sequences, and estimates of the importance of the genetic contribution of each of the original components.

The origin of the Melanesian is not a problem which can be considered in isolation without reference to paleontology, archaeology, geology, geography, population genetics, and evolutionary theory. Also relevant is the racial composition and history of the adjacent areas of Australia, Indonesia, and continental Asia. Although our investigation of the West Nakanai has been non-historical in approach, interpretation of our findings cannot be divorced from antiquity nor from historical considerations. In

SOURCE: Pp. 40–50 of Daris R. Swindler, *A Racial Study of the West Nakanai*. Philadelphia: University of Pennsylvania, University Museum, 1962. Reprinted by permission of the author and publisher.

the discussion to follow, we shall briefly review the geographical, geological, and paleontological considerations relevant to Melanesian racial history, and then evaluate existing theories in their light.

GEOGRAPHICAL CONSIDERATIONS

Acceptance of the importance of geography as a factor shaping man's culture or physique has waxed and waned through the years. Recently, Coon (1954, 1955) and Newman (1953, 1956), among others, have stressed anew the importance of a critical analysis of man's physical environment and its role in human evolution. These writers suggest that some of the racial variations in man may be due to adaptations to prolonged extremes of environment. Whatever personal predilections one may harbor, it is apparent that climate and geomorphology have played their part in man's history, and this is certainly true for the Pacific area. Speaking of this region, Oliver (1952:7) says, "the epic of Oceania can be understood only against its geographic setting."

For purposes of description geographers commonly divide Melanesia into two areas, Eastern Melanesia and Northern Melanesia (Coulter 1951). Although this division is convenient for heuristic purposes, there is much that is common to both areas.

Eastern Melanesia includes, from west to east, the Solomons, the Santa Cruz Islands, the New Hebrides, New Caledonia, the Loyalty Islands, and the Fiji Islands. These islands display many differences; some are volcanic, built up from vents in the ocean floor, while others are coral atolls only a few feet above sea level. There are several which have complicated structures due to uplifts and the action of earth building agencies. Most of the islands have fringing reefs which afford excellent fishing and thus offer the native a supplement to his vegetable diet. The larger islands are clothed with various kinds of forests, while the atolls support little natural vegetation other than coconut, pandanus, and shrubs. These islands have a uniformly warm temperature and generally heavy rainfall. The rainfall varies from archipelago to archipelago, and sometimes from one island to another in the same group. The southernmost islands are strongly affected by the trade winds, having rainy windward sides and drier lee coasts.

The composition of the soil differs from island to island, as in the Solomons, where it is high in granite on most islands, but Rennell and Bellona are raised limestone atolls. The importance of soil differences cannot be stressed enough inasmuch as Coon (1950) found that the natives of North Albania living on food raised on granite soil were significantly smaller than those living over limestone formations.

The islands comprising Northern Melanesia extend from the vicinity of the equator to 12° S. latitude, and from 130 to nearly 155° E. longitude (Bowman 1951). The more important of these are New Guinea and its western outliers such as Waigeo, Japen, and the Schouten group; its eastern outliers include the Louisiade Archipelago, the D'Entrecasteaux group, and lesser nearby islands, also the Bismarck Archipelago dominated by New Britain, New Ireland, and the Admiralties, of which Manus is the largest. The general description of the physical environment of the islands is again one of marked variability. The larger islands are rugged, with elevations up to 16,400 feet above sea level atop Carstensz Toppen in Dutch New Guinea. Some of the smaller islands, primarily those of volcanic origin, are hilly to mountainous, but many of the others are low, flat, and swampy, or else low, relatively flat, and sandy or rocky. The climate of the lower elevations (below about 3000 feet) is mostly warm to hot, and humid to wet. In places, equatorial heat is tempered by monsoon winds and land-and-sea breezes, as along the northern coast of New Britain. Within the intermediate elevations (3000 to 7000) the range fluctuates from warm to cool and from humid to wet, depending chiefly on the degree of exposure to wind and sun. Higher elevations (above 7000 feet) are likely to be rather wet, cloudy, and cold. Rain forest and swamp forest prevail in the lowlands and on mountain slopes up to about 5000 feet, except where native cultivations or commercial plantation enterprises have modified the indigenous plant associations.

The native fauna of Northern Melanesia is essentially a composite of Asian, Australian, and autochthonous elements. A complete inventory of the fauna would be exhaustive, but a brief ledger of the animals which preceded man into Melanesia includes cassowaries (the eggs of which are quite palatable); snakes; lizards, the most impressive being the iguana; beautiful plumed birds of paradise; wallabies; cuscus, a unique marsupial;

crocodiles; the "flying-fox," a kind of bat; and a myriad of lesser animal forms. Of course, fish abound in the waters and lagoons surrounding all these islands. Since it is assumed that the first settlers were hunters and food gatherers, animals such as these were probably important in their diet. Later, with the introduction of the New Stone Age cultural traits of polished stone implements, pottery making, and husbandry, these early inhabitants became sedentary agriculturists. Accompanying the Neolithic wanderers out of Asia were the pig, chicken, and scrawny dog. The principal cultivated plants introduced were yams, taro, coconuts, bananas, and breadfruit—all Asiatic in origin, and all present today in gardens throughout Melanesia (Oliver 1952). Taro (*Araceae* species) is so widespread and basic in so many isolated native cultures that Oliver (1952:31) believes "that it may well have been the first cultivated food plant introduced into the islands."

GEOLOGICAL CONSIDERATIONS

Many geologists believe that at one time continental Asia extended much farther into the Pacific. Indeed, this hypothetical southern continent is purported to have connected Australia, New Zealand, Fiji, the Solomons, New Hebrides, New Caledonia, and New Guinea with Asia. This archaic land mass may have begun sinking in the late Mesozoic era, and possibly the process continued to affect the fragments of the continent through the Cenozoic to the present day (Freeman 1951). Geologists do know that the principal rock underlying the sediments of continents is granite or one of its metamorphosed equivalents, and this is exactly what the volcanoes of the western Pacific extrude, in contradistinction to basalt, which is the common type in the islands that dot the central and eastern Pacific. Basalt is a heavier rock than granite and is the predominant constituent forming ocean basins. This petrographic difference affords the geologist a natural boundary which is termed the Andesite or sial line, a term proposed to emphasize the predominance of silica and alumina in continental rock (Nevin 1942:240). It traverses the Pacific in rather a north—south course, following the eastern edge of New Zealand, Fiji, the Solomons, Bismarck Archipelago, New

Guinea, Yap, the Marianas, Japan, Kamchatka, and the southern Aleutians. The islands lying west of this line are termed continental islands and possess wider varieties of climate and life than the volcanic islands to the east. The soils are rich. The high mountains, dense forests, broad expanses of kunai grass, and large rivers have encouraged the development of cultural and perhaps even racial diversity.

The continued submergence of this region has been offset by a series of eustatic changes of sea level during the Pleistocene. While the areas to the north were enmantled by continental glaciers, the ocean level dropped to the point where the shallow Sunda Sea became a land bridge permitting early man a dry passage to Java and beyond. The various fossil hominids of Java, such as Homo modjokertensis, *Pithecanthropus,* Wadjak, and Solo Man are usually attributed to one of these dry periods. De Terra (1949:13) observes:

> The fossil record of Early Man in Java seems to be controlled by both alluvial and volcanic processes as well as by the climate impact upon the ocean level whose fluctuations hereabouts worked like a trap door, admitting new migrant forms from the continent in times of low ocean level, or isolating the island in time of interglacial or interpluvial, submergence.

Hooijer (1951), however, points out that Van Bemmelen has raised some serious objections to this sort of correlation, since during the Quaternary epeirogenic movements were of the magnitude of several thousand feet, while the eustatic oscillations of the sea level were only a few hundred feet. Hooijer (1951:278) concludes that "in Java this method of Pleistocene chronology fails." The importance of this controversy centers around the dating of the early fossil faunas of Java, and, as such, does not concern the present problem. What is significant is the fact that the Sunda land bridge was available at different periods in the Pleistocene, and that early hominid forms were present in Java and perhaps on other islands as well. The Sahul Shelf uniting Australia and New Guinea was also dry land periodically, a fact which requires us to treat these two land masses as a single regional unit, especially during the terminal Pleistocene (Birdsell 1949, 1950). Water gaps were reduced and were probably only shallow streams with one notable exception, Wallace's Line. This imaginary line is a deep separating Bali and Lombok in the south and Borneo and the Celebes in the north. It also represents the farthest eastward extension of Asiatic fauna and was a moat which early man had to surmount in his eastward trek.

PALEONTOLOGICAL CONSIDERATIONS

The impression one gathers in reading most of the literature is that the early hominids, *i.e.*, *Pithecanthropus*, Solo Man, and Wadjak, did not contribute to the present populations and that the earliest migrants to Melanesia, as well as to Australia, were Negritos. This migration is attributed to the Last Glacial Period. In fact, Birdsell says, "there can be little doubt that Oceanic Negritos in relatively unmixed form did represent the first wave of human immigration into Australia, if it is assumed that *Homo soloensis* did not migrate beyond Wallace's Line" (Birdsell 1949:146, 150). As Birdsell admits, the evidence for this migration is non-archaeological and rests upon the patterning of the marginal distribution of genetic marker-traits. It seems to the writer, however, that since earlier hominids were present in Australasia prior to, or at least contemporaneously with, this postulated migration, they might just possibly have contributed a few genes to the emigrant Negritos. It must be remembered that a fossil isolated in time and space does not necessarily imply that it represents the beginning or termination of a phylogenetic line. On the contrary, the specimen is representative of a single individual from a group which certainly had time depth as well as geographical latitude. Robinson (1953:34) states this point rather clearly in a paper concerning the relationships of the Australopithecines:

> It is obvious—it is almost naive to mention it—that the Australopithecine group did not come into existence at the time the oldest (geologically speaking) known specimen in our collections lived. Nor did the group cease to exist at the time of death of the geologically youngest specimen present in our collections.

Undoubtedly the Negrito, or at least some small-statured

group, was present at an early date in Melanesia. Whether they enjoy the singular priority of being the first hominids to reach this region seems somewhat doubtful. Recently Robinson (1953) has shown that the East African *Meganthropus africanus* as well as Java's *Meganthropus paleojavanicus* were representatives of a once widely spread Australopithecine group. If these culturally denuded hominids had such a wide geographic distribution, it seems difficult to deny Solo Man or some other contemporary the price of the trip to Melanesia, if not literally at least *via* his genes. Admittedly, there is little fossil evidence to substantiate this thesis, but there has been little archaeological endeavor in Melanesia. The picture is somewhat brighter when one turns to Australia, although, to date, there appears to be no evidence suggesting a date prior to the Fourth Glacial Period (Birdsell 1950:148, quoting a personal communication from N. B. Tindale). In a recent physiographic and chemical analysis of the famed Cohuna skull, Macintosh (1953:296) states that "the cranium probably has at least moderate antiquity," although one is not sure how to interpret this rather cautious statement. The point to be made is simply that in any discussion of Melanesian origins, the early (Fourth Glacial Period) hominids of Java must at least be considered possible candidates. Indeed, Weidenreich (1943, 1945) suggested that there was an almost continuous phylogenetic line leading from the *Pithecanthropus* group through *Homo soloensis* to Wadjak Man and thence into the recent Australians and Melanesians. Perhaps this suggestion is an oversimplification, as pointed out by Montagu (1951), but it nevertheless indicates that these hominids warrant some consideration.

Fossil hominids present during the Terminal Pleistocene, such as Wadjak I and II from Java, the Aitape fragments from New Guinea, the material from the Upper Cave at Choukoutien in North China, and the Australian fossils, figure more prominently in Melanesian racial reconstructions (Weidenreich 1943, 1945; Sarasin and Roux, 1922). At the same time, there is a sizable amount of material exemplifying the morphologic characteristics of present day Melanesians derived from the Mesolithic and Lower Neolithic of Indochina, which has received a modicum of attention (Mansuy and Colani 1925; Mansuy 1931; Fromaget Saurin 1936). Weidenreich (1939) considers these to be bona fide Melanesians, whereas Birdsell (1949) believes the methodology employed by their describers and Weidenreich's reasons for accepting them to be fallacious. He therefore relegates them to limbo.

Along the north coast of New Guinea near the town of Aitape, Paul S. Hossfeld, later Senior Geologist of Northern Australia, found a fragment of the frontal and parietal bones of a human skull in 1929 (Fenner 1941). It was discovered on the east bank of Paniri Creek, near Barida village, about ten miles inland and some three hundred feet above sea level. The bony fragments were outcropping with pieces of carbonized coconut shell in the side of the stream bank. (The ultimate fate of the carbonized coconut shell is unknown to the writer; if still available, a C–14 dating would be recommended.) The fragment was overlain by four feet of undisturbed littoral marine deposits and an additional six feet of alluvial gravel. There were a number of fossil shells in association with the fragments, and Fenner says these indicate an Upper Wanimo (Pleistocene) assemblage. Thus, "it may be accepted as the first evidence from New Guinea of human remains of apparent Pleistocene age" (Fenner 1941:353). Fenner believes that the fragment is a portion of a female skull and that she was about forty-five years old at the time of death. He also notes that the specimen is too small for a positive racial diagnosis but does venture that "one might go further and suggest that its affinities are with the southern Australian type (type A, Fenner)" (Fenner 1941:353). Birdsell (1950) said it probably represented his Murrayian type, that is, a basically Archaic White Element. We are impressed with the development of the supraorbital region, the low forehead, and the great post-orbital narrowing, all of which recall the primitive morphology of the Australian phenotype. The previously mentioned Cohuna specimen from southern Australia also displays a similar appearance. Whether the Cohuna and Aitape material prove to have been coeval during the terminal phase of the Pleistocene or not, on the basis of the scanty evidence now available, they appear to have been morphologically quite similar. In any case, they demonstrate the persistence of the Australian phenotype through considerable time; this is especially true of the Cohuna cranium. (See Macintosh 1952:328, for comment concerning the Cohuna specimen.)

The fossil hominids from Indochina come from several sites, all of which are attributed to the Mesolithic or Neolithic, except a fragment of a left temporal bone and two lower molars which were discovered in Lower Pleistocene beds according to Fromaget and Saurin (1936). These authors ascribed *Sinanthropus* affinities to the teeth, but realized that evidence was slight and had to await further investigations before any definite conclusions could be drawn. The Tam-Pong site which yielded the above material also presents a Mesolithic to Neolithic stratification. A number of crania and cranial fragments, as well as numerous parts of the appendicular skeleton, have been uncovered from both horizons. The material from the Mesolithic resembled contemporary Ainu, Australian, and Melanesian populations. That from the Lower Neolithic apparently represented another racial group, exhibiting characteristics which led the writers to ascribe Negritoid affiliations to them. Present also was a Mongoloid element. The upper Neolithic contained individuals morphologically resembling the Negritos and Melanesians of today.

Mansuy (1931) described a cranial series from the Neolithic site of Lang-Coumn, near the Gulf of Tonkin. He stated that the Australo-Melanesians came from the lowest horizons before polished stones, and that the Indonesians appeared next, bringing with them the knowledge of polishing. The last element to appear was the Mongoloid. He also commented that the origin of the Melanesian remains largely unknown. In an earlier publication Mansuy and Colani (1925) described a Proto-Melanesian type as representative of the earliest Neolithic, while the Indonesians came from the later Neolithic.

Here again one comes up against the problem of methodology and interpretation. During the 1930's and earlier, it was common practice to choose a particular constellation of features of a given cranial series which were believed to be non-adaptive, either observational or metrical, and compare these with similar characteristics from other groups. If the selected traits proved to be similar, the groups were then believed to be racially related; that is, they were assumed to be biologically identical with respect to the traits selected. This is the typological approach. Within the past few years, a number of publications have appeared which have attempted to show the limitations and also the invalidity of the conceptual framework of this sort of analysis (Washburn

1953; Boyd 1952; Birdsell 1949; Weiner 1957). The exponents of this thesis refer to it as the genetic approach. Perhaps Washburn (1953:725–26) has expressed their position as well as any:

> The new strategy does not solve problems, but it suggests a different way of approaching them. The change from the old to the new affects the various parts of physical anthropology very differently . . . In evolutionary investigations the theoretical changes are of the greatest importance, and much of the anthropological work on race and constitution is eliminated by the rejection of the concept of type.

Certainly this approach has much to recommend it, but so far there are few traits outside of the blood groups which give unequivocal evidence of their genetic foundations. Indeed, the majority of traits employed in racial studies appear to be genetically complex, and as such are extremely difficult to elucidate (Neel and Schull 1954). And, of course, environment may also influence the final expression of the genes. As Boyd (1952:314) says, "A great many more pages could be written on the difficulties of genetic analysis of morphological and other characteristics which have been previously used or proposed for purposes of racial classification." He notes further, "Without exact genetic analysis we are not in a position to state how much one group differs from another group" (Boyd 1952:315). However, if one demands such exacting and exclusive use of characteristics with *known* modes of inheritance, racial studies and skeletal investigations in particular may be retarded many years. It will be a long time before human genetics can supply such precise information. In fact, Simpson (1945:6), in considering the importance of genetic data for phylogenetic studies, noted, "The limitations arise in part from the physical impossibility of making a really complete genetic analysis for any animal or of making a useful partial analysis for more than a very few laboratory animals." For the present, we must fall back on the available skeletal material to reconstruct the racial background of Melanesia.

There are a number of publications dealing with hominid remains from other Mesolithic and Neolithic sites in Indochina and contiguous regions. These are concerned essentially with dental features and are ably discussed by Hooijer (1950), whose paper the reader should consult for detail. He states his position succinctly as follows (Hooijer 1950:127):

> Migrations of Melanesoids and Australoids over the Malay Archipelago to their present habitat will certainly have taken place, but in my opinion it is entirely unjustified to use the large size of the subfossil teeth from the Malay Peninsula and Java in evidence. These teeth bear evidence only of the former existence of peoples with teeth bigger than those of the present natives, and do not necessarily belong to the Eastern peoples the living representatives of which happen to be characterized by large teeth. In fact, these large subfossil teeth are indicative of nothing but that Man, like the animals, has undergone a diminution in size in the course of the Quaternary.

This is the paleontological part of the story: an array of fossil hominids distributed in space from Indochina to Australia, and extending in time from the Second Glacial Period to the agricultural economy of the Neolithic. Certainly, there are obvious gaps in the record and no simple rectilinear progression is suggested, but with the acquisition of more data the importance of these fossils will become clear.

EXISTING THEORIES OF MELANESIAN RACIAL ORIGINS

When turning to the migration hypotheses and the racial components themselves, the impression is one of a kaleidoscope, in which the racial elements are ever blending and shifting in importance, till it seems virtually impossible to sort them out and fit them into a patterned schema. These basic racial elements have rejoiced under such epithets as Negroid, Australoid, Papuan, Paleo-Melanesian, and Negritoid. The terms have meant different things to different authors, and a great deal of confusion has resulted from misunderstanding in the use of terminology. Interpretation of the available data has also added to the imbroglio. Information has usually been derived from small samples, in many instances breeding isolates, which were not representative of the populations being studied. These data were then used as the cornerstone for constructing elaborate migration theories, as well as constituting the morphologic basis for ascertaining similarities and differences between extant populations. Historically, the first natives to be described were the coastal groups, and opinions and type concepts were molded accordingly. In 1911, the Tapiro pygmies were discovered living in the Nassau Mountains in New Guinea (Wollaston 1912). This was the first evidence of a true short-statured people within Melanesia. Henceforth, most physical differences were explained as the result of hybridizing between various coastal groups and the shorter people of the interior, and not infrequently the racial parameters were fabricated on extremely scanty material. Undoubtedly the processes of hybridization have produced new racial populations, but it also seems plausible that some of the racial diversity in Melanesia might be explained by such factors as adaptation, isolation, and genetic drift.

Sixty years ago, Deniker (1900) considered all the inhabitants of New Guinea and the neighboring archipelagoes to belong to one race, the Melanesian, which was part of his Negroid group. The Melanesian race was divided into two sub-races, the Papuan and the Melanesian. The former possessed elongated ovoid faces and hooked noses and were especially prevalent in New Guinea. The latter had squarer, heavier miens and occupied the rest of Melanesia. Seligman (1909) maintained that the term Papuan was unsuitable to describe the inhabitants of New Guinea since even in British New Guinea there were groups of people so little alike that they must be considered as racially distinct. He suggested that the term "Papuasian" should be employed for an inhabitant of New Guinea, while "Papuan" should be limited to the more frizzly-haired and often mop-headed, darker skinned peoples of western New Guinea. He then suggested the term "Papuo–Melanesian" for the generally smaller, lighter skinned, frizzly-haired groups of the eastern New Guinea archipelagoes and the eastern peninsula of New Guinea. According to Seligman, an undifferentiated Oceanic Negro or Proto-Papuan was the first comer to the islands. Somewhat later, the Melanesians came from the west and either gradually drove out or assimilated the pre-existing populations. Keane (1920:130) suggested a somewhat similar classification:

Owing to their linguistic, geographical, and to some extent their social and physical differences, it is desirable to treat the Papuans and Melanesians as two distinct though closely related subgroups, and to restrict the use of the terms Papuan and Melanesian accordingly, while both may be conveniently comprised under the general or collective term Papuasian.

Thus, while Seligman restricted the use of "Papuasian" to the inhabitants of New Guinea proper, Keane extended the term to include all of the natives of Melanesia.

A somewhat broader classification was suggested by Sarasin and Roux (1922) in their monograph on New Caledonia. They maintained that the Melanesian, Tasmanian, and Australian were closely related, but that each presented special features of development which they had undergone through time, although originally all had belonged to the same group. These three groups constituted their Austro-Melanesian designation. They also believed that the Wadjak material from Java represented a progenitor of the Austro-Melanesian. The pygmoid tribes were thought to have been derived from a pre-Negroid group which could have been antecedent to the pre-Austro-Melanesians. In his comprehensive work on the races of man, Dixon (1923) considered the oldest stratum to be represented by the Negritos (Palae-Alpine) of the interior of New Guinea. This racial element may also have been associated with the Proto-Australoids who came next, and who were in turn followed by Proto-Negroids. Haddon (1923, 1925) said that the earliest immigrants into this region were of several varieties. Some were very short, others were of short or medium stature, and all probably exhibited a tendency to vary in head breadth. These immigrants he termed Papuans, and he considered the short-statured groups among them (Negritos) to be simply an extreme variety of his Papuan type, and felt that both the shorter and taller varieties belonged to the Negro stock. Much later, a series of migrations composed of light-skinned, wavy or straight haired, and taller peoples spread eastward from Indonesia and hybridized with the dark, woolly haired, and shorter Papuans, resulting in the peoples he termed Melanesians. Subsequent migrations of the same type of people further diluted

the original Papuan, thus producing the present racial hetero-
geneity.

There are numerous other early investigations into the racial
anthropology of Melanesia. The present review would be remiss
if it did not mention the excellent contributions of Neuhass
(1911), Hagen (1898), Parkinson (1907), and Schlaginhaufen
(1914). Although usually invoking migrations to account for the
racial diversity they saw in Melanesia, these students did not
believe that hybridization was the sole answer and frequently
suggested that group isolation was influential in producing this
variability. Perhaps Bondy-Horowitz (1930:146) summed up
their position when she wrote, "Local variation, which consisted
of inbreeding, selection, and mutation can not be demonstrated
as migrations and cross-breedings can, but it must be accepted
as a conditioning factor." Today it is recognized that such factors
have had important consequences in evolution and it is of historical interest to note that the early German investigators were
thinking along these lines.

Within recent years the reports of Stirling (1943), Keesing
(1945), Howells (1943), and Birdsell (1949, 1950) have appeared. The first three studies espoused theories which recall
the racial elements postulated by the earlier students. In their
opinions, the area has sustained several migrations in the past,
which after a long period of amalgamation resulted in the present racial melange. Birdsell, however, has proposed a somewhat
different terminology, while differing but little with previous theoretical assumptions. He has suggested four migrations into Me-
lamesia, the earliest composed of the Oceanic Negrito. The next
migratory wave consisted of the Murrayians, who were followed
by the Carpentarians. Much later, the Mongoloids arrived from
Indonesia. Thus, "the so-called 'melanesian' populations are
quadrihybrid in nature" (Birdsell 1949:5). He diverges significantly from prior investigators in one major point: he maintains
that there is no full-sized Negroid element present in Melanesia,
but on the contrary, this phenotype is compounded from Negritic
and Carpentarian elements which are present throughout the
archipelagoes. Therefore, he proposes the term Oceanic Negri-
toids to designate these people. He also states that Negritic
genes form the basic genetic matrix throughout New Guinea and
Melanesia and that, "If there is any safe inference in the field of

racial anthropology, it is that the Oceanic Negritos must be considered as very closely related genetically to the Negritos of the Congo Basin in tropical Africa" (Birdsell 1949:3).

As is evident from this review of the anthropological literature dealing with racial elements in Melanesia, we are largely working in the dark. The main emphasis has been to explain Melanesia's present population as resulting from the differential hybridization of a few basic immigrant types, with differences of opinion as to what these types presumably were. Commonly expressed, also, is the view that at least one of these immigrant types had a close connection with Africa. Certainly, different components were involved in the Melanesian complex, but to identify them and to state in what proportion each occurs in a given population must by now be impossible. Melanesia's populations as seen today are the products of generations of racial churning, in which the evolutionary processes of mutation, migration, natural selection, genetic drift, and selective mating have effectively contributed to the racial diversity so demonstrable there today. Existing theories, moreover, have been based, in part at least, on observations whose accuracy our own data from the West Nakanai have given us grounds to question, as in the case of hair form. With the rather crude methods of analysis available, there is perhaps little more that can be done at the present time. Some progress is being made, however, by Simmons and his colleagues in Melbourne, utilizing information gained from numerous blood group studies throughout the Pacific. But these students admit that their knowledge is incomplete, and only the preliminary phases of blood genetic investigations have been performed. According to Simmons (1956:512), "The more critical investigations remain to be done, for the secrets of the racial origins of Man and his migration routes will be no easy task to solve."

Even at this stage, however, data are accumulating which call into serious question the theory that one of the racial strains in Melanesia is to be linked closely with Africa. In their recent publications, Simmons and his co-workers note that the African Negro gene A_2 is absent in the Pacific, that the phenotype Rh_0 has rarely been demonstrated, and that "it can be said with some degree of certainty that there is no blood genetic evidence that the African negro ever entered the Pacific" (Simmons 1956:506). Simmons (1956:507) also states that the Melanesian groups tested to date "have no blood characteristics suggesting any link with African pygmies." Gusinde (1955:4–5), utilizing morphological criteria, is also of the same opinion. There is, thus, growing evidence in support of the position taken years ago by Sarasin and Roux (1922) in their monograph on New Caledonia. Indeed, Simmons (1956:506) states, "The pygmies, the intermediates and the large physical specimens, whether on the coast or in the hills, are closely related members of one Melanesian family." And in a later publication (Semple *et al.* 1956:371) we read:

> In spite of the differences pointed out here, it is nevertheless apparent that all the populations of New Guinea and the Melanesian islands so far tested are of the same basic stock. However, the gene frequency data presented may well support the current anthropological conception of a predominantly Negritic stock with Papuan or Murrayian and Melanesian or Carpentarian elements superimposed.

It is not stated whether this Negritic stock is genetically related to the African pygmies or whether the differing blood group frequencies could have been caused by such processes as genetic drift.

How far it will be possible to go with this line of inquiry, however, remains to be seen. Brues (1954) has recently registered some serious doubts as to its meaningfulness in respect to illuminating problems of racial origins. In our opinion, Brues has presented a cogent argument demonstrating the effectiveness of genetic drift, one which does not vitiate current investigations but which must always be considered in discussing phylogenetic origins.

CONCLUSIONS

As we have seen, many previous investigators have depicted Melanesian racial history as represented by a series of migrations down the Malay Peninsula and onward to Australia or the eastward lying islands. The people representing the migrations have been given such designations as Proto-Australoid, Negritoid, and Carpentarian, to mention only a few. Such groups formed the unsullied original physical types from which the contemporary Melanesians are derived, and apparently these authors are able to detect these pristine elements in present-day Melanesians. We would like to suggest a somewhat different explanation regarding the peopling of Melanesia. We contend that centimeter or, in some cases, millimeter differences between the inhabitants of adjacent islands do not necessarily prove that migrations of different physical types have occurred or that miscegenation with roving bands of a more hearty seafaring folk is always the answer. In view of the recent work of Sharp (1956) it seems more likely that the Pacific islands were populated accidentally by small groups over a long period of time, rather than by deliberate, planned migrations.

The original racial ingredients which went to make up this mixture could have been represented by many polytypic populations slowly wandering out of Asia into Melanesia, populating the islands as they came, undoubtedly mixing with some neighboring bands and at the same time establishing rules of endogamy with respect to others. Whether this exodus was represented by three or four separate migrations or simply was a slow gradual dribbling of small groups is not known. However, the latter assumption seems more plausible. What fossil evidence there is, particularly that from the Mesolithic and Neolithic of Indochina, confirms the polytypic nature of these early groups. Further, these small polygenic communities would have afforded maximum opportunities for the operation of random genetic drift. Also, it was not necessary for these small groups to have differed markedly from the larger populations from which they became detached, since it is known that when a new closed population is formed, it develops a unique integrated polygenic system of its own. And once established, these genetic systems tend to persist (Glass 1956; Ryan 1953).

For these and other reasons discussed in the text, we feel that it is rather late to attempt to identify as particular genetic complexes the basic racial elements in Melanesia. In point of fact, what one is doing is trying to reconstruct history on the basis of data obtained, for the most part, from contemporary populations; and to paraphrase Simpson, one cannot be his own ancestor. Therefore, a more profitable approach would seem to be to view

Melanesia as a single geographical breeding unit, within which numerous breeding isolates integrate morphologically with one another and afford excellent opportunities for investigating the problems of racial dynamics.

R. T. SIMMONS[1]

3. Blood Group Genes in Polynesians and Comparisons with Other Pacific Peoples

The task allotted to me for this symposium has been to review the progress made in our knowledge of the blood group genes and their frequencies in Polynesians, and to make some attempt at comparisons with other Pacific peoples who may, or may not have contributed to their genetic make-up. A study of the Polynesians has been a pleasant occupation for many individuals of diverse disciplines over the years, and each has added to the fund of knowledge, but many questions concerning the Polynesians remain unanswered. The most recent comparisons of Polynesian blood group gene frequencies with others have been made by Graydon (1952), Mourant (1954), Simmons, Graydon, Semple and Fry (1955) and by Simmons and Graydon (1957).

The author and his associates have attempted over the years to place on record for all time more and more blood group gene frequencies, for more and more of the Pacific peoples, believing that what is unintelligible to us to-day may be perfectly obvious to scientists of future generations. For the purposes of record may I say that we have made some contribution to blood group gene frequency data for Ainu, Japanese, Chinese, Thais, Chenchu of South India, Indonesians, Filipinos, the peoples of Borneo, Celebes, Papua, New Guinea, Netherlands New Guinea, Admi-

SOURCE: Reprinted from *Oceania*, Vol. 32, No. 3 (1962), pp. 198–210, by permission of the author and publisher.

[1] Paper presented at the Tenth Pacific Science Congress, Honolulu, 1961, as part of the Blood Genetics Symposium in the Division of Public Health and Medical Sciences, by R. T. Simmons of the Commonwealth Serum Laboratories, Melbourne, Victoria.

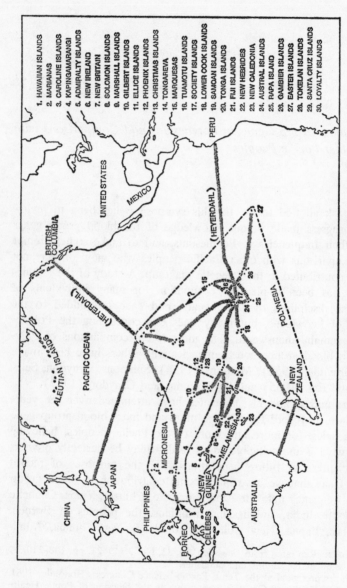

1. HAWAIIAN ISLANDS
2. MARIANAS
3. CAROLINE ISLANDS
4. KAPINGAMARANGI
5. ADMIRALTY ISLANDS
6. NEW IRELAND
7. NEW BRITAIN
8. SOLOMON ISLANDS
9. MARSHALL ISLANDS
10. GILBERT ISLANDS
11. ELLICE ISLANDS
12. PHOENIX ISLANDS
13. CHRISTMAS ISLANDS
14. TONGAREVA
15. MARQUESAS
16. TUAMOTU ISLANDS
17. SOCIETY ISLANDS
18. LOWER COOK ISLANDS
19. SAMOAN ISLANDS
20. TONGA ISLANDS
21. FIJI ISLANDS
22. NEW HEBRIDES
23. NEW CALEDONIA
24. AUSTRAL ISLANDS
25. RAPA ISLAND
26. GAMBIER ISLANDS
27. EASTER ISLANDS
28. TOKELAU ISLANDS
29. SANTA CRUZ ISLANDS
30. LOYALTY ISLANDS

FIGURE 1. The geographical areas of the Pacific and possible migration routes in relation to Polynesia.

ralty, New Britain, New Hebrides, New Caledonia, Loyalty, Australia, New Zealand, Fiji, Gilbert, Kapingamarangi, Marshall, Palau, Truk and the Polynesian islands referred to in this paper from the Cook Islands by devious routes to Easter Island. We have roamed far and wide for blood samples without ever leaving our laboratory, for we pioneered the long-distance transport of blood samples for accurate testing in a central laboratory with full facilities available.

Table 1 establishes the basic ABO pattern for Polynesia. The order of presentation is arranged generally in a west to east

TABLE 1.

ABO Frequencies in Mixed and Unmixed Polynesians.

Location.	Authors.	No. Tested.	A	B	O
Fiji	Simmons *et al.* (1945) and				
	Simmons and Graydon (1947).	310	0.206	0.106	0.688
	Walsh and Kooptzoff (1954).	100	0.273	0.081	0.646
Samoa W.	Cited by Boyd (1939).	51	0.24	0.10	0.64
Samoa Am.	Cited by Boyd (1939).	500	0.103	0.118	0.766
Tonga	Kooptzoff and Walsh (1957).	102	0.248	0.076	0.676
	Staveley and Douglas (1959).	200	0.284	0.062	0.654
Cook	Simmons *et al.* (1955).	269	0.314	0.039	0.647
	Douglas and Staveley (1959).	214	0.360	0.045	0.596
New Zealand[2]	Graydon and Simmons (1946).	267	0.352	0.004	0.642
	Simmons *et al.* (1951).	180	0.338	0	0.662
	Staveley and Douglas (1958).	241	0.295	0	0.705
Kapingamarangi	Miller (1950).	169	0.242	0	0.758
	Simmons *et al.* (1953).	46	0.25	0	0.75
Hawaii	Nigg (1930).	413	0.378	0.013	0.608
Tahiti	Shapiro (1940).	124	0.376	0.039	0.596
Tubuai	Simmons and Graydon (1957).	35	0.28	0	0.72
Austral	Shapiro (1940).	33	0.17	0	0.83
Tuamotu	Shapiro (1940).	176	0.315	0	0.695
Mangareva	Shapiro (1940).	29	0.36	0	0.64
	Simmons and Graydon (1957).	22	0.48	0	0.52
Marquesas	Simmons and Graydon (1957).	30	0.32	0	0.68
Easter	Rahm (1932).	63	0.47	0.03	0.50
	Shapiro (1940).	21	0.42	0	0.58
	Drapkins (1934).	158	0.363	0.029	0.608
	Wilhelm and Sandoval (1956).	199	0.366	0	0.634
	Simmons and Graydon (1957).	51	0.46	0	0.54

[2] The Maoris tested in these surveys were carefully selected. The results of other surveys on Maori soldiers are given by Mourant (1958).

manner, commencing with the areas of highest B adjacent to Melanesia and Micronesia. Group B is absent in unmixed natives in a number of island groups, but it has been demonstrated in low frequency in two of five surveys in Easter, in Hawaii, in one of three surveys in New Zealand and in Tahiti. The areas richest in B are Fiji, Samoa and Tonga. Without doubt Fiji, Tonga and Samoa show higher B as the result of gene flow from Melanesia and Micronesia, and in other areas where the frequency is very low it has resulted from recent admixture with peoples possessing the B gene. It is fair then to assume that the early Polynesian lacked the B gene entirely and in this respect was similar to other unmixed marginal peoples such as the Australian aborigines, American Indians and some of the Eskimo peoples.

The A frequency in Easter Island is the highest in Polynesia, varying in five surveys from 0.36 to 0.47. High A frequencies (0.3 or higher) prevail in Cook, New Zealand, Hawaii, Tahiti, Tuamotu and Marquesas. The lowest A is found in Samoa (0.10 and 0.24), Tonga (0.25 and 0.28) and in Kapingamarangi (0.24 and 0.25). The Kapingamarangi atoll just north of the equator (but not in Polynesia) is the home of some 500 typical Polynesians including a small element of recently added Micronesian stock. These people have been extensively studied by Dr. Kenneth Emory of Honolulu, who generously provided us with individual genealogies. There appears in Table 1 to be some evidence of a general gradient of A from east to west. The frequencies of A throughout Polynesia are higher than in Melanesia, Micronesia and Indonesia. Subgroup A_2 has not been found and proven in the Pacific people tested by the author, except in one family in the Eastern Highlands of New Guinea (Simmons, Graydon, Zigas, Baker and Gajdusek 1961).

In Table 2 it will be seen that S of MNS is present in Polynesians except Kapingas, as it is in all Pacific peoples except Australian aborigines and in isolated tribes in New Guinea. There are apparent contradictions in that the mixed Fijians and Tongans show the lowest S percentages (3.5%–8%). Cook Islanders show 10%–18%, Maoris 12%–13% and Easter Islanders 15.7% respectively. In New Caledonia the S positive percentage is 13.8 (Kooptzoff and Walsh 1955) and in the British Solomon Islands 10.3 (Walsh and Kooptzoff 1955), thus the Fijians and Tongans have only slightly less S than the New Caledonians and British

TABLE 2.
MNS Frequencies in Polynesians.

Location	Authors	No. Tested	m	n	S+ %	ms	mS	ns	nS
Fiji	Simmons et al. (1945) and Simmons and Graydon (1947).	310	0.326	0.674	8.0	0.347	0.013	0.618	0.022
Tonga	Walsh and Kooptzoff (1954).	100	0.5925	0.4075	3.9	0.585	0.008	0.395	0.012
	Kooptzoff and Walsh (1957).	102	0.587	0.413	3.5	0.569	0.023	0.406	0.002
	Staveley and Douglas (1959).	200	0.551	0.449	18.0	0.579	0.011	0.327	0.083
Cook	Simmons et al. (1955).	269	0.489	0.511	9.8	0.544	0.008	0.406	0.043
	Douglas and Staveley (1959).	214	0.525	0.475	12.2	0.500	0.014	0.438	0.048
New Zealand	Graydon and Simmons (1946).	267	0.478	0.522	13.2	0.476	0.028	0.479	0.017
	Simmons et al. (1951).	180	0.71	0.29	0	0.70	0	0.30	0
	Staveley and Douglas (1958).	241	0.33	0.67	15.7				
Kapingamarangi	Simmons et al. (1953).	46	0.50	0.50	13.6				
Easter	Simmons and Graydon (1957).	51	0.51	0.49	8.6				
Tuamotu		22							
Tubuai		35							
Marquesas		30	0.47	0.53	13.3				
Totals		138	0.435	0.565	13.0	0.412	0.023	0.520	0.045

Solomon Islanders. The S distribution because of its variability generally does not help, for example, in New Guinea S varies from 0–50% (Simmons *et al.* 1961).

The M-N pattern in Polynesia of moderate m tends to be distinctive compared with adjacent areas to the west and north-west of high n. Generally speaking, m in unmixed Polynesians is in the order of 0.5. More will be presented later on these points when comparisons are made in greater detail with other racial groups.

Table 3 shows the Rh gene distribution in Polynesia. The genes found have been mainly R^1 and R^2 with occasional R^0, R^z and r'. There appear to be quite definite gradients in the frequencies of R^1 and R^2 from west to east. Fiji on the Polynesian-Melanesian border has the highest R^1 frequency, 0.80–0.84, with correspondingly low R^2. New Zealand to the south has about equal R^1 and R^2, while Easter Island in the east has low R^1 0.34 and high R^2 0.66. This is the broad pattern and it appears to be true. It must be remembered when comparisons are made that gene frequencies we see have mostly resulted from the initial breeding of small numbers of men and women in isolation. Genes may not be present because the initial stock did not have them, or genes may be lost in small populations due to random genetic drift.

There is a low frequency of R^0 in most of the Polynesian groups. In Tonga, Cook and New Zealand a low frequency of R^z was demonstrated by the New Zealand workers Staveley and Douglas. In two different surveys in New Zealand a low frequency of the gene r' was found, however, in the first survey the Rh^0 variant (D^u) was not excluded, but it was in the second series tested later. The rare genes demonstrated will be discussed more fully in later comparisons made with other peoples.

Table 4 presents a summary of other blood group antigens and characteristics found in recent surveys in Maoris, Kapingas, Cook Islanders, Tongans and Polynesians of Central and Eastern Polynesia. The table shows the antigens not detected, and the percentages of those demonstrated; also the blood group with which the antigen is associated. Thus, A_2 of the ABO system, C^w and V of the Rh groups, Gr(Vw), Mg and He of the MNSs system, Kp^a of the Kell groups, together with Lu^a (Lutheran), Wr^a (Wright), Di^a (Diego), By (Batty), Js^a (Sutter) were not dem-

TABLE 3.

Rh Frequencies in Polynesians.

Location.	Authors.	No. Tested.	R^1 (CDe)	R^2 (cDE)	R^0 (cDe)	R^z (CDE)	r' (Cde)
Fiji	Simmons and Graydon (1947).	110	0.840	0.050	0.110	0	0
	Walsh and Kooptzoff (1954).	100	0.805	0.115	0.080	0	0
Tonga	Kooptzoff and Walsh (1957).	102	0.741	0.206	0.053	0	0
	Staveley and Douglas (1959).	200	0.690	0.2425	0.0625	0.005	0
Cook	Simmons et al. (1955).	267	0.516	0.459	0.025	0	0
	Douglas and Staveley (1959).	214	0.519	0.428	0.042	0.012	0
New Zealand	Simmons et al. (1951).	180	0.465	0.486	0.027	0	0.022
	Staveley and Douglas (1958).	167	0.476	0.450	0.060	0.009	0.005
Kapingamarangi	Simmons et al. (1953).	46	0.75	0.24	0.01	0	0
Easter		51	0.34	0.66	0	0	0
Tuamotu	Simmons and Graydon (1957).	22	0.43	0.57	0	0	0
Tubuai		35	0.47	0.51	0.02	0	0
Marquesas		30	0.62	0.38	0	0	0
Totals		138	0.449	0.543	0.007	0	0

TABLE 4.

Percentages of Other Blood Group Antigens and Characteristics of Polynesians[a]

Population	Authors	A$_2$	Cw	V	Gr	Vw	Mg	He	Kp^a	Lu^a	Wr^a	Di^a	By	Js^a	S.C.T.	D^u	K	Le^a	P$_1$	Fy^a	Jk^a	Kp^b	U	Vel	P.T.C.
		ABO	Rh	Rh	Rh / MNS	MNS	MNS	MNS	K							Rh						K	MNS		Tasters
Maoris	Graydon et al. (1946).	0																							
Maoris	Simmons et al. (1951).	0	0													0		29.0	71.7						91.7
Maoris	Staveley and Douglas (1958).								0	0	0					0	0–2.9	16.6	54.6	70.4	89.4			100	
Maoris	Douglas and Staveley (1960).					0	0	0						0							83.4	100			
Kapingas	Simmons et al. (1953).	0	0													0		45.0							72.0
Cooks	Simmons et al. (1955).	0	0													0.4	1.6	17.2	45.7	92.1					83.7
Cooks	Douglas and Staveley (1959).	0										0				0	0	19.2	59.8					100	
Tongans	Staveley and Douglas (1959).	0										0	0	0		0	0.5	23.7	35.5	98.5	72.5	100	100	100	
Eastern and Central Polynesians	Simmons and Graydon (1957).	0	0									0	0	0		2.2	0	14.5	39.1	87.3					92.1
Summary		0	0	0	0	0	0	0	0	0	0	0	0	0	0	0 / 2.2	0 / 2.9	14.5 / 45.0	35.5 / 54.6	59.8 / 98.5	72.5 / 89.4	100	100	100	72.0 / 92.1

[a] Staveley and Douglas have also shown that the Tongans are 100% Gm^a positive, and that neither the Tongans nor the Cook Islanders possess haemoglobins other than haemoglobin A.

onstrated. The S.C.T. (sickle-cell trait) was also absent. A very occasional example of D^u of the Rh system was found. One occurred in the Cooks, one in the Tubuai and two in the Easter Island samples. The blood group K (Kell) was generally absent, but did occur probably due to admixture in New Zealand, Cooks and Tonga varying from 0–2.9%. The P_1 group percentages varied from 35.5 to 54.6. Fy^a (Duffy) ranged from 59.8%–98.5%—the highest percentages being in the Cook Islanders and Tongans, both subjected to known Melanesian influence. The Jk^a (Kidd) group varied from 72.5% in Tongans to 89.4% in Maoris. Kp^b of Kell, U of MNS and Vel all proved to be 100% positive. The ability of Polynesians to taste phenyl thiocarbamide (P.T.C.) was recorded as 72.0%–92.1%.

Having established the broad blood genetic pattern of Polynesians scattered over thousands of miles of ocean in relation to ABO, MNSs, Rh, and other blood group systems, it becomes possible to attempt comparisons in a broad manner with the patterns available for Australian aborigines, the peoples of Melanesia, Micronesia, the aboriginal Ainu of Northern Japan and American Indians of North and South America. We are aware of the limitations of such comparisons, but as serologists who have provided much of the data without seeing the peoples concerned, and without the training of the specialist anthropologist, we ask you to accept our blood group phenotype and genotype frequencies as entirely objective, but our comments on them as pure speculation to provide you with subject matter for consideration and discussion. We would like your comments as to whether the serological data we have progressively provided over 25 years will provide any of the answers sought on the affiliations of man in the Pacific, or whether our data will, or may, provide the fundamental material for scientists of the future whose perception may be more acute than ours.

POSSIBLE MIGRATION ROUTES FOR THE COLONIZATION OF POLYNESIA

Six possible routes have been considered by various writers as providing pathways to the Pacific Islands.

The first which suggests itself geographically is from Indonesia along the northern coast of New Guinea and thence via New

Britain and the Solomons, New Hebrides and Fiji to Samoa and Tonga, and thence further east. This route involves relatively easy sailing stages, but it has been largely discounted by the lack of signs of racial admixture with the Melanesian populations en route.

The second and conventional route favoured by most anthropologists and by Weckler (1943) whose suggested migration paths have been incorporated in Figure 1, is from Indonesia through the area between the southern Philippines and the Moluccas some 400 miles from the Philippines to the nearest Caroline Islands and thence via Palau, Yap and Truk with one branch through the Marshalls to Hawaii, and the other from the Carolines via Gilbert, Phoenix and Tongareva to Society, and with still another branch via Ellice and Samoa to Society, and from there eventually to New Zealand and also to various other Polynesian islands to the east, south-east and south.

The third suggested route is from east to west with wind and current and Heyerdahl (1952) with five European companions proved the possibility of a drift voyage by raft from the coast of Peru, South America, directly to the Polynesian islands thousands of miles away. He has also suggested that another migratory stream drifted from the Northwest Coast (Canada) with the current to Hawaii and thence eventually to New Zealand. He discussed the Indians of the coast of British Columbia and claimed affinity between them and Polynesians. He suggested that the ease of a drift voyage made the affinity all the more probable. Hawaii could be settled from Eastern Polynesia, but the reverse could not apply due to prevailing wind and current. The best canoes in Hawaii were made from pine logs washed there from America (Sharp 1957) and a derelict ship once drifted from the South American coast to Eastern Polynesia. Accidental migration from much of the western American coast would have been possible if the inhabitants made coastal journeys.

It is said that the only firm evidence of direct contact between America and Polynesia is botanical. The sweet potato and cotton came to Polynesia by human agency from America. A variety of South American cotton probably introduced to Hawaii prior to the fifth century A.D. was found growing in a wild state by the early explorers. American cultivated cotton was found in Eastern

Hawaii and it is thought to have come from Central rather than South America. These cottons were probably brought in by one-way migrants. The pigs of Polynesia did not come from America, but from the East Indies, where the pig was native. Thus, again human agency for transport was essential, and we have certain contact with both the east and the west.

Sharp points out that there is no linguistic affinity between the American and Polynesian speeches, whereas there is between Polynesian, Melanesian, Micronesian and Indonesian showing that these four arose from a common speech area at the same time.

The fifth route is by the Japan Current to Hawaii, a current which sweeps from Formosa to California, and records show that in the nineteenth century a Japanese junk came on Hawaii with living seamen on board after an accidental voyage. However, this particular current would not assist the settlement of other parts of Polynesia.

The sixth and least likely route would be from Australia to New Zealand. The prevailing winds are westerly, but the aborigines of Australia were not a maritime people, and there are no suggestions of language or other ties between Australian and New Zealand natives.

The Polynesians have been credited with great navigational skill over long, as well as short distances, because of the apparent effective colonization of island groups within the triangle marked by Hawaii, New Zealand and Easter Island. However, Sharp (1957), who has made a study of the early Pacific from old literature and modern evidence, states that deliberate voyages of 200–300 miles were made within certain areas, for example Tonga-Fiji-Samoa and also Tahiti-Tuamotu, but no deliberate colonization was made of Fiji, Tonga, Samoa, Tahiti, the Tuamotus, the Marquesas, New Zealand, Hawaii and Easter Island. He quotes the records of Captain Cook's voyage of 1777, which state that when visiting Atiu in that year Cook's Polynesian interpreter found three of his countrymen from Tahiti 600 miles away on the island; they being the survivors of about 20 people blown away in a storm from near Tahiti when on a 100-mile canoe voyage. Cook as the result of this accidental journey said, this

Physical Anthropology

will serve to explain, better than a thousand conjectures of speculative reasoners, how the detached parts of the earth, and, in particular, how the South Seas, may have been peopled; especially those that lie remote from any inhabited continent, or from each other.

Sharp has collected considerable data from many sources on the movements of Polynesians. The evidence offers no support for considerable long and deliberate voyages of colonization, but supports Cook's belief that accidental voyages conveyed people and knowledge between distant islands, and that dispersal of man in general, and the Polynesians in particular, to distant islands was occasioned solely by accidental voyages. Both Cook and his official historian Anderson actively sought and recorded evidence of movement of peoples amongst the Polynesian islands. Sharp considers that the same fundamental facts apply to the peopling of isolated islands throughout the world.

COMPARISONS OF POLYNESIAN BLOOD GROUPS WITH THOSE OF AMERICAN INDIANS, AUSTRALIAN ABORIGINES, MELANESIANS, MICRONESIANS, INDONESIANS AND AINU

In Table 5 an attempt has been made to obtain an approximate picture of the range of variation in gene frequency and phenotype percentages, for some of the blood factors which could assist in the comparisons of the racial groups under discussion, namely Polynesians, American Indians, Australian aborigines, Melanesians of New Guinea, Micronesians of Palau, Truk and Marshalls, Indonesians of Java, Timor, Celebes, and Ainu of Northern Japan. It is obvious that there is a wide range of phenotype and gene frequency variations in people of the same race, when blood samples are collected from separate breeding groups, no doubt due to breeding from small numbers, inbreeding, and genetic drift. We have hoped for years that such comparisons could lead to identification of racial components, and to probable routes used for the migrations of the Pacific peoples.

We have looked for evidence of strong blood genetic links between Polynesians and American Indians, and between Polynesians and the peoples of Melanesia, Micronesia and Indonesia.

TABLE 5.

Approximate Range of Blood Group Gene Frequency and Phenotype Percentage Variations for Selected Polynesians and other Pacific Peoples.

Population.	O	A_1	B	M	S	R^1	R^2	P_1+	Le(a+)	Fy(a+)	Jk(a+)
Polynesians (Selected)	0.50–0.75	0.25–0.48	0	0.33–0.71[4]	0–15.7%	0.34–0.75	0.24–0.66	39–55%	14–45%	70–87%	83–89%
American Indians	0.80–1.0	0–0.2[4]	0	0.70–0.96[5]	30–67%	0.31–0.52	0.27–0.57	60–85%	0–12%	70–100%	70–95%
Australian Aborigines	0.35–0.85	0.08–0.65	0	0.14–0.31	0	0.53–0.72	0.06–0.38	32%	7%	99.7%	61–69%
Melanesians (New Guinea)	0.44–0.87	0.05–0.34	0.05–0.38	0.01–0.28	0–50%	0.73–0.99	0.004–0.204	37–50%	0–3%	100%	85–92%
Micronesians	0.34–0.75	0.14–0.38	0.10–0.28	0.22–0.39	1.1–22.6%	0.69–0.95	0.04–0.23	61–80%	8–25.9%	100%	—
Indonesians	0.62–0.84	0.07–0.22	0.08–0.20	0.38–0.68	—[6]	0.81	0.13	—	40%	—	—
Ainu	0.37–0.60	0.26–0.31	0.09–0.36	0.35–0.43	43–58%	0.56	0.21	72%	23–41%	96–100%	—

[4] Only the "Blood" and "Blackfeet" tribes in all America have a high frequency of A.
[5] The figures in italics indicate a basis for comparison with those figures for Polynesians.
[6] The "—" sign indicates that no data are available.

Here are a few points which emerge mainly from examination of the vertical columns of Table 5.

(1) The American Indians alone are almost uniformly of high O Frequency. The only exceptions seem to be the "Blood" and "Blackfeet" tribes, who have high A. (Matson and Schrader 1933; Levine, Matson and Schrader 1935; and Chown and Lewis 1953.)

The Indonesians also have a high frequency of O.

(2) Polynesians have possibly the highest A frequencies in the world, and the same tendency applies to most Australian aborigines except those of the Cape York Peninsula area near Melanesia, where A is exceptionally low (0.08). (The Bentinck Islanders of this area rich in B have no A at all.)

(3) Polynesians, American Indians and Australian aborigines of unmixed blood all lack the blood group B gene. The others listed all have low to high frequencies of group B.

(4) American Indians have the highest M and there is above average M in most, but not all Polynesians. There is also high M in Java reaching a figure comparable with that of the highest in Polynesians, while elsewhere in Indonesia M is higher than in Micronesians or Melanesians. Australian aborigines, Melanesians, Micronesians and Ainu have generally above average to very high N.

(5) S of MNS is completely absent in Australian aborigines over the entire continent, while elsewhere in other peoples there is considerable variation in S frequency. (It is regretted that our early surveys lack data for Indonesians for the S, P_1, Fy^a and Jk^a blood factors.)

(6) In the Rh types Polynesians and American Indians mostly shew raised R_2 (*cDE*) frequencies and a similar, but lesser tendency is also seen in Australian aboriginal groups of South Australia and Western Australia. In the others listed, high R_1 prevails, reaching a peak of 0.99 in some Melanesians, 0.95 in Micronesians, and 0.81 in Indonesians.

(7) The P_1 blood group also variable in frequency, provides no basis for comparisons.

(8) In the Lewis (Le^a) group variability prevails, Polynesians, Indonesians and Ainu reaching about 40% of Le(a+). In Melanesia, most groups are Le(a−), as are many American Indians.

(9) Of many Pacific peoples tested for the Duffy group (unfortunately no Indonesian data are available) nearly all are 100% Fy(a+). We have an unusual finding in that many American Indian and Polynesian groups are only in the order of 70% Fy(a+).

(10) The Jk^a (Kidd) blood group provides no basis for comparisons at this stage, and does not look promising.

From the total data I have collected I am expected to tell you the precise origin of the Polynesian and his relationships with the west or the east, depending on your personal preference. However, I would first like to discuss matters of a more general nature in the shape of a brief review entitled

THE ORIGIN OF RACIAL GROUPS IN THE PACIFIC, ESPECIALLY POLYNESIA

The peoples, as total groups within the geographical areas of Polynesia, Australia, Melanesia, Micronesia and Indonesia, each possess a general basic pattern of blood groups, for example in Polynesia there is high A, no A_2, no B, high R_2 and about 70% Fy(a+), and the findings in relation to areas other than Polynesia have been summarized by Simmons *et al.* (1953) and in subsequent papers. However, let it be noted that no individual could be placed within his correct racial group purely on the results of his blood group findings.

As we have seen in Tables 1 to 5, there are no fixed percentages for blood groups and gene frequencies for the members within any geographical area. Extremely wide variations of separate blood antigens and blood groups occur mainly, due I believe to breeding in isolation. Each group has progressively built up its numbers from a few individuals, and those individuals who varied (in the extreme) physically in stature, in skin colour or in other aspects often became outcasts, seeking refuge together and reproducing their own characteristics, but still showing a blood relationship to their sometimes nearby original family group. (Further, this is still happening even amongst our own people to-day.) A fine example of this is the true Negrito or pygmy types of New Guinea and elsewhere, for all are related to their immediate neighbours. While the pygmy sought and found refuge deep in the rain-forest, other coastal dwellers found safety on other islands, built up a population in numbers until the need for more food, or hostile neighbours drove some up the rivers into new valleys, or if a canoe-loving people, to other islands, and progressively further afield. In island areas, fate, in form of storms, winds and currents took man to every island, and if food and water were plentiful, man and woman survived and colonized again.

Possible migration routes have been mapped, and man has been credited with elaborate migrations made by daring adventurers in past centuries, but they probably never happened, except as accidents.

Men like Captain Cook and his historian Anderson of the eighteenth century had more vision than we, because they wrote that accidental journeys of men and women probably populated all the detached parts of the earth. Recent observers like Andrew Sharp of New Zealand and Kenneth Emory of Honolulu, have reminded us that the Polynesian story is not complex, but delightfully simple. As stated earlier, Sharp (1957) has produced a fine "Penguin" edition covering old literature and modern evidence of Polynesia, and Emory (1959), after years of study, considers that the Polynesians originated from a few people of diverse origins in the western archipelago about 1500 B.C., and subsequently moved eastward to the Tahitian archipelago and developed their own language and culture. They blended with occasional drift voyagers who came by raft from Peru, and progressively dispersed as far away as Hawaii, Easter Island and New Zealand after the beginning of the Christian era.

As stated earlier, blood grouping data show that all unmixed Polynesians to-day are basically of the same stock. Contributions to this stock have undoubtedly come from the west (Tonga and Samoa), the north-west (Indonesia) and the east (South America) to form a common gene pool and a different physical type. The original numbers were few and came (as others have said) in canoes, often at the mercy of wind and current. Just as we have shown that in isolated areas, for example New Guinea (Simmons *et al.* 1961), human types evolve with slightly different characteristics such as skin colour and an occasional gene mutation, so a blood pattern in one area differs slightly from those in isolation over the next mountain range, or in the adjacent inaccessible valley, or deep in the rain-forest. The variations in blood group frequencies we have shown in Polynesia from island population to island population, reflects again the results of small numbers breeding in isolation as in New Guinea, and in other parts of the world. It could be that the original limited numbers, or basic stock of men and women from the west or north-west lacked by chance the blood group B, and this nucleus with additions from the east (South America) also lacking B, but rich in the Rh genes R^2 (cDE) and M, increased in numbers and covered most of Polynesia. Group B was then only introduced in marginal areas, when numbers became sufficiently great many centuries later for the interchange of visits, mostly with Melanesians and Micronesians. It seems likely that the original men and women who entered Polynesia lived and bred in isolation for at least 1,000 years, dispersing to adjacent areas by design, but to distant areas by accidental voyages. Population additions from the coast of America would have represented a voyage of no-return, and these individuals made their contributions to the Polynesian way of life.

In conclusion, points of broad serological similarity may be drawn with Polynesians as follows:

American Indians:	No B, high M, high R_2, moderate Fy^a.
Australian aborigines:	No B, high A.
Melanesians:	Nil.
Micronesians:	Nil.
Indonesians:	High M.
Ainu:	Nil.

If one makes and accepts such comparisons with Polynesians, then there are four points of similarity with American Indians, two with Australian aborigines, one with Indonesians, and none with Melanesians, Micronesians and Ainu.

If the comparisons are valid, then American Indians and Polynesians shared in a common gene pool, more so than Polynesians and other races to the west and north-west.

After 25 years of progress, we serologists have mapped most of the known blood group genes for racial groups throughout the world, and while clear-cut gene markers are known in respect to some human races, it seems clearly evident that blood group genetical studies do not tell us the racial components of the Pacific peoples or their paths of migration. I believe that the blood grouping percentage variations demonstrates the impossibility of equating a component of one racial group, with the possible component of another some thousands of miles away. If the gene frequencies as calculated do hold the clues, then posterity alone will provide the proof and the answers.

It seems evident that there were no planned migrations into Polynesia, and that the Polynesian people spread mainly by accidental voyages to all the distant Polynesian islands. Blood group serology does not prove to us who they were or from whence they came. There is then no Polynesian problem, other than that created by ourselves, for it would seem that a handful of men and women from the east and the west, and not racial groups as we know them to-day, produced the Polynesian people as a distinctive entity amongst the races of Man.

C. LINGUISTICS

GEORGE W. GRACE

4. Classification of the Languages of the Pacific

INTRODUCTION

The languages with which we are concerned in the present discussion are those of the island areas of Micronesia, Polynesia, and Melanesia—including New Guinea. It is traditional, and convenient for the purposes of this discussion, to divide these languages into two groups: (1) those languages which are members of the Austronesian (or Malayopolynesian) language family, and (2) those which are not. The designation, Papuan, has traditionally been used for the second of these groups. However, some authors in recent years have preferred to substitute the term Non-Austronesian as more indicative of the fact that the group is negatively, rather than positively, defined. That is, the claim that a language is Papuan has traditionally represented a claim only that the language is not a descendant of Proto-Austronesian without any further commitment as to what its history is.

The geographical distribution of the two groups can be roughly sketched as follows. The majority of the perhaps five hundred Papuan languages are on the island of New Guinea. However, some are to be found on islands both to the east and to the west. In the Indonesian area to the west, Papuan languages are found in the northern part of the island of Halmahera, and on Timor and a few small surrounding islands. To the east there is a Papuan language on Rossel Island in the Louisiade Archipelago, several in New Britain, one in New Ireland, and a number on Bougainville. There are four scattered Papuan languages further east in the Solomons: on Vella Lavella, on Rendova, in the Russell

Islands, and on Savo (Savosavo). Moreover, it seems that the languages of Santa Cruz and the Reef Islands (except for a Polynesian language spoken in the latter group) can now be added to the list (Davenport 1962). Most of the island of New Guinea itself is occupied by Papuan languages. However, there are also a considerable number of Austronesian languages there. In general terms, the situation in New Guinea may be described as follows: there are no Austronesian languages on the south coast from a point near Kaimana in West New Guinea to a point near Port Moresby in the Territory of Papua. All of the Austronesian languages are found, interspersed with Papuan languages, in the remaining coastal areas of the island. Many are on offshore islands, and none is more than a few miles inland from the coast.

The Austronesian language family is one of the largest in the world both in its geographical extent and in the number of its languages. It extends well beyond the bounds of the Pacific, and probably includes at least five hundred languages. Except for the Papuan languages, of course, it includes all of the languages of Melanesia. It also includes all of the languages of Micronesia and Polynesia. To the west, it includes all of the languages of Indonesia, except the few Papuan languages to which we have referred, all of the languages of the Philippines, the aboriginal languages of Formosa, the languages of Madagascar off the coast of Africa, and—on the mainland of Southeast Asia—Malay and the Cham group of languages in Vietnam. The geographical extremes are Madagascar in the west, Easter Island in the east, New Zealand in the south, and Hawaii and Formosa in the north.

Interest in the classification of the languages of the Pacific has shown notable growth in recent years. Contributory factors have included, on the one hand, new developments indicating the feasibility of genetic classification from descriptive data of limited quality, and on the other hand, concrete support for such work from the Tri-Institutional Pacific Program under the leadership of George P. Murdock, Alexander Spoehr, and Leonard Mason. The first of the developments referred to was the publication of Joseph Greenberg's "Studies in African Linguistic Classification" (1949–54). This series, and subsequent papers by Greenberg dealing with methodology or presenting additional classifications, clearly indicated that further progress in discovering linguistic relationships was an attainable immediate goal. Although the most widely discussed methodological contribution of these studies is that concerning the proof of genetic relationship, they also deal extensively with the problem of subgrouping. The other development to which I referred is that of the technique of glotto-chronology, and subsequently of its derivative, lexicostatistics. The appearance of glottochronology on the scene may be dated from an article by Morris Swadesh published in 1950. However, it was another two or three years before its form had become established.

Glottochronology works with a standard list of two hundred meanings—represented by English words with certain qualifying instructions. The data are the "equivalents"—i.e., the words best representing each of these meanings—in the languages being studied. Studies indicated that approximately 19.5 per cent of the equivalents are replaced in any given language during each thousand years. An item is said to be replaced when there is a lexical substitution or semantic shift such that, at some point in time, the word which is the best equivalent of a particular item of the standard test-list is no longer historically the same word as the best equivalent at the starting point. An equivalent at the end of the period is said to be "retained" if it is historically the same word as the best equivalent at the beginning—i.e., if it differs only as the result of regular sound change.

Studies of historical materials had indicated that the rate of replacement in all languages fell within a narrow range around a mean of 19.5 per cent per millennium. If this were true, and if the choice of specific items for replacement were random, then it would be possible to determine how long two related languages had been developing separately on the basis of the number of test-list equivalents they still shared. Specifically, the divergence time in millennia was computed by dividing the logarithm of the percentage of shared cognates by two times the logarithm of 80.5 (the percentage of retentions expected per millennium).

Originally, the terms "glottochronology" and "lexicostatistics" were used interchangeably. However, subsequently the terms have diverged, and lexicostatistics no longer carries any implication of absolute dating. As doubts have arisen about the validity of the assumptions underlying glottochronology, lexicostatistical studies have increasingly tended to adopt the weaker assumption that *relatively* higher cognate percentages reflect *relatively* shorter divergence times without the assumption that absolute dating can be approximated.

AUSTRONESIAN CLASSIFICATION

Although there are many unresolved problems in the classification of the Austronesian languages, none is more fundamental than the problem of the position of the Melanesian languages. (I here use "Melanesian languages" in the accustomed sense of "Austronesian, but not Polynesian, languages of Melanesia.") As Wilhelm Milke (1962) puts it, there are two major schools of thought: "[the first] holds that the languages of Melanesia, Micronesia (Palauan and Chamorro excluded), and Polynesia form a subgroup within the Austronesian family and are derived from a common proto-language, termed by Dempwolff 'Ur-Melanesisch,' but preferably called 'proto-Oceanic'. The second . . . denies the first school's ideas and seeks to derive different languages within Melanesia, Micronesia, and Polynesia from different parts of Indonesia." More specifically, the second school holds that the Austronesian languages were introduced into Melanesia by colonies of Indonesians, and that Papuan languages were already spoken at the sites of the colonies. Apparently the Indonesian languages which were introduced are regarded as having diverged only slightly from Proto-Austronesian. However, some prior divergence is certainly assumed, because adherents of this school believe that the area of origin within Indonesia of particular groups of colonists can be determined on the basis of linguistic features attributable to particular subgroups of Indonesian languages. In any event, it is assumed that pidginized varieties of the Indonesian languages developed at the sites of the colonies, and that the grammar of the pidgins represented a simplified Indonesian grammar, while the vocabulary consisted of a core of (phonetically simplified) Indonesian words plus a large number of less basic words derived from the Papuan language. If I understand correctly, it is assumed that these pidgins were often subsequently themselves pidginized by Papuan speakers in areas more remote from the colonies, resulting in languages with even less "Austronesian content" (and that the

Austronesian vocabulary which survived these secondary transactions was typically even more phonetically distorted).

I will say little more about historical explanations proposed by
this school, as such, since they do not lead to linguistic classification in the usual sense, and in any event have not informed much
of the recent work. However, the leading proponents of this
school have had an impressive knowledge of the languages of
Melanesia. It is instructive to examine some of their remarks.
These remarks reflect a simultaneous appreciation of (1) a characteristic uniformity and (2) a remarkable diversity among the
Melanesian languages. Consider, for example, the following:

> The morphological patterns of MN [Melanesian] languages
> are generally fairly uniform; MC [Micronesian] structure is
> on the whole very similar. PN [Polynesian] departs a little
> more widely from the MN type, but is coherent to a very
> large degree within its own group. IN [Indonesian] lan-
> guages, however, diverge very widely from the MN
> type. . . . (Capell 1962b:387.)

> . . . we must expect a Papuan element in the languages
> which differs from island to island, and a Melanesian element
> which tends to uniformity. . . . (Ray 1926:25.)

> Complete vocabularies [for Melanesian languages] show
> that IN [Indonesian] words form only a small portion of
> the word-store of any single language. The very large num-
> ber of words which cannot be referred to an IN source can-
> not be shown to have (except to a very slight extent) any
> community of origin. (*Ibid.*, 597–98.)

> It is important to observe that IN words which have repre-
> sentatives in Melanesia are more numerous in certain regions
> than in others. Thus the languages of the Shepherd Group
> (Nguna), Central New Hebrides, Fiji, the Banks' Islands
> (Mota) and Central Solomons (Florida) show many more
> words of IN origin than the islands adjacent to them. (*Ibid.*,
> 37.)

> The great variation in the extent to which the Melanesian
> islanders have changed IN words seems to suggest that
> these words were introduced by colonists from Indonesia,

who effected a settlement on the smaller islands, imposing part of their speech upon the natives, and that this mixed speech influenced the native languages with which it came in contact, these latter adopting some of the IN modified speech, but changing it according to their own style of pronunciation. An IN word, for example, like *manuk* becoming *manu* in the colony, but *man, mon, men, min* in districts away from it. (*Ibid.*, 595–96.)

From these quotations and other remarks by writers in this tradition, the following picture emerges:

(1) There is a characteristic Melanesian grammatical structure (which is equally characteristic of most languages of Micronesia, and to a lesser extent, of the Polynesian languages), which contrasts with the characteristic grammatical structures of the languages of Indonesia. The main features of the supposed characteristic structure are briefly described in Ray (1926:597) and Capell (1940:60–67).

(2) There are a small number (300–350) of vocabulary items which are widely shared. Almost (but not quite) all have known cognates in Indonesian languages and can be reconstructed for Proto-Austronesian.

(3) Some languages retain appreciably more of these items than do others.

(4) In some languages (generally those which have retained fewer?) these retained items have undergone more pronounced phonetic changes than in others.

(5) Virtually all shared cognates (except in special cases of particularly close relationship—always accompanied by geographical proximity) among Melanesian languages belong to the set of items just described. The remainder of the vocabulary in each language is unique to it (except for a few identifiable borrowings in some cases).

(6) I am uncertain whether Ray would have agreed that the phonetic form of the words shared by Melanesian and Indonesian languages tended to differ in characteristic ways between the two groups. This may be implied in various of his remarks and in the fact that in presenting his list of the most common IN vocabulary in Melanesian languages (Ray 1926:596), he gave for each item "a characteristic MN and IN word." The kind of similarity I am

referring to here is a more subtle one which might not be apparent without systematic application of the comparative method. It involves like phonological developments in earlier stages of the history of the languages. Such similarities may be obscured by further developments at later stages so as not to be immediately apparent. The most extensive applications of the comparative method to Oceanic languages were made by Otto Dempwolff. He states (1937:164–65) that he has examined the material from all languages counted as Melanesian [note: for him this includes the languages of Micronesia as well, excepting Palauan, Chamorro, and the languages of Polynesian outliers], and, in particular, that from the twelve best-described languages. He notes a series of phonological developments common to these languages, but "found in no Indonesian language known to me." He continues, "They should suffice—even without examination of their grammatical relations—to classify the Melanesian languages together as a unified linguistic grouping. . . ." (1937:165). Dempwolff subsequently (1937:192–93) develops the argument that the Polynesian languages also can be assigned to this grouping on the same grounds.

Thus, as has been indicated, observers have been struck both by a tendency to sameness in some respects and a great diversity in others among the languages of Melanesia (and Oceania as a whole). As it has happened, the first school described by Milke has seized upon the uniformities as the object of explanation—postulating a common proto-language, descended from Proto-Austronesian, from which all are believed to derive. Adherents of this school have not as a rule been greatly concerned with accounting for the diversity. The second school, on the other hand, has seized upon the diversity and attempted to explain it as the result of widely divergent substrata.

As was noted above, the views of the second school, as described by Milke, do not inform any of the recent studies which will be mentioned below. However, since the publication of Milke's remarks, there are indications of the development of a third school. This new school has in common with the first that its objective is the construction of a family tree. It has in common with the second school the fact that its historical interpretations emphasize the diversity, rather than the uniformities, of the Oceanic (and, particularly, the Melanesian) languages.

The essential assumption of this third school is that the diversity of Melanesian languages results from long periods of independent development. This suggests that the earliest branching of Austronesian probably occurred in Melanesia, and that many of the resulting branches are represented today only by small groups of, or even single, Melanesian languages.

This is the interpretation implied by Isidore Dyen's (1965) lexicostatistical classification. Ward Goodenough was apparently indicating a similar historical view in his remark (1962:408): "The role of Melanesia in the history of the Austronesian languages appears to be central and ancient, not peripheral and recent." It can be seen, then, that the classification of the Melanesian languages, as regards both their internal and external relations, remains a very unsettled and lively issue.

SPECIFIC STUDIES

Isidore Dyen's (1965) *A Lexicostatistical Classification of the Austronesian Languages* has just been mentioned. The study is of monumental scope. It employed 371 lists, with a total of 214 languages (by my count) represented in the formal classification. The difference between the two figures is due to the facts that some lists represented Non-Austronesian languages, some represented the same language (often different dialects), and some were not complete enough to be judged adequate. The procedure for deriving a family tree from the cognate percentages was sophisticated, but may be described approximately as follows. Languages which had their highest percentages with each other were assigned to the same subgroup. If one of the languages in the group had a cognate percentage with a language outside the group which was within 2.5 percentage points of the lowest percentage connecting languages already assigned to the group, that outside language was added to the group. Languages continued to be added to the group as long as any were found which showed cognate percentages within 2.5 percentage points of the lowest percentage which had been used thus far in constituting the group. When, at any point, no more such languages were found, the group was closed.

Groups, once constituted, themselves became eligible to be members of larger groups. Such a group was classed as an "open group" if the lowest percentage used to form the group was less than 8.0 percentage points greater than the highest percentage between a member and a non-member. The percentage used in assigning open groups to larger groups was the highest percentage between a member of the group and a non-member. Otherwise, the procedure was identical to that described for individual languages.

However, beyond a certain point in the classification (i.e., as the groups became larger) it became impossible to maintain the requirement of a critical difference (i.e., difference between lowest percentage used in forming the group and highest percentage between a member and a non-member) of at least 2.5 percentage points. If this requirement had been maintained, no further groupings would have been possible. Therefore, for the apex of the tree, the requirement was dropped.

The resulting classification has the following features of note:
(1) Austronesian has forty branches, of which twenty-four consist of a single language each, and of which thirty-three are represented only in Melanesia. An additional four are represented only in areas adjacent to Melanesia (Micronesia and the Moluccas). Only two are restricted to areas distant from Melanesia (namely, a group of two languages on Taiwan and Enggano, off the coast of Sumatra).
(2) The largest of the branches, the Malayopolynesian Linkage, consists of one hundred twenty-nine languages. (Note that "Malayopolynesian" is given a new definition thereby, and is no longer synonymous with "Austronesian.") It includes almost all of the languages outside the Pacific area, and all of the Polynesian languages, plus eight Melanesian languages. The Melanesian languages are: Fijian; Rotuman; Efate and Mota of the New Hebrides; Kerebuto, Lau, and To'abaita of the Solomons; and Motu of the territory of Papua. These eight Melanesian languages plus the Polynesian languages constitute the Heonesian Linkage —one of the six branches of Malayopolynesian.
(3) Only two Micronesian languages are assigned to the Malayopolynesian Linkage. The two are Palauan and Chamorro, and each constitutes one of the six branches of Malayopolynesian. Yapese and Nauruan each constitute a separate branch of Austronesian, and the other Micronesian languages as a group constitute an additional branch of Austronesian.

(4) Of the Melanesian languages, eight belong to the Heonesian branch of Malayopolynesian, as noted. An additional three—all in the extreme west of New Guinea—belong to the Moluccan Linkage, another branch of Malayopolynesian. The remaining seventy-two Melanesian languages in the study constitute thirty-three of the branches of Austronesian—these thirty-three branches having from one to seven members each.

It is important to point out that Dyen does not regard this classification as definitive, and in fact discusses in some detail (1965:53–57) the possible interpretations. However, he does regard the concentration in Melanesia of relatively remotely related languages as a matter of particular significance.

I will turn now to a few recent studies in the tradition of the first school. In 1955, I published in the *American Anthropologist* the first tentative conclusions of my work under the Tri-Institutional Pacific Program. My views were further elaborated in a monograph in the *Indiana University Publications in Anthropology and Linguistics* in 1959 and an article in the *American Anthropologist* in 1961 (Grace 1955, 1959, 1961; cf. also Grace 1964). The principal points are: (1) There is a large subgroup, which I called "Eastern Austronesian" and now call "Oceanic." This subgroup probably includes all of the Austronesian languages of Melanesia, Polynesia, and Micronesia except Palauan, Chamorro, and some languages in the western part of New Guinea. (2) My 1955 communication identified nineteen subgroups within Oceanic. These should be regarded as representing only an approximation of the actual relationships. However, the necessary revisions in most cases will require careful research and more and better data. (3) Fijian, Rotuman, and the Polynesian languages constitute a subgroup. (4) That subgroup and the languages of Efate, Epi, and the small islands between (all in the central New Hebrides) constitute a larger subgroup. (5) The languages of Micronesia, except Palauan, Chamorro, and the languages of the Polynesian outliers constitute a subgroup. (6) The two last named subgroups plus all remaining languages of the New Hebrides and Banks Islands constitute a still larger subgroup, which is one of the nineteen subgroups originally set up within Eastern Austronesian.

In 1958, Wilhelm Milke (1958a) published in the *Zeitschrift für Ethnologie* a classification of the Oceanic languages. He dis-

agreed with my original definition of Oceanic only to the extent
of assigning to it certain languages in West New Guinea which
I had excluded. I now agree with him as regards some of those
languages. As regards the others, I am still uncertain.

Within Oceanic, the basis of his classification was the treatment of three Proto-Oceanic phonemes, *1, *d, and *R. This procedure determined three major groupings. One of his groups
resembles my New Hebrides-Banks group in that it includes Fijian, Rotuman, the Polynesian languages, the Micronesian languages, and the languages of the New Hebrides. We disagree in
that I include the languages of the Banks and Torres Islands,
which he excludes, and that he includes the languages of the
Admiralties and Western Islands (a string of small islands west
of the Admiralties) and of New Caledonia and the Loyalty Islands, all of which I exclude.

In a subsequent paper (Milke 1961), he presents a summary
of his historical inferences containing the following points:

(1) A Proto-Oceanic can legitimately be reconstructed.

(2) No Proto-Indonesian, exclusive of the Oceanic languages,
ever existed. However, smaller groupings are found in the Indonesian area.

(3) The speakers of Proto-Oceanic lived for an extended period
in contact with speakers of earlier stages of Philippine, Celebes,
and eastern Indonesian languages.

(4) After the breakup of Proto-Oceanic, the languages ancestral
to present-day New Guinea languages remained in contact with
languages ancestral to present-day eastern Indonesian languages.

Also in 1961, Ward Goodenough published in the *Journal of
the Polynesian Society* a paper on the linguistic position of the
Nakanai language of New Britain. He argued that Nakanai, and
by implication the languages of the Willaumez Peninsula of New
Britain, should be added to my Fijian-Rotuman-Polynesian
grouping. He suggested that the present geographical location of
Nakanai results from a back-migration from the east. In the light
of recent research on Pacific voyaging, such back-migrations
should not be regarded as inherently improbable. Goodenough
considered a wide variety of evidence—phonological, grammatical,
lexical, and lexicostatistical.

A particularly encouraging development in the last few years is
the beginning of systematic attempts at reconstruction within the

Oceanic group. I refer particularly to the reconstructions of Proto-Oceanic kinship terms in Milke 1958b, a series of additional Proto-Oceanic reconstructions in Milke 1961, a few additional ones along with a few reconstructions labeled "Proto-New Guinea Austronesian" in Milke 1965, and a series labeled "Proto-Eastern Oceanic" in Biggs 1965. Further work in this direction should soon begin to make clearer the true historical relations of the Melanesian languages.

INTERNAL POLYNESIAN RELATIONS

In the past few years dissent from the conclusion that the closest external relations of the Polynesian languages are with Melanesia, and presumably with eastern Melanesia, has virtually disappeared. (Note, however, Kähler 1951.) However, the relationships among the various Polynesian languages has continued to attract interest.

In 1953, Samuel H. Elbert published a paper reporting lexicostatistical comparisons of twenty Polynesian languages and dialects. He also considered phonological and morphological features, providing a table of sound correspondences which has been basic to subsequent comparative Polynesian research. In this study, most of the principal features developed more fully in more recent works were recognized or at least adumbrated. Subsequent work includes Emory 1963 and Dyen 1965, and, most recently, Green 1966 and Pawley 1966.

The last two have in some measure the character of companion pieces. Pawley deals with the first series of Polynesian differentiations, while Green's bold proposals concern subsequent developments in Eastern Polynesian. Both take previous studies into account. Pawley's study gives primary attention to grammatical features, while Green's considers particularly phonological and vocabulary innovations. The latter also discusses the relations to recent archaeological discoveries.

The family tree which emerges shows the following features:

1. The first split distinguishes Tongic (Tongan, Niue, and possibly Uvean) from Nuclear Polynesian.
2. Nuclear Polynesian subsequently splits to produce a Samoic subgroup (including Samoan, Futunan, Ellice, Tokelauan, Ti-

kopian, and possibly Uvean), and Eastern Polynesian. The position of the languages of Polynesian outliers in Melanesia and Micronesia is not clear, except for Tikopian. However, the best evidence at present suggests that most, if not all, probably belong within the Nuclear Polynesian subgroup, and possibly within Samoic.

3. The first split in Eastern Polynesian distinguishes Easter Island from Central Polynesian.

4. Central Polynesian splits into Tahitic (not further developed in much detail, but probably including Tahitian, Rarotongan, Maori, and some Tuamotuan dialects) and Marquesic.

5. Marquesic splits into Mangarevan and Marquesan.

6. Marquesan splits into Northwest Marquesan and Southeast Marquesan.

7. Southeast Marquesan splits into Hawaiian and (contemporary) Southeast Marquesan.

PAPUAN CLASSIFICATION

In general, studies of Papuan linguistics have lagged far behind Austronesian studies. One major reason for this fact is that, on the whole, the Papuan languages are situated in areas where extensive European contact came late. Another factor has surely been the apparent absence of large groupings of languages sufficiently closely related that systematic application of the comparative method seemed feasible. A few initial studies of sound correspondences within small groups of related Papuan languages have been carried out (e.g., Young 1962; McKaughan 1964; Healey, reported in Wurm 1965; Bee 1965), but such studies have not yet attained sufficient scope to affect the larger-scale classificatory studies. I will briefly summarize the results of some recent studies of the latter type.

In 1957 H. K. J. Cowan published in the Dutch journal *Bijdragen tot de Taal-, Land-, en Volkenkunde* an article entitled "Prospects of a 'Papuan' Comparative Linguistics" (Cowan 1957a). In this article he presented his conclusion that six languages of the western "Bird's Head" of West New Guinea were related to one another and were also related to the group of Non-Austronesian languages of northern Halmahera. The argu-

ment is based on forms in the languages being compared which
are similar in meaning and phonetic shape. To minimize the effects of borrowing, he restricted his comparisons to a list of
ninety-seven non-cultural items which Morris Swadesh had found
particularly impervious to borrowing. To deal with the problem
of chance similarities, he required that the forms being compared
agree to the extent of a complex of consonant-vowel-consonant.
Swadesh had calculated that the probability of chance agreement
on this basis was generally smaller than one in one hundred.
However, Cowan did depart from the latter rule to the extent of
comparing pronominal systems *in toto*.

In the same year Cowan published a second article (Cowan
1957b) entitled (translated into English) "A Second Large
Papuan Language Grouping in Netherlands New Guinea." This
paper appeared in the journal *Nieuw-Guinea Studiën*. In this
study, by means of the same method, he identified a grouping for
which he proposed the name "North Papuan Phylum." The languages involved are distributed in an area near the coast stretch-
ing from about 140 miles west of Hollandia (Sukarnapura) to at
least as far east as the border with Australian New Guinea. In
subsequent studies (Cowan 1957–58, 1960, 1963, 1965) he returned to the grouping of Vogelkop (Bird's Head) and northern
Halmahera languages, and assigned to it a series of additional
languages. It now includes all Vogelkop languages for which he
had data, three languages of the Bomberai Peninsula (across the
MacCluer Gulf from the Vogelkop), the single Papuan language
spoken on the island of Japen in Geelvink Bay, the northern
Halmahera languages, and the only three languages of Timor and
Kisar which he accepts as Non-Austronesian. To this grouping he
gives the name "West Papuan Phylum."

Stephen A. Wurm carried out an extensive field survey of the
languages of the three Highlands Districts of Australian New
Guinea in 1958–59. He published a classification based on lexicostatistical comparison in Capell 1962a:105–28. Subsequent
analysis of the materials with consideration of phonological and
grammatical relations has led to a revised classification, reported
in Wurm 1965. In this classification, Wurm recognizes an "East
New Guinea Highlands Stock," which is further subdivided into
five language families. There is found to be another family of
three languages and an additional three separate languages which

appear to be distantly related to—but not included in—the stock. The larger grouping, which includes the last six languages, has been named the "East New Guinea Highlands Phylum."

In 1959–60, Donald C. Laycock carried out a linguistic survey in the Sepik area. He reports (Laycock 1965) in considerable detail the evidence for a grouping of seven languages (the Ndu Family) spoken in the middle Sepik basin and north to the coast.

Alan Healey in 1961–63 studied the languages of the Telefomin area (in the center of the westernmost part of Australian New Guinea). He discovered a large language family, which he has named the "Ok Family," subdivided into two subfamilies. The first of these, the Mountain Ok Subfamily, is distributed through the highland area in the north and extends across the border into West New Guinea. The second, the Lowland Ok Subfamily, extends southward on both sides of the border from the Mountain Ok area. Healey has carried out systematic reconstruction in each of the subfamilies (reported in Wurm 1965).

In an earlier article, Wurm (1960–61) lists twelve numerically important Papuan groupings "now known, or seriously believed, to exist." These are:

(1) East New Guinea Highlands Microphylum.

(2) Maprik (Middle Sepik) Family.

(3) Huon Peninsula Group.

(4) Binandere Group (Northern District of Papua).

(5) Kukukuku Group.

(6) Koita-Koiari Group (Central District of Papua).

(7) Toaripi Group (Gulf District of Papua).

(8) Kiwai Group (Western and Gulf Districts of Papua).

(9) Telefomin Group (Highlands, overlapping the border of Australian and West New Guinea).

(10) Dem-Ndani-Uhunduni Group (eastern part of West New Guinea Highlands).

(11) Ekagi-Wodani-Moni Group (western part of West New Guinea Highlands, including the Wissel Lakes region).

(12) Kamoro-Sempan-Asmat Group (south coast of West New Guinea).

He notes further that groups 1, 3, and 10 are probably related to one another.

In 1958 Joseph Greenberg reported on a classification of the

Papuan languages based primarily on the published materials and extensive manuscript material on languages of West New Guinea provided by J. C. Anceaux. This report has not been published, and has probably not influenced any of the studies thus far reported. Greenberg's classification shows nine major groups in New Guinea and an additional five in the areas surrounding New Guinea. It is hard to interpret Cowan's West Papuan Phylum in such a way as to make it compatible with Greenberg's classification. Otherwise, except that Greenberg's groupings are often more inclusive, there seems to be little disagreement with those reported by others. I will take Greenberg's groups in turn, and show approximately how they relate to those groupings proposed in the other works described above.

1. Includes Wurm 1960–61 group 12, and much of Cowan's West Papuan Phylum. Does *not* include northern Halmahera, Timor-Kisar, or Japen languages, however.

2. Approximately identical with Wurm (1960–61) group 11.

3. Includes Wurm group 2, Laycock's Ndu, Cowan's North Papuan Phylum, and other Sepik District languages.

4. Presumably includes Wurm group 9 (= Healey's Ok) plus other languages extending southwest to the coast in West New Guinea.

5. Includes Wurm group 8 plus the languages of Frederick Hendrick Island.

6. Approximately identical with Wurm group 1 plus Wurm group 10.

7. Not mentioned in any of the other studies, approximately coterminous with the Madang District.

8. Approximately identical with Wurm group 3.

9. Includes Wurm groups 4, 6, and 7, and all Papuan languages in the southeastern part of Papua, including Rossel Island.

Greenberg was not able to classify the Kukukuku languages (Wurm's group 5) into any larger grouping. There was one other small group and still another language which likewise could not be classified into any larger grouping.

Outside New Guinea, Greenberg recognizes five additional groupings of Papuan languages, distributed as follows:

(1) British Solomon Islands
(2) Bougainville

(3) New Britain
(4) North Halmahera
(5) Timor-Kisar-Alor.

In the 1958 report, Greenberg commented that certain of these groups appeared certainly to be related to one another. Specifically, he noted an apparent relationship among 7, 8, and 9. He deferred setting up larger groupings, however, until it was possible to determine more precisely their membership. However, in a later report, also unpublished, he turned to the consideration of much more extensive relationships.

The later work to which I refer (Greenberg 1960) was reported to the Association for Asian Studies' annual meeting in 1960. In this report he recognizes a larger grouping, which he calls "Indo-Pacific," including the languages of the Andaman Islands and Tasmania as well as the fourteen groupings mentioned above. In addition, he informs me that there is a good possibility that the Australian languages may ultimately be found to constitute a seventeenth branch of Indo-Pacific.

In sum, research on the relationships of the Papuan languages has begun to acquire momentum on all levels. It is particularly encouraging to note the degree of compatibility among the independent results obtained by different observers.

D. CULTURE HISTORY

GEORGE P. MURDOCK

5. Genetic Classification of the Austronesian Languages: A Key to Oceanic Culture History

This is essentially an expository review article of Isidore Dyen's *The Lexicostatistical Classification of the Austronesian Languages* (New Haven, 1963). I consider it a significant work—one which may conceivably be as revolutionary for Oceanic linguistics and culture history as was the work of Greenberg (1949–54) for the interpretation of African languages and cultures. Since Dyen's monograph is apparently privately printed (it is copyrighted by the author, and no publisher's name appears on the title page), it may be very slow in attracting the readership it deserves. Moreover, it is addressed primarily to professional linguists, devoting much attention to methodological problems and introducing a plethora of new technical terms, so that a nonlinguist like myself can gain a clear conception of its conclusions only by the expenditure of considerable analytic effort. For these reasons, in addition to the potential significance of the work, it seems desirable to summarize its findings in a somewhat simplified form so that Oceanic ethnologists may be made quickly aware of them.

Dyen's study was initiated under the sponsorship of the Tri-Institutional Pacific Program (TRIPP), conducted between 1954 and 1963 jointly by the Bishop Museum of Honolulu, the University of Hawaii, and Yale University on grants from the Carnegie Corporation. It analyzes 371 Austronesian word lists obtained by Dyen and other TRIPP participants from the published literature, from extensive correspondence with missionaries and teachers

SOURCE: Reprinted from *Ethnology*, Vol. 3, No. 2 (1964), pp. 117–26, by permission of the author and publisher.

(especially by William Sturtevant), and from field surveys (especially by George Grace in Melanesia and by collaborators of the Summer Institute of Linguistics in the Philippines). These lists included 196 words and their glosses, based on the 200-word list of Swadesh (1952), from which four words, e.g., "snow" and "ice," were eliminated as inappropriate for the area. Their number was reduced from 371 to 245 by excluding lists from non-Austronesian languages and all lists containing fewer than 150 entries, as well as by combining duplicate lists and those representing mere dialects of the same language (defined as those revealing more than 70 per cent of shared homosemantic cognates). This total represents approximately half of all Austronesian languages, which are estimated to number nearly 500.

The 245 lists were analyzed to ascertain all probable homosemantic cognates, i.e., words presumably cognate in form and clearly similar in meaning, in two or more lists, using "a conservative judgment of cognation." Then, employing an IBM 704 computer, each word on every list was compared with those on every other list—a total of more than 7,000,000 pairs—to ascertain the percentage of homosemantic cognates between each list and each of the other 244.

The next step was to arrange all the languages into presumably genetic groups. Such groupings are called "closed groups" when the lowest percentage of shared cognates between any of its members exceeded the highest shared percentage between any member of the group and any nonmember language by a "critical difference" found significant at the 10 per cent level by a chi-square test, i.e., where the probability of the group's seeming discreteness being due to chance was less than one in ten. Where the significance was lower than this, and the probability that its apparent discreteness might be due to chance was greater, the group is called an "open group." Classifications involving open groups are, of course, to be regarded as highly tentative.

In summarizing Dyen's classification, it will be useful to indicate the different kinds of units of which it is composed. These are:

1. An isolated language, i.e., a language whose shared cognates with other Austronesian languages are few, or random, or otherwise do not warrant its inclusion in a group,

either open or closed, with any other language or languages.

2. A group, i.e., two or more single languages which Dyen's procedures indicate are more closely cognate with one another than with any other Austronesian language. A group will always be designated as "closed" or "open" when so indicated by Dyen.

3. A composite group, i.e., a grouping one or more of whose members is itself a group (or a composite group) according to the same procedures as those by which languages are combined into groups, i.e., treating component groups as though they were single languages. Composite groups will also be designated as "closed" or "open" whenever so specified by Dyen.

4. A possible cognate, i.e., a single language which barely misses being included in a group by Dyen's criteria but which nevertheless shows a particularly high shared percentage of homosemantic cognates with one other language or group, suggesting the possibility that further data and analysis might conceivably classify it with the latter.

Inspection of Dyen's data indicates that, in general, an isolated language has fewer than 15 per cent of shared cognates with any other language, that groups and composite groups are based on percentages usually in excess (and often substantially in excess) of 20 per cent, and that what I call a "possible cognate" normally exhibits a percentage of between 15 and 20.

The above four categories, it should be specified, are mine, not Dyen's. They are adopted to enable me to summarize his results in a simple hierarchical classification, which incorporates his many supplementary comments and suggestions without, I think, doing serious injustice to his many reservations regarding the validity of particular segments of his classificatory scheme. I shall treat the Austronesian languages as a whole as a linguistic "phylum," each of its primary divisions as a linguistic "family," each primary subdivision of a family as a "subfamily," each subdivision of a subfamily as a "branch," and each subdivision of a branch as a "cluster." At every superordinate level in the hierarchy, each unit is, of course, either a "group" or a "composite group" as defined above.

Dyen's major discovery deserves clarification before the classification itself is presented. He finds that approximately three fourths of all the Austronesian languages fall into a single enormous linguistic family with numerous subdivisions. Following his usage, I call this the Malayo-Polynesian family and treat it as a subordinate unit within the Austronesian phylum as a whole. All the remaining Austronesian languages break down into a large number of isolated languages or small groups, none as yet classifiable into larger composite groups comparable to those of the Malayo-Polynesian family and each thus constituting, at least potentially, an independent family co-ordinate with Malayo-Polynesian. These, moreover, are confined almost exclusively to Melanesia, being distributed from New Guinea in the west to the New Hebrides in the east. The Malayo-Polynesian languages are distributed in a great arc, encircling the non-Malayo-Polynesian area on the east, north, and west. This arc extends from Easter Island in the east to Madagascar in the west, thus spanning about 43 per cent of the earth's circumference, and from Formosa in the north to New Zealand in the south, spanning about 40 per cent of the distance between the North and South Poles. The explanation of this curious distribution must be deferred until after the detailed presentation of the linguistic classification.

I have rearranged the classification to highlight Dyen's conclusions and to incorporate his supplementary suggestions, and I have interjected occasional comments of my own. The non-Malayo-Polynesian units (isolated languages and groups) are listed by geographical regions rather than individually. Numbers in parentheses indicate the highest shared percentage of cognates with a language classified in another category.

AUSTRONESIAN PHYLUM

I. Divergent Languages and Groups (each is at least potentially an independent family co-ordinate with Malayo-Polynesian).

A. North Coast of West New Guinea. Four open composite groups: Bigic (15.8 with Philippine Ivatan), Bombarai (14.5 with Moluccan Kuiwai), Geelvink (14.6 with Moluccan Kuiwai), Hollandia (10.7 with Polynesian). Also one isolated language: Waropen (13.6 with Geelvink). Also two possible cognates with Moluccan Kuiwai: Fakfak (19.1 with Kuiwai), Kasira (18.9 with Kuiwai).

B. Northeastern New Guinea. Three isolated languages: Acira (7.3 with Yapese, the lowest shared percentage for any Austronesian language), Hapa (10.8 with Nubami), Nubami (15.2 with Heonesian Mota). Also two possible cognates with Malayo-Polynesian: Tami (18.7 with Palauan), Kairiru, which probably forms a group with Blubblub of the Schouten Islands (19.5 with Polynesian Futuna, 17.7 with Malay, 17.0 with Palauan).

C. Papua and the Massim Area. Two isolated languages: Panyati in the Luisades (15.2 with Massim), Ubir of Collingwood Bay (14.4 with Massim). Also one possible cognate with Motuan: Massim, called the "Tip cluster" by Dyen (17.2 with Motuan), an open composite group composed of two closed groups, Dobuan and Wedauan. Comment: Dyen's list includes so few of the languages of this region that further data are urgently needed before an adequate classification will be possible.

D. Bismarck Archipelago. Four isolated languages: Gunantuna of New Britain (16.4 with Willaumez Bakovi), Peletea of New Britain (16.0 with Willaumez Bakovi), Pililo of New Britain (10.6 with Polynesian), Tomoip of New Britain (11.5 with Rotuman). Also one closed composite group: Uvolic of New Britain (14.6 with Kerebuto). Also four possible cognates with Malayo-Polynesian, all of them isolated languages: Dang of New Hanover (17.4 with Palauan), Kilenge of New Britain (18.0 with Fijian), Mussau of New Hanover (19.1 with Mota), Nalik of New Ireland (18.4 with Fijian). Also one open group: Willaumez of New Britain (19.0 with Kerebuto), which includes Nakanai, Bakovi, and probably Kapore; this is likewise a possible cognate with Malayo-Polynesian, although Dyen specifically classifies it as an independent family co-ordinate with Malayo-Polynesian. Comment: It is unfortunate that Dyen had no lists from the Admiralty Islands, which might provide additional evidence of Malayo-Polynesian, or even specifically Heonesian, penetration of the area.

E. Solomon Islands. Three closed composite groups: Buka (13.6 with Banoni, 13.5 with Kerebuto), Choiseul (13.5 with New Georgian), New Georgian (17.2 with Kerebuto). Also three isolated languages: Banoni of Bougainville (13.6 with Buka), Mono (16.1 with Kerebuto), Zabana of Santa Isabel (9.6 with New Georgian).

F. New Hebrides. One isolated language: Tanna (11.2 with Fijian). Also three possible cognates with Malayo-Polynesian Heonesian: Aneityum (17.2 with Fijian), Male of Malekula (19.6 with Mota), Paama (19.6 with Fijian). Comment: The number of lists from this region is much too small for an adequate classification.

G. New Caledonia and the Loyalty Islands. One closed composite group: South New Caledonian (11.3 with North New Caledonian). Also one open composite group: North New Caledonian (11.3 with Kerebuto, 11.3 with South New Caledonian). Also one open group: Lific of the Loyalty Islands (13.4 with Polynesian).

H. Micronesia. Two isolated languages: Nauruan (16.1 with Carolinian), Yapese (16.1 with Kerebuto).

I. Indonesia. One isolated language: Enggano (12.6 with Murut), which Dyen thinks is probably Hesperonesian despite the low percentage of cognates. Comment: Lists are needed from Mentawei and Nias before the linguistic position of the islands fringing Sumatra on the west can be clarified.

J. Formosa. One closed group: Atayalic (11.8 with Central Formosan), which Dyen thinks is probably Formosan despite the small percentage of cognates.

II. Malayo-Polynesian Family

A. Heonesian Subfamily (21.9 with Hesperonesian Bareic).
    1. New Hebridean Branch. Dyen includes only Efate (28.9 with Fijian, 27.6 with Rotuman), but there are other possible cognates (see I.F above), and a full coverage of the region would doubtless reveal a composite group including Efate.
    2. Fijian (28.9 with Efate, 26.5 with Kerebuto).
    3. Rotuman (27.7 with Polynesian, 27.6 with Efate).

4. Polynesian Branch: This closed composite group shares 27.7 cognates with Rotuman, 27.6 with Efate.
    a. East Polynesian Cluster, including Easter, Hawaiian, Mangarevan, Marquesan, Rarotongan, Tahitian, and Tuamotuan.
    b. Maori.
    c. West Polynesian Cluster, including Ellice (with Ontong Java, Tikopia, and Fila and Futuna in the New Hebrides), Pileni of the Santa Cruz Islands, Rennell, Samoan, and Tongan (with Niue).
    d. Nukuoro, a Polynesian outlier in Micronesia.
    e. Kapingamarangi, another outlier in Micronesia.
5. Mota of the Banks Islands (29.5 with Bauro, 24.5 with Fijian).
6. Gilbertese (23.9 with Carolinian, 23.2 with Polynesian).
7. Carolinian Branch, including Kusaian, Marshallese, Ponapean, and Trukese (with Woleaian). This closed composite group shares 23.9 cognates with Gilbertese, 19.4 with Polynesian. Comment: Dyen merely suspects the affiliation of this group with Heonesian but does not actually include it as such because the percentage of shared cognates falls somewhat below his minimal criterion.
8. Southeastern Solomons Branch. Only one of the four languages listed below (Kerebuto) is included by Dyen in his primary classification, the others being added in supplementary notes. They probably nevertheless form a group.
    a. Bauro of San Cristoval (29.5 with Mota, 28.4 with Kerebuto).
    b. Kerebuto of Guadalcanal (28.4 with Bauro, 26.5 with Fijian).
    c. Lauic of Mala (24.5 with Kerebuto).
    d. Mahaga of Santa Isabel (28.0 with Kerebuto).
9. Possible West Melanesian Branch. Comment: The presence of a number of languages and groups in the Bismarck Archipelago and Northeastern New Guinea showing relatively high percentages of shared cognates with Kerebuto and other Heonesian languages

(see I.C and I.D above) suggests the possibility that one or more separate branches of Heonesian may ultimately be established in this region.

    10. Motuan of the Port Moresby region of Papua (22.1 with Kerebuto). See I.C for the possibility of additions to this branch.

B. Chamorro of the Marianas Islands (20.4 per cent with Hesperonesian Bareic).

C. Palauan (21.1 with Hesperonesian Bareic, 18.7 with Tami of Northeastern New Guinea). Comment: The fact that Palauan and Chamorro, though not particularly close to each other, are both closer to Bareic of Celebes than to any other Austronesian language suggests a connection between the Heonesian and Hesperonesian subfamilies through western Micronesia.

D. Hesperonesian Subfamily.

    1. Celebes Branch. An open composite group embracing two closed groups.

        a. Bareic or Toradja Cluster (23.0 with Philippine Ivatan, 21.1 with Palauan).

        b. Bugic Cluster, including the Buginese and Macassarese (26.5 with Bareic).

    2. Totemboan of north Celebes (21.6 with West Indonesian Batak). An isolated language.

    3. Sangir (39.9 with Philippine Cebuan, 36.0 with West Indonesian Malay and Sasak, 33.0 with Moluccan Sikkic). Comment: This language, from the Sangir Islands between Celebes and Mindanao, is possibly an important link.

    4. Northwest Branch.

        a. Gorontalic Cluster of north Celebes (27.2 with Philippine Cebuan). A closed group.

        b. Ilongot of Luzon (27.5 with Philippine Tagalog).

        c. Philippine Cluster. This is an open composite group embracing all the languages of the Philippines except Ilongot and, in addition, Dusun, Kalabit, Kayan, Kenya, and Murut of northern Borneo.

    5. Sentah of Borneo (26.1 with West Indonesian Dayak).

    6. Malagasy of Madagascar, including the Maanyan of

Borneo (23.9 with West Indonesian Dayak). Inferentially a closed composite group.

7. West Indonesian Branch. An open composite group, to which possibly Enggano also belongs (see I.I).
   a. Sundic Cluster (30.8 with Batak, 29.2 with Cru).
      1′. Dayak of Borneo, including Katingan, Ngadju, and Sampit. A closed group.
      2′. Balinese (33.8 with Madurese).
      3′. Sasak of Lombok (34.1 with Malay).
      4′. Javo-Sumatran, including Javanese, Sundanese, and Malay (with Achinese, Kerintji, Lampong, Madurese, and Minangkabau). An open group.
      5′. Gayo of Sumatra (33.7 with Malay).
   b. Batak Cluster (30.8 with Gayo).
   c. Cru of Vietnam (29.2 with Malay). Comment: It would be interesting to know whether other Malayo-Polynesian languages of this region of mainland Asia, e.g., Cham and Rhade, form a group with Cru.

E. Formosan Subfamily.
   1. Central Formosan Branch (20.1 with Hesperonesian Bareic), including Ami, Bunun, Paiwan, and Thao. An open group.
   2. Atayalic (11.8 with Central Formosan). See I.J for the problematic position of Atayalic.

F. Moluccan Subfamily (20.0 with Batak). An open group.
   1. Kuiwai of southwestern New Guinea (20.6 with Letic). See I.A for possible additional members.
   2. Sekar of western New Guinea (21.1 with Letic).
   3. Ambic Branch of Ambon and Ceram (23.8 with Buru, 21.4 with Sumba). A closed group.
   4. Buru (23.8 with Ambic).
   5. Fordatic of Kei and Tanimbar (27.3 with Tettum). A closed group.
   6. Letic Branch of Kisar and Leti (27.2 with Letic, 25.8 with Sikkic).
   7. Tettum of Timor (31.3 with Sikkic, 27.2 with Letic).
   8. Sikkic Branch of Solor and Flores (31.3 with Tettum, 25.8 with Letic).

9. Endeh of Flores (30.8 with Sikkic, 24.1 with Letic).
10. Sumba (23.2 with Sikkic, 21.4 with Ambic).

"There can be little reasonable doubt," asserts Dyen (1963:81), "about the implications of the lexicostatistical classification for the history of the [Malayo-Polynesian] migrations." The crucial facts, he points out, are three in number:

1. The concentration of closely related languages in the west. He advances several reasons for discounting the low percentage of shared cognates for Enggano and Atayalic (Dyen 1963: 82–83).
2. The concentration of closely related languages in the east, including all of Polynesia and most of Micronesia.
3. The concentration of relatively remotely related languages in Melanesia.

The first conclusion drawn by Dyen (1963:83) from these facts is "that the Malayopolynesian languages have their origin ultimately in some area of Melanesia." This is based on the hypothesis, first propounded by Sapir (1916) in assigning a northern origin to the far-flung Athapaskan family and generally accepted by linguists ever since (cf. the derivation of the Bantu languages from West Africa in Greenberg 1949:309–337), that the homeland of the ancestral speakers of any group of related languages is likely to have been located in or near the region exhibiting the greatest genetic diversity. In the instance of Malayo-Polynesian, perhaps the best case can be made for an original homeland in the vicinity of the New Hebrides and Banks Islands.

On the assumption of some such place of origin, Dyen (1963:83–84) postulates a series of specific migrations to account for the present enormous area of distribution of the Malayo-Polynesian-speaking peoples. These are:

1. A migration of Heonesian-speaking peoples northeastward into Polynesia, probably by way of Fiji.
2. A westward migration of the Carolinian languages through Micronesia.
3. A westward migration, implied but not expressly stated by Dyen, through the southeastern Solomon Islands to the Bismarck Archipelago and coastal New Guinea.
4. A westward migration of Moluccan-speaking peoples through eastern Indonesia as far as Flores and Sumba.

5. A northwestward migration from western Micronesia to Formosa.
6. A migration of Hesperonesian peoples via Celebes to the Philippines and Borneo, and thence to Madagascar, the Greater Sunda Islands, and the mainland of Southeast Asia.

This reconstruction obviously inverts all earlier theories of the migrations of the Malayo-Polynesian peoples, which invariably derive them from China, India, or Southeast Asia, through Indonesia, and then via either Micronesia or Melanesia to Polynesia. It disagrees less drastically with more recent hypotheses, e.g., those of Grace (1955, 1959). It is not my task to reconcile these discrepancies, or to either support or criticize Dyen's findings. It does seem worthwhile, however, to assume for the time being that Dyen's conclusions are essentially correct and, as an ethnologist, to indicate some of the modifications we would have to make in our current thinking to accommodate them.

First, we should presumably be forced to abandon attempts to discover genetic relationships between Austronesian and other linguistic families in Southeast Asia, such as Thai-Kadai. South China, the presumptive homeland of the latter, is altogether too remote from Melanesia.

Second, we shall have to find some way of filling the linguistic hiatus in Indonesia and the Philippines prior to the arrival of the Malayo-Polynesian immigrants. Perhaps we can fill it in part by an extension into the area of Negrito and Veddoid peoples speaking Mon-Khmer languages akin to the surviving Semang and Sakai of interior Malaya, which would be consistent with the survival of such "interior marginal" peoples as the various Negrito groups in the Philippines and the Caucasoid "Proto-Malay" groups inhabiting the interior of the larger Sunda islands, e.g., the Kubu of Sumatra, Punan of Borneo, and Toala of Celebes (see Kennedy 1942). And perhaps we can also people the region in part with peoples speaking Indo-Pacific languages—a linguistic phylum postulated by Greenberg in unpublished memoranda to include the Australians and Tasmanians, the Andamanese, the Papuans of New Guinea, and the non-Austronesian-speaking peoples in the Solomon Islands and in Halmahera and Timor in the Moluccas. Physical anthropological data on Timor in particular and the Moluccas in general seem consistent with the former extension of Australians and Papuans of Indo-Pacific speech into this region.

Third, we shall have to assume that Melanesia lacked agriculture at the time of the original differentiation of the Austronesian languages and even at the time of the westward migrations of the Malayo-Polynesian peoples, though not, presumably, at the later period of the migrations into Polynesia. Dyen has elsewhere (Dyen 1962:46) pointed out the great time depth of Malayo-Polynesian as compared with Indo-European:

> If we adopt the commonly suggested date 2500 B.C. as the beginning of the Indo-European spread, it follows that the Malayopolynesians began their migrations before this date and possibly well before it.

Even within the Hesperonesian subfamily in Indonesia, there is lexicostatistical evidence (Dyen 1953) that Maanyan had not become separated from Dayak and Javo-Sumatran in the general area of Borneo until about the end of the second millennium B.C., which would push back still farther the arrival of the Hesperonesians in the west. This must almost certainly antedate the spread of Southeast Asian agriculture and its major crops (bananas, breadfruit, taro, and yams) into Indonesia.

We must consequently assume that both the original Austronesians and the early Malayo-Polynesians had a subsistence economy based primarily upon fishing, shellfishing, and the gathering of fruits from plants like pandanus and the coconut palm whose spread into the Pacific did not require human intervention. Such peoples as the Gilbertese and Marshallese still live almost exclusively on these products. In parts of New Guinea and western Melanesia the sago palm would have provided an additional staple; even today, sago is nearly always gathered rather than cultivated.

To account for the Malayo-Polynesian migrations in the insular environment of Oceania, where islands are often separated from their nearest neighbors by long stretches of open water, the migrants would have had to possess a relatively complex culture, specifically one which included developed water craft and advanced navigational skills. The outrigger canoe, which is distributed from Polynesia to Madagascar (Dixon 1928:75–104), is probably the most seaworthy and maneuverable craft devised by man until recent times. Moreover, the Malayo-Polynesians command truly remarkable navigational techniques, such as the "stick charts" of the Marshallese (Winkler 1901) and the "star compass" of the Carolinians (Goodenough 1953), with which they travel with confidence over distances of hundreds of miles out of sight of land. It is by no means unprecedented for nonagricultural peoples to have seagoing canoes which they use for extended voyages, as is attested by the American Indians of the Northwest Coast (Drucker 1955:63–67) and the Chumash of aboriginal California (Kroeber 1925:550–568). The case of the Calusa of Florida (Goggin and Sturtevant 1964), indeed, demonstrates that it is even possible for a nonagricultural people to possess a complex political structure and to co-operate in the erection of monumental structures.

The mere possession of outrigger canoes and of advanced navigational techniques, however, could not account for the occurrence of extended migrations. There would have had to be, in addition, a very powerful motive to travel and explore. The most likely such motive would be trade. It is thus perhaps no accident that extensive overseas trade is reported very widely in the regions occupied by Malayo-Polynesian peoples. A few striking examples must suffice: the extraordinary development of local specialization and interisland exchange in the Santa Cruz Islands (Davenport 1964); the importance of the "kula ring" in the Massim area (Malinowski 1922); the flotillas of canoes which annually sailed the 400 miles from Woleai to Guam to trade for iron which the Chamorro had obtained from the Spaniards (Murdock *et al.* 1944:131–133); and the fact that the inhabitants of Borneo were trading with East Africa by the time of Christ and with China by way of the Philippines and Borneo even earlier (Murdock 1959:208–210, 214–215).

Finally, to reconcile Dyen's conclusions, it would be necessary to modify prevailing views as to conditions and events in Indonesia at and after the time of the arrival of the Hesperonesians. Since they themselves were preagricultural, as we have seen, their predecessors must also have been preagricultural or the newcomers could not have established themselves. We must assume that they did so on the basis of their superior maritime and mercantile skills. We must also assume that they traveled farther and, somewhere in Southeast Asia, encountered peoples of a different language and superior culture who were cultivating the root and tree crops of the Southeast Asian agricultural complex. From them they would presumably have borrowed these crops, together with domesticated pigs and fowl, and have carried them to Indonesia and the Philippines, and thence, through their network of overseas trade relations, to Melanesia, Micronesia, and Polynesia, where they thereafter became firmly established.

We would have to postulate further, on the basis of the recent racial, cultural, and linguistic complexion of the area, that the mainland peoples would have followed the trade routes established by the Malayo-Polynesians and have infiltrated Indonesia and the Philippines, bringing with them their Mongoloid ("Deutero-Malay") genes and such features of their more complex civilization as iron, rice, the water buffalo, and ultimately writing. This infiltration must have been a mere trickle at first, gradually swelling to greater proportions. It could not have been a sudden mass migration, for this would have introduced new languages—possibly Mon-Khmer or Thai-Kadai. The movement must have been sufficiently gradual so that the newcomers could absorb the speech, and to some extent the culture, of their Malayo-Polynesian predecessors.

Thereafter the picture is clear. Continued contacts with the Chinese disseminated fine porcelain wares, gongs, and other valued trade goods widely through the Philippines and Indonesia; contacts directly or indirectly with India introduced Hinduism and Buddhism; those with the Arabs introduced Islam; those with the European colonial powers brought increasing familiarity with the elements of Western civilization.

Speaking personally, as one who has had considerable experience in Oceanic ethnology, I feel that the readjustments in our traditional thinking about Pacific culture history, which the acceptance of conclusions like Dyen's would demand, present no necessarily insuperable difficulties.

EDWIN N. FERDON

6. Polynesian Origins

When the raft "Kon-Tiki" crunched down on the reef off Raroia atoll in 1946, the story made the front page. Later, the voyage was the subject of a best-selling book, and the moving picture of the expedition won an Oscar award. To the skipper of the raft, Thor Heyerdahl, these were fringe benefits, for the real goal had been to prove to a world of doubting and experiment-shy anthropologists that the prehistoric Peruvians, at least, had had seaworthy craft capable of taking them to Polynesian islands. The idea that American Indians might have reached, and even populated, some of the Polynesian islands was not new. However, the concept had been laid aside because it was believed, though not shown, that no adequate craft had existed in prehistoric America and that the American Indians lacked the necessary navigational skills.

If the joys of successful experimentation were pleasant, they were equally short, for with the publication of his theoretical book (Heyerdahl 1952), the skipper of the "Kon-Tiki" opened a Pandora's box of conservative, tradition-bound anthropological argument.

The controversy that ensued over East versus West as *the* source of the people and culture of Polynesia has tended not only to obscure the complexity of the problem, but to conceal the numerous other possibilities. Although this controversy has stimulated research on Polynesia, an unfortunate secondary effect

SOURCE: Reprinted from *Science*, Vol. 141, No. 3580 (1963), pp. 499–505 (Copyright 1963 by the American Association for the Advancement of Science), by permission of the author and publisher.

threatens the eventual results of these new and vigorous efforts. There is a tendency to interpret new knowledge in terms of the old East-versus-West argument, as if the twain should never meet, and as if no other interpretations were possible. To continue within this rigid frame will mean losing the healthy effect of re-vitalization which the initial controversy precipitated.

The origin, or origins, of the people and culture of Polynesia has been the concern of seafarers, missionaries, and scientists since the days of Captain Cook. The range of theories is only slightly exceeded by the variety of evidence mustered to support particular concepts. Mainland Asia, Indonesia, Melanesia, Micronesia, the Philippines, and the west coasts of the Americas have all been proposed as possible points of departure for one or more migration waves into this island world.

By the beginning of World War II, anthropological interest in Polynesia, especially as regards origins, had waned noticeably. Perhaps because the Bernice P. Bishop Museum in Honolulu dominated the field of Polynesian anthropology, the views of its director, Sir Peter H. Buck, were generally accepted as the best that could be arrived at from available data.

According to this widely accepted pre-"Kon-Tiki" concept, the Polynesians originally were a group of people of one composite race located somewhere in Indonesia (Buck 1960:26). They were thought to have broken away from their original homeland at some early date, and, with their then existing culture complex, to have migrated in one or more waves to their present island domain by way of Micronesia. According to other versions, they migrated along the north coast of New Guinea (Buck 1960:43). Except for minor Fijian influence in extreme western Polynesia and for certain food transmissions from Fiji (Buck 1960:310, 316), these people were seen as having evolved biologically and culturally in isolation until their discovery by Europeans.

Although broad, ethnologically based culture areas had been established for Polynesia, their existence had been explained as in no way reflecting occasional and varied outside influences but rather as the result of splinter migrations that broke away from the original migratory band. As a starting point for their own isolated cultural evolution, it was thought, these splinter groups had taken with them the bulk of the cultural content of the original band, plus the various elements which had evolved locally up to the time of departure. Thus, the difference between one culture area and another was considered to reflect the period when each broke from the main (or an ancillary) migratory body, the cultural inventory at the time of the break, and the internal cultural evolution of each splinter group after its isolation on some other island or group of islands (Buck 1960:309). It was recognized that there was cultural exchange, other than of domesticated plants and animals, *within* Polynesia, but apparent parallels in traits beyond this insular area were regarded as the result of independent invention or of parallel development.

So firmly entrenched was the foregoing concept that the lack of supporting evidence in subsurface archaeological excavations made before 1950 was brushed aside, with the simple statement that such deposits were too shallow and too recent to be of use. It was this archaeologically unsupported concept of a single group origin from one location and of isolated, independent development that Heyerdahl challenged, with his "Kon-Tiki" journey, and his theory of an American Indian origin. This challenge, however, was a case of the pot calling the kettle black, for Heyerdahl (1952:705–07), also without supporting archaeological evidence, concluded that two specific areas on the continent of South America, Peru and the northwest coast, were dominant sources of Polynesian population and culture.

Although parts of Heyerdahl's book suffer from his having been a novice in anthropology, his exhaustive coverage of the pertinent literature brought together a vast amount of widely dispersed information on the problem. Although some of his arguments could not be regarded as valid, others, if they did not wholly support his specific migration theory, certainly appeared to uphold a thesis that contact between prehistoric Polynesia and America had been made. Also, his trip aboard the raft had shown that the sailors and craft involved in such contacts were not necessarily Polynesian. If many of his arguments were not fully acceptable to anthropologists, his discussions of the weaknesses of other theories were sound enough. These discussions cast a brilliant light on the inadequacy of the existing data to support the thesis that the Polynesians were, racially and culturally, a single homogeneous group.

Of all the types of evidence yet brought to bear upon the question of human migration, probably the strongest has been lin-

guistic evidence. The Polynesian language has been placed by
linguists in the Malayo-Polynesian family. Peoples speaking these
related tongues are spread in a near-continuous pattern from
easternmost Polynesia westward through Melanesia (except for
the interior of New Guinea) and Indonesia and across the Indian
Ocean to Madagascar. Northward, related languages are spoken
by certain peoples in Southeast Asia and the Philippines (Kroeber 1948:215–16). Firm as this evidence would appear to be,
reflecting, as it must, a strong influence throughout Polynesia of
people speaking a common language related to languages spoken
to the west, we know that that language is culturally transmitted
and that, therefore, one language may be supplanted by another
in a variety of ways. Thus, although the linguistic proof of a connection to the west seems sound enough, it is not acceptable per
se as proof that no other people existed and that no other languages were ever spoken on any or all of the islands of Polynesia.

The use of genetic information was another approach through
which it was originally hoped the question of Polynesian origins
would be resolved. With the increasing use of blood typing in
genetic studies, it was felt that here, at last, was a biological
approach that might more clearly indicate the probable source,
or sources, of the Polynesian people. Contrary to the linguistic
evidence, the results of a study of blood groups and gene frequencies of the Cook Islanders, made by R. J. Simmons, J. J.
Graydon, N. M. Semple, and Ernest I. Fry (1955:687), prompted
these workers to state, "The blood groups and gene frequencies
presented here for the Cook Islanders do not invalidate the conclusions reached, that there is a close blood genetic relationship
between American Indians and Polynesians, and that no similar
relationship is evident when Polynesians are compared with Melanesians, Micronesians, and Indonesians, except mainly in adjacent
areas of direct contact." Later, after working with blood samples
from eastern Polynesia collected by the Norwegian Archaeological
Expedition to Easter Island and the east Pacific, Simmons and
Graydon (1955:365) concluded, "The results obtained are comparable with those previously reported for Maoris of New Zealand and Cook Islanders, and in a number of characters are
comparable with some South American Indian tribes. No such
similarity is evident when comparisons are made with Melanesians, Micronesians and Indonesians."

The results of this latter study have been challenged on the grounds that the blood samples taken by the Norwegian expedition were not from "pure" Polynesians (Suggs 1960:214), but such criticism is basically fatuous. In view of the two hundred years of contact with foreign sailors and travelers and the sexual license common in Polynesia, who could honestly expect, let alone prove, purity for any Polynesian sample? Of far more significance, granted the impurity of the samples, is the question of why the results showed apparent affinity with the American Indians. Obviously, as Robert C. Suggs (1960:35, 216) and E. Goldschmidt (1961:99), and more recently Simmons (1962:209), have pointed out, it is not enough to determine the present blood groups and gene frequencies for Polynesians, and for other surrounding racial groups, and from these comparative data draw conclusions about racial relationships. Processes of microevolution, such as genetic drift, mutation, and selection—especially those selective factors that have operated in historic times through the decimation of native populations by European diseases—must be determined and taken into account. Even if the difficulties originally encountered in determining blood types from prehistoric bone material should be resolved, the microevolutionary forces must be taken into account before much more can be said about the biological relationships of the Polynesian peoples.

While claims and counterclaims were being made, and the data were being said to support one theory or its opposite, one of the primary sources of basic evidence, subsurface archaeology, had been virtually neglected. Prior to World War II, only two excavations, one on Tonga (McKern 1929) and the other in New Zealand (Duff 1950), had been made. This lack of professional interest stemmed in part from the difficulty of access to the numerous islands. To a larger extent, however, it stemmed from a misconception, current as late as 1953: "sites are shallow, refuse is sparse, and there seems to have been relatively little change in culture through time" (Rouse 1953:58). However, with the revitalization of research in the Pacific, it was realized that, shallow or not, Polynesian archaeological deposits must be excavated, and that, for purposes of comparison, such activity must be extended into neighboring areas.

In 1950, as part of a University of Hawaii course in archaeological techniques, Kenneth P. Emory and several of his students undertook the excavation of a series of shelters on Oahu (Emory and Sinoto 1961). In 1953 Heyerdahl, with two archaeologists, conducted a brief expedition to the Galapagos Islands, where, to the surprise of everyone, prehistoric Peruvian pottery was found (Heyerdahl and Skjölsvold 1956). Two years later Heyerdahl moved his archaeological activities directly into Polynesia by organizing and financing a major expedition to conduct excavations on Easter Island and several other islands of eastern Polynesia (Heyerdahl and Smith 1961). No sooner had this expedition gotten under way than the American Museum of Natural History sent Suggs to the Marquesas (Suggs 1961); then, somewhat later, Roger Green undertook excavations in the Gambier Islands and the Society Islands. During this same period, New Zealanders became increasingly interested in what their country could reveal of Polynesian prehistory. They now are excavating on other Polynesian islands as well. Other excavation has been undertaken by archaeologists of various nationalities, in neighboring Melanesia and Micronesia. Today, more archaeological expeditions than have ever before been concerned with Oceania are either in the planning stage or already in the field.

As of today, it would be foolhardy to attempt to summarize our knowledge of Polynesian prehistory on the basis of the excavated record. The record is excessively spotty, and the sites are separated by hundreds of miles of ocean; moreover, the results of numerous archaeological excavations now being made are certain to alter the present view, which, at best, is a delicate and highly mobile frame of reference.

Thanks to dating by the radiocarbon technique, we now know that Polynesian prehistory goes back farther than had previously been estimated, and that it does evince change through time. A date of 122 B.C. has been established for human occupation in the Marquesas at the eastern edge of Polynesia, and a date of A.D. 9 has been obtained for Samoa, at the western extremity. An early date of occupation of 46 B.C. has been obtained for neighboring Fiji, and it seems reasonable to expect at least temporally comparable evidence of human occupation on Samoa. Far to the north, in Hawaii, a possibly valid date of A.D. 124 may indicate that this outpost of Polynesia was settled at about the beginning of the Christian Era. To the south, in New Zealand, where thirty-eight radiocarbon samples have been obtained, the earliest date of occupation so far obtained is around A.D. 1000 (Shutler 1961).

Because much of Polynesian material culture was of a perishable nature, the number of artifacts that have remained in the soil is quite limited. Pottery, which readily lends itself to change in form and decoration and is, therefore, especially useful in the finer cross-dating of one archaeological deposit with another, so far appears to be largely restricted to western Polynesia. However, the pioneering efforts of Roger S. Duff (1959) of New Zealand in classifying the numerous stone adzes of Polynesia will, as their stratigraphic relationship is gradually determined through excavation, aid in determining cultural relationships. Careful study of the stratigraphic sequence of fishhooks from excavations in Hawaii (Emory, Bonk, Sinoto 1959) has already shown that the fishhook is another artifact whose change through time may aid in determining island relationships at different periods. No doubt the stone *poi* (fermented taro root paste) pounders of central and marginal Polynesia will eventually prove of equal value. On Easter Island, where no deep culture-bearing deposits were found, archaeologists turned to excavation of the great ceremonial platforms called *ahu*. Here they found that, as with Mesoamerican ceremonial structures, various platforms had been covered or modified through time, so that the shape and variety of the architectural features provided a means of interpreting changing religious functions and of estimating relative dates (Mulloy 1961:93–180; Smith 1961:181–219; Ferdon 1961:223–29). Thus, although the available archaeological record is not so rich in Polynesia as in other parts of the world, nevertheless, the record in the islands can provide ample evidence on which to reconstruct the culture of Oceania.

PROBLEMS OF INTERPRETATION

Undoubtedly a mass of archaeological information will be revealed in the next several years, and thus the greatest problem facing the culture historian is proper interpretation of the data.

Anthropologists, being essentially landlubbers, have long interpreted the concept that an ocean is a formidable barrier to mean that it is an absolute barrier to all but a highly specialized few. Over the years this restricted interpretation has limited the search for potential sources of cultural inspiration for any given primitive group to other societies on connected, or immediately accessible, land masses. Thus, the anthropological search for possible prehistoric contacts between the Old World and the New, for prehistoric American-Polynesian contacts, and for prehistoric Asiatic-American over-water contacts has been restricted by insistence on the kind of proof that could be found only where a more or less continuous contact, or a series of chain-linked contacts, had occurred between two cultures over an extended period. I do not question the general validity of a requirement for proof of long-continued contact, but the requirement is unrealistic where the route of dispersal involves the crossing of great oceans, especially where one-way voyages may have occurred.

That one-way accidental voyages did occur within Polynesia has been amply documented by Andrew Sharp (1957) and G. M. Dening (1962). Also, historic records of derelict junks encountered in the north Pacific as far east as Mexico, many of which carried survivors after months of drifting (Stokes 1934), testify to the fact that accidental dispersal of mankind in the Pacific has occurred. This is not to say that there were no planned voyages into, and within, Polynesia, but, as Sharp has demonstrated from historic documentation, the Polynesians were largely limited, geographically, to island groups that they had the navigational ability to reach. Once the Polynesian mariner had passed these limits, as a result of storms, wind shifts, or other natural hazards, he was essentially lost, and his final destination was a matter of happenstance.

In addition to unplanned voyages into distant seas, there were probably planned voyages into the unknown, made for a variety of reasons, including the basic one of overpopulation. Unless there was cultural control of population, overpopulation could have become a cyclic phenomenon in this island world and thus have induced a series of migratory resettlements. That the Polynesians did make such planned voyages into the unknown, with the full knowledge that they did not have the navigational skill to return, and that only by chance could they do so, is indicated by the inventory of human and cultural cargo they carried on some of their voyages. This inventory appears to have included as much of the homeland cultural complex as possible, so that a new settlement could be made with the fewest possible adjustments (Buck 1960:39–41, 68–69, 99–100).

In terms of cultural diffusion into, and throughout, Polynesia, the two types of voyager—those who migrated intentionally and those who migrated unintentionally—are distinguished by the fact that the former carried with them as much of their human and cultural heritage as they could, whereas the latter brought to an island refuge only their personal knowledge and concepts of their original cultural world, and any objects which happened to be aboard the vessel when it was carried into unknown seas. Thus, the intentional landing of a group of immigrants on an uninhabited island assured the transplanting of a fairly complete cultural inventory of the parent complex. If the island were already settled, such a landing offered a choice of culture traits. This was a far greater cultural contribution than could be made by a solitary voyager who made an unplanned landing.

It appears likely that at least one population group which entered Polynesia and spoke a Malayo-Polynesian language developed, or maintained, a cultural tradition of intentional migratory voyaging. Because this tradition was probably maintained over several centuries, a basic language and culture were successfully implanted throughout the Polynesian islands. However, as new cultural information is revealed through excavation, it must be kept in mind that other population groups may have been equally successful at an earlier date and may later have been wiped out, subjugated, or amalgamated.

Because intentional migrants would tend to transplant a variety of trait complexes, the similarity of complexes between distant Polynesian islands has been accepted as proof of prehistoric contact and attendant diffusion. Where a variety of specialized developments on various islands do not fit into the total assemblage of interfunctioning traits, they have too often been interpreted as the result of independent invention. However, it is precisely this type of specialized characteristic, which seemingly does not fit into basic Polynesian culture, that could reflect the influence of single voyagers who made unplanned landings.

Although it is seldom realized, there is a parallel between the chance dispersal of animals and the chance dispersal of man onto Pacific islands. Just as faunal associations that spread to an island by the accidental transferal of occasional individuals exhibit an imbalance, so cultural influences that spread in a similar manner can result in the incorporation of one or more culture traits into an already existing, but wholly different, functional complex. Thus, individual components of such a complex may resemble components of a complex in another area of the Pacific and indicate contact and diffusion, even though the complexes are quite different. With cultural as with faunal dispersals of this accidental type, there is no reason to believe that such trait diffusion is not "relatively random or indeterminate." With man as with faunal associations, "groups that might cross do not necessarily do so; crossings may be long delayed and are scattered through time; and the sequence seems to depend in part on chance" (Simpson 1962:24).

Of course, the insular dispersal of prehistoric man does not wholly fit the pattern of faunal accidental dispersal. Unlike other animals, man has the power to set out intentionally upon the sea, to extend his period of survival by living off the sea, and, weather and currents permitting, to direct his course to the extent of his navigational ability. Because of these factors, the chances of man's reaching and occupying island after island, even in the vast Pacific, are considerably greater than the chances of faunal dispersal from island to island by natural means, and the time required would of course have been very much less.

ENVIRONMENT AND HUMAN DISPERSALS

The essential environmental requirement for the inception of either a migratory or an accidental voyage is a littoral where a maritime culture can arise. However, the factors that precipitate the two kinds of voyage are quite different. The planned voyage presupposes navigational knowledge, equipment for sailing on deep waters, and an urge to seek new lands. Ascertaining the possible points of origin of such planned voyages in the Pacific is basically a problem of determining the locations of prehistoric advanced maritime cultures bordering on the Pacific. In this respect the problem is one of anthropological interpretation and appraisal of circum-Pacific cultures. Such an appraisal has hardly been begun.

As for accidental voyages, these could originate within any maritime culture where there was any kind of seagoing craft. Thus, the possible points of origin of accidental voyages into Polynesia are much more numerous and cover a much greater geographic area than the possible points of origin of intentional voyages. The craft of many primitive maritime societies were suitable only for inshore cruising, but the fact remains that such craft could have been blown into open seas. Although the mortality rate would have been high, there would always have been a chance of survival. Animals have been able to survive on floating trees and other objects (Zimmerman 1948:57), and certainly primitive fishermen, with their knowledge of the sea and their ability to live off it, would stand a considerably greater chance of survival.

Although maritime cultures have developed around the greater

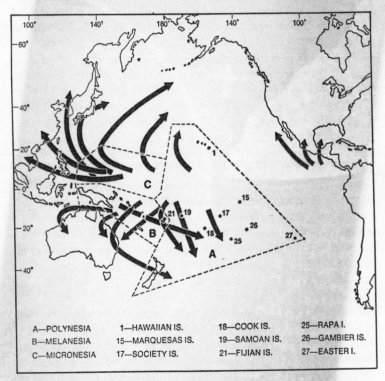

FIGURE 1. A greatly simplified representation of paths of hurricanes in the Pacific. [The generalized routes of the hurricanes were plotted from information in S. S. Visher, *Bernice P. Bishop Museum Bull. No. 20* (1924), and O. W. Freeman, in *Geography of the Pacific* (Wiley, New York, 1951).]

part of the perimeter of the Pacific, not all of these culture areas are equally likely points of origin of accidental voyages, because winds of the strength to blow a vessel into unknown seas occur less frequently in some of these areas than in others. Principal among such winds are hurricanes, or typhoons, and gales.

The dominant area of hurricane occurrence in the Pacific is in the western part, immediately to the north and to the south of the equator (Fig. 1). Most of the hurricanes that occur to the north of the equator develop over an area between 120 and 160 degrees west longitude. Passing to the north of New Guinea, the Celebes, and Borneo, some of the hurricanes move west and north, striking the mainland of Southeast Asia. Others move first to the west and then veer north and northeast, striking the coast of China, the Philippines, and Japan before advancing into the north Pacific.

To the south of the equator, hurricanes develop over an area from 160 degrees west longitude to 160 degrees east longitude. These pass over the southern islands of Melanesia, east of New Guinea; over the southwestern area of Polynesia; and, to the west, over Australia. Far less frequent but of equal importance are the hurricanes that occur off the Pacific coast of Guatemala and Mexico, as well as those that occur occasionally well off the coast of South America (Visher 1925:56–60).

Less violent than hurricanes, but capable of driving a ship into unknown seas, are gales with winds of 43½ kilometers (27 miles) per hour or more. Figure 2 shows the extreme equatorward distribution of those areas of the Pacific in which winds of this force, or greater, have made up 5 per cent or more of the wind observations (at 12 noon, Greenwich time) for any single month of the year.

The area from New Guinea to Borneo is largely free of such winds, as it is of hurricanes. However, the Asiatic mainland from Southeast Asia northward, as well as the islands of Micronesia and the northern Philippines to Japan and northward, is subject to such winds during at least one month of the year. To the south, the equatorward limits of winds of fresh-gale strength extend from, roughly, Cape Flattery, Australia, northeastward around New Guinea to the Solomon Islands, and eastward in a sinuous line to include most of the southern Polynesian islands south of 12 degrees south latitude. Along the coast of South America, the

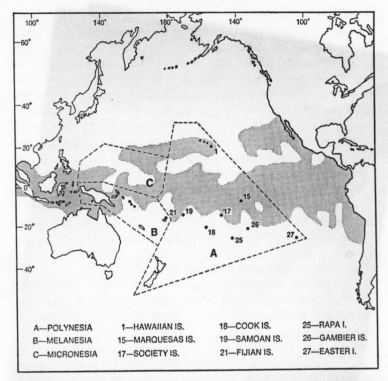

FIGURE 2. Average maximum equatorward distribution of gales of 43½ kilometers (27 miles) per hour, or more, in the Pacific. [The data were obtained from W. F. McDonald, *Atlas of Climatic Charts of the Oceans* (U. S. Weather Bureau, Washington, D.C., 1938).]

equatorward limits of such winds in the Southern Hemisphere is in the approximate latitude of Santiago, Chile. In the Northern Hemisphere the winds have a continuous distribution along the coast from Alaska down to the vicinity of Santa Barbara, California, and there is an isolated area of occurrence at, and to both sides of, the Isthmus of Tehuantepec.

From the premise that weather phenomena of this type are the principal cause of accidental voyages, we may logically reason that the likelihood of occurrence of such voyages is greatest in those areas of the Pacific where both hurricanes and gales occur. Thus we conclude that Southeast Asia, the Philippines, the lands washed by the East China Sea between Formosa and Japan, the lands touched by the Sea of Japan, the east coast of Australia, and Melanesia south and east of the Solomons are the most likely areas of origin of accidental voyages, as both typhoons and gales occur frequently in these regions. Almost as likely an area of origin, in the east Pacific, is the south coast of Oaxaca and Chiapas, Mexico. Hurricanes occasionally occur north of this region to Baja California, and gales occur along the West Coast of the United States and Canada, roughly from Santa Barbara northward, and along the south-central coast of Chile from Santiago to the Chonos Archipelago. Thus, these coasts might have been areas of origin of accidental voyages.

At this point one is tempted to postulate that the Asiatic areas where hurricanes and gales are most frequent are *the* sources of the people and culture of Polynesia. They may indeed be the dominant sources. However, the eastern coast of the Pacific has its area of storms, and since it is accidental dispersal that we are considering, these areas also must be considered.

Disregarding planned voyages, we can see that any Pacific-coast area where hurricanes or gales are frequent, and where man has had a maritime orientation, might have been a source of Polynesian culture. Whether or not it was, when (if at all) its influence was felt, and where the island that received this influence was located are matters that can be determined only through comparison of the culture history and cultural remains of these many coastal and island localities, and through study of the ocean currents and winds between these coasts and islands.

The course of a vessel on a planned voyage, as well as that of one accidentally sailing unknown seas, would have been largely dependent upon the natural elements. Ocean currents and major wind systems probably would have governed the course of the vessel that was lost and would have influenced the choice of direction in the case of a fully operational primitive craft. Heyerdahl (1963) has justifiably laid great stress on the effects of these systems in determining the principal over-water routes of prehistoric migrants. However, remarkably little attention has been paid to the opportunities presented by the monsoonal wind-shifts of the western Pacific and the spiraling winds that accompany the eastward passage of cyclonic storms in both hemispheres. In the Northern Hemisphere these winds blow in a counterclockwise path around the center of a low-pressure storm, so that winds on the equatorial quarter of a cyclonic disturbance tend to blow from the west or northwest—that is, in a direction opposite to that of the easterlies, which they frequently displace in the subtropics and higher latitudes of the tropics. In the Southern Hemisphere the circular path of cyclonic winds is clockwise, resulting in a similar displacement of marginal easterlies by westerly winds. Thus, in the subtropics of both hemispheres, in spite of opposing ocean currents and the normally dominant easterlies, a craft could be borne to the east by a cyclonic disturbance (Sharp 1957:88; Zimmerman 1948:57). Thus, the assumption that simple craft could have made a west-to-east crossing only in the cold, higher latitudes of westerly winds and currents is not valid. Because the dominance of the easterlies in the higher tropical latitudes is a seasonal matter, I have indicated in Figure 3, by directional arrows, those regions where easterly winds account for 60 per cent or more of the observations for every month of the year. These areas, then, may be said to be virtually dominated by the easterlies the year round; undirected craft entering these regions would normally follow the path of the arrows, while craft under sail could also move easily to the north or south. However, on the poleward edges of these easterlies, movement to either the east or the west would have been possible, depending upon the season. That primitive sailing craft could have made headway against the easterlies is not denied, but to do so would have been time-consuming, and it is obvious that, in sailing an unknown sea, the more ocean the vessel covers each day, the greater is the chance of discovering land and, therefore, the greater is the chance of survival.

Although one might reasonably expect those Polynesian islands that are closest (geographically, and from the standpoint of wind and current) to a continental mass to exhibit the greatest number of cultural parallels, islands are, of course, but dots in the Pacific. Migrants as well as involuntary voyagers might unknowingly pass them by and transplant themselves a thousand miles deeper into the Pacific. In this respect Polynesia differs from most other culture areas of the world, for the possible sources of human cultural influences, on any Polynesian island, are not necessarily influences from adjacent areas. For this reason, culture traits or complexes may not exhibit a continuous island-to-island distribution from their point of origin.

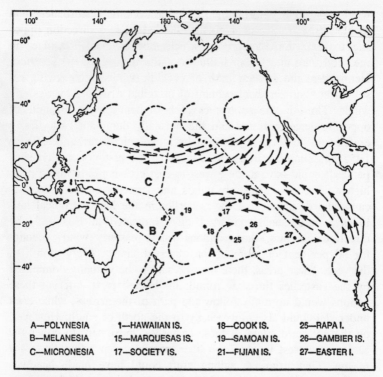

FIGURE 3. Map showing the approximate equatorward limits (curved, dashed arrows) of the westerly-wind effect from cyclonic storms in the Pacific during the period of low sun in each hemisphere. The solid arrows indicate the extent and the average direction of the easterlies during at least 60 per cent of every month of the year. [Data for the compilation of dominant easterly winds were obtained from W. F. McDonald, *Atlas of Climatic Charts of the Oceans* (U. S. Weather Bureau, Washington, D.C., 1938).]

Because there are many possible sources of Polynesian origins and many possible routes of travel, we can never expect to gain a complete picture of this maritime activity. We can learn a good deal, however, through greater understanding of the nature of such voyages and through appreciation of the fact that cultural changes attributable to an unplanned voyage were matters of chance, and that numerous, sometimes evanescent, factors governed the acceptance or rejection of ideas and objects transported in this manner.

Since voyagers, especially involuntary voyagers, may have implanted only fragments of their culture in Polynesia, the picture is a mosaic, and it will indeed be difficult for the culture historian to determine the sources of the pieces. Incorporation of a cultural component into a particular island culture would have resulted in new uses; the component would seem aberrant in its new association, and the culture historian would be likely to overlook it as evidence of cultural diffusion.

The problem of Polynesian origins and cultural diffusions is far too complex to be solved from immediately available evidence. The variety of possible sources and of possible routes is infinite. What routes were chosen, and what routes were forced upon what number of undirected vessels, can never be completely known. Only through a broad view, and an awareness of these facts, can we eventually arrive at a better interpretation of the meaning of the data derived from archaeological evidence, ethnographic collections, and historic and ethnological observations.

Although the results of many of the more recent excavations are still being compiled, a few have been published. Happily, many of these reflect the authors' understanding of the complex and nascent nature of Polynesian archaeology. Conclusions are limited to the problem at hand, and comparisons, if any, are made only to point up the need for excavations in other, possibly related, areas. Although the field still suffers slightly from pronunciamentos concerning Polynesian origins, the more thoughtful Pacific archaeologists are awaiting the day when enough excavated objects have been accumulated to provide a sound basis for the reconstruction of Polynesian prehistory.

E. ECOLOGY

JACQUES BARRAU

7. L'Humide et le Sec: An Essay on Ethnobiological Adaptation to Contrastive Environments in the Indo-Pacific Area

During the last few years, the relations between Nature and Culture have received some attention from the anthropologists (see for example Frake 1962; Haudricourt 1962, 1964). My purpose in the present essay is to discuss an aspect of these relations, namely Man's horticultural adaptations to his environment in the humid tropics of the Indo-Pacific area and, to some extent, the cultural implications of these adaptations. As an economic botanist accidentally involved in ethnological matters, I feel very much like a trespasser in forbidden country. It is therefore with deep apprehension that I present the following over-simplified and naturalistic approach to problems belonging mainly to the social sciences. Furthermore, I realize that some of the opinions expressed in this article are not necessarily shared by all. I present these notes, however, in the hope that they may stimulate thought, discussion and further research.[1]

I have given this paper a simple French title, "L'Humide et le Sec," the wet and the dry, because the relative excess or lack of water probably was one of the main ecological factors which determined Man's earliest horticultural adaptations to his environment in the Indo-Pacific area.

The largest part of this Indo-Pacific area belongs to the humid

SOURCE: Reprinted from the *Journal of the Polynesian Society*, Vol. 74, No. 3 (1965), pp. 329–46, by permission of the author and publisher.

[1] This article is a revised version of a paper presented at the Yale Anthropology Colloquium on April 8, 1965. The author wishes to express his warm thanks to N. Bowers, G. Condominas, H. C. Conklin, C. O. Frake and D. Rogers for their useful comments and criticisms.

tropics "where winter never comes" (Bates 1952) and where drought is unknown.

The original landscape of a large part of this Indo-Pacific area was most likely characterized by the *tropical rain forest* which, in a permanently humid zone, still occupies today large tracts of lands from the western Ghats of India to Fiji, through Indo-Malaysia and Melanesia [see Figure 1].

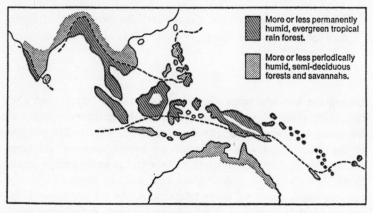

More or less permanently humid, evergreen tropical rain forest.

More or less periodically humid, semi-deciduous forests and savannahs.

FIGURE 1

This evergreen tropical rain forest with three tree layers is a plant-formation of remarkably constant structure, yet within such a forest there are ecological variations: thus, in New Guinea where the tropical rain forest occupies about 80% of the total land area, one can distinguish a floodplain form, a drained alluvium form, and a low hill form (Robbins 1961:24–29).

To the south and to the north, within the Indo-Pacific area, in zones not permanently but *periodically* humid, the tropical rain forest tends to give way to *seasonal forests,* which are semi-evergreen, semi-deciduous, or deciduous. Such forests are widespread in Northern India, Burma, Thailand, Viet Nam, Indonesia, New Guinea, and other Pacific islands, as well as in parts of tropical Australia. In places, these forests are found together with, or have been replaced by, *savannah woodlands* and *grasslands*.

This type of seasonal semi-evergreen or deciduous forest (also called *monsoon forest*) seems to be "a plagio-climax community whose existence has been permitted by a degree of burning and human interference" (Eyre 1963:218)[2] and these factors have also played a major role in the extension of the savannah woodlands and grasslands.

In other words, the tropical rain forest—a warm, wet, and shady environment—can be considered as the climatic climax[3] of the main part of the Indo-Pacific area.

To summarize, one can distinguish roughly within this area a permanently wet zone, the rain forest one, and a relatively dry one, the seasonal forest and savannah one.

The western part of this Indo-Pacific area, i.e. Indo-Malaysia and New Guinea, broadly coincides with the *Indo-Malayan centre of origin of cultivated plants* defined by Vavilov (1951:29), a region of floristic wealth where a large number of crops originated and where Carl Sauer (1952:24) located his *cradle of earliest agriculture,* an idea earlier suggested by Haudricourt and Hedin (1943:88, 139).

Among the herbaceous plants found in lowland tropical rain forests or on their edges, the *Araceae* are of particular importance for the purpose of this discussion. They grow in damp spots, near forest streams, or sometimes in open swamps. To this family belong some of the ancient food plants of the Indo-Pacific area such as *Alocasia macrorrhiza* Schott, *Colocasia esculenta* (L.) Schott, and *Cyrtosperma chamissonis* (Schott) Merr.; their starchy stems or tuberous rhizomes are still today important articles of food in the diet of the South Pacific islanders who grow these plants which, in ancient pre-rice days, may have been staple food plants in the whole of the Indo-Pacific area. This seems to be particularly true of the taro, *Colocasia esculenta* (see Figure 6), which as a cultivated plant was carried by man from tropical South-East Asia to the southern part of Japan, to eastern Polynesia, and probably to the Mediterranean shores (Porteres 1960:170–71). Taro seems to be "one of the oldest cultivated plants" (Hill 1939:113) and if one considers the whole of tropi-

[2] By plagioclimax, we mean a community apparently capable of perpetuation under the prevailing soil and climatic conditions, but which is maintained by continuous human activity.

[3] By climatic climax, we mean a community which is capable of perpetuation under the prevailing climatic conditions, and which represents the ultimate phase of ecological development permitted by these climatic conditions.

cal Oceania today, it is certainly the most characteristic of the basic food plants in that part of the world.

The progenitors of taro are not known with certainty, but they may have been similar to the wild variety *aquatilis* described by Hasskarl in 1848 from Indonesia (Porteres 1960:169) where it grows in swampy areas.

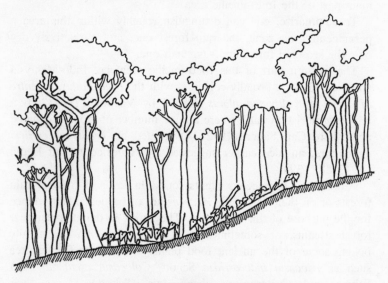

FIGURE 2. Taro garden in the rain forest.

In such an environment in tropical Oceania, particularly on the continental high islands of Melanesia, one can find the simplest form of cultivation of this aroid: a clearing or partial clearing of a patch in the tropical rain forest where taro cuttings—tops of corm bearing bases of petioles—are planted in holes opened with a digging stick in the soft, moist ground (see Figure 2). This represents a somewhat limited amount of interference with the environment, the only role of the gardener being to provide through clearing and weeding a larger space for the taro which is propagated vegetatively.[4] Of course, such simple gardening often

[4] Taro fruits and seeds have rarely been observed (Barrau 1959:436–438)—not that they are actually very scarce but mainly because they are often overlooked; they occur generally on plants escaped from cultivation and growing, for instance, in forest fallows or along streams; the natural seedlings when found by the gardeners are often the sources of new clones

seriously affects the vegetation due to the clearing operation. But for the most part, it is based on an almost direct use of the environment through simple management aimed at facilitating the multiplication and the growth of the plant. In these forest gardens, taro grows in ecological conditions rather similar to those of what we can guess was the habitat of its wild relatives.

Other methods of taro gardening imply various degrees of transformation of the environment.

The first and the simplest method in this category is the one consisting of land-reclamation in swampy ponds by building in such ponds mud ridges or mounds on which taro is planted. This can be seen today on many Polynesian high islands in the swampy depressions located between beach rampart and foothills (see Figure 3). This method is to a large extent similar to the one used in the case of the Mexican *chinampas* (see Schilling 1939; Coe 1964).

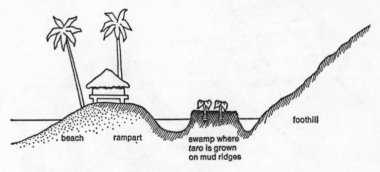

FIGURE 3

In the ancient days of incipient horticulture in the Indo-Pacific area, taro may have been first cultivated in such freshwater, swampy depressions between beach rampart or river bank and foothill or alluvium plain. As I have already mentioned, Carl Sauer (1952:23–24) has suggested that Southeast Asia may have been the "cradle of earliest agriculture" and that "the progenitors of earliest agriculturists" may have been "progressive fishing folk."

---

brought into cultivation. The same process of appearance of new clones in fallow, wasteland, and forest is also true of the cultivated yams (see Haudricourt 1964).

This idea was shared by the late Burkill who thought also that "dwellers on the banks of rivers of Southeastern Asia and of the coasts whose food consisted largely of fish, originated . . . cultivation . . . The river's spill or a beach provided a place for their house . . . Behind this mound or raised beach . . . a backwater where forest growth was made thin by the wet soil and its muddy approaches gave an area within which it was easy to plant *Colocasia* and other aroids . . ." (Burkill 1960:407).

The mud mounds or ridges, *chinampas*-like, might therefore have been an early method of growing taro just as the forest gardening I described earlier.

More elaborate is the method based on terracing with irrigation (see Figure 4); again I shall use the example of tropical Oceania as representative of the Indo-Pacific area and, perhaps, of its agricultural past.

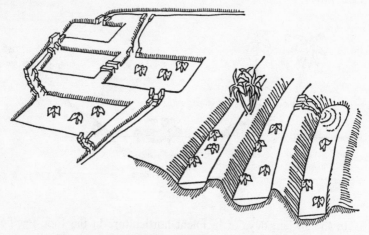

FIGURE 4. Irrigated taro gardens, New Caledonia.

In Oceania, terracing with irrigation is found from New Guinea to Fiji through the Melanesian arc and also in Polynesia, mainly in areas where monsoon forest, savannah woodlands, and grasslands are today the main plant formations.

Agricultural terracing, with particular reference to the Indo-Pacific area was thoroughly surveyed a few years ago by Spencer and Hale and it is not necessary to review their definitions here in detail. In some less humid parts of tropical Oceania, taro is grown under irrigation on terraces which belong mainly to two of the types defined by Spencer and Hale:

(a) the "linear contour, irrigable terrace" (Spencer and Hale 1961:10) of which some striking examples can be seen in New Caledonia, with or without stone walls;

(b) the "wet field terraces" (Spencer and Hale 1961:11–12) which are rather common on some Polynesian islands, Futuna, for instance.

In the grasslands of the New Guinea mountains, for example, in the Morobe district, one can find also "isolated, short, sloping field terrace" (Spencer and Hale 1961:9) where bamboo pipelines bring water from a nearby spring or stream. This represents a rather crude, primitive form of terracing with irrigation.

For the Oceanian gardener in growing taro with irrigation outside the tropical rain forest area, and far from coastal or riverine fresh water swamps, the main and constant subject of concern is water supply.

Earthworms can ruin and drain the irrigated terraces, and the New Caledonian gardeners when building or repairing terraces used to sing hymns of praise to the earthworms, in the hope of thus obtaining their benevolence (Leenhardt 1930:111).

Magical plants are grown on bunds and banks to protect these fragile constructions against all kinds of evil; thus, in New Guinea, a soft, juicy, dark purple variety of sugar cane is planted on terrace banks as a magical protection against droughts.

In New Guinea as in New Caledonia, taboos protect the conduits bringing water to terraces; interdicts limit walking along open ditches, prohibit touching bamboo pipelines or even approaching the fragile aqueducts crossing gullies; wood carvings representing protective spirits are placed at the most fragile points of the conduit. In short, water is worthy of a kind of religious veneration. Hence, this New Caledonian invocation accompanying a ritual offering of taro to ancestors to obtain from them the end of a dry season: "Bring the rain, leave the water flow, for it gives us joy for today and tomorrow . . ." (Leenhardt 1937:66).

In New Caledonian folklore, the association "taro-water" plays a role in all important myths telling the story of the origin of the island, of its springs and streams. In the same folklore, one can find curious legends giving an account of the arrival in ancient days of foreigners who taught the aboriginal population how to build terraces and irrigate them (Leenhardt 1930:112). Before, taro was grown on mounds or ridges erected in wet ground of the valleys.[5]

In the geography of tropical Oceania, there is a striking morphological and ecological contrast between the high islands and the low islands, a simple classification now adopted by all geographers dealing with the South Pacific Islands (see, for example, Cumberland 1954).

The *high islands* are the mountainous, continental or volcanic formations; the *low islands,* the low madreporic, coral islands; the most typical of these low islands is the *atoll,* a chain of sandy islets built on a reef surrounding a lagoon. The soil of an atoll is made almost entirely of calcium carbonate, and ground-water is salty or brackish except for a fresh-water lens in hydrostatic equilibrium in the ground, roughly at the centre of each of these coral sand islets (see Barrau 1957:257).

The latter constitutes an environment not particularly suitable for horticulture and yet, on many of these atolls, a plant of the taro family, *Cyrtosperma chamissonis,* is one of the staple food plants. This aroid originated in the lowlands of Indo-Malaysia, where its wild relatives, such as *C. lasioides* Griff., grow in swamps or on damp ground.

To grow *Cyrtosperma* on atolls, the islanders use an extremely elaborate method: a pit is dug in the central part of the coral islet down to the level of the fresh-water lens; gabions, bottomless baskets made of woven twigs, are placed on the muddy pit floor, filled with fallen leaves and all available organic material of vegetable origin; cuttings of the many different clones of *Cyrtosperma* (see Catala 1957:72–73) are planted in these baskets floating

[5] In the course of centuries, cultivated taro—an amphibious plant with adaptability to varying ecological conditions—has undergone a lot of variations. It is therefore not surprising to find today variants suitable to cultivation with or without irrigation. In New Caledonia, the popular nomenclature of taro clones used by Melanesian gardeners divides them into three main categories: irrigated taros, unirrigated taros, and "spring" taros, which are grown near springs and along streams in the forest shade while the first group grows on irrigated terraces and those of the other one can be grown without irrigation but on relatively moist soil (Barrau 1956:74–75).

on the fresh water mud. These pits almost perfectly recreate the natural habitat of *Cyrtosperma,* a striking adaptation to an environment where both fresh water, the essential fresh water, and the organic matter of the tropical forest are lacking (see Figure 5).

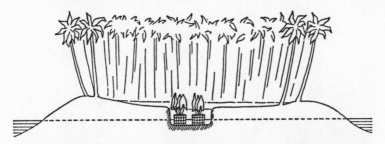

FIGURE 5. Sunken *Cyrtosperma* pit garden, Gilbert Islands, Micronesia.

This gardening method has been described by Spencer and Hale (1961) as "sunken, taro-pit terrace." One might perhaps discuss the adequacy of the word "terrace" here yet this technique fulfills the same purpose as the irrigated terraces I dealt with earlier to recreate the ecological conditions of the natural habitat of the species grown, in the case of *Cyrtosperma* the conditions of the humid tropical lowlands.

This "ethnobiological association" between water, tropical forests, taro and other aroids, so important in the history of Indo-Pacific agriculture, does not allow us to neglect other important food plants such as the yams which, in ancient days, also played a prominent role in the subsistence economies of this area (see Burkill 1951). They have retained this prominence on some of the islands of tropical Oceania which do appear, indeed, to be a kind of conservatory where are kept many useful plants of the ancient days of the old world tropics.

The most important of these yams is the greater yam (see Burkill 1951) *Dioscorea alata* L., a cultigen (see Figure 7) whose wild relatives seem to be two yams of tropical Asia, *Dioscorea hamiltonii* Hook, and *Dioscorea persimilis* Prain and Burkill (see Prain and Burkill 1934). Both species grow not in the tropical rain forest zone, but in the less humid zone of continental Asia (Burkill 1954:331) where monsoon forest is, or was, prevalent and where there is a seasonal variation of rainfall which is also noticeably less abundant than in the tropical rain forest zone.

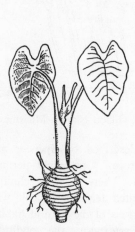

FIGURE 6. *Colocasia esculenta.*   FIGURE 7. *Dioscorea alata.*

Man transported the greater yam to Indonesia and probably improved it there far from its natural habitat (Burkill 1950:443). Such an acclimatization seems to have played an essential part in the domestication and the improvement or ennoblement of many cultivated plants, as shown by Helbaek in his work on the origin and domestication of cereals in the "fertile crescent" (Helbaek 1959; see also Braidwood 1960:8). Helbaek has clearly described the importance of this acclimatization process in the origin, domestication and diversification of wheat: "Since wild wheat grows in medium altitude, usually 2,500 to 3,000 feet above sea level, and preferably on dry and sunny slopes, it was necessary to move it down from its natural habitat. *This encroachment upon its nature increased the rate of mutation, while physiological and morphological changes began which eventually led to the formation of thousands of varieties and strains, with vast ability of adaptation"* (Helbaek 1959:186). Incidentally, one can find in tropical Oceania many more examples of such an acclimatization process in the origin of cultivated plants: Breadfruit (*Artocarpus altilis* "Park." Fosberg), *Cyrtosperma chamissonis* (Schott) Merr., and the *fehi* banana (*Musa troglodytarum* L.) are examples (Barrau 1962:221–40).

But let us go back to the greater yam: From Indonesia it spread to the islands of Oceania.

To cultivate this tropophyte[6] far from its centre of origin in conditions often differing from those of its natural habitat, special horticultural methods were devised: yams are generally grown on mounds or ridges built with loamy hand-broken soil; on these mounds the vine grows on poles, and the mounds are often surrounded by drainage ditches. Thus a larger volume of soil facilitates the growth and the harvest of the tuber while there is no excessive ground moisture.

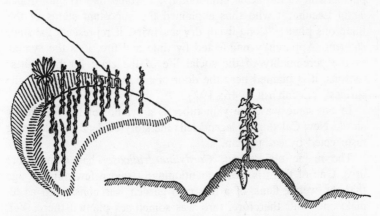

FIGURE 8. Cultivation of the greater yam, *Dioscorea alata*, New Caledonia.

In contrast with taro, the yam is therefore a relatively "dry" crop and, indeed, in the popular nomenclature of the Melanesian gardeners of New Caledonia, one finds a contrastive classification between "wet crops" of which the main one is taro, and "dry crops" of which the greater yam is the most important.

Sexual symbolism accompanies this ecological dichotomy: wet

[6] A tropophyte is a plant which can live under dry conditions during part of the year, and under moist climatic conditions during the other part.

crops are "female" while dry crops are "male." Leenhardt (1937:63) has masterfully analyzed this symbolism; to the phallic yam tuber is opposed the triangular taro which, according to this author, is considered by the New Caledonians as a symbol of the *genitrix.* Wet "female" gardens, dry "male" gardens are separate, and there is a division of labour between men and women for the care and management of these gardens.

Micro-environmental nomenclature also reflects this sexual symbolism: the wetter flank of a hillside yam garden is considered as female and a few taros can be grown there while the place of each yam clone on the mound is determined by the degree of soil moisture and depth; the "noblest" yams enjoy the privilege of growing in the dryest and deepest parts of the mound.

Magical plants associated with yam in the male plant category include *Cordyline fruticosa* (L.) A. Chev., a plant of utmost importance in Indo-Pacific ethnobotany. I would like to quote once again Leenhardt who thus explained the important status of this liliaceous plant: "Long-lived, dry and wiry, it represents the male element. Apparently unaffected by time and fire, it is the symbol of the perenniality of the social life of the clan; for both these reasons, it is planted near the door of the men's house and at the shrines" (Leenhardt 1946: 192).

In the same way, the yam tuber is a symbol of life and many an old New Caledonian legend tells the story of dead people being resurrected by eating yam.

The magic male plant, *Cordyline fruticosa,* has many more uses. One of them is worth mentioning: I said a few minutes ago that the wetter flank of a dry yam garden was considered as female and that, therefore, taro was sometimes planted there. Yet, often *Cordyline,* the male plant *par excellence* is also planted on the female side of the yam garden to neutralize the unwanted moisture and femininity.

By contrast with *Cordyline,* the plants associated with taro in the female plant category are trees with soft, aqueous wood such as *Erythrina fusca,* Lour., vegetables with tender mucilaginous leaves, such as *Hibiscus manihot* L., juicy sugar canes, etc.

In the rain making rites, *Erythrina* soft wood was burned and the "magicians" covered themselves with the charcoal and ashes as well as with black mushroom spores. In the sunshine making rites, hard, dry wood was burned, giving glowing red embers, red yam were eaten, leaves of red varieties of *Cordyline* were used.

So far, I have quoted only New Caledonian examples, but this symbolism associated with gardening and useful plants occurs on many other islands of tropical Oceania; Margot-Duclos and Vernant in their interesting and critical exegesis of Malinowski's work on the Trobriands have dealt at length with this subject and it is therefore not necessary for me to discuss it further.

As in most parts of the world, there is in the popular beliefs and rites of tropical Oceania, a close association between human procreation, plant reproduction and horticulture which has therefore an exceptional importance in social life.

As Margot-Duclos and Vernant have pointed out:

> In the Trobriands as well as in New Caledonia or even in pre-European New Zealand, in the detail of its operations and techniques, horticulture is controlled by the distinction 'male-female' and the notion of the sexes' respective roles: agrarian techniques and rites represent the various phases of impregnation, pregnancy, and birth: crops are procreated like children . . . The sexual order present in nature and horticulture is on one hand the consequence, on the other hand, the justification and the guaranty of the order established between sexes and lineages within the perpetuation of generations . . . (Margot-Duclos and Vernant 1946: 11).

For the Melanesian gardeners of New Caledonia and the Trobriand islands, yam and taros are assimilated to human beings. Fortune (1932:101) has shown that this is also true of yams in Dobu. One can find similar examples on the New Guinea mainland, for example in Abelam where, in addition, taboos associated with the ceremonial growing of large yams resemble those of New Caledonia (Lea 1964:111 ff.). To this enumeration, one might add the cases of Micronesian yam growers on Yap and Ponape where the above noted sexual symbolism is also associated with yam growing.

The similarities between beliefs and rituals of yam growers of Oceania are indeed striking and I would like to quote one last example of such similarities: Françoise Girard writes that, in the villages of the Buang, yam growers in the hills of the Morobe district of New Guinea, *Cordyline fruticosa,* the male magic plant associated with yam in New Caledonia, is "planted near the men's houses, the yam houses, around the villages and the gardens . . . The red variety of *Cordyline,* a symbol of life, plays an essential role in rituals and this red variety is the one planted at the shrines, near the men's house and near the yam houses" (Girard 1957:224).

Let us return to the initial environmental contrast related to this dichotomy wet and dry, female and male plants.

The Indo-Pacific area is divided *grosso-modo* in two main climatic zones:

(a) One "wet", that is, more or less permanently humid and characterized by the tropical rain forest;
(b) One "dry", that is, more or less periodically humid and characterized by monsoon forests, savannah woodlands and grasslands.

This basic, contrastive division has been confirmed by recent works on the climatic definition of the humid tropics, such as those of Garnier (1961) and Küchler (1961).

New Caledonia is located in the more or less periodically humid tropical zone: to be more specific, this island is located in the Southern trade-winds zone characterized by a contrast between a rainy and warm summer (from December to May), and a dry, relatively cool winter. We cannot here enter into details concerning the horticultural calendar of the New Caledonian Melanesians which corresponds to this seasonal variation, a calendar where we could find other aspects of the wet and dry, male and female dichotomy discussed earlier (see Leenhardt 1930:132; Margot-Duclos and Vernant 1946:29).

There is a point, however, which deserves some attention: if, in the Southern trade-wind zone, one can distinguish a wet and a dry season, unfortunately for the gardeners, a considerable variability in the quantity and the seasonal distribution of rainfall occurs. Adaptation to the environment is therefore a constant process and it might be of interest to consider in that connection the functions of "master of the wet crops" and "master of the dry crops" characteristic of the horticultural Melanesian societies of New Caledonia (see Leenhardt 1930:106–34; 1937:59–74). In charge of the rituals and taboos associated with each category of crop, these "masters" were also technicians and managers of gardening operations; they decided the horticultural activities of the community; to some extent, the small ritual, magical gardens of dry or wet crops they maintained near their houses played the part—if I may indulge in some over-simplification—of micro-experimental and meteorological stations materializing this constant adaptation to a variable climate which governed the rhythm of these gardeners' lives. Taking into account the obvious importance of gardening in the daily life of such a fundamentally horticultural society, these "masters", through taboos related to the various phases of taro and yam cultivation, regulated almost the whole life of the group, from children's games to the use of food and to sexual intercourse between husband and wife.

The *towosi* or garden "magicians" of the Trobriand islands had a role similar to the one of the New Caledonian crop "masters" (see Malinowski 1935, I:64–68).

In the course of this discussion, I have referred only to Melanesian examples, and it is about time to pay some attention to the rest of the Indo-Pacific area.

In the irrigated rice fields of the Philippines, taro is still cultivated today, and one can find it also in many other parts of Indo-Malaysia, Indochina, and tropical and subtropical China. Spier (1951) and Porteres (1960) have shown the extended past distribution of this cultivated aroid.

The Mnong-Gar who grow dry, upland rice in the mountains of South Viet Nam, ritually plant a yam, *Dioscorea alata,* on the site of their new rice fields in the forest (see Condominas and Haudricourt 1952:23).

According to Gourou (1923:71) the Bontok who grow irrigated rice in the mountains of the Philippines use taro for rituals associated with new rice planting (see also Keesing 1962:96); Igorot tales say that in the ancient pre-rice days of Northern Luzon, taro was a staple food crop (Keesing 1962:52).

Rumphius's *Herbarium Amboinense* (1741–1756) shows that at the end of the 17th century, taro and yam were still of importance in the sustenance economies of Eastern Indonesia.

The Yami of Botel Tobago island, 45 miles from the southern tip of Formosa, still grow taro in irrigated fields and terraces, and yam in dry gardens on hill slopes; according to Kano and Segawa "in contrast with the taro . . . cared for by the women, the yam is more often cultivated by the men . . ." (Kano and

Segawa 1956:152). This trait of Yami horticulture is, to quote these authors, "more Oceanic than Malaysian . . . Although widespread in Micronesia and Polynesia, taro is not especially important in Malaysia except in the Banggai archipelago east of the Celebes, and in Enggano and Nias west of Sumatra, both being marginal to what may be called rice-cultivating Malaysia . . ." (Kano and Segawa 1956:11).

In other words, many signs indicate that these vegetatively propagated, tuber-yielding perennials, taro and yam, were most likely the staple food plants in ancient Indo-Malaysia. They have retained some importance in some localities (see, for instance, Conklin 1957:130) but are no longer the basis of sustenance. Burkill (1951) has analyzed the reasons for the "rise and decline" of these tubers in the service of man in Indo-Malaysia. The main reason for this decline seems to have been the domestication and the spread of cereals, mainly rice (*Oryza sativa* L.) and also millet (*Setaria italica* L.).

With Haudricourt and Hedin (Haudricourt and Hedin 1943: 153; see also Haudricourt 1962:41), I feel that rice may have first appeared as a weed, as a "desired weed" (Oka and Chang 1959:115) in ditches of wet taro gardens in the tropical and continental part of the Indo-Pacific area, i.e., from India to Indochina. Rice's wild relatives there (the floating perennial *Oryza perennis* Moench. and also *Oryza sativa* L. var. *spontanea* Rosch, an intermediate form between cultivated rice and its possible wild progenitor) show the validity of this hypothesis. They are hydrophytes with a potential of genetic variability; moreover, they have, particularly *Oryza perennis,* a striking adaptability to changing ecological conditions, from hydrophytic to tropophytic. According to Morishima, Hinata and Oka (1962:1–11) cultivated rice varieties, dry (or upland) and wet (or irrigated) rices, have retained different aspects of this adaptability.

As Haudricourt points out: "It would be a mistake to consider upland, dry rice cultivation as an elder stage than irrigated rice cultivation. Wild rice is an aquatic plant. Probably it was first a weed in taro patches then a crop in these wet fields. Later, it gave birth to varieties able to grow without irrigation . . . Upland rice has replaced yam as it requires less work . . ." (Haudricourt 1962:41).

As a matter of fact, one can draw an interesting parallel between taro and rice: both come from an original swampy, marshy habitat and both have cultivated varieties adapted to either irrigated or non-irrigated cultivation.

Grist (1959:50) has stated that rice "is not however an aquatic plant, for the roots of aquatics produce but few branches and no root hairs, whereas the roots of paddy, whether grown as a dry land crop or in water are much branched and possess a profusion of root hairs." This is a somewhat misleading statement: Aquatics or hydrophytes[7] include: (1) submerged plants, (2) free floating plants, (3) amphibious or emersed plants (see Weaver and Clements 1938:424–36).

The root characteristics of aquatics listed by Grist (1959) are those of the submerged and the free floating[8] plants, except when they grow in mud (see Weaver and Clements 1938). These characteristics, however, are not those of amphibious plants such as the helophytes or marsh plants of which the perennial rice *Oryza perennis* is a good example. These amphibious forms are "the least specialized of water plants" (Weaver and Clements 1938: 433), their rhizome and root structure showing both hydric and xeric adaptations. Moreover, for some authors (see, for example, Copeland 1924:21) rice exhibits physiological characteristics of a marsh plant such as its nutritional requirement for both nitrates and derivatives of ammonia even when grown as a dry crop, a peculiarity of adaptation probably evolved through its original life in marshes.

From the humid tropics of the continental parts of the Indo-Pacific area, rice spread to China, where it was improved and to insular Malaysia where it might have been preceded by millet (see Van Steenis 1962:273), a "dry" crop probably introduced from continental Asia as a domestic plant; *Setaria* millet as a cultivated cereal seems to have originated in China (Vavilov 1951:21). Little is known about this cereal in the Western Indo-Pacific area where, particularly in insular Malaysia, its past and even present importance has often been overlooked. It is there-

[7] A hydrophyte is a plant growing wholly or partly immersed in water.

[8] To avoid misunderstanding, it may be useful to clarify here the meaning of *floating* when applied to rice: some perennial, amphibious wild rices such as *Oryza perennis* are called *floating* because their stems grow as the water level rises so that the leaves remain emersed; they are not however free floating plants like, for instance, the well known tropical water hyacinth, *Eichornia crassipes* Solms, Pontederiaceae.

fore difficult to formulate any acceptable hypothesis about the history of millet in the Indo-Pacific area.

However, it seems likely that "in Southeastern Asia, including both the continental and insular areas, rice culture might have been preceded by millet or taro culture, though with the probability that taro was followed by millet in various localities" (Kano and Segawa 1956:11). Millet invaded the then yam-and-taro-growing areas of Indonesia probably from the north, possibly through Formosa and the Philippines, and then spread to the eastern islands of Indonesia.

As far as irrigated rice is concerned, I wholeheartedly support Kolb's views (Kolb 1953) that irrigated fields and terraces were first used for taro growing and later, much later, for rice.

In the Indo-Pacific area, there is another striking case of agricultural adaptation to an adverse environment: the drained sweet potato (*Ipomoea batatas* [L.] Lamk) gardens of the New Guinea highlands (see Figure 9).

Sweet potato seems to be a relatively recent introduction, 17th century perhaps, in New Guinea. Better adapted than taro, yams and other tropical tubers to the ecological conditions of the New Guinea highlands, sweet potato has probably been the factor of a population explosion in the montane valleys of this territory (see Brookfield 1964:21–25).

These valleys are often marshy and the methods used to grow sweet potato there are very similar to those used in the case either of the *chinampas*-like taro gardens or the drained yam gardens I described earlier.[9]

The case of the sweet potato leads us to consider that of European introduced food plants such as the manioc, *Manihot esculenta* Crantz, or the yautia, *Xanthosoma sagittifolium* (L.) Schott. Often, they are not included in the traditional horticultural patterns and nomenclature. Even when they are in daily use, they

[9] Nancy Bowers (personal communication) has pointed out that the wet-female/dry-male distinctions do not seem to be valid in the case of the New Guinea highlands, above 5,000 to 6,000 feet in altitude. Indeed, these distinctions and their adaptive significance appear to be mainly associated with the horticulture and economic flora of the truly tropical parts of the Indo-Pacific area. Moreover, in the montane valleys of New Guinea, the introduction of the sweet potato has most likely led to a kind of economic and social revolution; it may have seriously modified the lowlands horticultural traditions and beliefs which, in pre-*ipomoean* days, had perhaps reached parts of these highlands.

are sometimes considered as low grade food as indicated by the following comment of a New Caledonian Melanesian about manioc: "suitable for the dogs." The *Xanthosoma,* however, due probably to its obvious botanical affinities with the noble taro, is somewhat better considered!

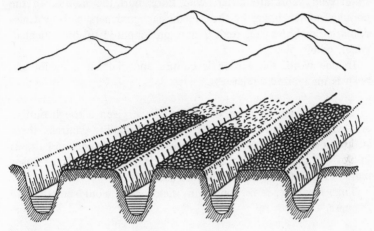

FIGURE 9. Sweet potato gardens, Baliem Valley (Irian Barat), New Guinea Highlands.

Taro and yam, irrigation and drainage, the permanently humid environment of the tropical rain forest and the periodically (and less) humid environment of the monsoon forest, wet and dry . . . these contrasts seem to me of considerable importance in the history of Indo-Pacific agriculture.

I also feel that, in this Indo-Pacific area and particularly in tropical Oceania where early forms of horticulture seem to have persisted, we have the possibility of finding some answers to the many questions concerning the origins of horticulture and agriculture as well as the ancient processes of plant domestication.

There are other ethnobiological or ethno-ecological contrasts worth studying in Indo-Pacific horticulture, for example, the dichotomy "garden vs. bush-fallow" to which Haudricourt (1964) recently drew attention. For the Melanesian of New Caledonia, the garden is the safe domain of the daily life where everything is known, foreseeable, rational . . . the clones of vegetatively propagated, edible perennials, taro and yams, always reproducing identical to themselves are the symbols of a comforting and civilized stability, the symbols of the established and accepted social order. The bush fallow or forest, is the domain of the unknown, haunted by ghosts of the dead; everything there is unforeseen, accidental, abnormal; escaped cultivated plants return to the wild state; wild yams are bitter; wild taros hurt the mouth. In the popular nomenclature of the Melanesian gardeners of New Caledonia, wild, bitter and toxic plants are opposed to domesticated, sweet, edible plants.

In one word, the garden is culture and civilization, while the bush is uncivilized wilderness.

These systems of ideas, of which I have given a rough outline and which seem to be related to a basic humidity contrast, these striking cultural analogies between horticultural beliefs and rituals in various parts of the Indo-Pacific area may have some resonance in the structure of Oceanian societies.

This, however, is no longer my field and I would not dare to trespass.

F. SOCIAL ORGANIZATION

WARD H. GOODENOUGH

8. A Problem in Malayo-Polynesian Social Organization[1]

Despite the wide differences in the social systems which now exist
among Malayo-Polynesian societies, Murdock (1948; 1949:228–
31, 349–50) offers convincing evidence that they are derived from
an original "Hawaiian" type of structure. The features characterizing this type include bilocal extended families, bilateral
kindreds, the absence of unilinear kin groups, and Generation-
Hawaiian kinship terminology.

Not considered by Murdock, because it was beyond the scope
of his immediate interests, is another feature characterizing the
organization of a great many Malayo-Polynesian societies: the
association of individual rights to land with membership in some
kind of kin group. It is so widespread as to suggest that it may
be an original Malayo-Polynesian pattern.

If Murdock's reconstruction is correct, the only two kin groups
with which land ownership could be associated were the bilateral
kindred and the bilocal extended family. Now a person's kindred
as defined by Murdock (1949:44, 56–62) includes roughly half
of the members of his father's and mother's kindreds, respectively,
coinciding with the kindreds of neither of them. This means that
there is no continuity of kindred membership from one generation
to the next. Kindreds, as so defined, cannot, therefore, function
as land-owning bodies. Bilocal extended families could so function, but this would require that all out-marrying members of a

SOURCE: Reprinted from *American Anthropologist*, Vol. 57, No. 1 (1955),
pp. 71–83, by permission of the author and publisher.
[1] This paper is a revised and expanded version of one entitled "The
Typology of Consanguineal Groups," presented at the annual meeting of
the American Anthropological Association, December 1952.

family lose membership in the land-owning group while all in-marrying spouses acquire such membership. Yet the present-day Malayo-Polynesian land-owning groups stress consanguinity as the basis of membership, not residence alone. Since, moreover, consanguineal ties are the normal basis for the transmission of land rights, consanguineal groups are more effective instruments of collective land ownership than residential ones. I find it difficult, therefore, to accept the idea that the early Malayo-Polynesians associated ownership directly with the bilocal extended family.

But what alternatives are there? The evidence for Murdock's reconstruction is too consistent to allow for any serious questioning of his conclusions. There is, however, the possibility that he has left something out, something which neither his data nor existing social organization concepts could readily have revealed.

A clue to what this something is may be sought in the current confusion as to what is meant by the term "kindred." In the literature it has two distinct definitions. Rivers (1926a:15–16) and Murdock (1949:56–62) both treat the kindred as a group of persons who have a relative in common, regardless of whether kinship is traced through men or women. Such people cannot all be related to one another. As just indicated, the kindred in this sense is ephemeral and cannot, therefore, function as a land-owning group. And it is in this sense that Murdock attributes kindreds to early Malayo-Polynesian society.

As defined in *Notes and Queries* (1929:55), on the other hand, the term kindred "should be limited to a group of persons who acknowledge their descent, genealogically or by adoption, from one family, whether through their fathers or mothers." Here, a kindred refers to people who have an ancestor in common as distinct from people who have a relative in common. In this sense a kindred has continuity through time and all its members are related to one another. As *Notes and Queries* defines it, a kindred is any nonunilinear descent group; as Murdock and Rivers define it, it is not a true descent group at all. The source of confusion has clearly been the feature common to both types of group: in both cases consanguineal connections are traced through either sex. The difference is that in the kindred of Rivers and Murdock these connections are traced *laterally* to a common relative, while in the kindred of *Notes and Queries* they are traced *lineally* to a common ancestor. I wish to suggest that the kindred in the latter sense must be added to the kindred in Murdock's sense as an element in the social organization of early Malayo-Polynesian society. Hereinafter, I shall reserve the term kindred for the bilateral group which Rivers and Murdock had in mind and shall refer to the group defined by *Notes and Queries* as a nonunilinear descent group.

As we shall see, nonunilinear descent groups may take many forms. We are, therefore, faced with the problem of ascertaining its probable form in the original Malayo-Polynesian group.

Logically, true descent groups, i.e., groups in which all the members trace descent from a common ancestor, may be of two basic types. The first type we may call an "unrestricted descent group," for it incudes *all* of the founder's descendants, whether through males or females. Such groups must of necessity overlap in membership, for each individual will belong to as many of them as he has known ancestors. The second type restricts membership to include only some of the descendants of the original ancestor. The unilinear principle, by which only the children of existing members of one sex are added as new members, is but one of several possible ways of restricting membership in descent groups. A second possibility is to include only those descendants who acquire certain land rights as their share of the original inheritance. If both sexes are eligible to inherit these rights, then the line of descent by which a member carries his genealogy back to the founding ancestor is likely to go sometimes through men and sometimes through women. A third way to restrict membership in a descent group is to include only the children of those members who after marriage continue to reside in the locality associated with the group. If residence is bilocal, then the line of descent will go sometimes through men and sometimes through women. Still another device is to make membership in the father's or mother's group optional depending on the individual's own choice of residence between the localities with which they are respectively associated. These are simple ways of maintaining restricted descent groups of a sort analogous to sibs and lineages, but not unilinear in structure. Such groups can readily function as land-holding units. What evidence do we have among Malayo-Polynesian societies for the presence of such nonunilinear descent groups either now or in the past?

Let us turn to the Gilbert Islands first.[2] Here we must distinguish formally and functionally between five types of kin group.

1. The *utuu,* a true bilateral kindred.

2. The *ooi,*[3] an unrestricted descent group including all the persons descended from a common ancestor, regardless whether through men or women. This group functions only in relation to property.

3. The *mweenga,* a household. Formerly it was an extended family unit. It was predominantly patrilocal, but matrilocal marriages kept it from being completely so.

4. The *bwoti,* a nonunilinear descent group based on land rights, functioning in connection with community meeting-house organization.

5. The *kainga,* a nonunilinear descent group based on parental residence. Now defunct, it formerly functioned in connection with some aspects of property organization, feuding, and some economic activities. The *ooi,* the *bwoti,* and the *kainga* are all of interest for this discussion.

As already indicated, the *ooi* functions only in relation to land, individual rights to which may be held by both sexes. When a man (or woman) dies, his land passes to his children. Each daughter who marries receives a small share of the inheritance. The bulk of it is divided among the sons, with a slightly larger share going to the eldest. Division among the sons may be delayed until their death, being subsequently accomplished by their heirs. If there are no sons, the daughters receive the entire inheritance. Since women also pass their shares on to their children, some of the land allotted among brothers and sisters comes from their father and some from their mother. If their mother is without brothers, they may get more land from her than from their father. As this process continues, a tract of land is divided and subdivided within

[2] Field work was conducted in the summer of 1951, when I was a member of a team making an ecological study of the Gilbertese atoll Onotoa, under the auspices of the Pacific Science Board of the National Research Council and the Geography Branch of the Office of Naval Research.

[3] I am not certain that *ooi* is the correct native term for this group. Literally, the word means "fence." It was only in the last two days of field work that I learned it referred to some type of kin group as well. Answers to last-minute queries suggested that it referred to the unrestricted descent group which I had already isolated but had thought to be unnamed. [Editor's note: *"Ooi"* is the author's corrected spelling of this term; in the previous publication of the present article, *"oo"* was used.]

various lines descended from the original owner. All of his descendants form an *ooi*. Some of them may not have acquired a share of this land, but are eligible to do so should present shareholders die without heirs. Since land may not be alienated from the *ooi* without the consent of its members, the several holdings of a person who dies without children revert for distribution among the nearest of his kinsmen who, like him, are descended from the original owner. Land which came through his mother cannot revert to kinsmen on his father's side; it can go only to those of his mother's kin who are her *ooi* mates with respect to that land. Membership in the *ooi* is not terminated by settlement in a different community or atoll. It lasts for as long as the genealogical ties are remembered. The Gilbertese *ooi* illustrates how an unrestricted descent group can be associated with land ownership. We must, therefore, enter this type of group as a candidate in our search for original Malayo-Polynesian social forms. Let us now turn to the *bwoti*.

Community meeting houses in the Gilbert Islands, as in Samoa,[4] have a highly formalized organization. Every member of the community has the right to sit in one or more of the traditional seating places under the eaves around the meeting house. Each seating place is named and together with the people who occupy it constitutes a *bwoti*. *Bwoti* membership is based on individual rights in certain plots of land. All persons who own a share in such a plot, if no more than one square foot, have the right to a corresponding seat. Since all persons holding a share in the same plot are theoretically lineal descendants of its original holder and thus members of the same *ooi,* all persons entitled to the same seat in the meeting house are *ipso facto* consanguineally related and so recognized. But not all members of the same *ooi* with respect to such a plot have actually inherited shares in it; they hold lands acquired from other ancestors. Not holding a share, they are barred from the associated seat, but must sit elsewhere as their present holdings permit. While all *bwoti* mates belong to the same *ooi,* only a segment of the *ooi* belongs to the same *bwoti.*

From his various ancestors a man may acquire shares in several plots, each entitling him to a different seat. He is potentially a

[4] The Samoan *fono* and Gilbertese *mwaneaba* (meeting house) probably have a common origin, for *mwaneaba* customs are attributed to Samoan invaders arriving in the Gilbert Islands several hundred years ago.

member of several *bwoti* at once, but can activate membership in only one. His children are not bound by his choice, however, and he, himself, may change his affiliation, either because he has quarreled with his mates, or because he wishes to help keep up the numerical strength or to assume the leadership of a *bwoti* in which he has the right of active membership. A man entitled to sit in two places may so divide his land holdings that one son acquires the right to sit in one *bwoti* while another son acquires the right to sit in the other. There are instances where brothers belong to different *bwoti*. Everyone has the right of membership in at least one; people divide their land holdings among their heirs in such a way as to insure this. Women pass on these rights to their children in the same way that men do. We have seen, however, that unless they have no brothers they traditionally receive smaller allotments of land, and then only at marriage. As a result men belong more often to their father's than to their mother's *bwoti*. It is understandable that this kin group should have been erroneously labeled "patrilineal" by such outstanding reporters of Gilbertese custom as Grimble (1933:19–20) and the Maudes (1931:232). In the light of existing concepts, this was the best label they could use.[5] The *bwoti*, then, is a common descent group whose membership is restricted, not by reckoning descent exclusively through one sex, but to those descendants of the common ancestor whose share of the original inheritance includes a portion of a particular plot of land.

Kainga appear originally to have had the same membership as *bwoti*, for in some instances their names coincide, and they often have the same founding ancestors. In time, however, they diverged, for the principles governing their membership differ. Like the *bwoti*, each *kainga* was a descent group associated with a tract of land. Its founding ancestor, also, was the original holder of the tract. Theoretically, the original ancestor established residence on his land. Those of his descendants who continued to reside there formed together with their spouses an extended family, or *mweenga*. Together with those who were born and raised there, but had moved away after marriage, they formed a *kainga*. Residence was commonly patrilocal but matrilocal residence was considered proper under some circumstances, as when a man's share

_____

[5] There remains the possibility, of course, that the *bwoti* are patrilineal on some Gilbertese atolls. On Onotoa, however, they are not.

of *kainga* lands was small while his wife's was large. While residence did not affect one's own *kainga* membership, it did affect that of one's children. It appears to have been the rule that if a person's parents resided patrilocally he belonged to his father's *kainga,* but if they resided matrilocally he belonged to his mother's. Since residence was predominantly patrilocal, most Gilbertese belonged to their father's *kainga.* Succession to leadership in the *kainga,* moreover, could descend only in the male line. Neither of these facts, however, made the *kainga* a true patrilineal lineage, for if membership were patrilineal then the children of men who went in matrilocal residence would still have belonged to their father's *kainga.* Patrilineal succession to its leadership was guaranteed by having the eligible successor reside patrilocally, so that his son would in turn be a member and eligible to succeed him. We seem to have in the *kainga,* then, a kin group resembling a lineage, but whose membership is determined by parental residence rather than parental sex. This membership principle is, of course, tailor-made for societies practicing bilocal residence.

Normally, each member of the *kainga* had a plot in the tract of land associated with it. If this tract had a corresponding *bwoti* in the meeting house, all the *kainga's* members would be eligible to sit there. The plots of those members of the *kainga* who moved away after marriage, however, went to their children, who belonged to other *kainga.* These children thus became eligible to membership in a *bwoti* other than that to which most of their *kainga* mates belonged. By this process members of the same *kainga* could and did belong to different *bwoti,* and, conversely, members of the same *bwoti* belonged to different *kainga,* even though both types of group were founded by the same ancestors. While each *kainga* tends to be associated with a specific *bwoti,* their respective personnel are not congruent.

To sum up, all three descent groups are somehow connected with land. An ancestor having established ownership of a tract was the founder of all three. All of his descendants form an *ooi.* Those in actual possession of a share in the land are eligible to membership in a *bwoti.* Those whose parents resided on it form a *kainga.* None of these groups is unilinear.

Because of its intimate connection with bilocal residence, we must look upon the *kainga,* like the *ooi,* as quite possibly an original Malayo-Polynesian form of kin group. The *bwoti,* too, despite its special function in relation to meeting-house organization, commands our interest on structural grounds. What indications are there of the presence of groups like the *ooi, bwoti,* and *kainga* among other Malayo-Polynesian peoples? Let us turn to the *ooi* and *bwoti* first.

Barton's account of the Ifugao indicates clearly that an unrestricted descent group of the *ooi* type occurs there. In describing the Ifugao "family," as he calls it, he leaves no doubt about the presence of bilateral kindreds (1919:15). When he talks of family-owned land, however, he is clearly talking about something else (pp. 39–41). He indicates that some holdings have been associated with a particular family for generations. They may descend through daughters as well as sons (pp. 50–55). When a person dies without children his property reverts for division not to his kindred as a unit but to the nearest of his kin who like him are descended from a former owner. Indeed, as far as the reversion of land to collateral heirs is concerned, Ifugao law is almost identical with Gilbertese law. Members of this land-holding family, moreover, have a voice in its alienation even though they possess no shares in the land. Clearly, when Barton talks about the family as a land-holding unit, he is talking about an unrestricted descent group like the *ooi*. The Ifugao are one of the societies considered by Murdock (1949:349) to preserve the original Malayo-Polynesian Hawaiian type of organization unchanged. If he is right, we must accept the *ooi* as one of its characteristic features.

Ulawa in the Solomon Islands is another society which exemplifies Murdock's (1949:349) original Hawaiian type of social structure. As reported by Ivens (1927:45–46, 60–61), the Ulawans live in hamlets whose members consider themselves kinsmen. Patrilocal residence prevails, but Ivens notes that commoners marrying into a chief's family may live matrilocally. In addition to extended families there is a kindred, called *komu*. Now, Ivens says that garden grounds and coconut trees belong to the *komu*, and adds that daughters as well as sons may acquire rights in them and retain these rights after moving away in marriage. We have already noted that a kindred cannot be a land-owning group. As such, the *komu* can scarcely be a true kindred. I conclude that the term *komu* must refer in fact to two kinds of kin group—one a kindred, the other a nonunilinear descent group associated with land rights. While the published evidence gives no direct clue as to how membership in the latter group is determined, it is enough to restrict the probabilities. I infer that it is an unrestricted descent group like the *ooi* or is restricted either on the basis of land shares like the *bwoti* or on the basis of parental residence like the *kainga,* for Ivens is emphatic about the absence of unilinear groups.

When we turn to Polynesia we find abundant evidence of nonunilinear descent groups. All authorities stress the importance of lineal descent, whether through men or women, in connection with social rank and land rights. Some authorities use the term kindred in the *Notes and Queries* sense for these nonunilinear groups.

Macgregor's account (1937:54) of Tokelau, for example, describes a kindred as all persons descended from a common ancestor, whether through men or women, indicating that it is an unrestricted descent group of the *ooi* type. He adds that "the land that was given to the heads of families [in the original settlement] became the common property of the kindreds descended from them. Each member of the kindred received the right to use a section of the land." Children thus acquired claims to a share of land in both their father's and mother's groups. Macgregor states that normally only one of these claims was activated, sometimes on the mother's side and sometimes on the father's. But he does not give the criteria for this choice. It could not have been parental residence for residence was regularly matrilocal, while leadership in the group descended patrilineally in the primogeniture line as in the Gilbert Islands. We can only conclude that in addition to the unrestricted descent group there was a restricted group comprising persons who actually possessed shares in the ancestral land, resembling in this respect the Gilbertese *bwoti.*

In his account of Uvea, Burrows (1937:62–68) likewise uses the term kindred to refer to two nonunilinear descent groups. One appears to be unrestricted like the *ooi,* its members having rights in ancestral land regardless of where they or their parents reside, though if membership is confined to those descendants who actually possess shares as distinct from the right to possess them it corresponds to the Gilbertese *bwoti.* Which is the case is not clear. A segment of this group is localized as a bilocal extended family. This more restricted group is analogous to the Gilbertese *kainga*. In fact, the Uveans use the name *kainga* for it, as well as for the larger group.

Burrows (1936:65–78) develops the same picture on Futuna, where the *kutunga* is either an unrestricted group like the *ooi* or a restricted group like the *bwoti*. Here the term *kainga* is reserved for that portion of it which is localized on *kutunga* land. Since residence is bilocal, membership in the *kainga* must be based on parental residence, as in the Gilbert Islands. Burrows calls the *kutunga* a kindred and cites *Notes and Queries* as his authority for doing so. Futunan society is another of those which Murdock (1949:349) regards as typifying original Malayo-Polynesian forms of organization.

The demonstrable presence of unrestricted descent groups associated with land in Ifugao and Gilbertese society, and their probable presence in Uvea, Futuna, and Ulawa means that either they developed independently in Indonesia, Micronesia, Polynesia, and Melanesia, or they were a part of original Malayo-Polynesian social structure. Of these five societies, three are represented in Murdock's survey. That each of them should be considered by him, for other reasons, to preserve the original social structure unchanged is not without significance in this regard.

Given the presence of unrestricted descent groups, it is evident that groups structurally similar to the *bwoti* readily tend to develop. All that is required is a distinction between those who as descendants have rights to acquire a share of ancestral land and those among them who actually have received such shares. If the latter are organized as a separate social group for any reason, they necessarily constitute a restricted descent group in which membership follows the *bwoti* principle. The conditions for its presence, therefore, may well have obtained in early Malayo-Polynesian society. The distributional evidence, however, is too limited to warrant any conclusion in this regard.

In the foregoing survey of possible examples of the *ooi* type of group, we have noted the simultaneous presence of the *kainga* type on Uvea and Futuna, where, too, it is called a *kainga*. This suggests that there may be linguistic as well as other evidence for considering the *kainga* type of group an early Malayo-Polynesian form.

The term *kainga,* together with its variant *kainanga,* has a wide distribution in Micronesia and Polynesia. This distribution cannot be attributed to borrowing because its various forms show the proper historical sound shifts as loan-words do not. While the meaning of the term is not always clear, it invariably has to do with land and/or some kind of social group. In Mangareva, for example, *kainga* refers to a section of land (Buck 1938a). It means a kinsman in Lau and Tonga (Hocart 1929), and a non-unilinear kin group together with its land in Futuna, Uvea, and the Gilbert Islands, while an ill-defined family group is called *'aiga* in Samoa. The variant form occurs as *'ainana* in Hawaii, where it refers to a local population of some kind. The cognates *kainanga* and *hailang* or *jejinag* refer to patrilineal and matrilineal sibs, respectively, in Tikopia (Firth 1936) and the Central Caroline Islands (Lessa 1950; Goodenough 1951). Clearly there was some kind of descent group associated with land in the society from which both Polynesian and Micronesian peoples are jointly descended. But how in the course of history could this ancestral descent group come to be nonunilinear in some places and unilinear in others? And where it is unilinear, how could it become patrilineal here and matrilineal there? If we start with the assumption that this group was originally, as in the Gilbert Islands, one in which continuity of membership derived from parental residence where the residence rule was bilocal, then the answer becomes clear. In those societies shifting to regular patrilocal residence, the group automatically became patrilineal. Where matrilocal residence became the rule, as in the Carolines, the group became equally automatically matrilineal. And in each case no one need even be aware that a change had in fact occurred. Where bilocal residence continued or tendencies to unilocality did not go too far, the kin group remained nonunilinear. If this is so, where else in addition to Uvea, Futuna, and the Gilbert Islands do we encounter nonunilinear descent groups based on parental residence?

The so-called patrilineal clans of the Lau Islands are definitely kin groups in which membership is based on parental residence. The accounts by both Thompson (1940:54) and Hocart (1929:17) make this clear. Hocart, for example, says: "Usually a man 'follows' his father's clan, but many men live with the mother's people, even though both clans may be in the same village, next to one another. If a man lives with his wife's people, the children follow the mother's clan." The importance of parental residence for *hapu* membership among the Maori has been noted by Firth (1929:99–100). For predominantly patrilocal Tongareva we have the suggestive statement by Buck (1932a:40) that "through matrilocal residence the children drop active connection with their father's kin and become incorporated and naturally absorbed into their mother's family and the organization to which it belongs." I suspect a similar situation in Tokelau (Macgregor 1937) and Manua (Mead 1930). Certainly it would be compatible with the meager facts reported there.

For patrilineal Tubuai, Aitken (1930:36) reports that in the absence of sons descent was carried through a daughter for one generation. This practice bears an obvious resemblance to *ambil anak,* or adoptive marriage, as reported for some Indonesian societies, where a patrilineal line may be continued for one generation through a daughter instead of through a son (Ter Haar 1948:175–76; Murdock 1949:21, 45). Here matrilocal residence is the social mechanism whereby descent through a woman is legalized. The daughter who will carry on the line stays with her family of orientation, her husband moves in and the bride-price is waived. In short, the children take their lineage affiliation in accordance with the residence of their parents. Looked at this way, Indonesian kin groups, where these matrilocal marriages are practiced, are basically like the Gilbertese *kainga* and the so-called clans of the Lau Islands. Historically, it would appear that a shift toward patrilocal residence made affiliation with the father's group so common that kin groups came to be viewed as properly patrilineal. Jural recognition of patrilineal descent then required a legal device for reconciling it with the less frequent but traditional practice of matrilineal affiliation under matrilocal residence. This was accomplished simply by adoption of the husband. Adoptive marriage, then, points to the former existence in some Indonesian societies of nonunilinear descent groups of the *kainga* type.

From Melanesia I have no clear example of kin groups corresponding to the *kainga.* There is a possibility, however, that they occur in Ulawa, as has already been noted. Rivers' account (1926b:71–94) of Eddystone Island shows bilocal residence. His one reference to gardening rights (p. 93) indicates that a woman retains a share of her parent's land if she and her husband live matrilocally, her children presumably inheriting from her, but she loses these rights if she lives patrilocally for then her children presumably inherit from their father. If the same principle applies to men, rights in land are based on parental residence. If those having such rights in the same section of land are organized as a group, it is very likely of the *kainga* type.

Melanesian possibilities aside, however, the demonstrable antiquity of the *kainga* for Polynesia and Micronesia, when taken together with the indications of its former presence in Indonesia, warrants the inference that this form of group was present in early Malayo-Polynesian society. Murdock's (1949:152, 228, 349) reconstruction of bilocal residence, without which the *kainga* is impossible, makes this inference even more plausible.

If we accept the proposition that descent groups like the *ooi* and *kainga* were both represented in original Malayo-Polynesian society, how can it help us to understand the processes by which some of the complex social systems among present Malayo-Polynesian peoples emerged? By way of introduction to answering this question, I wish to call attention to the peculiar form of the nonunilinear descent group in the community of Bwaidoga in the D'Entrecasteaux Islands, where I had the opportunity to collect some information in 1951.[6]

Bwaidoga consists of several hamlets, *kali:va,* strung along the coast. Each hamlet is associated with one or two kin groups called *unuma,* which are localized there in extended families. Several related *unuma* form a larger nonlocalized kin group, called *ga:bu.* Most men inherit a share of their father's *unuma* lands and reside patrilocally after marriage. Under these conditions a man belongs to his father's *unuma* and *ga:bu.* He may, however, choose to reside with his mother's *unuma,* receiving a share of its land from his maternal grandfather or maternal uncle. By doing this he loses rights in his father's land, unless he returns permanently to his father's *unuma* immediately following his father's death. If he remains with his mother's *unuma,* he forfeits these rights for himself and his heirs in perpetuity. By choosing to affiliate with his

[6] In November 1951, I spent two days at Bwaidoga, at which time, due to the generous assistance provided by the Reverend Mr. William Coates of the Wailagi Mission, I was able to obtain from a group of native elders the information presented here. The field work of which the survey of Goodenough Island formed a part was sponsored by the Museum of the University of Pennsylvania.

mother's *unuma,* a man automatically becomes a member of her *ga:bu* as well.[7]

The Bwaidogan *unuma* and *ga:bu* differ from the *kainga* in that residence is never matrilocal. The choice is between patrilocal and avunculocal residence. Men can acquire land from the *unuma* of either parent, and their choice of residence depends on where they can get the best land. As a result of this system, membership in *unuma* and *ga:bu* is traced sometimes through female and sometimes through male ancestors.

The avunculocal alternative to patrilocal residence suggests that the Bwaidogan *ga:bu* and *unuma* were formerly matrilineal, and that the *unuma* used to be localized as an avunculocal extended family. With a shift in favor of patrilocal residence, membership in the *unuma* became optionally patrilineal. The present system may be seen, then, as transitional from a matrilineal to a patrilineal form of organization. As such, it cannot be viewed as indicative of early Malayo-Polynesian forms. I mention Bwaidoga, however, not only to illustrate another kind of nonunilinear descent group, but to help point up a problem which I believe has played a major determining role in the history of Malayo-Polynesian social organization: the problem of land distribution.

In any community where cultivatable land is not over-abundant in relation to population, and all rights to land depend on membership in strictly unilinear kin groups, a serious problem must soon arise. Unilinear groups inevitably fluctuate considerably in size. The matrilineal lineages on Truk, for example, readily double or halve their membership in the space of one or two generations. As a result, one lineage may have twice as much land as its members need while another has not enough to go around. Unless devices are developed to redistribute land rights to persons outside the owning group, intracommunity conflict is inevitable.

As noted at the beginning of this discussion, Malayo-Polynesian societies characteristically vest land ownership in kin groups. Throughout their history, therefore, they have had to meet the

[7] The *ga:bu* seems to correspond to the totemic group described by Jenness and Ballantyne (1920:66–67) as patrilineal; and the representatives of such a group in one hamlet presumably correspond to the *unuma.* Their characterization of these groups as patrilineal apparently follows from the fact that patrilocal residence and consequent patrilineal affiliation predominated statistically.

problem of land distribution in the face of constant fluctuations in kin-group size. One of the simplest possible devices for achieving this end is to keep the land-owning groups nonunilinear. With the *ooi* type of group a person has membership in as many *ooi* as there are distinct land-owning ancestors of whom he is a lineal descendant. While he can expect little from those *ooi* which have become numerically large, he can expect a lot of land from those which have few surviving members. The overlapping memberships inevitable with unrestricted descent groups make them an excellent vehicle for keeping land holdings equitably distributed throughout the community.

As a restricted descent group without overlapping personnel, the *kainga* is also admirably suited for keeping group membership balanced in relation to its immediate land resources. With bilocal residence, as the size of one *kainga* decreases in relation to that of other *kainga,* more of its members remain at home after marriage; as its population increases, more move away.

How do these functional considerations help us to understand the development of other social forms?

In those societies where conditions came to favor neolocal residence, the *kainga* could not possibly survive. If the same factors promoted individual ownership of land, the *ooi* would also have been weakened, leaving only the bilateral kindred—as among the Kalingas of Luzon (Barton 1949), who now have a social structure corresponding to Murdock's "Eskimo" type.

In areas where there was an abundance of land, and slash-and-burn agriculture made the use of any plot a temporary matter, doing away with the need for permanent tenure, bilocal residence was no longer functionally advantageous. Unilocal residence rules could and did develop, and the *kainga* type of group became unilinear as a result. The large islands of Melanesia provided conditions of this sort, which accounts, I believe, for the high incidence of unilinear forms of organization there.

Tendencies toward unilocal residence and unilinear descent developed elsewhere also, as in the Caroline Islands and parts of Indonesia. These tendencies called for reliance on other devices for redistributing land. In the Carolines this was accomplished by separating use rights from membership in the owning group. Where formerly parental residence had been the basis for membership in the owning group, it now became one of several bases for transmitting use rights outside the owning group. I have shown elsewhere how the more complicated tenure system which resulted served to keep land use equitably distributed on matrilineal Truk (Goodenough 1951:44, 166–71).

Adoption of the land-poor by kinsmen in land-rich groups is another device for solving the land distribution problem. It is not mutually exclusive with other devices, and its wide practice is familiar to all students of Malayo-Polynesian societies. It is of special importance where the land-owning groups have become unilinear. We have already mentioned its wedding with the parental residence principle in Indonesia in connection with adoptive marriage there. Its elaborations on Palau in conjunction with financial sponsorship are so complex as to obscure almost beyond recognition the underlying matrilineal system (Barnett 1949).

The Bwaidogans provide an interesting example of a people whose landowning kin groups became matrilineal, but, under the stress of land distribution problems, could not remain so. They had to become nonunilinear again. With matrilineal descent and avunculocal residence as the immediate antecedents of this return shift, however, the result was the peculiar type of group already described, not the original *kainga*. Pressures of the kind at work in Bwaidoga may well lie behind the series of shifts which culminated in double descent in Yap (Schneider 1953:216–17) and the bilineal groups of the New Hebrides (Layard 1942).

I conclude, then, that in addition to the characteristics reconstructed by Murdock for early Malayo-Polynesian society, there were two types of kin group associated with land. One was an unrestricted descent group, while membership in the other was determined by parental residence. Because they stressed kin ties through both parents equally, these groups favored the simultaneous presence of bilateral kindreds and Generation-Hawaiian kinship terms as already reconstructed by Murdock.[8] The structure of both groups helped resolve land distribution problems. Where residence became patrilocal or matrilocal, these groups tended automatically to be transformed into patrilineal or matrilineal sibs and lineages. Where this occurred, greater reliance on adop-

[8] The reasons given by Murdock (1949:152, 158) for the association of Generation terminology with bilocal residence and bilateral kindreds, for example, apply with equal force to its association with nonunilinear descent groups of the sort herein described.

tion, adjustments in the land tenure system, or a subsequent return to optional bases of group affiliation led to the complicated and varied social systems now present in parts of Indonesia and Micronesia, as well as to such unusual ones as we find in Bwaidoga.

CHARLES O. FRAKE

Malayo-Polynesian Land Tenure

In a recent article[1] in the *Anthropologist,* Goodenough (1955: 81–82) proposes an association of kin groups with land tenure as a characteristic of early Malayo-Polynesian society. Without taking issue with Goodenough's analysis of similarities in principles of land tenure among certain contemporary Malayo-Polynesian peoples, an important contribution in its own right, I wish to submit an alternative explanation for their origin: kin groups became similarly associated with land tenure among different Malayo-Polynesian peoples as a response to comparable conditions met independently in the course of their history.

To reconstruct a phenomenon as Proto-Malayo-Polynesian, it is essential that it be sufficiently represented in Malaysia as well as in Polynesia and Micronesia. Goodenough draws the bulk of his examples from the latter areas, citing only one Malaysian society, the Ifugao of northern Luzon, as having kin groups comparable to the Gilbertese *ooi.* "The Ifugao are one of the societies considered by Murdock (1949:349) to preserve the original Malayo-Polynesian Hawaiian type of organization unchanged. If he is right, we must accept the *ooi* as one of its characteristic features" (p. 140).

It may well be that the Ifugao have not changed their structural type since Proto-Malayo-Polynesian times, but it does not follow that their kin groups have been associated with land tenure since that time. The great importance of land ownership to the Ifugao

SOURCE: Reprinted from *American Anthropologist,* Vol. 58, No. 1 (1956), pp. 170–73, by permission of the author and publisher.
[1] [The preceding article in this volume.]

Polanyi

145

Beacon

The Great Transformation

11-10-1

stems from that fact that they, unlike other interior peoples of
Malaysia, have, by means of an elaborate system of terraces,
adapted permanent-field cultivation of wet rice to their mountainous environment. Since Ifugao principles of land tenure are closely
integrated with this system of agriculture, their antiquity cannot
be immediately assumed unless it can be demonstrated that
permanent-field cultivation is equally ancient in Malaysia.

In actuality, permanent-field agriculture is comparatively late.
Its development depended upon the application of wet-field techniques to the cultivation of rice, which had previously been grown
by dry-field shifting cultivation (Burkill 1935:1595, 1600; Pelzer
1945:9). Indeed, rice itself seems to have been preceded in Malaysia by other grains, such as Job's tears and millet (Pelzer
1945:8–9; Burkill 1935:1999), and these by root crops. All of
these earlier cultigens were, and still are, grown in Malaysia on
dry fields by techniques of shifting cultivation.

If principles of land tenure found among contemporary
permanent-field agriculturists in Malaysia are to be considered
features of original Malayo-Polynesian society, similar principles
must be found among peoples who still practice prior forms of
agriculture. The data on Malaysian shifting cultivators reveal no
such similarities.

Among the Sindangan Subanun of Mindanao, whom I studied
in the field in 1953–54, land is a free good. Informal principles
govern the selection of clearing sites each year, but the local or
kin group affiliations of the original clearers of a tract have no
bearing on the issue. Clearing establishes rights to use for a *continuous* period, but once the field has been left fallow for refor-
estation all rights are abandoned, and cultivators make no effort
to preserve or remember the boundaries of particular plots. Usufruct rights to land are held only as long as crops are growing on
it, and only the crops—not the fields—are owned. Furthermore,
both ownership and usufruct rights are held by individuals and
by nuclear (or polygynous) families, never by wider kin groups.
Similar usages prevail among the Hanunóo of Mindoro (Conklin
1954:48). In Borneo and Celebes, where, unlike the Subanun
or Hanunóo, the shifting cultivators typically live in relatively
large nucleated settlements, villages appear to have rights over
delimited tracts of forested land for clearing purposes, but there
is no evidence that these rights are in any way associated with

descent groups (Provinse 1937:81–82; Leach 1950:82; Woensdregt 1928:149). As a matter of fact, the only areas for which I
can find evidence of kin groups having control over tracts of land
among Malayo-Polynesian shifting cultivators are in Madagascar
(Linton 1933:40) and Formosa (Mabuchi 1951:54) where *unilinear* kin groups have developed.

Goodenough (1955:81) ascribes the development of unilinear
descent in Melanesia to the absence, among shifting cultivators,
of kin groups associated with land tenure. But shifting cultivation,
as practiced in Malaysia, is fully compatible with bilateral descent
(Frake 1955). The central core of Malaysian islands remains for
the most part bilateral whatever the type of agriculture practiced.
This, in the face of extreme variations in subsistence economies,
makes it difficult to explain bilaterality in terms of systems of
land tenure.

It would appear, rather, that where land has become a form of
property among Malayo-Polynesians, similar systems of land tenure have developed from a common base of bilateral social organization. Group control of land has become a problem only
where, as among the Ifugao, permanent-field agriculture is practiced, or where, as in Polynesia and Micronesia, there is only
a very limited amount of land available. Prior to the Oceanic
migrations and to the innovation of permanent-field cultivation
in Malaysia, land must have been a free good. It is probable,
therefore, that similarities in systems of land tenure between Malaysian permanent-field cultivators and the peoples of Polynesia
and Micronesia are the product of convergence under conditions
of land scarcity and not of common cultural inheritance from the
original Malayo-Polynesian speech community.

WARD H. GOODENOUGH

Reply

Frake differs with me regarding the antiquity of nonunilinear descent groups, such as the Gilbertese *ooi* and *kainga* (Goodenough 1955), among Malayo-Polynesian peoples. It was my suggestion that one or both of them might have been characteristic of Proto-Malayo-Polynesian society and that they should be added to the other characteristics already deduced by Murdock (1949: 349–50).

I based this suggestion on three considerations. First, there appear to be nonunilinear descent groups among the same societies which Murdock for other reasons regards as preserving original Malayo-Polynesian social structure. Second, societies for which there is evidence of the existence or former existence of such groups are to be found in Indonesia, Melanesia, Polynesia, and Micronesia. Their distribution is discontinuous and not confined to any one subgroup or culture area. Third, most Malayo-Polynesian societies with which I am familiar have descent groups of some sort associated with land tenure. If we assume such association to be characteristic of Proto-Malayo-Polynesian society, we must suppose that the descent group involved was other than a bilateral kindred, which cannot function as a landholding group due to its discontinuity between generations and its different membership for every ego. Since Murdock makes a good case against the presence of unilinear descent groups in the proto-society, any landholding descent groups must have been nonunilinear, something like the *ooi* or *kainga* of the Gilbert Islands.

SOURCE: Reprinted from *American Anthropologist*, Vol. 58, No. 1 (1956), pp. 173–76, by permission of the author and publisher.

Frake makes the counter-suggestion that nonunilinear descent groups arose independently where there was strong pressure on the use of cultivable land, that there is, therefore, no need to attribute them to the ancestral Malayo-Polynesian society. This suggestion has merit in that it, too, is in keeping with the second consideration mentioned above: the discontinuous distribution of nonunilinear groups. To support it, Frake says that I am wrong in assuming an ancient association of landownership with some kind of descent group. He suggests that land was a free good not subject to private ownership by individuals or groups and that its status as such was consistent with the practice of swidden agriculture, which is not conducive to private ownership. According to this view, private ownership of land and functionally associated kin groups developed among those Malayo-Polynesian societies which adopted wet-rice cultivation or found themselves on small islands where the amount of cultivable land was limited. Those with shifting agriculture preserved the old system with free use of land. Frake develops this point of view by citing my own speculation that unilinear groups arose from nonunilinear ones in Melanesia where "slash-and-burn agriculture made the use of any plot a temporary matter, doing away with the need for permanent tenure" (Goodenough 1955:81). If we assume that Proto-Malayo-Polynesian society practiced swidden agriculture and inhabited a region where tropical forest land was abundant, the conditions would be like those in Melanesia; there would be no need for permanent tenure nor for any type of kin group with the functional advantages which I attributed to the nonunilinear descent group. I am thus apparently refuted by my own argument.

Frake's point is well taken. He catches me in an inconsistency of which I must confess I was unaware. Granting the inconsistency, however, is Frake's the only possible conclusion, or are there alternatives? Given swidden agriculture and an abundance of forest land, does it logically follow that there is no need for permanent tenure? I assumed so in speculating about Melanesia. Frake also assumes that it follows and cites the Sindangan Subanun as a case in point. It now appears to me, however, that we may have been wrong in making such an assumption.

Within the past year I have had the opportunity to make a field study of the Nakanai people of New Britain Island in Melanesia. They practice swidden agriculture and, like the Sindangan Subanun, do not seem to pay any attention to landownership in locating their gardens. Indeed, the several hamlets of a village garden side by side. Superficially it appears that land is a free good. The fact is, however, that land is owned by matrilineal lineages. While the owners do not necessarily make gardens on it, they must give their consent before anyone else, including their village mates, may do so. At the present time such consent is readily granted. Landowning lineages hold far more than they can cultivate over the fifteen- to twenty-year span that plots must lie fallow before they may be worked again. This means that formerly cleared land will revert to tall timber unless it is recleared within a reasonable time. Landowners do not want swidden land to revert to forest. Second growth is much easier to clear, whether with steel tools, as nowadays, or with shell and stone, as in former times. It is this second-growth land which is valuable as farmland, while virgin forest is not subject to individual or lineage ownership. One of the things that is particularly striking is the jealousy with which the Nakanai seek to protect their *title* to swidden lands, even though they are only too happy to have others use them. This is scarcely in accord with the idea that slash-and-burn farming fails to promote private ownership.

What has happened in the Nakanai case seems reasonably clear. Since the earliest European contacts there has been considerable population decline. At one time the amount of second-growth land per capita must have been far less than it is now. Jealousy regarding title reflects this past condition when gardening land was in greater demand, while willingness to allow others to use the land reflects the present concern to keep it valuable as property by not letting it lie fallow too long.

When the Indonesian and Melanesian islands were first settled, then, the early Malayo-Polynesians were faced with the problem of clearing virgin rain-forest. Cleared land was at a premium. As long as their descendants multiplied, cleared land continued at a premium. During the period of expansion of Malayo-Polynesian peoples, therefore, they were faced with precisely the same kind of pressures for access to readily cultivable land as Frake feels are unique to peoples practicing permanent-field agriculture or occupying small islands. What is important is not the type of agriculture but the amount of gardening land available to the existing population. The effort required to turn tropical rain-forest into gardening land is such as to make its results a significant capital gain, rights to which are not lightly to be granted to others but jealously preserved for one's descendants.

In deference to Frake's position, however, it should be noted that the degree of difficulty in clearing virgin forest varies from one locality to the next. In the high mountains of New Guinea's interior, for example, trees are less massive than in the lowlands. It is possible that in some areas possession of steel tools has made a difference, though, to the Nakanai, steel axes do not serve significantly to reduce the imposing dimensions of virgin timber, however much they help with secondary growth.

I conclude, then, that under some conditions slash-and-burn farming is capable of exerting considerable pressure toward private ownership. While Frake has rightly caught me in an inconsistency, it does not necessarily invalidate my conclusions as to the possible antiquity of nonunilinear descent groups among Malayo-Polynesian peoples.

I should point out, however, that the distributional evidence in support of my argument is far less convincing at present, in view of the recent findings by Grace (1955:339) concerning the subgroupings of Malayo-Polynesian languages. The bulk of my cases came from societies speaking Micronesian and Polynesian languages, which it now appears form together with Fijian and Rotuman a sub-subbranch of the New Hebridean subbranch of the Oceanic division of Malayo-Polynesian. This means that considerably more evidence for the occurrence of nonunilinear descent groups in Indonesia and Melanesia must be obtained if my thesis regarding their antiquity is to stand up. Frake may well be right that the Ifugao present a case of parallel development.

Because the nonunilinear descent group has not hitherto been one of the possibilities for which ethnographers were looking, it may exist in a number of societies which have been reported as bilateral or unilinear. What is important at present is to recognize the wider range of structural possibilities for descent-group organization. Reconstructing Proto-Malayo-Polynesian kin groups will have to wait. In the meantime, Frake has helped to clarify the alternatives.

MARSHALL D. SAHLINS

9. Poor Man, Rich Man, Big Man, Chief: Political Types in Melanesia and Polynesia[1]

With an eye to their own life goals, the native peoples of Pacific
Islands unwittingly present to anthropologists a generous scientific
gift: an extended series of experiments in cultural adaptation and
evolutionary development. They have compressed their institutions within the confines of infertile coral atolls, expanded them
on volcanic islands, created with the means history gave them
cultures adapted to the deserts of Australia, the mountains and
warm coasts of New Guinea, the rain forests of the Solomon

SOURCE: Reprinted from *Comparative Studies in Society and History*, Vol.
5, No. 3 (1963), pp. 285–303, by permission of the author and publisher.

[1] The present paper is preliminary to a wider and more detailed comparison of Melanesian and Polynesian polities and economies. I have merely
abstracted here some of the more striking political differences in the two
areas. The full study—which, incidentally, will include more documentation
—has been promised the editors of *The Journal of the Polynesian Society*,
and I intend to deliver it to them some day.

The comparative method so far followed in this research has involved
reading the monographs and taking notes. I don't think I originated the
method, but I would like to christen it—The Method of Uncontrolled Comparison. The description developed of two forms of leadership is a mental
distillation from the method of uncontrolled comparison. The two forms are
abstracted sociological types. Anyone conversant with the anthropological
literature of the South Pacific knows there are important variants of the
types, as well as exceptional political forms not fully treated here. All would
agree that consideration of the variations and exceptions is necessary and
desirable. Yet there is pleasure too, and some intellectual reward, in discovering the broad patterns. To (social-) scientifically justify my pleasure, I
could have referred to the pictures drawn of Melanesian big-men and Polynesian chiefs as "models" or as "ideal types". If that is all that is needed to
confer respectability on the paper, may the reader have it this way.

I hope all of this has been sufficiently disarming. Or need it also be said
that the hypotheses are provisional, subject to further research, etc.?

Islands. From the Australian Aborigines, whose hunting and gathering existence duplicates in outline the cultural life of the later Paleolithic, to the great chiefdoms of Hawaii, where society approached the formative levels of the old Fertile Crescent civilizations, almost every general phase in the progress of primitive culture is exemplified.

Where culture so experiments, anthropology finds its laboratories—makes its comparisons.[2]

In the southern and eastern Pacific two contrasting cultural provinces have long evoked anthropological interest: *Melanesia,* including New Guinea, the Bismarcks, Solomons, and island groups east to Fiji; and *Polynesia,* consisting in its main portion of the triangular constellation of lands between New Zealand, Easter Island, and the Hawaiian Islands. In and around Fiji, Melanesia and Polynesia intergrade culturally, but west and east of their intersection the two provinces pose broad contrasts in several sectors: in religion, art, kinship groupings, economics, political organization. The differences are the more notable for the underlying similarities from which they emerge. Melanesia and Polynesia are both agricultural regions in which many of the same crops—such as yams, taro, breadfruit, bananas, and coconuts— have long been cultivated by many similar techniques. Some recently presented linguistic and archaeological studies indeed suggest that Polynesian cultures originated from an eastern Melanesian hearth during the first millennium B.C.[3] Yet in anthropological annals the Polynesians were to become famous for elaborate forms of rank and chieftainship, whereas most Melane-

[2] Since Rivers' day, the Pacific has provided ethnographic stimulus to virtually every major ethnological school and interest. From such great landmarks as Rivers' *History of Melanesian Society,* Radcliffe-Brown's *Social Organization of the Australian Tribes,* Malinowski's famous Trobriand studies, especially *Argonauts of the Western Pacific,* Raymond Firth's pathmaking *Primitive Economics of the New Zealand Maori,* his functionalist classic, *We, the Tikopia,* and Margaret Mead's *Coming of Age in Samoa,* one can almost read off the history of ethnological theory in the earlier twentieth century. In addition to continuing to provision all these concerns, the Pacific has been the site of much recent evolutionist work (see, for example, Goldman 1955, 1960; Goodenough 1957; Sahlins 1958; Vayda 1959b). There are also the outstanding monographs on special subjects ranging from tropical agriculture (Conklin 1957; Freeman 1955) to millenarianism (Worsley 1957).

[3] This question, however, is presently in debate. See Grace 1955, 1959; Dyen 1960; Suggs 1960; Golson 1961.

sian societies broke off advance on this front at more rudimentary levels.

It is obviously imprecise, however, to make out the political contrast in broad culture-area terms. Within Polynesia, certain of the islands, such as Hawaii, the Society Islands and Tonga, developed unparalleled political momentum. And not all Melanesian polities, on the other side, were constrained and truncated in their evolution. In New Guinea and nearby areas of western Melanesia, small and loosely ordered political groupings are numerous, but in eastern Melanesia, New Caledonia and Fiji for example, political approximations of the Polynesian condition become common. There is more of an upward west to east slope in political development in the southern Pacific than a step-like, quantum progression.[4] It is quite revealing, however, to compare the extremes of this continuum, the western Melanesian underdevelopment against the greater Polynesian chiefdoms. While such comparison does not exhaust the evolutionary variations, it fairly establishes the scope of overall political achievement in this Pacific phylum of cultures.

Measurable along several dimensions, the contrast between developed Polynesian and underdeveloped Melanesian polities is immediately striking for differences in scale. H. Ian Hogbin and Camilla Wedgwood (1952–54) concluded from a survey of Melanesian (mostly western Melanesian) societies that ordered, independent political bodies in the region typically include seventy to three hundred persons; more recent work in the New Guinea Highlands suggests political groupings of up to a thousand, occasionally a few thousand, people.[5] But in Polynesia sovereignties of two thousand or three thousand are run-of-the-mill, and the most advanced chiefdoms, as in Tonga or Hawaii, might claim ten thousand, even tens of thousands.[6] Varying step by step with such differences in size of the polity are differences in territorial extent: from a few square miles in western Melanesia to tens or even hundreds of square miles in Polynesia.

The Polynesian advance in political scale was supported by

[4] There are notable bumps in the geographical gradient. The Trobriand chieftainships off eastern New Guinea will come to mind. But the Trobriand political development is clearly exceptional for western Melanesia.

[5] On New Guinea Highland political scale see among others, Paula Brown 1960.

[6] See the summary account in Sahlins 1958, especially pp. 132–33.

advance over Melanesia in political structure. Melanesia presents a great array of social-political forms: here political organization is based upon patrilineal descent groups, there on cognatic groups, or men's club-houses recruiting neighborhood memberships, on a secret ceremonial society, or perhaps on some combination of these structural principles. Yet a general plan can be discerned. The characteristic western Melanesian "tribe," that is, the ethnic-cultural entity, consists of many autonomous kinship-residential groups. Amounting on the ground to a small village or a local cluster of hamlets, each of these is a copy of the others in organization, each tends to be economically self-governing, and each is the equal of the others in political status. The tribal plan is one of politically unintegrated segments—segmental. But the political geometry in Polynesia is pyramidal. Local groups of the order of self-governing Melanesian communities appear in Polynesia as subdivisions of a more inclusive political body. Smaller units are integrated into larger through a system of intergroup ranking, and the network of representative chiefs of the subdivisions amounts to a coordinating political structure. So instead of the Melanesian scheme of small, separate, and equal political blocs, the Polynesian polity is an extensive pyramid of groups capped by the family and following of a paramount chief. (This Polynesian political upshot is often, although not always, facilitated by the development of ranked lineages. Called *conical clan* by Kirchhoff, at one time *ramage* by Firth and *status lineage* by Goldman, the Polynesian ranked lineage is the same in principle as the so-called *obok* system widely distributed in Central Asia, and it is at least analogous to the Scottish clan, the Chinese clan, certain Central African Bantu lineage systems, the house-groups of Northwest Coast Indians, perhaps even the "tribes" of the Israelites [Kirchhoff 1955; Firth 1957; Goldman 1957; Bacon 1958; Fried 1957]. Genealogical ranking is its distinctive feature: members of the same descent unit are ranked by genealogical distance from the common ancestor; lines of the same group become senior and cadet branches on this principle; related corporate lineages are relatively ranked, again by genealogical priority.)

Here is another criterion of Polynesian political advance: historical performance. Almost all of the native peoples of the South Pacific were brought up against intense European cultural pressure in the late eighteenth and the nineteenth centuries. Yet only the Hawaiians, Tahitians, Tongans, and to a lesser extent the Fijians, successfully defended themselves by evolving countervailing, native-controlled states. Complete with public governments and public law, monarchs and taxes, ministers and minions, these nineteenth century states are testimony to the native Polynesian political genius, to the level and the potential of indigenous political accomplishments.

Embedded within the grand differences in political scale, structure and performance is a more personal contrast, one in quality of leadership. An historically particular type of leader-figure, the "big-man" as he is often locally styled, appears in the underdeveloped settings of Melanesia. Another type, a chief properly so-called, is associated with the Polynesian advance.[7] Now these are distinct sociological types, that is to say, differences in the powers, privileges, rights, duties, and obligations of Melanesian big-men and Polynesian chiefs are given by the divergent societal contexts in which they operate. Yet the institutional distinctions cannot help but be manifest also in differences in bearing and character, appearance and manner—in a word, personality. It may

[7] The big-man pattern is very widespread in western Melanesia, although its complete distribution is not yet clear to me. Anthropological descriptions of big-man leadership vary from mere hints of its existence, as among the Orokaiva (Williams 1930), Lesu (Powdermaker 1933) or the interior peoples of northeastern Guadalcanal (Hogbin 1937–1938a), to excellent, closely grained analyses, such as Douglas Oliver's account of the Siuai of Bougainville (Oliver 1955). Big-man leadership has been more or less extensively described for the Manus of the Admiralty Islands (Mead 1934, 1937b); the To'ambaita of northern Malaita (Hogbin 1939, 1943–44); the Tangu of northeastern New Guinea (Burridge 1960); the Kapauku of Netherlands New Guinea (Pospisil 1958, 1959–60); the Kaoka of Guadalcanal (Hogbin 1933–34, 1937–38b); the Seniang District of Malekula (Deacon 1934); the Gawa' of the Huon Gulf area, New Guinea (Hogbin 1951); the Abelam (Kaberry 1940–41, 1941–42) and the Arapesh (Mead 1937a, 1938, 1947) of the Sepik District, New Guinea; the Elema, Orokolo Bay, New Guinea (Williams 1940); the Ngarawapum of the Markham Valley, New Guinea (Read 1946–47, 1949–50); the Kiwai of the Fly estuary, New Guinea (Landtman 1927); and a number of other societies, including, in New Guinea Highlands, the Kuma (Reay 1959a), the Gahuku-Gama (Read 1952, 1959), the Kyaka (Bulmer 1960–61), the Enga (Meggitt 1957, 1957–58), and others. (For an overview of the structural position of New Guinea Highlands' leaders see Barnes 1962.) A partial bibliography on Polynesian chieftainship can be found in Sahlins 1958. The outstanding ethnographic description of Polynesian chieftainship is, of course, Firth's for Tikopia (1950, 1957)—Tikopia, however, is not typical of the more advanced Polynesian chiefdoms with which we are principally concerned here.

be a good way to begin the more rigorous sociological comparison
of leadership with a more impressionistic sketch of the contrast
in the human dimension. Here I find it useful to apply charac-
terizations—or is it caricature?—from our own history to big-men
and chiefs, however much injustice this does to the historically
incomparable backgrounds of the Melanesians and Polynesians.
The Melanesian big-man seems so thoroughy bourgeois, so remi-
niscent of the free enterprising rugged individual of our own heritage. He combines with an ostensible interest in the general
welfare a more profound measure of self-interested cunning and
economic calculation. His gaze, as Veblen might have put it, is
fixed unswervingly to the main chance. His every public action
is designed to make a competitive and invidious comparison with
others, to show a standing above the masses that is product of
his own personal manufacture. The historical caricature of the
Polynesian chief, however, is feudal rather than capitalist. His
appearance, his bearing is almost regal; very likely he just *is* a
big man—" 'Can't you see he is a chief? See how big he is?' " (Gifford 1929:124). In his every public action is a display of the
refinements of breeding, in his manner always that *noblesse oblige*
of true pedigree and an incontestable right of rule. With his standing not so much a personal achievement as a just social due, he
can afford to be, and he is, every inch a chief.

In the several Melanesian tribes in which big-men have come
under anthropological scrutiny, local cultural differences modify
the expression of their personal powers.[8] But the indicative quality of big-man authority is everywhere the same: it is *personal*

[8] Thus the enclavement of the big-man pattern within a segmented lineage
organization in the New Guinea Highlands appears to limit the leader's political role and authority in comparison, say, with the Siuai. In the Highlands, intergroup relations are regulated in part by the segmented lineage
structure; among the Siuai intergroup relations depend more on contractual
arrangements between big-men, which throws these figures more into
prominence. (Notable in this connection has been the greater viability of
the Siuai big-man than the native Highlands leader in the face of colonial
control.) Barnes' (1962) comparison of Highland social structure with the
classic segmentary lineage systems of Africa suggests an inverse relation
between the formality of the lineage system and the political significance of
individual action. Now, if instances such as the Siuai be tacked on to the
comparison, the generalization may be further supported and extended:
among societies of the tribal level (cf. Sahlins 1961; Service 1962), the
greater the self-regulation of the political process through a lineage system,
the less function that remains to big-men, and the less significant their
political authority.

power. Big-men do not come to office; they do not succeed to, nor are they installed in, existing positions of leadership over political groups. The attainment of big-man status is rather the outcome of a series of acts which elevate a person above the common herd and attract about him a coterie of loyal, lesser men. It is not accurate to speak of "big-man" as a political title, for it is but an acknowledged standing in interpersonal relations— a "prince among men" so to speak as opposed to "The Prince of Danes". In particular Melanesian tribes the phrase might be "man of importance", or "man of renown", "generous rich-man", or "center-man", as well as "big-man".

A kind of two-sidedness in authority is implied in this series of phrases, a division of the big-man's field of influence into two distinct sectors. "Center-man" particularly connotes a cluster of followers gathered about an influential pivot. It socially implies the division of the tribe into political in-groups dominated by outstanding personalities. To the in-group, the big-man presents this sort of picture:

> The place of the leader in the district group [in northern Malaita] is well summed up by his title, which might be translated as "centre-man" . . . He was like a banyan, the natives explain, which, though the biggest and tallest in the forest, is still a tree like the rest. But, just because it exceeds all others, the banyan gives support to more lianas and creepers, provides more food for the birds, and gives better protection against sun and rain (Hogbin 1943–44:258).

But "man of renown" connotes a broader tribal field in which a man is not so much a leader as he is some sort of hero. This is the side of the big-man facing outward from his own faction, his status among some or all of the other political clusters of the tribe. The political sphere of the big-man divides itself into a small internal sector composed of his personal satellites—rarely over eighty men—and a much larger external sector, the tribal galaxy consisting of many similar constellations.

As it crosses over from the internal into the external sector, a big-man's power undergoes qualitative change. Within his faction a Melanesian leader has true command ability, outside of it only fame and indirect influence. It is not that the center-man rules his faction by physical force, but his followers do feel obliged to obey him, and he can usually get what he wants by haranguing them—public verbal suasion is indeed so often employed by center-men that they have been styled "harangue-utans". The orbits of outsiders, however, are set by their own center-men. " 'Do it yourself. I'm not *your* fool,' " would be the characteristic response to an order issued by a center-man to an outsider among the Siuai (Oliver 1955:408).[9] This fragmentation of true authority presents special political difficulties, particularly in organizing large masses of people for the prosecution of such collective ends as warfare or ceremony. Big-men do instigate mass action, but only by establishing both extensive renown and special personal relations of compulsion or reciprocity with other center-men.

Politics is in the main personal politiking in these Melanesian societies, and the size of a leader's faction as well as the extent of his renown are normally set by competition with other ambitious men. Little or no authority is given by social ascription: leadership is a creation—a creation of followership. "Followers", as it is written of the Kapauku of New Guinea, "stand in various relations to the leader. Their obedience to the headman's decisions is caused by motivations which reflect their particular relations to the leader" (Pospisil 1958:81). So a man must be prepared to demonstrate that he possesses the kinds of skills that command respect—magical powers, gardening prowess, mastery of oratorical style, perhaps bravery in war and feud.[10] Typically decisive is the deployment of one's skills and efforts in a certain direction: towards amassing goods, most often pigs, shell monies and vegetable foods, and distributing them in ways which build a name for cavalier generosity, if not for compassion. A faction is developed by informal private assistance to people of a locale. Tribal rank and renown are developed by great public giveaways sponsored by the rising big-man, often on behalf of his faction as well as himself. In different Melanesian tribes, the renown-making public distribution may appear as one side of a delayed exchange of pigs between corporate kinship groups; a marital consideration given a bride's kinfolk; a set of feasts connected with the erection

[9] Compare with the parallel statement for the Kaoka of Guadalcanal in Hogbin 1937–38b:305.

[10] It is difficult to say just how important the military qualifications of leadership have been in Melanesia, since the ethnographic researches have typically been undertaken after pacification, sometimes long after. I may underestimate this factor. Compare Bromley 1960.

of a big-man's dwelling, or of a clubhouse for himself and his faction, or with the purchase of higher grades of rank in secret societies; the sponsorship of a religious ceremony; a payment of subsidies and blood compensations to military allies; or perhaps the giveaway is a ceremonial challenge bestowed on another leader in the attempt to outgive and thus outrank him (a potlatch).

The making of the faction, however, is the true making of the Melanesian big-man. It is essential to establish relations of loyalty and obligation on the part of a number of people such that their production can be mobilized for renownbuilding external distribution. The bigger the faction the greater the renown; once momentum in external distribution has been generated the opposite can also be true. Any ambitious man who can gather a following can launch a societal career. The rising big-man necessarily depends initially on a small core of followers, principally his own household and his closest relatives. Upon these people he can prevail economically: he capitalizes in the first instance on kinship dues and by finessing the relation of reciprocity appropriate among close kinsmen. Often it becomes necessary at an early phase to enlarge one's household. The rising leader goes out of his way to incorporate within his family "strays" of various sorts, people without familial support themselves, such as widows and orphans. Additional wives are especially useful. The more wives a man has the more pigs he has. The relation here is functional, not identical: with more women gardening there will be more food for pigs and more swineherds. A Kiwai Papuan picturesquely put to an anthropologist in pidgin the advantages, economic and political, of polygamy: "'Another woman go garden, another woman go take firewood, another woman go catch fish, another woman cook him—husband he sing out plenty people come kaikai [i.e., come to eat]'" (Landtman 1927:168). Each new marriage, incidentally, creates for the big-man an additional set of in-laws from whom he can exact economic favors. Finally, a leader's career sustains its upward climb when he is able to link other men and their families to his faction, harnessing their production to his ambition. This is done by calculated generosities, by placing others in gratitude and obligation through helping them in some big way. A common technique is payment of bridewealth on behalf of young men seeking wives.

The great Malinowski used a phrase in analyzing primitive political economy that felicitously describes just what the big-man is doing: amassing a "fund of power". A big-man is one who can create and use social relations which give him leverage on others' production and the ability to siphon off an excess product—or sometimes he can cut down their consumption in the interest of the siphon. Now although his attention may be given primarily to short-term personal interests, from an objective standpoint the leader acts to promote long-term societal interests. The fund of power provisions activities that involve other groups of the society at large. In the greater perspective of that society at large, bigmen are indispensable means of creating supralocal organization: in tribes normally fragmented into small independent groups, bigmen at least temporarily widen the sphere of ceremony, recreation and art, economic collaboration, of war too. Yet always this greater societal organization depends on the lesser factional organization, particularly on the ceilings on economic mobilization set by relations between center-men and followers. The limits and the weaknesses of the political order in general are the limits and weaknesses of the factional in-groups.

And the personal quality of subordination to a center-man is a serious weakness in factional structure. A personal loyalty has to be made and continually reinforced; if there is discontent it may well be severed. Merely to create a faction takes time and effort, and to hold it, still more effort. The potential rupture of personal links in the factional chain is at the heart of two broad evolutionary shortcomings of western Melanesian political orders. First, a comparative instability. Shifting dispositions and magnetisms of ambitious men in a region may induce fluctuations in factions, perhaps some overlapping of them, and fluctuations also in the extent of different renowns. The death of a center-man can become a regional political trauma: the death undermines the personally cemented faction, the group dissolves in whole or in part, and the people re-group finally around rising pivotal bigmen. Although particular tribal structures in places cushion the disorganization, the big-man political system is generally unstable over short terms: in its superstructure it is a flux of rising and falling leaders, in its substructure of enlarging and contracting factions. Secondly, the personal political bond contributes to the containment of evolutionary advance. The possibility of their desertion, it is clear, often inhibits a leader's ability to forceably push up his followers' output, thereby placing constraints on higher political organization, but there is more to it than that. If it is to generate great momentum, a big-man's quest for the summits of renown is likely to bring out a contradiction in his relations to followers, so that he finds himself encouraging defection —or worse, an egalitarian rebellion—by encouraging production.

One side of the Melanesian contradiction is the initial economic reciprocity between a center-man and his followers. For his help they give their help, and for goods going out through his hands other goods (often from outside factions) flow back to his followers by the same path. The other side is that a cumulative build-up of renown forces center-men into economic extortion of the faction. Here it is important that not merely his own status, but the standing and perhaps the military security of his people depend on the big-man's achievements in public distribution. Established at the head of a sizeable faction, a center-man comes under increasing pressure to extract goods from his followers, to delay reciprocities owing them, and to deflect incoming goods back into external circulation. Success in competition with other big-men particularly undermines internal-factional reciprocities: such success is precisely measurable by the ability to give outsiders more than they can possibly reciprocate. In well delineated big-man polities, we find leaders negating the reciprocal obligations upon which their following had been predicated. Substituting extraction for reciprocity, they must compel their people to "eat the leader's renown," as one Solomon Island group puts it, in return for productive efforts. Some center-men appear more able than others to dam the inevitable tide of discontent that mounts within their factions, perhaps because of charismatic personalities, perhaps because of the particular social organizations in which they operate.[11] But paradoxically the ultimate defense of the center-man's position is some slackening of his drive to enlarge the funds of power. The alternative is much worse. In the anthropological record there are not merely instances of big-man chicanery and of material deprivation of the faction in the interests of renown, but some also of overloading of social

[11] Indeed it is the same people, the Siuai, who so explicitly discover themselves eating their leader's renown who also seem able to absorb a great deal of deprivation without violent reaction, at least until the leader's wave of fame has already crested (see Oliver 1955:362, 368, 387, 394).

relations with followers: the generation of antagonisms, defections, and in extreme cases the violent liquidation of the center-man.[12] Developing internal constraints, the Melanesian big-man political order brakes evolutionary advance at a certain level. It sets ceilings on the intensification of political authority, on the intensification of household production by political means, and on the diversion of household outputs in support of wider political organization. But in Polynesia these constraints were breached, and although Polynesian chiefdoms also found their developmental plateau, it was not before political evolution had been carried above the Melanesian ceilings. The fundamental defects of the Melanesian plan were overcome in Polynesia. The division between small internal and larger external political sectors, upon which all big-man politics hinged, was suppressed in Polynesia by the growth of an enclaving chiefdom-at-large. A chain of command subordinating lesser chiefs and groups to greater, on the basis of inherent societal rank, made local blocs or personal followings (such as were independent in Melanesia) merely dependent parts of the larger Polynesian chiefdom. So the nexus of the Polynesian chiefdom became an extensive set of offices, a pyramid of higher and lower chiefs holding sway over larger and smaller sections of the polity. Indeed the system of ranked and subdivided lineages (conical clan system), upon which the pyramid was characteristically established, might build up through several orders of inclusion and encompass the whole of an island or group of islands. While the island or the archipelago would normally be divided into several independent chiefdoms, high-order lineage connections between them, as well as kinship ties between their paramount chiefs, provided structural avenues for at least temporary expansion of political scale, for consolidation of great into even greater chiefdoms.[13]

[12] "In the Paniai Lake region (of Netherlands New Guinea), the people go so far as to kill a selfish rich man because of his 'immorality'. His own sons or brothers are induced by the rest of the members of the community to dispatch the first deadly arrow. '*Aki to tonowi beu, inii idikima enadani kodo to niitou* (you should not be the only rich man, we should all be the same, therefore you only stay equal with us)' was the reason given by the Paniai people for killing Mote Juwopija of Madi, a *tonowi* [Kapauku for 'big-man'] who was not generous enough". (Pospisil 1958:80, cf. pp. 108–110). On another egalitarian conspiracy, see Hogbin 1951:145, and for other aspects of the Melanesian contradiction note, for example, Hogbin 1939:81; Burridge 1960:18–19; and Reay 1959a:110, 129–30.

[13] Aside from the transitional developments in eastern Melanesia, several western Melanesian societies advanced to a structural position intermediate

The pivotal paramount chief as well as the chieftains controlling parts of a chiefdom were true office holders and title holders. They were not, like Melanesian big-men, fishers of men: they held positions of authority over permanent groups. The honorifics of Polynesian chiefs likewise did not refer to a standing in interpersonal relations, but to their leadership of political divisions—here "The Prince of Danes" *not* "the prince among men". In western Melanesia the personal superiorities and inferiorities arising in the intercourse of particular men largely defined the political bodies. In Polynesia there emerged suprapersonal structures of leadership and followership, organizations that continued independently of the particular men who occupied positions in them for brief mortal spans.

And these Polynesian chiefs did not make their positions in society—they were installed in societal positions. In several of the islands, men did struggle to office against the will and stratagems of rival aspirants. But then they came *to* power. Power resided in the office; it was not made by the demonstration of personal superiority. In other islands, Tahiti was famous for it, succession to chieftainship was tightly controlled by inherent rank. The chiefly lineage ruled by virtue of its genealogical connections with divinity, and chiefs were succeeded by first sons, who carried "in the blood" the attributes of leadership. The important comparative point is this: the qualities of command that had to reside in men in Melanesia, that had to be personally demonstrated in order to attract loyal followers, were in Polynesia socially assigned to office and

between underdeveloped Melanesian polities and Polynesian chiefdoms. In these western Melanesian protochiefdoms, an ascribed division of kinship groups (or segments thereof) into chiefly and nonchiefly ranks emerges— as in Sa'a (Ivens 1927), around Buka passage (Blackwood 1935), in Manam Island (Wedgwood 1933–34, 1958–59), Waropen (Held 1957), perhaps Mafulu (Williamson 1912), and several others. The rank system does not go beyond the broad dual division of groups into chiefly and nonchiefly: no pyramid of ranked social-political divisions along Polynesian lines is developed. The political unit remains near the average size of the western Melanesian autonomous community. Sway over the kin groups of such a local body falls automatically to a chiefly unit, but chiefs do not hold office title with stipulated rights over corporate sections of society, and further extension of chiefly authority, if any, must be achieved. The Trobriands, which carry this line of chiefly development to its highest point, remain under the same limitations, although it was ordinarily possible for powerful chiefs to integrate settlements of the external sector within their domains (*cf.* Powell 1960).

rank. In Polynesia, people of high rank and office *ipso facto* were leaders, and by the same token the qualities of leadership were automatically lacking—theirs was not to question why—among the underlying population. Magical powers such as a Melanesian big-man might acquire to sustain his position, a Polynesian high chief inherited by divine descent as the *mana* which sanctified his rule and protected his person against the hands of the commonalty. The productive ability the big-man laboriously had to demonstrate was effortlessly given Polynesian chiefs as religious control over agricultural fertility, and upon the ceremonial implementation of it the rest of the people were conceived dependent. Where a Melanesian leader had to master the compelling oratorical style, Polynesian paramounts often had trained "talking chiefs" whose voice was the chiefly command.

In the Polynesian view, a chiefly personage was in the nature of things powerful. But this merely implies the objective observation that his power was of the group rather than of himself. His authority came from the organization, from an organized acquiescence in his privileges and organized means of sustaining them. A kind of paradox resides in evolutionary developments which detach the exercise of authority from the necessity to demonstrate personal superiority: organizational power actually extends the role of personal decision and conscious planning, gives it greater scope, impact, and effectiveness. The growth of a political system such as the Polynesian constitutes advance over Melanesian orders of interpersonal dominance in the human control of human affairs. Especially significant for society at large were privileges accorded Polynesian chiefs which made them greater architects of funds of power than ever was any Melanesian big-man.

Masters of their people and "owners" in a titular sense of group resources, Polynesian chiefs had rights of call upon the labor and agricultural produce of households within their domains. Economic mobilization did not depend on, as it necessarily had for Melanesian big-men, the *de novo* creation by the leader of personal loyalties and economic obligations. A chief need not stoop to obligate this man or that man, need not by a series of individual acts of generosity induce others to support him, for economic leverage over a group was the inherent chiefly due. Consider the implications for the fund of power of the widespread chiefly privilege, related to titular "ownership" of land, of placing an interdiction, a tabu, on the harvest of some crop by way of reserving its use for a collective project. By means of the tabu the chief directs the course of production in a general way: households of his domain must turn to some other means of subsistence. He delivers a stimulus to household production: in the absence of the tabu further labors would not have been necessary. Most significantly, he has generated a politically utilizable agricultural surplus. A subsequent call on this surplus floats chieftainship as a going concern, capitalizes the fund of power. In certain islands, Polynesian chiefs controlled great storehouses which held the goods congealed by chiefly pressures on the commonalty. David Malo, one of the great native custodians of old Hawaiian lore, felicitously catches the political significance of the chiefly magazine in his well-known *Hawaiian Antiquities:*

> It was the practice for kings [i.e., paramount chiefs of individual islands] to build store-houses in which to collect food, fish, tapas [bark cloth], malos [men's loin clothes], pa-us [women's loin skirts], and all sorts of goods. These storehouses were designed by the Kalaimoku [the chief's principal executive] as a means of keeping the people contented, so they would not desert the king. They were like the baskets that were used to entrap the *hinalea* fish. The *hinalea* thought there was something good within the basket, and he hung round the outside of it. In the same way the people thought there was food in the store-houses, and they kept their eyes on the king. As the rat will not desert the pantry . . . where he thinks food is, so the people will not desert the king while they think there is food in his store-house (Malo 1903:257–58).

Redistribution of the fund of power was the supreme art of Polynesian politics. By well-planned *noblesse oblige* the large domain of a paramount chief was held together, organized at times for massive projects, protected against other chiefdoms, even further enriched. Uses of the chiefly fund included lavish hospitality and entertainments for outside chiefs and for the chief's own people, and succor of individuals or the underlying population at large in times of scarcities—bread and circuses. Chiefs subsidized craft production, promoting in Polynesia a division of technical labor unparalleled in extent and expertise in most of the Pacific. They supported also great technical construction, as of irrigation complexes, the further returns to which swelled the chiefly fund. They initiated large-scale religious construction too, subsidized the great ceremonies, and organized logistic support for extensive military campaigns. Larger and more easily replenished than their western Melanesian counterparts, Polynesian funds of power permitted greater political regulation of a greater range of social activities on greater scale.

In the most advanced Polynesian chiefdoms, as in Hawaii and Tahiti, a significant part of the chiefly fund was deflected away from general redistribution towards the upkeep of the institution of chieftainship. The fund was siphoned for the support of a permanent administrative establishment. In some measure, goods and services contributed by the people precipitated out as the grand houses, assembly places, and temple platforms of chiefly precincts. In another measure, they were appropriated for the livelihood of circles of retainers, many of them close kinsmen of the chief, who clustered about the powerful paramounts. These were not all useless hangers-on. They were political cadres: supervisors of the stores, talking chiefs, ceremonial attendants, high priests who were intimately involved in political rule, envoys to transmit directives through the chiefdom. There were men in these chiefly retinues —in Tahiti and perhaps Hawaii, specialized warrior corps—whose force could be directed internally as a buttress against fragmenting or rebellious elements of the chiefdom. A Tahitian or Hawaiian high chief had more compelling sanctions than the harangue. He controlled a ready physical force, an armed body of executioners, which gave him mastery particularly over the lesser people of the community. While it looks a lot like the big-man's faction again, the differences in functioning of the great Polynesian chief's retinue are more significant than the superficial similarities in appearance. The chief's coterie, for one thing, is economically dependent upon him rather than he upon them. And in deploying the cadres politically in various sections of the chiefdom, or against the lower orders, the great Polynesian chiefs sustained command where the Melanesian big-man, in his external sector, had at best renown.

This is not to say that the advanced Polynesian chiefdoms were free of internal defect, of potential or actual malfunctioning. The large political-military apparatus indicates something of the opposite. So does the recent work of Irving Goldman (1955, 1957, 1960) on the intensity of "status rivalry" in Polynesia, especially when it is considered that much of the status rivalry in developed chiefdoms, as the Hawaiian, amounted to popular rebellion against chiefly despotism rather than mere contest for position within the ruling-stratum. This suggests that Polynesian chiefdoms, just as Melanesian big-man orders, generate along with evolutionary development countervailing anti-authority pressures, and that the weight of the latter may ultimately impede further development.

The Polynesian contradiction seems clear enough. On one side, chieftainship is never detached from kinship moorings and kinship economic ethics. Even the greatest Polynesian chiefs were conceived superior kinsmen to the masses, fathers of their people, and generosity was morally incumbent upon them. On the other side, the major Polynesian paramounts seemed inclined to "eat the power of the government too much," as the Tahitians put it, to divert an undue proportion of the general wealth toward the chiefly establishment.[14] The diversion could be accomplished by lowering the customary level of general redistribution, lessening the material returns of chieftainship to the community at large—tradition attributes the great rebellion of Mangarevan commoners to such cause (Buck 1938a:70–77, 160, 165). Or the diversion might—and I suspect more commonly did—consist in greater and more forceful exactions from lesser chiefs and people, increasing returns to the chiefly apparatus without necessarily affecting the level of general redistribution. In either case, the well developed chiefdom creates for itself the dampening paradox of stoking rebellion by funding its authority.[15]

[14] The great Tahitian chiefs were traditionally enjoined not to eat the power of government too much, as well as to practice open-handedness towards the people (Handy 1930:41). Hawaiian high chiefs were given precisely the same advice by counselors (Malo 1903:255).

[15] The Hawaiian traditions are very clear on the encouragement given rebellion by chiefly exactions—although one of our greatest sources of Hawaiian tradition, David Malo, provides the most sober caveat regarding this kind of evidence. "I do not suppose", he wrote in the preface to *Hawaiian Antiquities,* "the following history to be free from mistakes, in that material for it has come from oral traditions; consequently it is marred by errors of human judgment and does not approach the accuracy of the word of God."

Malo (1903:258) noted that "Many kings have been put to death by the people because of their oppression of the *makaainana* (i.e., commoners)." He goes on to list several who "lost their lives on account of their cruel exactions", and follows the list with the statement "It was for this reason that some of the ancient kings had a wholesome fear of the people." The propensity of Hawaiian high chiefs for undue appropriation from commoners

In Hawaii and other islands cycles of political centralization and decentralization may be abstracted from traditional histories. That is, larger chiefdoms periodically fragmented into smaller and then were later reconstituted. Here would be more evidence of a tendency to overtax the political structure. But how to explain the emergence of a developmental stymie, of an inability to sustain political advance beyond a certain level? To point to a chiefly propensity to consume or a Polynesian propensity to rebel is not enough: such propensities are promoted by the very advance of chiefdoms. There is reason to hazard instead that Parkinson's notable law is behind it all: that progressive expansion in political scale entailed more-than-proportionate accretion in the ruling apparatus, unbalancing the flow of wealth in favor of the apparatus. The ensuing unrest then curbs the chiefly impositions, sometimes by reducing chiefdom scale to the nadir of the periodic cycle. Comparison of the requirements of administration in small and large Polynesian chiefdoms helps make the point.

A lesser chiefdom, confined say as in the Marquesas Islands to a narrow valley, could be almost personally ruled by a headman in frequent contact with the relatively small population. Melville's partly romanticized—also for its ethnographic details, partly cribbed

is a point made over and over again by Malo (see pp. 85, 87–88, 258, 267–68). In Fornander's reconstruction of Hawaiian history (from traditions and genealogies) internal rebellions are laid frequently, almost axiomatically, to chiefly extortion and niggardliness (Fornander 1880:40–41, 76–78, 88, 149–150, 270–271). In addition, Fornander at times links appropriation of wealth and ensuing rebellion to the provisioning of the chiefly establishment, as in the following passage: "Scarcity of food, after a while, obliged *Kalaniopuu* (paramount chief of the island of Hawaii and half brother of Kamehameha I's father) to remove his court (from the Kona district) into the Kohala district, where his headquarters were fixed at Kapaau. Here the same extravagant, *laissez-faire*, eat and be merry policy continued that had been commenced at Kona, and much grumbling and discontent began to manifest itself among the resident chiefs and cultivators of the land, the 'Makaainana'. *Imakakaloa*, a great chief in the Puna district, and *Nuuampaahu*, a chief of Naalehu in the Kau district, became the heads and rallying-points of the discontented. The former resided on his lands in Puna [in the southeast, across the island from Kohala in the northwest], and openly resisted the orders of *Kalaniopuu* and his extravagant demands for contributions of all kinds of property; the latter was in attendance with the court of *Kalaniopuu* in Kohala, but was strongly suspected of favouring the growing discontent" (Fornander 1880:200). Aside from the Mangarevan uprising mentioned in the text, there is some evidence for similar revolts in Tonga (Mariner 1827i:80; Thomson 1894:294f) and in Tahiti (Henry 1928:195–196, 297).

—account in *Typee* makes this clear enough (or see Handy 1923 and Linton 1939). But the great Polynesian chiefs had to rule much larger, spatially dispersed, internally organized populations. Hawaii, an island over four thousand square miles with an aboriginal population approaching one hundred thousand, was at times a single chiefdom, at other times divided into two to six independent chiefdoms, and at all times each chiefdom was composed of large subdivisions under powerful subchiefs. Sometimes a chiefdom in the Hawaiian group extended beyond the confines of one of the islands, incorporating part of another through conquest. Now, such extensive chiefdoms would have to be coordinated; they would have to be centrally tapped for a fund of power, buttressed against internal disruption, sometimes massed for distant, perhaps overseas, military engagements. All of this to be implemented by means of communication still at the level of word-of-mouth, and means of transportation consisting of human bodies and canoes. (The extent of certain larger chieftainships, coupled with the limitations of communication and transportation, incidentally suggests another possible source of political unrest: that the burden of provisioning the governing apparatus would tend to fall disproportionately on groups within easiest access of the paramount.)[16] A tendency for the developed chiefdom to proliferate in executive cadres, to grow top-heavy, seems in these circumstances altogether functional, even though the ensuing drain on wealth proves the chiefdom's undoing. Functional also, and likewise a material drain on the chiefdom at large, would be widening distinctions between chiefs and people in style of life. Palatial housing, ornamentation and luxury, finery and ceremony, in brief, conspicuous consumption, however much it seems mere self-interest always has a more decisive social significance. It creates those invidious distinctions between rulers and ruled so conducive to a passive—hence quite economical!—acceptance of authority. Throughout history, inherently more powerful political organizations than the Polynesian, with more assured logistics of rule, have turned to it—including in our time some ostensibly revolutionary and proletarian governments, despite every pre-

---

[16] On the difficulty of provisioning the Hawaiian paramount's large establishment see the citation from Fornander above, and also Fornander 1880: 100–101; Malo 1903:92–93, *et passim.* The Hawaiian great chiefs developed the practice of the circuit—like feudal monarchs—often leaving a train of penury behind as they moved in state from district to district of the chiefdom.

revolutionary protestation of solidarity with the masses and equality for the classes.

In Polynesia then, as in Melanesia, political evolution is eventually short-circuited by an overload on the relations between leaders and their people. The Polynesian tragedy, however, was somewhat the opposite of the Melanesian. In Polynesia, the evolutionary ceiling was set by extraction from the population at large in favor of the chiefly faction, in Melanesia by extraction from the big-man's faction in favor of distribution to the population at large. Most importantly, the Polynesian ceiling was higher. Melanesian big-men and Polynesian chiefs not only reflect different varieties and levels of political evolution, they display in different degrees the capacity to generate and to sustain political progress.

Especially emerging from their juxtaposition is the more decisive impact of Polynesian chiefs on the economy, the chiefs' greater leverage on the output of the several households of society. The success of any primitive political organization is decided here, in the control that can be developed over household economies. For the household is not merely the principal productive unit in primitive societies, it is often quite capable of autonomous direction of its own production, and it is oriented towards production for its own, not societal consumption. The greater potential of Polynesian chieftainship is precisely the greater pressure it could exert on household output, its capacity both to generate a surplus and to deploy it out of the household towards a broader division of labor, cooperative construction, and massive ceremonial and military action. Polynesian chiefs were the more effective means of societal collaboration on economic, political, indeed all cultural fronts. Perhaps we have been too long accustomed to perceive rank and rule from the standpoint of the individuals involved, rather than from the perspective of the total society, as if the secret of the subordination of man to man lay in the personal satisfactions of power. And then the breakdowns too, or the evolutionary limits, have been searched out in men, in "weak" kings or megalomaniacal dictators—always, "who is the matter?" An excursion into the field of primitive politics suggests the more fruitful conception that the gains of political developments accrue more decisively to society than to individuals, and the failings as well are of structure not men.

PART II. AREAL STUDIES

G. POLYNESIA

EDWIN G. BURROWS

10. Culture-Areas in Polynesia

Building upon the fact that neighbouring cultures usually resemble each other more than widely scattered ones, American ethnologists have developed the concepts of "culture-area" and "culture-centre." These are intended to express typical results of diffusion. Diffusion of culture is, of course, the process whereby useful or otherwise appealing human inventions are adopted by one community after another, so that their use spreads in all directions from where they were invented, as long as no physical or cultural barrier intervenes. A culture-area, then, is a region which by this process has come to share so many cultural devices ("traits, elements") that most cultures within it belong to a fairly definite common type. A culture-centre is a smaller tract where, to judge by the distribution of cultural devices, invention has been so active as to give character to the culture-area all around. Unlike the *Kulturkreise* or culture-cycles of central European diffusionists, culture-areas and culture-centres are not supposed to be universal in space or time, but are avowedly local and temporary. They have been associated to some extent, especially by Wissler (1926), with distinct geographic environments.

These concepts, like all tools devised so far for the study of human behaviour, have their shortcomings. One of the shortcomings of the culture-area concept is that the term "area" implies boundaries. Now cultural diffusion is such a variegated process that actually the boundaries of any culture-area are sure to be blurred.

SOURCE: Reprinted from *Journal of the Polynesian Society*, Vol. 49, No. 3 (1940), pp. 349–63, by permission of Mrs. Edwin G. Burrows and the publisher.

Similarly, the concept of culture-centre must not be used too rigidly. It should not be taken to imply that all devices character-istic of a region necessarily originated in the centre; only that the centre is geographically central to an area of similar cultures, and shares most of the devices characteristic of the area, so that many of them may well have originated there.

As long as it is recognized that culture-area and culture-centre are only abstractions representing a predominant course of diffu-sion, their validity will not be challenged by finding that now and then diffusion within the area has gone some other way. Since an invention may be achieved wherever its physical and cultural pre-requisites are available, and since diffusion is subject to contingen-cies of many sorts, it is likely that some devices will be restricted to part of any culture-area, not necessarily the centre, while others will overflow all boundaries suggested by the main run of distribu-tion. Such cases are better analyzed according to Beaglehole's concept of "cultural peaks" (1937), or Firth's similar one of "in-stitutional efflorescence" (1936), than those of culture-area and culture-centre. However, these conceptual schemes are not incom-patible. Thus, a culture-centre could be described as a point where many cultural peaks coincide.

There have been several attempts to apply the culture-area and culture-centre concepts to Polynesia. In any such attempt the first question to decide is what scale to use. If the criteria are of an or-der of magnitude like those that differentiate Wissler's culture-areas of North America (1938), then Polynesia is emphatically all one culture-area. If comparatively minute differences are chosen, culture-areas and -centres will, of course, multiply in number. Thus, Skinner (1929) has outlined several culture-areas within New Zea-land. Since the object here is to bring out the main regional sub-divisions of Polynesian culture, at approximately the time of first European contact, the scale of the cultural differences considered will fall in the main between that of Wissler and that of Skinner.

Another difficulty is that many of the cultural differences within Polynesia do not coincide with differences in geographic environment. According to geographic environment, New Zealand would be set off from the rest of Polynesia by its cooler climate and different flora and fauna. The rest of Polynesia would be sub-divided into high islands and atolls, because the two differ in soil and water supply, and hence in flora and fauna. Since high islands are as a rule not only richer in natural resources than atolls, but also larger in area, they can support far larger populations. Correlated with these differences are some differences in culture. So it would be possible to subdivide Polynesian cultures according to these geographic considerations. But the main regional variations within Polynesian culture do not coincide with geographic differences. The areas and centres to be discussed here, therefore, will follow differences that seem most satisfactorily explained in terms of invention and diffusion.

Finally, a recent book (Williamson 1939), in glancing at the point in view here, decrees that "the application of the method to Polynesia is justified neither by geographical conditions nor by ethnographic evidence. The isolation of the islands, the trans-oceanic routes which often passed by intervening areas of land, and the position of Polynesia in relation to its surrounding continents make it impossible to detect any 'centre of diffusion.' And, therefore, as we would expect, distributional studies of such diverse subjects as specific aspects of technology [Mead 1928d], kinship nomenclature [Firth 1936], decorative designs [Greiner 1923], and musical instruments [Roberts 1926], have failed to reveal anything corresponding to the American 'culture areas' which might enable us to infer a systematic process of diffusion in the past. As with the 'migrations' which were the vehicles of diffusion in the past, we list its directions and trends as asymmetrical, irregular, and lacking in temporal and geographic continuity" (Piddington in Williamson 1939:231).

Although the writer agrees with most of Piddington's conclusions in the work quoted, he is forced to take issue with this one. General acceptance of something like culture-areas in Polynesia is indicated by Mead's statement (1934:9): "Polynesian students have long treated Samoan and Tongan culture and parts of Fijian culture as a subculture area, including also Niue and the far distant but culturally allied island of Tikopia." Now if this were only a fallacious mental habit, it could be refuted by detailed empirical evidence, though hardly by a cursory dismissal like that given above. However, the empirical evidence in a study (Burrows 1938), too recent to have been noted by Piddington before his book went to press, has led to a nearly opposite conclusion: "What really stand out from these comparisons are not sharply defined cultural sub-areas within Polynesia, but two main centres, western Polynesia and central Polynesia. Some intermediate islands show no distinctly greater affiliation one way than the other. The marginal islands to the north, east, and south are all more closely related to central than to western Polynesia, which strengthens the showing of two centres of radiating influence" (Burrows 1938:91).

The object here is not so much to defend this conclusion as to illustrate and at one or two points amend it. The illustrations will be drawn from four kinds of cultural behaviour: technological devices, social arrangements, religious beliefs and customs, and (partly religious) mythology. Most of the information is summarized from the previous study just mentioned (Burrows 1938). A great deal of it was supplied in the first place by Dr. Peter H. Buck (Te Rangi Hiroa), who in the course of his extensive field-work in Polynesia has repeatedly been impressed by the cultural differences between western Polynesia and the central and marginal area. In these illustrations, islands of Polynesian culture adjoining larger Melanesian islands will not be included, except in a few instances.

TECHNOLOGICAL DEVICES

Variation in foodstuffs within Polynesia depended mainly upon geographic conditions, but variation in implements used for obtaining and preparing food clustered to a great extent around two culture-centres, western and central. Western Polynesia, for example, used one type of fish-hook almost exclusively—the composite bonito-hook with pearl-shell shank and lashed-on point. Central and marginal Polynesia had somewhat different types of bonito-hook, and used also simple or one-piece fish-hooks, while central Polynesia (and to a slight extent New Zealand) further shared with Micronesia the use of the specialized wooden *"ruvettus* hook." Absence of simple fish-hooks, then, is characteristic of western Polynesia (Samoa, Tonga, Futuna, Uvea) and the geographically and culturally intermediate island of Niue.

The distribution of *ruvettus* hooks has been shown by Gudger (1927) to coincide largely with that of the *ruvettus* or "castor-oil fish." In a letter Dr. Gudger has corrected my statement (Burrows 1938) that the *ruvettus* is absent from the waters about New Zealand, by citing a well-authenticated catch of this fish there. However, Kenneth P. Emory reports that in the Tuamotus hooks of the *"ruvettus"* type are made in different sizes and used for catching a number of kinds of fish. On the whole, the absence of *ruvettus* hooks in western Polynesia (except Tonga) supports the showing of regional specialization in hook-and-line fishing.

Another instance is the use in central and most of marginal Polynesia of laboriously-made stone pounders for mashing starchy vegetables. Western Polynesia was characterized by cooking starchy vegetables whole or in large pieces. For what little mashing was done, after cooking, only makeshift implements were used. Stone pounders have not been found in the western islands of Samoa, Tonga, Futuna, and Uvea, nor the intermediate islands of Niue, Tongareva, and the Tokelaus. Their use was universal in central Polynesia, and was shared by the marginal islands except New Zealand and Easter island. Their absence from these outlying regions may well be due to their comparatively slight utility for preparing the foodstuffs used there, which differed from those of central Polynesia. Another possibility, in this instance perhaps less likely, is that this type of food-pounder was invented in central Polynesia after the departure of the emigrants who settled New Zealand and Easter island. Either way, the distribution of food-pounders, like that of fish-hooks, shows different specializations about the two Polynesian culture-centres.

The making of bark cloth and some of the general processes involved were universal in Polynesia, except for atolls where neither the paper mulberry nor any other tree furnishing suitable bast would grow. Regional differences appear, however, in preparation of the bast for beating, joining the beaten-out strips to form large sheets, and decoration.

The practice of retting or long soaking of the bast before beating, and that of decoration by "watermarking" with a finely-grooved beater, were confined in the main to central and marginal Polynesia (Hawaii, Society islands, Cook islands, Austral islands, Rapa, Marquesas, Mangareva). Decoration by means of stamps dipped in dye was further restricted: Hawaii, Society islands, and Cook islands, all of which belong culturally (Burrows 1938) to central Polynesia.

Some other processes were exclusively western Polynesian (Samoa, Tonga, Futuna, Uvea). One such is joining the strips by pasting instead of the more wide-spread felting. Another is decoration by laying the sheets over a tablet bearing a design in relief and transferring the design to the cloth by rubbing over it a wad of old cloth dipped in dye. Thus, the western and central culture-centres were characterized by distinct techniques.

SOCIAL ARRANGEMENTS

Kinship-terminology has a common character throughout Polynesia (Burrows 1939), yet regional differences have been brought out by several authors, especially Rivers (1914) and Firth (1936). In detail these differences are rather complicated (Burrows 1938: Table 2). However, some of them clearly radiate from the two culture-centres. Central Polynesia (Cook islands, Society islands, Tuamotus, Hawaii) lacks special terms for mother's brother, father's sister, and their reciprocals (brother's child, woman speaking, and sister's child, man speaking). On the other hand, western Polynesia (Samoa, Tonga, Futuna, Uvea; in this case also Ellice islands, Tokelau islands, and Tongareva) lacks special terms for several relatives by marriage: parent-in-law, child-in-law, and parents of a child's spouse. These differences may be roughly summarized in two sentences. Western Polynesia laid greater stress on relationships that distinguish between the male and female ancestral lines of each individual, and supply a special link with the female line, the one less emphasized in a patrilineal system (Firth 1936). Central Polynesia brought about a similar linkage in another way, through emphasizing relationships by marriage.

Two conspicuous customs rooted in kinship illustrate the same regional differences even more clearly. One is the *vasu* or *fahu* status, apparently a local variant of the avunculate or special connection between a man and his mother's brother. The *vasu* relationship has not been reported anywhere in central Polynesia. In marginal Polynesia the kinship terminology includes special terms for mother's brother and sister's son, and in the Marquesas there was some overt recognition of special relationship, but not in the same form as the *vasu* of western Polynesia. That appeared only in Samoa, Tonga, Futuna, and Uvea. These same western islands, together with the neighbouring Ellice and Tokelau groups and Tongareva, also offered the only examples in Polynesia of formal avoidance between brother and sister.

Two customs expressive of rank were also peculiar to western Polynesia. One was the celebrated *kava* ceremony. This was practised only in Samoa, Tonga, Futuna, and Uvea. The other was the use of "chiefs' languages," or sets of respectful euphemisms used in addressing or referring to chiefs. This was found exclusively in Samoa, Tonga, Uvea, and Niue.

In central and marginal Polynesia rank was expressed in other ways, as by emphasis on the *mana* of chieftainship and on tabus associated with it. The difference between the two areas in the general framework of rank and land-tenure has been thus summarized (Burrows 1939): "In the western one, rank was delicately graded rather than stratified; and land tenure was fundamentally hereditary. In the more easterly one, rank involved class distinctions that, at least in general accounts by natives, were sharply drawn; and hereditary claims to land were subsidiary, as a rule, to the arbitrary authority of chiefs."

A study of the larger Polynesian social groupings (Burrows 1939) indicates independent change in the two centres from what was apparently an early arrangement throughout Polynesia. The apparently early arrangement was labelled in this study "coincidence of breed and border." That is, groupings on the basis of kinship ("breed") and on the basis of territorial boundaries ("border") were the same, because the territorial units were occupied by bodies of kinfolk.

By the time Polynesian culture came under the observation of Europeans, the principle of border dominated the larger groupings (village, district, and so on) in most of the more populous islands. Each of these large territorial units was populated by a population of mixed descent, according to the native genealogies. This arrangement has been called "intermingling of breed and border."

The geographic distribution of these two arrangements has been summarized as follows: "In general, types of alignment of breed and border in Polynesia had fairly distinct distributions. Coincidence of breed and border was found either in marginal regions (Marquesas, New Zealand), or in atolls with comparatively small populations (Tongareva, Manihiki-Rakahanga, Ontong Java). Intermingling of breed and border appeared in two separate areas; one western (Samoa, Tonga, Futuna, Uvea, Tokelaus), the other farther east (Society islands, Hawaii, Mangaia, Mangareva). Between these two areas stretched a continuous line of islands where breed and border either coincided (Tongareva, Manihiki-Rakahanga) or were aligned in unique intermediate fashions (Pukapuka, Niue). Two isolated regions, Easter island to the east and Tikopia to the west, also had intermediate alignments peculiar to themselves." This evidence of independent development in two centres is supported by the differing concepts of rank and land-tenure in the two areas, as outlined above.

RELIGIOUS BELIEFS AND CUSTOMS

In religious matters, several clear regional distinctions have been brought out (Burrows 1938). Tangaloa was the only primal god ("associated with creation and commonly with great regions as the sky or the sea") in Tonga, Futuna, Uvea, and Niue. Tangaloa was dominant in Samoa as well, although some mention of Tu has also been found there. By contrast, throughout central and marginal Polynesia there were, besides Tangaloa, three other gods of the same general type: Tu, Tane, and Rongo. The only qualification this statement needs is that from the Australs only three of the four have been reported. This is true also of Tongareva, but this accords with the rest of the culture and with the island's geographic position—intermediate between western and central Polynesia.

Sacred structures illustrate the division into two centres or areas once again. Throughout Polynesia there were sacred build-ings rather like dwellings. Universal, too, were level spaces open to the sky, where the people assembled. But in central and marginal Polynesia the buildings were adjuncts to the open-air meeting-places, which were strictly sacred. Their special character was emphasized by definite construction in stone, either as walled courts, terraces, or platforms. A definite elaboration of such struc-tures, characterized by a platform across one end, was used in the Society islands, Tuamotus, Cook islands, Austral islands, Rapa, Hawaii, Marquesas, Mangareva, Easter island, and toward the west in intermediate Tongareva.

In western Polynesia the open-air meeting-places had rather the character of village-greens than of sacred enclosures. They were not marked off, as a rule, with any stonework unless it were upright backrest stones for chiefs to sit against. Nor were the activities carried on there necessarily sacred, although the *kava*-ceremonies with which all formal assemblages began had an element of sanctity. The centre for religious activities in this area was typically the sacred building or god-house. It was not necessarily on or beside the village-green, and was decidedly not a mere adjunct of it. It was here that the people assembled for most of their religious ceremonies. This western emphasis in religious structures is reported from Samoa, Tonga, Uvea, the Tokelaus, and (less clearly) Futuna. Some islands adjoining the area of typical western culture —Ellice, Pukapuka, and Niue—seem to have had both types of sacred structures.

MYTHOLOGY

In the field of mythology, the areas about the two culture-centres are differentiated in several ways. One of these is the type of myth accounting for the origin of mankind. Characteristic of the west (Samoa, Tonga, Uvea, Niue, Pukapuka, and in this instance the Cook islands) is what has been called an evolutionary type, in which "the first human beings sprang from rocks or earth, either directly or through intermediate forms, as plants and maggots. If a deity is mentioned, it is as a spectator or at most an assistant, rather than a creator." Some localities merely trace back their genealogies to a primal couple, whose creation is left unexplained. But generally in central and marginal Polynesia (Society islands, Tuamotus, Hawaii, Marquesas, Mangareva, New Zealand, and Easter island) is found another type of myth, the procreative, in which "a male god brings mankind into existence either by copulation with a mass of earth or by forming a female being out of earth and impregnating her."

Legends of an underworld or a mythical island to the west were nearly universal in Polynesia. These, too, show the characteristic regional variation. In the islands most typically western in culture (Samoa, Tonga, Futuna, Uvea), the legendary place, whether conceived as an island to the west or an underworld, was called Pulotu. It was thought of as the home of certain gods and of the elect after death. The name Pulotu, in this sense, is not found in central or marginal Polynesia. In all the typically central and marginal islands, with the sole exception of Easter island, the name of a similar legendary place was Hawaiki. This, too, was sometimes thought of as an underworld, but more commonly as an island to the west. Hawaiki, however, was usually regarded as an ancestral homeland, rather than being peopled with the dead like Pulotu.

A comparative study of Polynesian hero-tales, starting with the

Maui-cycles, is nearing completion at the hands of Dr. Katharine Luomala, who has devoted several years to it. A brief preliminary report (Luomala 1939) brought out in all of them a common underlying pattern, like those evident in other aspects of Polynesian culture. Local variation within this general pattern is also apparent. In a recent letter, however, Dr. Luomala reports that broad regional groupings cannot be made out precisely in some instances. "The difficulty is that there is so little folklore material from the Society group. What we have are chants and the more religious type of literature."

In her analysis of the Maui cycle of tales, Dr. Katharine Luomala (n.d.) has divided Polynesia into two areas, according to the types of incidents ascribed to Maui. One of the areas is eastern, which corresponds to the "central-marginal" of this writer's subdivision except for the addition of Pukapuka, Manihiki-Rakahanga, and Tongareva, which I had called "intermediate." The other area is western, which corresponds to my "western" except, again, for the addition of some islands I classified as "intermediate," namely, the Ellice and Tokelau group and Niue. Dr. Luomala notes that from all of the islands where her classification differs from mine, accounts of the folklore are scanty.

The difference between the two classifications is not greater than that between some of the specific distributions shown on my maps. Dr. Luomala points out that in specific incidents of the Maui tales, the alignment varies. Her regional classification represents the predominant showing of the Maui material, as mine represented that of the practices whose distribution was traced in my study. In the main the two confirm each other.

A RECENT TEST

The regional subdivisions of Polynesia worked out in this way have recently been tested by Dr. Alfred Métraux who applied them to Easter island in his comprehensive and perhaps definitive ethnography of that Polynesian outlier (Métraux 1940). He concludes (p. 416): "All the essential features which characterize Polynesia as a whole are found on Easter Island. As appears natural from its geographical position, Easter Island is associated most closely with southeastern Polynesia and New Zealand. None of the distinctive traits of western Polynesia, listed by Burrows, was recorded on Easter Island. On the other hand, a great number of the features proper to central and marginal Polynesia formed part of its culture. These are: bark-cloth retting, direct outrigger attachment, carved human figures, Rongo as primal god, procreative myth of the origin of mankind, and nights of the moon. To this list established by Burrows could be added, the stone platform or *ahu,* widespread in marginal Polynesia though lacking in New Zealand. . . . There is no doubt that Easter Island belongs to the marginal sub-area of central Polynesian culture."

CONCLUSIONS

Let me say once again that the evidence presented here is only an illustrative sampling. If more is needed for a convincing demonstration that culture-centres and culture-areas (with the usual vagueness of boundary) exist in Polynesia as elsewhere, more is given in the longer study (Burrows 1938) already cited. From still other material, Buck (1939:34) has come to the following conclusion: "A comparative study of the myths, legends, traditions, genealogies, and historical narratives of Polynesia indicates convincingly that the cultural-centre corresponds with the geographical centre, the Society Islands." Elsewhere (Buck 1938b:68) the same author summarizes the character of this centre, and locates it more precisely: "An exuberant new life opened up in central Polynesia, and new adjustments took place, not only in the arts and crafts but in social and religious matters. The senior families and the most intelligent priests seem to have settled down in the Opoa district of Hawai'i (Ra'iatea of the Society Islands), which became the cultural centre of the group. A school of learning was established, and in the course of time, the school systematized the scattered fragments of myth and history that had been remembered by various voyagers from Micronesia. That systematization took place locally is borne out by the fact that the myths and legends were applied to the local area. The pattern established was ultimately carried by later voyagers in varying degree of completeness to the remote angles of the Polynesian triangle."

In these quotations Buck emphasizes one centre rather than two. A review of the evidence with this in mind shows that the western area does indeed differ in kind to a considerable extent from the central one. In the first place, it reveals no such sharply defined centre. In most cases inventions cannot be located more exactly than "Samoa or Tonga." Again, a count of the western and central-marginal characteristics ascribed to various historical processes (Burrows 1938:152–53) shows a decided difference between the two regions. Of the western characteristics, thirteen are ascribed to diffusion from Fiji, eleven to local development, and six to abandonment of old devices or rejection of new. Of the central-marginal characteristics, only five are ascribed to diffusion, in no case from Fiji; and in two of these, alternative possibilities seem about equally probable. Sixteen are ascribed to local development (including the two alternative possibilities just mentioned), and only one to abandonment or rejection. With all due respect for the limitations of quantitative measurement in culture, this substantial difference seems significant. Western Polynesia appears to have acquired its special characteristics to a great extent by diffusion from Fiji. This suggestion is supported by Mead's comparison (1934) of the western Polynesian kinship-pattern with that of the Melanesian Admiralty islands. In so far as western Polynesia has obtained its characteristics by "borrowing" from Fiji, it is a culture-province rather than a culture-centre. However, it remains predominantly Polynesian, so the term "culture-province" overstates the case. On the whole, western Polynesia seems best characterized as a Polynesian culture-area strongly influenced by Fiji.

Central Polynesia, or more exactly Opoa in Hawai'i, stands out as a more typical example of the culture-centre in the sense of a centre of inventive activity. Yet in the interpretation of regional differences, nearly as many cases of local invention are ascribed to western as to central Polynesia (western, 11; central, 14 to 16). This, together with the fact that all the marginal islands resemble central Polynesia more than they do western Polynesia, suggests one more explanation of the difference between the two areas; namely that central Polynesia, especially because it was less subject to Fijian influence, has retained more than western Polynesia of an old culture which was apparently that of all Polynesia before local differentiation became pronounced.

Criticism of the concepts of culture-centre and culture-area seems more effective when it raises other questions than that of the factual existence of such clusters of cultural resemblance. Demonstrably they do exist. Some limitations of the concepts, however, in addition to the difficulties discussed at the beginning, are revealed by an inquiry starting from this question: Granting that culture-area and culture-centre express typical results of diffusion, to what further conclusions can they lead? It is here that I find myself in substantial agreement with the comments of Piddington (in Williamson 1939).

If the purpose for which they are used is that of the archaeologist and historical ethnologist, to ascertain the temporal sequence of events, these concepts help a little, but not much. The trouble is that the evidence they afford hardly ever permits a confident decision among several alternative possibilities. As Boas insists, "It is well-nigh impossible to base a chronology of the development of specific cultures on the observed phenomena of diffusion" (Boas 1940:252).

If, on the other hand, the aim is a general understanding of just how diffusion works—not how it worked out once in the past, but how it may affect human cultures anywhere—classification by culture-areas and -centres again reveals something, but not nearly enough for an adequate solution of the problem. For that, the process of diffusion must be observed with a minuteness only possible where it is going on before the observer's eyes. Similarly, classification of culture-areas may be of service in working out the views of the American "configurationist" school. But a satisfactory analysis of the characteristic configurations of any culture again demands close study of the culture in actual operation.

Turning to the functionalists, culture-areas may help toward one of Radcliffe-Brown's objectives, the comparison of well-characterized types of social organization. But once again, adequate results demand scrutiny with a narrower and sharper focus. As for Malinowski's analysis of culture into institutions organized for the satisfaction of needs, the culture-area and culture-centre concepts seem to have only an indirect bearing upon that.

Classification of cultures by areas and centres, then, is useful for large-scale description. But for solution of the problems in which social science is most interested today, investigation of this kind can be no more than preliminary or supplementary to the main task.

ANDREW P. VAYDA

11. Polynesian Cultural Distributions in New Perspective

It has been an orthodox view in Oceanian anthropology that the pre-European Polynesians were capable of maintaining regular contacts between islands separated by more than 300 miles of open ocean and that the peopling of Polynesia resulted either entirely or predominantly from voyages of exploration and discovery followed by return voyages to the home islands and then by deliberate large-scale migrations to newly discovered lands. These reconstructions have been challenged by Andrew Sharp's impressively documented recent study (1956), which reviews the achievements and deficiencies of pre-European Polynesian voyaging and argues that Polynesia was peopled as a result of "accidental" landfalls of voyagers lost at sea. Although students, including myself (Vayda 1958), have proposed some modifications of Sharp's thesis, he may be said to have succeeded in shifting the burden of proof to adherents of the orthodox view to such an extent as to make it worthwhile to examine some of the new perspectives that his thesis provides for Polynesian anthropological research. That the thesis does have important implications has been recognized by a number of students (cf. Goodenough 1957; Luomala 1958; Oliver 1957). Some of its implications for the interpretation of Polynesian cultural distributions will be considered in this paper.

An appendix to the paper reproduces the list of cultural traits which have been used by Burrows (1938) for indicating or suggesting degrees of historical relationship among the various

SOURCE: Reprinted from *American Anthropologist*, Vol. 61, No. 5 (1959), pp. 817–28, by permission of the publisher.

Polynesian cultures. None of the listed traits represent complexes of behavior requiring large numbers of people, and therefore it may be said that the traits are likely to have been capable of being "conveyed" from previous homelands and perpetuated in new islands by parties of voyagers making accidental landfalls. Burrows' demonstration of two main Polynesian cultural groupings (a western and a "central-marginal" or eastern) may be made consistent with Sharp's thesis in the manner suggested by Sharp himself (1956:69, 106):

> The Cooks, the Tahiti-Tuamotu area, the Marquesas, Hawaii and New Zealand were worlds apart from Tonga-Samoa, and from one another, apart from occasional accidental arrivals. They derived their basic affinity of culture, including that more abiding cultural feature, basic vocabulary, from the western homeland. Yet the inhabitants of all these groups had common cultural features, including basic words, which were different from those of Western Polynesia. The only reasonable explanation is that these features were developed in an early centre of settlement somewhere in Eastern Polynesia, and were dispersed from there. It would be difficult to conclude otherwise than that this centre was somewhere in the central islands, and that the wide dissemination of these Eastern Polynesian cultural features took place because the maritime arts were developed for local inter-island voyaging, leading to many accidental voyages. . . . A concept of primary west-east settlement by occasional westerlies, with slow increase of population in each main group, followed by accidental settlement of the peripheral groups and islands of the Pacific, is compatible both with the divergences and affinities of language and general culture that existed.

If it is assumed that Sharp's reconstruction of the establishment of a culturally distinctive eastern Polynesian area is correct, a question may still be asked. Why was the cultural distinctiveness of the eastern and western areas not obliterated by people accidentally voyaging between the two areas and making landfalls on already inhabited islands at some considerable time after initial settlement? Sharp (1956:71) has suggested an answer: "No one lot of new arrivals would have sufficient impact to dominate the existing culture or language, but would be absorbed" (cf. Sharp

1956:123; Goodenough 1957:149). Certain exceptions to this statement will be noted later, but on the whole it seems reasonable. Population could expand considerably on the typical Polynesian high islands, and it is not likely that later accidental voyagers, arriving in small numbers at an island which already had relatively large numbers of people, would be successful in introducing variants of the kinds of culture traits which have been used by Burrows (1938) and others as the main diagnostics of the east-west cultural differentiation.

Some significant points may be made about the kinds of traits which have been regarded as diagnostic. Later arrivals at an island may well have succeeded in introducing certain new food plants or breeding stock (cf. Sharp 1956: Chapter 6) or ways of handling weapons (cf. Sharp 1956:43), since these can be obviously useful innovations. On the other hand, consider Burrows' traits. It should be noted that in most cases it is difficult to discern if a particular trait listed as "western" by Burrows is either more or less adaptive than a corresponding "central-marginal" or eastern trait. Is it manifestly better to mash cooked taro and breadfruit with heavy pounders, as in much of eastern Polynesia, or to eat the vegetables whole or grated, as in much of western Polynesia? Is it better to decorate bark cloth by stamping, as in much of the east, or by tablet rubbing, as in much of the west? Is it better to have right-angle plaiting or oblique plaiting, to have twining in kilts or not to have it, to have a direct or an indirect canoe outrigger attachment, to call the first-born sibling of the same sex "tuakana" or to call him "taokete," to say that the underworld is "Hawaiki" or to say that it is "Pulotu"? Definitive answers cannot yet be given to such questions, but this much may be said about the kinds of traits on Burrows' lists: it is very unlikely that there would have been strong pressures toward substituting traits brought by new arrivals for the traits already established among the local people. Indeed, the more likely tendency in general would be for the newcomers to adopt the prevalent usages of the island, although they might adhere for a while to at least some of their practices and might teach them to their offspring. Because of this last possibility, it would be not surprising if archeologists in one part of Polynesia were to find some isolated specimens of forms (e.g., in adzes) regarded as characteristic of the other part. However, it may still be said about the kinds of traits under consideration that the dominant or prevalent forms—possibly the only discernible forms in the ethnographic present—would in most islands probably be derived mainly from the culture of the early arrivals and their descendants rather than from the culture of later accidental voyagers.

Is it possible to generalize about the conditions under which this might not apply? A crucial consideration is the relative numbers of the new arrivals and the established local population. The statement has already been made that it is unlikely that later accidental voyagers, arriving in small numbers at an island which already had relatively large numbers of people, would be successful in introducing variants of the kinds of culture traits which appear on Burrows' lists. However, we must also examine the possibility of no very great numerical disparity between the newcomers and the local people.

The important question of the size of the accidental voyaging parties presents some difficulties. A party carried away while fishing often would have comprised only a few people. The numbers of people in parties carried away while going on a social visit or on a military expedition to a nearby island may usually have been greater and may occasionally have been quite considerable, at least at the outset of a voyage. Of course many people might die at sea, even in the case of accidental voyages which terminated in successful landfalls for some people. Evidence of high mortality in the course of "successful" accidental voyages may be found in Sharp's book.

The carrying capacity of the largest Polynesian sailing vessels is indicated in an account from early historical times that mentions a Tongan double canoe in which "two hundred and fifty souls," going on a military expedition, almost became lost at sea (Vason 1810:189–190). Elsewhere (Vayda 1958) I have shown that Sharp may have underestimated the role which exiles—people who may be described as deliberately losing themselves at sea—played in Polynesian "accidental" settlement, and I have cited Porter's account (1815:54) that the grandfather of a chief whom he met in Nukuhiva in the Marquesas in 1813 was said to have sailed with several families in four large canoes in search of land and to have not been heard of again. Yet if Sharp's views are accepted, it must be regarded as extremely unlikely that four such vessels would have made a landfall together after a long voyage. A passage by Sharp (1956:29) suggests how difficult it must have been for Polynesian canoes to keep together on the open ocean:

> Long journeys mean travel night after night with no assurance of fine weather. The ocean is too deep for anchors. How then could the vessels keep in touch at night in squalls, or when the sky was overcast? A practical test of this difficulty is to go out in similar circumstances on the sea in a small boat, or even to look out of the back door. The European sailing ships had the utmost difficulty in keeping together, even with high look-outs and telescopes and high masts to look for, and always used to appoint rendezvous at determined positions, so that when blown out of sight of one another they could come together again. The Spanish ships kept to an agreed line of latitude to facilitate their keeping together, having the advantage of quadrants to determine it, and yet were continually losing touch. Cook was separated from his second vessel on the second voyage, and did not see it again until both got back to England.

It is obviously not possible to make precise estimates of the usual size of the parties which survived or merely set out on accidental voyages in pre-European Polynesia. It can, however, be said that it is unlikely that there should have been many accidental landfalls by parties containing hundreds of people and, on the other hand, it is probable that some parties consisted of less than a dozen or so people.

Let us now consider the possibility of no very great numerical disparity between newly arrived accidental voyagers and established local people. A corollary of Sharp's thesis about the accidental nature of Polynesian long-distance voyaging is that long-distance voyagers would only rarely succeed in making landfalls (cf. Sharp 1956:123). From this it may be inferred that the initial accidental settlement of an island was not likely to be followed very quickly by new landfalls there. By the time that new accidental voyagers did arrive, the local population might have already swelled considerably from the original knot of settlers and might grossly outnumber the newcomers, even in the unlikely event that there were as many as 250 of the latter. Sharp (1956:48) has noted that conditions were particularly favorable for steady and progressive population increase from small beginnings in the high islands of Samoa, Tonga, Tahiti, the Marquesas, the Cooks, Hawaii, and New Zealand, for in these places there was room to expand and a sufficiency of food.

Conditions were different in the coral atolls and must be considered for suggesting the exceptions to Sharp's statement about the small impact of later arrivals to an island. Land and food supplies in the atolls were much more restricted than in the volcanic high islands. The latter have, in Goodenough's words (1957:152), "incomparably richer" soil, vegetation, and lithic resources. The possibilities of population expansion in the atolls were considerably smaller than in the high islands. Moreover, even when an atoll population had expanded to the limit set by the usually available food resources, it could quickly be reduced much more severely than could most high-island populations. Cyclones and tidal waves wreak considerably greater devastation upon the small, low, exposed atolls than upon volcanic islands. In general, the atolls are also much more subject to the effects of drought, since, unlike many volcanic islands, they do not have springs or rivers or soils with any substantial water-holding capacity. Moreover, they have no interior mountains which would push rain-bearing winds upward to cooler heights and thereby cause greater precipitation on the land than at sea.

Both traditional and European accounts mention the decimation of atoll populations. A tidal wave about 300 years ago is said to have reduced Pukapukan population to "two women and fifteen men with remnants of their families" (Beaglehole 1938: 386; cf. Beaglehole 1938:20–21). Mokil, a Micronesian atoll, was hit by a cyclone around the year 1775, and only 25 or 30 people are said to have survived (Weckler 1953:556). In historical times alone, many hundreds of natives in the Tuamotuan atolls have perished as a result of five separate cyclones of hurricane force (Danielsson 1955:24–27). The depopulating effect of droughts has also been noted for a number of atolls, such as the Polynesian outlier of Kapingamarangi (Fischer 1958:11, 22). The extinction of a pre-European population in Olosenga atoll in the Tokelau Islands is attributed by Tokelau traditional history to starvation resulting from drought (Macgregor 1937:23).

These various considerations imply that the numerical disparity between local populations and parties of newly arrived accidental voyagers was generally likely to be much smaller in the coral atolls than in the high islands. It may be well in passing to note one way in which the disparity might be even further reduced in the atolls. This would happen if, by chance, disproportionately more of the established local people than the recent arrivals were to perish as a result of a cyclone, tidal wave, or drought, or even as a result of being carried away and becoming lost at sea in the course of making off-shore voyages such as were regularly undertaken between the neighboring atolls of Manihiki and Rakahanga in the Northern Cook Islands (cf. Buck 1932:4). The loss of one or two canoe-loads of voyagers would not very significantly diminish the numerical superiority of an established high-island population, but the effect might well be otherwise in the case of the smaller populations of the atolls.

The sometimes very small size of a total atoll population, as well as the number of newcomers relative to established local people, is an important consideration. Many traits on Burrows' lists represent items of behavior which presumably would be taught to a child by members of his household, and in a small population certain variant culture traits could, just as certain mutant genes, become established mainly through the "accidents" of who mates with whom and how many children result. A child might get variant culture traits as well as mutant genes from a parent. It may incidentally be pointed out that incest prohibitions among the local people may have promoted intermarriage with any new arrivals. Danielsson (1955:124) recently found on Raroia atoll in the Tuamotus that seven of the nine unmarried women of nubile age were prevented by the incest restrictions from finding mates among the eleven "mature" youths on the island. Such prohibitions are likely to have had equal or even greater force in pre-European times, except perhaps when a people were confronted with the alternative of incest or extinction.

Let us consider a hypothetical example in order to bring out the implications of small population size and of the absence of much disparity in the numbers of newcomers and local people. Suppose that a party of about 20 accidental voyagers arrives at an atoll whose population is at a low ebb. The newcomers intermarry with the local people, and as a matter of course assume the responsibility for at least part of the socialization of their children or possibly their grandchildren. This will involve the teaching of certain items of behavior which depart from local usage. For example, the men among the newcomers may teach variant techniques of adze-making and canoe-lashing and describing the supernatural, while the women, if any, may transmit at least to their female offspring certain new ways of preparing food and plaiting and twining. The result may be that many or most of the children of a certain generation—or possibly most of the boys or most of the girls—will have learned the variant forms of certain traits, as taught by the newcomers, and will in turn transmit these to their own offspring. If the population builds up again and the descendants of the newcomers form a major part of it, certain of the introduced variant forms will be prevalent.

Fortunately we are not confined to mere speculation on these matters. The analysis of cultural transmission in small populations and the evidence of small and fluctuating populations in the coral atolls, taken together with Sharp's thesis about accidental voyaging, make possible certain predictions about the distribution of culture traits in the ethnographic present. If the premises are correct, we should find that in the coral atolls so situated as to be likely to receive voyagers from both western and eastern Polynesia, there would tend to be a more nearly equal representation of western and eastern traits than in the high islands similarly situated, since the later accidental voyagers would have been more able to introduce traits in the atolls than in the high islands. The expectation of a fair number of both western and eastern traits should apply also to coral atolls so situated as to be likely to receive voyagers not necessarily from both western and eastern Polynesia but rather from both western Polynesia and from other coral atolls so situated as to be likely to get both western and eastern voyagers. Consideration of geographical positions, wind and current directions, and the Polynesian voyages recorded in historical times (cf. Sharp 1956) makes our expectations applicable to the following atolls: Manihiki-Rakahanga, Tongareva (Penrhyn), and Pukapuka in the Northern Cook Islands, all likely to get voyagers from both eastern and western Polynesia; the Tokelau Islands, likely to get voyagers from western Polynesia and from the Cook atolls; and the Ellice Islands, likely to get voyagers from western Polynesia and from the atolls of both the Tokelau and Cook groups. The high islands which probably received voyagers from both western and eastern Polynesia include the Lower Cook Islands, the Society Islands, the Samoan Islands, Tonga, and Niue. The last named and also some of the islands in Tonga consist not of volcanic land but rather of coral-formed land which has been "raised." There are generally more environmental opportunities and diversity and certainly more land on such islands than on the typical low atolls.

The test of our expectations is provided by a tabulation that Burrows has made on the basis of the diagnostic western and central-marginal (eastern) traits given in the appendix to this paper. His reservations concerning the tabulation must be noted:

> For a number of reasons this list has no quantitative precision. First, the different traits are in no sense equivalent. Second, they have varying kinds and degrees of relationship to one another. Third, some of the traits classed as western or central-marginal in this simple dichotomy are more probably old Polynesian, superseded in one area or the other . . . Fourth, apparent absence of a trait in a given region may be due to incomplete data, as shown by the fact that the total number of traits listed differs for different regions. And real absence may be due to geographic environment rather than cultural factors. For example, regardless of cultural affiliation, the kava ceremony will not appear in an atoll where kava will not grow. Thus it is possible to count regional affiliations from the foregoing list in several different ways. The list below gives one of these. However, counting in other ways does not substantially change the broad grouping which is all the list can pretend to show (Burrows 1938:90).

The broad grouping is sufficient for an initial test of our expectations. Recent fieldwork in some of the islands (for example, my own work in the Northern Cooks) has suggested the presence of certain traits which Burrows, on the basis of incomplete data, had to regard as being absent, but even such new evidence does not appear to change the broad picture. In Burrows' tabulation (1938:91) reproduced here, the islands of special interest in the present context are indicated by asterisks.

With the single exception of Niue, our expectations are realized. In the coral atolls of the Tokelaus, the Ellice Islands, and the Northern Cook Group, there is a more nearly equal represen-

BURROWS' TABULATION OF WESTERN AND CENTRAL-MARGINAL
TRAITS IN VARIOUS POLYNESIAN ISLANDS OR ISLAND GROUPS

Region	Western traits	Central-marginal traits
Uvea	38	2
*Tonga	36	5
*Samoa	36	5
Futuna	33	5
*Tokelaus	18	12
*Niue	18	13
*Ellice	12	14
*Pukapuka	12	19
*Tongareva	10	21
*Manihiki-Rakahanga	10	24
New Zealand	8	27
Easter Island	6	23
Mangareva	6	25
Marquesas	4	34
Australs	0	26
Rapa	0	28
Tuamotus	1	33
*[Lower] Cook Islands	2	36
Hawaii	1	36
*Society Islands	1	40

tation of western and eastern traits than in the high islands of
Tonga, Samoa, the Lower Cooks, and the Society Group.

Less significance should be attached to the great preponderance
of western traits in Samoa and Tonga than to the great preponderance of eastern traits in the Lower Cooks and the Society
Islands. This is because traits have been identified as "western"
by Burrows largely on the very basis of their distinctive occurrence
in Samoa and Tonga; the only other "western" islands treated by
Burrows are Uvea and Futuna. The "eastern" traits, however,
can be characterized as such on account of their distribution in
quite a few islands, e.g., the Marquesas, Mangareva, the Australs,
and Rapa, excluding those under immediate consideration. This
means that the very marked preponderance of eastern traits in
the Lower Cooks and the Society Islands cannot be said to follow
simply from our having designated certain traits as eastern because they occur in the two island groups.

Niue is anomalous. Its 64,228 acres of coral-formed land give
it an area approximately 64 times that of some of the low atolls
under consideration. Yams and some other food plants not usu-

ally found on the low atolls could be grown on the island (cf. Buck 1945:7). However, the land in Niue was clearly much less productive than in the volcanic islands being considered (compare Smith 1902:84, 91 ff. on Niue with Sahlins 1958:260–266 on the Society Islands and Samoa) and at the same time the Niueans could harvest less from the sea than could the true atoll-dwellers. On the western side of Niue, the amount of fish that could be caught was severely restricted by the lack of any natural harbor, beach, barrier reef, or other shallow water; on the eastern side, steep cliffs made access to the sea precarious, while constant winds from the southeast caused continuously rough seas (Department of Island Territories 1957:82).

Moreover, Niue is visited by hurricanes about once in ten years, and a drought occurs nearly every year. According to Loeb's monograph (1926:6, 111) on Niue, the people of the island were always subject to periodic famine due to long droughts. A severe dry season was "a great calamity."

In the light of such facts, it becomes possible to suggest that there may have been some major reductions of population in the course of Niuean prehistory. It is not necessary to suggest that the population was ever reduced, as in some of the low atolls, to a mere 20 or 30 people. What numbers of people can be regarded as constituting "small populations" is a problem, and it may be said that for cultural as well as for genetic studies (cf. Li 1955: 325, 344 ff.) there is no clear-cut line between "large" and "small" populations. Here it is enough to suggest two things: first, that Niuean population may sometimes have been reduced to much smaller size than that to which the populations of the volcanic islands under consideration ever were reduced; and, second, that this smaller size may have been such that any relatively large parties of accidental voyagers would have made contributions to Niuean culture discernible in the ethnographic present.

In any case, the Niuean anomaly, for which there may be still other explanations, seems less significant than the fact that Burrows' tabulations agree so strikingly in all cases except the Niuean with the results predictable largely on the basis of the theoretical considerations which have been raised. This agreement seems significant indeed.

Before ending this paper, I should remark that Burrows presumably was working with the orthodox assumptions about Polynesian voyaging and settlement. That he has in spite of this provided a test for certain expectations or predictions derived from consideration of Sharp's thesis may be regarded as a welcome fortuity. Sharp's thesis, especially taken together with an analysis of cultural transmission in small populations and the evidence of small and fluctuating populations in the coral atolls, would lead us to look at—or look for—the data on the Northern Cooks, the Tokelaus, and the Ellice Islands even if they had somehow been omitted from Burrows' study of Polynesian cultural differentiation. It may be said that the importance of Sharp's thesis is that it leads us to ask new questions (or else to ask old questions more meaningfully than before) and sometimes to look for new data.

CONCLUSION

In this paper, I have tried to indicate some of the ways in which Sharp's thesis raises questions, particularly about cultural distributions within Polynesia. My discussion has been limited to cultural traits which probably could have been "conveyed" and perpetuated from one island to the other by relatively small parties of people making accidental landfalls. If Sharp's thesis is accepted, certain statements about such traits may be regarded as conclusions in light of the thesis.

(1) Inter-island similarities in the case of traits which would have been obviously useful innovations (e.g., certain subsistence techniques) cannot be relied on as evidence of a population's origins. The traits might have been introduced by later voyagers from a different area than the one from which the population originally came.

(2) Although due allowances must be made for the possibility of independent invention, similarities in traits which would not have been clearly useful innovations (e.g., most of the items on Burrows' lists) can be employed with reference to most islands as evidence (or at least as indications) of the general area (e.g., eastern or western Polynesia) from which the first permanent settlers came.

(3) However, even these similarities cannot be so employed with reference to some islands, such as the coral atolls, where the

population, after as well as during the early settlement period, may sometimes have been small enough so that new parties of accidental voyagers could introduce certain traits even if they possessed no marked advantages over traits which had been established previously.

Appendix: List of Western and Central-Marginal (Eastern) Traits (from Burrows 1938:88–90)

WESTERN	CENTRAL-MARGINAL
Absence of simple fish-hooks	Simple fish-hooks
Absence of *Ruvettus* hooks	*Ruvettus* hooks
Bonito hooks with proximal projection on point	Bonito hooks with simple point or distal projection
Absence of food pounders other than temporary makeshifts	Food pounders of stone or wood
Bark cloth beaten without retting	Retting bark cloth
Pasting bark cloth	Felting bark cloth
Absence of watermarking in bark cloth	Watermarking bark cloth
Decoration of bark cloth by tablet rubbing	Decoration of bark cloth by stamping
Right-angle plaiting in mats and baskets	Absence of right-angle plaiting in mats and baskets
Coiled basketry	Absence of coiled basketry
Absence of twining in kilts	Twining in kilts
Tangless stone adzes	Tanged stone adzes
Support of house ridge-poles by king-posts	Absence of king-posts in marginal Polynesia; a separate center of king-posts in central Polynesia
Rounded house-ends with parallel rafters or arched purlins	Absence of rounded house-ends in marginal Polynesia; rounded ends with radial rafters in central Polynesia
Canoe hulls with low ends, decorated with rows of toothed projections	Canoe hulls with upturned ends, ornamentally shaped and decorated in other forms than toothed projections

WESTERN	CENTRAL-MARGINAL
Flange lashing of canoe planks	Right-through lashing of canoe planks
Indirect outrigger attachment	Direct outrigger attachment in marginal Polynesia, mixed attachment in central Polynesia
Five or more outrigger booms	Two, more rarely three or four outrigger booms
Oceanic lateen sail	Oceanic spritsail
Absence of carved human figures	Carved human figures
Throwing club	Double-pointed club
Composite dart	Simple dart
Wooden slit-gong	Drum
Panpipes	Musical bow
Kava bowl and kava ceremony	Absence of western kava bowl and ceremony
Chiefs' language	Absence of chiefs' language
Kinship terms distinguishing father from mother	Father and mother equated in kinship terminology
Terms distinguishing son and daughter, man speaking, from son and daughter, woman speaking	Same terms for son and daughter, regardless of sex of speaker
Terms distinguishing mother's brother from father and father's sister from mother	Mother's brother equated with father, father's sister with mother
Terms distinguishing child, woman speaking, from brother's child, and child, man speaking, from sister's child	Woman's brother's child and man's sister's child equated with own children
First-born sibling, same sex as speaker, taokete	First-born sibling, same sex as speaker, tuakana
Affinal relative, same generation as speaker, maa; no other terms for affinal relatives	Affinal relative, same generation as speaker, taokete; terms for child-in-law, parent-in-law, and locally, parents of child's spouse
Brother-sister avoidance	Absence of brother-sister avoidance

WESTERN	CENTRAL-MARGINAL
Vasu privilege of sisters' sons	Absence of *vasu* privilege
Tangaloa the only representative of the "major pantheon"	Tangaroa, Tu, Tane, Rongo as primal gods
Evolutionary myth of origin of man	Procreative myth of origin of man
Pulotu as island in the west or underworld, home of gods and of the elect after death	Hawaiki as ancestral home to the west or underworld
God house	Sacred court with stonework
Vaimua, Vaimuli, Lihamua, Lihamuli, as month names	Pipiri, Hingaia, Erehu as month names
Absence of nights of the moon	Nights of the moon

12. A Note on Descent Groups in Polynesia

Now that the study of corporate descent groups is well advanced, and interest has been awakened in the existence and function of 'bilateral' systems, it seems appropriate to reexamine material from Polynesia.[1] In such a study it is simplest to start by consideration of the criteria conventionally assigned to lineage structures. Lineage is essentially a unilineal descent group with some corporate functions, normally related by segmentary process to other descent groups of the same type, and with them usually covering the entire society. Empirically, lineages in the African field have been treated as exogamous. Descent groups in Polynesia for the most part offer a contrast to practically every one of these criteria. In Tikopia they are unilineal but in most other Polynesian societies they are not. They are formed by segmentary process but the level of segmentation does not in itself necessarily have structural significance. In most Polynesian societies a person is a member of some descent group of some scale, but in at least one, Tonga, by no means every member of the society is a member of a 'lineage.' In no Polynesian society are the descent groups fully exogamous; even in Pukapuka, where the matrilineal sub-lineages are said to be exogamous, the lineages themselves are specifically stated not to be so.

Discovery of these facts is not particularly new. But the interest in the exploration of the varieties of unilineal systems has meant

SOURCE: Reprinted from *Man*, Vol. 57 (1957), Article 2, pp. 4–8, by permission of the author and publisher.

[1] I am indebted to a personal grant-in-aid from the Behavioral Sciences Division of the Ford Foundation for facilities in the preparation of this article.

that for the most part the more general significance of the Polynesian units as descent-group variants has tended to be overlooked. To use them effectively at this stage, however, some
reconsideration is necessary.

Two pieces of evidence may be revived here. In 1929 I drew
attention to the curious structure of the Maori *hapu,* pointing out
that it contravened the then generally accepted principle of unilineal transmission of membership of a descent group. I referred
to this group as ambilateral in type (Firth 1929:98; cf. Freeman
1956; Needham 1956). I pointed out that such a group had two
characteristics, that it was non-exogamous in distinction from the
current view of the 'clan' (which term had often been used to
describe *hapu*), and that it was not unilateral since both parents
were eligible for purposes of descent-group affiliation. In the same
year E. W. Gifford (1929:29 ff.) described for Tonga what he
termed 'lineages,' an equivalent for the Tongan term *ha'a,* which
previously had been described as 'tribe, class, family.'[2] Gifford
cited what he called the splitting of major lineages into minor
ones and likened the whole system of lineages to a tree with trunk,
limbs and twigs. He pointed out three interesting facts. One was
how a minor segment (a 'limb') becomes huge and flourishing
while a major segment (the 'trunk') ceases to flourish. This process was linked with chieftainship, since a succession of chiefs who
could command authority was necessary as a nucleus for the lineage. 'Without such chiefs it appears to wilt and die and its membership gradually aligns itself with other rising lineages.' The
second point was that not all members of Tongan societies in his
day belonged to lineages. Some commoners seemed not to be
aware of their lineage and even some modern descendants of former powerful chiefs were in this position. Thirdly, Gifford explained the mechanism of descent. He first described the lineages
as 'patrilineal.' But he qualified this by saying that though tracing
lineage through the mother was not considered 'appropriate,' it
did sometimes occur, usually when it gave greater prestige or
because the father was a foreigner. If a person were annoyed at
something, he might shift his allegiance from his father's to his

---

[2] Owing to the curious editorial practice of the then Director of the
Bishop Museum, all glottal stops were omitted from these publications. The
more correct way of writing this word would be *ha'a.*

mother's chief, which in effect would mean shifting his *ha'a*. More-over, he pointed out that the process of realignment of allegiance from a dying to a flourishing lineage contravened the theoretical rule of patrilineal descent.

Later, I took up this main theme in regard to the flexibility of Polynesian descent (Firth 1936:579–88, 596–98). In general, I noted how in Polynesia descent, *i.e.* membership of a named kin-ship group, is usually not unilateral, but is conditioned to a large extent by residence. For the Maori I stated specifically that de-scent and the formal structure of the kinship grouping can be understood only by reference to residence and land holding. I suggested that the patriliny of Tikopia may be correlated with a 'patrilocal' form of marriage settlement, whereas the ambilateral-ity of the Maori and the mechanics of absorption from female into male side of the house of Samoa and Tonga are correlates of the tendency to 'uxorilocal' settlement at marriage. I also used the generic term 'ramage' to describe the various Polynesian descent groups, primarily because of their branching character.

From the synoptic viewpoint one may organize the Polynesian material in various ways. But one of the most important distinc-tions is that between descent-group systems which do not allow choice in affiliation as regards membership through male and fe-male, and those which do. The former may be termed *definitive* descent-group systems, the latter *optative*. Taking as a criterion the rigidity of descent-group principle, one may single out two Polynesian societies of *definitive* type. One is the single unilineal system of Tikopia with patriliny as its established theory. Patriliny is indeed operative in practice for all normal occasions. The other is the double unilineal system of Pukapuka in which a set of matrilineal units ('lineages') operates in conjunction with a set of patrilineal units. Varying from these are *optative* systems such as those of the Maori, Tonga or Samoa, in which the major em-phasis is upon descent in the male line, but allowance is made, in circumstances so frequent in some societies as to be reckoned as normal, for entitlement to membership through a female. In such societies there are no purported matrilineal units. But looser analogy with Pukapuka is presented by Ontong Java, in which descent units with patrilineal predominance are combined with house-and-garden-owning units of matrilateral character and with normal uxorilocal residence.[3] A similar structure seems to exist in Tokelau (Hogbin 1934:109–14, 118–22; Beaglehole 1938: 221–33; Macgregor 1937:42, 46–48).

In considering Polynesian descent groups, there are three main concepts to be discussed. One is the concept of attachment to the group, the tracing of linkage with a particular descent group by the principle of *affiliation*. Another is the concept of the *constitution* of the group, the notion of what is meant when it is said that a person 'belongs' to a particular group, is a member of it. The third concept is that of the *formation* of the group, the process whereby new groups arise.

The principle of affiliation is of particular interest in Polynesia because of the relative lack of importance attached in most of the societies to the particular parent through whom it is traced. In theory as regards field of choice there are three possibilities:

(*a*) Unilaterality by tracing affiliation consistently through *one* kind of parent only to the exclusion of the other.

(*b*) Bilaterality by tracing affiliation through *both* kinds of parents equally and consistently.

(*c*) Ambilaterality, in which, in any one generation, *both* kinds of parents are feasible for affiliation but some selectivity is possible, with difference of emphasis.

This opens up a range of variants. If affiliation is traced through both parents who are themselves members of different descent groups, then their child is a member of these two groups. Such a claim may in fact be made, as often occurs among the Maori. A person will say that he 'belongs' to both Group A and Group B, or that he is half Group A and half Group B. In practice, however, the claim to membership of one group tends to be emphasized at the expense of the claim to membership of the other, either permanently or varying according to context. When affiliation is traced through one parent only but it is immaterial which, the descent-group membership established may be unalterable. But an alternative, as already indicated, is that a person may switch from one group to the other as circumstances dictate. Such reversible affiliation is probably more common than the unaltera-

---

[3] This specific matrilineal-group recognition in Pukapuka and Ontong Java suggests relationship with the recognized matrilineal descent groups of Micronesia—these islands are relatively close.

ble or irreversible type. I should doubt if irreversible affiliation occurs in the ambilateral field in Polynesia.[4] Finally, since exogamy is not characteristic of Polynesian descent groups, there is always the possibility that both parents may belong to the same descent group. The child thus has a double bond of affiliation. He does not need in such societies to emphasize one type of affiliation against the other, although for status purposes within the group he may stress the tie through father rather than through mother, or *vice versa*. (This gives a virtual though not theoretical bilaterality.)

One point about ambilateral affiliation is that a descent-group tie traced through the father in one generation may continue through the mother in the next generation and so on, using males and females as links without set order. The descent-group structure at any given moment looks like that of a lineage, as Leach has pointed out, though it lacks consistent unilineality.

In Polynesia, unilateral affiliation occurs in respect of the Tikopia *paito,* as also with the Pukapuka patrilateral *po* and *wakavae* and matrilateral *wua* and *keinanga*. Ambilaterality occurs among the Maori, the Tongans and the Samoans and also very generally in Polynesia.

As regards the constitution of descent groups, what are the implications of the choice found in ambilateral systems? A unilateral system of affiliation provides invariant group membership and presumably a less flexible group structure. An ambilateral system provides for variant group membership and presumably a more flexible group structure. This flexibility is seen, for example, in the Tongan situation where, taking advantage of the possibilities of choice, persons of relatively low status realign themselves with those of higher status and correspondingly give more impetus to the waxing and waning of lineage magnitudes. Again, the variant possibilities of group membership in the ambilateral scheme may tend to a more dispersed sense of responsibility. If not leading to divided allegiance, the possibilities of transferable allegiance in regard to one's descent group tend to modify the structural principle of the unity of the lineage group. What in unilineal de-

[4] That form of ambilaterality in which the choice of one parent for descent-group affiliation bars out affiliation through the other parent has been categorized by J. D. Freeman as utrolateral connexion. See J. D. Freeman 1955:5–7, and *cf.* Freeman 1956 and Needham 1956.

scent systems must be provided by conflicting ties of neighbour-
hood and political attachment, is given freer range within the very
structure of the descent-group system itself in Polynesia. The
ultimate outcome may not be so different, but the details of process are different. But the flexibility of Polynesian descent groups
has its limitations. For the most part, while an individual may
choose fairly freely the descent group in which he wishes membership, once his choice is made he tends to abide by it. Only
rarely does he change. His ties with other groups remain dormant
and in succeeding generations they tend to atrophy. With the
Maori there is traditionally a tendency for claims to descent and
land rights to 'grow cold' after a few generations if they are not
revived by residence. Hence the variant structure provided in
theory by ambilaterality is much less so in fact. The descent configuration is different from that of a unilineal lineage structure but
the operational effects are very similar (Leach 1948; 1950:61 f.,
72 f.).

From the point of view of an individual the mode of laterality in
descent affiliation is of first importance; he is primarily concerned
with the parent tie by which he is attached to the group. But from
the point of view of analysis of a social structure the mode of
lineality is equally important: group responsibility, claims and
rights are concerned with the lines along which membership is
transmitted from one generation to another.

Individuals are concerned with the principle of descent in their
societies, in particular as regards status and rights—when they
have to decide between competing claims or when they wish to
establish a special relation to someone in a previous generation.
But bearing in mind the need for economy in the handling of social
resources, it is highly improbable that persons will be allowed to
claim or establish membership in any wide series of descent groups
through both parents and their ancestors. In other words, bilaterality is a feasible operational procedure; consistent, complete
bilineality is not. It is for this reason that in speaking of 'bilateral
kin group' it has seemed necessary to distinguish by name as well
as in fact between two different types. One is the type illustrated
by the Tikopia *kano a paito,* which is bilateral—but not bilineal—
and is ego-oriented, having no persistence beyond the single generation. The other type of bilateral kin unit is of a corporate order,
with specific functions in regard to land holding, status rights, etc.

Here it is possible that completely bilateral groups may function for two or even three generations in descent from a common ancestor, both males and females consistently and invariably being reckoned in tracing membership. But unless birth and marriage are highly restricted or there is a high degree of endogamy, such bilinear continuity is unlikely. Unequal stress on the parental tie is necessitated by the ordinary conditions of living and handling resources. There may be a bias in favour of a tie with the male parent or through males generally and this patrilineal emphasis, though not exclusiveness, is characteristic of most Polynesian societies. Or again, the issue may be left to contiguity. Where the parents are from different villages residence tends to crystallize in one. It is clearly simpler to attach oneself to the group of the parent who is living in 'his own' village. Thus, a descent group behaving in most respects like a lineage tends to be formed.

I attach no great importance to terms as such. But considering the wide distribution of descent-group systems where there is some selectivity of parentage as a basis for membership, it would seem appropriate to have a set of terms to describe such systems. It would seem useful to include among such terms the following:

> *Ambilateral* for the mode of attachment in which both parents are feasible as links in group membership.
>
> *Ambilineal* for the maintenance of group continuity through the generations by using male or female links without set order.
>
> *Ramage* for the kind of group constituted by using both/either parents as links in group membership.

In former publications I have used *ramage* to include the Tikopia unilineal descent group. This, I think, is better described functionally as a lineage, keeping the term ramage for those descent groups which are not unilineal. Ramage would then be defined as a corporate descent group of a non-unilinear (ambilineal) character, membership being obtained ambilaterally, *i.e.* through either parent according to circumstances. Such a group ethnographically is normally found to be non-exogamous (cf. Sheddick 1954:18–19; Sahlins 1955:1047 ff.).

Now consider the constitution of such a group. What is meant by saying that a person 'belongs' to a kin unit? One such concept is that of *recognition,* in which the person himself and—of equal

importance—other members of the society, ordinarily speak of him
and regard him as properly associated with that group. (This is
essentially a process of social classification.) Such recognition is
commonly given by use of the group name. But the other concept
into which recognition is almost at once translated is that of rights
and obligations. The operation of status rights becomes one of the
conditioning factors in the working of ambilineal descent. While
most Polynesian societies, including those of the Maori and the
Tongans, allow membership in a descent group through females,
they attach greater importance for status purposes to descent
through males. The Maori stress the prestige of chieftainship, boasting of unbroken descent through a line of firstborn sons; they also
emphasize descent through males in the exercise of public privileges in oratory in general assemblies. Similar stresses in Tonga
explain Gifford's opening statement that in Tonga patrilineal descent theoretically and largely in practice determines 'lineage'
membership. As rank and status decrease, it becomes less important whether the individual's tie of membership is through male
or female, and in the idiosyncratic case of Tonga the tie may be so
reduced in importance that people of low status are ignorant even
whether it exists. (This is as far as membership in the major
named *ha'a* is concerned; they presumably belong to small unnamed descent groups.) From this point of view the Polynesian
ramage is a unit of political significance, though it usually also
involves ritual and other social rights, obligations and services outside the political field.

One question in regard to rights and obligations concerns the
lack of exogamy. It may be argued that the difference between
exogamous and non-exogamous lineage structures is not very important because with the latter there is always some degree of
incest ban on unions between close kin, and the distinction is, therefore, only a matter of degree. But where a person's mother's and
father's descent groups are identical there is a constriction upon the
social circulation of goods and services, which do not go out to
another group and therefore do not serve to enlarge and maintain
social ties. The whole system of pattern reciprocities may be affected. The Tikopia, for example, recognize this overtly (Firth
1936:339). Moreover, the absence of exogamy means that when
an intra-group marriage has occurred, the offspring will have a
more limited set of kin in typical roles. When a marriage has been

exogamous between Groups A and B, members of Group A provide the father's kin, those of Group B the mother's kin. When social support of any scale is needed and normally the parents' groups are mobilized, the child of a non-exogamous marriage has a more restricted field of support.

The importance of rights to group membership being associated with locality is now fairly clearly understood, and in respect of ambilineal groups has recently been reexamined and clarified by Goodenough (1955). But a distinction can be drawn between theoretical and operational membership of such a group. In a unilineal group system, a person living in one place may be regarded for local purposes, especially the exercise of land rights, as a member of a kin group, the rest of whose members live elsewhere (this is the situation in Tikopia). Residence is irrelevant as a determinant of descent-group membership, but residence is, of course, very important for operational purposes. People who have plenty of land tend to cultivate themselves those parts of 'their' lands which are nearer to their homes. In a completely bilineal group ('unrestricted bilateral' in Goodenough's term) the same is possible. But in an ambilateral group, a ramage, theoretical and operational limitations of land rights tend to coincide. Residence by itself does not give title to descent-group membership, but land rights established by descent-group membership tend to remain operational only through residence. Conditions here vary. In some communities several generations must pass before absentee land rights can be extinguished. Among the Maori, for instance, a change in residence traditionally implied a diminishing validity for a land claim. But it should be noted that in some Polynesian communities, *e.g.* Rarotonga and Maori, the institution of a new political and legal system has facilitated some change. New markets for products have given a more pronounced economic value to land. Peaceful conditions have allowed people to move about more easily and maintain multiple residence. Record of title has given a legal validity to what otherwise might have been disputable. The result has been to allow the operation of dispersed land rights to an extent apparently much greater than in traditional times. In this respect the land operations of ambilateral groups have tended to resemble those of lineages, though as yet there does not seem to be any sign that in the Maori system, for example, rights through women are tending to become more restricted than rights through men.

A few words about processes of group formation.

Anthropologists speak with confidence about the process of lineage segmentation, yet it must be remembered that most of the evidence is inferential rather than observed. It rests largely upon the interpretation of genealogical and other social data. Actual observation of changes that have taken place over a period of time during which documentary or other evidence about such segmentation was available has been scanty. One line of enquiry in the Polynesian field would be to take the classic material of, say, Elsdon Best on Tuhoe *hapu,* now nearly half a century old, and trace the changes in segmentation and rearrangement since Best's work. I discussed briefly 'progressive segmentation' among the Maori (Firth 1929:99), but it would be interesting to ascertain how far segmentation of Maori ramages is, in fact, progressive.[5]

One may distinguish here four concepts. One is the *segmentation model,* the anthropologist's description of what he understands to have taken place as a type of process. Then there is the *segmentation charter,* the local type of what the people themselves, or sections of them, regard as the 'historical' order of events. Then there is *operational segmentation,* the way the descent group splits for various social ends, recombining where necessary for other ends. Finally, there is what may be termed *definitive segmentation,* the irreversible process leading to the formation of new groups which do not then recombine. This process, progressive in character and sometimes described as 'polysegmentation,' may also be described as *gemmation,* referring to the way in which budlike growths become detached and develop into new individuals. This term might perhaps be most aptly used for those cases of segmentation in which connexions with the parent descent group are lost, so that what have been sometimes called 'truncated lineages' occur. This is a process which historically would seem to have taken place in many of the smaller Polynesian communities with the growth of population.

Segmentation is not a process which is difficult to understand. What is sometimes difficult is to relate the segmentation model of the anthropologist to the operational segmentation of the society—

[5] In Tikopia, after a generation, segmentation seemed to have occurred only at the lower levels.

the way in which the actual descent groups order their personnel for social purposes. Here it may be suggested that segmentation in any social structure is not an automatic process but is related to the available resources. The relation cannot be simple but it would appear that increasing pressure of population upon land is likely to lead to a speeding-up of the segmentation process for operational purposes, though not necessarily in terms of the structural frame.

13. The Analysis of Mana: An Empirical Approach

Despite sixty years of discussion and a bulky literature the controversies that have raged round the meaning of the Oceanic term *mana* and its related concepts are still far from settled. Much of the obscurity and confusion has arisen through the fact that elaborate theoretical discussions have been constructed on the basis of inadequate factual data.

In examining the meaning of the native term the investigators have tried to arrive at their results by varying combinations of the following three methods:

(a) By attempting an exact "translation" of the word concerned and trying to get a precise verbal equivalent for the native idea.

(b) By examining the relationship in native thought between the "*mana*-idea" and other concepts of the same native community;—that is, by obtaining linguistic explanations of the "*mana*-concept" from the natives themselves.

(c) By studying the actual usage of the word as employed in the course of normal behaviour and activities, and obtaining native linguistic comments on such usages.

The difficulty of obtaining any reliable empirical data in the last two categories makes it inevitable that nearly all armchair discussion has centred round the dictionary definitions supplied by the first category. The results have been unfortunate.

SOURCE: Extract from Raymond Firth, *Tikopia Ritual and Belief*. London: George Allen & Unwin Ltd.; Boston: Beacon Press, Inc., 1967. Reprinted by permission of the author and publisher. The article was originally published in *Journal of the Polynesian Society*, Vol. 49, No. 4 (1940), pp. 483–510.

Certainly in past discussions concerning *mana* nearly all the initial emphasis has been laid on trying to find some European verbal equivalent for the Oceanic concept. The diversity of the resulting translations may be an indication of the confusion that has arisen in fixing the meaning of the term. But it may also be a reflex of the assumption that there is in fact any general *mana*-concept that is common to all Oceanic communities. Such an assumption may be quite unjustified; there may be genuine significant differences of connotation between different communities.

The following selection from the various meanings (not all exclusive) that have been attributed to *mana* shows the confusion; it also illustrates the theoretical preconceptions of the various authors. *Mana* has been translated as:

Supernatural power; influence (Codrington).
Magical power; psychic force (Marett).
Impersonal religious force; totemic principle (Durkheim).
Divine force (Handy).
Effective; miracle; authority; prestige, etc. (Tregear).
True (Hocart).

Lehmann in his useful collection of material on the subject gives numerous other examples. More recently, Handy (1927:28) and Driberg (1936:4, 8) have sought an analogy for *mana* in electricity,[1] while Hogbin (1936:265) has compared it with luck.

The difficulty of describing the concept exactly is brought out by Hubert and Mauss, who characterize it as "not only a force, a being; it is also an action, a quality, and a state. In other words the term is at once a noun, an adjective and a verb."[2] This seeming

[1] Driberg likens *mana* to "an abstract Power of natural potency, formless as ether . . . It has been likened in its manifestations to electricity (though perhaps radium would provide a better analogy) . . ." "Like radium it gives out energy indefinitely without diminishing its own extent or potency, and each spark is capable no less of infinite sub-division without loss of potency." This sounds like a denial of the second law of thermodynamics, but even if the proposition could be defended by modern physics I doubt if it very much helps us to appreciate the meaning of *mana*.

[2] Hubert and Mauss 1904:108 et seq. Their otherwise excellent analysis is, however, obscured by a mystical element which they bring into it, thus:

"L'idée de mana est une de ces idées troublés, dont nous croyons être débarrassés, et que, par consequent, nous avons peine à concevoir. Elle est obscure et vague et pourtant d'un emploi étrangement déterminé. Elle est abstraite et générale et pourtant pleine de concret. Sa nature primitive, c'est à

grammatical confusion has been responsible for much laborious theorizing. The elaborate arguments that seek to determine whether the nature of *mana* is "personal" or "impersonal" seem to turn largely on the question as to whether it is more nearly correct to say that an object "is *mana*" or "has *mana*," though as Lehmann has pointed out this distinction is not material in many Oceanic languages. By some writers the notion of *mana* as "a vague and impersonal fluid" has been represented as in opposition to assertions that it is derived from spirit entities.

The type of inference drawn for anthropological theory from the material on *mana* has been almost as varied as the differences in translation. A. M. Hocart (1922) has made an important contribution to the study of *mana* by stressing that the Polynesian conception is a practical one connoting prosperity and success, and he has also drawn attention to the fact that *mana* tends to be attributed particularly to the leaders of the community, their chiefs and priests. His inferences, however, are essentially of an ethnological order. He is concerned to show the archaic character of the Polynesian idea and its place in the history of religion as intimately connected with the doctrine of the divinity of kings.[3] A. Capell, again, in a recent article (1938) has attempted to trace the linguistic history of the word, taking its primary meaning as "effective," with the general implication that the efficacy goes beyond that encountered in everyday life. With this one agrees. His conclusion is that *mana* is a prevailing Polynesian concept, but that "exactly similar ideas prevail amongst the American Indians, but naturally under a different name." He holds that the Polynesians

---

dire complexe et confuse, nous inderdit d'en faire une analyse logigue; nous devons nous contender de la décrire . . ." (p. 109); and again:

"L'idée de mana se compose d'une série d'idées instables qui se confondent les unes dans les autres. Il est tour à tour et à la fois qualité, substance et activité." The confusion and instability, however, seems to be the result of the anthropologists' analysis rather than a property of the native idea; indeed as this article will show the concept in Tikopia at least is entirely non-mystical, has always a concrete referent and is quite capable of being handled in a non-intellectual way. The complexity of the concept only begins to arise when anthropologists insist that *mana*—"c'est également une sorte d'éther, impondérable, communicable, et qui se répand de lui meme" (op. cit. p. 112).

[3] It may be remarked that such attempts at recovery of the "original notion" from which others have been derived rests implicitly upon a projection of a sequence in the mind of the analyst into the phenomena analyzed. This sequence may or may not have been followed historically.

brought the word *manan* with them from Indonesia, its incidence in Borneo and the Celebes being of particular significance here. He agrees also with Pater Schmidt that *mana* had its origin in and with mythology, developing in dependence upon an ancestor cult.

R. R. Marett, who by his own statement is entitled to rank among the "prophets of the gospel of *mana*," has stressed the view that *mana* and allied notions constitute the category that most nearly expresses the essence of rudimentary religion. His thesis that *mana* is the nearest expression of the positive emotional value which is the raw material of religion is too well known to need further discussion (Marett 1914:xxiii–xxvii, xxxi and *passim*).

Recently Ruth Benedict (1938:630) has revived this view in another form by stating that *mana, wakanda,* etc., have as their fundamental concept the idea of the existence of "wonderful power, a voltage with which the universe is believed to be charged," and always the manipulation of this wonderful power and the beliefs that grow out of it are Religion.

In contrast to these latter views is that of B. Malinowski (1926: 72–73). He argues cogently that on the empirical material the *mana*-concept is too narrow to stand as the basis of Magic and Religion, and holds that the concepts of *wakan, orenda,* and *mana* are simply "an example of an early generalisation of a crude metaphysical concept, such as is found in several other savage words also." He adds the very necessary warning that we have hardly any data at all showing just how this conception in Melanesia enters into religious or magical cult and belief. As will be seen, the argument of this article agrees in essentials with Malinowski's position. Controversy over the meaning of the term started soon after Codrington had published his somewhat abstract rendering of Melanesian ideas on the subject. This was a set of statements which he might never have given in this form if he had known that they would be treated as a classical text by distant scholars, subjected to microscopic analysis, and made the foundation of a system of primitive philosophy. The theoretical structures of Marett, Durkheim, Hubert and Mauss on this basis have in fact added much more to our understanding of primitive religion in general than to the clarification of the concept of *mana* itself.

Indeed, treated in this manner, the word *mana* becomes something of a technical term describing a specialized abstraction of the theoretical anthropologist and, as such, may have little in common with the same term as used in native phraseology. This fact indeed is appreciated (Marett 1914:99; Hocart 1933:185), but it is still assumed without serious enquiry, even by the latest writers on the subject (e.g., Radin 1937:13), that, quite apart from the technical usages of Anthropology there is in fact a *mana*-concept that is common to all parts of Oceania.

Scientifically speaking, any such general connotation of the term could only arise by inference as the result of the careful comparison of material from different communities; but in point of fact little adequate material exists. It is true that the term *mana* had been known from Polynesia long before it had received attention from the neighbouring Melanesian area.[4]

In the Maori literature in particular there are some data available which have received less than their due (for example, see Gudgeon 1905). F. R. Lehmann (1922) and E. S. C. Handy (1927) have analyzed the concept of *mana* from the available literary material on Polynesia.[5] But while this material is important, it is unfortunate that specific research into this problem was not carried further in the original field-work. Moreover, too often it is the European's own conception of the meaning of the term that has been placed on record and not an exact translation of texts spoken by the natives themselves. Again, the observation and analysis of actual native behaviour in situations where *mana* has been used as an explanatory concept is at a minimum. It is particularly to be regretted that Codrington, who knew his Mota people well, did not base his exposition on the analysis of examples which he actually recorded or observed, but instead composed some of them for his purpose. There always remains a doubt whether a native would really have thought out and performed an experiment in the way he describes.

The aim of the present article is to supply a body of empirical material from one particular area, Tikopia. By giving a contextualized description of the native usage of the *mana*-concept I hope to clarify its precise meaning at least for this particular community. By implication the material here put forward will also set certain

[4] W. Williams, *Dictionary of the New Zealand Language*, Paihia, 1844, where it is translated as "power, influence." A later edition by Bishop H. W. Williams (1917) gives "authority, control, influence, prestige, power, psychic force," and verbally "to take effect"; the causative *whakamana*, "to give effect to, to give prestige to."

[5] Some pertinent observations are also given in Williamson 1937:110.

negative limitations to the *mana*-concept in its more general connotation.

To my mind the proper understanding of the general notion can only emerge out of a careful consideration of particular usages such as are here recorded, and I would add that for our final appreciation of this general notion, if it exists, particular factual details may be irrelevant.[6] Thus for example the elaborate discussions that have been carried on by Codrington, Lehmann, Hocart and others as to whether or not *mana* is in the last resort dependent upon a spirit agency appears to me to be marginal to our understanding of the concept of *mana* itself.

I am concerned here first with the problem of definition of the term, and then with some other problems of the relation of the concept of *mana* to the economic and religious structure of the Tikopia.

In defining the meaning of the term I present material of three kinds: formulations obtained from men with whom I was specifically discussing the term, and to whom I put questions about it; citation of ritual formulae in which the term *mana* appeared incidentally as a standardized item in another context; and examples of the exercise of *mana* given in discussion of the behaviour and qualities of chiefs, comparison of past and present prosperity, illness, or other events in the life of individuals.

In presenting this material I give in translation the statements of my informants, as recorded in my notebooks in the original, and in addition, three long texts and several short ones as samples of the original material. Comparison of the translations with the texts will allow the accuracy of my rendering to be judged. It will be obvious that definition of such a term as *mana,* which is not the direct description of an act of behaviour or of a material object, must rely primarily on linguistic data. But it is important to note that this linguistic material is of varying value for interpretation. Statements given in response to direct questions of the order of "What is *mana?*" are acceptable only when reinforced, as in this case, by material of the other types mentioned above,

---

[6] Note . . . ". . . if it exists"; Hogbin's material from Ontong Java and Wogeo suggests that the *mana*-concept is far from being common to the whole of Oceania, and hence he questions the validity of attempting to build up any general theory of primitive religion on concepts of the *mana* type (Hogbin 1936:274).

where the formulation arises from the interest of the native himself in explaining or discussing another topic, and so is much more part of a standardized attitude than an abstraction.

MANA AND MANU IN TIKOPIA

It may be noted in the first place that the Tikopia use two words, *mana* and *manu,* for the one idea. The problem of definition is complicated by the fact that the sets of phonetic combinations giving *mana* and *manu* in Tikopia have a number of different equivalents according to the context in which they are used.

Mana may mean:
1. Thunder.
2. Father (a short for *tamana*).
3. For him, her, or it (pronounced with first vowel long).
4. Efficacious (equivalent to *manu* in the sense discussed in this article).

Manu may mean:
1. An animal, particularly a bird (the first vowel being stressed but short).
2. Efficacious, etc. (as here discussed the stress on the second vowel).
3. The name of an *atua,* a spirit-being resident in the heavens, identified with a star, and forming the subject of an important myth-cycle concerning storms.

As a preliminary explanation it may be pointed out that most of the Tikopia explanations of *mana* or *manu* are given by reference to the behaviour of their chief, and to prosperity, success, and welfare. A Tikopia chief is regarded as having a peculiar responsibility toward his people. He is considered to be able through his relations with his ancestors and gods to control natural fertility, health, and economic conditions, in the interests of his dependants.[7] Material evidence of his powers is given in native belief by the condition of the weather, of crops, of fish, and of sick persons whom he attempts to cure. Success or failure in these spheres are symptoms of his *mana.*

[7] See my *We, The Tikopia* and *Primitive Polynesian Economy, passim.*

I give now a series of statements in detail from natives to illustrate the empirical presentation of the idea by Tikopia. The views
expressed by Pa Rangifuri, eldest son of the chief of Tafua, may
be first considered. The subject arose between us during our discussion of initiation-ritual prompted by a case then in progress. He
said that initiation originated with the god of his clan and that in
olden times if the sun had shone fiercely for a long time then the
rite was performed to induce rain to fall—"to seek *manu.*" I en-
quired "what is this *manu* that is sought for?"

He replied, "If something is to be done indeed for the seeking of
manu (for example) you speak for the rain to fall; the rain falls
you sought *manu* by it; great is your *manu;* speech of praise is that,
praise for the man (to have it said 'great is your *manu*'); he (the
man seeking *manu*) speaks to his deity as my father is used to
speaking to the deity of Tafua, thus:

'I eat ten times your excrement, Rakiteua,
Drench down upon the land.'

That means the rain to fall; thereupon when we see that the rain has
come we say: 'the *manu* chief.' If we say also 'the chief is *manu*'
it is correct. If he asks for the breadfruit to come, for it to fruit, and
then it fruits, we say 'he has been *manu';* the asking of the chief
has been made *manu.* If no breadfruits fruit it is *mara.* He is
termed a *manu* chief, a *manu* man. He asks for different things,
manu!

"When we look at the land to which food comes constantly
then we say 'the land is *manu.*' But when we see that no food comes
that is the *mara.*"

I wished to find out if my informant regarded *manu* as something generally distributed, and inquired if it were to be found in
rocks and trees everywhere. He answered, "O! It is not there in
stones. It is not there in trees. It is there only in food and in fish.
We who dwell here, when we desire food, the chief requests the
god to give hither food for us. When we look upon the *taro* and the
yam which are living, and the breadfruit which has fruited there,
it has become *manu,* the *fakamanu* has come. It is not there in all
things, it is only in food and fish. When the fleet goes to sea and
brings hither fish that is the reef has risen (figurative expression
for the rising shoals of fish), it has risen and is *fakamanu.*"

Somewhat later Pa Rangifuri and I returned to the subject of *manu* and he began by discussing it in relation to the position of a newly-elected chief. He said, (Text 1) "The new chief beseeches the chief who has gone for some *manu* for himself, that he may crawl to the gods and the assemblage of ancestors. Indeed it is! That *manu* may come for him whatever may be done for him, the orphaned person cast down on that spot." (This is a technical phrase used of himself by a chief in addressing the gods to signify his humility and need.) "The chief who has departed, listens to the new chief, beseeching him indeed, calling out to him:

> 'I eat ten times your excrement
> You crawl to the gods
> For some *manu* for me
> My hand which touches a sick person may it heal
> (When he touches, that his hand may be *manu*)
> When I wail for anything that it may be *manu*'

Then the chief who has departed goes, performs his crawling to the god, and stretches out his hand to him 'Here! Give me some *manu* that I may go and give it to my next-in-line (successor).' It is given him by the god, whatever it may be, a bundle of leafage or the fruit of the coconut or a fish, or whatever be the desire of the chief who is beseeching him. Thereupon he comes again to sit in his place. He stretches out his hand to the new chief who is sitting among men (in the world of men). 'Here! There is your *manu*.' The *manu* is given hither after the fashion of gods; not a man looks upon it; he observes only the food which has become good, the *taro*, the yam, the coconut, all food has fruited well indeed."

Pa Rangifuri stated that when an old chief dies his *manu* goes with him—the sun shines, water dries up, food is scarce, and so on. This is the "parting of a chief." Hence the new chief whose vegetable resources have been cut off sends a request for *manu* for himself.

I put a question as to whether there could be *manu* alone independent of these material things. He said, "there is no *manu* alone of itself, there is *manu* of the rain, *manu* of the food, but no *manu* only. We look at the rain which has fallen, that is the *manu* which will come, come to the new chief." "*Siei se manu mosokoia, te manu o te ua, te manu o te kai, kae siei se manu fuere. Ono ko tatou ki te ua ka to, tera te manu ka u, au ki te ariki fou.*"

Some other explanatory material, obtained in other contexts, shows also this essential pragmatic aspect of the concept. Pa Rangi-furi on another occasion gave me a formula used in a net-rite which I had just seen. It appealed to a spirit, Kere-tapuna, to turn to the net, to act as sea-expert, that the net might be filled with fish, and ended *"Ke manu ko te kupenga."* When I asked for the meaning of the term *manu* he said "The *manu* canoe, the *manu* net, are those which catch fish. The canoe which has no fish for it, is not *manu."* *"Te vaka manu, te kupenga manu, e au te ika ki ei; te vaka sise ni ika mana, sise manu."*

Pa Motuangi, of Kafika, said of his mother's brother the Ariki Tafua *"Toku tuatina, matea na mana; ka fai te kava, ka to te ua; ka fai te kava ki te ika, ka tari mai; tari mai te ika."* "My uncle, great is his *mana;* if he makes the *kava,* the rain will fall; if he makes the *kava* for fish, they will be carried hither; carried hither are the fish."

Again, I was discussing with Pa Tarairaki of Kafika the canoe-rites of the Work of the Gods, and the celebration of what is termed "Evil Things," and offering to the gods of the fish secured. He said, *"Ka tu te vaka i te toki, au mai te ika e toto i te tunga te toki; ena na tunga toki. Tena e manu. Ko te toki e tu e manu, kae siei se tunga toki, e manu foki; te ika fuere e au mai te atua ke kai."*

"When the canoe is cut with the adze, the fish comes hither bleeding from the cut of the adze; there is its adze-cut. Now (it) is *manu.* The adze which cuts is *manu,* but if there is no adze-cut, it is also *manu;* the spirit simply brings hither the fish for food."

On another occasion, at a yam-rite in the Work of the Gods, I heard the Ariki Kafika ask for *manu* from the gods Pu-ma, that the breadfruit might "run," that is, that the fruit might be properly formed.

The term *manu* is used in a variety of ritual formulae in which spiritual beings are asked for practical results. Pa Rangifau gave the formula recited when the noose-method of fishing for *para* is used; in this he is an acknowledged expert.

> *Tou soa Ariki tautai*
> *Fatia tou mangai*
> *Ke rere o kai manu*
> *I tou raro vaka*
> *Inu tau poa*

Thy friend, sea expert chief,
Let thy tail be broken
To dash and eat in *manu* (fashion)
Below thy canoe
Eat thy bait

To explain here the significance of "friend," used in a special context implying that damage is sought, or the identification of spirit and fish, would demand a lengthy discussion. But the significance of the term *manu* is clearly the production of a practical result of securing the fish.

Again from Pa Vainunu I received the formula recited by a chief in investing a person with a cordyline-leaf necklet to secure his welfare

Te rau ti ka tutaki atu
Ki a ke, Pa e!
Tutaki manu
Motusia ki atea ko te fefea
Ma te urungaruru . . .

The cordyline leaf is being joined
To you, Father (his ancestor)
Join with *manu*
Be parted away things of whatever kind
And headaches . . .

"Things of whatever kind" refer here to the various types of illness or misfortune that might afflict a person. Karakiua of Taumako gave me the formula used by a chief to cure sickness. The chief calls on his father

"Au o fakamana i oku rima Pa e,
Ma te tauru rakau
Takina ki atea
Ko te kafo . . ."

"Come and make effective my hands, Father,
And the bunch of leaves
Be dragged away
The fever . . ."

Pa Fenuatara, eldest son of the Ariki Kafika explained *manu* as follows (Text 2): "In this land *manu* is there in the lips of the chief. In his speech whatever he may ask for, if a chief is *manu* then when he asks for fish, they will come; when he speaks requesting a calm it falls. That is a *mana* chief. But a chief who is *mara* there is no *mana* for him. The chief whose *kava* is wrong is *mara*. There is no *manu* for him. If he asks for a calm, no calm falls; if he asks for rain, no rain arrives; that is because his things (rites) are wrong."

I asked if *mana* lay simply in the chief as a man. My question made him laugh. He replied:

"No, friend. His *manu* is given hither by the spirits. When he asks it of the spirits, if the spirits wish to give it hither, they give it, and therefore I say that the chief is *manu*. A chief who is *manu* —the spirits just continually rejoice in their desire towards the chief."

I asked also if *mana* lay simply in the words recited. He replied:

"There is no *manu* in speech, it is simply asking. Now if I bewitch a man, I sit and look as to what may be his day upon which he may fall. If he is not ill that is the spirits are not turning to him, they do not wish my speech that I uttered. I am not *manu*." This too shows the dependence of *manu* on the will of the gods.

Several problems of definition are raised by these texts. The first is that of linguistic usage, as to whether *manu* and *mana* represent the same or different ideas. It will be seen in the texts above *manu* is used more frequently, but that *mana* sometimes occurs side by side with it. I asked Pa Rangifuri about this, and his reply was "A *manu* man, a *mana* man; a *manu* chief, a *mana* chief; great is his *mana* and great is his *manu*—such speech goes just the same; it is praising speech indeed." And Pa Fenuatara and Pa Motuangi also said that the two words meant the same thing.

A simple native assertion about the identity in meaning of the words could not be accepted without question. But I found that in actual usage by my range of informants, as can be seen from the texts, that either term is uttered with apparent indifference. The speaker switches from one to the other, obviously using them as synonyms.

A word closely allied in meaning to *manu* is *mairo,* though I heard it used mostly in reference to the healing of the sick. In discussing the "laying-on of hands" on a sick person the Ariki Kafika said "The hand of a chief is *mairo;* it touches and it heals. *Mairo* is *mana.* He is a *mana* man." He explained further that if the invalid rallied at the touch of the chief but then died when the chief had gone, the people would say, "Indeed, the hand of the chief, of course, was *fakamairo,*" meaning that it was this touch alone which had given the invalid sustaining power for the time being. Another statement points also to the equivalence of *mairo* with *mana.* "The hand of a chief is *mairo;* it touches a sick person, he gets well. He (the chief) calls to the gods to *fakamairo* his hand since he is going to the sick person."

Further material on the linguistic usage was obtained from Pae Sao. Our discussion began on the *kava*-ritual, which as an important elder he himself regularly performed. He spoke of chiefs and elders making appeals in set phraseology to their gods and ancestors to give them *manu.* He then proceeded to explain "The *manu*—that calm may come and rain may come, that the *kava* made to the gods may be *mairo.* The *fakamairo* indeed of the *kava* are the tokens of the *kava.* That is, it has become calm and it has rained." Later he added, "A ritual elder, a chief, is *mana,* is *manu;* the name of a chief is *manu* and *mana.*"

The position in Tikopia thus is that *manu* is the general term with *mana* as a synonym of it and *mairo* used less commonly, mostly in connection with healing. The usage of *manu* in Tikopia instead of or additional to the common Polynesian *mana* is puzzling. It is possible that the use of *manu,* in the sense we are discussing, is due to the fact that in this island *mana* is the ordinary abbreviation for *tamana,* father, with equal stresses also. This is speculation and I have no native opinion to support it.

Both *manu* and *mana* are quite flexible in syntax. Either can stand as a substantive or an adjunct, and can suffer some verbal modification. Some simple examples of the usage of *manu* may be given, extracted from the material quoted in this chapter.

> *Te manu ena i te ngutu te ariki.*
> The *manu* is there in the lips (of) the chief.

> *Na manu e sori mai i nga atua.*
> His *manu* is given hither from the gods.

> *Muna atu kuou te ariki e manu.*
> Speak away I the chief is *manu* (I say that . . .)

E faia toku mana ne manu, ne nofo ko ia, manu rei.
Because my father was *manu,* did live he, *manu* then.

Ku manutia ko te kaisianga a te ariki.
The request by the chief has been *manu.*

Ono tatou ki te mei kua fua, tera ku manu, ku au te fakamanu.
When we look on the breadfruit which has borne fruit, there
it has become *manu,* the making-*manu* has come.

An interesting verbal modification of the term *mana,* which has
a similar range, came from the spirit medium Pa Tekaumata,
who after giving me a formula he was in the habit of using said:
"Tena tenea nokofakamana ki oku nea." ("That is the thing used
to give *mana* to my affairs.") Here both frequentative and causative
prefixes have been attached to the word.

To students of Oceanic dialects this flexibility of the grammatical function of the word will be no novelty.

There has been some discussion as to whether it can be properly said that a man *"has mana"* or he *"is mana."* In Tikopia both
types of translation would be valid. If the flexibility of the word
in syntax be borne in mind, an analogous situation in English
would be of a man "having" success and "being" successful.

From the descriptive statements given above it can be seen that
manu covers a category of socially approved phenomena. It signifies positive results attained. So when a man is said to possess
or to be *manu,* this is a judgment in his favour. As Pa Rangifuri
said, this is "speech of praise."

Standing in opposition to this active and socially-welcomed
sphere of interest is the term *mara* which connotes absence of
visible results and is not a judgment of approval. A chief who
is *manu* is regarded as fulfilling his duty to his people and deserv-
ing their praise. A chief who is *mara* incurs their tacit censure
because the visible lack of fertility reacts upon their wellbeing,
which is his charge, and this is regarded as being due to some defect in his relations with his ancestors and gods. No action of any
kind is taken against such a chief; his people merely grumble and
speculate among themselves.

The alignment of *manu* with these positive effects might seem
as if *manu* signifies the activity-principle in nature. But it is correlated always with concrete situations, falling of rain, growth of

food, advent of calms, relief of sickness. In fact its very existence is inferred by such concrete results. Again and again I hammered away at my informants trying to find what was the meaning of *manu* itself apart from the evidence of it in crops, fish, and the like. But all my inquiries for the *Ding an Sich* came to nothing. Always it was insisted that the crops and the fish *were manu*. Now obviously my informants were not facing the logical and metaphysical issues squarely here, but their indifference to the existence of such issues is extremely significant. To the Tikopia, *manu* I am sure has not the connotation of an isolatable principle, a force, a power, or any other metaphysical abstraction—though it may be conceived of as a specific quality. The interpretation in terms of such abstraction can only be the work of the anthropologist. The Tikopia is content with concrete description of the results of activity and does not pursue the intellectual problem as to the nature of that activity.

It is well to reinforce this point by consideration of more material obtained not as the result of questions about *manu* but volunteered in an entirely different context.

When the seasonal dances were being performed in Marae, I participated in them. The songs chanted dealt mostly with the gods. When I asked why the dances were performed, the answer was given: "They are performed for the *manu* of the gods. All the chiefs sing to the gods that they may perform hither the *manu* for the land to be well." It might seem here that we are dealing with a native concept of the physical activity of man giving a stimulus to the activity of nature and using the theme of appeal to the gods as a medium of expression. But reference to the tradition of origins of the dances and to the beliefs about the gods show that though this be true as a sociological abstraction it is unjustifiable if put forward as a native idea. In Tikopia belief the gods give *manu* when the dances are performed because they see that the traditional ways of behaviour which they instituted are being faithfully followed; and they are pleased. Moreover, dancing is their primary amusement in the heavens and they are moved to interest and approval—and even to active participation when they see this practice being observed on earth (see Firth 1940).

Another linkage of the idea of *manu* with physical activity is given in the formula which is recited when a sacred adze is being used on a new canoe being built by a chief. From the Ariki Taumako and from a number of other people at different times, I was given texts of the formula and the explanation of it.

> "*Manu!* for your *marie*
> *Manu!* for your *para*
> *Manu!* for your *varu*
> *Manu!* for your bonito
> *Manu!* for your flying fish
> *Manu!* for all your fish on the starboard side
> *Manu!* may an orchard stand for you on the reef
> *Manu!* let them rise from the foam of the ocean
> *Manu!* flick behind harmful things."

Here again the pragmatic context of the term *manu* comes out very forcibly. The primary function of the canoe is to be an aid in securing fish and the kinds of most important fish are mentioned. The *marie* is a species of shark, while the *para* and *varu* are also types of highly prized large fish. The "orchard" is a metaphor for the fishing bank, and again it is fish which are adjured to rise from the ocean foam. The last line is an exhortation to ward off those spirits of the ocean which are evilly disposed. Although it is not stated in the formula, this is an invocation to the tutelary deities of the vessel and of the sacred adze. The best translation of *manu* here is "be effective" or "be efficacious." This example illustrates the use of the term *manu* in practical association with the citation of its material manifestation, the belief in the spiritual beings who vouchsafe it and a manual act of canoe-making—all this in a ritual context.

Another manual act believed to be accompanied by *manu* was described to me by Pa Fenuatara in connection with the initiation of a boy of rank. The chief of his clan pours some oil into his hand, announces it to one of his deities and then rubs it on the boy's chest. This is to take away his fear of the approaching operation. Pa Fenuatara said of his own case "I felt his hand strike my vitals. I was frightened but I felt as though he had given me food and that I was full. Great is his *mana*. Then my fear quite left me." In this case the Kafika chief was a very old man and so did not attend the lad's initiation. The ceremony was performed by the Ariki Fangarere instead.

Other material was obtained in discussing traditional events. Pa Torokinga, an old man, was telling me about his ancestors, the chief of the ancient group of Na Faea, who were driven off to sea by their enemies. He said, (Text 3): "Great was the weight of my ancestor the chief. His hand pointed to a man, the man slept down below (in death). His god indeed abode in his hand. He was *manu*. When he went down to the reef-waters and called to the fish to come to land they came—the *ature* (mackerel, which are netted on the reef). Long was the abiding of the fish; the land ate and ate and ate. He went and waved his hand at them to go; they went. Great was his weight. He spoke to a tree, the tree died. He spoke to the breadfruit, it came, it fruited." Pa Torokinga told me that this ancestor, on the day he went out to sea (driven away) loaded his canoe with food, took down a length of bark-cloth, beat the sea with it, and tied it trailing to the stern of his canoe. "The drawing away of the fish to go out to sea. The fish went completely. The reef was bare, there were no fish."

From Pa Motuangi of Marinoa I was told of the time when two rivals both occupied the ritual position of elder of the house at the one time. In this dual reign both performed their own *kava*-ceremonies and both sacralized their canoes for sea-fishing. When the rival fleets went to sea, fish were caught by the vessels of one elder named Vaiangafuru (my informant's ancestor) while those of the other caught nothing. "He made fish for his own fleet but not for the fleet of Pu Fangatafea which came in bare from the ocean. That is, Vaiangafuru was *manu*." I asked what was this *manu* and got the answer "A man who is not slept upon by the gods, that is a man who is not *manu*. It is exactly alike (*tau fangatasi*), the *mana*, the *manu*."

Pa Vainunu of Kafika was one day describing to me various types of ritual-chant, and gave as example one composed by his father, a former chief. The song referred to the "making bitter" of the lake. At certain times, apparently, the lake-waters became affected so that the fish rose to the surface in large numbers, died, and were collected by the people who carried them home to cook. Pa Vainunu with filial loyalty maintained that this did not happen nowadays, whereas in former times it occurred, because his father was *manu*. "The lake which stands there is not bitter in these after days because another chief has dwelt. When my father used to live it was bitter, from time to time it was bitter, because my father was *manu* as he dwelt, he was *manu* then. When he disappeared among the gods he disappeared with his own *manu*, and the land which stands here has become different. Because he called to his god; but they who dwell here do not know. The two of them, he and his god, have the same name. The name of the god is Mourongo, and my father has Mourongo as his second name. My ancestor Mourongo sat at the *kava* bowl as an *atua,* and prepared the *kava.* He listened to my father calling out among men but he himself heard him from the realm of spirits. My father called out:

> 'You Mourongo,
> I eat your excrement
> Turn hither to me who am calling out
> Shake the *kava* pith into the lake
> To be bitter that the land may eat.'

Then the *kava*-bowl was prepared and shaken into the lake; it was shaken in the realm of spirits. And my father the chief called upon the god and therefore his calling was *manu.* The fish went and sucked the *kava*-pith, went to drink of it, sucked, were poisoned, and died."

Pa Vainunu gave another incident after this to illustrate his father's *mana.* He said, "My father, great was his *manu.* He called out to the gods and his words were true. Look you upon me; I will tell you. It was his building of the sacred canoe which is drawn up there, Tafurufuru. As his building was going on the people went to hew out the vessel and he called for the fish to run hither. They ran then on the day on which the vessel was hewn out. The fish ran hither and the canoe was hewn while people went to bring hither the fish from the sea. They awoke on another day and brought them hither, awoke on another day and brought them hither, while the vessel continued to be hewn. The canoe was finished, but the fish continued still to stand. But when the chief who dwells here stood in his place he did not act thus and the fish did not run hither."

Here we have the recital of a miracle performed as an accompaniment to an important act of a chief—for the hewing of one of his sacred vessels is one of the marks of his career.

In the above text reference is made to the *truth* of the words of a chief when he called upon the god. The meaning of this is that his appeals to them were validated by results, not falsified by lack of results. The association hinted at here is between correctness of the formulae used, influence with the gods, and validity of one's case. Such association was illustrated by a discussion I had with Pa Motuata and Kavakiua who spoke of their father's brother the late chief of Taumako. They said: "Great was his *mana,* because he did not speak in lying fashion. He used to speak truly only; he spoke for calm—it fell; he spoke for rain—it rained at that moment." From the first part of the sentence it seems as if the possession and exercise of *mana* were contingent upon the practice of truth and the leading of a virtuous life. From the remainder, however, the actual position is clear that the truth is an inference from the results of the appeal and not a prior condition to those results.

This series of examples, drawn from a range of informants in different social groups, show how any Tikopia explanation of *mana* is presented in concrete terms, and on the other hand how concrete results which are more than those produced by ordinary efforts are interpreted in terms of *mana.* In all these examples as mentioned already the reference to *manu* was introduced in the course of explanation of the particular circumstances.

One question which arises is that of the origin of *manu.* From some remarks of the Tikopia it might appear that they believe that it was essentially an attribute of human beings. Pa Rangifuri said "The *manu* is there in you, there in your hand which touches and your outer lips." And, as mentioned earlier, Pa Fenuatara said "in this land the *manu* is there in the lips of the chief."

The statement that *manu* resides in the lips and hands is an explanation of its immediate location. It is there for the time being because these are the agencies through which it is liberated. It is the lips which utter the formulae, the hand which is laid upon a sick person.

To the Tikopia the only real source of *manu* is in the spirit world. *Manu* does not mean the exercise of human powers but the use of something derived from gods or ancestors. One further example is the case of an ancestor of the Fangarere people named Rakeimaitafua. He was a *tama tapu,* sacred child, of Tafua clan, that is, his mother was of that group. One of his descendants Pa Fenumera described him to me thus: "The coconuts came through him, his *manu;* the breadfruit and the chestnut. Things of the earth, the *taro* and yam, rose up above by his *manu.* He was *manu,* he sprang hither from Tafua, therefore the breadfruit and the coconut rose through the *atua* of Tafua; he made *mana* for his sacred child." This point of the origin of *mana* from the gods was made over and over again in different ways by my informant. Pa Porima, for instance, asked the question, "Kafika is *mana* through what?" And answered himself immediately, "It is *mana* through Tafaki and Karisi who used to be chiefs among men, who used to be chiefs formerly in Kafika." These two are the principal deities of the clan. The statement of Pa Rangifuri about *manu* being handed over by a dead chief to his successor has already been quoted. Pae Sao discussing the same point from another angle, that of the relation between a dead elder and his son, said that sometimes the father out of pique would withhold his *mana*. "It is clenched in his fist, the *manu* of the *kava* is denied to his son. The *manu* is clasped by his father and diverted away by him that it may not enter to his son." This, Pae Sao pointed out, is proven by the fact that no rain falls and the sea remains rough, hence the son knows that his father is displeased with him and so addresses him in deprecatory fashion to induce him to relent. The *manu* of the *kava* may be affected in other ways, as by some imperfection in the form of the invitation or in the list of names invoked. It is held that an ancestor or deity whose name is omitted turns his back in anger upon the performer of the *kava* which is thus rendered ineffective. In other words he refuses *manu* to it. Pa Rarovi complained to me that when his father died he was only a child. He got his *kava* from the Ariki Taumako and Pae Ava-kofe. But he was not sure if he received it rightly or not. He imagined that certain names were hidden from him because at first his *kava* was not satisfactory. Later, on the advice of Pae Sao he inserted other names into his lists and received good results in the shape of rain, or clear skies, when he demanded them.

When we were discussing the relation of a chief's activities to the state of the wind and of the weather Pa Fenuatara said "A chief who is wrong in his *kava* is *mara;* there is no *manu* for him. He requests a calm, but none falls; he requests rain but no rain arrives. That is because his things are wrong." The expression "to be wrong in the *kava*" means to omit from the list of deities in-voked some important names, or to use expressions incorrectly. A reason given for this is that before his election the future chief has not listened properly to the instruction given him by the reign-ing chief or other elders. He may have been too intent on fishing,

or on work in the cultivations. Then, when he performs his *kava*
and omits a name, the spirit concerned is offended, turns his back
and refuses to hand on *manu* to him—that is, to give any practical
results to his invocations.

An example of a chief calling upon his dead father for *mana*
arose when Pa Rangifuri gave me a formula used by the Ariki
Tafua in cases of illness:

> *"Fokimainiteni!*
> *Koke ono mai ki toku rima,*
> *Ke fakamana i toku rima,*
> *Ka po ki te naenae*
> *Ke tu fakamaroi*
> *Ke laui ki te naenae."*

> "Fokimainiteni!
> You look on my hand
> To give *mana* from my hand
> When it touches the sick person
> That he may stand firmly
> That the sick person may be well."

The method whereby *mana* is conveyed to a chief is described
thus: "The gods take and place it on the head of him who has
asked for the *mana* to be given to him." Hence according to this
theory the *mana* lodges in the top of the head of the man. According to the Tikopia it never resides in the belly.

But the native ideas are not very clear on the matter of the
relation of *manu* to the spoken word. On the one hand it is said
that *manu* resides in the lips and might thus be expected to go
out in speech, to exercise its effect. On the other hand, as just
stated, it is held that the spoken word which invokes the gods
is only a request for them to give *manu*.

This position can be resolved by the thesis that a man first
asks his gods for *manu* which, vouchsafed to him, he then emits
on other occasions to do its work.

A summary of the native statements quoted will help to bring
the Tikopia concept of *manu* into relation with the points discussed in anthropological theory. To the Tikopia nature does not
work independently of man; fertility is not merely a concatenation
of physical factors but depends on the maintenance of a relation-

ship between man and spiritual beings. *Manu* is discussed largely in terms of concrete results, natural phenomena such as crops, fish, and recovery from disease. Not only is its presence judged by material tokens, but at times it is represented as being in itself a material object—as when a dead chief hands it over to his successor or keeps it clenched in his fist. On the other side *manu* is connected with the personality of human beings, and is exercised through human agencies. It is not spoken of as a universal force inhering in all natural objects. The native view of *manu* may be regarded as an element in a theory of human achievement. Its thesis is that success above a certain point, the "normal," is spirit-given. It connects an end-product empirically observed with a set of human desires by a theory of spirit-mediation and a technique of verbal utterance. To the Tikopia the end-product is frequently equated in summary statements with the means whereby that product is obtained. "We look at the rain which is about to fall, that is, the *manu* which will come." But the separation of means from ends is also done. "The *manu* of the rain," "the *manu* is given after the fashion of gods; no man sees it," "one observes only that the food has become good."

The difficulty of rendering a term such as *manu* in translation is that of comprising under one head a number of categories which we ordinarily separate. Uncertainty in natural phenomena, differential human ability, dependence upon spirit entities, are the three primary factors in the *manu* situation. A possible translation of *manu* or *mana* in Tikopia would then appear to be "success" or "successful," which can embody reference both to the ability of man and to tangible results. This term is valid only if it be remembered that for the Tikopia success is not merely a matter of human effort. It is essentially success in certain spheres, those which affect human interests most vitally—food, health, and weather-control, but in ways with which ordinary technique cannot cope. Another possible translation of *manu* is "efficacy" or "to be efficacious."[8] Here the emphasis again is on the fact that the activity works, that it performs the function for which it was intended. But since the efficacy is believed to be only partly due to human endeavour, any translation must also by implication embody a reference to the extra-human causes of the result. The

[8] The translation given by Bishop Williams (1917), "to take effect," appears to be an appropriate one; his *whakamana* is also apt.

difficulty lies in comprising in the one term both the result of activity and the native theory of the reason for it. Any single word in English cannot therefore express the fullness of the native concept.

Most of the translations proposed for *mana* fail to give the reality of the native attitude, because of their abstract nature, and their introduction of categories which may have no counterpart in the native system. "Supernatural power" for instance does represent one aspect of the concept but it leaves out of account the essentially material evidence of such power, and directs attention to the means rather than to the end-product. It ignores also the vital factor that such power does not exist in vacuo but is exercised by human beings or personified material objects, for human benefit. "Psychic force" is a highly intellectualized rendering of the same idea and neglects the native theory of origins.

I could not find in Tikopia any secular connotation of *mana* as "authority" or "influence." Where this meaning occurs, as it apparently does among the Maori, it appears to be secondary, an inference from the more basic significance already discussed. The possible difference of meaning of *mana* in the various Polynesian communities may lead some critics to the conclusion that the *mana* or *manu* of Tikopia is a typical concept. But this is not a justifiable view until a body of empirical evidence comparable with that here presented has been analyzed for these other communities. From the material already available it seems to me that the same factual definition of *mana* of Tikopia probably could be applied elsewhere in Polynesia, though in some cultures there is an extension of meaning into the social sphere. However this be, it is clearly inappropriate to talk of *mana* at this stage as if it represented an identical system of ideas for the Oceanic field.[9] So far as Tikopia is concerned however, we have now arrived at a factual definition of *mana* (*manu*) in terms of the following characteristics.

1. *Material events,* e.g., crops, fish, death of bewitched persons, cure of sickness, relief from fear.

[9] My recent research in Kelantan, Unfederated Malay States, has shown that a very similar factual definition can be given to the Malay word *keramat,* translated by R. J. Wilkinson (1932) as "saintly; working miracles . . ." That it also can bear meaning akin to *mana* is shown from the remark of a Malay friend of mine to me "I think Tuan must be *keramat*—Tuan said 'tomorrow you will get fish'; and I did."

2. As a *personal attribute* of chiefs; though by way of illustration an informant may refer to himself.
3. The *volition* of spiritual beings who grant to or withhold the *manu* from the chiefs.
4. *Value.* In contrast to *mara, manu* and *mana* always have a positive connotation.

The concept of *manu* as being a personal attribute only of chiefs raises the problem of the relation of the concept to political and religious organization. To what extent does currency of this concept tend to maintain the organization and in particular the role and status of chiefs?

Viewed from one angle the linguistic concept of *manu* is a means of formulating the responsibilities and privileges of chiefs; it gathers into a single concept a series of disparate occurrences:— material events, and the acts and influence of chiefs. The *manu*-theme is thus part of the definition of a chief's job.

But the metaphysical control said to be exercised by the chief over goods and production by virtue of his *manu* must be correlated with the factual control exemplified by the chief's receipt of first-fruits and baskets of food, and with the ritual-control exemplified in his priestly functions.

On the one hand the concept of *manu* tends to sustain the role and status of chiefs and to exaggerate their actual power:—it is associated essentially with chiefs, it is there in his lips and in his hands, it is given to him (and not to others) by his chiefs and ancestors. In this manner economic and social results which in a great part at least arise from natural phenomena—(e.g., seasonal change, recuperative powers of the human body, etc.)—are concentrated upon the person of the chief and thus redound to his credit.

But on the other hand, in contrast to this, material failure as well as success is projected on to the person of the chief and his reputation may suffer through events entirely outside his control. Thus though a man may be, from the outsider's point of view, an effective chief, with a sense of responsibility to his people, hard working and keen to give a lead to the economic affairs of the clan, and assiduous in the performance of ritual, yet so far as the possession of *manu* is concerned he may be put at a disadvantage merely through a succession of bad seasons. Thus from the practical point of view the *manu* of a chief is no thorough test of his efficiency. I say no *thorough* test because, as with the Ariki Tafua, attribution of *manu* to him by reason of large catches of fish may well be based in reality on his better powers of organization, or his superior judgment of place and time for fishing.

It may be noted also that even where a chief is rated low in *mana* this value-judgment is not implemented in economic terms; there is no refusal, for instance, to give him the customary first-fruits or other food-acknowledgments. One reason for this is that his condition is not necessarily permanent; he may become *manu* again soon. Another reason is undoubtedly the social repercussions which any such refusal would involve. Thus projection of failure on to the person of a chief does not endanger the institution of chieftainship as a whole; all chiefs are not suspect because one is *mara*. It may be postulated that a breakdown of chieftainship in Tikopia from this angle would need a fairly thorough demonstration that success in agriculture, fishing, and medicine could be obtained on a wide scale in the face of resort to gods and ancestors.

APPENDIX

Text 1.

"Te ariki fou e tangi ki ni manu mona ki te ariki ko ia ne lavaki, ke nai torofia ko nga atua ma te kau firifiri. So ko ia! ke au ko se mana mona, pe nia ko ia ke faia mai ki tenea fakaarofa ne peia ki te ngangea na. Fakarongo ko te ariki ku lavaki ki te ariki fou e tangi atu ki ei, so ko ia, o karanga atu ki ei

> 'Kau kaina fakaangafuru ko ou tae
> Koke totoro atu ki nga atua
> Ki ni manu moku
> Toku rima ka po ki te ngaengae ke maroro'
> (. . . ke po atu ke mana ko na rima)
> 'Kau tangi atu kuou ki nia, ke manu.'

Tera poi ko te ariki ku lavaki, fai torofanga ki te atua, kae ropa atu ko tona rima ki ei. 'Ia! Sori mai ko ni manu moku kau poi o sori ki toku tau tafanga.' Sori mai e te atua, pe sea, te tauru rakau, pe te fua o te niu, pe tefea te fifia o te ariki e tangi ki ei. Tera au foki o nofo i tona ngangea. Ropa atu ko na rima ki te ariki fou o nofo i a tangata: 'Ia! ou manu kora.' Te manu e sori fakangatua mai; sise ono se tangata ki ei; mataki fuere ki te kai ku laui, te taro, te ufi, te niu, te kai katoa ku fua laui ko ia."

TEXT 2.

"I fenua nei te manu ena i te ngutu te ariki. Tana taranga ka muna pe ki nia, te ariki e manu, tera kaisi ki te ika, au; muna rei kaisi ki te ngaio, to rei. Tera te ariki mana. Ka te ariki mara, siei se mana mona.

Te ariki e sara tana kava e mara; siei ni manu mona; kaisi ki te ngaio, siei se ngaio ke to; kaisi ki te ua, siei se ua ke oko; tera e faia e sara ko ana nea."

(In laughing answer to the question whether *mana* lay simply in the chief as a man) "Siei, soa soa e! Na mana e sori mai e nga atua. Kaisi ki nga atua, fifia nga atua ka sori mai, sori mai; tera muna atu kuou te ariki e manu. Te ariki ka manu, nga atua e vakai mau fuere fifia ki te ariki."

(In answer to the question if *mana* could lie simply in the words recited) "Siei se manu ena i te taranga, te kaisi fuere. Tera ka tautuku kuou ki te tangata, nofo o ono pe tefea na aso ka to, sise e ngaengae, tera nga atua sise tafuri mai, sise e fifia ki toku taranga ne fai. Kuou sise manu."

TEXT 3.

"Matea te mafa toku puna te ariki. Na rima e tusi ki te tangata, ku moe ki raro ko te tangata. Na atua tonu e fare i tana rima. E manu.

E fakato ki roto tai, karanga ki te ika ke au ma te fenua, au rei—te ature. E roa te nofo o te ika; ka kai, kai, kai ko te fenua. Ka poi o pui atu ki tana rima ke poi, poi rei.

Matea na palasu; e muna ki te rakau, maro ko te rakau; e muna ki te mei, au, fua rei ko te mei."

14. The Samoans

The Samoan people inhabit a group of islands in the southwest of Polynesia, and are divided into three groups, the large islands of Upolu and Savai'i, the island of Tutuila, and the three small islands of Tau, Ofu, and Olosenga which constitute the Manu'a group—population 2,200. This account is based upon field work in the Manu'a group in 1925 to 1926, checked against earlier manuscript records for Manu'a and a large amount of published material for the entire group. Protected from the sale of their land and from indentured labor, isolated from the main impact of white contact in the Pacific, the Samoans, in spite of having been Christianized for about ninety years, have nevertheless maintained the body of their culture intact, softened somewhat in accordance with missionary teachings and to meet governmental edicts against war, intervillage brawls, feuds, etc. Their economic life has been expanded to include the growing of copra for sale, and the purchase of cloth, iron, soap, lanterns, and kerosene. But they have not lost the knowledge and control over their own methods of production, and in any emergency the native community is still self-sufficient. In a hierarchal form of government, alterations at the top do not seriously affect the functioning of the groups below, and therefore this statement of native forms is based also on a study of the present functioning of local units.

The Samoans lived in a closed universe, conceiving the some 60,000 members of the Samoan people as all members of one

SOURCE: Chapter 9 of *Cooperation and Competition Among Primitive Peoples*, Margaret Mead, ed. Boston: Beacon Press, Inc. Reprinted by permission of the author and the Beacon Press, Inc. Copyright © 1937 by McGraw-Hill Book Co., Inc.

organization. Although these people lived on island groups separated by canoe voyages of several days, and the experience of the bulk of the population of each island cluster was limited to its own part of the archipelago, yet conceptually the Samoan people were one. The symbol of their unity was an ideal arrangement of all of the highest titles of the entire group. This seating plan conformed to the form of a Samoan round house, in which all councils are held. The form of this giant all-Samoan council, which was called the Great *Fono* and had never met in the history of the group, was preserved in a series of phrases called the Great Fa'alupega. (The fa'alupega were the phrases of greetings recited by the orators at the opening of a fono.) The Great Fono itself took its sanction, somewhat inarticulately, from the gods, the chief of whom was Tangola, who had delegated most of his authority to the chiefs and was himself mainly concerned with heavenly matters. When titled men died they went to become posts in the fono house of the gods.

These titles were hereditary within definite lineages within villages. Each village, each cluster of villages, each large island, or group of small islands, had its own council (fono), composed of its most exalted titles. The local village council was represented in the next largest council for the island or district by a few of its higher titles, and through them took part in deliberations affecting the larger geographical units. These deliberations were mainly concerned either with large-scale ceremonials or with war, for the great mass of judicial and legislative decisions were made within the village council in terms of the needs of that particular village.

The Great Fono represented the upper limits of Samoan society, and provided the frame into which these permanent titles were fitted in carefully noted ranking order. The other limit, the base of the society, was represented by the land, the ground plan of each village to which the family lines were firmly attached. This land was guarded by the ancestral ghosts. All individuals who were descended from those who had owned it before had a residence claim. By the exercising of that claim, of living within the village unit, they became subject to the corporate power of the village, expressed in the village fono. Each village had its own high chief, its own series of talking chiefs, its own princess, the *taupou*—a virgin of the chief's lineage who occupied a title which was an attribute of the title of the high chief—and a prince, a

manaia, a titled youth who held another of the titles attached to
the High Chief. The talking chiefs were of an order complimentary
to the chiefs and made the speeches and provided food for ceremonies, while the chiefs were ornamental and executive and made
presents of valuable mats and pieces of bark cloth to the talking
chiefs. The village as a whole acted as the bilateral family of the
chief, reproducing on a village-wide scale the operations which
surrounded the birth or marriage of an ordinary person. The honor
of the chief was the honor of the village; any man committing
adultery with the chief's wife was put to death by village edict.

Each household—which might range from eight to fifty persons
—was under the direct control of a *matai,* a headman. He held a
title of either chiefly or talking-chief rank, had a seat in the village
council, and was directly responsible to the council for all those
beneath his care.

Theoretically the matai had the power of life and death over
members of his own household, but this was only exercised in the
case of very delinquent minors. The council had full authority over
the inhabitants of the village. Usually the fullest sanction which
the council ever exercised against an adult was banishment, in
which a man's house was razed to the ground, his pigs were killed,
his breadfruit trees cut down, and he himself was chased from the
village. Only occasionally, however, was this exile for life. For
minor offenses the council imposed fines, work for the village,
small painful expiations like sitting all day in the sun tossing a
sting ray in the bare hands. Such punishments were really a test
of the culprit's desire to remain in the village because as each
offense was regarded as against the village, it was only necessary
to flee to another village to find sanctuary. The number of villages
to which a refugee could go was limited only by the ramifications
of his genealogy. This was limited only in the case of individuals
whose ancestors had married within the same village for generations or in the case of residents upon small islands. In the matter
of offenses too small for the official cognizance of the council,
such as laziness or indiscreet and complicating love affairs, the
matai of the household acted. But again the culprit who wished
to escape discipline needed only to leave that household and attach himself to another. His continuance within the next household depended entirely upon his good behavior there.

The main tie which held an individual within his own household and within his own village was his better position in the social structure there, and the greater chance of succeeding to a title held in his direct lineage than to one in collateral lineages. Succession to the titles was not by primogeniture, nor even by direct descent, nor was there a rigid insistence upon patrilineal descent. The most able youth from the entire family connection was eventually chosen by the family group to hold their matai title—and this choice was approved or vetoed by the distaff side of the family and finally ratified by the council.

The ground plan of the council, in which each position represented rank, privileges and obligations to the whole were often formulated as a duty to the High Chief, who represented the whole. This ground plan was reproduced three times in the village: The first was in the organization of wives of matais. The second was the *aumaga*,[1] the organization of the sons of matais and of all the untitled men, in which the manaia acted as the chief and the heirs of the principal talking chiefs as masters of ceremonies. The third was the *aualuma,* a less formalized group of young unmarried girls, wives of untitled men, and widows and divorcees who were gathered about the taupou. Each of these groups had a definite ceremonial life of its own, and each derived its form from that of the fono, or council.

The ceremonial meeting place of the village was the *malae,* the village plaza, the name of which was always mentioned in the fa'alupega. Additionally the chief always had a large council house, and in a sizeable village, chiefs and talking chiefs of high rank would build council houses also. The fono and the other organizations might meet in any one of these houses. The importance of the meeting place was defined by the importance of the group which met within it. When the fono was meeting, all near-by noise and casual activity were forbidden in the village. Women and young people only could approach the outer edge of the circle on specific errands and, kneeling there, present a request or deliver a message. In all its formal meetings the fono was served by the aumaga, who cooked the food for its feasts and served at the banquets. In many villages, the fono ate one large daily meal in common. The members always ate together if there was any work on foot in which they were participating. Similarly when the wives

---

[1] g in Samoan orthography, as developed by the early missionaries, should be pronounced as *ng.*

of matais gathered formally, for instance in order to carry stones for the floor of a new council house, the village was theirs and the men stayed far away from the scene of action. The evenings were the time when the aumaga gathered, and the members of the fono, by their absence and abstention from any interruption, expressed their respect for the integrity of the young men's groups.

The minutiae of rank is observed throughout Samoan life. It is not an attribute of the individual himself, but it is always observed as an aspect of the situation in which an individual is temporarily or sometimes permanently placed. This is in striking contrast to the Maori, among whom status is an inalienable attribute which can be lost only when one is captured and taken away in slavery from one's land. A shadow of this attitude is preserved in the special sanctity which the Samoans allowed to the first child born to the Tui Manu'a, the high chief of all Manu'a, *after* he had assumed his title. The child was allowed to have sanctity as an attribute, but this was dependent upon his father's *assumption* of a title. So the Samoans recognize status in any situation. The lover who calls on a girl is treated by the father of the girl, who may far exceed him in rank, as a chiefly visitor. In any group of untitled young girls, one will be treated as the taupou; in a traveling party in which no one has rank, some will be designated to act as talking chiefs, etc. This tendency to reinterpret each situation in terms of a heirarchy is most conspicuous in the case of skilled craftsmen. The skilled carpenter or canoe builder becomes, by virtue of his mastery and control over a given piece of work, a chief for that occasion, and must be addressed with all chiefly honors, although once the occasion is past, he may be only an untitled youth. Conversely a high chief who wishes to call upon a taupou who is visiting his village, may explicitly lay aside his title and resume the title of a young manaia. As such he may behave as he could not were he holding the title of a chief. This separation between the individual and his role is exceedingly important in the understanding of Samoan society. The whole conception is of a ground plan which has come down from ancestral times, a ground plan which is explicit in titles and remembered phrases, and which has a firm base in the land of the villages and districts. The individual is important only in terms of the position which he occupies in this universal scheme—of himself he is nothing. Their eyes are always on the play,[2] never on the players, while each individual's task is to fit his role.

The circumstance that each village, and almost every family line, has more titles than it ever uses in a generation gives to this fixed pattern an expansiveness, a sense of spaciousness, and mutes competition. The custom of conferring titles within the lineage becomes stricter as the importance of the title increases. Every girl in the village is not eligible for the title of taupou, the preference goes first to the distaff line of the chief, then to his own male line; and the great majority of village girls do not come within the possibility of competition (see Mead 1928a:51–53). But in a large village there are lesser taupou titles also, around which small groups of related girls cluster. All these are seldom used. Competition for matai[3] titles is further muted by the fact that the matai rank is of two orders, chiefs and talking chiefs, and that the requirements and privileges of each complement the other. Every large family has titles of both kinds in its possession. If in a given generation no one measures up to the title, the title is not given, but its presence is still allowed for in the fono seating plan and the phrases which embody that plan.

Competition between holders of titles is covert and always expressed as the manipulation of the rank of a title, not as any overt alteration which affects the individual. If a holder of a title is not ineffective enough to be removed, which can be done by the fono's acting with the family line, but still does not adorn the title which he holds, the talking chiefs may, slowly over time, depress the importance of his title and rearrange the small interrelationships between titles within a village fono. This is done very slowly, without any sense of suddenness, almost in spite of the knowledge of the lackadaisical holder of the title which is being depressed. So the Samoans preserve their sense of a fixed structure but do not permit it to trammel their activities.[4]

[2] When I entered the village of Fitiuta under a taupou title, the people of the village spread the news that such and such a taupou with an Upolu title was staying at the guest house and neglected to mention that I was white, although there had not been half a dozen white women in Fitiuta throughout the course of history.

[3] For ways in which competition within a household operates during the years before the choice for a titleholder is made, see Mead 1928a:51–53.

[4] The importance of this flexibility in relation to social change is discussed in Mead 1928c.

ECONOMIC BACKGROUND

The Samoan life is based upon an economy of plenty. They depend primarily upon agriculture, taro, bananas, yams, sweet potatoes, breadfruit, supplemented by fish, shellfish, pigs, coconut crabs, coconuts, and greens. There is more than enough land, even with the system of rotating garden sites over long periods of fallowness in order to restore fertility to the land. Land is owned by the household groups, and the matai is a trustee for the land, presiding over the planting and harvesting, superintending the work of all the men and women who live beneath his authority. The gardens are worked by the household as a group, with the exception of the work which is limited to an age grade and which is performed jointly by the aumaga or the aualuma. Men clear and fence, women plant and weed, both sexes harvest; the fruits of the harvest belong to the household, subject to the levies made upon each household by the village. Each household has to provide for its own needs, for affinal exchanges in which it may become involved during the years, either as the group of the wife, in which case gifts of bark cloth and finely woven mats will be in demand, or as the group of the husband, in which case an extra supply of food, especially pigs, and in some cases woodwork, such as kava[5] bowls, will be needed.[6] If the household plans to build a new house, provision must be made for feeding the group of carpenters. Each household will also have to contribute during the year to village feasts, to the entertainment of guests, and to exchanges made in the name of the high chief, the taupou, and the manaia.

Whether we examine first the organization of a household cooking group or the organization of a village fishing expedition, we find the same principle exemplified, a number of individuals arranged in a hierarchical order, who contribute differentially according to their rank, age, sex, and skill, to a total result, in which the whole group share, either directly—as in eating the food from the family oven—or indirectly—as members of a household or village whose prestige has been enhanced by the result of the labor

[5] Kava, the ceremonial drink of Polynesia, is made by pulverizing the root of the kava plant and mixing it with water.

[6] For further discussions of the organization of affinal exchanges see Mead 1930:75–76.

which all have expended. All work is conceived of in this way, as something to which a number of people of different status make a contribution, which is increasingly important in proportion to the rank of the individuals involved. So a man who builds a house for himself with the help of the young men of his household is engaged in an activity which is on the same plane as cooking in an earth oven, in which he and the members of his household participate. If, however, he calls in a master carpenter and that carpenter's associates and apprentices, then the situation immediately becomes much more important, and he as the *taufale,* "the owner of the house to be built," takes on new rank, in relation to the rank of the *tafunga fai fale,* the master housebuilder. Food must now be cooked in a more ceremonial fashion and far more etiquette observed, although the result may be a house of about the same size.

In making an oven for a household, the entire household participates; and the oven is only made about twice a week, everyone eating cold cooked food in the intervals. The matai does the most important work, butchers and stuffs the pig if there is one, if not, laces up the largest fish into coconut leaf covers; the young men grate the coconuts and mix the coconut puddings; the women grate the rinds off the breadfruit, peel the taro and bananas; the children fetch salt water, leaves for seasoning, etc. The smallest child assists, each performing the task to which his skill and strength and age entitle him. There is no feeling in Samoa that a task is beneath a person's dignity; the emphasis is the opposite; an individual is strong enough, or skilled enough, to do something which requires his special ability and to leave the simpler tasks to his juniors and inferiors. When the oven is opened, containing an oversupply of food for the entire household for several days, gifts of food are sent to any relatives who may be visiting in the village, or to visitors who are staying in the house of a chief. Thus even the family oven is knit into the life of the village.

If we consider the other end of the scale we find that there is the same kind of division of labor within the village.[7] But the

[7] The village is the largest effective economic unit in Manu'a and in most of Samoa. There are a few exceptions; every village in Manu'a, except Tau, where the Tui Manu'a (the High Chief of Manu'a) lived, had to contribute breadfruit to the great breadfruit pit of Tau, in which breadfruit was stored against the famine periods which followed the ten-yearly hurricanes. The villages of Ofu and Olosenga also brought fish to the Tui Manu'a.

village frequently acted as a corporate whole in economic undertakings, in road making, council-house building, and community fishing, in preparation for feasts, in intervillage feasts, as a village ceremonial visiting party which goes to another village, and at all the *rites de passage* of the high chief and his family. The corporate activity had various degrees of intensity. It might consist of a tabu upon the use of more than a certain number of coconuts by any household, so that there would be an adequate supply for a feast which was three months off. In some villages special titles carried with them "the power over the land"—*i.e.,* to tabu land products for a communal end, and another title would carry the "power over the sea," to tabu certain fish or shellfish so that many would accumulate. Or community control in another economic field might extend only to determining seasons; thus no one could pick breadfruit until the fono had formally eaten a feast of the first breadfruit of the year. It might be a ceremonial levy upon a large fishing catch, so that from a turtle, a shark, or any other very large fish certain parts went to the high chief, and to the taupou. Other activities were initiated by a feast and a group starting to work together. This was so for the *taloloa,* the village taro plantation which was phrased as a group activity of the aumaga, but in which each young man planted a patch which would be weeded and harvested thereafter by the women of his household. Thus for the village paper mulberry patch, from which the bark cloth was made, the aumaga cleared the ground as a group; they were then feasted by the aualuma, after which the aualuma planted the paper mulberry from which each household drew their own supplies. Village cooperation might take the form of a requisition for contributions of food, and these contributions were harvested or fished for by individuals, using individual techniques. When there were guests in the village, the talking chiefs who were masters of ceremonies would assign to each household the provision of so many baskets of food, each one of which would contain fish and shellfish, caught by individual men and women, land crabs which might have been caught by children, and various cooked foods from the family oven to which every member of the household had contributed. The emphasis was never upon what an individual did, neither upon his skill nor upon the size of his catch or harvest, but always upon its place in a larger social situation.

This emphasis is displayed most sharply in the building of a village council house or in village fishing-fleet organization. When a village council house, said to be the house of the high chief, was to be built, a fono was held and orders were given for the planting of gardens to provide food to feed the carpenters. Bark cloth and fine mats were either made or obtained by exchange or begging from relatives (in other villages) to pay the carpenters, and sennit, the coconut fiber from which the string was made to tie the house together, was braided. To each household was assigned a given amount which was often less than the largest household could provide with ease and enough to make a small household strain a little. The largest household, which was almost automatically the household of a matai of high rank, would usually make an additional contribution because the higher the rank of a man the more he had to contribute to the village, through his payments to the talking chiefs who represented the village. To each household would be assigned the task of providing a section of the round house, wood for one or two posts, wood for the rafters, the weaving of the Venetian blinds which hang between the posts, the growing of the sugar cane—this is a prerogative of married women, each one of whom has a sugar-cane patch—and the sewing of the leaf of the cane into thatch for a section of the roof. In this form of division of labor the principle of hierarchy is abandoned and the village is conceived as made up of co-ordinate units, which make identical contributions to the common end, but each of the identical contributions are themselves split up into sections involving contributions of both sexes, and differential strength and skill.

The continual recombination of units in a cooperative hier-archical scheme is characteristically Samoan, so two cross-cousins may have one relative rank within the fono, and a different relative rank within the descent group (see Mead 1930:21 ff.). The fono has two kinds of divisions, one according to the classification of the title, as high chief, grouped higher chiefs, lower chiefs, high talking chiefs, supervising talking chiefs, small talking chiefs, etc., and the other according to another plan of subdivision, in which titles of different orders may be represented and the whole sub-division have a duty to perform such as the duty of acting as scouts in wartime.

The organization of village fishing is carefully controlled. Both men and women do many kinds of individual fishing, contributing their catch directly to the joint meal of their household, or to their household's contribution to the village. But for fleet fishing—especially for bonito and for shark—and for the surrounding of fish in the lagoon with long woven leaf fences, the most careful organization is followed.[8] In each village, or occasionally in each section of a large village, there is a chief fisherman, who rules over the sea, both in tabuing fishing at certain periods and in organizing and leading the fishing fleet (Buck 1930:517-19). Even a high chief if he join the bonito fleet must act as a private individual under the control of the *tautai,* his rank recognized only by the ceremonial gift of the first bonito caught. The fono decides when the fleet is to set out, the tautai taking the lead in the council. He selects the fishing ground to be visited and decides on the movements at sea. When he considers the fishing over, he gives the signal to return, and before the fleet reaches the shore, he makes a levy upon each canoe, a set proportion of the catch. This levy is not for himself but for a community feast for the fishermen in which the unsuccessful member shares equally with his more fortunate fellows. The tautai makes no levy, however, on the canoes with a very bad catch. If any fisherman fails to report accurately on his catch, and this is subsequently discovered, his bonito canoe is broken up and his fishing gear is confiscated to the tautai. The specific nature of the tautai's authority is shown by the rule that if a matai sends an individual canoe out after the fleet has departed, although that canoe may subsequently join the fleet, it is not an organic part of it, and does not have to contribute to the levy for the feast. Fishermen on returning to the shore have to give a portion of their catch to anyone they meet in the lagoon or on the shore, thus further socializing the catch.

In net fishing, the whole community contributes to the finished net; for example, the rule in one village (Buck 1930:487) was for each matai to contribute two arm spans plus an additional arm span for each male child in his household. These are then woven together into the net which the whole village uses. The explicitness of this ownership of nets is revealed by the instance (Buck 1930: 488) of a village which was divided into two parts, separated by a stream. A turtle net was owned by the two parts, and between turtle fishing seasons was kept in two sections, being reassembled

[8] Based on account given by Buck (1930:418-523, *passim*).

for each fishing. There is another instance (Buck 1930:487) of a net which one village, acting as a unit, gave away to another village.

When the leaf fencing for a lagoon trap (Buck 1930:429) is to be made, a fono is held, and a number of fathoms of leaf fencing are assigned to each matai as his household's share. Then the head of each family sends the young men of his household to the bush to get the required number of fathoms of vine. Meanwhile the other members of the household collect and strip coconut leaves. When the young men return, the matai ties knots in the vine, measuring off the required number of fathoms, the vine is tied between two trees, and the exact space between the two knots filled in. Each household coils its ten fathoms, and the next day they are combined and used with a net which the tautai and a few assistants have set in the reef. The whole village takes part in the drive that follows, and at the end of the catch the fish are divided among the households.

Bonito fishing, in which a single canoe is manned by three men, or occasionally only two, a steersman-fisherman, a bowman who is lookout, and a middleman who paddles and bails, is an example on a smaller scale of cooperative activity (Buck 1930:508). The canoe is usually owned by a matai and three young men of his household, or occasionally one from another household, will make up a more or less permanent team. In the distribution a share of the fish is given the canoe owner.

OWNERSHIP OF PROPERTY

Property may be classified into *toga,* dowry property, *oloa,* bride-price property, and *fanua,* land, which in occasional instances may be used as either toga or oloa (see Mead 1930:71). Toga must be given away with the bride in each marriage and is matched by a return of oloa. Toga is all made by women, consisting of mats and bark cloth, while oloa is primarily made, or grown, or otherwise collected, by men, such as pigs, other food, woodwork, and, in Western Samoa, red feathers. Not only marriage, but the birth of a child, visits of one spouse to the kin of the other, and funeral ceremonies require the exchange of the two kinds of property. Any given household can be said to be in a fortunate or unfortunate economic position in terms of the balance which it is able to preserve between laborers of both sexes, and affinal relationships which call for the two kinds of property. A household in which there are too many young people of one sex is in a doubly difficult position, because each time a female marries, the household becomes indebted in perpetuity in terms of the proceeds of female labor, and each time a male marries the opposite is true. Every object in Samoa, except the crudest household utensils, the tools of a craftsman, and the simpler articles of costume, such as a grass skirt or bark-cloth G-string, is continually changing hands in these toga-oloa exchanges. Property is valued for its mobility, for its power of validating ceremonial and increasing prestige; there is no hoarding and no great benefit given one generation by any accumulation of capital goods by the preceding generation. There is more land than is needed, and houses last only six or seven years.

The exchange of toga and oloa between affinal relatives is reflected in the exchanges between chiefs and talking chiefs, in which the chiefs always give toga and the talking chiefs give oloa. In intervillage alliances, in which a taupou marries a high chief or a manaia, the entire village mobilizes and contributes one kind of property. When a matai assumed his title, if he was a talking chief he had to feast the village; if he was a chief, or a chief giving a taupou title to one of his young female relatives, he had to distribute toga to the talking chiefs. All these interchanges were strictly reciprocal and returned in exact amounts (see Mead 1930: 75–76). In intervillage exchanges following a royal marriage, the fine mats and pigs were exchanged point for point until one side ran out, a point of shame for the village which was first exhausted.

Behind these strict interchanges lay the wider kinship group, which transcended village lines and within which mutual helpfulness was the rule. This cannot be said to be cooperation because no individual contributes to an end in which all the contributors are interested. Instead there is a continuous begging, borrowing-lending relationship going on between all relatives to meet the strictly formalized demands for a certain kind of contribution from a given household. If fine mats are demanded for the dowry of the taupou, each household may have to contribute a given number, and it will make up its quota by borrowing in other villages, and these loans will be returned in kind, not in the opposite class of property as is the case in the formal scheme. There are always definite limits to the formal cooperating groups, the household, or the aumaga of a village or of a section of a village, or the village itself; in any case the group is defined and limited, and each individual's part is specified in terms of the whole. But within the wider relationship group the most diaphanous claims may be honored, either of blood, affinal relationship, or adoption; anyone calling another *aiga*, relative, has claims of requisition if he is of higher rank, of effective pleading if he is of lower rank. So that every Samoan may be said to live a kind of double life, one part of which is defined in terms of a social situation, the other part of which is given in terms of the multiplicity and inalienability of his kinship ties. If a Samoan is presented with a statement of a legal or social dilemma in which an individual has violated rules, or outraged his present cooperative group, the answer always is, "He will go to another relative." Only in rare instances (see Mead 1928a:173–78) does the kinship group become exhausted. The memories of individuals are quickened in proportion to rank in Samoa, the higher a man's rank, that is, the more important his role in his cooperative political group, the greater security lies behind him in the number of aiga who will be glad to remember their relationship to him. The social organization may be said to be forms of highly cooperative but optionally composed groups. These groups are optional from the standpoint of both the individual and the rest of the group who may, if they wish, expel an uncooperative member. One of the strengths of Samoan society may lie in this dual emphasis. The commoner form of organization is that found among the Maori, in which one's membership in a cooperative group is a birth claim, and the effort of the cooperative group to discipline its members is continually tempered by its inability to expel someone who is felt to have an inalienable claim to protection, sanctuary, and food. But in Samoa when an individual fails in any cooperative group, either in his own terms or in theirs, his relationship claims will always give him a new chance in a new cooperative group; if he fails in this, it is the group and not his kindred who have turned against him.

Another strength lies in the continuing redefining of the cooperative situation, so that no individual plays continuously a fixed role, except the high chief, whose role is so hedged about with etiquette, procedure, and lack of any real executive authority that he is not likely to overstep his bounds. But most individuals play a series of parts of differing importance in a series of differently organized activities; a man's attention is focused upon his behavior in relation to a situation, as host, as guest, as matai, as member of the council, as member of a matai working group, as a fisherman beneath the tautai, as a member of a war party in which his role is determined by his division membership in the village, as a giver of toga and a receiver of oloa, as a giver of oloa and receiver of toga, as the heir in his patrilineal line, as the *tamafafine,* the cross-cousin with a veto, in his mother's family, as the ranking member of one group, as the man of lowest rank in the next group he enters, as the chief to whom a young man kneels as he gives a message at noon time, and as the father of a daughter upon whom the same young man, who must now be received courteously, calls in the evening. Such a man does not develop a fixed response to others which is definitely either dominance or submission, leadership or discipleship, authoritarian insistence or meek compliance, exhibitionism or refusal to play any public part; the multiplicity and contrast between his roles prevent any commitment to one personality type from developing. Whereas in a different kind of society, it is possible to predict what a given individual A will do as compared with a given individual B, in Samoa it is much more possible to predict what a series of men, A, B, and C, will do in a given situation.

THE PLACE OF SKILL IN SAMOAN SOCIETY

The skilled artisan in Samoa was honored, and he was permitted to defend his position, by being given a place in the fono. There were three main types of artisans, the housebuilders and canoe builders, who were classified in a wider group as the *Sa Tangaloa,* the Household of Tangaloa, the chief high god; the tattooers; and the fishermen. All these men, however exalted their prestige within their crafts, also participated as ordinary members of the community, and most craftsmen of note were matais and administered large households, although they themselves might give most of their time to their crafts. In each craft apprenticeship was recognized, young men usually choosing to serve under a relative, and it was usually a rich relative who gave a young aspirant craftsman his first chance at a real contract. The apprentices acted as assistants to the master craftsmen and were fed by them and shared in the distributions of presents given by the contractors for houses, canoes, or tattooing. The fishermen tended to be leading matais in sections of the community. When engaged in his craft the chief craftsman occupied the rank of a chief, and the rules of that craft had to be strictly observed. Payments were made at different stages in housebuilding or canoe building, and if they were regarded as insufficient, the craftsman might refuse to continue the work. If he did so, no other craftsman could take up the unfinished job unless the contracting would-be owner started the whole series of payments again from the beginning. Any craftsman who violated this rule was severely disciplined by the young men with the approval of the fono; his tools were taken away from him and he would never be allowed to practice as a carpenter in that village again. If the final payment for a contract was unsatisfactory, the craftsman might brand the house owner as stingy by removing one rafter, or take a more insidious revenge against an owner of a canoe by leaving a concealed wedge which would render the canoe unlucky (Buck 1930:416). The participation of the fono in preserving the sanctity of the contract and upholding the craftsmen in disciplining either a refractory member of their craft or a man who failed to meet the contract, socializes a potentially competitive situation. The craftsmen of each village were independent of the craftsmen of other villages, except that a visiting craftsman would be invited to any feast which was being given to a member of his craft, and he would be lent tools.

Skill in oratory is a function of the talking chiefs; if a young man discreetly displays such skill (see Mead 1928a:54–56), it will be regarded as a strong claim on a talking chief title. Chiefs may not display skill in oratory without coming under the ban of social disapproval and possible loss of adherents and of prestige. Wives of talking chiefs are forced to develop the skill after their husbands have succeeded to the title; they have no opportunity to acquire proficiency beforehand. The sons or probable heirs of talking chiefs have a chance to display such skill in the meetings of the aumaga which is a training ground for fono life. Good memories for genealogies and for history and proverbs are also requirements for talking chiefs, and men holding talking chief titles will start very early to train their sons or some other bright and favorite child in such lore. The balance here between training to hold a position, recognition of skill which is followed by the

award of a position, and the requirement that because a given
position is held the skill must appear (as in the case of the wives
of talking chiefs) or must be inhibited (as in the case of chiefs),
represents in fair measure the balance in Samoan estimation between the emphasis which should be laid upon native capacity as
opposed to social role.

There are a few skills which are limited to experts, midwifery,
the knowledge of certain medicines, and the practice of divining
by supernatural possession.[9] Payment for all these was small, and
mainly a matter of etiquette; the individual practiced through pride
in virtuosity and, in the case of the *taula-aitu* (the shamans),
probably for the influence which their oracular sayings yielded
them. Bark-cloth making and fine mat making, ordinary fishing,
gardening, sennit making, and the simpler carpentry skills were
known to everyone of the appropriate sex. Such experts as were
singled out—even in the case of the tattooer, as many people could
do simple tattooing—were those who were far better at the practice of a common skill than their fellows, who could make nine
ornamental lashings where the average man could do only one,
make ten kinds of hook where the average man could make only
one or two; and the special position of these men had to be defined in terms of each situation. A tautai was of no more account
than any other man of his age and village rank, except when communal fishing was under way.

RIVALRY ACTIVITIES

Samoa relied to a very slight degree upon group rivalry as a
cohesive force within the group. Rivalry attitudes were highest
between districts. Manu'a claimed to be more sacred than any
other part of the Samoan islands, a claim which the other parts
reluctantly admitted in various ceremonies, when they had to ex-
claim: "Tui Manu'a, thou art my Lord." But such claims were
also accompanied by a great deal of mutual vituperation and
abuse, by abusive songs about the other islands or districts, and
by insulting proverbs. Rivalry between districts was therefore

---

[9] The material on these shamans is most inadequate. They were possessed
by spirits of the dead or family deities, answered questions about causes of
illness or death, and demanded amends in the name of the offended spirit
or deity.

firmly entrenched in ceremonial usage, and when a *malaga*—a formal traveling party—entered Manu'a from another part of Samoa, a clubbing match between champions was held at the beginning of the visit. Western Samoa had worked out a scheme by which all five districts might agree to bestow a title upon the high chief of one, who thus became a kind of king. The Manu'a Islands were regarded as one district in which the Tui Manu'a reigned supreme. Within one district there theoretically should not have been war, or the theft of a taupou—a method by which the aumaga of one village displayed its superiority over the aumaga of another village—nor should there have been clashes between the aumagas of two villages within a district. All these did sometimes occur, however, but they were regarded as rather lamentable. Standardized competitive situations between two villages in the same district might be set up and ceremonially recognized, as in the case of the villages of Tau and Fitiuta, both of which claimed that they were the original capital. The two villages duplicated some of their most important ceremonial features. Inverted rivalry may also occur, as when the village of Ofu at present claim with pride a talking chief title which was given it originally to symbolize a defeat in war by the island of Tau.

All this intervillage rivalry and ceremonial—and occasionally real hostility—lacked any basis in material circumstance, and sprang from no scarcity of land or crowded fishing grounds. Within the village, each individual, no matter how exalted his sense of his own importance, had to mute continually any expression of this sense in conformity to the demands of the village. Of a high chief who made his daughter taupou, it was said, "He has given her to the village. She now belongs to them to dispose of as they will." So when a high chief died, half of the watching by his corpse was done by his relatives, but the other half was the privilege of the talking chiefs, representative of the village. As one high chief phrased it to me: "The Samoan had two gods, Tangaloa and the village, and the greater of these was the village." At the same time that the expression of any individual claims ran counter to the will of the village, the craft group, the fishing fleet, or the household were sternly muted, a touchiness in regard to the honor of the group as a whole was not only permitted to develop, but was even encouraged. It was this touchiness, this sense of the group's position in regard to other groups, which formed a kind of edge about the otherwise loose and noncohesive cooperative groups, in which voluntary continuance had been substituted for any strict relationship bond. This was expressed actively in the theft of the taupou of one village by the aumaga of a rival village. The young men, once having got the taupou safely away, would go and sing the news through the injured village. This theft was not motivated by any desire for a particular girl, but was merely a village gesture. This same touchiness was expressed by the over-sensitivity of any group to the hospitality which it was receiving; a ceremonial traveling party might leave a village if the coconut spines were not arranged correctly in the coconuts which they were given to drink; a group of carpenters might refuse to go on with their work because there was a stone in a fowl's gullet.[10] This touchiness, whether within the village, as between house owner and craftsmen, or between villages, was always phrased in group terms. But it was actually a way in which individuals who did not subordinate individual honor to group honor could make the group cause their own. In all these instances, it was not obligatory upon anyone to protest, there was merely a pattern within which protest was possible, just as there was a pattern within which insult was possible—for some insurgent member of the host village was responsible for misplacing the spines in the coconuts origi-nally. That such behavior is the overflow of individual aggressive-ness into group pride is shown by the fact that it is merely permitted to occur, whereas all aspects of intergroup relationships which the Samoans consider essential, such as the prolonged ar-guments between owner and carpenters whenever a payment is made, or the clubbing matches between champions of host and visiting village, are definitely provided for. The rivalry situation in which each village seeks to outdo the other, in some feat, in some sensitivity to insult, in some giving of insult, is strongest between districts and next strongest between villages; it occurs in some patterned situations within the village, most strongly when there are two divisions of the aumaga, based not upon age, but upon residence in two parts of the village; and it occasionally occurs between households.

In large villages the young people are worked into a final group plan slowly; they grow up in small neighborhood gangs, across

[10] Buck, personal communication.

which relationship ties operate more and more strongly as they grow older, and are sometimes welded first into two aumaga, which will sometimes but not always combine into a whole. These two aumaga groups perpetuate the neighborhood-gang hostility. They hurl insults, are rivals in their group work, and occasionally even break out into acts of depredation such as destroying the taro plantation of the other aumaga. Acts such as these are severely dealt with by the fono, on a semisupernatural basis in which the whole village has to celebrate an expiatory kava ceremony, but they form the basis for village splits. In the dual village of Tau-Siufaga there were two well-defined and competitive aumaga, and the fono was beginning to split, the split increasing each year as the younger men, accustomed to the hostility of the aumaga split, assumed titles and became members of the matai group. Where the opposite form of division occurs in the aumaga, into a tattooed and untattooed group, no such rivalry can occur, because rivalry can occur by definition only between equals, and the tattooed group are older and so outrank the untattooed group.

These illustrations will show the two tendencies in Samoan social organizations, the tendency to place each individual, each household, each village, even (in Western Samoa) each district in a hierarchy, wherein each is dignified only by its relationship to the whole, each performs tasks which contribute to the honor and well-being of the whole, and competition is completely impossible. The opposite tendency, the rebellion of individuals within the units against this subordination to a plan and their use of a place in a component unit to foment trouble and rivalry with other units, while not so strong, is always present.[11]

[11] This latter trend shows up sharply if compared with Tonga, an adjacent group in which the whole people were organized in a strictly hierarchal scheme, with a *Tui Tonga* at the top, and no village communities made any pretense at autonomy. Instead lineages numbering many thousands of people, owed direct allegiance, through their chiefs—with primogeniture and heredity—to the national kingship. The quarrels which took place in Tonga were quarrels between contestants for these major positions. *Cf.* Gifford 1929: *passim*. At the other extreme is the Polynesian community of Ontong Java, which lacks Samoa's cohesive villages and in which the joint family was the major cohesive unit, with a late development of kingship. *Cf.* Hogbin 1934: *passim*.

WAR

War in Samoa was part of the ceremonial rivalry between villages and was fought for no gains other than prestige, nor were there any important rewards for individual warriors. On the other hand, the role which one had to play in war was carefully laid down, as the people said: "How can a *Tauleá leá* (an untitled man) be brave? He would be killed for going ahead?" Warfare between villages was over the theft of the taupou, over slights delivered by one village to another, especially on traveling parties. It was fought at appointed spots after a great deal of speech making and mutual exchange of courtesies, and casualties were low.[12]

Households within the same village could become involved in hostilities if the honor of one was infringed by a member of the other, particularly if the offender was of lower rank than the offended. The principal cause of offense was liaison between the wife of a matai and a matai of lower rank, or a young member of another matai's household. In such cases, if the adultery was discovered, the principals could fight, a procedure of which the whole village disapproved but was not always able to prevent in the case of very strong households; or there might be an *ifoga,* a ceremonial reparation, in which the matai of the offending household—whether or not he was the individual who committed the offense—with his entire household, had to sit with bowed heads all day outside the house of the offended man, covered with fine mats, which the offended would finally accept as amends. Women, if one had seduced the husband of the other, could demand an ifoga also. If a matai refused to ifo or refused to accept an ifoga and inaugurated a blood feud, the fono would ultimately stop it, sometimes by exiling one or both participants.

Competition within the crafts was muted by the distribution of contracts upon a kinship basis, by the fact that all carpenters in

[12] This applies particularly to Manu'a and to a less extent to Tutuila. Our records for the Western Islands are complicated by the presence of white men of different nationalities who themselves continuously incited the natives to trouble and supplied firearms to them, so that it is difficult to obtain any picture of the normal course of life before white interference. The reverberations of international rivalry did not reach Manu'a importantly, so the material there can be used with more credibility.

a village participated in any large building, and by the strong sanctions against any active scabbing on the part of an individual craftsman.

SANCTIONS

We have described the way in which any cooperative group, the village, the household, the fishing fleet, the craft guild, could take definite and summary action against a recalcitrant member so that continuance within any of these groups depended upon strict conformity to the rules of cooperation within it. There was also a series of sanctions of another order which controlled an individual's loyalty to his blood kin, and these were for the most part supernatural sanctions, but sanctions which worked indirectly rather than in producing immediate action, as in Manus. The material on Samoan religious life is very poor, but all illness and death, with the exception of diseases contracted by thieving from magically protected gardens, was laid to the spirits of the ancestors, sometimes informed by the curse of a living relative (particularly the sister), sometimes merely the result of the spirit's sense of having been wronged during life or having been given an inadequate funeral, sometimes due to ghostly wrath over quarrels among living relatives. The indications, based upon very slight hints in the literature and in the memory of informants and also upon comparative material from related cultures, seem to be that the shamans acted to interpret the cause of death, sometimes to explain illness, and demanded ceremonial, not practical, expiation. Whereas in Manus, if a quarrel were given as the explanation of an illness, the quarrel would have to be made up at once under directions given by the medium, in Samoa the cause and effect relationships were less direct. If, however, a family had many deaths and also was involved in an intrafamily conflict, these two would be connected in conversation and sometimes in shamanic possessions, and would exert gradual pressure to heal that particular quarrel and also to deter other families from entering upon or continuing quarrels in flagrant disregard of the rules of kin amity. While the cooperative groups enforced efficiency, honesty, amity, and conformity, with secular sanctions, the kin group, which underlay the cooperative groups and crosscut them and which provided each individual with his final security, took its sanction from the spirits of the ancestors.

RELIGION

Religion played a very slight role in Samoa; the gods were conceived as having resigned their sacredness to the chiefs, who still retained enough of the divine essence so that to touch the clothing of a Tui Manu'a brought dire illness which could be removed only by the touch of his foot. Still the sanctity surrounding chiefs in Samoa was minimal for the Polynesian area, and almost every infringement of the *tapu* of a chief could be removed with a very slight ceremony. The emphasis was all upon the danger to the offender. There was no longer any sense that the chief's personal sanctity had been endangered by contact with commoners. There is some record of village gods, occasionally represented by fetishes which were carried about in war and guarded by specially titled men, whom the early missionaries described as "priests." Additionally each family had a family god, a *tupua,* which was embodied in some bird, fish, or animal. This tupua provided a convenient shamanic alibi when no family quarrel or possible curse could be invoked to explain illness. The sick person would be accused of having inadvertently insulted the tupua, through one of its embodiments, and ceremonial expiation would be demanded. But as compared with other parts of Polynesia, the Manu'a Samoans gave the slightest attention to religion; there were no temples, for the house of an officiant in a village in which a fetish was occasionally kept hardly deserved the name, and there were no religious festivals. The most important groups were the villages, and their importance was enforced by purely secular means. As a result the major dichotomy in Samoa was not between the sacred and the profane, but between work, which was solemnly undertaken by a recognized group, and all other irregular, unrecognized individual activity. There was only one ceremony —the process of preparing a certain kind of dye—in which the officiant worked alone. For the rest all group activities became more solemn, in proportion to the rank of the participants; all individual activities became less important, shading off into the actually non-respectable, the less related they were to some group end.

THE SAMOAN IDEAL MAN

The ideal Samoan man is always more conscious of his position than of his personal desires or motives. He is able to make his behavior conform in the slightest details to the particular exigencies of any situation, he wears at all times an armor of courteous, reserved consciousness of social form. As will appear in the discussion of education, the great Samoan sin is *tautala lai titi,* to talk above one's age, or rank, and this is a sin which even the highest chief could commit were he, for instance, to behave like a talking chief, and make his own speeches in the fono. To know one's place and to exercise that position wisely, and above all gracefully, without any discordant note or false emphasis, is the important point. The disallowed persons are the over-violent, those who take defeat personally, those who commit themselves too violently to a given end, those who foment trouble and discord and so break through the even texture of the social pattern.

EDUCATION

Samoan education is based upon the theory that small children are unimportant, aggressive, and in need of discipline and progressive muting, and that they become steadily more important as they grow older and display their ability to fit without friction into the social pattern. Children are desired. Under the economy of plenty and the grading of all household activities in terms of relative strength and skill, children are useful members of the household by the time they are six or so. Furthermore, conception is believed to be the result of a long period of intercourse; conception among the unmarried is a sign that the pair have loved each other enough to continue faithful for a long period, and this attitude with its accompanying affect is carried over into married life. No rigorous tabus surround pregnancy, although the old women disapprove of intercourse during the last months of pregnancy. There is no lactation tabu, and it is frequent for a woman to have to wean her child because she is pregnant again. Suckling is regarded as a pleasure for the mother, and a woman may be censured for her self-indulgence in suckling a child too long. This removes any element of guilt or strain in the mother's attitude toward weaning, which is accomplished with lemon juice or aromatic herbs. Children are frequently suckled by other women of the household or of related households and become accustomed to a number of "mothers" whom they see every day.

The training of the child from the time that it can crawl until it is five or six is conditioned by two facts, that the nurses are all little girls of from five to ten or eleven, and that *sense* or *judgment,* designated as *mafaufau,* is conceived as developing very slowly and that nothing positive can be done by the community to encourage it. Violence, aggressiveness, destructiveness, contentiousness are all qualities which show lack of judgment. These the infant is born with. The process of early education is a matter of keeping these manifestations down and waiting, with what grace one can, for the more desirable social virtues to develop. Meanwhile, the life of the community must go on in as graceful and undisturbed a fashion as possible. The children must be fed and taken care of in a way which will not interfere with the occupations of their elders. So that most of what a child learns during its first three or four years can be phrased as a series of avoidances of places, of situations, and of kinds of behavior which are frowned upon. It learns that it must never stand up in the house, that it must go outside the house to urinate or defecate, that it must not touch the pillow or possessions of the chief or the matai of the household, that it must not touch the kava bowl, that it must not go where grown people are solemnly gathered, that it must not create a fuss or disturbance. At first most of these misdemeanors are prevented by the small nurses simply dragging the child out of earshot of its elders, for when the child offends, it is the older child-nurse who is reprimanded or slapped by an adult. As a result the little nurses do everything in their power to keep the babies quiet, contented, and out of mischief. They carry them most of the time, discourage them from either crawling or walking, and do not particularly encourage them to talk. The babies are carried on the small girls' hips, often on the hips of little nurses who would not be strong enough to lift them in their arms.

Samoan children are made conscious of age from the very beginning, and even the little babies tend to be placed in an age group, because their small nurses are near of an age and cluster together. As these babies emerge from infancy, they play together under the supervision of their older sisters and cousins until they are five or six. By this time they have learned a certain number of social aptitudes; they can talk, walk, and swim well, carry loads, split open coconuts, climb coconut trees, gather land crabs, carry water, borrow fire, and carry messages—one of the most important activities of children in Samoa. They are permitted to play rough-and-tumble games among themselves and they are likely to be stopped from quarreling, not because their small nurses disapprove of quarreling but because screams will draw the unwelcome attention of the adults. The emphasis is never upon the act itself but upon the way in which it fits into a social situation; two children far away on the beach with only older children near may quarrel if they wish, or shriek and scream, but if they approach a group of matais, they must be hushed at any cost. This develops, in both mentors and charges, alertness to the social situation; even a child of three or four acts always with an eye to possible spectators.

Shame,[13] in Samoa, which is a potent force for control of individuals in the interests of conformity, is not connected with the bodily functions, nor with sex, but with social relationships, and comes from calling attention to oneself unsuitably, from speaking out of turn, from presumption, and also from awkwardness, fumbling for words, lack of skill, if these ineptitudes are specifically commented on by others. The greatest shame is aroused by the accusation tautala laititi, "talking above your age," a shame in which the parents share. For consonant with the emphasis upon form, upon each individual's slowly fitting into a decreed pattern, there is a great disapproval of haste or precocity, and the standard is the standard of the age grade. People remember the relative ages of children, and children in a neighborhood play in gangs. In these gangs the pace is always set by the slowest. This is the child to whom everyone will point with pride, and those who far exceed this slowness of pace will bring blushes to their parents' cheeks and will be constantly nagged and disapproved of by the older children.[14]

[13] This however is much slighter than the American Indian form.

[14] The attitude toward precocity in Samoa is best illustrated by the way it has affected the attempts to introduce European ideas of schooling. The missionary schools conformed to the Samoan pattern; the boy who entered first had to graduate first, regardless of how stupid he might be or how intelligent his competitors who had entered the school later. This effectually barred out competition and had a dulling and discouraging effect upon the brighter

In understanding the role which age plays in the life of a Samoan child, it is necessary to bear in mind the large households in which—with the rarest exceptions, exceptions which have definite reverberations in personality development (Mead 1928a: 141–44)—no child for long has a fixed status as the oldest, the only child, or the youngest. Rather each child begins life at the bottom spoke of a wheel which slowly revolves until in middle age he is at the top only to slowly descend again toward old age and a position near the ground. The pressure of the children whose births soon after his own rapidly rob him of the position of youngest, push him slowly upward in the relative scale, until at adolescence a girl or boy is near the center of pressure, with as many younger people who can be ordered about and disciplined as there are older people who can order him about and discipline him. What is the most difficult age in our society becomes in Samoa, because of this point of relativity, the age of maximum ease partly because it is the age of most equal pressure.

Up to adolescence, although the pressure decreases, there is a long period of discipline, which differs for boys and girls. The early years before six or so have developed children who are aggressive whenever the situation permits it, but who have learned never to act spontaneously, even in anger, but always after reviewing the social scene and the possibilities of disturbing their elders. These little children play hardly any group games. They play with pin wheels, make palm-leaf balls, stick little sticks in the sand, and form a parasitical group about their young nurses, about whom they surge and stumble in an unpatterned kind of play. Then, at six or so, the little girls become baby tenders, the little boys become fags for bigger boys; the girls are disciplined by responsibility for those much younger than themselves, the boys are disciplined by having to fag for an arbitrary group of adolescents. The care of the babies ties the little girls down, makes group life less possible, keeps them from wandering far afield, keeps them in the village where they are always liable to be requisitioned for some household task by any older relative, makes

students. In the modern schools under the United States Government, ordinary American ideas of "skipping grades" had been introduced, which were resulting in a very genuine conflict. The children were taught at school to be proud of effort; when they, however, returned home to report that they had been skipped ahead of their former companions, their parents hung their heads in shame.

their play time more sporadic and precious to them. The boys on the other hand can go fishing. They can range the bush or far-away reefs with the older boys. They become more adventurous, acquire more outdoor skills, and learn to cooperate with each other, for the older boys object to having the services of their juniors interfered with by jealousies and fist fights. Similarly the earlier obstreperousness of the little girls is muted, not because the adults really care whether they fight or not, but because if they do fight their infant charges are neglected and scream with fear, which immediately brings the rage of some adult down on the little nurses' heads.

From this age on, sex differentiation is very marked. The brother and sister tabu between all siblings—blood, affinal, and foster siblings being included in this wide range—is set in motion when at about this age the young child becomes self-conscious about this point. From that time on, all the members of the opposite sex fall into two categories, tabu siblings, and members of an opposing group any one of whom may in the future be one's lover. But from six to adolescence, the opposing groups see each other only as groups. Within each household, brothers and sisters never talk to each other, nor sit near each other, nor use each other's things. In the village, if no adults are near by, the two sexes go about in play gangs and throw sticks and stones at each other. This play becomes more vigorous after dark, when opposing gangs can actually give battle without disturbing their elders. Any child who deserts these sex-solid gangs and plays with the opposite sex is regarded by adults and children with great disapproval (Mead 1928a:178–80). These children's play gangs, although their hostilities are chiefly taken out upon the opposite sex, not upon other gangs of their own sex, give ample training for the rivalries and hostilities which in later life crop up between different aumagas and between village groups. The girls' solidarities are however, broken down after adolescence, when they cease to associate in neighborhood groups and turn more and more to relatives, who can be better trusted in love affairs. The break-down into groups of twos and threes, according to degree of sex experience, is followed by marriage and the absorption of the girl into her husband's household, often in another village, where her status will depend upon his rank, not upon any affiliations of her own.

The aualuma never becomes as integrated and continually functioning a group as the aumaga, but remains a pale reflection of the women's group on the one hand and of the activities of the aumaga on the other. This whole educational situation is reflected in the behavior of the women, who are more individualistic than the men and more jealous, and who engage in more quarrels. Occasionally rivalry situations occur between young men in the free love-making which precedes marriage, but it is notable that these have the same unrealistic character as the rivalries which occur between villages. The quarrels result not because one youth wants a girl and the other youth gets her permanently, but because one youth boasts to another that he was admitted to the favors of a girl with whom the other had slept earlier the same night. It is the slight upon the first suitor's virtuosity which is resented, just as villages compete for no prize but merely defend their respective reputations and honor. Women, on the other hand, especially married women, will quarrel over the actual possession of a man, and even come to blows or bite each others' noses or ears. Men, however, do not resent a wife's leaving them and marrying another, provided that this second husband is not below them in rank. It is this latter rule which occasionally makes the castoff wives of chiefs occupy the position of prostitutes in the community, where no one is of high enough rank to marry them. Here again the chief merely defends his honor; he does not compete for a prize which only one may have.

Throughout the whole educational system, even extending into love affairs, runs the thread of the *tautala laititi* prohibition. The girl or boy who makes love too young, or the man who has an affair with the wife of a man whose rank is higher than his, is guilty of this. Steadily the precocious, the combative, the ambitious are muted, nagged into dullness, until by the time that the household is ready to choose the matai, the slowest and steadiest man has gained self-confidence, the gayest and most brilliant has been steadied into reliability, and the choice does not in any case endanger the continuous working of the pattern. Throughout the whole educational process the Samoans wait for the development of mafaufau, judgment, they discourage any tautala laititi and they disapprove of all unusual behavior as *fua,* or uncaused, that is, occurring for an idiosyncratic and socially unrecognized reason.

THE CHANNELING OF OPPOSING TENDENCIES

If the Samoan emphases are summed up as the subordination of the individual to the pattern, as the subordination of the younger to the older, of the commoner to the chief, and in lesser degree but no less surely, of the woman to the man, then we find in one Samoan activity—the dance—a reversal of all these attitudes. Every child learns the dance rhythms before it can walk, as it sits in its mother's lap. By the time it is three or four, its dancing is highly stylized. And in a Samoan dance, the whole usual order of society is reversed, the individual is important, and no two individuals are conceived as dancing alike. Every dance is believed to be idiosyncratic within a series of known patterns, and uniformity or mimicry of other's styles are never recognized as occurring. The taupou's dance is the most important, and the talking chiefs honor her by becoming clowns. The dance begins with the smallest toddler and ends with the chief. The dreaded tautala laititi is never heard on the dance floor. Instead each mother pushes her youngest forward and the whole group approves the baby's hesitant steps. Within the confines of a well-learned form, every individual is given a maximum chance to exhibit his own individuality and skill. There is a dance for the hunchback, for the dwarf, for the mad feeble-minded boy, for the deaf-mute. And significantly the one girl I found who suffered most from what would be designated in our society as a "feeling of inferiority" was a girl who could not dance; whose failure was in the one field in which individual display and success are permitted.[15]

[15] For a fuller discussion see in Mead 1928a: ch. VIII.

H. MICRONESIA

LEONARD MASON

15. The Ethnology of Micronesia

Whenever anthropologists undertake to describe the cultures of a major portion of the Pacific, they feel impelled to draw lines on a map. These are traditional boundaries that culturally distinguish one Oceanic region from another. Anthropologists for generations have acknowledged the existence of these "culture areas," commonly labeled Micronesia, Polynesia, Melanesia, and Indonesia, and they have detailed the distribution of racial, linguistic, and ethnographic traits in support of this classification. Even today the custom persists. But increasingly the tendency is to deny the reality of these areas and to draw boundaries with only limited and quite specific associations.

For a moment we shall continue to observe custom. We shall define Micronesia quite literally as the "small islands" of the western Pacific, and identify them as the Mariana, Caroline, Marshall, and Gilbert archipelagoes, plus two isolated islands, Nauru and Ocean (or Banaba). The first three groups lie entirely north of the equator, as does the northern half of the Gilberts.

So far this conception of Micronesia is more geographic than anything else. If it is approached in terms of art, language, food technology, kinship practice (to name but a few categories on which to base classifications), the region must be dissected further and in multiple ways. The more peripheral cultures then appear at times to have more in common with cultures in Polynesia or Melanesia, or even Indonesia in the far west. In a word, the concept of Micronesia as a culture area loses its utility when confronted with the cultural and linguistic diversity which exists therein and which often obscures the putative borders.

So-called Micronesians, then, must be regarded as heterogeneous by nearly every standard, especially if compared to the peoples of Polynesia to the east. Such variation, however, pales into insignificance when viewed against the kaleidoscopic character of Melanesian cultures in the larger and more heavily settled islands of the southwest Pacific.

THE ENVIRONMENTAL SETTING

It is an anthropological truism that habitat limits but does not dictate the nature of a culture. To know the ecological diversity of Micronesia is to understand some of its cultural variation. In the peopling of these islands, the advantages for human occupancy depended importantly on such factors as island size, topography, soil, climate, water supply, marine life, and the flora and fauna, provided by nature and assisted by human agency.

The estimated 2500 islands in Micronesia account for just over 1000 square miles, but they are lost to view individually in the great expanse of ocean that in its extent matches the continental United States. Guam, with 209 square miles, is the largest island. The smallest ones are sand bars on the atoll reef.

TOPOGRAPHY

"High" islands are commonly distinguished from "low" islands or coral atolls. The first are volcanic in origin, few in number, and soon identified: all of the Marianas (Guam, Rota, Tinian, and Saipan in the south, to Pagan and Agrihan near the north end) and five of the Carolines (Palau, Yap, Truk, Ponape, and Kusaie). The highest of these is Agrihan at 3199 feet.

The rest of the Carolines and all of the Marshalls and Gilberts are coralline, constructed through aeons of time by lime-secreting organisms in the shallow waters surrounding submerged volcanic peaks and ridges. The atoll consists typically of a salt-water lagoon ringed by a limestone reef, and dry land areas (islets) rising above the reef. Islets may number more than a hundred on one atoll, reach a height of twenty to twenty-five feet above sea level, and average less than a thousand feet in width. The lagoon at

Kwajalein, largest atoll in the world, measures 80 statute miles in length and 840 square miles in area.

The unique complex of islands known as Truk is an "almost-atoll," with coral islets on a limestone reef, an enclosed lagoon, plus six large and many smaller volcanic islands rising out of the lagoon. "Raised atolls" are another type of island topography, e.g., Nauru, Ocean, and some western Caroline islands. These usually have no lagoon, although an inland depression may suggest an atoll origin. Their valuable phosphate deposits have resulted from consolidation of centuries-old accumulation of sea-bird droppings.

SOILS

The requirements of island horticulturists focus our attention on soil quality. The coralline soils of most atolls are infertile, shallow, and too porous to hold moisture. Atolls with high rainfall tend to be enriched with humus from plant debris. The complex soils of volcanic islands vary according to parent materials, weathering conditions, and land use methods. The fertile soils of Truk, Ponape, and Kusaie are derived from heavy basaltic lavas. Yap and Palau combine lighter granitic materials with ancient metamorphic rocks which evidence a continental tie with Asia in ages past; these soils possess mineral elements either rare or absent elsewhere. Volcanic soils in the Marianas are fairly good, but coralline soils from the raised terraces of ancient reef derivation are not unlike those in the atolls.

CLIMATE

Micronesian climate is tropical and oceanic. Temperatures average about 80° F. and show more diurnal variation than seasonal. Humidity is also fairly constant, about 80 per cent. Trade winds predominate in most of Micronesia and blow briskly from the northeast (southeast, if below the equator) most of the year. The seasonal monsoon winds of the western Carolines alternate direction between Australia and Asia. Annual rainfall of 120 to 150 inches between 2° and 9° N. is fairly well distributed during the year. It drops to 40 or 50 inches as the latitude increases either side of the equator. Seasonal deficiencies then develop in the months when the trade winds are strongest. Typically, the windward side of high islands, which intercept the prevailing winds, get more rain; the leeward side may receive as little as 20 to 30 inches. In the thermal belt, which lies mainly north of the equator, frequent calms develop and at times may affect Nauru, Ocean, and some of the Gilberts. Here, heat and humidity intensify, and droughts have lasted as long as two or three years. Typhoons originate in the central and eastern Carolines and, moving west, cause greatest damage in the Yap-Woleai-Guam area.

WATER SUPPLY

Permanent streams are relatively few and limited to the high islands. Fresh water is frequently a serious problem. Torrential rains create temporary freshets or pools, which in more porous soils quickly disappear below ground. Low-island dwellers depend on rain-water catchment or wells that tap underground lenses of fresh to brackish water.

PLANT LIFE

The major portion of Micronesia's flora has been established by natural means (seeds and fruits carried by wind, water, and birds) or as a consequence of human migrations. The primary source of materials lay in the southwest Pacific and Southeast Asia. The limited amount and variety of vegetation in the atolls has resulted from poor soils, brackish ground water, and salt spray. More recently, Europeans have introduced species from other major floras of the world.

The drier atolls and raised coral islands present the greatest challenge to human occupancy. Here the vegetation is mainly vines, coarse grasses, and a few hardy shrubs and trees. Introduced coconut and pandanus trees are principal food plants. In the wetter atolls, especially inland on larger islets, humus-enriched soil and ground-water reserves of low salinity permit a moderately dense vegetation, including additional food plants, such as breadfruit, taro, and banana.

Weathered volcanic islands with abundant rainfall are characterized by a greater number of plant zones. The strand flora that is common to the atolls is here supplemented by mangrove and nipa palm in brackish mud flats. Primary and secondary forests take over in valley bottoms, coastal plains, and hilly slopes. Rich soil and rainfall produce a veritable jungle of tangled vines, ferns, shrubs, and trees of all sizes. The rain forests of Kusaie and Ponape are good examples. Somewhat similar conditions exist on Yap, Palau, and the southern Marianas, save that interior uplands may appear as open woodland and grassy savanna, possibly due to poor soils, lack of rain (in leeward areas), or to Micronesian practices of burning forest land to acquire new cultivation acreage.

Land Fauna

The varied fauna of "continental" islands south and west of Micronesia is reflected only faintly in the oceanic islands. Land bird and insect species are best represented. The fruit bat thrives in the southern Marianas and western Carolines. A few land snakes and the crocodile are known from Palau. The atolls are only rich in migratory shore and sea birds, e.g., pigeon, plover, curlew, frigate bird, booby, tern.

The native rat must have first entered Micronesia with humans. Pigs and dogs, less ubiquitous in island cultures, probably arrived later. In modern times poultry, cats, and the European house rat have become fairly common, the last as a serious pest. Cattle, goats, and carabao (a draft animal) are kept in small numbers on some high islands. Familiar to all islanders are geckos, skinks, hermit and coconut crabs, centipedes, scorpions, spiders, and many insects, such as ants, termites, beetles, cockroaches, fleas, lice, houseflies, and mosquitoes (although malaria is not present). Recently the rhinoceros beetle has been destroying countless coconut palms, and the giant African snail has invaded gardens in many high islands.

Marine Resources

Micronesia shares with other regions of Oceania a basic similarity of marine life, owing to a common western Pacific origin and a wide distribution by ocean currents. Islanders depend on marine resources for much of their daily needs. The food potential of reef and lagoon, unquestionably more important than that of the open sea, varies greatly from island to island, and relates to many complex factors, such as reef physiography, lagoon size and conformation, and the number and location of open passes whereby tides, waves, and currents circulate the water between lagoon and ocean.

To describe this wealth of marine biota is impossible here. Some atoll environments support several hundred species of tropical fishes, e.g., angelfish, butterfly fish, demoiselle, parrot fish, puffer, triggerfish, wrasse. Associated denizens are clams (including the giant Tridacna), cowries, snails, poisonous cones, spiny lobsters, pearly oysters, sea urchins (stings from their spines may be deadly), squid and octopus, sea cucumbers (famed in the China trade as trepang), and giant turtles like the hawksbill. Beyond the reef, Micronesians troll for bonito, tuna, wahoo, dolphin, and other large fishes. They may trap an unwary whale, or some of a school of playful porpoises. Apart from the dangers presented by sharks, barracudas, and sting rays, a considerable hazard to native health exists in poisonous fishes, often known by their species and then avoided, but others may be dangerous due to changes in food habits and be eaten without suspicion.

THE CHANGING WORLD OF MICRONESIANS

The description of traditional culture presented here does not imply that things are the same today, or that custom in aboriginal times never changed. Any cultural system undergoes constant modification as the society's members respond to changes in habitat and population, to contacts with other societies, or to the very process by which a person learns his culture. In Micronesia each cultural configuration is the product of an evolutionary continuum, which did not end when Micronesians first met Europeans in 1521 upon the occasion of Magellan's historic landing in the Marianas.

In the more than four centuries following, islanders came to know in varying degree other explorers, missionaries both Catholic and Protestant, whalers, beachcombers, traders, blackbirders, and officials of five nations—Spain, Germany, United Kingdom, United States, and Japan, who at different times established control over one group or another. These contacts ushered in a new era, not without bloodshed, population dislocation, and cultural atrophy. But it did introduce a new technology, a system of exchanging local products for imported goods, a religion not incompatible with Micronesian orientations toward the spiritual world, medical treatment for endemic and introduced diseases, schools for learning foreign ways, and governments that outlawed civil war and alleviated the crises periodically created by typhoons and droughts.

Spain abandoned her island holdings in 1898, leaving Guam to the United States, and the rest of the Marianas and the Carolines to augment Germany's possessions in the Marshalls and Nauru. Britain already controlled the Gilberts and Ocean Island. The first World War saw the Germans evicted by the Japanese. After the second World War, Japan was forced to withdraw. In 1947 the former Japanese holdings became a United Nations trusteeship and, with Guam, were governed by the United States. Australia, New Zealand, and the United Kingdom shared the jurisdiction over Nauru, which had been taken from Germany in 1914. The Gilberts and Ocean Island continued under British rule.

The keynote of island administration in mid-century was provided by the United Nations' emphasis on trusteeship, on the progressive development of island peoples economically, socially, educationally, and politically. Self-government was the stated goal, with recognition that it could be achieved only by further economic advancement. It was inevitable that the older Micronesian customs would continue to disappear with each passing generation. Nevertheless, Micronesians themselves stood in the forefront of those who cried "Progress!" Despite this seeming rush toward assimilation, much of Micronesian tradition is still viable, as in food technology, language, kinship practices, political structures, and the covert aspects of native supernaturalism.

What follows is a review of Micronesian customs as they functioned prior to intensive Western exposure and as they continue in some degree today. Much of this is necessarily reconstruction, based on the reports of late nineteenth- and early twentieth-century German observers, and supplemented importantly by American ethnological research since 1945. The style is that of the "ethnographic present"—from the conviction that culturally the contemporary island societies are still more Micronesian than anything else. To describe their traditions in the past tense would be a distinct disservice to the living generation.

THE EXTERNALS OF DAILY LIFE

Think of an orange. Let the rind represent the outward manifestations of a Micronesian culture as any outsider might view it. His first insights will be cued by the sights and sounds, and smells, of daily activity in the island community. Now remove the rind (the observer perfects his communication and rapport). The peeled orange (non-manifest culture) reveals many characters not suggested in the first instance. These segments or aspects of culture carry the deeper meanings of cultural behavior that are implicit in family and kinship, property and exchange, power and authority, and the symbolism of supernatural belief. In the following review of Micronesian cultural patterns, we shall first consider the rind, that is, the externals of daily life, and then proceed to a more careful examination of the segments wherein lies the true quality of the Micronesian designs for living.

SHELTER

Family dwellings, associated cook huts, and canoe sheds occupy sites that are dispersed along or just back from the shore. Each household communicates with its neighbors by water or by paths, which are frequently sanded or stone-paved. Houses tend to be small, rectangular, and without partitions. They are built directly on the ground or elevated on wood posts, stone pillars, or rock-walled mounds. An elongated hexagonal floor plan is customary on Yap and adjacent atolls. Gabled roofs are thatched with pandanus, coconut, or nipa palm leaves, as is often true of the walls. Dirt floors may be covered with a layer of water-worn coral pebbles and mats. Bamboo poles or wood planking furnishes flooring and walls in sturdier construction. House timbers are firmly lashed together with sennit, although Palauans carpenter their timbers to fit without other fastening.

FOOD

The household gathers at dusk for a substantial meal prepared in a ground oven. Otherwise, fresh food is eaten as snacks or cooked quickly over an open fire. In the westernmost islands, clay pottery permits boiling. Inhabitants of the drier atolls subsist on coconut, pandanus, arrowroot, and fish, but on the wetter islands breadfruit, banana, and Cyrtosperma are also available. High islanders add to these resources yams, taro, and sugar cane, to name the more important. Fresh beverages include palm toddy and coconut milk. Kava is made only by Ponapeans and Kusaiens. Western Micronesians use betel nut, but tobacco was first introduced by Europeans. Pigs, poultry, and young dogs figure mainly as feast food.

Drop-line fishing from small canoes is more common than trolling outside the reef in sail canoes. Other techniques are spearing, netting, reef-collecting, and lagoon drives with coconut leaf sweeps. Fish may be trapped in stone weirs or stupefied with plant poison.

Shell or wood fishhooks, wood spears, basket traps, and sennit line, in combination with shell knives and scrapers, stone or shell pounders, coconut graters, a variety of wooden bowls, digging sticks, and a shell-bladed hoe make for a relatively simple technology. Irrigation and fertilizers other than compost are not known. In order to conserve food, low islanders dry their surplus pandanus and breadfruit, and most Micronesians from Truk eastward preserve large amounts of fermented breadfruit in earth pits.

DRESS

The scant clothing of Micronesians is compensated for by its quality. Some of the region's finest artistry appears in the loomed wrap-arounds worn by Carolinian women east of Yap, and in the plaited dress mats of the same sex in the Marshalls. Women elsewhere, and some men, wear skirts of pendent fibers; in some islands, men prefer a snug breechclout. Hibiscus and banana plants provide weaving material, and plaiting is best accomplished with leaves of a fine-textured pandanus. Unusual displays of personal ornament appear on festive occasions. Examples are flower garlands, shell necklaces, earrings, belts, plaited arm bands, and wooden combs. Ears are pierced and various parts of the body are tattooed in locally unique patterns. The most varied and spectacular adornment is found in the islands from Truk to Yap. (Early Spanish accounts suggest that natives in the Marianas wore no clothing at all, neither were they tattooed.)

THE PROCESS OF BECOMING

To speak of one becoming a Micronesian has no meaning. One really becomes a Palauan, a Chamorro, a Gilbertese. The process of growing up, of becoming fully participant, of internalizing the values of one's group, is given real meaning only when the several Micronesian cultures are examined and compared. To attempt generalizations for the entire area is to rob each island society of its special flavor. Yet there does exist a commonality which permits the observer to "feel at home" in most, if not all, communities in Micronesia.

We continue in this section to be concerned with the more visible aspects of a Micronesian's environment, namely the *household,* which in his early years is his primary reference group. Residence and kinship are the relevant principles of household organization. Interpersonal relations are further determined by distinctions of age and sex. These four factors are the bonding fibers, embedded in the circumstances of nativity, which shape the social destiny of every Micronesian. This lesson is first and most intimately presented in the household. Years later as an adult he will come to assume his proper place in the rank and prestige systems which are extensions from the household to other and more important kin groups and to the larger residential community.

The household varies greatly in size and composition but is usually an extended family, representing up to three or four generations or its nuclear units joined by a sibling tie. Generally one cooking place is shared, although nuclear components of the group may live in separate adjacent dwellings. The household functions adequately as a production group when its age and sex ratios are in balance, and is commonly the principal consumer of its own produce.

Micronesians are born into such a group without fanfare or ceremony, save the postnatal observance of taboos by mother and baby. Offspring of high-ranking parents, or the firstborn in some islands, may be publicly recognized by feasting and gift exchanges. Weaning occurs at two or three years of age, or when the mother again gives birth. Adoption is widespread, the arrangements usually being made in infancy or even prior to birth. The motives, many and complex oftentimes, range from satisfying the wants of childless couples to strengthening existent kin ties or creating new fictive relationships.

In childhood the islanders acquire some basic skills, the boys learning to fish and climb coconut trees, the girls to cook, tend house, and care for younger siblings. They begin to distinguish sex in their dress, and to segregate in play activities. Peer groups are established. Fathers show much affection for their children, but, since they are away from home more, the relationship is less intense than the mother's. At the onset of menstruation girls are temporarily secluded, and in some islands the event is marked with considerable ceremony. In the westernmost islands boys at puberty leave the family dwelling for the men's house. Throughout Micronesia brother-sister relations become more formal and more restrained. The transition to adolescence is generally easy and, for both sexes, leads to perhaps the most free and pleasurable period of their lives. Premarital sex play is encouraged in nearly every group, but definitely not in the Gilberts, where virginity must remain inviolate until marriage.

At this age Micronesians are often reluctant to enter upon marriage. In places like Yap and Truk adult responsibility is postponed unduly in a kind of prolonged juvenility. Even marriage may not provide the settling experience, but the birth of a child does finally usher in the need for adult maturity and the game is over. Henceforth the wife, now mother, must be blameless in her behavior; indeed, she has little time for dalliance. The new family relationship carries with it important obligations to kinsmen on both sides. A new social unit has emerged in extension from the parental families. In a few islands this status transformation is recognized by exchange of food and other goods. The young parents now begin to seek their niche in the social, economic, and political matrix of their society.

Postmarital residence rules seem to possess little significance in most villages and hamlets. Patrilocality has been reported for Yap,

Palau, and the Gilberts; elsewhere matrilocality is the stated rule. Adherence to the ideal is not strongly supported by quantitative observation, however, and other factors evidently support alternatives. Local endogamy and the small size of communities mean that the newly married couple is never far from the other parental residence. A great deal of moving about among relatives seems to take place in any case. Divorce is easily obtained if there are no children; otherwise kinsmen apply pressure to keep the marriage intact.

The sexual division of labor in the household is usually drawn rather strictly. Men do the heavier work, clearing land, preparing the soil, building houses and canoes, fishing in the lagoon and outside the reef. They also plant trees and harvest the fruit, fashion artifacts from wood, shell, and stone, and engage in warfare. Older men may become experts in navigation and the curative arts, or more generally spend their time in the councils of clan and community, scheming to improve their individual rank and prestige along with that of their respective kin groups. Women have less spatial mobility, and remain close to home and garden. They look after the children, cook the daily food (men prepare feast food), weave textiles and plait mats and baskets, and collect shellfish in the reef shallows. Exceptions do occur, of course, and in eastern Micronesia the men more often take over the cultivation of taro and other garden crops.

KINSHIP AND KIN GROUPS

Outside the household, Micronesians resort to a wide range of kinship ties in dealing with other persons. Remarkably few labels are needed to refer to these relatives, since the kinship systems are broadly classificatory. Reference terms are mainly those applied to members of the nuclear family: father, mother, brother, sister, child. These tend to cue similar patterns of interpersonal behavior when extended to the many other biological relationships. Generally the brother-sister bond is the strongest, marked by affection, obligation, and restraint. The tie between siblings of the same sex, also strong, is frequently the structural basis for extended families. (The husband-wife link is correspondingly weak and brittle, except in places like Yap and Palau where nuclear families display more autonomy.) Relative age of siblings is generally important (the elder has the advantage) and this distinction is frequently reflected in an "older-younger" designation.

The "Hawaiian" or generation type of kinship system is most widespread, being reported for the Gilberts, Kusaie, Palau, and Carolinian atolls except the Mortlocks and Ulithi. Nuclear terms are typically extended to relatives of the same sex and generation. Thus, sibling terms are applied to cousins on both sides of the family.

A second system, undoubtedly derived from the "Hawaiian" type, occurs on Yap, Ulithi, Truk, the Mortlocks, and Ponape. This is the "Crow" type, in which relatives in a female line of descent are emphasized and generation is ignored. In cousin terminology, the speaker refers to his father's sister's children as "mother" and "father" and, reciprocally, applies the term "child" to his mother's brother's children. His other cousins are classed as siblings. Micronesian practitioners of either system sometimes give further importance to the maternal tie by special terms for mother's brother and sister's son.

Another matrilineal modification of the Hawaiian system is the so-called "Iroquois" type, practiced in the Marshalls and Nauru. Special terms exist for mother's brother and sister's son, but also a difference appears in the cousin terminology. Children of father's brother and mother's sister are regarded as siblings, and, where the opposite sex is involved, this relationship carries the same restraint and sexual avoidance as for real siblings. A different term is used for cousins of opposite sex when they are the children of father's sister or mother's brother, and then the prescribed behavior is quite unrestricted.

Out of this web of kinship, Micronesians have conceived a variety of kin groupings that are larger and generally more important than the household. Most of these groups express some priority for maternal relatives, and are organized as matrilineages and matriclans. This is not true, however, in the Gilberts or the Polynesian outliers. In the last-named—e.g., Kapingamarangi—there are bilateral kindreds as well as smaller, largely localized, economically sufficient, corporate bodies organized on the same bilateral basis. The situation in the Gilberts is more complex. Bilateral descent groups or ramages segment into localized cores that control portions of the ramage estate. These segments are overlapping and quasi-patrilineal, owing to the options for affiliation and the fact that related males tend to associate with a particular landholding.

LINEAGES

Almost universally the lineage is more important than the clan. It is usually a corporate body, with common landholdings, formalized hereditary leadership, and a core of members resident on the ancestral homestead. Sometimes unnamed, lineages more often bear the personal name of a living or recently deceased progenitor. Lineages are exogamous and function in feasting, gift exchanges, ceremonial observance of life crises, and inheritance of titles. They grow by natural increase and fission along lines of seniority, and they become extinct when lineal issue fails. Membership is determined biologically, usually through one's mother, but in a few places spouses and adopted children are admitted. In Yap and Palau, the definition of lineage is less traditional and allows certain other features. The Yap lineage is essentially patrilineal, that in Palau is more matrilineal but with paternal features; in both areas one is reminded that nuclear families are stronger than is customary among Micronesians.

CLANS

Lineages are usually specific segments of more diffuse clan memberships. In some islands, however, lineage and clan are unrelated, in fact one or the other may be totally absent. The clan is almost always non-localized, at times overriding linguistic boundaries. Descent is always matrilineal. Clans are named, often with a place-association or suggesting some totemic character, and they have traditional histories. In times of war they provide sanctuary within the membership, and in peace there is a guarantee of hospitality. Marriage is regulated by the rule of clan exogamy. Although the clan is non-corporate and usually lacking in real property and political authority, it frequently provides the essential unifying influence to counteract the fissive character of lineages and other local groups.

While unilineal descent groups predominate in Micronesian society, some compensatory mechanisms do exist, more or less organized, in the numerous bilateral relationships that can be called upon in need. The full significance of this equilibrium function still requires more research in Micronesia.

RIVALRY IN RECIPROCITY

Examination of Micronesian property and exchange systems soon leads one to question their primarily economic nature and the reciprocity that appears to underlie them. To what extent, one asks, is the fundamental motive more that of rivalry toward social or political ends? The truth lies somewhere between for most island societies. The principle of co-operativeness for social and economic integration is present everywhere in some degree. The essence of competitiveness is rather subtle in some islands and may lie just below the surface; in other societies it obtrudes openly, even blatantly, for all to see and applaud.

PROPERTY SYSTEMS

The observation that land is the heart of Micronesian property systems should not be surprising in islands where arable acreage is so scarce. Land is the basis of subsistence for the household and extended family. It functions as an integrating principle for lineage and ramage. And it provides the means for ranking both individuals and kin groups in village and district hierarchies.

Real property includes house sites in the village, garden plots, parcels of coconut and forest land, reserved sections of reef and lagoon where these are scarce resources, and untended or waste land. All land is owned collectively by lineages, ramages, clans, or in the case of unused land and unlimited reef and lagoon, the district. Parcels of kin group territory, often widely scattered, are allocated to localized lineage segments, nuclear families, or even individuals for active maintenance, and the corporate kin group usually retains some sort of residual rights. Trees and garden crops generally go with the land, but in Truk and a few other places they are treated separately. Where class privilege prevails, ownership and usufruct are often differentiated and are inherited by upper- and lower-class kin groups respectively.

Inheritance of real property usually proceeds from one generation to the next without disruption of corporate group control. Every person, according to local practice, acquires a right at birth to expect certain liberties and privileges in land from the parental generation, mostly from his mother (or father, or both). Alternatively—e.g., in the Gilberts—he has an option in later life to affiliate with one or more properties available to him through different descent lines. Again, local custom may admit a lifetime or possibly more enduring claim to land by exchange, gift, or lease to in-marrying spouses, adopted children, non-lineal kinsmen, or unrelated persons. Tenure rules are specific for each society, and to attempt more than a few generalities here becomes impossible. The rivalry aspect of land ownership and usufruct appears most obviously in the ostentatious display of produce from the land on public occasions, and in the exercise of suprafamilial authority, which will be reviewed shortly.

Other property includes houses, canoes, household furnishings, domesticated animals, personal articles, titles, special skills, and reserved knowledge. The ownership of most of these is commonly associated with a nuclear family or an individual. Such property can be transferred as gift, bequest, loan, or sale without the larger group's approval. Western concepts of private property apply more directly to Micronesian practice in these categories than is possible with real estate.

EXCHANGE SYSTEMS

As noted earlier, the household is a self-sufficient unit in production and consumption. The entire range of essential resources is typically present in the land and lagoon areas controlled by a house group. There is little need for economic exchanges between such extended families. The one important exception is a periodic demand for more labor than a household commands, as in building and thatching a house, constructing a seagoing canoe, clearing land, excavating taro pits, conducting fish drives, and going on overseas expeditions. Reciprocity is plainly evident in these principally male activities. The work effort of the larger kin group or neighborhood is individually contributed to get a big job done quickly, and will be reciprocated individually at a later date.

Another kind of exchange stresses reciprocity but serves more of a social function. This is the gift exchange that marks life crises, homecomings, and the completion of certain projects. In the giving and receiving of cooked food, mats, textiles, and sennit, nothing changes hands that all participants do not already possess. The aim then is to maintain and strengthen the social integrity of the larger kin group, i.e., lineage or ramage. One important exception to this statement is the exchange of bead money and other valuables between Palauan families at life crises, which contributes to the integration of clan and village but is equally dedicated to the manipulation of native wealth for the advancement of personal and family rank, prestige, and power. This sort of competition between kin groups is reflected to a lesser degree in Yap with the exchange of shell and stone money.

Exchanges of food and other goods accompany public feasting. The principle of co-operation continues to operate in the production and accumulation of quality goods by kin groups, but the competitive drive emerges prominently as rival groups seek public acclaim and notice by high-ranking officials through conspicuous display. The biggest yams or taro corms, the largest fish, the finest mats, the most valued currency are put forward, usually with humble mien, but the truth is there for all to behold—this is a man (or his family) who is industrious, hard-working, generous, possessed of special skills and knowledge, and, therefore, someone to be seriously reckoned with. The exchange is no longer economic, although the food contributions are divided among those present and taken home to be eaten later. Rather it connotes rivalry and symbolizes the continuing struggle for prestige in the community, either by validation and maintenance of a title or other ascribed status, or by advancement within the limits of mobility permitted in Micronesian hierarchies.

Some comment must be injected here about interisland trade. The Marshall atolls and those lying between Yap and Truk are well known for the magnificent sailing outrigger canoes and the specialized knowledge of wind, wave, and stars that insures successful navigation over hundreds of miles of ocean. Trade among the low islanders themselves is either a kind of gift exchange among kinsmen, already described, or it is simply part of the hospitality practiced among clansmen. In a more economic sense, trade is conducted between the low and high islands where each environment offers as surplus that which is scarce to the other. Thus, low islanders produce mats, sennit, coconut oil, textiles, toddy, and shell ornaments in exchange for turmeric, timber, giant swamp taro, preserved breadfruit, basalt rocks for earth oven cookery, and other things that may be absent or in poor supply in the atolls.

HIERARCHIES OF POWER

Political organization in Micronesia, as elsewhere, is concerned with the differential possession of power, the ability to influence, organize, or dominate others. Micronesian rights to power are primarily ascriptive, i.e., they derive from rank and prestige systems structured on the birthright of sex, relative age, and lineal descent. Yet within customary limits, an individual or his family group can better their status by concentrating available resources and talents in achievement activities. This constant effort to move upward in the system, even though it be but one step, is the essence of political activity in Micronesia.

As we have already seen, the institutional basis of rank and therefore of power is twofold: 1) the lineage or some other corporate kin group, and 2) the estate that is owned or managed by the group. Internally the kin group as a collectivity relates to its land as a principal means of subsistence. In its external relations the group's numerical size and activity, together with the traditional history of its estate, rank it appropriately in the village or district hierarchy. This participation of propertied kin groups in territorial organizations—i.e., village and district—is the principal theme of this review of political power and authority systems in Micronesia.

The authority systems by which Micronesians acquire and use differential rights to power vary considerably from place to place. Land as an index to rank is in some islands overshadowed by a preoccupation with ranked titles, class or caste privilege, or accumulation of wealth in the form of quality artifacts. Such substitutive indices, however, are ultimately associated directly or indirectly with access to land. Another manifestation of power priorities is chieftainship, which depends on membership in ranking descent groups. Chiefly authority not uncommonly bears the supernatural sanction of divine ancestry or spiritual communication. Chiefdoms are usually no larger than an island or a section of an island, but at times they have been extended far beyond that by aggressive warfare or supportive alliances among villages and districts. Rarely is the chief's power absolute; in most islands it is contained by the presence of a council of elders, kin group leaders, who manage the bulk of a community's jural problems.

SOUTHERN GILBERTS

The simplest form of political organization is practiced in the southern Gilberts, which have no chiefly authority or stratified class structure. Customary law is maintained primarily by the authority within each kin group. Communities are autonomous, each governed loosely by a council of elders who represent the community's landed kin groups. Seating location in the council house is prescribed by consanguineal ties with the founder. An important function of the council is the redistribution of kin group contributions of food among those attending community feasts. Council decisions on intergroup conflicts are reached by consensus.

TRUK AND THE CAROLINIAN ATOLLS

In most Carolinian atolls and the high-island complex at Truk, some form of chiefly authority supplements the council organization. The chief is usually the eldest male in a senior landholding kin group. In theory, at least, he exercises eminent domain within his jurisdiction. He receives food gifts from his constituents, including a first fruits presentation, but these are hardly tribute. He frequently directs the distribution of food resources when the whole community has engaged in the activity, such as the catch from a fishing expedition. His rulings are generally based on accepted custom, and in any case are subject to review by the council of elders. In the Polynesian outliers, where descent groups are bilateral, there is both a hereditary chief and an elected priest. Mokil, Pingelap, and Ngatik are patrilineally oriented and show some influence from Ponape in a kind of title system. The rest of the islands are matrilineally organized, including the atolls from Puluwat to Ulithi, which have superimposed upon them a political structure from Yap.

MARSHALLS AND NORTHERN GILBERTS

Chiefly power in the Marshalls demands tribute in services and goods from subject families who cultivate lands owned by the chief's matrilineage. The spiritual aura which surrounds the paramount chief's person and extends to his close relatives provides a basis for an aristocratic class as distinguished from that of the commoners. Stability is lacking in the many, autonomous chiefships, since their fortunes change easily with warfare and political intrigue. In the northern Gilberts the high chief and his descent group stand somewhere between the chiefly families of the Marshalls and those in the Carolinian atolls in having only moderate powers and lesser privilege as an aristocratic class. Land is held in common by ramages of both classes and succession to chiefship is patrilineal.

Political sophistication reached a peak in Micronesia at Ponape, Palau, and Yap, and in each place the elaboration is unusual. Kusaie appears to have many of the same political forms as Ponape, but details are missing because of the early Christianization of this island. In the Marianas the ancient Chamorros seem also to have achieved political maturity, but its true character remains obscured by the Hispanicization of the group after the sixteenth century.

PONAPE

Ponape is divided into five districts or petty states, although at one time the island may have been ruled by one dynasty, as is the case in Kusaie. In each district two parallel lines of titled men serve as a council, and the same pattern applies to sections within a district. Titles are ranked and are the property of certain matriclans. The leading title in one line, Nanmariki, is held by the district chief, whose person is regarded as sacred and requires special behavior and respect language by others in his presence. The principal title in the other line, Naniken, is nearly as important, and its occupant serves as primary counselor and spokesman for the district chief. Succession is restricted to titled men in the same line. To be appointed to a title a man must first belong to an appropriate clan, and further demonstrate his worth to the chief by evidence of his skill and industry in yam production and other competitive activity at public feasts.

PALAU

Palau's authority structure is well institutionalized and highly stratified, households ranked within lineage, lineages within clan, clans within village, and villages within two major confederations. Competition flourishes at every level and emphasizes the duality of Palauan society. Power relationships can be seen most clearly in the organization of the village council. This body is composed of two rival sections of chiefs who are the senior male titleholders from the major matriclans in the village. Each of the ten titles is differentiated historically and assigned a specific seating place in the council house, the rank order alternating on each side. The top title is held by the village chief, the next by the chief-designate. These and the next two titles contain the basis of authority within the village. Women are organized along similar lines, but their participation is limited in the political arena. Competition between clans and between villages is aided by warfare and shamanistic activity, but rests mainly on manipulation of wealth exchanges, particularly of bead money. The wealthiest Palauans represent the upper ranks of society and come close to being a formal social class, but mobility and intercourse between upper and lower ranks keep the situation quite fluid.

YAP AND THE EMPIRE

Yap villages are aggregations of unrelated and largely autonomous patrilineages, ranked in relation to their landholdings and sharing only a common territorial, class, and caste affiliation. These villages are organized into eight districts and three impermanent alliances. The leader of each territorial unit is the highest ranking of those who head its components—e.g., the village chief is the top-ranking lineage head and represents the village in its external relations. Crosscutting this hierarchy is a ranked nine-class system further divided into upper and lower castes. Each village has its place within the system, all of its members belonging to one class and one caste with prescribed rules of behavior and rights to property according to its rank. Matrilineal clans, being widely dispersed in membership, are not organized politically and lie completely outside the rank hierarchy. They do function, however, in the application of supernatural sanctions, and through the wide-ranging ties of clanship help to relate Yap territorial units, whose chief concern is to raise their rank competitively through property exchanges, warfare, and access to chiefly favor.

The Yap district of Gagil is unusual in that economic, political, and even religious bonds have been established with Ulithi and other atolls as far east as Puluwat. Gagil's upper-caste, landowning lineages play a "father" role in respect to Ulithian lineages and those farther east, which calls for regular exchanges of food with their "children." Ulithian lineages are likewise "father" to those in the atolls between Woleai and Puluwat, with corresponding exchanges, although these occur with less regularity. The district chief of Gagil is also priest of a most powerful sacred place and annually receives mats, sennit, and textiles as tribute, along with food offerings for the local spirits. Ulithi acts as intermediary in this "empire" relationship by passing along orders from Yap and assisting the eastern islands in forwarding lineage gifts, tribute, and spirit offerings to Yap.

THE SUPERNATURAL

In this review of Micronesian ethnology we have moved from the physical, the natural, and the visible which require little or no interpretation, to the complexities of the economic, the social, and the political which can be clothed with meaning only after painstaking examination and analysis. This summary is possible only because of the careful fieldwork and interpretation of field data that have reached publication in very recent years, as attested by the appended bibliography.

As we now move on finally to consideration of the supernatural in Micronesia, the task is made difficult by two principal factors. One is that Christianity has been accepted in most of the islands for at least half a century. The other is that anthropological researchers have had little occasion or interest to inquire into the deeper qualities of Micronesian supernaturalism. And too, it must be admitted that religion in Micronesia is traditionally less emphasized or elaborated than in other parts of Oceania.

In the material presented this far, religion and the supernatural have been mentioned only in passing, obliquely, as if they hardly existed for Micronesians. We have been aware of the relationship to ceremonial observance of life crises, and as sanctions for the exercise of authority by political leaders. But no mention has been made of the place of religious belief in the daily life of Micronesians, of its efficacy as magic or sorcery in interpersonal relations, of its value in providing Micronesians with a whole view of life and the world in which they live, of its application to the understanding and treatment of illness, or of its resolution of questions which arise at death and in anticipation of it by the aged as well as those who are left behind to mourn and fill the emptiness created by death. Much of this aspect of Micronesian culture and personality remains to be investigated, and it still can be in spite of the inroads made by Christianity.

In a general way we can say that Micronesians conceive of a personal soul, a spirit separate from the mortal body, which after death seeks its fortune in the spiritual world. Preparation of the corpse, its interment, and appropriate mourning rituals are prescribed according to local custom. The idea that ghosts of the dead may tarry to haunt the living is sufficient to ensure that custom will be observed.

With the emphasis upon lineal descent that is emblematic of Micronesian societies it is to be expected that some form of ancestor respect or worship should prevail as it does. The recently departed are generally regarded as still participant in affairs of the living and are conceptually provided for in the structure and functioning of lineages. Additionally, the immediate surroundings of the islanders—the sea, the air, the land, and various forms both animate and inanimate—are peopled by them with a host of nature spirits. In some islands, named legendary deities stand at the apex of a spiritual hierarchy, prepared to render assistance in mortal affairs or bring down destruction and death as conditions necessitate. In the islanders' communion with the spirit world they are assisted by shamans, part-time specialists in divining, doctoring, counseling, or working the magic of love, fertility, jealousy, and revenge. The people are convinced of the effectiveness of charms, amulets, and fetishes. Sacred places, although not common in Micronesia, are surrounded with attitudes of awe and reverence and restrictions of access. Priests and shrines are present in a few islands, but are generally not characteristic. Taboos on behavior and property are enforced in support of natural conservation, protection of private interests, and most frequently, the respect and observance of chiefly roles.

Despite the relatively slight development of religion in the formal sense, Micronesians have achieved a conceptual unity of their world in which they make no separation of the physical and social from the supernatural.

SUGGESTED READINGS

Preparation of this chapter was made easier by such published summaries or reviews as Freeman (1951b: chapters 8, 9, 10) and Wiens (1962a) on island environments, Fischer (1957) on the eastern Carolines, and my own work on social organization (1959) and art (1964). Particularly useful studies of the high-island cultures are Spoehr (1954, 1957) and Thompson (1945) on the Marianas; Force (1960) and Osborne (1966) on Palau; Schneider (1962) on Yap; Goodenough (1951) and LeBar (1964) on Truk; and Bascom (1965) on Ponape. For the Carolinian atolls, attention is directed especially to Lessa (1966), Alkire (1965), Burrows and Spiro (1953), Weckler (1949), and Bentzen (1949). Buck (1950) and Emory (1965) provide excellent coverage of a Polynesian outlier, and Wedgwood's work (1935–37) is one of the few authoritative sources on Nauru. Spoehr (1949) and my own field notes are the principal basis for the Marshall Islands' treatment. The Gilbert Islands have become better known recently through the publications of Lambert (1966), Lundsgaarde (1966), and Maude (1963). From the extensive German literature, the Thilenius series (1913–36) must be cited as absolutely essential to any review of Micronesian ethnology.

LEONARD MASON

16. Suprafamilial Authority and Economic Process in Micronesian Atolls

Circumstances in societies with a garden economy, by comparison with those among hunting and gathering peoples, encourage the rise of larger and denser populations. The interests of the larger society, in competition with the demands of component kinship groups, are better served by some form of suprafamilial authority (Hoebel 1954:321). The development of such authority (sometimes attended by social stratification) appears to be related to the production of food surpluses, i.e., to the degree in which food-producers in the society share part of their necessary reserves with a non-food-producing elite (Harris 1959:198). Institutionalized chieftainship, a common form of suprafamilial authority in the Pacific Islands, is seen as depending upon control of the distribution of food and other produce. Command over the distribution process is in turn related to authority in the organization of goods production and in the allocation of rights and privileges pertaining to the utilization of natural resources (Sahlins 1958:249).

One critical factor in this matter is the potential a given habitat presents for production of economic surpluses within the technological limitations of the culture. In environments that are characterized by low productivity due to severe restrictions in the resource base, one can examine more rigorously the nature and extent of suprafamilial authority as related to the production of food and other surpluses and to their distribution beyond the kin-

SOURCE: Reprinted from *Humanités, Cahiers de l'Institut de Science Economique Appliquée* (Paris), Ser. V, No. 1 (1959), pp. 87–118, by permission of the author and publisher.

ship group. The atolls of Micronesia, occupied by Malayo-Polynesian peoples who combine gardening with fishing, are commonly regarded as areas of low productivity permitting only small, even infrequent surpluses.

This paper is an exploratory effort to compare seven atoll societies in Micronesia with special attention to the functional relationships between suprafamilial authority and the economic processes of production and distribution. The evolution of this authority will not be considered here, mainly because historical documentation is exceedingly meager and any attempt at reconstruction would be highly speculative. Neither will the limits of this paper permit close examination of the cultural ties that link these atoll societies with certain high islands. Ecological conditions on high islands such as Palau, Yap, and Ponape foster the production of larger economic surpluses. Societies on these islands exhibit more complex cultural systems than do those which inhabit atolls in the same area. At least some of the features of suprafamilial authority among atoll populations in Micronesia can be explained by reference to the cultural heritage derived from previous adaptation to a high-island setting.

MICRONESIAN ATOLLS

The atolls selected for comparative study are Onotoa in the Gilberts, Arno in the Marshalls, Mokil in the eastern Carolines, Lukunor in the central Carolines, Ifaluk in the west-central Carolines, Ulithi in the western Carolines, and Kapingamarangi, a Polynesian outlier.[1] They are given here in order from east to west, except Kapingamarangi, which lies to the southeast of Lukunor and somewhat apart from the rest of the Caroline Islands. They are representative of those districts of Micronesia which contain atolls.

An atoll usually consists of an attenuated, coral reef-platform

[1] This paper could not have been written without the many reports made possible by the Coordinated Investigation of Micronesia (C.I.M.A.) and the Coral Atoll Research projects sponsored by the Pacific Science Board of the National Research Council—National Academy of Sciences (Washington, D.C.) and the United States Office of Naval Research. All reports published in the *Atoll Research Bulletin* (Pacific Science Board) are based on field investigations which were part of these programs.

surrounding a salt-water lagoon. At intervals on this reef variously
sized islands of coral sand and gravel have been produced by
erosive action of ocean waves at the edge of the reef barrier. In
places the reef may be interrupted by channels or passes, often
deep enough to permit entry of large ships. All atoll islands are low
and rarely rise higher than twenty or thirty feet above high-tide
level. Shore areas have poor soil, lack fresh ground water, and are
constantly exposed to salty spray. In this zone the only domesticated plants are coconut and pandanus. Farther inland, conditions
improve and support cultivation of a wider range of plants, including breadfruit, arrowroot, banana, and various wild species.
In the interior of larger, inhabited islands one encounters swampy
regions with soils enriched by nature and by human agency. Taro
and other aroids are generally planted in such localities. Water
supply depends on rainfall catchment or on wells sunk in the sand
to tap a fresh ground water reserve.

The relative size of atolls in this study is presented in Table I,
in order of their respective land areas.

TABLE I

Land and Lagoon Areas of Selected Micronesian Atolls*

Atoll	Total Land Area (sq. mi.)	Lagoon Area (sq. mi.)
Onotoa	5.21	21.00
Arno	5.00	130.77
Ulithi	1.80	183.14
Lukunor	1.09	21.25
Ifaluk	0.57	0.94
Kapingamarangi	0.52	22.01
Mokil	0.48	2.61

* Freeman, Otis W. (ed.). *Geography of the Pacific* (New York: John Wiley &
Sons, Inc.), 1951, pp. 237–38, 273–74.

Agricultural production and marine activity are affected seasonally by minor changes in climate. Rainfall is usually more than
adequate, averaging 120 inches a year, except that Onotoa and
Kapingamarangi lie in drier areas and are subject to extended
droughts. Strong trade winds prevail most of the year in central
and eastern Micronesia. Only Ifaluk and Ulithi fall within the range
of Asiatic monsoons. Typhoons threaten at infrequent intervals,

causing death and destruction when accompanied by high seas that inundate the low-lying islands.

Although most Micronesian atolls support about the same range of plant species, each human population has come to favour a distinctive pattern of economic resources. Some groups have selected breadfruit or pandanus for primary emphasis, while others prefer taro or the aroid Cyrtosperma as the main staple. All make considerable use of the coconut. Land products are supplemented by a varied use of marine resources. The several patterns of subsistence economy reflect differences in technique and work organization. These differences appear to correlate with variations in certain non-economic practices, e.g., family and household composition and settlement plan (Alkire 1959).

In view of the more limited resources of atoll communities it is remarkable that lower densities of population are reported from the high islands. (In 1949 Palau, Yap, and Ponape numbered 34.6, 69.7, and 46.4 persons per square mile respectively, according to estimates made by the U. S. Navy Department.) Table II provides the basic data for comparison of the variations which occur today among the atolls reviewed in this paper.

TABLE II

Population Density in Selected Micronesian Atolls*

Atoll	Total Land Area (sq. mi.)	Population	Density (persons/sq. mi.)
Onotoa	5.21	1,491	286.1
Arno	5.00	1,068	213.6
Ulithi	1.80	421	233.9
Lukunor	1.09	804	737.6
Ifaluk	0.57	220	372.9
Kapingamarangi	0.52	540	1,038.5
Mokil	0.48	355	739.6

* Land area and population for Onotoa: Gilbert and Ellice Islands Colony, *A Report on the Results of the Census of the Population, 1947*, Suva, (n. d.). Data for other atolls: United States Navy Department, *Report on the Administration of the Trust Territory of the Pacific Islands, for the Period July 1, 1948 to June 30, 1949*, Washington (D.C.), 1949.

ONOTOA[2]

This largest atoll in the study lies in the southern Gilberts, an area subject to periodic droughts. When a dry spell extends beyond one or two years, the coconut trees, mainstay of Onotoan economy, cease to produce nuts and toddy. Without the abundant reserves of fish and shellfish the islanders could not have survived. Fruit of pandanus trees constitutes the third staple of importance. In normal years when rainfall averages forty inches, breadfruit may also be had from trees carefully planted and tended in the habitation areas. Settlements are located on the three largest of the atoll's seven islands, which line the eastern and southern margins of the twelve-mile-long lagoon. Inland on the principal islands Onotoans have for centuries maintained deep pits, laboriously excavated and composted, for cultivating Cyrtosperma, whose roots yield starch. This *babai* seems to have greater significance, however, in social exchanges than as a food resource.

Traditional working units are the household (*mwenga*) and the extended family (*kainga*). These kin groups formerly lived directly on lands belonging to their members. This meant a more dispersed distribution of the population than exists today, when, with urging from the Administration, Onotoans live in seven villages of from 150 to 300 persons. Women, as co-operating members of a kin group, tend the children, prepare all food, engage in reef fishing, and make matting and leaf skirts. Men's contribution to the common effort includes canoe and house building, lagoon and deep-sea fishing from canoes, maintenance of *babai* pits, collection of fish traps and fish ponds. Food, as available, is gathered only to meet current needs. More than that, as when an excess

[2] Principal sources for Onotoa summary: A. H. Banner and J. E. Randall, *Preliminary Report on Marine Biology Study of Onotoa Atoll, Gilbert Islands*, Atoll Research Bulletin 13 (1952); René Catala, *Report on the Gilbert Islands*, Atoll Research Bulletin 59 (1957); Ward Goodenough, "A Problem in Malayo-Polynesian Social Organization," *American Anthropologist* 57 (1955):71–83; Arthur Grimble, *The Migrations of a Pandanus People*, Polynesian Society Memoir 12 (1933–34); H. C. and H. E. Maude, "Adoption in the Gilbert Islands," *Journal of the Polynesian Society* 40 (1931):225–35; E. T. Moul, *Preliminary Report on the Flora of Onotoa Atoll, Gilbert Islands*, Atoll Research Bulletin 57 (1957).

results from the seasonal harvest of pandanus, is preserved and stored against future emergencies.

The daily consumption pattern mainly concerns the household and extended family, the units responsible for production. On special occasions, presents of food and various artifacts may be exchanged by family groups. Visitors are entitled to hospitality in material needs by reference to kinship ties, however attenuated these may be. Food in larger quantities is shared by many families when they convene for feasting in the *maneaba,* or communal meetinghouse. Certain foods, such as *babai,* pigs, pond fish, and porpoises, will then be added to the usual fare, although normally they are of secondary importance in the subsistence economy.

The Onotoan is basically dependent on his land and defends his title with great vigour. Real property is defined as parcels of land and associated *babai* pits and fish ponds, as well as offshore reef and lagoon areas. Rights to property are normally inherited from either parent, although sons receive preference, especially the eldest. Use of inherited resources is restricted by the individual's subordination to interests of his kin group. Trespass by outsiders is punishable by extreme action of the owner.

One type of landowning group is the *kainga,* an extended family in which membership is based on parental residence. Since a man usually raises his family on his father's land, children are more likely to belong to their male parent's *kainga.* This group controls a number of land plots and functions mainly in economic production and in social exchanges. It normally comprises several households (*mwenga*), although in-marrying spouses are not included. Each *kainga* recognizes certain totems and food tabus. Leadership is determined patrilineally.

Another social unit associated with land is the *bwoti.* Each *bwoti* tends to be congruent with a particular *kainga,* if patrilocal residence and patrilineal inheritance rules have been practiced. Members of a *bwoti* are descended from the same ancestor and possess rights in common to certain parcels of land once owned by their progenitor. They also share a named sitting place in the communal meetinghouse. Composition of the *bwoti* is not affected by residence practices since it is strictly a consanguineal group.

Suprafamilial authority on Onotoa is exercised within the *maneaba.* Here all elements of the community have a right to be heard through their *bwoti* representative. Discussion in the *mane-aba* is controlled by a group of old men (*unimani*), chosen for their superior knowledge and wisdom. These elders have the support of public opinion in interpreting the right of any man to speak in public meeting. This support is strengthened by popular belief in supernatural sanctions extended to decisions of the old men.

ARNO[3]

Arno appears in striking contrast with Onotoa. The atoll, located within the climatically favoured southern Marshalls, receives about 150 inches of rainfall well distributed throughout the year. Such humid conditions favour rapid plant growth. The food economy, therefore, is well founded on the ever-provident coconut, extensive reserves of seasonally maturing breadfruit and pandanus, and supplemental stocks of arrowroot. Cyrtosperma (*iaraj*) is cultivated only halfheartedly and is of little consequence economically or otherwise. This abundance of food is the more remarkable because Arno's total land area, approximately the same as that of Onotoa, is fragmented into at least one hundred separate islets. Only eighteen of these are large enough for permanent habitation. Arno's lagoon, on the other hand, is more than six times the size of Onotoa's, and with the many miles of fringing reef provides an almost inexhaustible supply of sea food.

The principal co-operative work unit on Arno is the household, or complex of related households, that occupies a single, named land parcel (*wato*). Each *wato,* usually about four or five acres, crosses the island from lagoon to ocean and encompasses a complete range of plant resources. Households, scattered as they tend to be, are part of settlements which are normally defined by an island's borders. Such settlements average about fifty persons, although in a few instances this number exceeds 150. Large work parties are sometimes organized for enterprises such as house

[3] Principal sources for Arno summary: R. W. Hiatt, *Marine Zoology Study of Arno Atoll, Marshall Islands,* Atoll Research Bulletin 4 (1951); Leonard Mason, *Anthropology-Geography Study of Arno Atoll, Marshall Islands,* Atoll Research Bulletin 10 (1952), also unpublished field notes, 1950; E. L. Stone, Jr., *The Agriculture of Arno Atoll, Marshall Islands,* Atoll Research Bulletin 6 (1951).

building or fishing surrounds, and include unrelated neighbors as well as kinsmen. Women traditionally tend the children, cook all food for daily consumption, aid the men sporadically in reef fishing, and fashion mats and clothing from pandanus leaf fiber. Men are the only ones who work with wood, fish from canoes, plant food crops, and harvest the yield of same. On the large islands men devote some of their time to the maintenance of *iaraj* pits. Both sexes contribute labour to the preservation of seasonal surpluses of breadfruit, pandanus, and arrowroot.

As on Onotoa, members of an Arno household or extended family share the produce of their co-operative labour. Similarly, both atolls feature exchanges of food and other artifacts as gifts in celebration of certain life crises. On Arno, only marriage is not ceremonially recognized as it is in the Gilberts. No communal meetinghouses exist on Arno, and public feasting is therefore conducted on the land of the host group. At such times, the daily fare is abundantly supplemented with food preserves and with pigs and chickens raised for this purpose. The further distribution of produce is carried out within the context of tributary obligations of commoners, working on the land, to their overlords, who enjoy upper-class status.

Land is power, and access to land reflects status in a system of ranked authority. Trees and other crops go with the land, but (in contrast with Onotoa) adjoining reefs and lagoon areas are not restricted. Property rights are inherited only from the mother and must be shared with certain matrilineal relatives. This matrilineage (*bwij*) is the basic unit in land matters. Members of this group are lineally descended from the same woman, who lived within the memory of the oldest generation. Marriage is forbidden within the *bwij*, and thus a man is always "stranger" to his wife's kin. Although residence after marriage is generally matrilocal, circumstances permit a woman to follow her husband. The head of each lineage is an elderly male who is called *alab*. He is empowered to direct the economic labors of all persons resident on *bwij* lands, even those individuals who came to the land by marriage or adoption.

Workers on the land, having inherited only usufruct rights, belong to the lower class (*kajur*). Above them are the *iroij,* an upper class that enjoys the benefits of controlled worker production. At the top of the authority pyramid is the paramount chief (*iroij-lablab*), head of the lineage that holds exclusive rights of ownership to the land of Arno. Certain lineages close to the royal *bwij* have *bwirak* rank and are regarded as upper class. A special group of commoners (*atok*), raised by royal favour to a kind of *bwirak* privilege, aid the chief in supervising the *alabs* of worker lineages.

The upper class is served in all things by the lowly *kajur:* food, manufactures, water transport, and war service (in pre-European times rival chieftains settled their territorial claims in battle). Life and liberty of the commoner are by tradition subject to the will of the *iroij*, whose behaviour is sanctioned by popular belief in supernatural power vested in the elite. Special foods are reserved by tabu for use of the *iroij*, and first fruits harvested in season are borne with dignity to the chief's house. In past decades, before the *iroij* power had been curtailed by foreign administrations, the high-born reciprocated *kajur* support by leading them in defense of their lands, providing relief to victims of typhoon and tidal wave, and generally maintaining order when interfamilial disputes among their subjects threatened to disrupt community life.

MOKIL[4]

A disastrous typhoon in the 1770s severely damaged the land resources of this smallest atoll of our study and drastically reduced its population. However, Mokil lies in the same climatic zone as Arno, and its annual rainfall of one hundred inches has permitted a remarkable recovery. Agriculture is the mainstay of this eastern Carolines community. The most dependable crop is Cyrtosperma (*mweng*), which is grown mainly in a swampy depression on Karlap, the largest island. Everywhere on the three islands of Mokil are the useful coconut trees, interspersed in more fertile places by stands of breadfruit, which is highly prized locally as food but

[4] Principal sources for Mokil summary: Conrad Bentzen, *Land and Livelihood on Mokil, Part II*, C.I.M.A. Report No. 25, Washington (D.C.) (1949); Raymond Murphy, "The Economic Geography of a Micronesian Atoll," *Annals, Association of American Geographers* 40 (1950):58–83; J. E. Weckler, "Adoption on Mokil," *American Anthropologist* 55 (1953): 555–68; J. E. Weckler, *Land and Livelihood on Mokil, Part I*, C.I.M.A. Report No. 11, Washington (D.C.) (1949).

is limited by its seasonal habits of production. Pandanus trees are common enough, though Mokilese value them more for the fiber of their leaves than for the fruit. Despite the atoll's favoured location, the extremely small areas of Mokil's lagoon and islands present a serious economic handicap. It is the abundant wealth of vast reefs around the islands and of the sea beyond that spells the difference between starvation and security.

The entire population resides on Karlap in a compact settlement between the *mweng* swamp and lagoon. Here the basic social and economic unit is the extended family (*paneyney*). Each family centers its activities in its canoe house, located near a long rock wall with canoe ramps that edges the shore. Nearby are thatched cook huts and sleeping shelters. Women of the *paneyney* prepare food, make thatch and mats from pandanus, and help their men with reef fishing, *mweng* cultivation, and collection of plant materials on the main island. Excess breadfruit in season is preserved and stored in pits for use in later months. Men are responsible for heavier work, such as excavation of *mweng* pits, repair of the boat pier, and house and canoe building. They also spend much time in trolling for deep-sea tuna and bonito, and periodically they visit Urak and Manton Islands for supplements of food and fiber. Surplus fishes are kept alive in storage wells deep in the lagoon wall. Tasks which may require more manpower than one *paneyney* can muster are undertaken by reciprocal arrangements between related families.

The one substantial meal daily is taken in the evening, and consists of fish and *mweng* or whatever is in season. Smaller units of an extended family may eat independently, although often the total membership congregates about a common oven. Informal exchanges of food occur continuously among the various *paneyneys* and constitute the principal means of distribution in the atoll. If some family is short of a certain product its request to another group with more ample supply is freely granted, except that *mweng* tends to be hoarded within a *paneyney* because of the very considerable labour spent in its cultivation. Co-operative work parties are given food by *paneyneys,* who compete for the prestige of supplying a bounteous repast, but workers generally take the food home with them when their labour is ended. Visitors to the atoll are given provisions by their Mokilese kinsmen during their sojourn. Another method of distribution is the feast, such as accompanies a funeral, at which time pigs, *mweng,* green coconuts, chickens, and other valued produce are featured. Most *paneyneys* contribute to these "feasts," though actually little or no consumption of food takes place. The main activity of participants consists of bringing prepared food to the festive place, dividing it among those present, and later carrying it away in baskets to be eaten at home.

Prior to the destructive typhoon noted above, all products of land and sea appear to have been the property of an atoll chief known by the title of Nanau. First fruits of the season were presented to him for blessing before the rest of the crop could be harvested. Other produce was gathered freely by one and all (except that *mweng* pits were closely administered) and its distribution was controlled by the Nanau. In the half century before the copra trade was established in 1875, Mokilese are said to have been able to produce a comfortable surplus, sufficient at least to barter frequently with whalers who stopped at Mokil.

Individual holdings in the open land planted with coconut and other tree crops and in the *mweng* gardens are usually inherited from one's father. Rights to plant *mweng* on another's land may be granted, but the owner can reclaim the property after the tenant has harvested his crop. Exploitation of these land strips is ultimately controlled by the head of the patrilineal *paneyney.* The status of each *paneyney* depends on the collective land wealth of its members. Although earlier some form of communalism under the Nanau was apparently practiced, a new system of tenure was evolved after the typhoon. Only three *paneyneys,* less than thirty persons, survived that disaster. All land was then divided among the three families, with individual holdings designated within each group. The properties of each *paneyney,* scattered though they may be over all three islands of Mokil, tend to be maintained as a unit from one generation to the next. An eldest son succeeds his father or paternal uncle as head of the *paneyney,* and, since he receives the major share of the inheritance, is able to exercise authority over the use of resources on holdings of his close kinsmen. New *paneyneys* are created by fission of expanding membership accompanied by division of the land. Small parcels of *paneyney* land are transferred as dowry for out-marrying females, who are expected to join their husband's *paneyney* and need some form of security in the male-dominated group. *Mweng* land is particularly useful as dowry, because, even though it passes to the *paneyney* of the groom, the woman has the right to plant and harvest a crop of her own.

In public meetings, held on the main island, any male adult is privileged to speak his mind freely, but more respect is given to the words of *paneyney* heads. However, it is the atoll chief, the Nanau, who administers the debate. Although he has less to do with organization of production and distribution than in the era before the typhoon, he plays an important role in the maintenance of community peace and security. Here, though, is none of the social class privilege associated with the authoritarian *iroij* on Arno. The atmosphere is more like that on Onotoa, but with the difference that the titled chief of Mokil is replaced by the Onotoan council of old men.

LUKUNOR[5]

Lukunor Atoll is one of the Mortlock group in the central Carolines. Its twenty islands add up to only one fifth of the land area of Onotoa, although its lagoon compares quite favourably. Located in the same latitude as Mokil and Arno, Lukunor receives sufficient rainfall to insure steady production of Cyrtosperma (*pula*). On the larger islands bush areas yield an abundance of coconuts, breadfruit, and pandanus (the last is planted mainly for its leaf). *Pula* is always available as food, though it is quickly abandoned when the more desirable breadfruit comes into production from May to September. The main island, named Lukunor, supports slightly more than half of the atoll's population, the rest living on Oneop Island across the lagoon on the leeward side. The principal center of *pula* cultivation is the seventeen acres of rich swampland in the interior of Lukunor Island. However, this island is less favoured with regard

[5] Principal sources for Lukunor summary: John L. Fischer, *The Eastern Carolines*, New Haven, Human Relations Area Files, 1957; Augustin Krämer, "Inseln um Truk," Vol. 6(1), Series II-B, G. Thilenius (ed.), *Ergebnisse der Südsee-Expedition 1908–1910*, Hamburg, 1932; Bert Tolerton and Jerome Rauch, *Social Organization, Land Tenure, and Subsistence Economy of Lukunor, Nomoi Islands*, C.I.M.A. Report No. 26, Washington (D.C.) (1950).

to marine food, since its windward setting hinders deep-sea fishing during the trade-wind period. Its residents then have to depend upon reef and lagoon, or trade their surplus *pula* for fish from Oneop.

On Lukunor the basic work group is the extended family. Its core is the lineage and it usually comprises several primary families. Thatched sleeping houses and associated cook huts are located in random manner on lineage lands near the lagoon. Men of a household spend much time in the *pula* gardens, often working alone. This is a very prestigeful occupation and demands both skillful and arduous application. Men are almost exclusively responsible for fishing, an activity that is permeated with magic and ritual as if to surmount the uncertainty of this source of food. Prior to a fishing expedition, men must be continent and therefore retire to the clan's clubhouse to sleep. Male members of a lineage, sometimes of an entire clan, work together on such projects as house or canoe building, thatching the massive men's house that dominates the dwellings of constituent lineages, fishing drives, and clearing of land they own in common. A man may have assistance from his wife when collecting plant food. Actually, a wife contributes little to food production, even in the net fishing she does on the reef. Her main jobs are child care, cooking of food, and manufacture of mats, baskets, and loom-woven textiles.

Lukunor folk say that plant food should be balanced against fish. Distribution of food within and between lineal kin groups converts this value into practice. Property rights are structured so as to provide resources for meeting socially defined obligations. Productive holdings include portions of *pula* swamp, strips of tree land, sections of reef, and lagoon locations for fish traps. Named building sites are the ancestral loci of matrilineal clans (*ainang*) and matrilocal lineages (*mwala*). Although land is owned collectively by such lineal relatives, usufruct rights adhere to individual members, and the trees a man plants are his own. In addition to properties transmitted for generations through the female line, some lands are the subject of frequent interlineage exchange. When marriage is consummated by birth of a child, the father's *mwala* presents fish and land to the mother's *mwala* in return for cooked taro or breadfruit and other land. By rule of exogamy the lineage of mother and child is always different from the father's. The resulting relationship (*ofokur*) commits the maternal lineage of the child to certain services, and reciprocally, the father's lineage is expected to transfer additional land to the child when he grows up. Unrelated *mwalas* may exchange food and other wealth in competitive feasts in which each attempts to acquire prestige through material display.

Every lineage and clan has an administrative head who is normally succeeded by a younger brother or a sister's son. In each clan its several *mwalas* are ranked according to their distance from the senior lineage. Heads of junior *mwalas* dutifully present first fruits to the clan chief (*samol-en-fel,* chief of the clan men's-house, *fel*). Further, clans within each of Lukunor's independent districts are ranked in traditional order of their settlement. In the principal district, for example, clan heads periodically bring tribute to the chief of the Sor clan, the first to occupy land there. This practice is recognition of gifts of land made originally by the Sor ancestor. As district chief, better known as *makal,* he administers his Sor kinsmen by the rights and obligations that pertain within the *ainang,* and he rules the districts at large by reason of his prestige and association with superior ancestral spirits. Because of his supposed descent from heavenly beings, avoidance as well as respect and obedience are the lot of one of *makal* status. In his inability to mingle freely with his subjects, he is assisted by his sons and his sisters' husbands in supervising annual harvests, placing tabus on resources to be conserved, and initiating dances and other ceremonial activities.

The district chief on Lukunor is more powerful than the paramount chief of Mokil, and his subordinates are ranked more elaborately than the *paneyney* heads of the latter atoll. The administrative superstructure, however, lacks the temporal authority and cohesiveness of social class that set the *iroij* apart from *kajur* on Arno. The special privilege of Lukunor's highest office is dependent in the last analysis on the interaction of clan and lineage members within an extremely involved system requiring constant exchange of food and other property.

IFALUK[6]

One of the far-flung Woleai group of atolls in the west-central Carolines, Ifaluk is remarkably small and has only four islands. The entire population lives on two large islands, Falarik and Falalap, in more than a score of homesteads spotted along the lagoon shore in the lee of the land. A heavy and well-distributed rainfall insures against drought. The islands are thickly planted with coconut and breadfruit, the latter in season producing sufficient to become the principal food and to allow pit preservation of a sizable surplus. In the off-season Ifaluk's productive center shifts to the immense swampy depression in the interior of Falalap where Cyrtosperma (*pulax*) is cultivated assiduously. This abundance of the land, normally restricted only by the labour supply, is threatened from time to time by typhoons, which are more frequent here than to the eastward. An investment of years of work may be wiped out in a few hours by wind and salt water. The small areas of reef and lagoon have been exploited to the limits of reasoned conservation with the aid of varied fishing techniques. Deep-sea trolling from canoes for bonito and tuna is carried on whenever surface conditions permit, but the catch is unpredictable.

The most common co-operating unit on Ifaluk is a matrilocal household, a cluster of smaller families bound to one cooking place and directed by the senior female and her husband. Men sometimes form larger work groups, coming together from several households associated with a single canoe house. Here friendship and neighborliness complement kinship as the labour tie. As a rule, fishing is a man's job, and then he avoids female associations for magical reasons. Men plant trees and collect their products, including coconut toddy. They are the builders of canoes and of houses and do other work in wood and shell. Women's work revolves about the home and the *pulax* gardens (from the latter, men are excluded entirely). Women cook and preserve food,

[6] Principal sources for Ifaluk summary: Marston Bates and Donald Abbott, *Coral Island, Portrait of an Atoll,* New York, Charles Scribner's Sons, 1958; Edwin G. Burrows and Melford E. Spiro, *An Atoll Culture, Ethnography of Ifaluk in the Central Carolines,* New Haven, Human Relations Area Files, 1953.

watch over the children, plait mats, sails, and baskets from pandanus (and thatch from coconut leaf), weave cloth from banana and hibiscus fibers, and at low tide wade over the reefs, collecting shellfish. In more communal activities male participation predominates and women supply only supplementary service, such as cooking food for the workers. Such enterprises are generally organized within one or another of Ifaluk's four districts and are supervised by one of the chiefs.

Each household is self-sufficient because use rights to all types of productive land are vested in its membership. The catch from communal fish drives, a principal source of marine food, is always divided among households represented in the enterprise. Exchanges between households are less likely to be made in goods than in labour. Only small gifts are presented at funerals and to formalize adoption or marriage. Every man, since he lives matrilocally, is obligated to serve two households, that of his wife and her children and that of his sisters and their children. Practically no gifts or services are rendered to Ifaluk's chiefs, but for generations token goods have been sent as offerings to chiefly lineages on Yap. Every two or three years a canoe from Ifaluk joins others from the Woleai atolls, all bearing coconut oil, rope, mats, and fiber loincloths to intermediaries at Ulithi Atoll, in return for which they are given various food products, bamboo, red turmeric, and combs.

Ifalukians are divided among eight exogamous matrilineal clans (*kainang*) which provide for inheritance of chiefly titles but have no other economic significance. In each clan are several ranked lineages. These are the landowning groups whose members share a named house site and other parcels of land. This lineage is not formally conceptualized but is the core of the matrilocal household. In-marrying spouses are not admitted to its membership, but the ghosts of recently deceased lineal ancestors are included. The senior lineages in four of the *kainangs* carry the chiefly titles of Ifaluk, the relative importance of each title signifying the rank of the clan. The main islands are divided into four districts (*gapilam*), each of which is controlled by one of the chiefs (*tamol*). Reef and lagoon areas are the property of a district, and therefore fishing parties from the canoe houses are directed by the appropriate *tamol*. In matters of community interest the chiefs act together and conduct their deliberations in a large men's-house (*fannap*) near the southern end of Falarik. The *fannap* and land around it are highly respected and constitute the most conspicuous symbol of rank on the atoll. Ifalukians detour the vicinity or stoop deferentially as they walk by.

To be a *tamol* is a part-time occupation. There is little to distinguish him from the common man. The *tamol* of highest rank does have the exclusive right to butcher the sea turtle, most of the meat being given to his clan relatives. Yet young people intermarry freely without regard for clan rank, observing only clan exogamy. As a group the chiefs form no social class, since their titled status is defined individually. They have no forceful means to support their orders and have to depend on their prestige and personality. They claim no divinity. Direction of religious ceremonial is the responsibility of a priest whose position comes to him from his father.

In Ifalukian society personal rank is highly valued but is manifested only on formal occasions. Here, on this atoll, suprafamilial authority appears to be only a little more elaborated than on Mokil or Onotoa.

ULITHI[7]

This farthest-west atoll of the series lies between Ifaluk and Yap in the western Carolines. A quite irregularly shaped atoll, Ulithi has more than thirty islands, nine of which were inhabited prior to this century. In land area it exceeds Lukunor, and its lagoon is the largest in the Carolines. Rainfall amounts to 120 inches annually. Coconut is very important in the economy, plantings of this tree being more than ample. Breadfruit, though highly prized as a food, yields barely enough for immediate use during the latter weeks of the monsoon season. The chief source of plant food is the gardens on Falalop, Mogmog, and Asor, where true taro (*ioth*) and Cyrtosperma (*bwolokh*) are both carefully cultivated. These two, with the sweet potato (*komoti*), introduced in 1850, give some protection against famine after a typhoon. In

[7] Principal sources for Ulithi summary: William A. Lessa, *The Ethnography of Ulithi Atoll*, C.I.M.A. Report No. 28, Los Angeles (1950); William A. Lessa, "Ulithi and the Outer Native World," *American Anthropologist* 52 (1950):27–52.

1907, however, the atoll's population was nearly halved by death and emigration following a most destructive blow. Fish is the main meat source as on other atolls, but even the large lagoon and abundant reefs of Ulithi do not guarantee a steady supply of marine food.

Most work is carried on at the level of the nuclear family, to which a few relatives may be added. Residence after marriage is patrilocal. Although a dozen persons may sleep under one roof, the average is much less. Women of the family usually work as individuals, yet often in the company of others, at gardening, reef gathering, and production of mats, baskets, and fiber cloth. Men's work, more frequently co-operative, includes canoe and house building, fishing, and collection of fruit and toddy. Sedentary tasks such as netmaking are undertaken by males in the social atmosphere of their canoe houses. A few families or as many as a hundred people may constitute a village (*hapelam*), restricted in area to an entire island or a part of it. In the community are brought together in daily contact many unrelated persons. Communal working parties are organized by a council of elders, one for men and one for women, for fishing drives, communal house building, visits to smaller islands for supplemental food, fiber, and wood, and (for women) sailmaking for ocean canoes and communal house thatching. No food is prepared for the workers on these larger projects. Labour is valued for its own sake, even the councilors setting an example for others by their active participation in productive work.

Constant circulation of produce occurs within the family circle and between kin groups in a community-wide system of mutual obligations that is more social than economic. Birth, puberty, marriage, and death are publicly ceremonialized by large gifts of food from the families most immediately concerned, and the invited village participates in their consumption. Twice a year the women of a village present cooked plant food to the men; the latter, weeks later, reciprocate with the catch from a communal fishing expedition. Every household contributes labour on these occasions and receives a share when the men's council divides the food in front of the men's house (*metalefal*). Daily consumption of edibles is carried out by groups of related persons from several households. This larger kin aggregate leads us to consideration of the basic unit in Ulithian social structure, the matrilineal lineage (*hailang*). Descended from a remembered female ancestor, each *hailang* is identified with certain landholdings scattered over the island and with a traditional house site in the village, all bearing the same name.

Every lineage on Ulithi belongs to one or another of six land districts. Bush and village land as well as taro gardens and fishing areas in the lagoon make up the district. It is headed by a chief (*tamol*) who is also leader of the senior lineage. Out of respect for his title and its implied right of eminent domain other lineages in the district bring him offerings of first fruits (breadfruit, first coconuts after a typhoon). This food is divided by the men's council and redistributed among the lineages. No further tribute is demanded of the "tenants." The *tamol* appears to have little or no formal authority in land matters, for lineages engaging in disputes over property are expected to work out their differences by themselves.

Landholdings in reality are owned by individual *hailangs* and are maintained by matrilineal inheritance. Plots of land are assigned in usufruct to smaller segments of the *hailang* (taro land is held only by individual women) who work the soil as their own. The lineage headman (*mal*) and the oldest female (*fefel*) administer the economic and other activities of their sex and represent the kin group in the two village councils. Usufruct rights may be transferred by members to other members, to sons or wives of males of the group, even to unrelated persons, but only after the headman has given his permission. In such transfers the lineage retains its rights of ownership for as long as it survives.

Land ownership is believed by Ulithians to rest in the final analysis with more than a score of patrilineal lineages (*tabinauw*) in the Gagil district on Yap. The relationship (*sawei*) is not that of tenant and owner but is symbolized in appropriate kinship terminology. Yapese are "father" to their Ulithian "children," and both parties behave accordingly. Each year the senior *hailang* of a *sawei* district on Ulithi (these are different from the land districts described earlier) transmits certain goods to the Yapese *tabinauw* with which it traditionally is paired. These gifts are accompanied by religious offerings (*mepel*) to the ancestral ghosts of the parent lineage. Ulithian visitors to Yap are received like children and their needs are met. When they return to Ulithi their canoes are loaded with additional goods, generally things which are scarce or lacking on Ulithi. In like manner, Ulithian *hailangs* act as "father" to certain matrilineal groups in the Woleai region to the east. This relationship, however, is much less formal and rather tenuous. The total effect of these exchanges, though not conducted for material reward, nonetheless plays a significant role in Ulithian economic security.

On Ulithi a political authority higher than the village council rests with the chiefs of eight ranked districts. Each district consists of one or more islands and is headed by the eldest male of the area's senior lineage. Apportionment of the atoll in these terms differs from that which pertains to land ownership or *sawei* exchange with Yapese lineages. The head of the ranking political district is paramount chief of Ulithi. His principal function is to take orders from the paramount chief of Gagil district on Yap and to transmit these to other atolls within the Yap "empire" and through the descending hierarchy of Ulithian district chiefs. Such orders call for tribute—fiber textiles, rope, mats, and food—from subject peoples for delivery to Gagil through the paramount chief of Ulithi. This tribute (*pitigil tamol*) is not to be confused with *sawei,* the goods which are exchanged between paired lineages of Ulithi and Yap.

District chiefs (*tamol*) exercise no local authority except within the tribute system that is oriented toward Yap. In routine affairs of the village the *tamol* defers to the head (*metang*) of the men's council. Law and order are assured by kinship obligations, public opinion, and supernatural sanctions. Relative social status depends on the individual's birth, i.e., older persons take precedence over younger, males over females, and first-born lineages over junior ones. Although Ulithians visiting their *sawei* counterparts on Yap are relegated to low caste position within the discriminatory structure of Yapese society, no caste or class distinctions are recognized among Ulithians at home. In effect, Ulithi appears to be organized as democratically as Ifaluk, Mokil, or Onotoa, with a superficial overlay of political posts because of Ulithi's role in the historically derived chain of command extending eastward from Yap.

KAPINGAMARANGI[8]

This Polynesian outlier, almost on the equator and isolated from the rest of the eastern Carolines, has the densest population in the study series. While its lagoon is moderately large, comparable to Onotoa's and Lukunor's, its total land area is small, less than Ifaluk and little more than Mokil. All thirty-three islands, only a third of them inhabited, lie on the eastern reef. Most of the population resides on the islands of Touhou and Werua. Foremost in economic importance is coconut, which grows everywhere. Next come breadfruit, heavily planted inland on larger islands, and Cyrtosperma (*puraka*) in numerous pit excavations both large and small on Werua, Hare, and several smaller islands. Pandanus is raised extensively for both fruit and leaves. With existing fishing techniques, the ecological balance of reef and lagoon environments is barely maintained. Tuna and bonito are sought with some success in the open sea beyond the passes. Kapingamarangi lies south of the typhoon belt but is subjected to severe storms with frequent damage to crops from wind and wave. More restrictive are the droughts which when extended reduce critically the supply of breadfruit and coconut. The more resistant *puraka*, together with fish, is the mainstay of existence.

On larger islands the lagoon shore is a scene of constant activity. Near the water large thatched structures shelter outrigger canoes and fishing gear. Farther back under the trees are numerous smaller buildings for sleeping, cooking, and fuel storage. Each household (*hare*, or house) includes several related nuclear families occupying as many dwellings and sharing a cookhouse and a canoe house. This group is the basic economic unit, and its members work under the direct supervision of its *taki*, or head. Women perform all work in the *puraka* gardens, preserve surplus

[8] Principal sources for Kapingamarangi summary: Kenneth P. Emory, *The Kapingamarangi People*, (in press); Te Rangi Hiroa (Peter H. Buck), *The Material Culture of Kapingamarangi*, Bernice P. Bishop Museum Bulletin 200, Honolulu (1950); Herold J. Wiens, *The Geography of Kapingamarangi Atoll in the Eastern Carolines*, Atoll Research Bulletin 48 (1956). [Editor's note: Emory's monograph was published in 1965 as *Kapingamarangi: Social and Religious Life of a Polynesian Atoll*, Bernice P. Bishop Museum Bulletin 228, Honolulu.]

breadfruit and pandanus in season, cook for the household and for male working parties, plait mats and baskets, and watch after the children. Men are responsible for all fishing, construction of canoes and houses, collection of tree food, and manufacture of bark-cloth and loom textiles for clothing. Much of their work demands co-operation, and working parties are then supervised by community leaders or by specialists. Even when their work can be done individually, men tend to gather for social intercourse in the canoe houses. Fishermen in a communal drive receive equal shares of the catch. At the close of day all members of a household are again united when they eat together in the open near the cook-house.

Another important social unit is the extended family, or *hakahitinana,* which differs from a household in that the former includes out-marrying sons and daughters but excludes adopted children and spouses. As a corporate body this group inherits rights to land and other property. Its members gather in the event of illness or death within the family. It functions at time of marriage in the exchange of gifts and the provision of food for public feasting. When two persons marry they may live with either parental group and thereafter shift residence from time to time. The *hakahitinana* is not a unilinear descent group. Its membership includes the children of both sons and daughters. The term used actually refers to a relationship between mother and children, but the word is applied to families characterized by descent from the father as well. The head of the family is called *taki.* He functions in granting use of specific parcels to individual members, giving permission to others to use the products of family land, and naming his successor.

Family land consists of a number of named parcels which are located on one or several islands. *Puraka* plots are more precisely designated for individual inheritance, probably in view of the greater labour required for their maintenance. All land on Kapingamarangi is family-owned, except for a cult center on Touhou, two communal canoe-house sites on Touhou and Werua, and three small islands reserved for sacred use. A larger kin group than *hakahitinana* exists in the bilateral kindred (*matawawa*). All members are descended from the same though distant ancestor and trace their inheritance back to a traditional house site. Otherwise this group appears to serve no economic function.

Touhou Island is the politico-religious center of the atoll. The highest authority on Kapingamarangi rests with a high priest (*ariki*), who is charged with keeping the gods content in order to avert disaster and to insure an abundance of food and children. In the cult house (*Hereu*) the *ariki* is aided by carefully chosen attendants. If drought threatens he is held accountable and may be ousted from office. The new priest is selected in a meeting called by the secular chief. A necessary qualification for priesthood is identification as *tautonu*, as distinct from *tauihara*, both being statuses which are inherited from one's mother.

The secular chief has no title except the descriptive *tangata-e-putu-tana-herua* (he who serves his people). His position is hereditary in the male line and carries with it responsibility for knowing all genealogies and landholdings. His authority is limited, his privileges few. He is ordered by the *ariki* to initiate such communal activity as a fishing drive, and he superintends distribution of the catch. There is no intermediary between the *tangata* and the *takis* who represent the numerous family groups. The last enjoy a great deal of autonomy outside the realm of the sacred. Peace in the village is upheld largely by the weight of public approval and tabus enforced by supernatural penalties.

In Kapingamarangi we have come nearly full circle. At Onotoa, in the beginning, we viewed a community in which family groups, democratically organized, conducted their affairs with a minimum of supervision from above. Where suprafamilial authority was needed, the council of old men met with the heads of families in the communal meetinghouse. Here, on Kapingamarangi, the secular power is no greater, and supernatural controls are only organized with more formality.

PRODUCTION IN A LIMITED ENVIRONMENT

The foregoing summaries present seven Micronesian atolls as they were prior to European acculturation. Certain shared features characterize them as a cultural type. Small sedentary populations depend on subsistence production of tree crops and Cyrtosperma, supplemented by fishing. Most economic effort is organized within the household. Occupational specialization occurs mainly along age and sex lines. Land rights are inherited within a consanguineal grouping, use rights being assigned to members as individuals. Community life emphasizes the interaction of kinship groupings, especially in celebration of life crises. Limited authority is extended to a hereditary chief or a council of elders. Warfare and social stratification are absent. Spirit worship and shamanistic practices provide controls for social behavior. Significant exceptions to this characterization will be discussed below.

Meggers, in reference to aboriginal peoples in South America, has suggested that "the level to which a culture can develop is dependent upon the agricultural potentiality of the environment it occupies" (1954:815). Since we are interested in the development of suprafamilial authority within marginally productive atolls, it will be worth our while to determine what possibilities, and limitations, have been established by Nature. Despite important differences among the island cultures, it is evident from our review that each population, within the limits of its technological facility, has learned to exploit its resources to the maximum. As an environmental type, the seven atolls generally are limited by small land area, soil deficiencies, poverty of plant species, a dearth of land fauna, and geographic isolation. Contrasting patterns derive principally from such variables as amount and distribution of rainfall, extent and seasonal availability of marine food, and exposure to typhoon and tidal wave.

It will not do to evaluate economic potential simply by computing averages for the above factors; in any case quantitative data for statistical comparison are lacking. Man is still an organism and as such must find his ecological niche even though his culture has given him an advantage over other biological species in adapting to environmental limitations. Liebig's Law of the Minimum, as restated by Taylor (1934:378), tells us that "the growth and functioning of an organism is dependent upon the amount of the essential environmental factor presented to it in minimal quantity during the most critical season of the year, or during the most critical year or years of a climatic cycle." Observations of atoll living bear this out. Onotoa and Kapingamarangi have undergone crippling droughts. Lack of rain for extended periods and the consequently depleted fresh-water reserve below ground kills breadfruit trees, retards coconut production, and among the Kapinga people eventually brought about the abandonment of true taro in favor of the coarser but more drought-resistant Cyrtosperma. Equally destructive in most Caroline atolls are the typhoons, which in a few hours level tree plantations of long standing. Accompanying tidal waves fill the Cyrtosperma gardens with salt water and deeply erode or completely remove the sparse soils of the low-lying islands.

According to studies of crop production in Midwestern United States, the optimum region is that in which highest average yield is combined with the smallest degree of variation, i.e., fewest crop failures (Klages, quoted in Odum 1953:34). Support for this generalization in our island sample is best illustrated from the Marshalls. The consistently humid atoll of Arno features a wide variety of economic plants, seasonal surpluses for preservation, infrequent typhoons, and no droughts. Significant in this connection is Arno's neglect of Cyrtosperma as an important food source, because this root crop is regarded everywhere in the Carolines as the principal protection against famine following a typhoon or a long dry spell. Onotoa falls at the other extreme. It has the lowest annual rainfall and besides is most liable to extended periods of even drier weather, conditions which cause the usually reliable Cyrtosperma to yield only poor and small returns.

Variability in marine resources is another critical factor in our assessment of economic potentialities. Size of lagoon, extent of reefs, access by canoe to the open sea, and seasonal variation of wind and wave patterns combine in different ways to define the relative availability of this essential source of protein. Weather conditions seem to favour the eastern atolls. Arno with its already abundant plant foods has an even more provident marine source. For the agriculturally deficient Onotoa and Mokil, however, the sea is a lifesaver. Farther westward, fishing returns appear to be less reliable, and we find that marine activities are notably permeated with an elaborate magical lore and ritualistic tabus aimed at securing more effective control of this vital source of food.

ORGANIZED PRODUCTION AND DISTRIBUTION

In economic production the organization unit is usually an extended family, household, or localized lineage, groups of perhaps ten to thirty persons bound together by heredity, marriage, and adoption. Each group enjoys use rights to all or most of the complete range of local resources, and works the landholdings under the supervision of the family headman. As a productive unit the family manifests considerable independence. Women generally require no extrafamilial assistance, since their tasks are mainly those of food preparation, child care, craftwork, and swamp gardening. The same is true of a great deal of men's work, namely tree-food collection, artifact production, and certain types of fishing. Other male activities, however, are necessarily co-operative and include house and canoe building and expeditions to exploit fishes running in schools. These larger labor forces are directed by an appropriate specialist, sometimes a chief. Here we have the first instance of suprafamilial authority.

While family groupings incline toward autonomy in productive enterprise, they are less independent in other matters. They always form part of a larger community, the settlement, which may comprise as many as 300 residents. Contacts within the settlement are nearly as frequent and personal as those observed in the extended family, since the latter interacts with others through the channels of marriage and adoption. A community of this type may rarely coincide with the entire population of an atoll, as on Mokil. Generally the settlement is only one of several within an atoll and is apt to be confined to a section of one island. At this level exists the framework for organizing some of the larger co-operative work parties noted in the preceding paragraph. Suprafamilial authority, vested in a chief or a council of elders, functions to a greater degree, as we shall see, in the distribution of goods than in their production.

The most frequent pattern of food distribution is collection by the extended family from its own properties for immediate consumption by its members. This is especially true for coconut and Cyrtosperma, which are always available, for breadfruit and pandanus in season, and for reef fish caught by one or two or three individuals. Only enough is taken for the day's needs. Seasonal surpluses of breadfruit on Arno, Mokil, Ifaluk, and Kapingamarangi, and of pandanus on Onotoa, Arno, and Kapingamarangi, are regularly converted into preserves and stored by members of a family for their future use in off-season months or as insurance in the event of famine.

The principal reason for distributing food and other goods beyond the family circle is gift exchange between kin groups in observation of the birth of a child, adoption, puberty, marriage, or death. Usually the exchange has a warm and binding quality, but in some atolls the spirit is more of competition and rivalry to outgive the other party. Generally each family has the same resources to draw upon as the next group. Reciprocity, therefore, is less economic than it is a social recognition of the respective rights and obligations of participating families. Exceptions do occur, as on Lukunor, where the residents of the main island trade Cyrtosperma for fish from Oneop Island in order to relieve chronic shortage in each area. Kin groups on Ulithi and Ifaluk through *sawei* exchange with lineages on Yap obtain desirable high-island products in return for atoll manufactures.

When numbers of men from many families engage collectively in a fish drive on the lagoon reef or an expedition at sea for bonito, large amounts of food may become available for distribution. This is where suprafamilial authority functions importantly. Having to some extent initiated or directed the project, the chief or council of elders publicly manages the division of the catch in such a way that each family in the community will receive an equal share. Ordinarily the portion for any one family does not exceed the possibility of immediate consumption. The significance of whatever share may be set aside for the chief will be discussed later.

The first-fruits ritual formalizes the special position of those in suprafamilial authority. Heads of extended families present to the chief baskets of the first breadfruit or pandanus of the season, sometimes supplemented by other products from the land. It is worth noting that Cyrtosperma, which is constantly available and requires an inordinate amount of individual labor in production, does not figure prominently on these occasions. The chief makes appropriate comments about the offerings and then, either by himself or with the aid of subordinates, redistributes most or all of the food among the families represented. This constitutes public validation of the reciprocal bond between the people and authority. Generally this tie derives support from the popular belief that the office of chief symbolizes the source of food, e.g., the land on which it was grown may have been settled originally by the chief's ancestors, and his family by tradition now exercises a nominal right of eminent domain. Presentation of first fruits does not carry the implication of rent or tribute from tenant to owner.

Tribute, properly speaking, is rendered to suprafamilial authority on Arno in the Marshalls and from the Caroline atolls of Ulithi and Ifaluk to the paramount chief of Gagil district on Yap. Not only food but manufactures of wood and fiber are presented on demand with no return gift to the producers. On Arno the tribute relation between chief and commoners is strengthened by a first-fruits ritual during which some redistribution of the food offering is made to the people. The paramount chief stands at the head of all production and distribution, and exerts a strong influence on the behavior of his subjects. On Ifaluk and Ulithi nothing is received by the people in return for the *pitigil tamol* presented to the Yap authority. The separately administered *sawei* exchange involves neither the paramount chief on Yap nor the chiefs in the atolls. Internal affairs in the low islands are supervised mainly at the village level, by the council of family heads on Ulithi and by titled chiefs with little power on Ifaluk, in a manner resembling the custom on other Caroline atolls. Arno remains the sole instance in our sample where suprafamilial authority enjoys more than a token control of production and distribution of goods.

SURPLUS PRODUCTION AND SUPRAFAMILIAL AUTHORITY

Production in the atolls is maintained primarily for two reasons: survival, and the social satisfaction which comes from gift exchange. Neither requires a surplus. Beyond that, first fruits may be offered to the office linked symbolically with a food source, e.g., land. Where possible, a small surplus is offered as payment for specialist services. Master craftsmen and fishermen, navigators, shamans, and chiefs are the principal recipients. As administrator the chief co-ordinates certain production and distribution activities and serves as arbiter in disputes between kin groups. Where surpluses are restricted by the environment, administrative specialists usually obtain no material advantage from their work. To rise above this limitation, the chief must demonstrate the value of his services to the point where the community will be willing to share its limited produce with him.

Land, the essential source of sustenance, is the key to suprafamilial authority in the atolls. With land restricted as it is, conflicts arise when dwelling and cultivation sites become crowded by increases in population. Disputed use rights within the landowning group can usually be resolved under the guidance of the family head. Between kin groups, disagreement concerning inheritance and boundaries requires the intervention of suprafamilial authority if physical strife is to be avoided. The council of family heads in atolls like Onotoa and Mokil affords an opportunity for public airing of disputes in a less disruptive manner. In other places the chief participates in the settlement proceedings according to the degree of authority vested in him. His right to do so stems either from his role as intermediary with heavenly beings whose patronage insures productivity of the land, or from a traditional relationship with the first settlers of the island. Up to a point the populace appears willing to delegate this authority to the chief, but a check on his actions is provided by informal pressure from the elders.

If the extent of suprafamilial authority depends upon surplus production and if the latter is limited by the environment, let us proceed first to arrange the seven atolls on a continuum in relation to their estimated economic potentialities. The accompanying chart is an attempt to do this in a very general and necessarily subjective fashion. The superior position of Arno is readily perceived. Ulithi and Lukunor follow, the first being more subject to typhoons, while Lukunor has a smaller lagoon and less rainfall. Mokil holds only a slight advantage over the three remaining atolls. Ifaluk is handicapped by a small land area, a small lagoon,

TABLE III

Factors Influencing Economic Potentiality in Selected Atolls

Atoll	Rainfall	Land Area	Drought	Typhoon	Lagoon
Arno	heavy	large	no	some	large
Ulithi	heavy	moderate	no	frequent	large
Lukunor	moderate	moderate	no	some	moderate
Mokil	moderate	small	no	some	small
Ifaluk	moderate	small	no	frequent	small
Kapinga	light	moderate	yes	no	moderate
Onotoa	very light	large	very much	no	moderate

and frequent typhoons. Kapingamarangi and Onotoa, in that order, are distressed by lack of rainfall and extended droughts.
Onotoa's large land area has lessened significance because the
restricting climate permits less to be done with it.

The next step is to identify those structural and functional features in each culture which reveal the extent and importance of
suprafamilial authority. Data are drawn from the atoll summaries
and are presented in Table IV.

TABLE IV

Cultural Features Identified with Suprafamilial Authority[a]

Features	Arno	Ulithi	Lukunor	Ifaluk	Kapinga	Mokil	Onotoa
Distinguished by class	X	—	—	—	—	—	—
Applies force to orders	X	—	—	—	—	—	—
Displays rank insignia	X	X	—	—	—	—	—
Restricted from working	X	X	X	—	—	—	—
Accorded un- usual respect	X	X	X	X	—	—	—
Receives first fruits	X	X[b]	X	—	—	X	—
Initiates com- munal work	X	X[c]	X	X	X	—	—
Directs commu- nal sharing	X	X[c]	X	X	X	X	X[c]

[a] Paramount chief, unless otherwise indicated.
[b] Land district chief, not political district chiefs.
[c] Council of elders.

Once more Arno and Onotoa lie at opposite ends of the continuum. Chieftainship is elaborated most in the very culture best
supported by economic abundance, and the one least endowed by
Nature is the only group in the series without chiefs. Ulithi and
Lukunor appear in the same order in both tables, after Arno. The
position of the remaining atolls (Ifaluk, Kapingamarangi, and
Mokil) in relation to each other is not the same in the two analyses, but as a group they fit similarly into the general pattern of
both. This remarkable correlation lends support to the hypothesis
that institutionalized chieftainship as a form of suprafamilial authority is directly related to the production of surplus food.

Rationalization for the relationship is shown in the frequency with which such authority functions in the distribution of food at the communal level, the initiation and direction of productive work by groups larger than the family, and the link with the land in the first-fruits ritual.

Only on Arno has chiefly power emerged relatively free of popular check. The use of force, as demonstrated in the confiscation of goods, eviction of unsatisfactory tenants from their land, and the conscription of labor for state interests, is combined with a fully developed distinction between aristocracy and commoners. Nowhere else in the atolls is feudal organization associated with warfare that is aimed at the aggressive acquisition of new lands. Onotoans are equally well known as fighters in eastern Micronesia, but their economy cannot support the luxury of a chiefly superstructure. It may be noted, however, that Gilbertese populations in the ecologically better-favored northern part of the archipelago are reported to have paramount chiefs and a tribute system not unlike those of the neighboring Marshalls (Grimble 1933–34).

WILLIAM A. LESSA

17. The Social Effects of Typhoon Ophelia (1960) on Ulithi

On November 30, 1960, Typhoon Ophelia struck Ulithi, an atoll in the southwest Pacific, leaving the island groups a mass of devastation. It was the worst tropical cyclone to strike the atoll since 1907, when a similar catastrophe laid waste the land,[1] but Ophelia differed from this earlier typhoon in being perhaps less intense in surface wind speed and much more violent in the wave action it churned up, resulting in severe damage to nearly all beaches and inundation of the interior of Falalop Island. Moreover, over half a century of change had rendered the human circumstances different.

A disaster of this kind has certain special conditions. When a rotary storm strikes a native community on a small island there is little recourse to defensive measures and no possibility of escape, and there is the danger of unlimited destruction. Immediate help from external sources is not forthcoming and in any event is not available for preventing destruction. The inhabitants have minimal control over the situation. Another special condition is that a typhoon involves a relatively short period of intense impact, followed by a post-impact period of long duration.

The enduring effects of this particular typhoon lie in the impe-

SOURCE: Reprinted from *Micronesica*, Vol. I Nos. 1 and 2 (1964), pp. 1–47, by permission of the author and publisher.

[1] The typhoon struck on March 29, 1907, and was accompanied by a tidal wave. The German government dispatched a vessel, SMS *Planet*, which arrived from Saipan on April 14 and helped in the rehabilitation of the atoll. The ship took 100 natives from Ulithi to Yap. See Reichstag, Germany, 1908:4122.

tus it gave to changes inherent in the acculturative situation. Had the people of Ulithi not hitherto been drawn into the world orbit, with inevitable consequences to its economy, political system, religion, and values, the storm would merely have created temporary dislocations without changing the *modus vivendi*. True, there would have been a severe decimation of the population due to the sudden loss of available foodstuffs, but in the precontact setting the typhoon would have been absorbed without appreciably changing the nature of the society or the culture.

This is the thesis of my analysis, and it is my intention to substantiate it with observations made before Ophelia and afterward. In 1947 and again in 1948–1949 I studied Ulithian society as it then was—relatively unchanged and unchanging. Then in the summer of 1960 I examined it largely with an eye to noting the effects of American custodianship. Finally I saw it, albeit lamentably briefly, as it was after the autumn typhoon. Opportunities of this kind rarely present themselves to the social scientist.

My return to Ulithi to study the impact of Ophelia was made at the suggestion of the Pacific Science Board and the Disaster Research Group of the National Research Council. I arrived on the atoll on January 18, 1961, in company with Charles G. Johnson of the U.S. Geological Survey in Honolulu and the late David I. Blumenstock of the U.S. Weather Bureau, also in Honolulu. They stayed seven days; I remained fourteen. The islands I visited were Mogmog, Asor, Falalop, Fassarai, and Lossau, as well as the uninhabited island of Potangeras.

BACKGROUND

Ulithi's location at 10°05′30″ N and 139°43′15″ E (on Mogmog Island) places it geographically in the Caroline Islands archipelago of Micronesia. It is 85 miles east-northeast of Yap and about 380 miles southwest of Guam. Fais, a raised island 45 miles to the east, is its nearest neighbor.

The atoll proper consists of a group of thirty-odd islands of small size, most of which are clustered around a large lagoon about 19 miles long and 10 miles wide. Only five of these islands are at present inhabited. The total land surface of the atoll is a mere

1.80 statute square miles. The largest island is Falalop, but this is only one mile long and less than that wide.[2]

Being in the doldrum belt near the equator, the atoll has that region's characteristic climatic features of heat, great cloudiness, and high humidity. The velocity of the winds varies greatly: the period from May through July is one of great calms and the rest of the year experiences intermittent trade winds. Typhoons incubate in this general area and sweep on to the Philippines, China, and Japan. Winds rather than temperatures distinguish one season from the other.

Precipitation is heavy, averaging about 120 inches a year, with a pattern of relatively dry winters and wet summers, but there is some inconsistency in this respect. Droughts do not constitute much of a threat, although owing to the porosity of the soil, water drains down through the ground by percolation; hence there can be a shortage of potable water in less than two weeks' time. Wells are few and in any event are brackish, so for their drinking water the natives depend mostly on the flow of rain off the roofs of their dwellings.

The islands are distinctly coralline, with all that this implies for limiting the growth of vegetation. They are low-lying, with a high point of only about 22 feet on Falalop island, although it should be borne in mind that many atolls elsewhere in Micronesia are perceptibly lower than this. Characteristically, the surface of individual islands is slightly higher on the shores bordering the open sea, and lower on the beaches bordering the lagoon. Ulithian villages are always built along the lagoon. Slight depressions producing a certain degree of swampiness are to be found on the islands of Falalop, Mogmog, and Mangejang, thus permitting the cultivation of certain plants that require muddy soil.

The number of cultigens supported on the atoll is relatively small. Coconut palms grow very well indeed. So do two aroids, *Alocasia macrorhiza* and *Cyrtosperma chamissonis,* but another aroid, *Colocasia esculenta* or true taro, can only be grown in special pits on certain islands. Breadfruit trees grow moderately well, as do banana plants. Three crops that were very common

[2] Technically, the island of Falalop is a separate element outside the atoll, but for all practical purposes its location makes it an integral part of it. Figure 1 does not show certain Ulithian islands east of the atoll, none of which have been inhabited at least since 1904.

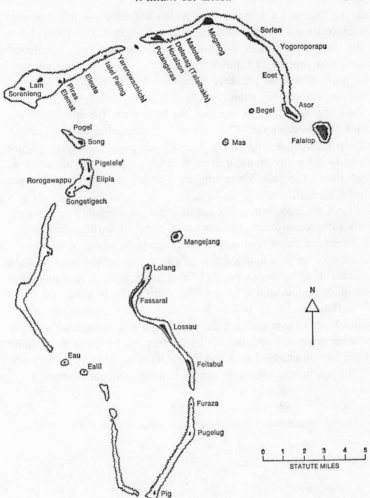

FIGURE 1. Map of Ulithi Atoll. The names of some islands are Japanese versions of Ulithian words.

and valued in the early postwar period—squash, sweet potatoes, and papayas—have for some inexplicable reason almost disappeared from the local scene, possibly through neglect, possibly from the salt spray of several typhoons during the 1950's.

Aside from the dog, which is not ordinarily eaten, the only two domesticated animals are the pig and the chicken, with an occasional cat, and a few carabao, which are very recently acquired additions used as draft animals and seemingly out of place. More pigs are needed than are now raised but there are insufficient scraps to support the number required to supply a steady source of pork. Chickens are kept in a semi-feral condition; their eggs are not customarily eaten.

Of the rodents there are only the brown rat, the small gray rat, and the house mouse. The only other mammal is the fruit bat or flying fox, eaten only rarely. Lizards are numerous and on some islands there are monitor lizards introduced by the Japanese to get rid of the rats. There are few species of land birds, but sea birds abound.

Fish, shellfish, and other sea animals are abundant and numerous in species. Such crustaceans as crabs of various species and lobsters are eaten, and so are many kinds of molluscs.

According to a detailed census that I took of the atoll in 1949 (Lessa 1955), there were 421 inhabitants, with a preponderance of older people and a masculinity ratio of 90.5 males for every 100 females. In 1960 I took another census (Lessa and Myers 1962) and discovered that the population had risen, after a steady decline since the opening of the century, to 514, the masculinity ratio having changed to 106.4. The following table (Table 1) will be of use in understanding some of the subsequent discussion.

TABLE 1

Population of Ulithi by sex and residence, July 1, 1960.

Island	M	F	T
Mogmog	86	89	175
Asor	28	31	59
Falalop	81	70	151
Fassarai	64	54	118
Lossau	6	5	11
Total	265	249	514

Obviously, such pre-existing factors as social structure, kinship, the locus of formal and informal power, work patterns, and the like are pertinent to an understanding of the impact of the disaster. They may be briefly reviewed at this point, with later elaboration when necessary to clarify the process and content of change.

The people of Ulithi constitute a very small society, with inevitable consequences for social and political organization. They are agriculturalists and fishermen, with some interest in raising chickens and pigs. Women traditionally do the gardening, cooking, weaving, and lighter work, while men do the fishing, coconut gathering, carpentry, sailing, and heavier work.

On the five inhabited islands the people live in small villages. The houses, with plank walls and roofs of plaited coconut leaves, are built on rectangular coral platforms surrounded with pebbles and sand. They are shaped in the form of an elongated hexagon, with the inside area divided by walls into several compartments.

Land is never owned privately; it belongs to lineages which parcel out plots for the use of certain kinds of land-use groups. Although most of the gardening is done by women, men nevertheless spend time in agricultural activity when they are not otherwise engaged in fishing.

Canoes are an extremely important part of the material paraphernalia of the Ulithians, being owned by lineages and used for fishing, transportation, and some recreation. Without them, activities are circumscribed and a source of food almost eliminated, for most fish are caught from them. Like all Carolinian canoes, they are unusually speedy, with outrigger and huge sail-spread.

Social organization, apart from the nuclear family, centers around matrilineal lineages which control much in the way of property, marriage, political activity, social behavior, and, formerly, religion. Each lineage has a male chief, who succeeds to his position by virtue of seniority in the group, and on his death he of course cannot be succeeded by his son, who belongs to his wife's lineage. Some chiefs function as district heads as well as lineage heads. The oldest man from a certain lineage, the Fasilus, automatically succeeds to the "kingship," an office now without great authority except in inter-island matters.

Political structure is not exactly simple. The most important everyday institution is the village council, composed of the senior men of the village, who meet frequently to decide matters of everyday concern, as well as to deliberate on questions occasionally raised concerning the whole atoll. Super-village councils are held when the need arises. Each village council is presided over by a *metang,* a kind of chairman who owes his position to his membership of a designated lineage. There is no formal mechanism by which a man becomes a council member.

The island of Yap, 85 miles to the southwest, controls a far-flung empire extending hundreds of miles to the east (Lessa 1950). It does so through chiefs in Gagil district. Ulithi is part of this domain. Yapese consider Ulithians to be low caste with respect to their own caste system, and require the payment of annual *sawei,* a kind of rent for the use of the Ulithians' own land. Ulithi is also required to contribute religious offerings and political tribute. It holds a special position in the Yapese empire in that it is superordinate to all the other islands, which must pay three-fold tribute not only to Yap but to Ulithi also. These other islands, which we may refer to as The Woleai, are low caste with respect to both Yap and Ulithi, but they are so closely related to the latter by kin, linguistic, and other ties that the relationship is a benign one. For economic reasons their relationship to Yap is often advantageous, but when the Yapese are displeased they are capable of retaliation.

Social control is chiefly through public opinion, gossip, ridicule, and other informal mechanisms. There is no law, in the strict sense. Punishment for transgressions is in the hands of one's kin group, whether the family or the lineage, although it should be noted that physical violence or chastisement is almost absent.

The native religion until recently was a kind of paganism embracing belief in celestial and terrestrial deities; in spirits of minor character but often greatly feared in everyday life; and in ancestral ghosts. In actual practice, the ancestors were the really important spirits, being protective as well as paternal in matters of behavior. When taboos were broken, punishment could come from any supernatural source in the form of illness or other misfortune.

Magic in various forms, and for many purposes, once held an important place in Ulithian life, being especially prevalent in disease, navigation, the weather, fishing, and divination. There used to be numerous part-time specialists in magic, although ordinary persons also had some knowledge of the simpler everyday rituals.

By 1960, however, the native religion has disappeared to such a degree that for all practical purposes it had been replaced by a simple Christianity. Undoubtedly, some magic, both white and black, still persists, but the old recourse to magic for divinatory, meteorological, erotic, horticultural, medical, and other ends is minimal.[3]

THE TYPHOON

An appreciable amount of information concerning the history of this cyclone and its physical effects is available from the U.S. Weather Bureau, native informants, Coast Guard personnel stationed on one of the islands, and the studies by Mr. Johnson, the geologist who accompanied me on my trip.

The *Mariners Weather Log* (U.S. Weather Bureau 1961:75) gives us the basic essentials. Ophelia started as a small LOW south of Kwajalein and as it moved westward it gradually intensified. At 1200 (GMT) on November 21 the cyclone was southwest of Eniwetok and the first tropical depression warning was issued, but soon after this warning the system began to weaken and warnings were discontinued at 0600 (GMT) on the 24th. But when the cyclone reached northwest of Truk and 300 miles southeast of Guam, warnings were resumed at 0000 (GMT) on the 27th. The depression increased to tropical storm intensity by 1800 (GMT) of that same day and to typhoon intensity by 0000 (GMT) on the 29th.

Ophelia's track followed a semi-sinusoidal pattern, and the typhoon passed directly over Ulithi at 1200, local time, on November 30. The pressure reportedly reached a minimum of 939.4 millibars, and maximum gusts attained 125 knots. Thenceforth, the typhoon took a northwest course and later a northward one, but we need not be concerned with its career after leaving the atoll except to say that it ended on December 6.

[3] One of the major magicians was the *serawi*, who was carefully trained and highly respected by the community, whom he served. He uttered lengthy incantations and defied the wind with gestures involving a spear, a triton shell, and young palm leaves. Another magician, the *tolo*, was used to subdue the waves. As he recited his spell and jabbed at the waves with a ritualistic spear, he was assisted by two men who held a rope tied around his waist to keep him from being engulfed. Specialists in the interpretation of meteorological signs portending a typhoon were called *tohomal*, and used natural clues rather than divinatory ones. They made an appeal to certain spirits, praying over a spider web. A fuller account of Ulithian culture as it existed prior to the typhoon is contained in my mimeographed report to the Pacific Science Board (Lessa 1950).

Ophelia's behavior over Ulithi can be further described from the point of view of the persons on the atoll at the time.[4]

The Coast Guard on the island of Falalop was first notified of a possible tropical disturbance two days prior to the actual typhoon. No action was taken at that time by the personnel other than to observe on a chart of the area the progress of the storm. The next day the station was notified from Guam that it was to take certain safeguarding precautions. While the personnel was engaged in this activity, the winds picked up so noticeably that the local commanding officer notified the Coast Guard section on Guam that it was going to move every last item of equipment, personal gear, and emergency rations into a concrete shelter.

The typhoon hit the following morning, November 30, sometime between 0900 and 1000, local time. The winds were from the northwest or north-northwest, and a reading on the station anemometer seemingly indicated a velocity of 70 knots. The major damage that was to be inflicted on the station took place at this time, owing to the washing away of the nearby seawall, which had been erected during the war by piling up rubble on the west side of the island. The surge of water over this part of Falalop was initially between three and four feet, and then subsided to about two feet. Many trees were downed.

During the period when the eye of the typhoon passed over the atoll, starting about 1500 or 1600 that afternoon, there was no wind and no rain, but the island of Falalop was inundated up to about two feet, at least near the station.

After the eye had passed, the winds began picking up again at about 1700, the velocity now being at its height; but the greatest damage to the station had already occurred, owing to its location on the west shoreline of the island. The anemometer reading indicated a velocity of 74 knots, but later investigation revealed that the rotor had been broken and only one cup was making it revolve. The true velocity was probably between 120 and 135 knots. Further buildings and equipment were lost or damaged, and the small airstrip was badly mauled, a good deal of it being washed away. The winds did not begin to subside until about 2200 hours that night.

[4] My chief sources of information are certain natives, especially Hathokhomar, Iamalamai, Ithuerung, and Tathokh, as well as BMC R. L. Tovani of the U.S. Coast Guard LORAN station on Falalop.

The natives did not at all expect the typhoon. Two of the villages had received no warning from the Coast Guard on Falalop, but even the three villages that had been notified were inclined to accept the threat without special anxiety because no sense of urgency had been conveyed to them. The M/V *Erroll,* a small vessel belonging to the Trust Territory, had been in the lagoon for three days and had left for Yap on November 29 without imparting any news of imminent danger. The presence of the ship proved in the end to have had disruptive effects because so many men had been preoccupied with loading copra on it that when they returned to their homes they had almost no time to take precautionary measures. As the wind began to gain in strength some canoes were pulled inland, but most could not be moved in time; nor could dwellings and canoe sheds be secured. Many families were caught with some of their members away on other islands, unable to return.

The chief measure taken to insure safety was to find shelter from flying objects, particularly from corrugated iron sheets ripped from houses and military installations still standing since World War II. When a house was threatened by winds and waves, it would be abandoned in favor of a dwelling that promised greater protection. On Mogmog the villagers had from the start been summoned to the large concrete church by the missionary, who was there at the time. On Asor the people finally retreated to the wooden church there. These two structures stood firm. On Falalop the church, which had barely been completed, was too close to shore to invite refuge, and on Fassarai the wind was not sufficiently menacing to induce the natives to turn to the church. Lossau had only four old people on the island when the hurricane struck, and they managed to find adequate shelter in one of the dwellings.

The only persons who ventured outdoors were some of the younger men, who went from house to house inquiring into the needs of the occupants and helping the aged and weak to move to places of greater safety. During the storm the people usually remained huddled, frequently praying and occasionally commenting on the wind and the wetness. A few people complained of hunger and cold.

Johnson's (MS) field examination of the geomorphology of the atoll indicates that "the major effects of Typhoon Ophelia were the erosion of the lower slopes of beaches, and the deposition of much of the detritus as boulder or sand sheets onto the island slopes of the beach ridges of the islands." Johnson notes that although water crossed some of the islands, erosion by scour action was minor and was seen on only two of the islands he investigated. He states that the net geomorphic effect of the typhoon was to heighten the islands, remove beach materials temporarily exposing the underlying beach rock, steepen temporarily the beach scarps, and slightly lengthen or shorten the ends of the islands.

The islands of Falalop, Asor, and Mogmog, and other islands at the north end of the atoll were most affected, while Fassarai, Lossau, and other islands at the south and east side were least affected.

Waves pushed seawater into the central depression of Falalop by topping the marginal ridges of the island at most points, but at no time was the entire island awash. Great changes took place at the southwest beach of the island, waves having approached from the south during and after the period of the southwest winds. Waves reached a depth of six feet over the high beach ridges south of the village. The force of the wave action can be further gauged by the fact that sand was moved inland for at least 700 feet at one point, causing several taro pits in the interior of the island to be filled.

Asor was not affected very much by the swells preceding the storm because it was protected on the east by Falalop. The greatest change was produced by the waves generated by the southwest winds of the second phase of the cyclone. The northern tip of the island was shortened by about 150 feet, with erosion taking place everywhere at the lower slopes of the beaches.

Mogmog, farthest north of the islands composing the atoll, was less damaged than Falalop and Asor; its southerly beaches were protected by the lagoon. The northern or seaward beach, which reaches up high, was eroded on its lower slopes, with the boulders and cobbles being deposited on the high beach ridge as a boulder sheet up to 100–150 feet wide.

The island of Potangeras was also examined by Johnson, who noted among other observations that the changes made on the lagoon side were less than those on Mogmog and Asor, but as on these islands, sand accumulated at the west end, increasing Potangeras' length by about 200 feet.

The largest of the southern islands, Fassarai, was not greatly affected geomorphologically because its position sheltered it from all the seas except those coming from due east.

Johnson was unable to visit Lossau, the most southerly of the inhabited islands, but I can state from my own brief visit there that the wave action was small; in fact, the sandy beach facing the lagoon seemed to be intact.

The effect of the typhoon on the ground water of the island of Falalop was studied by Johnson, who observed that the low central basin was inundated by several feet of seawater diluted to some extent by rainwater. By draining to the water table it mixed with or displaced the fresh water of the Ghyben-Herzberg lens, causing a salinity that Johnson reckons must have ranged upwards to near seawater.

After the typhoon, during the period from December 1, 1960, to January 20, 1961, 6.25 inches of rain was recorded at the LORAN station, and samples of water taken by Johnson from six wells on January 20 and from a taro pit on January 21 indicated a chloride content of from 960 ppm to 4,200 ppm, as compared to about 35,000 ppm for seawater. However, these wells have little importance for the natives, who do not depend on them. The damaging effects of salinity were therefore confined to taro pits, as far as the natives were concerned, and it is significant that the chloride content of the ground water in the lone taro pit sampled by Johnson was very high—3,790 ppm.

Circumstances did not permit a precise inventory of the damage to property created by Ophelia. However, I did come to a crude estimate through interviews and my own visual assessment, and these are presented in Table 2. I must emphasize that this table includes many approximations, although it is not without value.

Casualties were relatively slight: two small boys of the ages of nine-and-a-half and eight were killed when the house in which they were staying collapsed and pinned them down so that they were unable to flee from the huge waves coming in from the south shore of the island of Falalop. Their bodies were washed inland. Flying sheets of corrugated iron injured a man on Mogmog and another on Asor, neither injury being serious. On Falalop there were three slight injuries.

But damage to property was enormous for a population so reliant on its own limited resources. There is no doubt that without outside assistance the greater portion of the population would have

TABLE 2.

Damage to inhabited islands by Typhoon Ophelia, 1960.

Category		Mogmog	Asor	Falalop	Fassarai	Lossau	Total
Deaths		0	0	2	0	0	2
Injuries		1	1	3	0	0	5
Pigs (58):	lost	1	1	0	0	—	2
	saved	20	6	20	10	—	56
Chickens:	lost	10	4-5	most	few	few	few
	saved	most	most	few	most	most	most
Carabao (2):	saved	—	—	2	—	—	all
Dwellings (126):	destroyed	7	3	8	8	3	29
	repairable	27	12	6	13	6	64
	intact	8	6	12	4	3	33
Council houses (6):	destroyed	1	1	2	1	0	5
	repairable	0	0	0	0	1	1
Menstrual houses (7):	destroyed	1	2	2	1	1	all
Stores (4):	destroyed	1	1	1	1	—	all
Canoe houses (44):	destroyed	14	6	13	4	3	40
	repairable	0	0	0	3	0	3
	intact	0	0	0	1	0	1

Canoes (59):	destroyed	3	3	11	3	1	21
	repairable	13	2	3	4	0	22
	intact	6	2	1	4	3	16
Dispensaries (4):	destroyed	1	1	1	1	—	all
Medical supplies:	destroyed	75%	100%	100%	100%	—	75-100%
Schools (4):	destroyed	1	1	1	1	—	all
Coconut trees:	severely destroyed	20%	20%	25%	20%	15%	ca. 23%
	moderately damaged	40%	40%	50%	40%	30%	ca. 45%
	damaged	40%	40%	25%	40%	55%	ca. 32%
Taro:	destroyed	100%	100%	100%	25%	—	almost all
Other plant foods:	destroyed	<100%	<100%	<75%	>50%	?	most
Fresh water sources:	availability	moderate	moderate	moderate	moderate	moderate	moderate

perished from starvation because of the great ruin to crops and the destruction of so many of the canoes so vital to fishing.

The domesticated animals fared well. I did not make a check on Ulithi's dogs and cats, but feel confident they rode out the storm.

Damage to building structures was severe. One fourth of the houses were wrecked entirely, one half were damaged severely but repairable, and one fourth were left habitable. All the council houses, except a small one on Lossau, and all the menstrual houses, dispensaries, and schools were lost.

Well over two thirds of the outrigger canoes were completely destroyed or severely damaged; only sixteen remained operable for transportation and fishing. Falalop was hardest hit, being left with but a single canoe for about 150 people. Of the six big ocean-going canoes included in the above atoll-wide totals, one was lost, three damaged and two saved—a stroke of fortune for a people so dependent on them for making distant voyages and carrying heavy cargo.

The damage to economically useful plants varied from island to island, but some general estimates can be made. Almost all growing sources of food were either destroyed or temporarily eliminated. Coconuts were wrenched by the wind from the trees and those in mature condition were immediately laid aside for eating; but about two thirds of the trees were totally destroyed or severely damaged, with only one third left reasonably intact, except for their blossoms and nuts. Severe ocean spray, inundation by waves, and burial by sand ruined almost all the taro (*Colocasia esculenta*), which was concentrated on Falalop, Mogmog, and Asor. Other aroids, namely *Alocasia macrorhiza* and *Cyrtosperma chamissonis,* survived to a minor degree. Banana plants and breadfruit trees were rendered temporarily useless, although for the most part in a recoverable condition.

Fresh water for drinking and cooking remained available. With the considerable amount of rain coming on the heels of the storm there was an adequate supply for all villages.

Two months after the typhoon the economically useful plants that seemed to be making the quickest recovery were the *iabwuch* (*Allophylus* sp.), a tree used for food, medicine, and loom shuttles; the *iar* (*Premna integrifolia*), a tree used for leis, medicine, amulets, and firewood; and the banana. None of these has much economic value and they contribute little to the diet. Those coconut trees that had been damaged by Ophelia but not destroyed had begun to show signs of slow recovery, with the possibility that by September, 1961, some coconuts would have grown to maturity, although the prediction for a return to normalcy was two years in all—an estimate by the natives which I learned from later correspondence to have been accurate.

Leaching-out of the salt water in the taro pits had not progressed far enough in January of 1961 to permit the replanting of any crops. Part of the delay may have been due to lack of time needed for removing debris and silt.

REACTIONS UNDER STRESS

In the face of imminent danger the people of a community are emotionally agitated, but the manner in which they react is not always predictable, being dependent on the circumstances. Certainly they are jarred out of their customary routines and patterns of interaction. When the danger strikes, and after it has passed, there is a drastic alteration in behavior patterns on both the individual and societal level. The form assumed by the human experience cannot always be known in advance, but observation has taught us that certain possibilities may be looked for.

Ideally, the psychological effects of stress should be analyzed according to differential behavior among various status groups; practically, this is not possible where a population is small and relatively undifferentiated. For the most part, therefore, we shall be constrained to treat the stress reactions to Ophelia as generalized rather than individual reactions. Our attention will be devoted to community-oriented questions rather than individually-oriented ones.

Not unexpectedly, there was a diffuse kind of fear among the people, except for the children, who were generally unable to comprehend the gravity of the situation. Some of the older women confided their apprehension over the possibility of dying, although for the most part there was little verbalization of the concern that was felt by the adult portion of the population.

The effects of fear on behavior in the kind of situation with which we are dealing can be multiple in form and varied in intensity. One psychological phenomenon whose possibility immediately comes to mind in connection with disaster is shock, and it was my particular concern to explore the incidence of this reaction.

The first reference to shock came unexpectedly in the course of an interview with an intelligent young man whose nine-and-a-half-year-old son had died during the typhoon. He volunteered the information that he could recall little about the storm as it raged about him on the island of Falalop, where he huddled with his family in his dwelling on the south shore. He said it was as if he were in a dream. Questioning brought out the existence of a native term, *samawel,* for the state he felt. The term suggests a kind of paralysis, but only in the sense that one might black out from fright. Discussion with an older informant present during the interview brought out another term, *ruschealokh,* allegedly a "bigger" word for the same thing. Examples were elicited and it seemed to be borne out that both native terms refer similarly to a state of shock. Ulithians do not speculate on the mechanism producing this state.

Having been directed by my first informant to other natives whom he said had had an experience similar to his own, I interviewed the father of the other young Falalop boy who had died in the storm. This man, forty-one years old, said he had been forewarned of the typhoon, and when it struck he was told that his son, who had been staying with his adoptive parents, was missing. He wanted to go out and search but became confused out of concern for his pregnant wife, who was very ill during the storm. Moreover, his six other children were crying. He was unable to decide whether to look for his missing boy or stay and look after his wife and children. He strained to think out the best course but was unable to do anything.

A third man, also of Falalop, who was said to have been stunned was seventy-five years of age and had experienced the great storm of 1907. It is not clear from my notes when it was that he felt the state of *ruschealokh,* although he did recall taking his wife and the rest of the family to another man's house farther inland after he saw a huge wave coming up on land, followed by another. But at some point he was distinctly unable to think or act. Parenthetically, it should be remarked that at the time of the interview he felt concern that another typhoon might be brewing because the weather had not cleared up as he thought it should. His worry was evidenced by his scanning the skies each morning after he arose. He said he had lived through five bad typhoons, including not only the great one of 1907 but another going back to the time of the famous trader Captain O'Keefe during the Spanish period. One might speculate that he had been so sensitized to the dangers of typhoons that this latest one caused him to experience shock, but this is too simple an explanation, for others of his age had not had the same sensation.

Interviews with two or three other Falalop men confirmed that they too had experienced a degree of *ruschealokh,* but nothing indicated that the community as a whole underwent shock. No instances at all were reported for the other islands of the atoll. It is interesting that no women were known to have gone into shock, but this may in part reflect the fact that in this society women are not expected to show much initiative and consequently would not be put to the test as much as a man.

If that explosive psychological state, panic, overtook anyone, it has not been revealed through an examination of the interview records. Everyone, as might be expected, experienced some degree of concern, but it was not panic fear and apparently no one lost control of himself. Father William Walter, the missionary for this area, who was on Mogmog during the typhoon, says that about 175 people gathered in his church and during the storm only one eleven-year-old girl cried, demanding food and not reacting ostensibly to fright. Elsewhere in the atoll, hunger and cold similarly caused some children to cry. Some adults, too, are reported to have cried, but out of fear for the safety of the boys who had just departed on the *Erroll.* It is true that everywhere men ran from house to house shouting, but they did so deliberately and systematically. Says one informant: "Some of the men hollered because they want to take care of people in the typhoon, and maybe they say, 'Let's us go there!', and, 'Maybe I think will be safe there!', or maybe, 'This much people go to there and live [stay] there!' "

If you do not shout in a typhoon, you are apt not to make yourself heard, and if you do not move when your roof collapses or your floor is awash, you are inviting trouble. Of course, there is not much room for flight on a small island, and it would have been madness to have set out to sea. So movement could in no event have been manifested by the kind of exodus we usually associate with the word "flight." But even if we ignore the factor of distance, the fact remains that those who fled did not do so in panic.

The lack of panic may be attributed to a variety of causes, one being that in the several typhoons since the war there was always the realization that the Coast Guard station on the island of Falalop had contact with the outside world, including the Navy and Trust Territory, so that the events on Ulithi would not remain unnoticed. The presence of the missionary, with his access to both material resources and a powerful and protective God, provided further and substantial reassurance. Added to all this, the natives had experienced enough storms to realize that there was nothing to be gained from panic. Many Ulithians have expressed themselves on this matter, so my statements are not so much speculation on my part as a repetition of interview remarks.

Spontaneous leadership will of course emerge in most disasters, depending among other things on the need for leadership. During the impact period of the typhoon there was a relative absence of leadership because the situation was such that it was not needed. Self-preservation depended more on individual or family measures than on concerted action under a leader. No leader was necessary to give direction to the whole community, even in the pre-impact stage. During the storm, individuals emerged with attributes of initiative, force, and confidence. For the most part they were situational rather than institutional leaders. Their roles were limited to maintaining communication and giving directions for moving to places of safety, although their ability to take charge undoubtedly inspired calm and confidence in the rest of the people.

Leadership was more important during the period of rehabilitation, for during that time it could play a more effective role than in the impact situation when it was less vital for survival. Spontaneous leaders were as important as institutional ones even though the force of tradition tended to deny recognition of their informal status. Leadership in this phase of the disaster will, however, best be analyzed in a subsequent discussion of the effects of the storm on the social system.

The emergence of altruistic leaders was not a manifestation of the kind of diametrically opposed reactions often referred to as "polarization." It is true that under conditions of severe stress, where overwhelming danger or severe deprivation assail the individual, latent characteristics may become intensified in opposite directions, but on Ulithi the catastrophe was not seen as insurmountable. The absence of panic and the deeply ingrained feeling of responsibility toward one's kinsmen and neighbors precluded the development of unreasonable egocentrism. Conversely, the situation did not call for heroic sacrifice. People went about their business in accordance with their basic patterns of motivation, even though their responses were not uniformly conditioned by a sense of social responsibility.

The behavior of Ulithi's four psychotics under the impact of the storm has some interesting facets. I ought to preface my remarks by saying that cultural conditioning seems to be strongly reflected in psychosis on Ulithi and that the psychotics I have known do not seem to have lost complete touch with reality.[5] Of the four psychotics living in 1960, I saw and had pleasant relations with two whom I had known since 1947. A third was a blind man whom I had known only slightly in the past and who had deteriorated as he approached old age, and I sensed that the natives thought it just as well that I not see him. The fourth was a youth who was the only clearly violent psychotic I had known about, and here again it was obvious that the people were not especially anxious that I should meet him, although I had seen him when he was a boy.

The subject of the behavior of the psychotics during the storm was volunteered by a reliable informant, leading me to feel that his remarks were prompted by a conviction that here was something of special merit for my study. Another good informant corroborated and enlarged upon his observations.

It appears that during the storm a sudden improvement was seen in Mai, a thirty-three-year-old man.[6] In the wet church where the people of Mogmog were huddled against the wind and rain he acted quietly and rationally—praying, inquiring about the weather, acting solicitously toward the women and children, and showing no signs of aggression. The first informant comments: "After the typhoon I saw Mai working hard and also help people for their work [on their] house, and going to fishing. And he eat with people and also once a while he came to each family and ask how they are. He's been all right." The other informant imparted the in-

[5] One young man who used to experience manic periods knew well enough, when passing by my house outside the village proper, to pause in his shouts of defiance and pass by quietly, only to start up again when at a little distance beyond. This was in 1947–1949. The strong hand of conformity shows itself in many ways on psychotics, who are treated almost as if they were normals, although of course the people know the difference and never misapply the term *bwuch,* which is used to designate them.

[6] He is the man alluded to in note 5.

formation that Mai had only twice "hollered" since the typhoon, and had done so with some restraint, in his own house instead of in the village as he customarily did. He had become a hard worker in the ranks of the men's work groups, and begun to carry on conversations. No one claimed that he had rid himself of his dementia, but obviously it was felt that the shock of the storm had had a salutary effect.

Improvement of a gradual rather than a quick nature appeared in Iourmar, an older man of fifty-seven. When I had first known him in 1947 he had appeared outwardly rational and very friendly, but soon after that, while I was gone, he had had a sudden collapse, and when I saw him in 1948 he was pale, immobile, and withdrawn, hardly recognizing me. In 1960, before the storm, I again saw him after a lapse of several years and he had so improved that he was active in the community. Iourmar's behaviour during the crisis itself was even more lucid and cooperative. He helped other people. He prayed, and unlike a few people who said the typhoon was a punishment sent by God for the people's misconduct, he made no attempt to place the blame. During the post-impact period he gradually slipped back in the direction of his former but improved condition, once again becoming highly critical of the way people did their work and making bungling efforts to correct it. His recovery, then, was not sustained.[7]

The blind old psychotic, Iakhomo, living on Fassarai was moved during the storm to a certain house for safety, and then he steadfastly refused to leave it when the others with him took refuge elsewhere. Although he had shown some violence about four years previously, during the crisis he was merely recalcitrant. He insisted on meeting the storm in his own way, alone, and apparently emerged from it none the worse for the experience. No enduring improvement in his condition was reported.

The only truly dangerous psychotic in the atoll had in 1949 at the age of eighteen killed two men on the island of Asor with a carbine left behind by American troops after the war. Up to then,

[7] It is interesting that Iourmar was one of a party of six men who lost their way in an effort to sail eastward to nearby Fais in April, 1963, and eventually landed almost a thousand miles westward on the island of Samar in the Philippines. It is noteworthy that he was even taken along on the trip, on which a much younger kinsman served as the navigator. Apparently Iourmar emerged none the worse for the harrowing six weeks at sea. For an account of the voyage, see Boykin 1963.

no one within living memory had ever been murdered on Ulithi. The unfortunate young man had been taken away for treatment and then had been returned to his family when it was realized that his case was hopeless. On Asor he was always dangerous and was kept in a barred hut, but during the storm he was removed and taken by his sturdy brother to his father's house as a protection against the typhoon. No one fled from him but the children were nevertheless afraid. He told everyone to pray. He showed no fear of the typhoon and was fairly quiet. He asked for food and tobacco, which was given him by his brother. His mollification did not persist, however, for after the crisis he reverted to his old condition.

Thus the typhoon served as a kind of shock therapy, being unevenly beneficial and unevenly enduring.

No apparent increase in sex activity, marital or otherwise, took place as a result of the disaster. In their anxieties and pressures there apparently had been no effort by the people to turn to sexual outlets. One informant attributed this to the weariness experienced from the hard work of rehabilitation. There may have been a practical deterrent, too, for the storm removed much of the protective concealment in the form of trees and shrubs needed by clandestine lovers for their nocturnal encounters.

Reference has been made to the question of blame for the storm, but the nature of the disaster precluded the encouragement of blaming. In the old days one could always attribute the storm to the machinations of the Yapese. The currently accepted view that typhoons are natural phenomena left no place for scapegoating; at most there was a diffuse feeling that God might be punishing the people for their sins. It would have been easy to blame the Coast Guard for not having provided more positive assurance that a major storm was impending, but apparently no one thought that their troubles lay in this direction, especially since it was obvious to everyone that the Coast Guard itself had been taken by surprise despite some earlier radio warnings from Guam.

One might expect that the typhoon, coming on the heels of two severe tropical cyclones in 1953 and 1958, with lesser ones before and after, would have prompted some desire for relocation. Inquiry brought out the fact that a few people had indeed spoken loosely about moving to Yap, Palau, or Saipan, and even the Philippines —the last being remembered with fondness by Ulithians who had on several occasions been canoewrecked there—but such talk quickly died down. It was mostly the younger men who had thought of the possibility of leaving, preferably to a place where they felt they would be welcomed by the inhabitants. The older men and women did not wish to bestir themselves. It is interesting that in 1948, when I tried to ascertain if any sentiment prevailed for resettlement in a place where there was a greater abundance of land, food, facilities, and opportunities, it appeared that the younger people were willing, provided the entire population left in a body. Similar questioning after the storm made it clear that the people did not wish to budge. I was not able to establish if the events of the ensuing dozen years had given them a glimpse of the outer world that was not altogether rosy, or if the typhoon had drawn them closer to their cherished homeland. A combination of these two alternatives as well as others is of course possible. Ulithians have often expressed to me a sentimental pride in their islands, and I cannot help but feel that the typhoon caused them to rally around their land rather than abandon it.

THE ACCELERATION OF INCIPIENT CHANGES

Interesting as the psychological consequences of Typhoon Ophelia may be, its greater importance lies in the field of social and cultural dynamics. The storm did not initiate change as much as it accelerated processes already under way. Most likely if there had been no acculturative influences or contacts with the outside world, the disaster would have had little effect in altering the existing way of life. In a system essentially closed in character the condition of equilibrium to which the society would tend to return would be essentially the old one. Direct data are not at hand to test this assumption against the consequences of the great typhoon of 1907, but there is every reason to believe that aside from the relocation at that time of some of the inhabitants to other islands, there was no introduction of new elements and therefore no achievement of a new type of homeostatic condition. Ophelia disturbed a system that now was no longer closed—a system already off balance by virtue of its enmeshment with the great world beyond the seas. The catastrophe increased the imbalance and dictated that any return to a state of equilibrium or near-equilibrium would have to be on a different level.

The shattering of the atoll's isolation had at first been trivial, then moderate, and finally rapid and irrevocable, as a brief survey of the history of contact will reveal.

Early European explorers arrived in the western Carolines over four centuries ago, and it may be that Ulithi was discovered either in 1525 or 1543. Except for an ill-fated mission established on the atoll in 1731 and wiped out six months later, there was virtually no contact with the outside world until the last century. The extent of cultural influence on the people of the atoll was minimal. During the German administration of the Caroline Islands from 1899 to 1914 there was still only weak influence, but somewhat more when the Japanese took over in the latter year. Yet even then the natives were left much to their own devices until the arrival of the American armed forces in September, 1944. In a year's time more than one million men passed through Ulithi, which had become a secret advance base for the invasion of Okinawa and the Philippines. The isolation of the island was shattered severely and dramatically, yet there was little contact between the people and the military personnel because of a deliberate governmental policy of protective segregation. Thus the population was saved from being overwhelmed. After the withdrawal of the military a LORAN station was left behind, operating until 1952 on the island of Potangeras, and since 1949 a Jesuit American missionary, Father William Walter, has made his headquarters on the atoll (but he spends much of his time visiting other islands of the west central Carolines).

The acculturative process, which had been relatively slow during the Spanish, German, and Japanese regimes, gathered great momentum only after World War II. The typhoon did not so much introduce change as speed up and consolidate what already had been initiated.

The most obvious indications of acculturation are ordinarily seen in the material items adopted by a native population, and so we may start with them. They are overt and scarcely open to the kind of conjecture necessary in dealing with ideologies, values, and other imponderables. Moreover, on Ulithi they were innovations that for the most part had been deliberately and consciously embraced, whereas economic, political, and other social changes had come about almost unwittingly, despite the reverberations they were destined to cause.

In precontact Ulithi the clothing of the people had been fairly scant. Men had worn loincloths woven out of banana fibers on a true loom. Starting with German and Japanese contact, but especially after the United States took over the administration of the atoll, cotton loincloths had largely but not entirely replaced the native ones. Women had worn no more than a brief wraparound skirt woven out of a mixture of hibiscus and banana fibers. This was kept in place with a belt, usually constructed with much care out of hundreds of small beads carved from coconut and sea shells. Up to the time of the typhoon, no woman beyond her early 'teens had worn a skirt made of the foreigner's cloth, although occasionally women would wear a skirt woven on a native loom but employing nylon threads. Prepubertal girls were still wearing "grass" skirts made of shredded coconut leaves, but it was becoming increasingly common for such children to adopt a simple cotton cloth wraparound, held in place by a twist of the upper border.

Almost furtively both men and women had begun after the war to drape a shirt of cotton cloth over their shoulders when out at sea in a canoe and exposed to the sun and wind. While stopping at uninhabited islands they would often cover themselves in the same way and for the same reasons, with the additional incentive of protecting themselves against mosquitoes. But it was forbidden for anyone—man, woman, or child—to wear an upper garment while in a village. There undoubtedly was a growing recognition that the foreigner's garments and cloth had their advantages but no one was willing to concede that an open break should be made with tradition. The prestige and at the same time the unacceptibility of Western clothing was brought home to me in 1948 when two young men who had just returned to Ulithi after a period of schooling on Guam asked to have their photos taken wearing their shirts, ties, trousers, belts, and shoes. It was necessary to retire to an isolated spot on the island of Mogmog to take the pictures. Although the older people of the atoll would not permit open capitulation in matters of dress, they had already begun to breach tradition when away from the villages. The king himself set the example. He seemed to relish the military shirts he donned at sea.

The incipient use of clothing was not at all inspired by growing modesty, for the missionaries had never deprecated the native dress and certainly not encouraged the belief that it was indecent for women to expose their upper bodies. Women have always attended Mass wearing no more than their customary wraparounds. Protection, then, has been most responsible for the trend toward Western clothing, and to it must be added the desire to emulate the prestigious foreigner, who is seen in his full splendor in magazines and the occasional motion pictures viewed by the natives.

After the typhoon the women are said to have petitioned the chiefs to be allowed to wear an upper covering.[8] Perhaps this was not a complete innovation, for apparently in old times a covering in the form of a pandanus cape was sometimes employed by men and perhaps women. The argument used by the women was that since most of the trees and virtually all of the leaves had been blown down, they could find no shelter from the sun while working outdoors, particularly in the moving of debris, the digging of pits, and other work connected with rehabilitation. The chiefs quickly gave their assent. It does not take too much to suppose that the people were already on the verge of open flaunting of the old standards and that this provided an easy justification for the transition. And so, six weeks after the typhoon, young women and old ones alike were wearing whatever shirt or cloth they could lay their hands upon, and in this respect had available some upper garments that had been obtained largely through the local missionary. Men now began to wear shoes and trousers without feeling guilt.

A process that otherwise might have been slow and painful thus suddenly became quick and easy. The grass skirt now disappeared among young girls in favor of cotton wraparounds. Women continued to wear their woven fiber skirts, but I can report that among some gifts I received from Ulithi in 1963 there was not, for the first time, a single skirt of hibiscus or banana fiber; all had been woven

[8] There is some disagreement as to whether the women actually requested permission to wear shirts. Coast Guard personnel maintain that they were told King Malefich had given his consent, but in view of his virtual withdrawal from the community the story does not ring true. One of my most reliable informants says it is his feeling that after the storm some of the more prestigeful members of the men's council on Mogmog began wearing hats and otherwise breaking with tradition within the village limits, and that other people, including women, took this as a cue. I am inclined to accept this explanation, for although it is possible that the events on Falalop were as depicted by the men at the LORAN station, anything happening on Mogmog, the "capital" of the atoll, would most likely give sanction to changes elsewhere.

out of nylon threads. It requires no clairvoyance to predict that it will not be too long before the native loom falls into disuse. Should it do so, it would release women from a good deal of time spent in preparing fibers and laboriously weaving them.

Hats had never been worn by Ulithians except when outside the village, although ethnohistorical sources do indicate that in the past an umbrella-shaped pandanus covering for the head had been worn. After World War II some of the younger men would occasionally don a European hat to protect themselves, as they explained, from the sun; but again I feel that the hat was prized more as a symbol of Westernization than as a source of shade, for it was seldom that a man lacking a Western hat would bother to make a substitute out of palm leaves, which can be done with ease.

Suddenly, after the typhoon, both men and women began to wear whatever European-style hats were available. In keeping with the spirit of things, the young children now began to wear palm leaf hats, although adults continued to avoid such hats even when they would have been their only means of protection. Palm leaf hats are, admittedly, bulky and cumbersome, yet, if the need for shade had been as pressing as the natives maintained, they ought to have been more common; after all, together with pandanus hats they had served Ulithians and other South Sea Islanders for centuries.

The traditional barefootedness persisted until shortly after the war, when on rare occasion a man could be seen wearing a pair of military shoes while walking on the reef. In the course of time, some of the younger men who had been on Palau, Yap, and other centers of American influence began sporadically to wear Japanese sandals or zoris, made of rubber. Now suddenly with the typhoon such footgear became almost *de rigueur,* owing partly to the increased danger from rusty nails and corrugated iron and partly to the discomfort from walking on the gravel and coral rubble that had been churned up in unaccustomed places. Under the old conditions the soles of the feet were tough enough to withstand any threatened laceration or abrasion, so one is led to wonder if the already established trend had not received an impetus from the desire to emulate the foreigner.

The native-style hut had persisted without change for centuries, but when I first visited the atoll in 1947 some inroads had already been made. This was especially true of the island of Falalop, and the way this came about is interesting. A disaster in the form of a firebombing of the native village by American planes in 1944 had leveled many houses, and in rebuilding, the people had adopted a crude bungalow-like rectangular design that bore little resemblance to the traditional hexagonal hut. To what extent they had been influenced by Japanese or other outside influences I cannot say. Even the island's two new council houses, rebuilt after the fire, though retaining some flavor of the Ulithian style, had nevertheless for the first time used milled lumber, nails, corrugated iron, and paint. Elsewhere in the atoll the changeover was slow. After the American forces had left Ulithi in 1946, abandoning a good many supplies, the natives took every opportunity to roof both their old and new houses with the abundant corrugated iron that had been left behind. The change was slow because there had been virtually no damage from the war. When I made a survey in 1948 of all the dwelling structures on the island of Mogmog twenty-four were of basic Carolinian design and sixteen were partly or entirely of the Westernized style; but when I revisited the same island in 1960 virtually every new house that had been built during the ensuing twelve years had capitulated to the new trend. Traditionalism, then, had succumbed with hardly a struggle even before the typhoon.

The tropical cyclone blew down most of the houses, old and modern alike, and when the population began to occupy itself with the reconstruction of new shelters, it turned out that the native design had been abandoned for good. All recent houses have iron roofs and are built in a rectangular rather than hexagonal shape. They are no longer built on stone platforms, although many are raised on piles for protection against ground moisture. Admittedly, the materials brought in by the government and the missionary are all of European type, but there is no doubt that enduring seeds of change had been planted long before. The natives are of the conviction that their traditional houses do not have the strength, efficiency, and comfort of the new ones, so they willingly embrace the change. However, I am not entirely sure that the old houses did not have some special merits, especially in their utilization of local materials. One of the main drawbacks was that it took so long to build them. It may well be that the typhoon proved the strength of concrete in the eyes of the natives, for the two concrete-block churches built by Father Walter withstood the wind and floods.

After the storm there was an expressed desire on the part of the people, the government, and the missionary to exploit the possibility of building with concrete.

Ophelia hastened what will be a permanent change in dietary characteristics. During the war when the American forces were in Ulithi there had been a temporary but significant alteration in the diet. The natives had been kept alive largely through military rations, so they had already experienced some of the changes that were to come later. But for a large part of the period when the Americans occupied Ulithi, most of the able-bodied men were on Yap, having been forcibly moved there by the Japanese to work on military installations. A number of Ulithian students had also been stranded on Yap during the war. Thus the new foods of the Americans had not been available to a large segment of the population. Moreover, children born after the war had not seen much of this kind of food because military rations were no longer being dispensed. However, trading ships offered some continuity, and in addition those young men either working at the local LORAN station or staying at government installations on other islands of the Carolines were able to experience a new diet.

But habituation to new foods was by no means the result of the military period alone. Rice had already been introduced by at least the time of the Japanese regime and was especially familiar to boys who had gone to Japanese schools on Yap. Well after the war flour had been introduced, apparently having been encouraged by the local missionary. By the summer of 1960 corned beef and such other canned foods as tuna, sardines, and evaporated milk had become popular. Soda drinks, although expensive, were purchased when possible, adding free sugar to the diet.

Refined sugar had steadily gained in importance over the postwar years; in fact, by 1960 it was painfully obvious that it had brought about an appalling incidence of dental decay among a people whose teeth I had examined in 1947 and found to be singularly free of caries. The postwar use of sugar found application in a variety of ways, of which the most pernicious from the point of view of health was in the manufacture of a beverage called *fifi*. Traditionally, *fifi*, which is a drink consumed daily in large quantities by children and adults alike, uses a coconut sap base to which various herbs and other plants are added. Ulithians claim that it is their main food. But the important thing is that nowadays sugar has largely replaced this palm toddy as the basic ingredient.

By 1960 sugar had also come to have widespread use in sweetening bread. It was being used as a frequent substitute for fresh palm toddy in preserving leftover foods, in making a kind of coconut candy, and in taking the bitterness out of aroids, breadfruit, and *iabwuch (Allophyllus* sp.). Three or four years previously it had come to be used in a newly manufactured alcoholic beverage called *habwolokh,* or "yeast" (one of its ingredients), which, however, was not so popular as fermented palm toddy. Even though the natives were paying seventeen cents a pound for sugar, they eagerly sought it, largely because it saved considerable time as compared with the procurement of palm toddy.

Now, suddenly, as a result of the typhoon virtually all traditional foods were denied the people and they had to depend on the foreigners' foods, to which they of course had already become somewhat accustomed. A few days after the storm the M/V *Erroll* arrived with 290 cases of "C" rations from military stores on Guam. These contained canned meat stews, sugar, candy, coffee or chocolate, chewing gum, cigarettes, and biscuits. At the same time the ship left sixty 100-lb. sacks of rice, twenty-seven 60-lb. sacks of sugar, and twelve 50-lb. sacks of flour. Evaporated milk for babies had become common after the war; now it was being imported, along with dried milk, in increasingly large amounts.

Undoubtedly, this impact on the diet could not be sustained at its original pitch. Many natives came to express some distaste for the new foods, particularly the military rations, and yearned for the coconuts, aroids, breadfruit, and fish that pleased their palates. To some extent their appetites were soothed by the importation, largely through missionary efforts, of traditional foods from nearby Yap.

There can be no doubt, however, that permanent changes have taken place, and rice, sugar, flour, condensed milk, canned meats and canned fish have found a wider usage than ever. For the first time coffee became a beverage through its introduction in the "C" rations. Natives have expressed a liking for this drink and it most likely will remain. This would be a minor blessing if it replaced toddy, either sweet or fermented; unfortunately, however, a good deal of sugar is stirred into it.

Eating in traditional commensal units was temporarily suspended by Ophelia. Customarily, even though a nuclear family may be domiciled under one roof, its members may eat separately in other units. In 1948 I ascertained that in the village of Mogmog there were twenty-six commensal units averaging 5.2 persons in each group. The composition of these units varied from complete nuclear families to mixed and extended families, with occasional non-relatives included. As soon as the storm subsided, the natives gathered together what food supplies they could muster. For about a week, on Mogmog at least, they would assemble as one community in front of the church and partake of their meals in common. There was no hoarding or effort to conceal supplies; instead, cooperative sharing dominated the consumption of food. After a week had passed, the people reverted to the old eating patterns, for by this time sufficient supplies had begun to arrive from outside sources.

Less objectively identifiable than the foregoing are the effects of the typhoon in the economic and social spheres. It can be stated from the outset that certain social institutions either underwent little or no change as a result of the storm, or at least were not susceptible to detection in the two-month period following the disaster. For instance, there is nothing to show that the family and lineage systems underwent immediate change, as indeed they had not to any appreciable extent previously, despite the impingement of the outside world. The system of land tenure, enormously complex, remained steadfast, despite the fact that forces had long ago been set in motion that must inevitably transform its character. Patterns of social control were in some respects superficially changed for the moment but gave no indication of being transformed.

Since it is with change rather than stability that we are concerned, we ought to turn to this aspect of our survey, and a fruitful way to begin is by considering what Ophelia did in the economic sphere.

Traditionally, goods within the atoll had always been distributed through gift and ritualistic exchange, and outside the atoll barter had customarily been resorted to in addition to these methods. Cash began to make an appearance during the Japanese administration, although even then and for several years after the war it was never used within the community, except occasionally, as in the purchase of a pig. Most income came from the sale of copra, with a trickle coming in from the sale of handicrafts and employment with American governmental and military units. A great and sudden increase resulted from the collecting of trochus (*Trochus niloticus,* Linné), a mother-of-pearl shell of value in the manufacture of buttons. This happened in 1956, after the local missionary announced to the people that the shells were present on the reef and should be sold to traders. Trochus had been seeded several years before by the Japanese, who had never had the opportunity to return to gather the shells. The foreign goods that were in demand were rice, canned meats and fish, tools, textiles, kerosene, matches, flashlights, soap, dyes, fishline and fishhooks. A great impetus to the use of cash in the community came about when local stores were set up about 1956 on Mogmog, Asor, Falalop, and Fassarai. Money was sometimes used when a person wanted to rent a canoe to transport his copra. By 1960 Ulithians were using cash to purchase canoes from other islands, and it appears probable that some occasional selling of canoes was taking place within the atoll itself. In addition to all this, the people were making sporadic purchases from Guam and the United States through the good offices of the missionary and Coast Guard personnel.

All these stores were wiped out by the storm, but it is easy to see that they had become so deeply entrenched in the economic structure that nothing could stop their reappearance. They had become not only a symbol of change but an instrument as well. The storm dramatized the importance and indispensability of the local stores in the new order of things, and if they had not been reinstituted by February of 1961, it was only because there had not been time to do so.

A digression into the origin and subsequent history of the stores is not without interest and will help make clear the role they will play in the future. A forerunner was set up in 1945 at the instigation of the Navy medical officer who was staying on Fassarai to look after the people of the atoll who had been placed there. It was designed to assist the natives in selling their handicrafts to the military personnel who visited there once a week. Afterward, owing to the conservatism of the king, all efforts on the part of the Trust Territory to induce the natives to maintain stores failed. On January 3, 1949, for example, an atoll-wide meeting of the chiefs was held on Mogmog to consider the invitation of the Trust Territory to institute local stores. My advice was sought, and although

I endeavored to show the advantages and disadvantages of the idea, it was apparent that the traditionalist elements resisted the proposal. No action was taken. After Wegelemar, the king, died on September 26, 1953, new efforts to institute stores succeeded, the first one being opened on Mogmog around 1954. It was owned by about a dozen or more "stockholders" who had accumulated enough capital through the sale of copra. The chief of the island headed the company, and two storekeepers took turns in conducting sales at sporadic hours. Prices were set by the Island Trading Company, a government-operated firm which sold merchandise to the store. Other goods were acquired through the kindness of the missionary and Coast Guard personnel, and other means. Sales were excellent, with profits varying between ten and fifteen percent. In time, however, some suspicion of dishonesty arose. Later, the islands of Asor, Falalop, and Fassarai started their own stores. The two on Asor and Falalop were cooperatively owned and were successful and the one on Fassarai that had been established along the lines of the one on Mogmog ran into much difficulty and mistrust. Eventually, Mogmog gave up its privately owned store and replaced it with a cooperative one, which in 1960 was operating in a highly satisfactory manner, having accumulated about $2,000 in profits for its sixty-odd owners, who constitute the adult male population. The cooperatives apparently solved the two problems of profit and honesty, probably because they fit into the strong pattern of community cooperation that had always been a dominant characteristic of the society.

The adjustment that Ulithians have made to cash purchasing in these stores has necessitated an alteration in native values and patterns of exchange. There is general agreement, even among the older people, that the stores permit wares to be more readily available and more varied than heretofore, and at the same time have ended the long delays and shortages attendant upon direct purchases from the infrequent ships that stop briefly to pick up local copra. In 1960 there was a move to supplant the private Yap Trading Company, which had replaced the government Island Trading Company, with a Ulithian organization that would make it possible to make direct purchases from Guam and thus eliminate the profits of the Yapese middlemen.

The typhoon merely stopped temporarily a development that the storm itself could only accelerate by creating a shortage of goods. The demand for replacement of supplies lost in the wind and water became acute, and at the same time pointed up the need for a local retail outlet that would expedite purchasing. The typhoon gave the new stores, once they could come into being, an opportunity, owing to new needs, to stock a greater variety of goods. Overcoming the objections of the conservatives, the younger men had already by 1960 been very successful in their introduction of such new items as scissors, knives, penknives, watches, cigarette lighters, and carpentry tools. These young managers could now take advantage of a fluid situation further to implement their policy of providing any goods that might be in demand.

Another effect of the trend away from the native system of exchange and toward the new cash economy was in the alteration of old work rhythms. The urge for money constrained the natives to employ greater speed and energy in all their work activities, thus reducing the time for lounging about in the canoe sheds and council houses. An amusing example of the new spirit was the pronouncement of the chief of Mogmog that the women of that island must return home sooner from the menstrual houses after their periods had terminated. (Women often spent an inordinate amount of time there.) Contrasting the situation in 1947 with that in 1960, one could readily observe that the manufacture of copra had suddenly become an energetically pursued activity rather than a desultory one, with large kin groups hacking away and gouging at an unaccustomed pace. Some of the older men complained about the frenetic tempo that had begun to push aside the leisurely attitudes of the past, wondering out loud if it were at all worth while.

The traditional role of women in the economy was conspicuously altered by the new economic order. In the summer of 1960, before the storm, I made specific observations on this score. The most obvious change was the active participation of women in the manufacture of copra. Indeed, on one island four women were each operating alone, and even though two of them were married, none of them worked as part of a family team, as had been customary. Each sold her copra directly to the trading company and received payment for herself. The husbands of these women seemed to be content with the arrangement and made no complaints about any possible neglect of their spouses' domestic responsibilities. We can assume that any cash acquired in this fashion went into the family pool, but it is nevertheless interesting that a certain degree of independence must have resulted from the women's enterprise.

Women had also begun to turn to other cash-producing activities. They found it especially lucrative to gather the trochus, a valuable income-producing shell. Unmarried women rather than married ones took up the fishing. Mostly the shells were collected on the reefs, but some women undertook to dive down deep for them, always separated from the men, however, for reasons of modesty. Women had also turned to the making of handicrafts for sale to the Yap Trading Company, the Coast Guard, and occasional visitors. The motivation behind all this was always the desire to purchase trade goods, especially after the local stores had opened and made items at once available; it had nothing to do with any drive for female emancipation.

The new striving for money helped produce changed attitudes toward sharing. By 1960 the great force of kinship had already been diminished to the extent that people questioned their obligation to support individuals who were lazy and therefore unproductive. A trend toward advancing the interest of the nuclear family had begun to develop, although it would be a mistake to suppose this had been brought about by economic factors alone.

Another effect of the drive for cash was the creation of inequalities in wealth hitherto suppressed by kinship patterns. The ability of some men to accumulate more cash than others through the manufacture of copra and the gathering of trochus became readily apparent. Actually, most men worked in cooperative economic groups of no fixed composition, and they divided their incomes; but it is nevertheless true that some men showed an ability to participate more actively than others, and these were the ones who had gained a reputation for being better off than others.

Still another effect was to heighten the value of land. The traditional system of land tenure does not allow individual ownership of land but it does convey usufruct tenure to men and women. With coconuts in greater demand than before, efforts to control parcels of land became greater than ever, with disputes increasing noticeably.

There is an obvious circularity in the whole process of acquiring cash. Ulithians work for money to enable them to purchase trade goods. This withdraws them from their customary economy so that they reduce their usual fishing, gardening, weaving, and other economic pursuits, thus creating a vacuum which can be filled by purchasing foreign goods, and so on and on. Having been drawn irrevocably into the world orbit, the natives now have a suddenly increased commitment to extend changes that some of the older folk had already begun to view with misgivings. At any rate, when the typhoon struck it hit an island community that had already taken more than the first tentative steps toward a new economy. And the way in which the natives dealt with the storm reflected many of the changes that had taken place in recent years.

These, then, were some of the economic changes that were underway at the time the typhoon roared in from the east, and it seems apparent that they were hastened perceptibly by it.

After the storm, women began to do unaccustomed heavy work —digging, chopping, hauling, and even carpentering. Somewhat clumsy in their efforts, and obviously unused to such sustained exertion, they nevertheless showed considerable zest in the restoration of their lands and reconstruction of their houses. To the younger women, this activity was something of a pleasurable game, but whatever their motives, both they and the more mature women cast aside the restraints of centuries and often put some of the men to shame with their doggedness. No doubt to a large extent they had been conditioned by their recent entry into the manufacture of copra and the collecting of trochus shells, but the typhoon broke wide open what had hitherto been a modest incursion into new avenues of activity. One used to seeing Ulithian women, seemingly glued to the ground after reaching adulthood, never again to arise, could not help but be astonished at seeing them on their feet in the performance of their work.

The work of the women was part of a larger, unprecedented plan in which three kinds of fatigue parties, composed separately of men, women, and children, gave their services to the community for three days of the week. Communal labor has always been traditional on Ulithi but the uses to which it was now being put after the typhoon were novel. The plan had been deliberately conceived by some of the younger men and had found widespread acceptance. Children for the first time performed labor, and were made to look upon their contribution as not only a useful obligation but a sport. The atmosphere in which everyone worked was characterized by a gaiety never before manifested so openly, unless it was at the group dances. Singing, chanting, and laughing were exercised without the usual restraints of propriety. Pre-existing hostility patterns could not help but be repressed in the pervading spirit of *camaraderie*.

Some of the new work patterns are probably among the more evanescent of the changes wrought by Ophelia. With the reestablishment of orderliness, the re-building of shelter, and the return of gardening and fishing, children will undoubtedly have reverted to their old carefree days, although it is possible that their new-found energies may be directed toward helping in the making of copra, an activity in which they had already begun to play a small part. Women will have returned to the less strenuous aspects of the daily round, but again there is the possibility that they will direct their new emancipation toward intensification of their cash-producing activities. The obligation for adults to donate three days of labor a week for the common good will by now have vanished into thin air, without implying, however, that the private and the community labor parties of tradition will be abandoned. Most likely the force of tradition will cause a return to some of the decorum of the past, with children especially being enjoined from shouting and racing through the villages; yet it is probable that a less restrained atmosphere during work will henceforth prevail through the society.

One effect of the storm on the economy—a changing agricultural procedure—had not had time to manifest itself by 1961, but there can be no doubt that impetus was given to a better conceived and implemented agricultural improvement program. Since the advent of the American administration, and to a lesser extent that of the Japanese before it, efforts had been made on the part of the government agriculturists to improve the variety and yield of the local plant crops. It is doubtful that these had ever had more than superficial effect. When, after the typhoon, the Trust Territory administration sent in a special agricultural advisor and he remained for some weeks, returning again at a later time, he naturally was in a better position to provide more specific, detailed advice than had previously been available from either the Yap administrative district or the central administration on Guam. This agriculturalist planned a systematic revision that without doubt must by now not only have helped in recovery but produced a lasting imprint on the nature and quality of the crops.

A partial realignment of political power resulted from the disaster. The political structure and hierarchy of authority prevalent for centuries had been perceptibly altered under the German and Japanese administrations, although the changes were principally in external relationships, especially in the necessary accommodation to foreign authority and the concomitant weakening of the bonds to Yap. Internally, the form and function of the native political system had not undergone great change, unless it was in the prestige of the king, who now no longer enjoyed the kind of support he had formerly enjoyed when paganism held full sway.

To appreciate the nature of the changes to come it is necessary to review the traditional system. Each Ulithian village has a council of elders made up of men who are close to middle age or older. Men are admitted to membership in a completely informal way, the only implicit criteria for membership aside from age being a reasonable sense of responsibility and degree of intelligence. Those who are excluded, again aside from age, sense that they are not encouraged and so refrain from attending council meetings except as observers sitting discreetly in the background. Young men accept the fact that power is in the hands of the elders and do not particularly resent the situation.

With the typhoon, informal leadership dramatically encroached on the formal authority of the men's council. During the storm itself, younger men took a good deal of initiative in supervising aid and organizing evacuations. After the storm it was again young men who showed the way to reconstruction and rehabilitation. The older men seemed to accept and even welcome the assistance of the younger ones, especially since it was felt that the new generation was wiser in the ways of the outside world on which so much reliance was now being placed, especially in providing material assistance. Thus an old pattern became weakened. To the credit of the younger men it should be pointed out that they assumed their authority with great tact and little disturbance. They continued to show the traditional deference required toward older people. But when for the first time they began to speak up in council meetings, as I observed in 1961, it was obvious that an old order was passing for good. New criteria, only superficially reflecting youth but in reality fashioned ultimately by experience with the outside world and all that this implies, are forcing the change. In addition I would suggest that younger men, with their preoccupation with copra-making and trochus-fishing, have attained an overall economic position that cannot help but be reflected in the council meetings.

The typhoon did much to lessen the authority of the reigning king, Malefich. To understand how this came about it is necessary to understand the background of his assumption to office. When the former king, Wegelemar, died in 1953 there was for the first time an inclination to depart from the traditional line of succession to the position, which was filled by the oldest competent member of the Fasilus lineage. The old man who technically headed the lineage had pleaded to be released from his obligation on the grounds that he felt incapable of meeting the exigencies of the office. His lineage mate, Malefich, was next in line but similarly begged off. As a consequence, a man who was highly respected for his navigational skills and general competence, but belonging to another lineage, was selected by an inner circle of elders, and he agreed somewhat reluctantly to assume the position. But at the last moment, before the decision could be communicated to Yap for approval by the Gagil chiefs, Malefich had a change of heart and agreed to become king after all. The previously selected candidate, who was a pagan, retired gracefully.

Malefich was weak from the start, and in 1960 it could be observed that his authority had long before been taken over by the old *metang* on Mogmog. When the typhoon came raging over the island, Malefich showed considerable ineptness. At this time the old *metang* was hospitalized on Yap, but a high chief on Falalop, where Malefich lived, became the de facto king, at least as far as that island was concerned. This man, named Mara and belonging to the Limat lineage, was the one with whom the Coast Guard and other authorities came to deal. Fairly young at forty-one years of age, he showed quiet confidence and initiative, contrasting markedly with the king, who was conveniently indisposed after the storm with an infected foot and went into virtual seclusion.

Thus, it can be seen that prior to the typhoon the first tentative steps away from the traditional succession to the kingship had been taken, but the typhoon, with its demand for vigorous and effective leadership, forever shattered the notion that the heads of the atoll had to be drawn from the Fasilus lineage.

A somewhat parallel replacement of a de jure chief by a de

facto one took place a few years ago on the island of Asor, where the head of the village had become so functionless, through senility and ineptitude, that a man in his thirties took over his responsibilities. The acting chief admittedly belongs to the same lineage as the retired one, but he is not next in the line of succession. However, he is a man of some force and intelligence, and as a youth not only attended Japanese schools on Yap but acted as a canteen clerk there. In 1961 the acting chief had solid authority on his island, undoubtedly due in part to his ability to command the situation during and after the storm. This example reinforces the view that a new type of person is needed to hold political office.

Although the storm did not strike all communities equally, there can be no doubt that much of the difference in recovery on one island as compared with another was the result of leadership. Mogmog, long known for its strong political chiefs and councils, fared far better than Falalop or Asor, where the men holding positions of authority are traditionally reputed to exercise it less effectively. Fassarai was hit less hard than the others but in any event not only had a competent chief to supervise recovery but also several young men capable of initiating practical steps toward rehabilitation.

How did the typhoon affect relations with Yap, the traditional overlord of Ulithi and a string of other islands extending farther east? The complex relationships in the miniature empire controlled by Gagil district chiefs in Yap has withstood the concerted disapproval of three successive foreign administrations, including the American, and it seems obvious that something more than the threat of force has kept the system together, even though on a greatly diminished scale. Now Yap must be seen as having little political control; instead, it retains a strong economic and sentimental influence over its subjects. Viewed from the point of view of an American, the system is contrary to democratic principles, but the economic advantages of being in good favor with Gagil are substantial enough to cause Ulithi to go along with the arrangement, much as it may be deprecated by officialdom. Yap, as the "parent" of Ulithi, has obligations toward its "child" in the east. This was dramatically brought out on January 7, only five weeks after the storm, when the M/V *Erroll* arrived in the lagoon with 200 baskets of taro, yams, and Polynesian chestnuts sent by the people of Gagil to the people of Ulithi. Accompanying the cargo were two Yapese, one of them actually part Ulithian. The food was distributed to all the islands of the atoll without regard to the complicated *sawei* system, involving as it does a reciprocal relationship between lineages on the respective islands. The elders of Gagil had held a meeting in Gatchapar village and made the decision to assemble and ship food. The gesture was a humanitarian one but it had overtones of moral obligation.

Ophelia, then, did nothing to hasten the deterioration of the traditional vassal-like linkage, but rather allowed it to express itself in a new form and thereby gain continued life. The *sawei* system of reciprocity was based on the notion of an upper caste landlord lineage dominating a lower caste tenant. It carried many benefits to the tenant, for reasons that are too involved to go into here. Under American administration it had perhaps become outmoded. Yet Ulithians have need to turn to Yap for some of their important supplies, and in addition to this they are bound by diffuse ties originating in a variety of factors. The dispatching of foodstuffs to Ulithi on an island-to-island basis rather than a lineage one had more the character of the strictly political relationship known as *pitigil tamol* than *sawei*. It must be obvious, however, that whatever the form, the obligation of Yap to help its "child" was still being exercised. Ulithians are not apt to forget soon the expression of assistance made by Gagil.

Without doubt the place of Christianity in the lives of the people was considerably enhanced by the typhoon.[9] The church structures, where possible, were used as both shelters and rallying places and stood firm against the elements. The people, no matter where they were, kept praying aloud, throughout the storm, and gained considerable comfort thereby. The presence of Father Walter on the atoll did much to reassure the people that they would be protected by Providence, and his subsequent help in obtaining food and materials, as well as interceding with the Trust Territory and Coast Guard, could scarcely have gone unnoticed.

One may assume on principle that some magical beliefs and

[9] The old paganism had begun to decline in the late 'thirties, when two missionaries based on Yap began to make periodic visits to Ulithi. During the war they were beheaded as spies by the Japanese. The spiritual needs of the people were attended to during the time of the military occupation by Father James E. Norton of the Marine Corps. In 1949, about eighty percent of the people were Christians, and in 1960 the figure had risen to ninety-seven percent.

practices were still extant at the time of the typhoon, but certainly they were minimal. People refused to concede that sorcerers on Yap might have caused the typhoon, and if a few old people persisted in this belief, they did not give voice to it. Recourse to magic in the treatment of illness had virtually disappeared; in fact, the rapidity with which modern medicine had replaced it was little short of phenomenal. The white man's medicine worked—that was obvious. During the war it had wholly eradicated all the cases of yaws in the atoll. After the cyclonic storm, when the dispensaries had been destroyed and the drug supply virtually ruined, the main concern of the male nurse and the "corpsmen" had been the procurement of penicillin, sulfa drugs, aspirin, and other drugs to which the people had become accustomed. If the storm did not visibly increase faith in modern science in the treatment of disease, it certainly gave testimony of the extent to which it had come to be embraced.

The way in which Ophelia modified centuries-old taboos is interesting. Ulithians refer to any prohibition as an *etap,* a word etymologically related to "taboo," but used in so loose a sense as to include secular interdicts. Some of these restrictions are hardly more than ritualistic expressions of decorum, while others are derived from religious considerations lingering on from pagan times. Their origins frequently are obscure or completely forgotten, although it should be noted that often an *etap* may be instigated by highly practical and sensible considerations, such as a desire to protect the food supply or to regulate the presence of outsiders arriving from other islands within or without the atoll. Some loosening of the old taboos had begun after the war and even before that, but most *etap* had continued in force even where their original basis was no longer clear. The typhoon had a varying effect on the observance of taboos. We have already noted that the attitudes toward garments were so changed as to permit the use of items previously frowned upon.

Taboos relative to menstruation were noticeably relaxed. Changes had already begun to take place before Ophelia. By the summer of 1960 women were being allowed to leave the menstrual house to attend services at the church and to visit the dispensary. All but a few had ceased to remain there for the customary three full lunar months after delivering a baby; indeed, some were having babies delivered by the native male nurse at the dispensary, where they would remain eight or nine days and then fill out one postpartum lunar month at the menstrual hut. Men, previously enjoined from visiting their wives or seeing their babies because of the proscription against trespassing on the grounds surrounding the hut, were now able to enter the area to speak to their spouses and look at their infants. Schoolgirls were already being allowed to attend school during their menstrual periods, although to reach the building they had to be sure to avoid the village and walk along the beach to get there.

The long postpartum sex taboo between a woman and her husband had in recent years gradually been lifted, so that instead of waiting for the child to be able to walk to the beach and dip its head in the water before they could resume coitus, the parents were at liberty to do as they pleased. The old belief had been that if marital relations were to be resumed sooner than this it would make the infant weak, thin, diarrheic, and unable to walk. Other restrictions between spouses had broken down completely, and as a consequence it is said that coition between them was more frequent.

The effect of the storm was to consolidate and still further encourage the erosion of the sexual taboos. All the menstrual houses had been either partly or completely destroyed, although some semblance of segregation was still in effect six weeks after the disaster. On Mogmog women were continuing to use a hut that had collapsed and was resting precariously on its eaves. On Fassarai a small new hut had quickly been built, and on Falalop two were in the process of reconstruction. There was no talk of abandoning menstrual houses, but it was obvious that the old order was being flouted in many ways, especially since women were badly needed to help in the work of rehabilitation and could not be allowed the luxury of lounging about in the huts. Apparently only a few of the older generation seemed to mind the loss of the old restrictions. Men moved about freely in the vicinity of the huts, and women moved unselfconsciously away from it. The sense of boundary had faded even before this, when the menstruants in the huts had been led during the storm into the churches for protection and had for the first time mingled freely with the other villagers. Before this typhoon, women in the houses used to be moved to safety by following a prescribed path to previously selected houses, where they continued to live in isolation, but the new attitude probably forever precluded this.

Some taboos relating to canoes continued to be maintained in force after Ophelia. While these may seem to be mere courtesies, they have practical applications and will therefore be continued in use. One of these requires that a canoe arriving at the reef off an island shall lower and dismantle its sail and mast. This certainly prevents rash young men from wrecking their craft. As the canoe is being poled or paddled in, no one may stand—a taboo that has no apparent rationale but which may in some way be more than a gesture of courtesy to the "old men" who lounge about in the great council houses always located near the shore. On coming ashore, the leader of the canoe, or his representative, must go to the men's house and make a formal declaration of any "news" that the canoe may bring, as well as a statement as to the composition of the passengers. Failure to make this declaration is viewed as a grave offense, punishable by the destruction of the canoe.

It would be interesting to see how other taboos have fared. Women who have not borne a child have traditionally been forbidden to enter the sacred taro patch, probably because their barrenness might affect the crops. Those persons who have defecated during the morning or had sexual congress during the night are similarly excluded, for reasons never made explicit. The taro patches were temporarily ruined by the inundation of waves and salt spray, and I would venture to guess that with their reconstruction the attitudes toward them will have become greatly altered. Christianity has already alleviated any fear of punishment by the female spirit, Lachokhlubwol, and so if the observance of the taboos had in 1960 become merely routine it could scarcely survive this latest assault. Another taboo, minor in importance but previously observed assiduously, forbids the carrying of a certain large shell fish through the village, ostensibly because it suggests the female pudenda; it will probably persist for reasons of delicacy.

The site of the former atoll-wide council house has up to now been considered sacrosanct and had to be avoided by all persons not performing some ritualistic obligation. The house itself was not rebuilt after its collapse many years ago, but the location continued to be used to invest new kings, as well as to perform the ritualistic killing and distribution of sea turtles. Its political and religious implications have persisted for some time, even though the original basis for these had been destroyed by the undermining of the old religion. The outward forms, at least, continued to be observed with respect to the site until 1960, when I observed a turtle ritual there (Lessa 1962). Probably the destruction of the buildings in the area, including the council house that had still been standing alongside the site of the old house, will cause a reconsideration of the taboo. Among other considerations, the appreciable expansion of the population of the village on Mogmog may demand that the unused land be turned over to new housing.

The effect of Ophelia on the children of the atoll was to provide them with unaccustomed opportunities for gaiety and freedom, and at the same time inculcate a certain degree of discipline, cooperation, and responsibility. Two months after the devastation they could be observed shouting, laughing, and singing in unwonted fashion. The landscape had been considerably altered, creating a novelty to be exploited much in the fashion of an American child playing in the snow after a blizzard. Dwellings had to be repaired and rebuilt and in assisting their elders the children went about their work as an exciting game. Trash had to be removed, but this was viewed as play rather than work. All the atoll seemed to be alive with hyperactive children, for without doubt their elders had not communicated to them any feeling of despondency or concern. For the moment, at least, life had assumed the character of a prolonged holiday, embellished with the gay colored clothing and frilly foods of the foreigner.

If one were to guess at the long-term effects of the storm on the children, one might say that perhaps the freedom from traditional behaviour that they had already begun to experience through schooling, church influence, and contacts with the Coast Guard station on Falalop, where they could see motion pictures, was further promoted by the storm. In the old days, although children had been raised with much permissiveness and solicitude, they had nevertheless been required to observe proper decorum by keeping down their voices and not racing through the villages. Now silence was no longer so demanded of them, and they could move about more freely from one place to another. This is not to imply that control over them had broken down; instead, it means that greater tolerance of their animal spirits was assumed by their elders. Another enduring effect might come from their "regimentation" in the work parties that were established formally and for the first time after the windstorm. Even though the children regarded their projects as a kind of sport, they willingly submitted to the necessary restrictions attendant upon them. Finally, the general plasticity in the social behavior of the adults could hardly have escaped influencing the children's conditioning.

A kind of "urbanization" that has been taking place over the years in Ulithi, in that the population has been tending to concentrate on fewer and fewer islands, is worthy of comment. Once, twelve islands were inhabited, but by 1904 only nine. Then a general depopulation set in, and by 1949 only five islands were inhabited. After that there was a sudden and steady upsurge in population, yet the villages on Asor and Lossau began to diminish in numbers, with those on Mogmog, Fassarai, and Falalop increasing. Mogmog is steadily becoming the center of population, even though it is not the largest of the islands; in 1904 it had 95 inhabitants, and in 1960 it had 175. There appears to be no single reason for the population shifts. Sorlen and Pigelelel, which once supported 70 and 79 persons, respectively, are reasonably fertile and comfortable, yet both have been unpeopled for decades.[10] If impressions have any value, I would like to venture the suggestion that the places being abandoned are villages with little opportunity, activity, and excitement, whereas those that are expanding offer advantages in trade, education, medical facilities, and recreation. Some of this new focus on certain islands is due to historical factors and some to geographical ones. Yet a place such as Falalop, where an air strip is located and a Coast Guard station is maintained, continues to decline in numbers, despite the fact that it is easily the largest of the islands and has a big taro field, while smaller Mogmog becomes more crowded than ever. In any event, the fact is that after the typhoon one more island, Lossau, was abandoned. Mogmog showed signs of expanding more than ever.

These, then, were the overt manifestations of Ophelia's impact on the atoll. They are manifestations observed during a brief period of two weeks, but they gain greater significance by our knowledge of the 1947–1949 baseline as a means of gauging the

[10] For details on the distribution of the population by islands for the years 1904, 1949, and 1960, see Lessa and Myers 1962:246.

degree and direction of change. It now remains to see what wider implications can be derived from their interpretation.

CONCLUSIONS: DISASTER THEORY

The foregoing is an essentially empirical report on a collectively experienced stress situation, and it is hoped that it may in some measure contribute to the urgently needed kind of cross-cultural and interdisciplinary research necessary for the emergence of a theoretical frame and conceptualization of disaster. If nothing else, it emphasizes that individual and group reactions to situations of extreme shared stress must be studied in their particular context.

While the psychological effects of the 1960 typhoon on Ulithi have been described, the consequences to custom and social pattern have been given greater emphasis because from the anthropological point of view they were clearly more important. Anthropology as a discipline is more concerned with cultural and social dynamics than with individual or social psychology.

The function of disaster as a catalyst of change is not a newly recognized role, having been emphasized by Prince, Carr, Sorokin, and to a lesser extent Spillius; but perhaps specific recognition of it has seldom been given for a tribal society. Catastrophe does not, however, always lead to permanent social change, for in any system that is virtually closed, a great impact in the form of disaster will simply mean that after recovery there will be more or less of a complete return to the old pattern without enduring change. But where a society is already undergoing change, a disaster will accelerate the already existing processes. This is true of the modern industrial community, and in attenuated form it is true of a society such as Ulithi, which has now been linked irrevocably with the outside world beyond the Carolines. At the time that Ophelia hit the atoll, the society was already in a state of mild flux. It had lost the approximate homeostasis that had endured for centuries when exposure to the great nations had not intruded. When calamity came, disequilibrium came with it, but since the social system was no longer a relatively static one, it regained an approximation to equilibrium within a new context.

The innovations that the people of Ulithi had already begun

to accept in the pre-impact period were seen by them as not simply change for the sake of change but as an aspect of progress. The natives envisioned the adoption of certain foreign ways as not merely inevitable but desirable as well. True, some of the older people counselled against the abandonment of the old way of life, but the majority of the population saw merit in change and welcomed the typhoon as an instrument for more readily achieving their goals. The principal aspect of the new orientation centered on economics and material things.

Our discussion has suggested the importance of knowing the social system involved in a given disaster, not only for an understanding of how it adapts to the catastrophe but also how it influences the emergence of a new social system. Thus, for example, the strong cooperation during the post-impact phase had its roots in the strong sharing and cooperative pattern dominating Ulithian economic effort. To give another example, the acceleration of the acculturation process could only be understood from a knowledge of the dynamic factors that were conducive to change.

The questions that we have dealt with on a psychological level have been essentially social, but some individually-oriented reactions have been given notice. No pretense can be made that the psychological reactions to Ophelia reflect universal human reactions, as the following review of our findings will affirm.

In a disaster any intense feeling of helplessness and disability will sometimes paralyze either or both the individual and the community. Obviously, no such sensation gripped the Ulithians, except for a few individuals who found the pressure too great to cope with in their particular situations. We see that personally disorganized behavior occurs only under special conditions and is not a frequent consequence of disaster.

The intensification of basic values and consequent division of behavior into diametrically opposed forms, under stress, has been called by some writers "the polarization of behavior" and by others "U curve reaction." The latter designation graphically symbolizes the statistical distribution of this phenomenon. In other words, crises tend to bring out the best in some persons and the worst in others. Ophelia, however, did not elicit any polar reactions, probably because cultural conditioning by recurrent typhoons appeared to have minimized fear, panic, and despair. Instead, the basic values of cooperation, interdependence, and mutual trust, which are so imperative for survival, prevailed in the stressful situation, so that if anything behavior was pushed in the direction of only one of the possible polar extremes.

The spontaneous leadership so often reported in the literature in connection with disaster did not emerge during the course of the typhoon itself, mostly because there was no need for it beyond the level of the household. Young, emergent leaders did appear in the post-impact period when the hurricane had passed and task-oriented leadership was more important than formal leadership. The new leaders did not emerge haphazardly and unexpectedly, for they had already been partially prepared by virtue of their education, mechanical skills, and experience with the world of the foreigner, on whom so much of rehabilitation depended. It can be assumed that given the changing situation in which succession to chieftainship finds itself, the formal leaders will reassert their authority only nominally and will relinquish it to the younger men with good grace, if not through the attrition of death and old age. In the wider context of disaster studies, the Ulithian example demonstrates that situation factors are all-important in the emergence of spontaneous leadership and will determine whether such leadership will indeed arise at all, and if it will be enduring or transitory. It would be difficult to envision any spontaneous leaders of the 1907 typhoon, for example, as having had permanent effects on the political system as it was in those relatively static times.

As a reaction to disaster an effort may be made to fix blame, but as the example of the Ulithians' feelings about Ophelia shows, such a reaction does not necessarily arise nowadays. A few individuals on Ulithi suggested that the storm was the work of a displeased God; but most accepted it as a natural event. In the old days, the misfortune would have been attributed to the machinations of Yapese sorcerers commissioned by their chiefs to wreak retribution on their recalcitrant underlings on Ulithi. Fixing blame can of course be a logical process without overtones of illogic or hostility; it depends on a variety of factors, including the way in which the cause of the disaster is regarded. The people of Ulithi saw Ophelia as something beyond their power, because they regarded it as an impersonal act of nature in the tradition of the many typhoons besetting the Carolines annually.

If we think of scapegoating as a way of transferring blame to others, then this too was obviously absent in the reaction of the people. Scapegoating is an irrational process that thrives in the presence of latent aggression and social tension. Such factors were not present on the atoll to any serious extent; moreover, in the absence of any idea of blame itself, there could be no effort to transfer it.

Psychiatrists would be better qualified than I to decide if the typhoon acted as a kind of shock therapy. In gross terms, all four psychotics on Ulithi appeared to have been jarred temporarily to a greater or lesser degree out of their condition. It would require long and expert study to reveal the mechanisms involved.

The winds and waves of the November typhoon, then, not only caused widespread physical changes on the tiny atoll but also dramatically transformed the social organization and traditions of the islands. They swept away old ways as well as trees. In doing so they stimulated social changes already in progress before the storm and at the same time provided a more dynamic way of life to cope with the program of reconstruction.[11]

[11] I acknowledge with gratitude the assistance and hospitality shown me during my field work by Lt. George P. Vance of the local Coast Guard detachment, as well as several men under his command. The natives of the atoll cooperated in the same generous fashion as always. The manuscript has benefitted by readings on the part of Geoffrey Ashton and Rita Ventura Loeb.

JOHN L. FISCHER

18. Folktale in the Eastern Carolines

There is a great variety of folktales still to be found in Truk and Ponape Districts. A simple division of tales into those told for amusement and those which are purportedly true is universal throughout the Micronesian islands of the area (that is, all except Kapingamarangi and Nukuoro which are Polynesian), although the assignment of tales to one or the other category often seems arbitrary to Western listeners. Prominent among the tales told for amusement are tales of encounters with supernatural beings and monsters, often cannibalistic, romantic love stories, and animal stories, the latter especially for children. The subjects of the allegedly true stories are often similar to those of the tales told for amusement but also include legends of the origin of clans and the first peopling of the islands, legends of wars and the development of political units, myths about the activities of the native gods, the origin of magic and medicine, and about the formation of local landmarks.

The tales told for amusement are considered to be "lies" of little value and the principal reluctance to tell them is based on a desire not to waste the hearer's time. There is also a belief among the Trukese that telling many tales will cause the group listening to break up, and a belief among the Ponapeans that telling tales in the daytime will hasten nightfall and thus interfere with work. The Ponapean belief at least is not a very gross exaggeration.

SOURCE: Excerpt from pp. 200–03 of *The Eastern Carolines* by John L. Fischer, with the assistance of Ann M. Fischer. New Haven: Human Relations Area Files (Behavior Science Monographs), 1957, 1966. Reprinted by permission of the author.

Neither of these beliefs are taken seriously enough to interfere much with the collection of tales.

Many of the tales considered to be true are treated as valuable private knowledge. The general outlines of these tales are often widely known but the full versions are often known only to a few experts. In the past these experts would not reveal their knowledge to someone outside of the family without receiving considerable payment for the instruction. At present some but not all experts are willing to divulge their knowledge to the public at large. Even those willing may desire payment.

For Ponape many of these valued tales were received by the German anthropologist Paul Hambruch in 1910. Hambruch's collection of tales is very good and by far the best published from the area but more complete and probably more accurate versions of many of his tales could still be collected from living Ponapeans.

Folktales of native origin appear to be most highly developed in Truk Lagoon, and next on Ponape Island. On Kusaie folktales of native origin have mostly been forgotten although apparently at one time there was a large body of tales. Foreign folktales have also largely displaced native tales in the Mortlocks.

Each of the various culture areas in the two districts gives its own twist to tales found widely in the Pacific Ocean area. For instance in a common Polynesian and Melanesian tale a man goes to chop a tree down to make a canoe; each morning he finds the tree standing again in full foliage; finally he makes the appropriate offering to some nature spirit and is able to complete his work. This tale is also known in Ponape but here the cause of the inability to fell the tree once and for all is that the canoe-maker has failed to apologize for his poor work to an insignificant looking passerby who was really a supernatural being. The emphasis on the need for speaking modestly is characteristically Ponapean.

Stories resembling part of the Oedipus myth of Greece are found in the Pacific area: a man orders his wife to kill any boy baby born, fearing that the son will be dangerous to him; the wife bears a boy baby which is secretly kept alive and later returns to supplant his father. In a Trukese version the hero is not the man's own son but rather his sister's son. The man's sister's son is his matrilineal successor. It would appear that much of the suppressed tension which normally exists between father and son in societies where the son is the father's heir is transferred to the maternal uncle-nephew relationship when a man's sister's son is in line to succeed to important rights of the man, as in Truk.

The proportion of "amusement" tales to the total body of tales appears to be especially high in Truk Lagoon. The proportion of allegedly true tales appears to be higher on Ponape. Among these Ponapeans are especially fond of tales of oppressive chiefs who meet retribution for their misdeeds, also of tales which explain the origin of their more elaborate political system. Trukese tales are often quite lengthy and contain many incidents, some of which are rather loosely connected. Ponapean tales tend to be shorter and more tightly organized.

As in our own culture a distinction is made between tales which it is suitable for children to hear and those which it is not. The line between the two is not the same as in our culture however and the original versions of Trukese and Ponapean children's tales sometimes contain references to bodily functions which would not be permitted in tales for American children.

Both children's and adults' folktales contain much violence, as do folktales in most cultures the world over. Ponapean tales are perhaps more violent than Trukese. In one popular Ponapean tale a king sets fire to the house of his mother-in-law (who happens to be a monstrous lizard); his wife jumps into the flames to die with her mother, and the king jumps to join his wife. In another, one chief sends a man and his son to get some bananas from another chief; the second chief secretly wraps up the corpse of a pregnant woman instead; when the boy reaches into the basket for a banana as they are paddling home he grabs the breast of the corpse instead; the corpse arises to devour him but the father throws it into the water; in revenge for this trick the first chief sends a school of sting rays which lure the second chief out of his house at night and then whip him to pieces with their tails.

Not all stories are as gruesome as these but at least these should serve to illustrate the point that there is no possibility of protecting islander children from notions of violence by carefully screening English reading material or movies. They will get the violence in the home anyway; although the specific techniques of violence will often be different.

DAVID M. SCHNEIDER

19. Abortion and Depopulation on a Pacific Island

THE PROBLEM

THE PRACTICE OF SELF-INDUCED ABORTION

Before the coming of the first European explorers to the Pacific Island of Yap, its 39 square miles supported an estimated population of more than 50,000 people. By 1945, when American troops landed on Yap, the island's population had fallen to about 2,500. This spectacular decline in population has had far-reaching consequences for the people of Yap and their mode of life.

The people of Yap had developed a social system predicated on a relatively large population. While the population continued to decline, the form of their organized groupings changed but slowly. Today people bemoan the fact that there is a constant scarcity of individuals to hold the offices and perform the necessary jobs. Political organizations calling for a staff of 150 officials have only four or five men available to fill these posts. Present-day Yap society, with its several thousand people, is still geared to a population 20 times that large, and it is with deep regret that people contemplate the spectacle of unfilled positions and depleted organizations. As they express the situation, something should be done "to have more babies."

In the face of this dramatic population shrinkage and the keenly felt need to refill the thinned ranks of their society, Yap women

SOURCE: Chapter VIII of *Health, Culture and Community*, Benjamin D. Paul, ed. New York: Russell Sage Foundation, 1955. Reprinted by permission of the author and publisher.

engage in a practice that produces results exactly opposite to those desired. Evidence indicates that self-induced abortion is widely practiced by Yap women precisely during the years of maximum fecundity. This lowers the fertility rate in a situation where a higher rate is urgently desired. Moreover, the methods of inducing abortion are such as to expose women to the risk of infection. Abortion is widely condemned on moral grounds. A Yap woman will tell of other women who have induced abortion but never admit having done so herself. The admission would create serious trouble with her husband or, if she were single, it would impair her chances of making a good marriage.

In view of the unfavorable consequences of abortion, as well as the moral strictures against it, why do women persist in this practice? Could the very methods devised by the people of Yap to stabilize the population at the optimal level have produced results that defeat their own ends? The enigma of abortion has roots deep in the history of Yap and its people. It is not an isolated practice that can be understood by itself, but is bound up with the totality of Yap culture, its values, moral standards, social organization, and the aspirations of its people.

THE SITUATION

FERTILITY AND CULTURAL VALUES

As part of a four-man team of social scientists studying the problem of depopulation on Yap in 1947 and 1948, I became interested in cultural factors relating to the low birth rate. In the course of ethnographic research, I was particularly struck by the fact that 34 per cent of Yap women between the ages of twenty-six and fifty who were interviewed claimed that they had never given birth to a child. In seeking to account, at least in part, for this high incidence of infertility, I began to accumulate information pointing to the prevalence of self-induced abortion. It was next to impossible to get direct evidence. Morally disallowed, this practice was performed in secret. Women readily told about *other* women who had induced abortion. Their knowledge of the precise details of technique, however, left little doubt that this information was based on more than indirect experience. The facts that emerged on the illicit but widespread practice of self-induced abortion are these.

SELF-INDUCED ABORTION ON YAP

Abortion techniques fall into three classes. One consists in a series of magical manipulations with little apparent efficacy. These were universally recited to me as "ways to abort, but they don't always work." Doubtless they are tried from time to time, however. The other two techniques are empirically more effective. One of these is drinking boiled concentrated sea water. Women described the effect as a general feeling of illness accompanied by vomiting and severe cramps.

The other technique consists in introducing a thin rolled plug of hibiscus leaves (which expand when moist) into the mouth of the cervix and then injuring and scratching the mouth of the cervix with a bit of stick, stone, iron, fingernail, or other sharp object until blood is drawn. Women informants generally agreed that injuring the area about the mouth of the cervix was necessary in addition to inserting the plug; the plug without injury or injury without the plug was subject to failure. The boiled sea water technique was held to be less reliable than the plug-and-injury method, and therefore the less common of the two techniques. One technique common on the Pacific islands of Melanesia and Polynesia, that of massage, was never mentioned by Yap informants and is apparently unknown on Yap.

Induced abortion fits neatly into the Yap way of life, for a woman who knows how to induce abortion can usually do so without the fact ever being discovered. Yap women customarily repair to a special area during their menstrual periods. There they sit within a small but comfortable hut on their voluminous skirts of dry banana leaves and other grasses. When the peak of the flow is over, the woman is free to move around within the menstrual area, and she busies herself with making her new skirt, cleaning up the area, and such basketry work or other appropriate occupation as may come to hand. At the conclusion of her menstrual period, she places her soiled skirt in a place reserved for that purpose in the menstrual area; these old skirts are burned when the pile is great enough to warrant it. She is then free to return to the village and resume her daily life.

It is customary for a woman to keep pregnancy a secret for the first three months at least, for both she and her child are considered to be most vulnerable to sorcery at that time. So whether or not she is actually menstruating, she will repair to the menstrual area about the time she would normally have expected her period to begin. So far as the rest of the world can tell, she is not pregnant and is menstruating regularly. A young woman who becomes pregnant is thus in an excellent position to keep her condition secret and to induce abortion without discovery if she so wishes and knows how.

Contraception, in certain of its forms, is known on Yap but hardly ever used. Coitus interruptus was reported by some male informants to have been learned in relatively recent times from Japanese occupation personnel. It is something some women try once or twice but abandon quickly; men will not tolerate it, and a woman finds that it defeats her own ends in that it drives lovers away. Condoms were made familiar by the Japanese; they were known to be effective in preventing pregnancy, but Yap men were not motivated to use them for this purpose, preferring to make excellent slingshots out of them instead. Other forms of contraception are unknown.

Abortion induced by the plug-and-injury method is likely to produce infection, which in turn may possibly lead to some lasting impairment of a woman's reproductive capacity. On the other hand, it seems clear that more serious consequences of the plug-and-injury method are unlikely, though they may well occur in individual cases. Yap women live in their microbiological environment all their lives without the protection of antiseptics or the habits of cleanliness and hygiene common among us. Consequently, the resistance to infection on the part of those who survive is generally quite high. This does not mean that they never become infected. It only means that were an American woman to try to abort by the plug-and-injury method she would very likely incur a serious if not fatal infection, where the typical Yap woman probably incurs only a mild, localized infection. Medical experts have made actual observations of this sort.

As already mentioned, deliberate abortion is considered "wrong" and immoral on Yap. A husband who discovers that his wife has resorted to abortion may beat her or divorce her, or do both. A woman who becomes known among men as one who practices abortion jeopardizes her chances of a stable marriage. Men are interested in having children, and a woman who destroys her unborn child is viewed as a woman who "throws her child away."

Because Yap abortion techniques are in fact effective, the practice has a critical bearing on the fertility rate. However, the low rate cannot be attributed entirely to the practice of abortion. In all likelihood, there are additional important causes. Although the evidence remains inconclusive, there are good indications that gonorrhea or some other low-grade infection is present and contributes to the low fertility on Yap.

But the practice of abortion by itself is a problem of sufficient gravity to cause concern on the part of American officials charged with the responsibility of administration and on the part of natives themselves. The problem of devising effective means for dealing with abortion requires a searching look at the whole complex of circumstances that surround it. Only by understanding this problem can one hope to plan suitable countermeasures.

THE ISLAND OF YAP

Yap is a large, eroded mountain top of 38.7 square miles surrounded by a reef and rising to about 500 feet at its highest point. It lies 451 miles southwest of Guam; it is approximately 10° north of the equator and 138° east of Greenwich. Yap is a western member of the Caroline Islands, which in turn are part of a widespread group of small islands and island clusters known as Micronesia. In 1947 Yap had a population of 2,600 living in more than a hundred villages.

Although Yap was discovered by westerners in the sixteenth century, its contact with European and American peoples was sporadic until the last three decades of the nineteenth century, and even so the direct effects of foreign contact on Yap culture have been minimal. Nominal and ineffective administration of Yap by the Spanish lasted until 1899, when the whole Caroline Islands, from Ponape in the east to Palau in the west, were sold to Germany. In 1914 the Japanese took over the former German South Seas Colony in Micronesia and continued effective administration of Yap until 1945, when the American Navy gained control of the islands. Soon after, they became the Trust Territory of the Pacific Islands ultimately under United Nations control but administered first by the Navy Department and later by the United States Department of the Interior.

American administration of Yap since the fall of 1945 saw the introduction of health and sanitation measures, the erection of a hospital and dispensary for the natives, isolation of all known lepers, and the dramatic eradication of yaws. This last task alone, completed before my visit in 1947, went far toward enlisting native support for medical and hygienic suggestions emanating from the American administration.

Yap is known as one of the most conservative islands in Micronesia. After more than fifty years of occupation by a succession of foreign powers—Spain, Germany, Japan, and now the United States—the Yap way of life has altered very gradually, if at all. Missionary efforts are a good example. In the late 1800's, Spanish soldiers and missionaries alternately tried to establish stations on Yap. At first, they were treated with direct hostility, and some missionaries and soldiers were killed. Later Spanish forces were augmented and became sufficient to maintain their position, and fear of retaliation prevented violence from the Yaps. Toward the end of the period of German administration in the first decade of the twentieth century, there were some 60 Capuchin missionaries on Yap, and their published report lamented the fact that for all their work and for all their numbers, but 15 natives could be counted as converts. At the time of my visit in 1947 many natives felt it a gesture of friendliness toward the Americans to claim to be Christians, since in their view all Americans were Christians. In fact, however, the number of regular church-going Christians who had more than a vague notion of what Christianity was, did not far exceed the number cited by the German missionaries.

DEPOPULATION AND ITS BACKGROUND

One change of major importance that has taken place over the past hundred or more years is the severe depopulation of the island. Precisely when this depopulation started is unknown. The best guess is that it probably began sometime before 1850, although how long before is unknown. For the people of Yap, a whole series of alterations and adjustments have followed in the wake of the decrease in numbers. The reduction in available personnel simply prohibits certain activities and restricts others to a scale which distorts their meaning and function. Yet these activities of an older day are still thought to be the proper and good ways, while the restricted ways of today are seen as unavoidable compromises to be rectified at the earliest opportunity. It is in this latter sense that the Yap way of life has changed but little; the ideal patterns, so to speak, appear to be unchanged, while their necessarily inadequate realization is universally deplored.

The traditional table of organization for the government of a village lists so many political offices ranging from village chief down to the janitor of the old men's clubhouse that nowadays one man alone may hold four or five out of the 12 or 15 political offices in a given village, while in other villages the complaint is that "everybody is a chief." Such focusing of political function in the hands of one man and such diffusion of offices throughout the whole population distort the concept of evenly balanced political powers implicit in traditional Yap political organization. Furthermore, this situation defeats the traditional intent of restricting the governing function to a selected segment of the society. The Yaps are well aware of this and insist that the time-honored ideal pattern remains "right" but that the present undesirable arrangement is unavoidable because of the shortage of people.

Although the complete history of Yap depopulation is impossible to recover, certain inferences can be made with reasonable confidence. The depopulation trend started during a period of acute overpopulation. According to a careful estimate based on a study of abandoned house sites, the population at one time was in the neighborhood of 51,000 with a density of approximately 1,300 persons per square mile, a figure 20 times that of the present, but no greater than the present density of some other Micronesian islands, according to official sources:

Island	*Density per Square Mile*
Nama	2,093
Losap	1,892
Eauripik	1,477
Yap (estimated)	(1,300)
Pingelap	914
Kapingamarangi	892

At no time during the depopulation of this island did genuine social disorganization take place. Yap is highly conservative with respect to change of any kind. It is even possible that conservatism increased precisely as depopulation progressed, since barrenness, death, and disease are essentially believed by the natives to be supernatural punishments for breaches of custom and taboo. The frequent occurrence of such departures might well have made the Yaps feel that compulsive observance of customary modes of action was essential to avoid these evil consequences. Associating misfortune with improper behavior is not uncommon elsewhere in the world. The combination of conservatism and absence of severe social disorganization helps to explain why Yap culture, as a blueprint for how life should be lived, remains today in many ways the same culture as obtained during the period of overpopulation. In brief, Yap culture is one that is geared not only to a large population, but in important respects to overpopulation.

If the practice of abortion began during a period of overpopulation, it was at that time a successful adaptation to a pressing problem. These circumstances could account for the origin of the practice of abortion on Yap, and a simple explanation for its current prevalence in spite of a drastic change in population would be that it is a "survival," a custom that has lost its utility but persists of its own inertia. Such an explanation would fail to take account of the interrelated nature of the components that comprise a society's culture. The values and institutions that arose in past response to overpopulation became linked to form a fairly coherent cultural totality with powers of persistence greater than those of the constituent parts.

THE YAP WAY OF LIFE: YOUTH AND LOVE AFFAIRS

Insight into the motives that impel abortion can be gained by examining the childhood and youth of Yap men and women. A man's life goes through a protracted period of childhood, lasting well into the late teens, without many responsibilities, without duties of any serious kind, and with a predominant interest in play. As a youth, he has begun to take love seriously, to learn the elaborate code and ritual of love affairs, and has perhaps had one lover and is going on to a second. He has learned that Yap girls are hard to get and harder to keep; they demand much and they are not constant. If he can talk the girl into coming to live with him, he has a firmer hold over her, though her affection is still likely to wander.

Even a married man with a wife and child, however, has few responsibilities. He will have built a house for himself on his father's land (but well apart from his parents' dwelling) when he was between fifteen and twenty. At that time plots for his yams and pits for his taro and trees for his coconuts will have been set aside from those of his mother and father, for he may not share with them food grown on the same land, cooked over the same fire, or in the same pot. He may share food only with men or women of his age-group. A man's wife cultivates and cooks his vegetable food, and the man should provide her with coconuts and fish, and betel nut for chewing; and these he provides as the need arises or as the spirit moves him. Beyond these duties he has but one other, to provide his father-in-law with fish or other gifts from time to time. Otherwise the care of the child, house, and garden falls almost entirely on his wife. She should help her mother-in-law in the house and in the garden and with any small children her mother-in-law may have.

A man's serious responsibilities and obligations do not begin until he is in his late forties or early fifties when, as head of his kin group, he takes part in the councils and the serious political affairs of his village.

A woman's life need be no different from a man's with regard to responsibilities and work. As a young girl she celebrates her first menses with a year-long residence in a specially designated area outside her village, usually near the inland grassy region. There her friends come to visit and play with her, and she begins her love affairs in earnest. According to the cultural rules, no man can have exclusive claim on her affections during this year, even if she is married, and she spreads her favors widely. After this year she returns to the village, living in a house her father builds for her not far from her parents' dwelling, unless she is married. Except for the fact that she has put on the black neck cord of a mature woman, she continues to lead the life she led as a girl. Her primary interests are in play, in love affairs, and in sociability.

If a woman comes to live with her lover, she is regarded as married, but except for the fact that she is expected to be faithful to him, her life is not radically altered. True, she should do his cooking eventually, but for months after arriving at her husband's house, his mother will still cook for him, and she will share his food. Properly the right to cook her husband's food should be ceremonially transferred from the man's mother to his wife, but since young women do not particularly like the chore, they postpone this ceremony. Often it is just as well, for the couple frequently decide, after a week or a month or a year, that they would rather terminate the marriage. Young people do not get married in the sense of solemnly undertaking the responsibilities of home and family; for them, marriage is in effect a special arrangement to make a love affair easier. When married, they no longer have to meet secretly at night.

The procrastination of the very few ceremonies which are supposed to attend a marriage reflects the instability of this period. There are only two ceremonies, and as often as not one or both are never performed. Besides the ceremonial transfer of cooking privileges, there is supposed to be a small gathering of the bride and groom's immediate families and an exchange of food between them. In this last ceremony the groom's father always makes a little speech which dwells on the hope that the couple will get along together and not fight, will stay together and have children.

There is nothing to prevent the separation (which is divorce) of a couple if they so desire, provided no children have been born. The girl simply goes back to her father's house, taking with her what property she brought—her skirt, her basket, and the knives and jewelry she carries in it. There is no ceremony marking this separation.

On the other hand, considerable social pressure is put on a woman to remain in the marriage if she has borne a child and if the child is alive, for on divorce a child remains with his father unless the child is still nursing, when he will go with his mother until weaned and then return to his father. The mother's parents, her husband's parents, and public opinion bring pressure to bear to keep her with her child. The whole burden of the appeal is laid squarely on her relationship with her child. She is not asked to stay with her husband. She is not appealed to on the ground that she owes her husband's kin group anything, either through her work or her fertility. She is only asked to stay with her child who needs her. It is considered the gravest misdeed for a mother to separate herself from her child and, indeed, the very few children whom I saw whose mothers had been divorced after the child's birth, suffered markedly from the sense of abandonment engendered in Yap in such a situation. A woman who does this is said to have "thrown her child away" and her reputation is badly damaged.

When there are no children divorce is simple, practically without repercussion and consequences; divorce after children are born is a very serious matter and occurs relatively rarely. Out of a group of 28 married women who had each borne one live child, nine had never been divorced at all, 15 had been divorced before the birth of their first child, while only four had been divorced after the birth of their first child.

Thus, when a woman bears a child, her position changes radically. She is primarily responsible for the care and feeding of the child, and she must be with him almost all the time. She will take him with her to the gardens and she will take him along when she goes visiting, but she must be with him. Although her husband shares most of the pregnancy taboos with her and helps with the actual delivery, his responsibility toward the child duplicates his responsibility toward his wife—providing coconuts, fish, and betel. He is not constantly tied to the child the way she is, and a husband's extramarital affairs are not sharply curtailed as are a woman's when she has a child. A woman with a child cannot go "playing about," with her husband or anyone else, at night or by day. A woman becomes tied to a man when she bears a child, and young women on Yap do not like to be tied to one man.

Women up to the age of thirty do not want children because they would no longer be free to fall in and out of love, to attract lovers, to have and break off affairs at will, to practice the elaborate games of love and sociability that appeal to young Yap men and women. They do not want to be tied to a child and to a husband when they are in the best position to gain and enjoy the rewards of being unattached. It is one thing to want to avoid having a child, and something else again to actually do so. Wishing alone will not suffice. On Yap the standard and available means of avoiding children is to induce abortion when pregnancy occurs.

THE YAP WAY OF LIFE: ADULTHOOD AND PRESTIGE

When a woman is about thirty, her attitude changes. She begins to want children. Women say that they want children then because they are lonely and need someone to talk to. This is another way of saying that they find it hard to attract and keep lovers. At this time a woman will have a child if she can. If she cannot, she will resort to a host of magical aids, medicines, prayers, and whatever else promises to bring the child she now desires. If all of her efforts fail, she will try to adopt a child. Adoption is a common practice on Yap, but the supply of children for adoption is, of course, insufficient to meet the demand.

Although women over thirty give as their main reason for wanting babies that they are "lonely" and are tired of running around, it is significant that at this age a woman leaves the age category of "youth" by Yap standards and enters the status of "adulthood." This social transition has important consequences for the people of Yap. Different kinds of rewards are available to people in different age-groups. Older men and women are less dependent on the gratifications that arise from love affairs and sexual conquest and can turn instead to new activities that now become appropriate and available. The reasons for this shift are connected with the basic values of Yap culture.

The dominant value of Yap culture is prestige. People are ranked and assigned differential prestige in almost every conceivable way. Family groups are ranked within a village, and the villages themselves are ranked into a nine-class system divided into an upper and a lower group. This is crosscut by a formal "war organization" now oriented primarily to political ends. Districts are ranked within three major alliances, and these three alliances continually jockey in the political arena for temporary dominance. Organization within the family itself is conceived as a rank system with father taking precedence over mother, mother over children, and older children over younger. Each plot of land within the village has its inherent, almost inalienable rank, and the highest ranking piece of land validates its owner's position as village chief, while lower political statuses inhere in lower ranking plots of land.

Older people, men and women, have more prestige than younger, and the responsibilities which go with age are seen as privileges appropriate to the older people's prestige. It is the old men, the heads of family groups, who sit around in conference, planning large and ostentatious exchanges of valuable shells or exhibitions of dancing by the men or women of the village. Old men and heads of families achieve the available political statuses of chief, subchief, magician, messenger, and so forth. Owing to depopulation, chieftainships today are often inherited by young men and boys, and when this happens a trusted relative of advanced age is often called in to act as regent for them. In the past when population was at its peak, it was only the oldest who could hold such offices, who were admitted to the old men's clubhouse, who could sit with the council of family heads. The young men were the warriors and fishermen, with time on their hands and without important responsibilities.

Closely related to the fact that age, prestige, and responsibility go together is the conception that a man is still a "young man" until he is about forty or fifty years old. Technically a "young man" becomes a "man" when he succeeds to the head of his kin group. Since succession to the position of "leader of the kin group" goes from a man to his next oldest brother, through all brothers in order of descending age, and then to the oldest male among the sons of all the brothers, it was unlikely in the past that a man would succeed to that position until he was nearly fifty. Depopulation has now accelerated this progression, but it has not changed the rules of the system.

Although this elaborate system of ranking is stable, as far as its rules and regulations are concerned, it has a degree of flexibility in that the rank of any particular unit (family, village, district, alliance, plot of land) is not necessarily fixed permanently. Families, villages, districts, and alliances all vie with each other according to prescribed and orderly rules for legitimate improvement in their position; magic, sorcery, and pure chicanery are often used to hasten this necessarily slow process. But whatever the position held by any social unit, the aim is to increase its prestige and better its position.

Prestige on Yap is not correlated with such powers or privileges as make daily life precarious for some and easy for others, as in the United States. For all practical purposes food is now and was in the past equally accessible to all, regardless of rank. High prestige groups do not have the right to exploit the labor of low prestige groups except in ways which are primarily symbolic. Thus, certain families within the upper groups have the right to demand that their roofs be repaired by persons from lower groups. This amounts to a token expression of ranked relationship rather than a continuous work obligation of great magnitude. So far as can be discovered now, depopulation affected all social classes on Yap equally, for all social classes had equal access to the necessities of life and no social class was disadvantaged by being overworked or otherwise penalized in any but symbolic ways.

WHY ABORTION PERSISTS

I have shown that Yap women induce abortion because they do not want to be tied down with children during a time when they feel they would be better occupied in love affairs and in sociability. In terms of our own standards we might feel that such an attitude was morally "wrong," but they would insist that it was morally "right" and such indeed is the Yap cultural premise in terms of which they act. Young people *should* spend their time in love affairs and in nonresponsible pleasures. But Yap women also feel that they should have children and care for them. The problem is one of timing; after their period of love affairs is over, women want to have children and care for them, but they do not want the children earlier to interfere with the game of love. Yet it happens that children often come before they are wanted.

Yap standards of behavior for young men and women differ from our own standards. This is a matter of cultural relativity, but more than relativity is at issue. What is also involved is the fit between one part of culture and the rest of the cultural totality. Let us suppose that young Americans in their twenties emulated Yap and consistently preferred to engage in love affairs than to assume adult responsibilities. Quite apart from morality, such a shift would set in motion a series of other changes disrupting what we regard as our way of life. Conversely, if young men and women on Yap suddenly decided to settle down in their twenties and rear families, a host of other changes would ensue and the Yap way of life would similarly be disrupted.

I have said that the dominant values of Yap culture center around gaining and keeping prestige. Fundamental to any prestige system is the fact that a kind of scarce commodity (prestige) is differentially distributed; some have a lot and some have a little, but all cannot share equally. For such a system to work, there must be rules and regulations governing who has prestige and who has not, how it can be gained and how it can be lost. These rules must be obeyed if they are to prevent the chaos which would follow a disorderly scramble after the coveted values. One important consequence of such rules is that people must wait, often for long periods of time, before they can obtain the ultimate rewards, and in the nature of such a system some people will be destined never to achieve them. Waiting, along with the possibility of never gaining valued ends, is difficult for human beings. Accordingly, the prestige system of every society has built into it devices that will make waiting bearable and will make the fact that all cannot attain the highest goals a tolerable if not a happy situation. One such device is embodied in proximate rewards, rewards which can be achieved during the waiting period as substitutes for the ultimate goals.

It is likely that characteristic features of Yap culture—nonresponsible early adulthood, love affairs during youth, and induced abortion—originated during a period of ample population. At that time these practices were undoubtedly effective in keeping down the birth rate. When young men and women spent their time avoiding the responsibilities of adulthood, they did not press closely on the high prestige statuses of the old people. When young women were strongly motivated to postpone reproduction until their later years by inducing abortion, they shortened the time span within which they could reproduce and thus limited the overall number of births on the island.

Today, however, underpopulation rather than overpopulation is the dominant problem, and shortening the reproductive span of a woman's life by inducing abortion during her younger years serves instead to aggravate the imbalance. Why, then, does abortion persist? Because they cannot become chiefs or heads of kin groups, women can never achieve the same rewards from the prestige system that the men do. For them, the pattern of repeated love affairs provides pleasure and reward; resort to abortion makes it easier to maintain this pattern of behavior. For men, who must still mark time before assuming positions of prestige and responsibility, protracted love-making offers interim rewards. These practices persist, not merely as useless holdovers from a past era of overpopulation, but as vehicles that continue to serve useful purposes and give psychological gratifications.

IMPLICATIONS

Should anything be done about abortion on Yap? Answers to this question must be predicated on the realization that the abortion problem cannot be considered in isolation but is tied to other aspects of Yap culture. If anything is done, it must be done in a responsible way or not at all. Responsibility implies many considerations. One of these requires asking whether the Yap people feel a need to have something done. The answer is both yes and no. On the one hand, the people of Yap—particularly the men—clearly feel the need to do something about the low population. If they were convinced that eliminating abortion would increase their numbers, they would incline to support such a policy. On the other hand, the felt need of the women depends on their age. After thirty they want children, but eliminating abortion and providing no substitute method would work counter to the felt needs of women under thirty.

Another aspect of the responsibility problem concerns our own moral evaluation of the Yap situation. Among all their felt needs, and there are surely many, which will we try to meet? A program to eliminate induced abortion would have to ponder the problem of introducing another form of birth control to take its place. This inevitably enmeshes us in our own moral values. However we choose to resolve this sensitive issue, we will necessarily become involved in a related one, namely, the responsibility for anticipating the indirect consequences of an action program. Assuming that we were able to increase population by eliminating abortion, could this increase be controlled and kept within practical limits? Yap is a small island in a wide sea, and its resources are limited. At least once before it has suffered from overpopulation, so that food was scarce and people were hungry. Can we responsibly take action that will tend to reverse the population trend without considering the danger of once again bringing about overpopulation? Any program of population control must aim toward a balance adjusted to available or possible food resources.

Overpopulation could be a major undesirable consequence of a well-intentioned but unwise policy. On the other hand, there are other less obvious consequences more difficult to evaluate. Let us assume that we find a means to eliminate induced abortion in such a way as to preclude overpopulation. Mechanical and chemical devices are not and cannot be manufactured on Yap. They would have to be imported and someone would have to pay for them.

So far, the Yaps have scarcely become involved in a money economy. They like tobacco and good steel knives. Today they gather a bit of copra and sail it along the coast to the settlement at Yaptown where they exchange it for money to buy tobacco and knives. But they gather the copra only when they want to, not when the price is right. Germans, Japanese, and Americans have all found the Yaps undependable as a labor force. They far prefer asking for tobacco than to work for the money to buy it with; they assume that any decent human being who has tobacco will share it with those who have none.

If they are to have birth control devices, either they will have to pay for them or the goods will have to be supplied free of charge. The cost of this item alone would not be sufficient to force them into full-time wage labor, but this could become one of a series of conditions that might produce such results. Is this to be seen as a favorable consequence or an inevitable consequence, or as something for a program planner to worry over in advance?

Another facet of the responsibility problem is to foresee to what extent a new item will remain available and a new practice remain possible. If birth control materials could be brought to Yap and successfully introduced, what provision could be made for maintaining the supply over a long-time span? It would be irresponsible to say in effect, "Here is a five-year supply of materials. After the fifth year you will have to figure out some way of getting them yourselves." It is hard to picture how a responsible program could in fact guarantee a continuing supply of materials. Yap has been governed in turn by the Spanish, Germans, Japanese, and Americans. Administrations and policies within administrations have changed time and again. The international situation is not such that we can say that things are now settled. With more certainty, we can say that even within the brief period of American administration there have been some major changes of policy at the upper levels and an interminable series of "shake-ups" at the local level. Would it be wise to initiate a program with far-reaching consequences in view of the likelihood that administrative changes might force its cancellation after people have come to count on its continuance?

PROBLEMS OF POLICY

A sound program to halt abortion would initiate only those changes acceptable to the Yap, would anticipate the major consequences of such a program, and would entail responsible planning, execution, follow-up, and control over ensuing changes. The introduction of some appropriate form of contraception would meet most of these policy requirements and at the same time prove practical.

The outstanding problem is that of the women who do not want children at one period of their lives. To challenge this motivation directly would be futile. It would also be unethical, in the writer's view. A form of contraception that does not cause infection would be an ideal substitute for the current and possibly harmful technique of abortion. During that period of a woman's life when she did not want to bear children, she could safely avoid pregnancy. This plan would substitute one device for another without alteration in motivation or in pattern of general behavior.

The danger of eventual overpopulation would be minimized since contraception is a form of population control. Moreover, the rise in population level would probably be gradual, since only the later years of a woman's fertility span would be involved. Readjustment to increasing population would be easier if the rise were gradual rather than precipitous.

It might be supposed that putting contraceptive devices in the hands of women would increase their power and thus disturb the pattern of interpersonal relations between husbands and wives. I think that this would not be the case. In the first place, the present abortion technique is already in the hands of the women. In the second place, Yap is no fanciful patriarchate in which the men have so subdued the women that a social revolution would follow female emancipation. Yap women do not enjoy precise equality but their status is close to that of men, and women have distinct minds of their own which they do not hesitate to use. A man can abuse his wife only once; she would leave, and her kinsmen would begin vigorous inquiries.

Substituting contraception for abortion would cause very little social change, but two practical problems would arise: the cost of the program and responsibility for maintaining the supply of materials. Continued contact with western European culture almost inevitably will introduce more and more of our standards including a money economy; but it need not be the task of a health action program to initiate these changes. Assuming their inevitability, these far-reaching changes should be the responsibility of the island's civil administration, as part of a carefully planned program including medical service; they should not be tied directly to the tail of a particular health project. The cost of a long-range culture-change program must either be borne by agencies outside Yap or financed with a view to receiving repayment sometime after introducing a money economy on the island.

PROBLEMS OF IMPLEMENTATION

To implement a birth control plan such as suggested, the sequence of action, the timing, the phrasing, the channels of communication, would all require point by point collaboration between anthropological and medical personnel. Experience has shown that this is more easily projected than accomplished. Two major aims of the project would be to establish the relevant medical and cultural facts on Yap and to generate an atmosphere of trust and rapport. To these ends the program should begin with a period of joint preparatory study by selected members of the anthropological and medical teams. Study and establishment of rapport go hand in hand, provided the study is conducted tactfully and with due attention to the concerns of those studied. Three to four months of preparatory work should permit the action program to begin with favorable prospects of success.

Anthropological research already conducted on Yap points to a number of areas of potential difficulty. Difficulties would probably be encountered; first, in explaining the presence of the persons involved; second, in clearly communicating the objectives in terms understandable to the Yaps; third, in exploring the areas of resistance; and fourth, in minimizing these resistances.

One probable area of resistance will concern medical examination. Yap women are loath to submit to genital examination, and their husbands are even more opposed to letting them be examined. The Yaps have very vivid and bitter memories of medical field work carried out by the Japanese. They were forcibly stripped in mixed groups, subjected to public examination, and several Japanese men sometimes held consultations over the exposed women. Obviously, the job need not be done in this way. In 1947 a conscientious and tactful American medical officer was able to persuade quite a few women to have their children delivered in the Navy-supervised native hospital, although resistance to this suggestion was considerable when he first undertook the task. His success suggests that genital examination could be accomplished. Clear explanation of the necessity for the examination would reduce resistance. The explanation should be made in terms that Yaps can understand, giving assurance of privacy and stressing the desired end of having more babies. Contrary to expectations, employment of female personnel as examining assistants would probably arouse resistance, since Yap women implicitly view any other woman of whatever age as a potential rival for men's attentions. Yap women feel that the worst thing that can happen to them is to expose their genitals, the source of their competitive power, to another woman.

It should not be too difficult to convince the women that contraception would be more desirable than abortion. Once they are past the very early years of their adolescence, Yap women treat sexual relations in a straightforward manner, if the discussion is private and with a man. Women distrust other women, considering them unreliable competitors. While they view sexual relations as pleasurable and desirable in their own right, they also regard them as means to further ends. On Yap a woman's genitals are likened to a man's land; they are her real asset in terms of which she maintains her position in the all-embracing Yap hierarchy of rank and prestige. A woman relies on her genitals to get what she wants: lovers, attention, and the power over men that protects her against being put in a subservient position. At first, she tries to get lovers, and does so by judiciously withholding and granting sexual favors; later, these same sexual powers should provide the children that secure her position as an important and irreplaceable member of a family. Treating sex as a means to an end, not alone as a form of direct gratification, enables women to exercise a high degree of control. The rational appeal to young women to substitute contraception for abortion in their own self-interest would not fall on deaf ears.

A program for the introduction of contraception would probably encounter opposition from the Yap men, from the resident Catholic missionary, and from religious groups outside Yap who exert influence on the administration. Yap men would have to be dealt with directly, for they are all concerned as fathers, brothers, husbands, and potential husbands of the women. I do not believe that Yap men recognize the high incidence of induced abortion. By Yap standards, a man who discovers that his wife has induced abortion would be justifiably violent. Knowing this, any Yap woman who aborts will not tell her husband if she can avoid it. Men have very strong feelings about discussions of sexual matters between their wives and other men. In their view extramarital intimacy, even of a nonsexual nature, constitutes adultery and is punished as such. Further, it is men's conviction that they cannot really exert control directly over the women but can only keep other men away from their wives. A man who suspects his wife of infidelity vents his anger on her, to be sure, but he feels that the only effective remedy is to stop the other man. It would thus be necessary to dissociate consultation between young woman and physician from the sphere of adultery, taking pains to convince the men that the relationship was a purely medical matter.

However, the men are acutely aware of the depopulation problem. In certain respects it has raised more havoc with their concerns than with those of women. It is the male political organization, oriented toward prestige values, which has become extremely difficult to maintain. "Everybody is chief now," they say ruefully. Men are always willing to discuss ways and means of having more babies. Presented to them in this context, a program for contraception would receive a careful hearing. They believe that pregnancy is due to the beneficence of ancestral ghosts and the cooperation of a certain spirit. Older people firmly believe that coitus has nothing whatever to do with conception, except that coitus at the wrong time or place or with the wrong person will offend the ghosts and spirit, and these in turn will deny pregnancy to an offending woman or to the wife of an offending husband. The younger people, having come under Japanese influence, are not so sure about this. Young people believe that the ghosts and spirit have much to do with conception, but that coitus is probably important too. Both older and younger men alike are realists and will try a new proposal if it seems to show any promise at all.

For example, the German and Japanese administrations both treated yaws without success, as did the native magicians, except that the magicians occasionally claimed cures. As the Yaps saw the situation, no one but the spirits could cure yaws. Notwithstanding these beliefs, they tried the antibiotic treatment offered by American Navy physicians and were happily surprised when it worked. They still believe that no one but spirits can cure yaws; but they argue that where the Germans and Japanese and their own magicians had all failed to influence the spirits, American medicine knew the secret. This secret was so powerful that American doctors could gain the cooperation of the spirits without going through the series of ritual steps ordinarily required—payment of shell "money," offering of prayer, and observance of taboos.

Whichever way the Yaps may decide to rationalize the role of contraception in raising the birth rate, they could probably be convinced that it is worth trying, that the doctors' "directions" are a potentially effective ritual. I can see no harm in permitting men or women to regard the mechanics of any contraceptive technique as a ritual; it will be treated far more respectfully and carefully if the "ritual" instructions are clear and simple. On the other hand, I foresee only confusion and resistance if the whole matter is treated in a purely rational or "scientific" way. It will not endear the doctor to his patients if he insists or implies that their beliefs are unfounded and that only his own science is right; they will have a hard time understanding his science and will be offended by his disdain for their beliefs.

The problem of conveying the skills and techniques of contraception and of inculcating the habits necessary for the effective use of contraceptive materials is perhaps the biggest single problem of any such program. Much would depend on the particular contraceptive technique chosen. To be most successful on Yap, the technique should have certain characteristics. First, the technique must be in the hands of the women, not the men. Second, it should be as simple as possible. Dangers of misuse should be minimized even at the expense of a degree of failure to prevent conception. Like most nonwestern European peoples, Yaps do not have the sense of time and routine which we have developed so highly. Third, the materials should be cheap, easy to replace and, as indicated earlier, they should remain available. Fourth, the instructions must be clearly communicated and simple to follow, and there should be routine ways to check that they are understood.

SUMMARY

Induced abortion is a problem on Yap. It is a factor in keeping down the fertility rate and in prolonging the underpopulated state of the island. The practice of abortion cannot be understood apart from its cultural context. Until about the age of thirty, women who become pregnant are motivated to induce abortion, relying on a method that involves at least temporary injury to themselves. But after thirty, women have an intense desire for children. Older men, too, bemoan the low production of babies.

Young women resort to abortion because they have no other reliable means to prevent the birth of unwanted children. They do not want them because children would complicate the most highly valued pursuit available to young men and women on Yap, namely, elaborate and intricate love affairs involving a succession of lovers. The high value placed on love affairs is consistent with the fact that the Yaps consider adult responsibilities as appropriate only to people in their more mature years.

Up to the age of about thirty, Yap men and women are assumed to be "youths" rather than adults, and on Yap the proper behavior for youths is engaging in love affairs. The protracted period of youth is related to the fact that Yap is a stratified society in which positions of high rank are few in number and reserved for the older generation. The rewards of life prized above all others on Yap, the achievement of prestige and high status, are all found in late adulthood and old age. Freed from many of the responsibilities that are thrust upon men and women shortly after physiological maturity in many other parts of the world, young men and women on Yap can afford to preoccupy themselves with lovemaking. This preoccupation makes the long wait for high status tolerable and rewarding.

With the knowledge now on hand, it is difficult to estimate how much of the partial sterility on the part of women who are over thirty and who desperately want children is due to complications arising from abortions induced before the age of thirty when children are not wanted, and how much is attributable to the venereal infection of both sexes. But whether, in the interest of repopulation, one is primarily concerned with the control of abortion or with the control of venereal disease, he must recognize the significance of the love-making pattern and its relationship to the entire way of life on Yap. He must be aware that the needs and motivations of a Yap individual vary according to age. He must also realize that the introduction of any one change such as mechanical contraception, if not properly planned, can do as much to disturb the equilibrium as to correct it.

I. MELANESIA

B. MALINOWSKI

20. Kula: The Circulating Exchange of Valuables in the Archipelagoes of Eastern New Guinea[1]

In this article is described a special system of trade, obtaining over a widespread area and possessing several features remarkable in their bearing upon questions of primitive economics, as well as throwing some new light on native mentality.

The distant and perilous trading expeditions of the South Sea islanders are a well-known feature of their tribal life. We possess especially good descriptions of such voyages in Dr. Seligman's *Melanesians*. In that book, the *Hiri,* the seasonal voyage of the Montu to the Gulf of Papua, is treated in a brilliant monograph by Captain Barton, and Dr. Seligman himself gives an excellent analysis of the trading routes between the various islands of the East End of New Guinea (Seligman 1910: Chapters VIII and XL).[2]

All these trading systems are based upon the exchange of indispensable or highly useful utilities, such as pottery, sago, canoes, dried fish, and yams, the food being sometimes imported into islands or districts which are too small or too infertile to be self-supporting. The trading system, however, which will be described in this paper, differs in this and many other respects from the usual Oceanic forms of exchange. It is based primarily upon the circulation of two articles of high value, but of no real use. These

SOURCE: Reprinted from *Man,* Vol. 20 (1920), Article 51, pp. 97–105, by permission of the publisher.

[1] Some results of the Robert Mond Ethnological Research work in British New Guinea.

[2] For the trading system of the Mailu, a tribe living midway between Port Moresby and the East End of New Guinea, see Malinowski (1915).

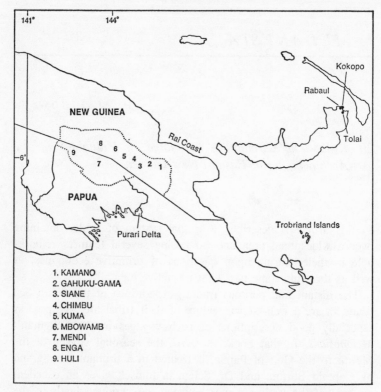

141°   144°

NEW GUINEA

Ral Coast

Kokopo

Rabaul

Tolai

8
6
9   5 4
7   3 2 1

-6°

PAPUA

Purari Delta

Trobriand Islands

1. KAMANO
2. GAHUKU-GAMA
3. SIANE
4. CHIMBU
5. KUMA
6. MBOWAMB
7. MENDI
8. ENGA
9. HULI

Sketch map of Melanesian tribes and places mentioned in the text.

are armshells made of the *Conus millepunctatus,* and necklets of
red shell-discs, both intended for ornaments but hardly ever used,
even for this purpose. These two articles travel, in a manner to
be described later in detail, on a circular route which covers many
miles and extends over many islands. On this circuit, the necklaces
travel in the direction of the clock hands and the armshells in
the opposite direction. Both articles never stop for any length of
time in the hands of any owner; they constantly move, constantly
meeting and being exchanged.

This trading system, the *Kula,* embraces, with its ramifications,
not only the islands off the East End of New Guinea, but also the
Louisiades, Woodlark Island, the Loughlans, the Trobriand Archipelago and the d'Entrecasteaux Group. It touches the continent
of New Guinea and extends its indirect influence over several

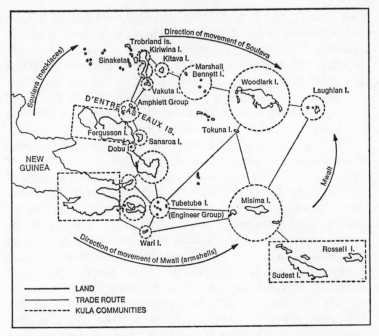

Sketch map of *Kula* showing the area, trade routes, and communities of the circular exchange. The dotted circles represent the *Kula* communities, the dotted squares represent the districts indirectly affected by the *Kula*.

outlying districts, such as Sud-Est Island, Rossell Island, and stretches of the northern and southern coast of the mainland.

A glance at the map will show the enormous geographical extent of the trading system, and the statement may here be anticipated that the *Kula* looms paramount in the tribal life of all the peoples who participate in it. These peoples belong to that branch of the Papuo-Melanesians whom Dr. Seligman calls the Massim, and whom he has characterised in the above-mentioned work (Seligman 1910: Introduction and Chapters XXXIII–LV). Some of them, living on big islands, have a very highly developed agriculture, and they harvest each year a crop amply sufficient for their needs and with a good deal to spare. Such are the natives of Woodlark Islands, of the Trobriands, of the d'Entrecasteaux Group. Others, again, who live on very small islands, like the volcanic Amphlett Rocks, Wari (Teste Island), Tubetube (Engineer Group), and some of the Marshall Bennett Islands, are not self-supporting as far as food goes. They are, on the other hand, specialised in certain industries, notably pottery and canoe-building, and they are monopolists in intermediary trade. Thus it is evident that exchange of goods had to occur between them. The important point about it, however, is that with them, and notably according to their own ideas, the exchange of utilities is a subsidiary trade, carried on as an incident in the *Kula*.

The *Kula* has been called above "a form of trade." The usual a priori notion of savage trade would be that of an exchange of indispensable, or, at least, useful things, done under pressure of need by direct barter, or casual give and take of presents, without much ceremony and regulation. Such a conception would almost reverse all the essential features of the *Kula*. Thus, first, the objects of exchange—the armshells and strings of shell-discs—are not "utilities" in any sense of the word; as said above, they are hardly ever used as ornaments, for which purpose they could serve. Nevertheless, they are extremely highly valued; nowadays a native will give up to £20 for a good article, and in olden days their value was an equivalent of this sum, if we take as a common measure such utilities as basketfuls of yams, pigs, and other such commodities. Secondly, the exchange, far from being casual or surreptitious, is carried on according to very definite and very complex rules. Thus it cannot be performed between members of these tribes taken at random. A firm and lifelong relationship is always established between any participant in the *Kula,* and a number of other men, some of whom belong to his own community, and others to oversea communities. Such men call one another *karayta'u* ("partner," as we shall designate them), and they are under mutual obligations to trade with each other, to offer protection, hospitality, and assistance whenever needed.[3]

Let us imagine that we look at the whole system from one definite point, choosing the large village of Sinaketa in the Trobriand Islands. An old chief in that village would have, say, some hundred partners southwards, and about as many again to the north and east, while a young commoner would have only a few on both sides. It must be remembered that not all men in a village

---

[3] *Karayta'u* is the word for "partner" in the language of Kiriwina, in the Trobriand Islands. All the terminology in this paper will be given in the language of the Trobriands, from which district the *Kula* has been studied.

take part in the *Kula,* and some villages are out of it altogether.

Now another definite rule is that the armshells must always be traded to the south, and the necklets of shell-beads to the north. The word "traded" is, of course, only a rough approximation. Let us suppose that I, a Sinaketa man, am in possession of a pair of big armshells. An oversea expedition from Dobu in the d'Entrecasteaux Archipelago, arrives at my village. Blowing a conch shell, I take my armshell pair and I offer it to my overseas partner, with some such words, "This is a *vaga* (initial gift)—in due time, thou returnest to me a big *soulava* (necklace) for it!" Next year, when I visit my partner's village, he either is in possession of an *equivalent* necklace, and this he gives to me as *yotile* (restoration gift), or he has not a necklace good enough to repay my last gift. In this case he will give me a smaller necklace—avowedly not equivalent to my gift—and will give it to me as *basi* (intermediary gift). This means that the main gift has to be repaid on a future occasion and the *basi* is given in token of good faith—but it, in turn, must be repaid by me in the meantime by a gift of small armshells. The final gift, which will be given to me to clinch the whole transaction, would be then called *kudu* (equivalent gift) in contrast to *basi*.

This does not exhaust the subtleties and distinctions of *Kula* gifts. If I, an inhabitant of Sinaketa, happen to be in possession of a pair of armshells more than usually good, the fame of it spreads. It must be noted that each one of the first-class armshells and necklaces has a personal name and a history of its own, and as they all circulate around the big ring of the *Kula,* they are all well-known, and their appearance in a given district always creates a sensation. Now all my partners—whether from overseas or from within the district—compete for the favour of receiving this particular article of mine, and those who are specially keen try to obtain it by giving me *pokala* (offerings) and *kaributu* (solicitory gifts). The former (*pokala*) consists, as a rule, of pigs —especially fine bananas and yams or taro; the latter (*kaributu*) are of greater value: the valuable "ceremonial" axe blades (called *beku*) or lime-spoons of whale's bone are given. There are further complications as to the repayment of these solicitory gifts, into which we cannot enter here, and the *termini technici* of the transactions are by no means exhausted by the words so far given.

But this is sufficient to make clear that the *Kula* involves a complicated system of gifts and countergifts, in which the social side (partnership), as well as the rules of give and take, are definitely established and regulated by custom. It must also be emphasized that all these natives, and more especially the Trobrianders, have both a word for, and a clear idea of, barter (*gimwali*), and that they are fully aware of the difference between the transactions at the *Kula* and common barter. The *Kula* involves the elements of trust and of a sort of commercial honour, as the equivalence between gift and countergift cannot be strictly enforced. As in many other native transactions, the main corrective force is supplied by the deeply engrained idea that liberality is the most important and the most honourable virtue, whereas meanness brings shame and opprobrium upon the miser. This, of course, does not completely exclude many squabbles, deep resentments and even feuds over real or imaginary grievances in the *Kula* exchange.

As said already, the armshells and shell-strings always travel in their own respective directions on the ring, and they are never, under any circumstances, traded back in the wrong direction. Also they never stop. It seems almost incredible at first, but it is the fact, nevertheless, that no one ever keeps any of the *Kula* valuables for any length of time. Indeed, in the whole of the Trobriands there are perhaps only one or two specially fine armshells and shell necklaces permanently owned as heirlooms, and these are set apart as a special class, and are once and for all out of the *Kula*. "Ownership," therefore, in *Kula* is quite a special economic relation. A man who is in the *Kula* never keeps any article for longer than, say, a year or two. Even this exposes him to the reproach of being niggardly, and certain districts have the bad reputation of being "slow" and "hard" in the *Kula*. On the other hand, each man has an enormous number of articles passing through his hands during his lifetime, of which he enjoys a temporary possession, and which he keeps in trust for a time. This possession hardly ever makes him use the articles, and he remains under the obligation soon again to hand them on to one of his partners. But the temporary ownership allows him to draw a great deal of renown, to exhibit his article, to tell how he obtained it and to plan to whom he is going to give it. And all this forms one of the favourite subjects of tribal conversation and gossip, in which the feats and the glory in *Kula* of chiefs or commoners are constantly discussed and rediscussed.

But the tradition of the *Kula* is not limited to the recounting of recent or historical exploits. There is a rich mythology of the *Kula*, in which stories are told about far-off times when mythical ancestors sailed on distant and daring expeditions. Owing to their magical knowledge—how they came to it no one knows distinctly —they were able to escape dangers, to conquer their enemies, to surmount obstacles, and by their feats they established many a precedent which is now closely followed by tribal custom. But their importance for their descendants lies mainly in the fact that they handed on their magic, and this made the *Kula* possible for the following generation.

The belief in the efficiency of magic dominates the *Kula*, as it does ever so many other tribal activities of the natives. Magical rites must be performed over the seagoing canoe, when it is built, in order to make it swift, steady, and safe; also magic is done over a canoe to make it lucky in the *Kula*. Another system of magical rites is done in order to avert the dangers of sailing. The third system of magic connected with overseas expeditions is the *mwasila* or the *Kula* magic proper. This system consists in numerous rites and spells, all of which act directly on the mind (*nanola*) of one's partner and make him soft, somewhat unsteady in mind, and eager to give *Kula* gifts.

In order to form a better idea of how the magic is woven into the many practical activities incidental to the *Kula,* it will be necessary to give a concrete outline of a trading expedition, and thus to supplement the set of rules and features enumerated above somewhat *in abstracto*. It will be best again to adopt a definite starting-point in our geographical orientation and to imagine ourselves again in Sinaketa, one of the main industrial and trading centres of the Trobriands.

Glancing at the map we see a number of circles, each of which represents a certain sociological unit which we shall call a *Kula* community. A *Kula* community consists of a village or a number of villages, who go out together on big overseas expeditions and who act as a body in the *Kula* transactions—perform their magic in common, have common leaders, and have the same outer and inner social sphere, within which they exchange their valuables. The *Kula* consists, therefore, first of the small, inner trade within a *Kula* community or contiguous communities, and secondly of the big overseas expeditions in which the annual exchange of articles takes place between two communities, divided by sea. In the first, there is a chronic, permanent trickling of articles from one village to another, and even within the village. In the second, a whole lot of valuables, amounting to over a thousand articles at a time, are exchanged in one enormous transaction, or, more correctly in ever so many transactions taking place simultaneously.

I will describe the normal and typical course of such a big overseas expedition as it takes place between the *Kula* community of Sinaketa with its surrounding villages and the Amphlett Group and Dobu districts to the south. Such an expedition would take place about once a year, but only every second or third year would it be carried out on a really big scale. On such occasions big preparations take place. First of all the large seagoing canoes must be made ready. As a rule a few new ones have to be built to replace those worn out and unseaworthy, and then those in good order have to be overhauled and redecorated. The building of a canoe, which cannot be described in this place in detail, is a big tribal affair. A series of magical rites have to be performed by a specialist or specialists, who are versed in the art of constructing and carving—the magic being considered indispensable to both arts. The magical rites aim successively at the expulsion of a wood spirit (*tokway*) from the tree to be felled; at the imparting of stability, swiftness and good luck to the canoe, and at the counteracting of evil influences cast on the canoe by direct sorcery or by the unwitting breaking of taboos. The rites—some performed in a simple manner by a magician alone, some ceremonially with the attendance of the whole community—are carried out in a series, associated with the various activities, inaugurating some, accompanying others. The magic is always interwoven with the technical operations and is to the native mind absolutely indispensable to the successful accomplishment of the task. Another important feature of canoe-building is the communal labour, which is always used at certain stages and for certain tasks, as for sail-making, the piecing together and lashing, caulking and painting of the canoe. The owner of the canoe has to pay for the work by gifts of *vaygu'a* (valuables) and distribution of food, and the expert magician-constructor directs the work.

The building and overhauling of canoes lasts for about six

months, for it is done slowly in the intervals of other work. As the expeditions take place usually in February–April, the canoe work begins some time in August or September. When all the canoes are ready, there is a big gathering from the whole district, and the canoes are launched ceremonially, and races and general festivities take place. Some days later all the canoes start on a preliminary trip to the neighbouring districts, that is, in the case of Sinaketa, to the northern half of the island, to Kiriwina proper. There is a custom, called *kabigidoya,* of ceremonially presenting a canoe, and the owner receives gifts, which form part of the subsidiary trade, to be used on the big expedition. More subsidiary trade is obtained by barter (*gimwali*), especially from the manufacturing districts on the north shore of the lagoon. Wooden combs, fibre armlets, baskets, mussel shells, and other articles, abundant here and rare in the Amphletts and in Dobu, are thus acquired in great quantities. On this preliminary trip the Sinaketans also obtain a number of armshells from Kiriwina by inland *Kula,* and with their wealth thus replenished return to Sinaketa.

A period of taboos and initial magic now obtains as the immediate preliminary to main departure. The owner of each canoe is subject to the most stringent restrictions—mainly referring to sexual relations—and he also performs all the magic. On an evening he goes into a garden and uttering a spell he plucks a spray of aromatic mint, which he brings home. Then he prepares some cocoanut oil, anoints the mint with it, and, putting some oil and the mint into a vessel, he medicates it all with another spell. The vessel—in olden days a contrivance of roasted and thus toughened banana leaves, now a small glass bottle—is then attached to the prow of the canoe. This magic aims at the softening of the Dobuan's mind, so that he may be unable to resist any appeal made to his generosity. This aim is explicitly stated by all natives, and an analysis of the magical spells reveals it also as their leading idea. But the magic is full of mythological allusions, of side ideas and of references to animals and birds, and it contains interesting metaphorical circumlocutions of the aims to be attained.

Other spells, all expressing more or less the same ideas, are used in the magical rite performed over a special bundle of valuables and goods, called *lilava,* which is placed in the centre of the canoe and must not be opened before the arrival in Dobu; also in the rite over the cocoanut leaves lining the canoe. Again, in the rite over the provisions of food taken on the journey, the main aim is to make it last long.

After the rites are finished and the expedition is ready, many people from the neighbouring villages assemble, the departing chiefs enjoin chastity to their wives and warn all the neighbouring male villagers to keep off Sinaketa, and prognosticate a speedy arrival with much *vaygu'a* (valuables). They are assured that they can depart in safety as no one will visit their village surreptitiously. Indeed, during their absence, the village should be kept tabooed, and if a man is found loitering about the place, especially at night, he is likely to be punished (by sorcery, as a rule) on the chief's return.

The fleet now sails south; but the first stage of the journey is short, as the natives halt on a sandbank some ten miles off Sinaketa, where they have a ceremonial distribution of food, which imposes an obligation on the *usagelu* (members of the crews) towards the *toliwaga* (owners of canoes) to carry out the expedition even in the face of contrary winds and bad weather. Next morning several rites are performed over the canoes to undo all evil magic and to make them swift and steady.

The open sea now lies before the fleet with the high, distant peaks of the d'Entrecasteaux mountains floating above the haze. In very clear weather the nearer Amphletts can be seen—small steep rocks, scattered over the horizon, misty, but more material against the faint blue of the distant land. These far-off views must have inspired generation after generation of Kiriwinian sailors with zest for adventure, wonder and desire to see the much-praised marvels of foreign lands, with awe and with superstitious fear. Mixed with it all—associated in the native mind with the allurement of the distant *koya* (mountains)—there was the ambition to return with plenty of *vaygu'a*. In myths, in traditional legends, in real stories and in songs, *Kula* expeditions were and are described and praised and there is a definite complex of *Kula* tradition and mythology, governed perhaps by two dominating emotions: the desire to obtain the *vaygu'a* and the dread of the dangers to be encountered.

These latter are real enough, as the wind in the N.W. season, when the expeditions take place, is changeable, and violent squalls obtain, and the sea is full of reefs and sandbanks. But the natives have added to that from their store of myth-making imagination, and have surrounded the real dangers with a fabric of imaginary perils and modes of escape. There exist for them big, live stones, lying in wait for a canoe—they jump up when they see one, and smash it to pieces and destroy the sailors. There is a giant octopus, which will take hold of a canoe and never let it go, unless a sacrifice is made of a small boy, adorned and anointed, who is thrown overboard to the *kwita* (octopus). There may come a big rain, which smashes and submerges the canoe. But the greatest danger comes from flying witches, who, whenever they hear that a canoe is drowning—and they possess the capacity of hearing it at enormous distances—assemble and wait till the men are in the water, and then fall on them. There is a deep belief that shipwreck in itself would not be fatal—the men would float ashore, carried by the *débris* of the canoe—unless the flying witches were to attack them. A whole cycle of beliefs centres round this main idea, and there is a system of rites which are always practised in shipwreck, and which, if carried out properly, would ensure safety to those shipwrecked.

One part of this magic is directed towards the flying witches; it blinds and bewilders them and they cannot attack the men in the waves. Another part is chanted by the *toliwaga* (master of the canoe) whilst he and his companions are drifting, suspended on the float of the outrigger, and it attracts a giant fish (*iraveaka*). This beneficent animal arrives and pulls the float and the men ashore. This is not the end; the shipwrecked party have to go through a series of ceremonies intended to make them immune from the flying witches, and only after that may they return to their village. This interesting account of a potential shipwreck and the magical rites referring to it I have obtained from several sets of independent informants. There are also a few definite traditions about actual salvage from death by drowning, through the carrying out of the magic.

The normal expedition, however, sails in one day with good following wind, or in several days if the wind is weak or shifting, and arrives at its first stage, in the Amphletts. Some exchange is done here, as well as on the further two intermediate halts in Tewara and Sanaroa and the concomitant magic has to be performed here. There are also several mythologically famed spots in these islands: some rocks from which magic originated—how, the myths do not relate distinctly—and other rocks, formerly human beings, who travelled to their present sites from very far, and to whom the natives offer *pokala* (offerings in order to have a propitious *Kula*). The island of Gumasila in the Amphletts, that of Tewara, and places on Fergusson Island, are important mythological centres.

But the main aim of the expedition is the district of Dobu, more especially the north-east corner of Fergusson Island, where on the flat and fertile foreshore, among groves of cocoanut, betel-palms, mangoes, and bread-fruit trees, there stretch for miles the populous settlements of Tautauna, Bwayowa, Deidei, and Begasi.

Before approaching them, the whole fleet stops on a beach called *Sarubwoyna,* not far away from the two rocks, *Atu'a'ine* and *Aturamo'a,* which are the most important, perhaps, of the rocks to whom *pokala* offering is given. Here the final magic is performed. All the *usagelu* (members of the crew) go ashore and collect leaves for magic. Spells are pronounced over them by the members of each canoe and everyone washes with sea-water and dries his skin with the medicated leaves. Then spells are uttered over cocoanut oil, red paint, and aromatic herbs—and the natives anoint and adorn themselves, the magic making them beautiful and irresistible. A spell is uttered into the mouth of a conchshell and the canoes get under way. The last distance, a few miles only, is traversed by paddling; and powerful spells are uttered by several men in each canoe, who recite them simultaneously, and the medicated conchshell is blown. These spells have to "shake the mountain"—that is, to produce a deep agitation in the minds of the Dobuans, and impress them with the arrival of the newcomers. One more important rite is uttered to prevent the Dobuans from becoming fierce and angry and to suppress any attempt at attacking the visitors.

Finally the party arrive, and it is the custom for the Dobuans to meet them with *soulava* (shell-disc necklaces) in their hands. The conchshells are blown and the necklaces are ceremonially offered by the Dobuans to the newcomers. Then the party go ashore, every man going to the house of his main partner. There the visitors receive gifts of food, and they again give some of their minor trade as *pari* (visitors' gifts) to the Dobuans. Then, during a several days' stay, many more *soulava* are given to the visitors. Often it is necessary for a Kiriwinian to woo his partner by gifts, solicitations, and magical rites, transparently performed, if the latter possesses a specially good and desirable article. All the transactions are carried out according to the rules set forth above.

Side by side with the *Kula,* the subsidiary trade goes on, the visitors acquiring a great number of articles of minor value, but of great utility, some of them unprocurable in Kiriwina, as, for instance, rattan, fibre belts, cassowary feathers, certain kinds of spear wood, obsidian, red ochre, and many other articles. This subsidiary trade is carried on by means of gifts and countergifts with one's own partners; by means of barter (*gimwali*) with other people; whereas certain articles are procured directly. Among the latter, the most important is the spondylus shell, fished by Sinaketans in the lagoon of Sanaroa, again under the observance of many taboos, and with the aid of magic, private and collective, simple and ceremonial. The shell called *kaloma* is, on their return home, worked out into the red shell-discs, which serve for making the *soulava* necklaces.

All the transactions in Dobu concluded, the party receive their parting gifts (*talo'i*) and sail back, doing the spondylus fishing just mentioned in Sanaroa, trading for pots with the Amphletts, and receiving additional *Kula* gifts and *talo'i* (parting gifts) in all the places where they go ashore on their return journey.

In due time, after a year or so, the Dobuans will make their return expedition to Sinaketa, with exactly the same ceremonial, magic, and sociology. On this expedition they will receive some armshells in exchange for the necklets previously given, and others, as advance gifts towards the next *Kula* transaction.

The *Kula* trade consists of a series of such periodical overseas expeditions, which link together the various island groups, and annually bring over big quantities of *vaygu'a* and of subsidiary trade from one district to another. The trade is used and used up, but the *vaygu'a*—the armshells and necklets—go round and round the ring.

We have here a very interesting form of tribal enterprises. In a sense they are *economic,* for the natives carry out their organised purposeful work under the stimulus of a desire for wealth, for ownership. The conception of value and the form of ownership revealed through the *Kula,* are different from those current among us, and this shows how necessary it is to apply a more detailed analysis to their economic ideas.

Again, the *Kula* presents a type of intertribal relationship of unprecedented magnitude, the standing partnership linking together thousands of people scattered over an immense area.

In this short preliminary account I have been able barely to touch upon the essentials of the *Kula*, and to give a summary account of one of its typical concrete manifestations—the expeditions from Sinaketa to Dobu. A more detailed and thorough description, which I trust will soon be forthcoming, will allow me to show many more of its important features.[4]

[4] Editor's note: In 1922 was published Malinowski's classic and full account of the *Kula*, his *Argonauts of the Western Pacific*.

REV. GERARD A. ZEGWAARD

21. Headhunting Practices of the Asmat of Netherlands New Guinea

The inhabitants of the swampy areas of southern Netherlands New Guinea have won a reputation for their headhunting practices. Because these practices were carried out even in the Australian Territory of Papua, which caused the Australian Government to protest, the Dutch Colonial Administration was forced to establish the first police post in Merauke with the Marind people (1902). The Jaqai have been forced to stop headhunting only since World War II; and the Asmat (at present thought to number about 25,000) still continue the practice.

During my stay with the Asmat (1952–1956; I had been with the related Mimikan tribes from 1946 to 1952) I had ample opportunity to study their headhunting practices on hundreds of occasions, as I was the first white man to take up residence among them and there was no representative of the Dutch Colonial Administration to enforce the ordinances against headhunting that were carried out elsewhere.

Though we may expect that even with the Asmat headhunting will gradually decrease and finally vanish, it is worth while to analyze the ideologies from which this practice originated. For, even when the Asmat people will no longer hunt heads, they will have these ideologies.

Because it is impossible to mention in detail all the differentiations that occur in the various districts among the different tribes of the Asmat area, I shall limit myself to the coastal area, notably

SOURCE: Reprinted from *American Anthropologist*, Vol. 61, No. 6 (1959), pp. 1020–41, by permission of the author and publisher.

to the inhabitants of the village of Sjuru, at the mouth of the Utumbuwé river near Flamingo Bay.

It may be mentioned in passing that the Asmat have associated headhunting with cannibalism. I had many an opportunity to observe this, but this exposition may make it clear that cannibalism is not the objective of headhunting (as far as the Asmat are concerned), but only a subsidiary part of it.

I will first give the mythical origin of the hunting feast and describe the ritual as taught in the past and executed by following generations. This mythical background was told to me by Warsékomen, elderly chieftain of Sjuru, an extremely clever man with a remarkable memory (he knew nine past generations of all clans in his tribe; in many instances I was able to check the correctness of his information against other sources). In his description of the myth he typically mixed the myth and the reality as experienced by him.

In the second part I will describe a number of customs and rituals that have a more or less close connection with headhunting, and the actual headhunting raid. In the third and final part I will attempt an explanation of the headhunting practice, in which we will meet with several factors that may have influenced the Asmat simultaneously, but not to the same extent.

1. THE MYTH BEHIND HEADHUNTING (AS TOLD BY WARSÉKOMEN)

There were two brothers. The senior was called Desoipitsj (*deso*—wound; *ipitsj*—man: man with wound) and the junior Biwiripitsj (*biwir* or *bewor*—many colored parrot: parrot man). Because of his physical condition the elder brother had always to stay indoors and the younger had to go out to support him. One day, returning from a hunting trip, Biwiripitsj brought home a pig. He cut off the head and thrust a dagger into the throat so that the point came out through the neck. The dagger was a sharpened cassowary thighbone. With the point of the dagger Biwiripitsj pinned the head of the pig to the floor of the hut, which was covered with bark. The elder brother had been watching and after some time remarked: "Bah, a pig's head is but a pig's head. Why not replace it with a human head? That would be something,

I think." But the younger brother didn't like the idea at all. "What are you talking about? Besides, where could I get a human head?" (The story presupposes that just the two brothers are around.) The older brother insisted, and proposed: "Well, you can have my head." But the younger wouldn't hear of this and refused emphatically. However, Desoipitsj continued to argue and in the end succeeded in persuading his younger brother. Biwiripitsj thereupon killed Desoipitsj with a spear, cut into the throat with a bamboo knife as far as he could, and pressed the head forward until the vertebrae of the neck cracked. He then removed the head from the body. The loose head, however, was able to speak and it gave instructions to Biwiripitsj, who obediently executed the orders given by it.

(1) To begin with, the head of Desoipitsj taught Biwiripitsj the technique of butchering (*nao*). He was told to make a deep cut with a bamboo knife from the anus to the neck in such manner that the cut went through one side of the trunk to the armpit and from there went by the collar bone to the throat. He was instructed to make a similar cut on the other side, but now from top to bottom. Through these openings he had to break the ribs with a sharpened palmwood stick (*om*) or with a stone ax (*si*). Then he put his hand underneath the chest, which could now be lifted easily and put aside. Arms and legs were first loosened, then cut off. Now Biwiripitsj took the entrails as in a bundle and removed them from the backbone with a vigorous jerk. Only the backside remained. The various parts, including the entrails, were placed in the fire and roasted. The upper part of the body and the arms were at once ready for consumption, but the lower part and the thighs had to be mixed with sago (a starch prepared from the pith of the sago palm) which had to be made in the form of long sticks, whereupon these too could be eaten. [Preparation of sago in the form of long sticks is often the usual way of preparation in the rest of southern New Guinea, but is done by the Asmat only on ritual occasions.]

(2) The second lesson related to the triumphant return of the men from a headhunting raid to their village, which was a prelude for the initiation rite of a young man. [Here we note how our informant, Warsékomen, unconsciously shifts from myth into reality; in the myth there was only Biwiripitsj, here Warsékomen and his men from Sjuru are in action.]

Biwiripitsj blew a bamboo hunting horn to make known the success of his raid. On the way home the "paddle song" was sung. But he had also explained how those who had stayed behind—the old men, the women, and the children—had to act. The eldest man was to ask the headhunters approaching on the river in their dugout canoes: "How did you get along? What did you accomplish?" Whereupon the leader of the headhunters, who meanwhile arranged their canoes side by side in battle array, was to answer: "I, Biwiripitsj, have been to the Islands river this night. I killed a man, a big man. The flesh lies in the canoe." From the river bank would come the question: "What is his name?" And the answer: "His name is Desoipitsj." That caused the people on the river bank to jump and howl, while the canoes covered the remaining distance at a tremendous speed. The women had adorned themselves with ornaments and were beside themselves, cheering and dancing in honor of the warriors.

Biwiripitsj showed them how the oldest brother of the mother of the boy who was to be initiated, had to submerge the decapitated head for a while under water and then run with it to the bachelors' house. [Pubescent Asmat boys are separated from their families and live in the bachelors' quarters, which serves also as clubhouse for the men.] Meanwhile the spectators sang a long-drawn "e-e-e-e-h" and sounded bamboo horns. Then the singers had to harmonize with Biwiripitsj and sing a song alluding to the pose of shame that had been assumed by the initiate. The mother's oldest brother had to pin the head to the floor of the bachelors' house near the fireplace, with a cassowary-bone dagger, so that it might dry partially.

(3) As the head was to play a principal part in the initiation of a son or a younger brother of the headhunter, Biwiripitsj now demonstrated the role of the initiate and at the same time the role of the mother's oldest brother. The latter made a mat and filled it with *eram* (magic) twigs. The initiate took the mat under his arm and walked out of the bachelors' house. He went to a canoe, put the mat on its bottom, and acted as if he returned to the place from whence the decapitated man came. He then apparently changed his mind and went back to the bachelors' house, after some water had been poured over his head. After entering the bachelors' house he sat down on the floor, lowered his head, did not look up, and paid no attention to what happened

around him. He assumed the pose of one who is ashamed, a taboo pose.

The initiate, acted by Biwiripitsj, received the name of the victim—that is, of the elder brother, Desoipitsj. The Asmat call this name the *nao juus* or decapitation name, often also referred to as *owam juus* or bamboo name (after the bamboo breast-plate that is later worn as a substitute of the hunted head). The new Desoipitsj persevered in his pose of shame for several days. Now and then the bystanders tried to upset him, but he sat tight. In this way he was to make clear that he was going to be a determined, fearless warrior.

He was subjected to various food limitations—the same taboos that rule the lives of new-born babies—for example, fish with thorns (a form of sympathetic magic: to avoid harm in the future).

The mother's oldest brother held the head long enough above the fire to scorch part of the hair. The ash of this burnt hair was mixed with some of the blood that had been collected in a mussel shell when the victim's head was cut. The mixture of blood and ash was smeared on the head, shoulders, and body of the initiate and thus the identity between the initiate and the victim was effected. Whereupon the initiate was adorned by his mother's oldest brother.

The ritual of identification and adornment had to take place in the afternoon or evening following the raid.

As instructed by the talking head of Desoipitsj, the whole body of Desoipitsj junior was painted with red ochre [burnt earth from the interior]. Alternating black and white stripes were painted on the face with wet ash and chalk. The hair of the initiate was lengthened with sago-leaf fibers, made in curls; a piece of mother-of-pearl had to hang on his forehead; on the back of the head were placed two big tassels of cassowary feathers; in the septum was placed a beautiful open-work swine-bone or wooden nosepin, decorated with beads or Job's tears; around the arms, wrists, calves of the legs, and the ankles, belts of finely split rattan were attached, and in one arm-belt was placed a carved human bone or a cassowary bone [dagger]; across the chest and the shoulders was put a crossed band; on the abdomen a triton shell; around the hips a sago-leaf-fiber apron [otherwise exclusively worn by married women]; and on the back the bamboo plate or *owam.* The bamboo plates are at first worn on the back and later shifted to the breast. [The breast is the more prominent place, as shown by the fact that it is the privilege of the great head-hunters to wear their ditty bag, *bilum,* on the breast, whereas lower persons wear it on the back.]

There are several plates. First, a bamboo lath, *bakar-owam,* about twelve inches long and one inch wide, with pointed tips; next, a combination of two or four shorter and narrower laths that are bound side by side, *owam pa,* and then another combination of still narrower but somewhat longer laths, arranged in such a way that they fill three-fourths of a circle (almost as the spokes of a wheel). The three types of bamboo plate are all used during the initiation; afterwards one type can be used as a common adornment on the occasion of festivities or warfare. Instead of the third bamboo plate a string of dogs' teeth may be used (*juur sis owam*).

When the initiate had been invested with the bamboo plates, the *mbipitsjin* (the skin of the victim that had covered his nose and upper lip) was hung over the plates, after it had been dried above the fire. (This piece of skin is removed separately during the scalping.)

(4) In the next instruction, the head of Desoipitsj taught Biwiripitsj and all future generations how to handle the decapitated head. In the evening the head should be roasted; during the night it should be kept on some sort of loft; and in the morning it should be scalped. But in the actual case of the first Desoipitsj this process was put off until the end of the whole ritual, because he had to continue his instructions. The treating of the head of the victim was again to be the function of the mother's oldest brother.

The next morning the head was to be taken down from the loft and the nose-skin was to be taken off first. Then the jaws had to be removed. The brothers of the initiate's mother worked in turns according to their age. While cutting and carving they would comment on the victim's past actions; for example, while taking the skin off the mouth one would say: "Yesterday this mouth ate fish on the bank of the river; today it is dead."

A cut had to be made with a bamboo knife or a shell across the head from the root of the nose to the nape of the neck. Thus the skin could be torn off in two pieces toward the ears.

The jaw bone had to be thrown outside; those interested could take it. It was eagerly seized and used as an ornament on the breast of a boy or woman who had to participate in the initiation rite.

The preparation of the head went on. It was held above the fire so that the flames touched the temple and the back. Then a hole was cut into it with the narrow side of a stone ax. The ax had been decorated and had been named after the victim [initiate]. The brains were then shaken out through the hole and caught in a mat. The mucus that came out first was at once removed. The brains were deposited in an *an,* a vessel made of the leaf-sheath of a sago palm. The remaining bits of brain were scraped out with a bamboo knife. About midnight the brains, mixed with sago prepared in the form of long sticks, were eaten exclusively by the old men.

After the eating of the brains, the leaves in which the sago had been wrapped were put in the *eram okop,* the magic mat. Into this mat also went the inedible parts of the body: eye balls, genitals and the like. [Information about the contents of the mat was whispered into my ear by Warsékomen.]

Thereupon the skull was painted with ash, ochre, and chalk, and then decorated with tassels of cassowary feathers, beads, and so forth. The nose was filled with resin, and a net was drawn over the whole head to facilitate attaching the ornaments. The decorated head was laid between the spread legs of the initiate, who meanwhile had been sitting on the floor of the bachelors' house in his pose of shame. In the myth the head of Desoipitsj was placed against the groin of the initiate. The head had to remain there for two or three days, and the initiate had to look at it incessantly. He could take food only stealthily, when no one watched him.

During these days the women of the celebrating community had to collect young pith of the sago palm, and each time they came home in the evening they had to announce their return by blowing bamboo hunting horns.

(5) One or two days later the ceremonies were continued according to the next instruction of Desoipitsj. Every villager had to adorn himself, and the canoes too had to be freshly painted with ochre and chalk. Everyone boarded the canoes. The initiate stood in the canoe of his relatives, and the skull was placed before

him on the bottom of the canoe. The brothers of the initiate's mother were to stand in front of him; later they would squat. Like an old man, the initiate would lean on a stick on which was set a disk with a hole in the center so that a few inches of the stick would show above the disk. The initiate would hold the stick with two hands somewhere in the middle. Slowly the canoes, manned with drumming and singing villagers, began to move down the river toward the sea—to the west, to where the sun sets.

The initiate acted like a worn-out old man; he appeared to become weaker and weaker, the farther westward they went. After a while he began to lean on the shoulder of an uncle and finally collapsed and lay down on the bottom of the canoe.

At that stage he was lifted by one of his mother's brothers and, together with the skull, was immersed for a while in the sea. After he was hauled back into the canoe, all his ornaments were taken off and put in the magic mat; they were never to be removed from it. From this moment on, the skull was no longer used by the initiate; he had to hang it on the breast of a woman, who had asked the owner-hunter for this favor.

While singing, all turned back toward the land, to the east, to where the sun rises. When they reached the shore, they entered the tide-flooded forest to look for crabs. The initiate joined them, but he had to be careful not to break off the pincers of a crab, as that might cause the death of the headhunter.

The initiate now acted as a new-born babe, and then as a child who did not know how to handle a paddle. He acted as if he did not know the name of the river and its tributaries, or the names of the trees. But gradually he seemed to learn more and more. At every tributary his name was called and he answered with his bamboo horn.

Back again in the village he did not enter the bachelors' house, but went to the house of his family. There he was again decorated from head to foot, and now the bamboo plates were hung on his breast while all present sounded a long-drawn "é-é-é-é-é-h." Henceforth the initiate acted as a young man, full of vigor and admired by all.

(6) After the submersion rite there were a few days of rest. The next instruction called for a ceremony in the sago-woods. While the whole community watched, the brothers of the initiate's mother cut down a sago palm and removed the bark. The initiate

looked on, together with the woman to whom he had handed the skull. Somewhere near the middle of the palm trunk a *gaba-gaba,* sago-leaf-stalk, was planted by his mother's brothers. By loosening the rind, except at the top and bottom of the stalk, they could bend the middle part so that an oblong hoop was formed.

First the woman with the skull approached and swung with a sago pounder through the opening of the hoop at the sago palm without touching it. She handed the pounder to the initiate, who in the same manner swung at the tree. Meanwhile the onlookers sang: *"Amus jene, amus jene . . ."* [sago pounder, sago pounder], following with the same song that was sung on occasion of the preparation of the head.

After this ceremony, everyone went in search of palm pith. The woman with the skull found palm pith for the initiate, who repaid her with pith that he had found. The woman also prepared some sago in the shape of a stick and gave a few pieces to the boy. Other pieces were put in the magic mat.

The ritual ended with the brothers of the initiate's mother decorating him once again.

The night after the sago-pounding ritual there was a dance in the bachelors' house, with drums providing the accompaniment. The following morning all lengthened their hair with curled sago-leaf fibers. For the last time the initiate and the skull were decorated for the final ceremony, which was to take place the next night. The skull was hung in the center of the bachelors' house. At night a fire was built in front of the house, and singers and dancers sat in groups in solemn silence. Then the initiate came out of the bachelors' house, carrying the magic mat under his arm and in his hand the richly decorated skull. The men carried shields which they moved up and down, toward them and away from them, while a song was intoned; the dance began and the initiate joined the men, swinging the skull. The songs which were sung during the preparation of the head and during the sago pounding were repeated.

This dance, which with some breaks lasted until dawn, completed the *nao pokmbu,* the headhunting and initiation festivity.

In the myth the head of Desoipitsj was at this time roasted and scalped, as described earlier, after it had once more emphatically ordered that in the future all should obey its instructions.

Warsékomen ended his description of the myth with this apologetic remark: "If Desoipitsj had not pressed the headhunting and butchering on his brother Biwiripitsj, we the people of the Asmat would never have been headhunters."

Additional remarks on the mythical procedures. Thus, in the myth, the headhunting festivity came down from Desoipitsj, who instructed his younger brother in everything connected with the festivity.

The first ceremony was the butchering. The method described above is also applied when a cassowary, pig, crocodile, or big lizard is slaughtered. Throughout New Guinea we find regional instructions on the slaughtering of animals, and these regional methods are faithfully executed on both animals and human beings.

The actions of both the headhunters and those who stayed behind are also regulated; they consist mostly of certain traditional songs.

The heads acquired are intended for the initiation of sons and younger brothers, nephews and cousins. At times it is hard for a hunter to decide who is to be favored. All the different sections of the village, grouped around the bachelors' houses, have claims and those who have treated the others expect a feast in return. Often the claims of the different clans would lead to altercations and sometimes to bloodshed. On such occasions the corpses of the headhunting victims would be the subject of fights, would be taken and retaken by the different factions. It has happened that village unity has been permanently damaged by such fights.

Young boys are the proper candidates for heads, but, in what seem abnormal circumstances, older males and even women may be favored. The pose of the initiate, acting as if he were the decapitated victim, has a special meaning. The informants emphasized repeatedly that the initiate is smeared with the ash of the burnt hair and with the blood of the victim. This is explained by the fact that the initiate assumes the name of the victim. This identity between victim and initiate will later prove very useful. When meeting the initiate, even after many years, relatives of the murdered person will always call him by his assumed name, the victim's name, and treat him as their relative. They dance and sing for him and give him presents. It is strictly forbidden to kill people from other villages who, because of their ritual names, are related to one's village. These people are often chosen to be negotiators. On my tours I frequently hired them to be my guides to tribes hostile to their community. More than once I witnessed persons with the adopted names of headhunting victims being enthusiastically welcomed by relatives of the victim, especially on our Mission station where we had visitors from all parts of the district. Cases are known of the killing of such people but it is considered a very serious breach of the taboo law, and violators were said ultimately to meet their punishment, for example by the extinction of the whole family by disease.

There are definite regulations governing what is to be done with the head and how the scalping, removal of the brains, and decoration of the skull have to be performed. It should be noted that the initiate is absolutely excluded from the cannibalistic meal, in which the brains are consumed. It is certain that only the head is taken to the bachelors' house (social and ritual center of the neighborhoods), where it must undergo the ritual treatment. The flesh of the body is distributed at once after the butchering, according to the traditional scheme, among relatives and friends; after the return to the village it is taken to their homes. Even the women and children get their share. The bones are for the dogs.

For a considerable time the skull must rest between the thighs of the initiate, almost touching his genitals; thus there is thought to be a relationship between the skull and the genitals of the youngster, whose initiation marks his entry into manhood.

The immersion rite is clearly a rite of passage, with a ritual death and ritual rebirth. A cosmic event—the daily course of the sun—seems to have suggested this ritual: a parallelism in which sunrise is thought of as birth and sunset as death.

The sago pounding and the nightly dance with the decorated skull need not be interrelated, as may be gathered from the lapse of time between these phases. It is possible that the ritual sago pounding is a later addition for it seems to be associated with the following myth, which was related in the form of a song in a bachelors' house of Sjuru on the occasion of the inauguration of that house in the Ar section (December 26, 1953): *omo Faitepi omo.* . . . (*Fait* is the name of a river, southeast of the Asmat area; *ep* is the mouth of the river; *om* is a club, used by those who have no axes, to uproot the soil around a tree and also to remove the rind from a trunk.)

Biwiripitsj [this name appears in many mythical stories] went with his wife and children to the river Fait to pound sago. Near the mouth (*ep*) of the river he felled a palm that was in full flower and with his rooting stick he removed the rind, beginning at the *umu* (part of the trunk where the branches begin) and cutting toward the *mopan* (the thick part near the roots). Biwiri-pitsj then called his son and ordered him to lie prostrate on the bare trunk of the tree. The boy did so. The father [according to some versions the mother] took a sago pounder and struck the boy's neck with force. The head, decorated with hair-lengthenings, was separated from the body and with a few jumps landed in a *jimemmut* tree, where it became entangled by the hair. Blood from the head trickled down the trunk. The chin pointed upward and the hair-lengthenings hung down. The father [or mother] struck again and again with the pounder and smashed the body. Blood and flesh were entirely mixed with the pith of the sago palm, and the entrails splashed high into the surrounding trees. When the mother began to work the pith, it proved to be very easy to knead. She rejoiced and said: "Before it was very hard to knead sago and wring it out, now it's extremely easy." The son, however, was not completely dead, for the head began to talk. He taught his father the songs that have to be sung at the decapitation festivities: the songs on the way home from a raid, at the arrival in the village, when shaking out the brains, and so on.

2. CUSTOMS AND RITUALS CONNECTED WITH HEADHUNTING

Ancestors' cult. Before we discuss the various ceremonies in detail, it will be necessary to indicate first the relation between war (in the form of headhunting) and other rituals. Almost every larger festivity or public ritual presupposes a headhunting raid. The festivities occur at regular, short intervals and generally last for several months. Often the festivities are organized at the same time or with a short interval in the various neighboring villages.

The main festivities are: (a) the celebration at the building of a new bachelors' house, (b) the festivities on the occasion of the carving and the erection of an ancestor pole, and (c) the weaving of masks, followed by a solemn mask dance. On the occasion of any of these celebrations the spirits of the dead are supposed to come back to the community of the living.

When celebrating the building of a bachelors' house, grubs of the sago beetle are gathered and solemnly poured down from a loft into a cylindrical basket of sago-leaf ribs (*gaba-gaba*). The basket (*samu mini: samu* is the name for the spirits of the decapitated, spirits without heads; *mini* means a straight basket), which may be five to seven feet long, is filled to the brim and taken apart after the ceremony.

In the case of the ancestor pole, the spirits are carved in wood —for example, on the prow of a canoe.

The masks too represent the spirits of the deceased. However, on each occasion (celebration of the bachelors' house, the ancestors' pole, the masks) the spirits are allowed to stay for just one night. Then they are terrified and attacked without mercy. Thus, it seems that all festivities have the same object: to drive away the souls, who are forced to migrate to the *safan,* the realm of the souls, beyond the sea.

These rituals revive the memory of the dead and their revengeful feelings. But there is more: when we try to find out which spirits seem to play a part in the rituals, we discover that they involve largely the spirits of decapitated people—in other words, spirits who have a special reason to be angry or who, when living, had proven that they were not to be mocked at; spirits who may harm the community. Even these spirits are urged to leave and to cross to hades. When they have received the satisfaction of revenge they are more easily induced to go away.

The names of these spirits are passed on to other persons who will take over their duties and functions, and thus it is made quite clear to them that they are no longer needed.

On similar occasions the neighboring Kamoro (in Mimika) tell the spirits that they are indeed excellent boar hunters or warlords, but that the survivors can easily get along without them, because there are still good hunters and war-lords left in the community. In fact, the Asmat and Kamoro tribes have much in common, both in language and culture.

As headhunting appears to be a part of the big rituals and because those rituals aim at driving away the spirits, it may be inferred that headhunting is also practiced to get even with and to satisfy the spirits. Thus it is practiced to urge the spirits to retreat.

Therefore, such rituals are not foreign to the general frame of Asmat religion in which the spirits of the deceased play the predominant part; on the contrary, they are an integral part of the religion. New canoes, new houses, spears, paddles, breast- and back-bags, strings of dogs' teeth, and even domestic dogs and pigs are named after the dead. The ornamentation of the mentioned objects can be understood in terms of this attitude and it is not surprising that human figures—either realistically or idealistically represented—are the essential pattern of Asmat art. And in the mind of the Asmat, they are real, they live. All these objects are generally called *etsjo pok,* things that make great. They serve to kindle thoughts of revenge and may be given to others who, by accepting such gifts, bind themselves to cooperate in the retaliation.

On one occasion, after a murder occurred in Sjuru, one of the relatives of the murdered man gathered a bundle of fire-wood and gave it the name of the deceased. He kept the wood in the loft of the bachelors' house, and after some time offered it to people of the other sections of the village. Those who accepted agreed to help him retaliate.

In the bachelors' houses the posts, roofbeams, central beam, walls, and the like, are named after the fathers and the brothers of those who occupy the houses. In the newly-erected bachelors' houses, the walls would not be placed until the *fo mbufum* ritual had been performed, that is, until the new canoes (again named after the spirits of the deceased) had been publicly put into use by removing the mats which concealed the ancestors' figures.

The Asmat, therefore, is surrounded by *etsjo pok,* objects named after the deceased, which remind him of his duty of revenge. The etsjo pok are not limited to private property (canoes, private houses, paddles, spears), but include public property as well (bachelors' houses, masks, ancestor poles).

Ceremonials connected with headhunting. First there is the *firao wu* ceremony, which opens the celebration for the construction of a new bachelors' house. A pole of palm pith (*firao wu*), which must end in a thick knob, is cut with ritual paraphernalia. The pole is decorated and carried in procession to the canoe. The accompanying ritual is similar to that of the return from a headhunting

raid: bamboo-horn blowing, singing of the paddle song, the loud
reception in the village where the oldest man will ask: "What did
you bring?" And the reply of the senior man in the canoe: "We
have killed a big man, he lies in the canoe." The pole is carried
into the village where the knob (*kus*—head) is cut off. This ritual
is performed either before or after the headhunting raid. Mention
may be made of a similar ritual among the Kamoro of Mimika,
in which some people act as pigs and are "killed" in a mock killing; this is in preparation for a headhunting raid. After this ritual is
over, the leader of the "pig men" declares that the headhunting
raid will be successful.

Another ritual is that of the *eram asan* or magic trunk. When
a new bachelors' house is inaugurated, the lower part of a thin tree
trunk is smeared with some mixture. The kind of tree and the
ingredients of the mixture are known only to the performer of the
ritual. During the night, fires are solemnly built in the new fire-
places. One of the leaders holds the pole in the fire; burning of the
mixture produces a smoke that has a penetrating smell. One of
the components of that mixture seems to be cassowary fat. The
performer conjures the *namjipi,* the souls of the enemies, who
are much feared, and invites them to come and eat the smell of
the mixture. (Namjipi is the name for the soul of a body that is not
yet dead.) The intention of this performance is to bring about
some sort of enchantment of the enemies. The Asmat are convinced that the souls of the living can leave the body when a person
is sleeping. This happens in particular when the head is in an un-
comfortable position, for in that case the soul (thought to reside
in the head) is more inclined to leave and roam around until daybreak. If that soul, on its wanderings, eats of the smell of roasted
pig or of some other things, its owner will be killed not many days
later by the inhabitants of the village where his soul was a guest.

On one occasion I witnessed the ritual butchering of a pig in
Sjuru; the namjipi souls of some enemies were called up in that
manner so as to be destroyed.

There is a myth about two heroes, Beweró and Tasjim, who
died because their souls had eaten of the smell of roasting meat in
a hostile village the night before their death.

If a person sees the roaming soul of a friend, disaster may be
averted if that friend is warned in time. The one who is warned
must reward his friend with a present.

A third ceremony is what the Asmat call the *dewe natakan* (in some communities the *naan atakan*), which is performed on various occasions. The achievements of the headhunters are called out. They boast: "I killed a big man on such and such river; I killed a big woman on such and such river; I killed another man . . . ."

I heard the most detailed dewen when I traveled on several rivers which were unknown to my rowers. At every tributary (also at whirlpools, which are thought to be entries to the underworld) all the men were bragging about their achievements.

On other occasions only the most important headhunters get a chance to do their boasting—for example, at the first stroke of the ax in the carving of an ancestor pole, or when the long basket is opened in which the grubs of the sago beetle had been placed, or when new warriors are inaugurated. The foregoing indicates that the dewen is always performed in awkward situations, for on all these occasions the people are confronted with something new and all that is new is dangerous because of the new spirits connected with it. In the same situations, the neighboring Kamoro speak of a *kaipiri,* a condition to which one is new, so that one is more subject to the harmful influence of the spirits.

It is entirely in accordance with the general attitude of the Asmat to cope with the frightening situation by over-awing the forces behind it by bragging about themselves. According to Asmat tradition, even after death the deceased will, at his arrival in the realm of souls, tell hair-raising stories of wars and fights in which he was the hero. Ordinary wounds and scars are bragged about as having been received during such fights. The enumeration of achievements on headhunting raids may be seen as an attempt to make the spirits more cautious, and thus it is regarded as a means to safeguard both the person who calls the dewen and those who join him.

Toward the end or after the bigger festivities a *fo mbufum* may be organized. This is the solemn unveiling of the carved memorial prow of a canoe, named after some one who has died. The brothers-in-law of the deceased are the performers. They receive a long stick stuffed with the grubs of sago beetles and also a large ball of sago. They take the food into the new canoe, and row toward the hostile place where their relative was killed. Most of the time they do not go beyond the spot where the tributary river, on which their relative had been killed, branches off. There they make a small rack on which both the stick and the ball are deposited,

after offering them to the soul of the deceased by a gesture toward
the place where the soul is thought to dwell. A few grubs are
dropped into the river. The Asmat intend this food to be eaten by
the souls. The food is uncooked; the souls do the opposite of what
the living do, and thus eat uncooked food. After the food has been
brought away and offered, they remove the mat which had hidden
the figure on the prow of the canoe from the eyes of women and
children. The food is taken back into the canoes; at home it will
be roasted and eaten by the brothers-in-law. The day of revenge
is not far away: the ceremony of the fo mbufum is considered a
threat.

Threats are expressed in various ways, mostly in the form of
arrows or other implements of war, placed in conspicuous spots.
A favorite method of frightening enemies and keeping war
psychosis alive is inventing and spreading lies and using tricks to
confuse the enemies and make them nervous. I was often in contact with tribes which were hostile to each other, and traveling (for
which I needed rowers) became very difficult as a result of these
lies and false stories. The *nao piri* (lie connected with headhunting) is sometimes concocted by the entire group in the bachelors'
house. They appoint someone who can visit the hostile village
without being harmed—for example, because his decapitation name
(bamboo plate name) is from that village, or because his mother
or relatives came from there, or perhaps because he was given by
the village as ransom or in reconciliation. He is sent to spread some
rumor, for example, that village A is going to move to river B to
catch fish. Thus the inhabitants of village C will have a chance to
gather sago in the part of their territory adjacent to the territory of
A. If village C believes this story, its inhabitants will be attacked
and possibly slaughtered by A. Before the man who has to spread
the story leaves the bachelors' house, all men present eat a lump
of sago with which they have rubbed his body. Sometimes this sago
is mixed not only with his sweat but even with his blood, taken
from a scratch made for the purpose.

In several communities there is a ceremony which the Asmat
call *ai tes* (probably means: new ornaments). New spear bearers
are inaugurated after being decorated. Sometimes they must stand
for two days and are subject to numerous taboos. They must plunge
into the river and are then covered with a cloud of chalk which is
thrown over their heads. In the Islands River area, the ai tes cere-

mony is considered an indication that a village will soon be going on the war path. A related ceremony is that of the *bajip,* the public decoration of two youngsters on the occasion when they wear their triton shells for the first time. This triton shell is a very precious and important ornament and is worn on the abdomen by the warlords whenever they are performing their duties.

Background and Preparation for Headhunting. There are many variations of the work preparatory to the actual headhunting raid. At times there is no preparation at all, because the Asmat avail themselves of an opportunity—for example, they kill their guests or people who ventured too far from home. Thus headhunting raids with a ritual preparation, planned to be large and to involve alliances, are relatively rare.

It often happens that visitors are cordially welcomed and treated but later killed, especially in their sleep. Such visitors may even be given presents and later attacked as they are leaving. They may be under the special protection of some family which may try to protect them but is defeated by the majority. This, of course, is a humiliation to the protecting family. After one such occasion in Sjuru, a war lord and his group broke away from the other clans and built a new bachelors' house at another spot.

Since headhunting is associated in the origin myths with the ancestors, who were the great leaders and instructors, every village has its own peculiarities. But the main background of headhunting seems to be safeguarding the territory and therefore the food supply. For, according to the origin myths, the prime function of the ancestors is the protection of the tribe's economic prerogatives. The origin stories do not account for the origin of the world (creation), but they do emphasize the fact that the ancestor selected a definite territory for himself and his progeny. As the Asmat live exclusively on the products of nature without cultivation, ownership of village territory is vital to them. The ancestor of the tribe taught men the use of arms to protect their territory. While the men form a protective ring, the women can pound sago, catch fish, and gather mollusks in the tide-flooded woods. The men scout the area, the women follow and begin work.

Each ancestor left to his tribe his special magic objects which are kept in a bag, *eram ésé.* Some have played a part in the life of the ancestor or his wife: a round stone, a flat disk, a string of dogs' teeth. Some were brought by the ancestor from his native land (mythological world): the tusks of a wild boar, the teeth or the gall of some serpent. Most of them are also mentioned in the origin myth. These objects are called *omer pok,* things to frighten with. Before an attack on the enemy they are used to frighten the enemy and to make him an easy prey.

Ornaments worn in war have the same function as ornaments used for festivities (which are similar to the war ornaments). These festivities are a kind of war, aimed at driving away the spirits. The sago palm is widely used on both occasions. It seems to be no coincidence, but a result of Asmat thinking, that the same words are used for the ornaments of men and for the blossoms of plants and trees. A man with all his ornaments reminds the Asmat of a tree, and especially of the sago palm, in full blossom.

Another group of ornaments (red ochre, white chalk, black ash, bones of bears, bones and feathers of the cassowary, human bones, nose shells, white-parrot feathers, tree-rat skins) are also symbols of strength and courage, which aim to frighten. The ornaments not only display these qualities, but cause them too. For the Asmat, ornaments are equipment and armament. They are not allowed to wear them when on a friendly visit, for this would be demonstrative and would in fact invite trouble. In the Agats district the breaking of this rule caused frequent fights.

The chalk used for decoration is mixed with pulverized leaves and makes the men brave. The chalk thrown at the enemy is of a different composition and aims to frighten. Furthermore, chalk makes "hot" and throwing chalk is a challenge. To "warm up" for an occasion, the Asmat eat the leaves of the stinging nettle (for example, when erecting a bachelors' house) and also a kind of ginger.

In the village of Biwar the men sat around the stone disk which the ancestor-mother had worn on her abdomen. By moving their bellies toward the disk while sighing, they hoped to participate in the courage of the tribal mother who had foretold that her offspring would have the ferocity of the serpent while the neighboring Atsj would have the ferocity of the saw-fish. These qualities can probably be explained as totemistic, for the respective Mother and Father of the two tribes possessed the qualities of the mentioned animals in a high degree, namely, slyness and brute force. One preparation for a headhunting raid by the Asmat is to draw the imprint of a cassowary foot on their soles, calves, and thighs. The same drawing is found on the new canoes and on the stone axes. To the Asmat the cassowary is the symbol of swiftness and strength.

Immediately before the attack, the leader of the headhunting raid addresses the sun and asks for courage for his fellow warriors and for fright in the enemies. Enemies are lured into an ambush with the collar bone of a turtle or with a forked bough. The war-leader makes gestures indicating "come this way." During the night preceding the raid, sorcerers go to the village of the enemies to charm it from nearby. They blow water through a loop or throw it toward the enemy.

Shortly before the raid the *onam so,* the song of the clouds, is sung, at least in the Bismam villages around Flamingo Bay. This song was sung by the ancestors of the Bismam when they rowed down from the mountains to the coast. It tells of the inhabitants of the "world above," of the ancestors of all villages who live there (every village on earth has a parallel village in the world above); it mentions all those who are mad, crippled, deformed, charmed; it tells about the misers, the roughnecks, the lizards, the thunder-men, the light-men, the white-cloud men, the black-cloud men, the ant-men, the gnat-men, the spider-men, the wasp-men, the mantis religiosa men, the worm-men. Of all these people it is said *ae mira fenaoa* (archaic language, seeming to mean: they harm us). People of the world above, abnormal people, outstanding people, men of the natural phenomena, men of the insects and the lizards, annoy the inhabitants of earth. This is a striking resemblance to the neighboring Kamoro people who, at the end of the "kaware" festivity, organize a ritual war against the spirits that embitter their lives.

The "song of the clouds" sings of the spirits that set all sorts of traps for men, manifesting themselves in all forms, not only in abnormal and deformed persons (abnormality and deformation are ascribed to the presence of spirits in the body), but also in the animals that annoy people. In the Asmat way of thinking, spirits take the shapes of crocodiles, birds, mice, and fireflies. The spirits have hindered man in various ways and thus he became weaker and weaker; that is why man needs rejuvenation.

The second part of the "song of the clouds" is an enumeration of scores of trees of the species that grow on plankroots, which are the favorite abodes of the spirits, and also of scores of grasses and reeds. From these hiding places the spirits steal upon man, molest him, make him ill and weak.

Next comes the *é'so* in which the different parrots are mentioned. *Bewör [parakeet] araotsj-o tsja tsjem-a tamoranése ajua.* ("Younger brothers [araotsj-o] of the Bewör [etc.] to whose house will we be going tomorrow morning?") The Opet, Jür, Sokor and all kinds of parrots are sung of in turn. The text runs as follows: Each line puts the same question to a different group of parrots. (Warriors call themselves the younger brothers of the parrots.)

They continue by addressing the tree-kangaroo (*fatsj*) and different kinds of squirrels.

Parrots and squirrels are famous fruit eaters, as noted in songs and stories, and men about to go headhunting feel a relationship to these beings and call themselves their brothers. (Remember the parallelism between the human body and a tree, the human head and its fruit.)

The song is repeated many times and sung softly so that the singers can not be heard by the women and children, who are sleeping in the family houses.

In Sjuru a swine hunt was organized on the eve of the headhunting raid. The swine was butchered on an open space between the war canoes that were lined up in two rows on the river bank. The head of the swine was offered to the leader of the raid. The people of Sjuru believe that the mythical swine that lured the ancestors of the Bismam group to the earth traveled with them to the coast hanging beneath the prow of a canoe. This swine is believed to join the raid in the same manner, causing a short curved swell (resembling the tusks of a swine) with its growling. This swell will get the enemies into trouble. The Amberep, I was told, had the custom of having the women dance before the men go on a headhunting raid. One of the women would tie the head of a swine on her buttocks. The older men, watching this dance, were supposed to remark that it would be better to have a dance with human heads. (Recall the beginning of the myth of headhunting.)

Another example of the preparations for a headhunting raid is this: The men gathered in the bachelors' house want to know if the raid will be successful. A sorcerer smears his right hand with chalk mixed with pulverized leaves; he rubs the hand faster and faster and so vigorously that blood trickles down from it. That is what the men have been waiting for: there is to be bloodshed! The sorcerer gets wilder, he takes his right hand in the left and swings both hands through the air. He runs up and down the bachelors' house in a trance. Suddenly he runs to one of the men and gesticulates as if cutting off a head and cutting a body into pieces. He becomes rational again after holding his hand in the fire. That is the end of the ceremony.

On one occasion, Jisinamakat of Sjuru performed a pantomime. He imitated a woman who was ready to pound sago and was looking for her pounder, sieve, and bags. Then he imitated a man who was to accompany his wife, looking for his paddle, bow, and arrows. Jisinamakat showed how husband and wife walked to the canoe and went off to the sago woods. After this performance the men needed no more hints. At once they rowed to the Seper river and laid an ambush. Shortly after that two men of Amberep entered the sago woods; they were attacked and killed. Their wives who had followed at some distance managed to escape.

Had Jisinamakat only foreseen the coming of the Amberep people or had he caused them to come by means of his magic? The Sjuru people are inclined to believe it is the latter.

The Headhunting Raid. The headhunting raid proper normally takes place in the early morning, shortly before daybreak. The participants, exclusively men, are divided in three groups: leaders who only give advice and commands, archers who open the attack by shooting from a distance, and spearmen and shieldbearers who attack from close by and do the actual killing.

The leaders are old men, the seniors of the families. The archers are strong men of middle age, who distinguished themselves on former occasions. They also hold the bows and arrows of the others in reserve. The spearmen form a semicircle at the back of the village, waiting for the frightened villagers to take to the woods when attacked from the front by the archers.

After the headhunting party has approached as near to the enemy village as possible in their canoes (the villages are all close to the river), they go ashore and take their positions. Then some one makes a noise. From one of the houses some man will call: "Who is that?" The answer is: "Your husband, Sjuru" (where Sjuru is the attacker). As a result of the sudden attack, panic breaks out; women and children flee into the woods or try to get away in canoes. The men may also try to escape, or they may put up a brave fight, sometimes after feigning flight. For that reason the invaders have every reason to strike quickly. Conditions are not altogether in their favor and the fortunes of war may easily turn.

The young people among the attackers are given the best chance for renown and priority to enable them to prove themselves, but there are always some middle-aged men who want to increase their prestige. In exceptional cases a woman or child is spared. If a raider wants to keep a captured woman or child alive, he has to make this quite clear, as the killing will often turn into an orgy. Such a woman or child will be taken to the attackers' village to start or expand a family. When a village has a shortage of women, their abduction may be the sole objective of a raid.

The young man who has cornered his victim will say: "Fathers, brothers, the women of our village never took any notice of me. I'll take this woman home." Or: "Fathers, brothers, I want an *asé pitsua* (a dagger of cassowary bone, worn on the hip as proof of being a great headhunter)." One who wants a decoration of this sort has to kill.

The success of the attack is announced by blowing the bamboo hunting horn. As soon as a victim is overpowered the *kus jetet* begins: a wild outburst of joy which is at the same time a reaction to tense nerves. The victims are seized, beaten, pushed around, and generally ill-treated. The head of the victim is particularly subjected to torture. The victorious raider yells constantly: "My head, my head won in the raid."

It is imperative to discover the name of the victim. Usually some one knows the name, especially when the raid was not too far from the home village. If the name is unknown, the hunters may use a trick to find out what it is. In 1954 three men marked for killing were received in a certain village as guests, and when a song was intoned in their honor they were asked to give their names so that they could be mentioned in the song. They could then be killed.

Only when the raiders are in a hurry are the victims killed at once. Then, only the head and thighs may be taken. Ordinarily the victims are dragged to the place where the raiders left their canoes, and placed in a sitting position in the bottom of a canoe with their hands and chest hanging over a pole. Then the invaders set out for home.

Somewhere on the way they leave a sign for the relatives of the victims, a man's ornament or a woman's skirt, placed in a conspicuous spot. There is no reason to suppose that the female victims are raped (my informants denied that rape took place and I never found evidence of it in the many cases which I investigated) but they are stripped and, like the men, ill-treated in many ways.

The most lugubrious sign left behind was done by the men of Puér, who tied parts of the intestines together and hung them across a small river.

On one occasion I saw a sign composed of an arrow point, a red fruit, and some hair of the victim. The arrow point and fruit were intended to attract attention, and the hair of the victim was identification for the family members who had not yet discovered their loss.

The victims are beheaded one after another at the confluences of rivers or at river bends (places where living spirits are found). The beheading is done by persons with special skill for it; the butchering and the distribution of flesh are done in the manner already described. After the festive home-coming, the raid celebrations, *nao pokmbu* (as taught by Desoipitsj) begin.

3. EXPLANATION OF THE HEADHUNTING PRACTICE

In this part I will attempt to draw a conclusion from the accumulated facts and account for the headhunting practices of the Asmat.

The Asmat is not a philosopher and cannot explain his behavior. He lives almost exclusively in a world in which his activities are regulated by customs that have become traditional in his community. Only on rare occasions will he make a more rational decision; as a rule he does what is done by everyone else in his environment and because it is done by everyone else. He will explain his actions by referring to the *o nditsjür,* the ancients, the ancestors. This does not mean that the Asmat has no convictions of his own, basic to his actions. Though most of the time he does not seem to be conscious of his motives, we would not be justified in assuming that he always acts without reason and is only directed by the traditional pattern of life. While comparing the different myths and stories, I discovered that changes in actions had taken place and are taking place all the time, and that such changes are the result of individual, contemporary thinking, of which the people are themselves unconscious.

The practice of headhunting is complex and rather confusing, many factors simultaneously and consecutively contributing to its origin and continuance.

Among the important factors are (1) the cosmology of the Asmat (or rather, the influence of cosmic events on their lives), but this has now lost much of its significance; (2) the economic demand, sago-gathering and its cult; (3) fear of the spirits, expressed in the ritual of expelling the spirits as a characteristic feature of both large and small festivities; and (4) the need of prestige on the part of the male population, the desire for fame and the urge to impress the women of the village. We will examine how these elements are associated with headhunting.

There appears to be a definite association between headhunting and cosmic events though it is not possible to determine whether the Asmat are themselves aware of it. I have already noted the invocation of the sun just before the actual attack in order to get courage for the hunters and spread fear and confusion upon the enemy. The sun is often taken as a witness to an oath of vengeance or to strengthen a solemn statement. Many mysterious things are said of the sun and admiration is expressed when they say: *nambir apok*, the sun never dies. There is probably some identity between the sun and the tribal ancestors. A wide and colorful sunset glow is a sign of a big headhunting raid somewhere, its red being the blood of the victims. A man of Sjuru is called *jomes omer*, afraid of the evening glow, expressing contempt for his lack of courage. The initiate's immersion in the water parallels the solar cycle—the sinking in the west, submersion in the sea, and rising in full glory on the eastern shore. The usual time of attack is toward sunrise (though this may be for practical reasons). Some ornamentation (perhaps not all) seems originally to have been symbols of the sun, moon, and clouds: red ochre—light of the sun; white chalk—light of the moon; black ash—rain cloud.

Cassowary and human bones, used as daggers, resemble the crescent moon, as do the shells worn in the nose, the dogs' teeth, and the boar tusks. (The Asmat have one and the same word for crescent moon, dogs' teeth, swine tusks, and clitoris, *okos.*) The white parrot feathers which adorn the head and the spears may be considered symbols of light. Spear and sunbeam are associated in myth and song and in colloquial language.

The technique of butchering victims suggests the image of the slowly decreasing moon, the picture of gradual scooping out. After the moon is full, it is exposed to the rays of the sun, for she (the Asmat would say "he") has not set before sunrise. Every day the moon falls further behind and is more annoyed by the sun. The moon is pictured in myths as a man wounded in the foot, unable to get away. In the myth about the origin of headhunting, the victim was called "the man with the wound."

The technique of scooping out (beginning at the top and progressing slowly) occurs frequently in Asmat life: when pounding sago out of the palm, when cutting canoes, and shaping eating-bowls. The same is done when butchering pigs (or prehistoric monsters in the myths).

Again, the Asmat may not be conscious of the relationship between the sago cult and headhunting, but there is no doubt in my mind of such relationship.

The account of the origin of the sago palm relates how the hero, Biwiripitsj, sinks in a morass one night while on his way home. In the night, after a thunderstorm, a magnificent sago palm appears on the spot where Biwiripitsj disappeared. Biwiripitsj's head is found in the bud of the palm, his arms in the branches. We have already had the story of the boy stretched out on a felled sago palm who was smashed to death by his father (mother); the sago pith, mixed with the blood and pounded flesh of the boy, proved to be more kneadable—an important economic factor, as more flour could be produced from that palm.

The prominent place of the sago palm in Asmat life is shown by the fact that sago-leaf veins are frequently used to make ornaments and that many names of people are allusions to the sago palm. Such names show that these men were beautifully decorated, and thus had distinguished themselves as great warriors, for only great warriors are entitled to wear sago-palm decorations.

One of the initiation rituals took place in a sago wood and consisted of the ritual pounding of a stripped trunk. The myth states a relationship between headhunting and sago by recording how the son of Biwiripitsj was killed to improve the sago pith. The ceremony of the *firao wu* uses the pith of the palm as a symbol of the human body.

Headhunting is required for the bodily development of young men and for their sexual maturation. The Asmat is inclined to consider that things having a similarity in shape or otherwise to be related, as a younger or older brother. He uses the same word for many things that resemble a sickle. Stars, flowers, and fireflies come also under the same name, because they show and hide their color alternately. Similarly, the human body is associated with a tree: the legs compare to the plankroots, the trunk to the human body, the arms to the boughs, the head to the top (often with the fruit that sits in the top). In the related Kamoro language, the word for head is *wé-éke,* fruit of man, for the human head also has a hard shell which protects the core, like the coconut. We recall that the raiders call themselves the younger brothers of the fruit-eating birds, fruit-gathering squirrels, and tree-kangaroos; the headhunting raider goes in search of human fruit: heads. After a raid the heads are tied together in a bunch and hung on the door post or near the fireplace; *kus fé* is a bunch of heads.

The decapitated head of a victim is laid between the out-spread legs of the initiate, almost touching the genitals of the boy who is about to mature sexually. I have repeatedly been told that after this ceremony the boys grew very fast. The ritual is connected in their minds with the growing of the boys. As the fruit contains the germinative power, for the Asmat observe time and again how a new sago palm grows from a fallen fruit, and as the human head is associated with fruit, the Asmat expect that the germinative power of the head (fruit) will be transferred to the boy's genitals by the ritual of placing it between his legs, and thus that it enables him to reproduce.

More than once I noticed decapitated heads hanging near little banana plantations, coconut groves, or sugar-cane fields long after the rituals were over. The head evidently was expected to stimulate the growth of those plants. At times there was a triton shell in lieu of the head.

When I discussed the health of the children with the chieftain of Sjuru (two out of three children die before reaching their first birthday), the chief remarked that many children are weak and feeble despite the fact that they eat plenty (quantity but no quality). Therefore the parents have to go for heads to make their children strong and healthy.

The murder of a relative arouses feelings of revenge, and the Asmat see warfare as retaliation. The brothers-in-law are insulted and stirred up by their wives, and have to band together in planning revenge in order not to lose their prestige. Thus revenge is one of the motives behind headhunting.

I have already pointed out how the big celebrations aim at driving away the spirits of the deceased, and numerous other customs do the same.

Immediately after someone dies, the women undress and wallow through the mud; the men smear themselves with clay, as a protection against the spirits. A layer of clay, especially in the armpits and groins, prevents bodily smells from being strong and saves people from detection by the spirits, who have a keen sense of smell. (Swine hunters do the same in order to approach the swine undetected.) Keeping bones and skulls of the deceased is another effective way of keeping the spirits at bay. A spirit cannot stand the sight of his own bones or skull. In places the deceased had frequented, signs (arrows and the like) may be placed to frighten away the spirit. Most burial customs can be explained in the same manner. When a death has occurred in a village, there is a temporary prohibition of drumming, singing, and yelling, so that the spirit will be led astray as to the whereabouts of the living. The larger rituals are influenced by the same fear of spirits. To some extent, a feast may be considered a war against the spirits, as it is connected with war against living enemies.

Perhaps the nocturnal ritual dance (during the initiation rite) when the decorated skulls are brandished, is also to be explained as an attempt at over-awing the spirits. The shields are moved up and down, forward and backward, indicating the direction which the spirits should take. This was the explanation given to me on one such occasion.

Attempts to overawe the spirits are frequent; the *dewen atakam* (enumeration of achievements) is one. The faked attack in several rituals, as at the erection of an ancestor pole and the mask dance, are other examples. In certain villages a very demonstrative fight was staged during the mask dance to impress upon the spirits that they should seek safety in flight. In another village the masked persons were "killed" in a mock killing in the bachelors' house.

The desire for prestige as a motive for headhunting is certainly significant, but headhunting would not confer so much prestige if it were not already important for other reasons. The motives for headhunting are many, and they are undoubtedly interwoven.

In Asmat society all prestige, and therefore all authority, is ultimately derived from achievements in war. It is impossible to be a man of social standing without having captured a few heads. A bunch of skulls at the door post is a measure of status. When distributing food on the occasion of a feast, it takes wisdom to give everyone the share proper to his rank and achievements. Successful headhunters enjoy many privileges: they are entitled to wear their ornaments as distinguishing marks; they can expect an extra portion of food when relatives return from a food-searching party; they need not exert themselves with heavy work; they are to be consulted in the meeting of men; they stand better chances with the women.

Out of a hundred proper names in the community of Sjuru, 75 proved to have some relation to warfare: "Our iron-wood tree," "Our flowering sago palm," "Man with the hot belly," "Man with the fierce look," "Our gall," "Man with a body like a *jo*-tree," "Arrows with sharp points." Such were names for heroes. But the unheroic had their own names, too: "Man that stayed home for fear," "Man that did not venture far from home," "Man that paddled away for fear," "Man that did not contribute to the list of achievements," "Man that never blew a raiding horn," "Man that was afraid of Asiwetsj [people along a river]," "Man without ornaments," and so on.

It is impossible to compliment someone without referring to his achievements. The usual titles are: *juus aptsjam ipitsj,* man with soul, courage; *aretsjar ipitsj,* great man; *nao pimir ipitsj,* man of frequent killing; *kus fé juro ipitsj,* man with large bunch of skulls; *tsjesesema ipitsj,* good shot. These names indicate social standing. Many times I and other foreigners were given these flattering titles.

Headhunting is not a necessary prerequisite for marriage. An Asmat can marry without having acquired a single head, even without initiation, but he will be constantly reminded of his nothingness. His opinion will not be asked in the bachelors' house; his own wife will pay little attention to him. When his wife wants to hurt him, she calls him *nas minu,* piece of meat; she declares that he is only meat, that he has no soul, no courage. The nas minu is the milksop, the spineless fellow, the duffer. He is not considered a real man; he belongs to the category of the women and children. He is not entitled to wear ornaments, has no share in the festive meals, stands no chance with other women. He constantly feels the contempt of the community; he is always the odd man out. As a result, he may work himself into a frenzy and go out and kill. Then he can look eye to eye with the other men and has the admiration of the women and children, for he has proven that he too has a soul.

Bravery not only assures a career in this earthly life, but it will secure an important place in the realm of the spirits as well. When the soul of the Asmat has crossed the big river (the sea), he is at once surrounded by a number of ancestors and relatives who had seen him coming. They will ask his name and how he died. He will tell them in glorious detail about his fights and the raids he was in; his wounds and scars will prove his story. In the realm of souls, as in the bachelors' houses, strong stories—real and imaginary alike —are accepted.

There is also a vague relationship between headhunting and sexual intercourse, which seems to follow from the manner in which headhunting contributes to manliness. Mention has been made of the cry of the headhunters at the beginning of the attack: "I am your husband from Sjuru." It seems to me that the enemy is called woman for more than one reason. But undoubtedly, head-hunting is drawn into the sexual sphere. There is a story telling how some men were decapitated and how their heads were miraculously restored, but this was a secret that the women were not to know. When the secret was given away by a child, the men were unmanned and transformed into dolphins (which have a hole in the nape of the neck and a skull that shows a striking resemblance to the human skull).

4. CONCLUSIONS

The motivation for headhunting is indeed complex; as headhunting appears today, it must be understood in the light of all the factors taken together.

Evaluating the different factors we may perhaps conclude by saying, in Scholastic terminology: "the finis operis," the objective, is the rite of passage, the initiation; but the intention and goal of the headhunters, "the finis operantis," is revenge, acquisition of social position through prestige, and attainment of the ideal of perfect manliness.

PAULA BROWN

22. Chimbu Tribes: Political Organization in the Eastern Highlands of New Guinea[1]

The 60,000 natives known as Chimbu make up the largest language and cultural group in the Eastern Highlands of New Guinea, and one of the largest in the Territory. The Chimbu are not a single political unit, but are composed of numerous autonomous groups linked in shifting alliances. Before the discovery of the Wahgi valley populations in 1933 and their subsequent pacification, fights within and between tribes were frequent. Chimbu political units are of a larger size and result in a larger scale of political organization than has been reported in other parts of New Guinea. In 1959, an even larger unit was formed in the Waiye Native Local Government Council composed of four tribes, with a total population of about 10,000 people.

Some features of Chimbu social organization can best be explained in terms of the particular conditions of the area. But in many respects, the Chimbu are typical of the Highlands natives. Their staple food crop is the sweet potato, which is cultivated on square plots surrounded by drainage ditches. This practice, and terracing, permit the gardening of slopes of over 50°. One or more crops are taken from the garden, and then a fallow period, under grass and planted trees, is allowed before the land is recultivated.

All garden land is claimed by individuals and inheritable patri-

SOURCE: Reprinted from *Southwestern Journal of Anthropology*, Vol. 16, No. 1 (1960), pp. 22–35, by permission of the author and publisher.

[1] This paper was read at the 34th Congress of The Australian and New Zealand Association for the Advancement of Science in Perth, August, 1959. It is largely based upon field research carried out by the author in 1958, as a Research Fellow of the Australian National University.

lineally. In some other societies, this has led to a rigid pattern of land holding by agnatic groups; but in Chimbu an individual has land claims in several parts of his subclan's far-flung blocks of land, and garden land is quite often transferred to kin and affines in other clans. In the past, land could be lost or gained in warfare.

Two distinct types of settlement are found in the Highlands of Australian New Guinea: scattered houses from Chimbu westward to beyond Wabag, and villages east of Chimbu and at Telefomin. In Chimbu, and in most of the Highlands societies, there is also a residential separation of the sexes. Each woman, with her unmarried daughters and sons under about six, lives on her husband's land, either near a current garden or in a pig forage fallow area. (One of the feminine domestic tasks is the care and feeding of pigs.) With a population density of over 300 per sq mi, few women are beyond calling and visiting distance of other women's houses, but there is no aggregation of dwellings. In the areas which are mainly under cultivation, several women's houses are sometimes near a men's house, but they may be quite isolated in the fallow stretches. Men's houses are also scattered, but these are communal: the average men's house contains four men and their sons. East of Chimbu, the men's house seems to be a permanent subdivision of the village. But there are many factors in Chimbu which serve to make the inmates of a men's house a fluctuating group. A man normally lives in one of the houses of his subclan, convenient to land which he is currently gardening. The passage of the cultivation and fallow cycle, which is only partly coördinated among the claimants of neighboring garden plots, the gatherings at the ceremonial grounds every six to ten years for large-scale pig feasts, personal inclination to live separately or with friends, kin or affines in neighboring groups, and the limited lifetime of the buildings, all affect residence. The men's house group is by no means a patrilineage; in fact, close agnates live apart more often than they live together, and most houses contain men who are not agnatically related to any members. The Chimbu men's house group often has a stable core, but actual residence is quite variable.[2]

There is a superficial appearance of similarity in the reported ethnography of these Highlands societies, because of the use of

[2] Further detail on these features of Chimbu will be found in Brown and Brookfield 1959.

the terms subclan, clan, phratry, and tribe.[3] But the same term has been used to describe groups of quite different sizes and functions. For example, the average Enga clan is three times the size of those in Gahuku. Also, these units have a very wide range of sizes in any particular society: Kuma clans, for example, vary from 100 to 1700 persons. All of these societies have some sort of a hierarchy of patrilineal groups, and it is often possible to discern stages of segmentation. There appears to be a peculiar fluidity and mobility in these New Guinea Highlands social structures; they lack the genealogical base,[4] ancestor concern, and ritual attachment to land which is associated with unilineal descent groups in other non-centralized horticultural societies.

I will briefly describe the groups which I call subclans and clans before turning to the main subject of this paper, Chimbu tribes. Genealogical ties are not far extended in Chimbu, and the relations between subclans and clans which claim common origin are in terms of mythological ties of brotherhood. The membership is recruited primarily by birth: children of both sexes are regarded as members of their father's subclan, clan and tribe. Marriage is patrivirilocal, and the persons who live permanently on a subclan territory are the natal male members, their unmarried daughters and their wives. Adoption occurs, most often when a widow takes her young children to live with her brother and they remain with him. In the Naregu tribe of central Chimbu where our work was based, the subclan has an average population of 123 including men, their wives and children; it ranges from 36 to 243.[5] The

[3] The use of "clan" in New Guinea Highlands ethnography generally follows that proposed by Murdock (1949), that is, the clan is both a residential group and a unit based upon unilineal descent. Some confusion may arise from this usage, as the residents of a clan-village or a clan-territory include: (1) males who are natal members of the patrilineal descent group; (2) their unmarried daughters and sisters who will leave at marriage; (3) their wives, whose natal membership in another community is recognized, and who form links between groups; and (4) men and boys who are non-patrilineal kin or affines, and who may become incorporated or adopted members. In discussing the Huli descent system, Glasse (1959) uses "clan" for a non-territorial descent unit with little co-activity; such a group has not been reported elsewhere. Using Murdock's criteria, some Highlands groups composed of several "clans" might also be called a "clan," but "phratry," "tribe," or other terms have been used. On this larger group level, the distinction I draw between "tribe" and "phratry" in Chimbu shows that local and descent groups do not necessarily correspond.

[4] Variations in genealogical depth are discussed by Salisbury 1956b.

[5] Population figures are taken from the 1957 census.

subclan is named; its territory is made up of a number of blocks of garden land scattered through the clan territory; the only joint subclan land is a plot in the ceremonial ground, burial grounds, and perhaps forest on slopes too steep for cultivation.

There are often groupings of subclans within a clan, but these are variable and realignments are possible. The clan, however, is a distinct unit. Although the government census does not always allow us to discover the clan groupings, there appears to be a range in population size from less than 200 to over 1200, with a mean of about 700. Each clan has a name, and most of its land lies in a territorial block. Furthermore, the clan is exogamous; within the clan, all persons are expected to help and support one another on certain occasions, but they may not marry. Outside the clan, there are many ties of kinship and affinity derived from present and past marriages, and persons help one another according to these personal ties. As most marriages are between neighboring clans, the clans are stitched together by a large number of ties between individuals.

The Chimbu clan is larger than clans elsewhere in the New Guinea Highlands; it is perhaps more comparable to the exogamous groups which are parts of phratries or subtribes in the terminology of other ethnographers. I use "clan" for the exogamous unit, because I want to reserve the terms "phratry" and "tribe" to describe important and different social groups in Chimbu. Put briefly, the *phratry* is a group of clans linked by a tradition of common descent; the *tribe* is an alliance of neighboring clans.[6] In order to

[6] The terms as used by ethnographers writing about these societies do not correspond to the most common American usage. This is particularly true of "phratry": it is a group of clans linked by a tradition of common descent, which may have some other characteristics such as a territory. The largest exogamous group is called a "clan" by most New Guinea Highlands writers. However, the Mbowamb "great clan" ("Grossippe") and "tribe" ("Stamm") are exogamous (Vicedom and Tischner 1943–48); Read (1952, 1955) uses "subtribe" for the Gahuku-Gama exogamous unit, while Salisbury has called this both a "subtribe" (1956 a,b) and a "phratry" (1958). In using "phratry" as defined above, I follow Meggitt (1957, 1958) and Reay (1959 b,c). The term "tribe" has been used by Vicedom and Tischner, Read, and Salisbury for a territorial unit composed of several clans; it may have various other characteristics, such as common military or ceremonial activities or a tradition of common descent. The Berndts (1953, 1954, 1955) use "district" for such a unit, while Ryan (1959) has called the larger groups in Mendi a "clan cluster."

understand the larger units, we must look into the traditions of origin, fights, and migrations.

A general tradition of origin is found throughout Chimbu, and includes some of the surrounding groups who have a slightly different language and culture. All trace their source to Womkama, a place about two-thirds of the distance up the Chimbu River from the confluence of the Chimbu and the Wahgi. In the origin story, there were at first three people: a man, his wife, and another man who represents a group different from that of the husband. This other man taught the woman and her husband some basic Chimbu techniques, such as making fire. The husband became suspicious of this too-knowledgeable man. They fought, and the husband was forced to flee. In the various versions of the tale, the men represent different groups, so that each group identifies itself as one of the original men, and may explain its present location by winning the fight and remaining at Womkama or by being forced to flee. But this tale explains only the common origin and the first of a series of group moves. Each group also has a set of traditions to account for its present territorial claims and relations with other groups, describing alliances, fights, and migrations. Many of these merge with living memory, so that the last moves of the group can sometimes be described from the personal experience of the older men. Since 1933, no large fights or group migrations have taken place. After pacification, some displaced persons returned to their home territories.[7]

The traditions help us to understand the present organization, but we must distinguish between the traditions of common descent and the local alliances even though clans may be joined by both processes. Chimbu phratries are composed of two to eight clans with a tradition of common origin. It is often said that the phratry was once a single exogamous clan; by growth and segmentation, the present clans developed. The Chimbu, like other Highlands peoples, commonly visualize parallel segments as "brother" groups: each clan in a phratry is said to have been founded by a brother. The name of a clan is the name of one of these brothers, with a suffix meaning agnatic descendants. If the Chimbu had unlimited space for expansion and did not conquer land in war-

[7] Patrol reports of the Chimbu area, which were most generously made available to us by the Department of Territories, contain accounts of the traditions of origin from various tribes and also report these movements.

fare, we might find a territorial phratry derived from the growth and segmentation of clans. But such expansion could not take place in a confined valley such as the Chimbu, and in fact we find that most phratries are more or less dispersed.

In the upper Chimbu valley, population densities are over 600 per sq mi. The traditions throughout Chimbu state that this has been an area of out-migration. The groups which are now found on the western fringes of Chimbu—in the Koronigl valley and beyond—usually bear names which are also found in the Chimbu valley and claim a common origin with these people. For some time after the migration of part of a clan, the two widely separated sections of the clan may continue to recognize common clanship. Groups which are larger and have been longer separated still retain a tradition of common origin, but have little contact with one another. Prolonged separation makes the ties of clanship meaningless: visiting ceases, coöperation is not possible, and, as the occasions for courting and marriage do not arise, the exogamic rule is not invoked.

The prevalence of fights and warfare in the Highlands is well known. Land conquest has been reported among the Enga, Mendi, Mbowamb, and Chimbu, but not in other societies. In Chimbu, at the frontiers between group territories, gardens were subject to burning, pigs to theft, houses to attack, and persons to murder. Such acts were part of the prevailing hostile relations; occasionally they gave rise to a larger fight. Intermittent warfare, sometimes involving hundreds of men, occurred on the frontiers between traditional enemies. The immediate causes of fights were these hostile acts and disputes over women, land, sorcery accusations, or payments. There are frequent disputes between neighbors, especially where the smaller social units do not form territorial blocks. Thus when a pig breaks through a fence and destroys part of a sweet potato crop, or a man extends his garden into a fallow area claimed by another, or a man visits his neighbor's wife, or a child dies in circumstances where sorcery is suspected, neighbors quarrel. Within the subclan and the clan, no permanent hostility is possible, because men must pass through one another's land to assemble, neither side can enlist a large group of allies, and there is pressure by fellow-clansmen to settle disputes.

When neighbors are not bound to one another by common clanship, each party may be able to mass support for a fight at a clan boundary. Interclan fights did occur, with the occasional result that land was conquered and the defeated were forced to flee. There were several possible forms of this: sometimes the defeated were invited to return, compensation exchanges were made, and a boundary was reëstablished at or near the former one; at other times some of the defeated fled as individuals or small groups and found refuge with kin and affines, to be later absorbed into these groups; a third outcome, group migration, is responsible for the scattered distribution of many clans and phratries.

So far, we have seen that clans are likely to be solidary units, but we have not yet seen how this is achieved in larger groups. We must first point out that commonly part of a phratry is found as a territorial unit. Clan territories within a local phratry are not single continuous blocks; they often occur as a main block, with isolated islands of land within the territory of other clans of the phratry, or between the land blocks of other clans of the phratry. Interdigitation of clan territories is greater in Kamanegu than in Naregu, and it is greater still in the upper Chimbu valley where settlement, land conquest, and other land transfers have been going on longer than in the Naregu area.

Because of this interdigitation of land, opposing forces within the phratry could not be readily mobilized or, once mobilized, could not maintain permanent hostilities. The land between these phratries or part-phratries, on the other hand, is not always fully occupied, so that some sort of a buffer zone is often found. Within the main area of phratry settlement, communication among the clans is possible by the Chimbu practice of ululation and shouting from hilltops. When a boundary was attacked, the land and houses of more than one clan were endangered, and the threatened groups combined to resist the attack or launch a counter-attack. There are many reasons why these clans formed a military unit: aside from the way that land is distributed among the clans, there is the multitude of personal ties between individuals. We noted earlier that marriages usually take place between neighboring clans: furthermore, neighboring clans within a local phratry intermarry more frequently than do neighboring clans outside it. There is much mutual aid, sharing of houses, and transfer of land among kinsmen and affines of neighboring clans within this group. And a man who is temporarily living with his sister's husband becomes involved in his problems; he may bring some of his clansmen in to help when an outside attack occurs.

These local phratries, or parts of phratries, were relatively peaceful units. When there were internal fights, they did not last long, and compensation was paid for men killed. In the course of fights, adoptions, migrations, disease, and the uneven growth of population, some phratries became large and powerful, while other phratries and clans declined in population. The members of these remnant groups were at a disadvantage in the defense of their territory, and they could not maintain a position in the large-scale exchanges and group gifts. Our accounts of fights and alliances describe them as shifting to support or oppose the larger groups surrounding them. This ambivalent relationship could not continue for long; the group was subject to attack from all sides by more powerful neighbors.

Some such groups have probably completely lost their identity. Members of a group which was forced to disperse as individuals and in small groups would be absorbed by their hosts. In the absence of long genealogies, their separate origin would not long be recorded in tradition: their children and grandchildren would not be distinguished from those of their hosts. Sometimes, a remnant group could build up its numbers by adopting refugees and thus occupy its land more successfully. Other remnant groups could survive in a more permanent alliance with one of the powerful neighboring phratries. When such a remnant group has been incorporated, names and traditions record the event. The incorporated group does not become another clan in the local phratry; it frequently has phratric ties with other clans elsewhere. I call this local alliance of clans a tribe.

By this process, we often find that the core of a tribe is a group of clans forming a phratry. Frequently, a part of the phratry migrated at some time in the past, so that the tribal core is in fact a local part-phratry. The stability of these tribes composed of part-phratries and incorporated groups can no longer be tested, because fights and migrations have ceased.

It is, however, possible to distinguish some stages in the incorporation of groups. At the time of first European contact, some of the smaller groups were clearly attached to a larger neighbor. Others, however, were fluctuating in their alliances or perhaps were in process of migrating to consolidate with detached sections of the clan or phratry. Their position has remained ambivalent: while they are politically allied with the larger group, they have remained independent in some other matters, such as ceremonial activities. This relationship has also been fostered by Administration, since the small groups are no longer in danger of losing their land in warfare, and thus being forced to choose a permanent ally or leave the area.

If these phratries or local parts of phratries, plus small remnants of other groups, were the only form of Chimbu larger organization, it would not be necessary to use an additional term, tribe, for these units. We would simply have a form of political organization in which the dependence of small groups upon large ones was accommodated by partial incorporation. There are other reasons why the phratry must be distinguished from the tribe. One is that the traditions of origin and movements record the dispersal of some phratries, and the widely separated groups often maintain social relations by visiting and the retention of clan exogamy. They may combine to give or receive a large-scale food distribution. The relations between the dispersed parts of a phratry do not involve military alliance, which was a most important tribal activity. Secondly, intraphratry fights sometimes led to tribal fission and migration. The Endugwa phratry is composed of three tribes which were formed after such fights. They are quite distinct even though two of them have a long common boundary.

Some Chimbu tribes are alliances of equal partners belonging to two distinct phratries. Many of these tribes are known by the names of the two groups so allied. The pairing of two nouns in juxtaposition is a common feature of the Chimbu language. For example, Siambuga-Wauga tribe is composed of part of a very large clan in Siambuga phratry and two Wauga clans; although their traditions record a fight about forty years ago, this was followed by a peace exchange, and since then the two sections have formed a unit, first in military and ceremonial activities, and, since 1934, as an administrative unit which has more recently accepted a single Luluai as its leader. The Siambuga-Giraigu tribe in the upper Koronigl valley is a similar case, composed of another Siambuga clan and part of the Giraigu who trace their origin to the Chimbu valley. Several tribes in the upper Chimbu valley also carry such names. This form of alliance is not always recorded in tribal names: Kamanegu tribe consists of four clans of Umbanegu phratry and a large Simbaigu clan. These alliance-tribes are composed of two groups of nearly equal size. It is only in alliance that they could face the neighboring tribes on terms of equality, successfully defend their territory and make an adequate presentation of food and goods in exchanges.

It does seem that a certain size of political unit was general in the Chimbu area, and this is larger than the clan. Tribal size varies, within certain limits, and it is not always possible to place a small fluctuating clan in one or another of its neighboring tribes. Thus any simple calculation of average tribe size would have little meaning. The largest tribe seems to be the Gena, a group which is spread over a considerable area, and whose northern fringe is high forest on the flanks of Mt Wilhelm. Gena is unusual because it is a phratry as well as a tribe, and has a total population of 4500. The bulk of Chimbu tribes, however, have a population of 2000–3000.

The Chimbu distinguish between phratries and tribes, even though the same group names are sometimes used. The tribal name is, in fact, often a phratry designation which does not take account of the names of small incorporated groups. However, the distinction is made when referring to the relations within the groups. Thus a group which is regarded as composed of the patrilineal descendants of a man is called *nem-angigl,* meaning "father-brother"; *nem-angigl* is used for groups of various sizes —the subclan, clan, and phratry, but always to connote common agnatic descent. The two groups of separate origin which are joined by an alliance are, on the other hand, referred to as *angigl-angigl,* or "brother-brother." The Chimbu kinship term "brother" may be extended very widely on occasion, and does not refer to agnatic relations in all of its usages; thus "brothers" are not nec-essarily sons of the same father. For example, a man may call any of his approximate contemporaries "brother" within the phra-try. Older men, however, are addressed as "father" within the clan and as "mother's brother" in other clans of the phratry.

It is not possible to assert great stability for these tribal units which are alliances of two groups of independent origin. The tra-ditions which we collected lead to a view of Chimbu larger-scale organization as in a constant state of shifting alliances and fre-

quent dispersal and migration. The settlement of the western part
of Chimbu territory, reaching into the middle Wahgi valley, cannot be dated in its earlier stages, but some of this occurred
within living memory. Twenty-five years of administration using
these units may well have given them a stability that they could
never achieve when warfare was frequent. A small remnant clan
which may have been loosely attached to a tribe has often been
included in the new administrative unit, termed a "group." This
"group" has a number of common responsibilities. The Government has appointed one or, occasionally, two Luluais for each
such group, and this has further stabilized the units. It is notable
that when a man has been placed in charge of a group outside his
tribe, he has rarely succeeded in maintaining his authority there.
Under Administration, boundaries between tribes have been
marked with lines of trees and cordyline plants, a procedure which
is always accompanied by disagreements between the bordering
tribes, but which has resulted in giving the tribes a fixed territorial block.

It will be interesting to compare Chimbu structure with that
of other Highland peoples. For many of these, the population
is only roughly estimated and the political structure is as yet
unstudied. For those societies concerning which we have some
ethnographic data, however, some comparisons can be made.[8]

To the east of Chimbu, where village settlement prevails,
villages are grouped into local tribes whose population seems
never to have exceeded 1500, and many of these are smaller than
1000. West of Chimbu the organization is more variable, and a
unit including several clans has been termed by the several writers a tribe, great clan, phratry, or clan cluster. Of these larger
units, only the Mbowamb of Mt Hagen have tribes of over 3000
members, and the average tribe is smaller. In most of these societies, the clan is the main political unit. Thus Enga localized
phratries average 1020–1330, but it is the clan rather than the
phratry that is the important political unit, and clans number a
few hundred persons.

Although we might be tempted to explain the larger groupings
in Chimbu as a product of high population density, comparison
with other areas does not support this. The Enga are the second

[8] Much of the material presented here has been published since Read's
(1954) study.

TABLE 1

People*	Group	Size	Composition	Territory	Common descent	Exogamous	Ceremonial unit	War unit	Internal warfare
Enga	Phratry	1020-1330 av.	6 clans av.	+	+	–	–	occasional	occasional
	Clan	280-360 av.	2-8 subclans	+	+	+	+	+	limited
Huli	Phratry			–	+	occasional			
	Clan			–	+				
Mendi	Clan cluster		2-4 clans	+	in part	in part	+	+	limited
	Clan		2-6 subclans	+	mainly	+	+	++	–
Mbowamb	Tribe	700-3500	6-27 clans	usually	+	+	+	occasional	limited
	Great clan			+	++	++			
	Clan	38-395		+	++	++	+	+	prohibited
Kuma	Phratry	300-600 av.	2-9 clans	–	+	–	–	–	occurred
	Clan	100-1700 range		+	+	+	+	+	–
Chimbu	Tribe	1500-4500	2-8 clans	+	some	–	+	+	occasional
	Phratry	1200-4500	2-9 clans	few	+	–	local section	local section	occasional
	Clan	700 av.	2-6 subclans	+	+	+	+	+	limited
Siane	Tribe	400-1500	2-9 clans	+	+	–	–	–	–
	Sub-tribe or phratry								
	Clan	250 av.	2-3 clans / 2-4 men's house groups	+ village	++	++	++	++	–

									prohibited
Gahuku-Gama	Tribe	500–1000		+	+	−	+	+	−
	Sub-tribe	200–500	2 clans	+	+	+	+	+	−
	Clan	100	1 or more villages	+	+	+	+	+	+
Kamano, etc.	District	200–700	several villages	+	−	+	+	+	+
	Clan		village	+	+	+	+	+	+

+ indicates that the characteristic is present, e.g. that the group is a ceremonial unit, etc.
− indicates that the characteristic is absent, e.g. there is no internal warfare, etc. Where no information is available, the space is left blank.

* The groups are arranged roughly from west to east in the Western, Southern, and Eastern Highlands Districts of Papua-New Guinea. This table is based as follows: Enga: Meggitt 1957, 1958; Huli: Glasse 1959; Mendi: Ryan 1959; Mbowamb: Vicedom and Tischner 1943–48; Kuma: Reay 1959b, 1959c; Siane: Salisbury 1956a, 1956b, 1958; Gahuku-Gama: Read 1951, 1952, 1954–55, 1959; Kamano, etc.: R. M. Berndt 1954, 1955; C. H. Berndt 1953.

In writing about the Chimbu, whom he calls Kuman, Nilles (1943–44, 1950, 1953) uses a different terminology from that presented here: his "subclan" is my "clan," and his "clan" is my "tribe." He does not distinguish between tribe and phratry, although some groups are shown as found in several locations.

most densely settled Highlands people, with small effective political units, and the Mbowamb density is much lower although the tribes are large.

The larger Highlands groups are usually unified by a tradition of common origin, whether these have been called phratry or tribe. These are usually territorial groups as well; only Kuma, Huli, and Chimbu have dispersed phratries. The Chimbu distinction between tribe and phratry has not been reported elsewhere. Mendi clan clusters resemble Chimbu tribes in some respects, but are not primarily military alliances.

In the Highlands, when a group of clans claim common descent, this does not always make the inclusive unit exogamous. The exogamous group, whatever its composition, is usually also a territorial, ceremonial, and military unit within which internal warfare is restricted. Affines, the members of neighboring exogamous groups, are often ceremonial exchange partners, recipients of distributions, and military enemies. But in Chimbu, almost half of the marriages take place within the tribe, and these intratribal affines are more often collaborators than opponents in ceremony and war.

Group expansion in Chimbu involved the migration of small groups out of the Chimbu valley. The resulting fragmented groups were unable to maintain and defend their territory. The smallest groups were incorporated, while larger ones formed alliances on more equal terms. I am inclined to conclude that the Chimbu have tribes as well as phratries because a local alliance protected the smaller groups against the large neighboring phratries.

PAULA BROWN

23. Social Change and Social Movements

Social and cultural change is continuous in all societies. The changes which take place in an isolated non-literate community are largely inaccessible to scholars; archaeology and the analysis of traditions provide limited information, but this work has hardly begun in New Guinea. For the most part, we discuss social change as it occurs in communities which are in contact with vastly different societies or are in transitional periods of revolutionary or especially rapid change. But the description of change we might attempt for an isolated community has to be concerned with somewhat different problems, problems like population growth and decline, adaptation to environmental variations, diffusion of the relatively small stock of ideas taken from other communities, and the acceptance of internal discoveries and inventions.

Our lack of knowledge about social change in pre-contact New Guinea cannot be remedied. Even if we were to discover and study a hitherto isolated community, our very presence there would be a source of change. Many cultural descriptions by anthropologists assume that a relatively static situation preceded discovery and contact with Western society. The ethnographic description is of a timeless pre-contact way of life. When we talk about social change, we talk about those changes which have occurred since discovery by Europeans, and sometimes that which has taken place during some specified period. Changes which follow contact between greatly different societies and cul-

SOURCE: Chapter VIII of *New Guinea on the Threshold*, E. K. Fisk, ed. Canberra: The Australian National University Press, 1966. Reprinted by permission of the author and publisher.

tures are of a more traumatic kind than those which take place either within an isolated community or within a complex Western society. These changes can be viewed in the context of colonization, and for our purposes we can contrast two broad types, without attempting to include all possible colonial situations.

1. Colonists occupy the land and the aboriginal population becomes a dwindling minority with a decreasing proportion of fullbloods, as has been the case in North America and Australia. Such colonies develop from the standard of the immigrants, and rapidly become economically advanced and politically independent.

2. Where the area has a dense indigenous population and/or is unattractive to the colonists they enter in small numbers and establish a few settlements, plantations, etc. They assume political control and introduce Western techniques, economic forms, religion, and culture. The aboriginal inhabitants mostly remain in their own communities. They become the objects of educational, medical, and administrative activities and religious missions. Often large-scale changes are introduced, such as economic development programmes to raise the standard of living. This has been the form of colonization in most of Africa, southern Asia, and the Pacific. Many of the former colonies of this type have now achieved independence with an economic and cultural standard far different from that before their discovery and colonization. But most of them have higher birth, mortality, and illiteracy rates, lower incomes and standards of living than Europe or former colonies of the first type.

The Territory of Papua and New Guinea is one of the second type, a dependent country; it is one of the backward parts of the world, largely undeveloped and primitive. There are still a few New Guineans who have never seen a white man. I shall not examine the historical, political, or economic reasons for this backwardness. But I shall ask whether there are any special characteristics of the people of New Guinea and their communities which help to account for it. My principal interest is in social movements as organized efforts to change social conditions. Cargo cults will be discussed as a form of social movement, and I shall suggest some reasons why they occur in New Guinea and the conditions under which they may disappear.

New Guinea societies

Many writers have remarked upon the very large number—
many hundreds—of distinct languages in Papua-New Guinea. The
exact number may never be known, since some will have become
extinct before they can be recorded, and linguists will disagree
about the distinction between language and dialect. However,
the counting of languages and differentiation of language families
is a side issue; what is significant is the separateness of native
communities. Melanesia is notable for the small scale of indigenous political organization, the absence of any central authority
or formal legal procedures within a tribe or even a village, the
constant intertribal and intratribal warfare. These conditions prevailed even in areas where tens of thousands of people spoke the
same language and shared the same culture. In the highlands of
New Guinea the largest language and cultural groups of Melanesia are found, but even there the largest unified group which
restricted internal warfare and joined together in occasional ceremony was a tribe of a few thousand people. And in these no
central authority could prevent internal conflict and fighting.

The small local community, rarely more than a few hundred
people, was normally the largest effective political unit. Beyond
this, most people had relatives and partners in trade and ceremonial exchange. Outsiders were on the whole regarded with
suspicion; one did not travel among strangers. Intervillage and
intertribal raids and attacks might occur at any time.

There were no great differences in forms of political organization between New Guinea communities; none was differently
armed, more productive, or stratified so as to achieve domina-
tion over another group; there were no states, no slaves, no rulers
or ruled. However, there were some differences in the size and
area of community and in the number of people who combined
to fight or to hold a ceremony.

Colonial administrations in Africa and Asia have had to overcome established systems of local authority and privilege to form
a Western style of administration on the large scale necessary
for a modern nation. They have had to meet organized conservative resistance to innovation, and have had to substitute other
selective procedures for hereditary privilege. In New Guinea these

problems do not exist. There were no centralized states, no hereditary positions of political authority, no competing organized systems of government. Some local leaders in a few parts of Papua-New Guinea were called 'chief', and there was a 'Paramount Chief' in the Trobriand Islands, but these did not have officially established power nor any important legislative, judicial, or executive functions.

Such absence of indigenous political structures has given the colonial power no foundation on which to build modern government; but it has also relieved it of the necessity, so common elsewhere, of breaking down the old hereditary system and transforming it into a modern one (Brown 1963). Once tribal warfare is stopped, larger associations can be introduced. It does appear that regional alignments may precede a national one, but there does not seem to be resistance to the idea of a central government.

There is, in some respects, a kind of sameness about these small and separate New Guinea communities. Before the Europeans arrived all these communities were technologically at more or less the same level, using stone, wood, and occasionally bone or shell for tools, making pottery in only a few places, working vegetable fibres into clothing, belts, and containers, cultivating tubers, bananas, sugarcane, and vegetables, raising pigs, building houses of wood, reeds, leaves, and grass, and using bow and arrow, spears, and occasionally clubs and shields to fight. However, there are striking regional differences: the advanced agricultural techniques of the highlanders as compared to shifting cultivation in the lowlands and sago gathering in the coastal swamps; specialization and trade in food or other products between coastal fishing and inland gardening communities; large villages in the Eastern Highlands and dispersed houses in the Western; and arts, cosmological beliefs, myths, rituals, and magic were distinctive in different areas. The people were generally disinterested in tradition, myth, genealogy, and other ways of preserving the past. Thus in some places cults were adopted, spread, and abandoned as soon as new cults were introduced (Ryan 1961; Williams 1930).

Subsistence did not fully occupy the time and energies of the people; they had leisure to fight, to trade, and to celebrate. A dominant interest throughout New Guinea is material wealth— not only in the possession of it but in its use for exchange. In the absence of fixed hereditary positions of authority or the accumulation of heritable property, prestige is gained by participating in the exchange system. Essentially, a man gains prestige by his application and shrewdness in exchange relations; he arranges marriages and ceremonial distributions, takes a leading part in group activities, adopts younger men who become his dependants and supporters, takes several wives, who produce food and raise pigs for distribution, and enters into exchange relations with his wives' brothers and his sisters' husbands.

Leadership fluctuates as men's fortunes and activities wax and wane. A young man has not the productive resources, the accumulation of exchange partnerships and credit, to be a leader; an old man has no longer the energy to keep up his obligations. Achievement is the result of hard work and intelligent investment. Native ideas of power and wealth are concerned with gaining supporters and dependants within the local community to help the leader hold a successful ceremony or win a single battle. There is no permanent accumulation of power or wealth, no inheritance of privilege. The valuable goods—shells, stone axes, bird of paradise feathers, etc.—circulate within and between communities through a complex exchange system based upon personal ties of kinship and marriage.

REACTIONS TO CONTACT

New Guinea was discovered early in Pacific exploration, but until the late eighteenth century there were no European settlements. Explorers, missionaries, and commercial companies preceded administration in many places. Only in the late nineteenth century was administration at all regularized, and this was restricted to the coastal fringe and smaller islands. Administration changed from British to Australian in Papua and from German to Australian in New Guinea long before the interior was visited and patrol posts were established.

Interior New Guinea was explored in the present century, with a more advanced technology than in the exploration of Africa, Asia, or America. The first view of Europeans that most inhabitants had was of a well-equipped patrol composed of one or two Australian officers, a native police force, and a line of native carriers. Many such patrols carried radios and cleared areas for aeroplane landings or airdrops of supplies. The dominance of the European, his wealth, and his material possessions have been evident from first sight. The Australian differs enormously from the Melanesian in power and wealth. The unschooled native knows nothing of the history of Western technological, political, and economic development. He sees the European in possession of material goods, but he sees no mine or factory; he may only know that these goods arrive from outside in ships or aeroplanes. In remote government stations nowadays several planes arrive daily, carrying passengers, mail, and a great range of goods, from frozen foods to power equipment, for the station officers. Native prisoners unload the planes and crowds gather. The plane then departs for unknown places to reload and bring further supplies. The European does no menial labour to obtain these things; he sits in an office and sends messages by letter or wireless.

The goods and power of the European (and of the natives associated with him as assistants, police, etc.) are very attractive to New Guineans. Cloth and metal are eagerly sought, and, while they are very rare, confer prestige on their possessors. They are often incorporated into the system of valuables used for prestige-giving exchanges. Money becomes a valuable, a vital part of ceremonial payments; European goods such as knives and axes replace native manufactures in ceremonial exchange at marriage and death. But European manufacturers are also a coveted part of a rising standard of living—clothing, tools, and domestic hardware are quickly incorporated into daily life.

New Guineans can obtain none of these things as easily as the Europeans seem to get them. Only small quantities come through hard work, often as a plantation worker far from home, or by trade. Not only does the white man own many of these things, but he sets the terms of trade and the wages whereby the natives can get them. Only occasionally does he introduce a cash crop or other source of cash income, and these incomes are often pitifully small. A high value is attached to European goods, and people want them. At first they may be just novelties, but later they are incorporated into daily life as luxuries or even as necessities.

SOCIAL MOVEMENTS

Movements, cults, and protests have been reported in many parts of Melanesia. Only a few of these have been reported in any detail by scholars who have remained in the communities long enough to gain the confidence of leaders and participants and compile a description, history, and analysis of beliefs and actions. Several writers have attempted to state the general characteristics of cults. Here I draw upon some accounts of social movements, my own experience in New Guinea, and the general discussions, to determine the place of movements in general, cargo cults, and protests in the changes now occurring in Papua-New Guinea.

The feelings of the indigenous people towards Europeans have been aptly described as 'hopeless envy' (Mair 1948:67). The people are not always content to wait for the ordinary processes of education and economic advancement to reach them through the slow expansion of services by the Administration. In a number of places, at different times since the 1890s (Hogbin 1958:207), native-led social movements have had as their goal the quick acquisition of European goods, and often also of power. I consider cargo cults to be a kind of social movement.[1]

A great deal of attention and concern has focused upon 'cargo cults' in New Guinea, and this shows no sign of abating. Jarvie (1964) devotes a book to the problem of explaining the cults, and a number of studies have appeared in recent years (Schwartz 1962; Burridge 1960; Worsley 1957; Lawrence 1964). Most of these have emphasized the bizarre nature of the beliefs and the behaviour of the adherents—destruction of property, trembling, credulity. They are often regarded as phenomena quite apart from social developments, retrogressive, fantastic, hysterical, led by insane or pretendant prophets. Some writers have directed attention to the political and economic factors and the problems of the people undergoing change in Melanesia (Stanner 1953; Worsley 1957; Hogbin 1958): their tensions, crises, and their poor

[1] King (1956:27) presents an appropriate definition of social movement: 'A group venture extending beyond a local community or a single event and involving a systematic effort to inaugurate changes in thought, behaviour, and social relationships.'

and apparently hopeless plight in comparison with Europeans. The general situation is comprehensible, but the appearance of a cult at a particular place and time is more difficult to explain (Inglis 1957). It depends upon certain common conditions as well as upon the presence of an outstanding leader who may have visions and the gift of prophecy. It also requires acceptance by the community.

Stanner (1953:63–64) lists six common characteristics of cargo movements:

1. Leadership—the initiative of distinctive personalities.
2. Contact with the spirit world; visions, swoons, etc.
3. Orders, charters; systematic instruction of followers. These vary and may include positive or negative exhortations and the abandonment of old ways.
4. Prophecies: the arrival of a ship or plane sent by the spirits with a cargo of non-traditional wealth for the natives.
5. Mass demonstrations, often hysterical or eccentric.
6. Symbolic Europeanism in articles and forms of organization.

Of these characteristics all but the second occur in social movements which are not cargo cults.

Many movements with goals similar to those of cargo cults have occurred in Papua-New Guinea. They have a number of characteristics in common with cargo cults: a leader, moral reforms with orders and charters, co-operative community effort, expectations of wealth, mass demonstrations, symbols of Europeans in the form of books and papers, and quasi-military discipline. They often bring together members of a number of communities, former enemy villages and tribes, and sometimes several language groups. A common feature is the re-siting and re-building of villages with new architectural styles.

An example of this, the Tommy Kabu movement in the Purari Delta of Papua, has been well reported (Maher 1958, 1961). Tommy Kabu returned from wartime work with Australians in 1946 and began a programme of change. 'The aim of the movement was to establish the Purari economy on a co-operative tribal basis so far as productive effort and its returns were concerned, but what was produced was to be sold for cash on European or native markets in Port Moresby' (Maher 1961:58). The economic programme 'was only part of what was planned and attempted. The already tottering ceremonial system was swept away . . . Christianity was held up, at least in name, as the proper religion for the new order' (ibid.:59). 'Villages formed their own police force, raised a flag and copied military ceremonies some of the people had seen in Port Moresby' (ibid.). 'Wherever he established a more or less permanent headquarters, he had an "office" set up with tables, chairs, and official-looking papers which he had gathered from various places' (ibid.:60).

> Given the strong and common desire for change, the negative aspects of the program were rather easily accomplished
> . . . the rejection of the old, both real and symbolic, could be done, or at least appear to be done, with desire and a moment's action, but the construction of the new required continuing activity and a knowledge of specific techniques which were also essentially new (ibid.:61).

New village sites and new architectural styles replaced the old. The Kompani, with contributions from the people, purchased a boat in which produce of the Purari Delta was to be transported to market. The scheme foundered because the specific knowledge and techniques were lacking, the boat was lost in a fire, account books were not kept, the distribution centre in Port Moresby was inefficient and expensive, and the business was badly run. The movement brought together in one organization for the first time a number of Purari tribes, but it did not obtain help from the Administration, and the necessary management skills were not acquired. Although the Kompani continued, it had much reduced support and few achievements. 'As failure became apparent, disillusionment with the Kompani spread but the Purari's interest in "doing business" remained strong' (ibid.:73). Tommy began a much more modest business venture in 1955, but except for this there was no further organized effort.

Maher suggested that the failure of the movement might be followed by apathy and stagnation, or by a cargo cult for which some ideas were present (1958, 1961). The second alternative has not been reported, but it has been a later phase of other movements in New Guinea. Paliau and Yali began as leaders like Tommy Kabu; their early efforts for practical programmes were quickly re-directed into cargo cults. Guiart (1952a) describes a 'borderline type of cargo cult' in Malekula, in the New Hebrides.

In order for people to join any movement for social change, their wish for a different life must be strongly held. Their wishes can vary greatly in content. They can wish to return to the golden age of the past (as in the American Indian Ghost Dance); they can wish for a somewhat better standard of living in the present (a labour movement); or they can have millennial dreams of a perfect age and salvation. In its common Melanesian form the wish is for the achievement of European wealth and power. These feelings are often linked with resentment at the native's present position. 'The white man shall go' is a common, though not universal, element; nationalism is often involved as well (Guiart 1951).

There have been many types of movement in other parts of Melanesia (Kouwenhoven n.d.; Allan 1951; Guiart 1951, 1952a), and indeed in undeveloped territories everywhere. Movements and cargo cults are not restricted to Melanesia, although some of their features may be distinctive. Goals other than European goods may be sought (for example in North America, the religious movements of Handsome Lake and the Shakers, and African separatist churches).

In Papua-New Guinea few adults are literate and fully trained for any sort of clerical employment. The majority have had at most a few years in a mission school under poorly educated teachers. This ignorance makes it impossible for the prominent men to understand the administration, economy, and technology in which they live or towards which they are moving. Yet some of them are remarkably adaptable and enthusiastic for economic and political development. One such man is Kondom, a Chimbu who was a boy when the first Australian patrol explored the New Guinea highlands in 1933. Without any formal schooling, he has during the past twenty years, with administrative support, been a *luluai,* member of the District Advisory Council, observer at the pre-1961 Legislative Council, observer at conferences of the South Pacific Commission, President of a Native Local Government Council, and elected member of the Legislative Council for the Highlands 1961–64 (Brown 1963). He failed to be elected to the House of Assembly in 1964, but is President of the newly-formed Co-operative Society in Chimbu. He led the local people in developing cash crops and growing coffee, and in 1954 built a large hall of woven bamboo with a thatched roof and instituted meetings to encourage reform and development. A sort of record was kept of points made in these meetings either by a native recorder or government officer attending. The introduction of cash crops and problems of processing coffee and marketing produce were the main matters for discussion. A set of rules was put forward:

> My name is *luluai* Kondom. The meeting is about the government laws. I want the natives to hold these laws. These are the rules:
> 1. Man must not kill other human beings.
> 2. Man must not commit adultery with young girls and old women.
> 3. Men must not burn the house.
> 4. Men must not steal someone's property.
> 5. Men must listen to their head man or *Luluai* or *Tultul*.
> 6. The women must not kill the young child that was born.
> 7. Man must not play with someone's wife.
> 8. The best and most important one is education.[2]

Meetings I attended in 1958 were of a similar character. An agenda in Pidgin-English was put on a blackboard, with items on cash crops, schools, taxes, prohibition of fighting, and the beginning of local government. On these occasions leading men spoke in favour of progress, and the audience cheered, expressing unanimous approval. In 1959 a Local Government Council was established in central Chimbu. The councillors elected were, in comparison with the previous appointed officials, young, progressive, and mostly fluent in Pidgin-English. The monthly meetings of the Council are held in a building of timber and corrugated iron; members sit on benches facing the President, who wields a gavel and proceeds formally through an agenda, with the help of the clerk and supervising officer. Members stand to address the chair, propose motions, vote, form committees, and so on; the ritual of procedure is more or less learned, but it has no meaning beyond being the white man's way of conducting Council meetings. The main Council business concerns the use of the

---

[2] From a notebook given to me by Kondom, with spelling corrected; entry dated 19 July 1954.

few thousand pounds' tax: proposals for expenditure on certain projects, estimates, and calculations are made by the supervising officer. Chimbu Council meetings are occasions for government officers to speak to Councillors and announce new developments. The Councillors raise questions of interest to them—such matters as payment for work on roads and the sale of coffee. The Council is more of a centre for complaint and information than an organ of government in the terms of the Ordinance.

The confusion of the people can perhaps be conveyed in a few examples. One Councillor bought a cow, and then at a Council meeting asked the government to provide a milking machine. In discussing the high price of locally raised chickens and the relatively low price of imported tinned chickens, Kondom remarked that the tinned ones are cheaper because they are made in a factory. Although the decline in world coffee prices was responsible for lower payments for coffee beans in Chimbu, this explanation was never accepted by the people; lower prices were responsible for much anti-European feeling.

Such an atmosphere of ignorance is a fertile field for the Melanesians' belief that the desired manufactured goods may be delivered to them by their ancestors. 'Cargo' beliefs and incipient cults are common in Melanesia; many of them fail to attract sufficient followers to become a cult, or are stopped by government officers, or die out before many communities are involved (Salisbury 1958; Read 1958; Berndt 1952–53; Burridge 1960, on Manam). Firth (1955:131) calls them 'prototype cargo-cult phenomena.' He says there can be a 'cargo'-cult type of behaviour, without its attaining the organized coherence of a movement or cult development.

CULTS

The desire for social and economic improvement may be expressed in social movements which include confused and mistaken beliefs about money and the manufacture of goods. A 'cargo' cult is one form of such a movement. A message is communicated in a dream or vision, the prophet foresees a millennium of prosperity and plenty, nearly always of European goods. To attain this the believers carry out rites, often destructive of traditional property; they may appear hysterical, entranced, etc.

Other common beliefs are that the Europeans have the secret of obtaining wealth which had been withheld from the natives, and that the ancestors or spirits have now sent a ship or aeroplane loaded with cargo for the natives.

> During the time the white man has been present in our land, so it was told, we have seen the many 'good things'—steel tomahawks, steel knives, laplap [cloth], saucepans, etc., and the good foods, which have all come to our country from outside . . . these good things have always been sent to us by our predeceased forefathers, but instead of finding their way direct to us, the white man knew how to intercept them and did so. Then instead of passing the goods on to us, they put them into trade stores, and we had to work very hard to get even a part of them. However, our predeceased forefathers have found out what has happened to all these goods and now they will be bringing them direct to us.[3]

A few studies have traced the origin and development of such movements. Lawrence examines traditional beliefs and the several stages of contact, including elements of Christian belief.[4] His study of Yali, a cult leader, first shows him being supported by the Administration in his efforts to raise the standard of living in his area of the Rai Coast, Madang District. At that time there was no cargo cult dogma involved, but later some members of the Letub cult group took charge of the movement and it became a cargo cult with Yali as its figurehead. Lawrence concludes, 'Although Yali was the accredited leader of the pagan Cargo Cult, I do not believe that he was its sole or true originator' (1955:12).

Yali seems to be a different sort of man from Mambu of Bogia, who had an entirely mystical programme in which the secret of the white men was revealed; Mambu performed miracles and produced money. However, in the stories of their followers, both Yali and Mambu were mythical figures, 'symbols which focus ideas in Cargo. . . . So far as they exercised political authority in accord with the myth-dream, they were as divine kings' (Burridge 1960:207).

Perhaps the fullest documentation to date on any movement in

[3] From Report: Lieut. R. J. Stevenson, P.O., Akuna Police Post, 28 October 1944 to D.O. Bena Area; Patrol Report, Bena No. 8 of 1944/5; Agarabe area, p. 12. Quoted in Berndt 1953:231.

[4] Lawrence's major study (1964) was published after this paper was written; these remarks are based upon his earlier work (1955).

New Guinea is on the one led by a man named Paliau in the Admiralty Islands. Several phases were observed and reports and analyses were given by Mead (1956) and Schwartz (1962). The people of Manus were greatly affected by troops stationed there during World War II; American Negro soldiers especially impressed them. After the war their discontent with the old way of life was expressed both in social movements and in cult. In his monographs on the Paliau movement, Schwartz distinguishes various phases:

1. Local phase: secular and partial programmes of change were organized independently by leaders in their own villages to eliminate certain aspects of the old culture.

2. Initial movement: Paliau instituted a programme of social, economic, political, religious, and cultural transformation in a movement for all Manus. This rejected the old culture and drew on Christian belief for new goals.

3. First cult: during the events which are known as 'The Noise' people destroyed their property and had convulsive seizures. The cult spread rapidly and collapsed rapidly in many villages. The first cult maintained Paliau's original goals; Schwartz characterizes the belief system as sparse, underdeveloped, unstandardized.

4. Organizational phase: the movement was in the forefront, and the development of a council, native courts, and co-operatives was anticipated by new forms of organization. New villages were built on the beaches, government recognition of new forms of organization was sought, and government schools were requested.

5. Plateau phase: a period of imposed waiting, drift, and decline in morale, and conservatism.

6. Second cult: the main emphasis was on ghosts and the reconstruction of cemeteries. This developed at a time when establishment of a council and of a co-operative were expected shortly. However, these were considered to require hard work. The cult was a short route to Paradise.

7. Officialization phase: the council was established, and a co-operative was to be instituted. This phase has not yet been reported upon by Schwartz or Mead.

The people of Manus wanted the sort of wealth they saw among the American troops. Several local leaders had small-scale pro-grammes to achieve this. Then Paliau developed an inclusive pro-gramme. After this, cult and movement alternated: the movement demanded hard work for modest rewards; the cult promised easy success. It may be that the obviously slow progress of secular cul-tural transformation produced strains and impatience which in-clined the people towards the immediate rewards promised by the cult. Collapse of the first cult was followed by a more practical programme, but morale declined with delays, and yet another cult spread through the area.

Schwartz's account is the fullest yet available, and we can only inquire whether this alternation of movement and cult is usual. Reports of cults in Biak (de Bruyn 1951), the Vailala River (Wil-liams 1934), Tanna (Guiart 1952b), and Buka (Worsley 1957) show that cult beliefs often persist after the ritual stops and that the cult behaviour may recur. 'The persistence of these movements on Buka shows that mere failure of a prophecy is no assurance that a cult will lose its hold on the people' (Worsley 1957:122). Descriptions of Melanesian traditional religious cults with the aim of increased food, pigs, shells, etc. suggest that they have many characteristics in common with cargo cults (Williams 1930; Blood 1946; Ryan 1961).[5]

Attempts to understand and direct the course of social change in Papua-New Guinea have been bedevilled by the consideration of cargo cults as enigmatic phenomena and evidence of primitive gullibility, suggestibility, and credulity (Williams 1934). Officers and settlers are apprehensive of any suggestion of the presence of cargo beliefs and cults. But while only some of the movements have as their aim the ousting of the Administration, missionaries, or settlers, many Europeans assume that all the cults are anti-European. However, some movements, for example Marching Rule (Allan 1951), John Frum (Guiart 1952b), and the 'Johnson movement', merely want to replace the present administrators with other Europeans.

[5] The belief systems involved in New Guinea cults have been studied by only a few scholars; the accounts of Schwartz (1962) and Burridge (1960) should be compared with one another and with that of Lawrence (1964). Further examination of the similarities and differences between cults and social movements would be of interest; so would a study of those Melanesian communities which have neither. The influence of traditional beliefs and Christian teaching on modern beliefs also needs to be studied.

The destruction of property and neglect of subsistence, the refusal to pay tax, the mass hysterical demonstrations and false hopes are indeed serious matters for the Administrators who must restore order. Overt cult manifestations can be stopped by police action. However, cult belief pervades even where no ritual is observed. Cults thrive on ignorance and wishful thinking. Cults may alternate with secular movements or with a rather static and apathetic state. Movements which are practical both in their ends and in their means may incorporate the sort of false beliefs which are common in cults, for example members of his movement believed that 'Tommy Kabu was married to a daughter of the king of England and that they had two children' (Maher 1961:61).

OTHER FORMS OF POLITICAL AND ECONOMIC CHANGE

The movements which have been discussed are on a fairly large scale for New Guinea, bringing together several communities in a secular movement or a cargo cult. There have been many small-scale communal enterprises led by local men with a little education and entrepreneurial ability, such as Numbuk of Erap (Crocombe and Hogbin 1963), Gulu at Amele, and Simogun at Dagua (Anon. 1951). Other community projects have had no single leader but a small group of men have taken charge, as at Milne Bay (Belshaw 1955), or a group of villages have joined together, as at Sissano Lagoon. Such undramatic enterprises, with or without official support, are a common form of development in all colonial territories.

In Papua-New Guinea the government has sponsored Native Local Government Councils, rural progress societies, co-operative societies, agricultural extension projects, marketing projects, and other political and economic programmes. Most are still in their early stages, and without detailed studies it is difficult to assess them. The best known and apparently most successful of these has been the development of cocoa as a cash crop, combined with advances in education, health, and local government, among the Tolai of the Gazelle Peninsula, New Britain.

From time to time New Guineans demonstrate against government-sponsored activities. They may refuse to support a project or to pay a tax. These actions are sometimes attributed to cargo cult beliefs, but they are nevertheless protests: they are organized oppositions to the Administration. Our knowledge of their origin, leadership, and organization is unfortunately slight. They seem to be short lived and do not become social movements.

Papua-New Guinea has had few associations of employees or trade unions. Several organized political and economic actions have taken place or been led by police or military groups. Twice, Rabaul has been the locale of a strike. In 1929 a one-day general strike was organized by the police and extended to include other employees. It was quickly suppressed. In June 1964 the native police in Rabaul went on strike for some hours for better working conditions and pay. The Pacific Islands Regiment has also demonstrated against its rates of pay in recent years. The structure of these groups, the skills and continuous service of their members give them the basis for organized action which has not developed in labour lines on plantations or among the employees of small private firms. When such a group strikes, their action may be viewed as disloyalty rather than as the expression of a labour grievance.

The labour movement in New Guinea has barely begun. When the Public Service was reorganized in 1964 there was an immediate reaction against discriminatory salary scales. But as work associations develop, employees must be expected to strike or protest to demonstrate their views.

CULTS AND OTHER MOVEMENTS

In his discussion of the Mansren cult, de Bruyn (1951:3–5) makes some significant general points about these movements. He says the movement is

> a communal expression of the renunciation of the struggle for life. It symbolises the efforts of a people to re-order and re-organize its way of life as a result of changed conditions. . . . Such movements, although they sometimes show strongly religious, syncretic features, are, I believe, merely psychological reactions to existing situations. They are the people's attempt to gain relief or release from their distress, through the intervention of supernatural powers in the efficacy of which they firmly believe, which powers either belong to the indigenous religion or are an element in an alien religion with which the people have become familiar. . . . There is no essential difference between these mystical and religious cults,

and the aggressive movements whose political nature is becoming more and more prominent. From the psychological point of view both types of movement are the same.

Social movements are common in Papua-New Guinea; the Melanesian type of movement is most often directed towards obtaining an improved standard of living, including the accumulation of European goods in quantity, and often the obtaining of political power. It is a form of 'revitalization' movement: 'a deliberate, organized, conscious effort to construct a more satisfying culture' (Wallace 1956:265). It is not nativistic or revivalistic, but reformative and/or millenarian (Voget 1959).

Movement and cult have many common characteristics, but, as in any historical event, each phase of a movement or a cult is in some ways distinctive. The overthrow or departure of Europeans is not always part of the programme. Nor need it include destruction of property. In both the secular and cult movements the programme commonly includes a list of reforms—leaders urge the people to reject their old evil ways and become tidy, peaceable members of the new society. The rejection of the past is accompanied by a strong desire for a future in which the people have wealth and power. The preparation for the arrival of new property may include the re-siting of villages, new community plans, and new buildings. The new property may be expected to arrive as cargo gift from ancestors or as a result of community enterprise.

Various attempts have been made to pick out the defining features of cults. From Stanner's list we might select three: contact with the spirit world, prophecies, and hysterical mass demonstrations. But these characteristics are not limited to cults. Prayer is a common preliminary to political meetings in New Guinea; when a co-operative society was discussed in Chimbu, increased wealth was prophesied as the result; and Kondom's meetings were a mass (but not hysterical) demonstration of a desire to change.

Hogbin (1958:215) has advanced a somewhat different set of common characteristics of cults: the belief in the cargo, the ceremonies, the feasting, the constructional work, the emergence of leaders with their codes of correct behaviour. But while the belief that cargo is being sent is a defining feature of cargo cults, ceremonies and feasting can be part of any cult ritual; and leaders and codes of correct behaviour are as characteristic of social movements in general as they are of cults.

Margaret Mead distinguishes cult from movement while noting that they can occur in combination. She concludes that:

> The essential features of a cargo cult manifestation are these: An innovator, inspired by a supernatural revelation, announces . . . the arrival, by supernatural agency, of a cargo made up of a large assortment of objects emanating from the world of the European; at the same time, the invading whites will go away. . . . The inauguration of the new order may be accompanied by some natural hazard . . . those who will be its beneficiaries are urged to prepare themselves for the millennium by destroying their property. . . . Acceptance of the prophecy usually is followed by a period of great excitement, often accompanied by convulsive seizures of a contagious nature (1964:194–5).

> Movements . . . include programmes of directed change, modeled on Euro-American culture, that call for local autonomy, political identity and the adoption of real (not merely symbolic) aspects of modern culture (ibid.:196). Sometimes cargo cults and movements have occurred in association; at other times they have occurred separately. But they do have several features in common . . . both are future-orientated. . . . Leadership also is very important. . . . Whereas cargo cults had become endemic in the New Guinea area, political movements were epidemic in the immediate post-war atmosphere. Cargo cults depended on supernatural means of bringing about an immediate Utopia, and thrived on dreams, visions, and suggestibility. In contrast, movements depended on politico-economic means of realisation and thrived in the political atmosphere in which colonialism was being abandoned (ibid.:197–8).

Jarvie (1964:64–6) summarizes the distinctive features of cargo cults under eight points:

> 1. Cults are founded and led by a single prophet who receives the revelation and propagates it.
> 2. Prophets are hardly educated and are misinformed about the workings of society outside Melanesia.

3. Cults borrow European rituals, both secular and religious. They have a charter of systematic instruction.

4. New beliefs are grafted on to older local beliefs.

5. Cults predict the coming of a millennium in the very near future, and in material form: the cargo will be of non-traditional wealth.

6. There is organized activity of gardening and building, and various kinds of collective hysteria—visions, seizures, dancing, manias, etc.

7. The area is colonized but economically underdeveloped, isolated, politically acephalous and not given to violent resistance to white rule.

8. There have been attempts to Christianize the natives by missionaries.

This, too, is a mixed aggregation of criteria. The fourth, seventh, and eighth are true of nearly all rural communities in New Guinea; the second characterizes all members of the community, not merely prophets. The other characteristics are true as well of secular movements, when the non-magical, non-supernatural, and abnormal are removed. Thus movements have leaders with programmes, not revelations; movements use European rituals and make new rules of behaviour; movements state that the people will obtain non-traditional wealth; movements organize their adherents into working parties for construction and gardening. In fact these things —leadership, new procedures, expectation of material improvement, communal activity—are common to any ordinary development programme, but enthusiasm and conviction may be lacking.

The distinctive features of cargo cults are the dream or vision of the prophet, the belief in access to supernatural beings, miracles, the swoons, and seizures of individuals, and massed dancers, etc. —those elements of belief and behaviour which are magical, supernatural, and abnormal.[6]

---

[6] Sinclair (1957:44) sees the cults as 'a false belief . . . a resulting dislocation of normal thinking and activity with its replacement by abnormal thinking and behaviour of an hysterical nature.'

Conclusion

The natives of Papua-New Guinea are going through a difficult transitional period. They have a strong wish for the power and wealth which they see held by the white man. Their own traditional beliefs, and some of the Christian influences which have reached them, sometimes make them expect wealth as a gift from gods or ancestors. Few natives have even now reached a standard of education to comprehend Western culture; beliefs in sorcery and other unscientific notions of causation are prevalent among schooled and unschooled. Dreams and visions told by prophets are readily accepted, especially when no alternative mode of attaining the unsatisfied desires has succeeded.

New Guineans lack both the general education to understand Western history and technology and also the training for skilled or professional work. They depend upon Europeans, mostly officers, but to some extent missionaries and settlers, for all of their information about the outside world. Only a limited number are now receiving the education which will give them this understanding and skill; the majority of today's youth will become illiterate subsistence farmers with very small cash incomes. Their longing for power and wealth is not likely to be satisfied by political means; their envy is likely to remain hopeless. In this situation they may find the rate of change unbearably slow. Their ignorance of technical processes, combined with their awareness of the inequalities of wealth and power between Europeans and themselves, produce movements aimed at social and economic improvement, millennial cults, and social protests. If these are to become increasingly realistic and progressive, it will be necessary to introduce a practical programme which will include fundamental education under enlightened leadership. One most important requirement of this programme is that its results be visible to those people of New Guinea who are supposed to benefit from it.

RICHARD F. SALISBURY

24. Early Stages of Economic Development in New Guinea

Much current discussion of indigenous economic development in the Territory of New Guinea and elsewhere is of how individual enterprise is held back by outmoded "group pressures," and of how "individualization" (e.g. of land tenure) is needed to realize the full indigenous economic potential. Material presented here on the early stages of development among two currently prosperous and progressive groups tends to show that the first stage of successful development was not the breaking down of group solidarities, but the building up of larger groupings with more effective political control by emerging leaders. Only after political consolidation did production increase markedly, and with it investment (both private and corporate) and consumption standards. The suggestion would be that current attempts to increase native cash crop production through registration of individual land titles, for example, is likely to be most successful in areas where it takes place within the framework of an effective indigenous local political organization.

The two histories of development are those of the Siane of the Eastern Highlands between 1933 and 1953 (based on the author's field study in 1952–53) and of the Tolai people of New Britain between 1870 and 1914 based on published material and records, especially those of the Sacred Heart Mission.[1]

SOURCE: Reprinted from *Journal of the Polynesian Society,* Vol. 71, No. 3 (1962), pp. 328–39, by permission of the author and publisher. Government and mission reports and similar periodicals cited in the article are listed immediately following it.

[1] The Australian National University supported the Siane fieldwork. The Tolai study has been supported by the University of California Institute of

The history of the Siane people can be given in brief outline since an extensive treatment is available (Salisbury 1962). Enough will be given here to permit a comparison with the Tolai growth process. The Siane number some 15,000 individuals who live in the mountains west of Goroka. An exploring party crossed their territory in 1933, but found an easier route to the west, skirting the north of Siane, which all later travellers from Goroka to Chimbu used until 1944–45. Europeans settled in nearby Benabena and in Chimbu, but did not re-enter Siane, although their goods did, traded in through native channels of exchange. This period of indirect contact was one of considerable political consolidation in Siane.

Before 1933 Siane society was very atomistic. The people lived in villages of about 200 individuals, and each village was nominally a unit for making war and for making ceremonial payments of shells to other villages at occasions such as weddings. The largest group that commonly combined for work or for the collection of payments was only a section of a village, however—a "ward". More commonly still, individuals or small lineages worked independently, as few men could spare the time to attend the ceremonies or help in the work of men not of their own lineage. Producing enough food, when stone axes were the only tools used, took 80 per cent of a man's time. No one except lineage heads had much authority, and they commanded the support of only five or six men each. Men who were active in contributing to ceremonial payments were termed "big men" (*we namfa*) and their word carried some weight in informal discussions. One big man represented his ward in disputes or ceremonies involving more than one ward; as there was no indigenous term for such a man, I shall follow current practice and refer to him as a *bosboi*. No single individual was a permanent spokesman for the whole village, on occasions when members of different villages met together. Whichever *bosboi* was appropriate to the particular occasion performed this task. Travel too was restricted by the permanent inter-village hostilities, and men left their villages only to attend ceremonies

International Studies and by the U. S. National Institute of Mental Health Small Grant No. M-4427A. The Sacred Heart Mission, Münster, Germany, granted invaluable assistance and facilities. This is an interim report and does not utilize material obtained in 1961 in New Britain. This material confirms and amplifies the present discussion and will be published subsequently.

as a group, or to exchange gifts when visiting matrilineal relatives as private individuals. The gifts exchanged were luxury commodities such as pandanus nuts and oil, and salt.

The introduction of steel axes, traded in as part of the ceremonial payments received from groups nearer to European settlements, reduced the time needed to do the work previously done with stone axes. Cutting jobs now took only one-third as long, and men needed to spend only 50 per cent of their time in the tasks connected with food production. The surplus of time was spent in increased fighting, attendance at ceremonies and visiting. A negligible amount was devoted to increasing the already adequate food supply. Both the fighting and making of payments placed more power in the hands of the big men, while the village now emerged as the effective unit in ceremonials, as men eagerly seized the opportunity to attend whatever ceremonials took place. Increasingly one particular *bosboi* in each village began to assume an office of permanent village representative. By 1945 large wars had become common, though inter-ward brawls had decreased in frequency; there was increased competition among the big men, each of whom tried to increase his status by contributing to as many ceremonial payments as he could, so that he would gain influence in the ensuing political discussions; each *bosboi* strove for the office of village representative, and the growing pre-eminence of one particular *bosboi* merely increased the pressure of competition among the others. As an immediate result of the technological change, the Siane had become more leisured, they had larger and more elaborate ceremonials, and the number and size of ceremonial payments had increased about threefold. Politically, although the form of groupings and the activities involved were unchanged, larger aggregates were working together and the authority of the leaders was more autocratic and covered a wider span. Political unification and centralization was under way.

A dysentery epidemic in 1944–45 resulted in a climax of fighting, as sorcery accusations were made on all sides. This induced some native leaders to seek European help, thereby beginning the second phase of change. Government recognition of village spokesmen as *luluais* and the treatment of villages as the administrative units stabilized the new political organization. Patrols paid for their food with such consumer goods as tobacco, European salt, beads, and cloth *laplaps* which had previously been unknown in Siane.

The developing Siane taste for such luxuries was further satisfied by gifts from sophisticated matrilateral relatives living closer to European settlements. In 1948 a small group of young men, under-employed at home now that wars had ceased, went to the coast as indentured labourers. They returned in 1950 and brought back shells and other valuables for use in ceremonial payments, a few novel goods like flashlights, hurricane lamps and footballs, and also many luxuries such as tobacco, newspaper for rolling cigarettes, salt, face-paint and peroxide. About three-quarters of their earnings they distributed to their lineage brothers and to the big men. The remaining quarter gave them the nucleus of a bride-price, luxuries to last a few months, some new durable goods and a few shillings with which to buy more luxuries. Shillings, in fact, became "luxuries" suitable as gifts to departing guests. Pound notes, although usually used immediately to buy gold-lip shells at £1 apiece, came to be regarded as equivalent to a shell "valuable" and to be used as such in ceremonial payments.

The next batch of labourers, numbering some ten per cent of the Siane labour force, returned in 1953 and brought even greater wealth which they distributed as before. Pound notes could no longer buy shells as the price of shells had trebled in the meanwhile. More notes were retained as such and were used in bride-prices. On the other hand, the later returnees were visited more by distant relatives, all sophisticated enough to expect to be offered trade tobacco to smoke and to be given shillings or trade goods on departure. Many returned labourers had to change their "valuable" notes for "luxury" shillings to meet their obligations. This meant that for them the accumulation of capital in the form of "valu-ables" was hindered by the rising demand for consumer "luxuries"; the consumer demand also prevented the maintenance of durable goods brought back by them. Thus, for example, no labourer after six months in the village had enough cash to buy kerosene for his new hurricane lamp. What capital was accumulated was mainly in the form of traditional valuables, such as headdresses of small nassa shells, or in the form of cloth *laplaps,* although some productive capital was added at this time in the form of bush-knives.

In 1953 the major form of novel capital investment in Siane was corporate public investment. With minimal pressure (and no supervision) by Government officers, Siane villagers under their *luluais* cleared roads on Mondays, a day they set aside for Government work. Unfortunately, three mile stretches of drivable road through progressive villages alternated with rough tracks through others, and no connections were made with the Highland jeep road. Some 6,000 workers with minimal supervision levelled an airstrip for DC-3's in a few months, working again as village units under their *luluais*. Three progressive villages laid out coffee nurseries, and then coffee plantations, using co-operative clan labour. The tighter village organization seemed to have found an outlet for productive activity.

Individual capital accumulation in Siane was possible only for the few who could evade the pressure from relatives to dissipate earnings by luxurious entertaining. Most of the 25 such individuals (out of about 6,000 Siane surveyed) were Government police or medical assistants. One police corporal who had spent several years in Port Moresby had enough in two savings accounts to buy a truck when his period of service ended. Others hoped to open trade stores. The investments they planned were all in service enterprises, however, and not in primary investment which was left to corporate investment.[2] Neither investment had begun to yield returns in 1953, but it is clear that at that time the incentive to make increased investments was being provided by the demand for increased consumption of luxuries.

The Tolai,[3] whom I wish to compare with the Siane, live near Rabaul on the Gazelle Peninsula of New Britain. They are a group of matrilineal peoples now numbering some 35,000. Indigenously they lived mainly in small hamlets of 30–50 individuals, grouped into clan-parishes averaging about 200. Inter-marrying and neighbouring parishes sometimes combined as "districts" for defence, and were referred to by outsiders using group names. The occasions for co-operation were rare, however, and the district groups had no feeling of solidarity. The hamlets had as their cores, small matrilineages each with its own senior male member called a *lualua*. He had considerable authority over matrilineage property, and his position was hereditary. Within the parish one or two

[2] Private investment in coffee plantations in Siane began later, in 1955.
[3] This summary of indigenous Tolai organization is based primarily on Parkinson (1887) supplemented by an analysis of other first-hand reports. Later reports (e.g. Parkinson 1910) differ slightly, but in most cases the differences can be seen as reflecting the changes analysed in this paper.

lualua were marked out by their possession of large stocks of shell money (*tabu*), and were called *ngala* or "big men". They represented their parishes in such political matters as the making of marriage payments, but had little say in everyday matters of garden work or market trading which were individual or lineage concerns. Under the *ngala* were war leaders termed *luluai*, who were often younger men, although in some instances an individual was both a *ngala* and a *luluai*.

Travel was extremely limited since districts were permanently at war with each other, and fights between neighbouring parishes and even hamlets were common. Parishes of the same district that wished to contract marriages would temporarily seal the peace by exchanging shell money. Despite this there was an extensive system of inter-parish trade. On appointed days the women of neighbouring parishes would come to the boundaries of their territories, each bringing specialty products, and would exchange them, under the watchful eyes of their heavily armed husbands. Such markets were only about three miles apart, as is shown by the report of an expedition into uncontacted areas that passed through seven in the course of a 15 mile journey (N. 88:156). In this way inland taro was exchanged for coastal fish, shells, lime and bananas, while products such as Baining stone clubs and feathers from the southern forest also entered into the trade. It is clear that each parish traded both on its own account and as middlemen in long distance trade. Shell money was used as a medium of exchange in this trade. This money consisted in numbers of small nassa shells threaded on lengths of rattan cane. Small lengths were the standards used in trade; rolls of 50 or more fathoms and skeins of ten fathoms formed the units for ceremonial payments. Only one group of western Tolai knew where the shells came from; the remainder knew vaguely that they came from the west, but the inhabitants did not dare to sail beyond the first foreign villages of the Baining people. This fear did not worry the offshore islanders who obtained most of the shells and made them up into ropes, thereby compensating for the lack of arable land on the islands.

In summary, although the first travellers described the Tolai area as extremely fertile, life was precarious because of the incessant fighting and cannibalism. While the north shore of the Rabaul peninsula appeared like a park of banana groves interspersed with coconuts, other areas were covered with *kunai* grass, as all trees and gardens had been destroyed in the incessant fighting. Truces and markets were uneasy interludes marked by suspicion and attempts to outsmart the other man.

Several Europeans sailed near the coast after Carteret discovered St. George's Channel in 1767, but they visited only the offshore islands until 1872. The firm of Godeffroy then expanded its search for labour for its Samoan plantations, and several traders and recruiters visited in the coast in the next few years. They included among them the well-known W. T. Wawn (cf. Wawn 1893). They found a coastal people generally uninterested in work abroad,[4] although some youths did volunteer. More were kidnapped and many were forced to go by their *lualua* who received gifts of guns or tobacco. The coastal people were more interested in trade and in exchange for guns, ammunition, steel axes and knives would give as many coconuts as were asked (Parkinson 1887:85), while for a stick of trade tobacco they would give 25–30 nuts. The guns and axes were for use in wars against the inland people, the axeheads being mounted on six foot long poles for use as battleaxes.

This picture of native wants at the time of first contact applies to the whole Tolai area. All areas in due course passed out of this phase of development and into a second phase, but the dates of this transition vary from area to area. The northern coastal peoples, living between what is now Rabaul and Cape Livuan, were the earliest exposed to traders and passed into the second phase in about 1883. The people on the shores of Blanche Bay near what is now Kokopo entered their second phase in 1894, while the more inland peoples near Toma did so in 1902. For lack of space I shall discuss only the first two groups, treating the phases separately rather than retaining a chronological narrative.

In the first phase on the north coast, the people there, thanks to their initial monopoly of weapons, drove inland peoples further inland and stole their shell money and coconuts. More peacefully, coconuts began to be regularly traded from inland to the coast, despite the existence of palms on the coast. The coastals then

[4] But recruiters found and continued to find a ready interest in New Ireland. Thus in 1883–84 recruiting on New Britain was almost to a standstill (Parkinson 1887:27), yet 2,200 labourers were obtained from the rest of the Bismarck Archipelago—principally New Ireland. In 1890 1,044 workers went from New Ireland as against 130 from New Britain (N. 91:14). In 1893 only 39 of 798 labourers recruited for work in New Guinea were Tolai (N. 94:25).

traded the nuts with Europeans for trade goods. They then had a monopoly of these articles for trade with groups further inland. Within a short time the increase in native marketing seems to have brought most of the coconuts of the whole Tolai area to the coast for trade, greatly enriching the coastals with a minimum of work on their part. Coconut palms take ten years to come into full bearing, yet already by 1879–80 an estimated 1,000 tons of copra were exported (Z. 86). The number of coconuts needed to produce this tonnage must have been available before the advent of European traders, and in fact would represent the yield from the Tolai area if each person in a population of 20,000 owned only four trees. This figure seems in accord with early descriptions of the numbers of palms around each hamlet. It would seem that the Tolai merely ate less nuts as relish with their other foods, and now carefully collected nuts which had previously been left to rot (as is specifically recorded by observers as happening on New Ireland) (B. 02: 89). The arrival of European traders enabled them to cash in on an already existing but imperfectly utilized resource.

Few coconuts were planted, as is attested by the reports that new native plantings were only just coming into bearing in 1896 (N. 96:30). The absence of extensive new plantings also appears in the figures for copra exports from the Bismarck Archipelago. By 1883, although traders had meanwhile extended their operations to other islands, exports from the whole Archipelago had risen to only 1,350 tons (Parkinson 1887:35, 40). They rose to 1,550 tons in 1885 (Z. 88) and to an annual rate of 1,703 tons in eighteen months of 1892–93 (N. 94:20–25). By 1896 2,437 tons were exported (N. 96:31), but Schnee (1937:202), later the chief judge of the Territory, estimated that one-quarter of this production came from European plantations, or about 1,800 tons only were native grown coconuts. The annual increase of about 1.5 per cent per annum during these 13 years would probably be fully accounted for by the expanded operations of the traders. If it resulted from increased Tolai plantings, the latter would still represent a planting of three palms per capita in thirteen years. Any sizeable amount of new planting would be represented by a rapid and continuous rise in exports. In fact exports rose sharply after 1896, indicating that planting did not begin until the second phase, after 1883.

The coastal riches were not distributed to the ordinary people, nor spent in clothing or luxury consumption, with the exception of tobacco. As late as 1889 the residents of some Nodup hamlets remained completely nude, putting on bunches of leaves only when talking to missionaries (H. 89:5). Against this, as early as 1883 the *ngala* of other Nodup settlements had obtained enough rifles to equip every man of their groups. Goods, which represented a source of power, were overwhelmingly concentrated in the hands of the *ngala*. Not merely did these own weapons obtained from traders, their monopoly of trade goods enabled them to drain the inland people's supplies of shell money and to become rich in the native tokens of power. But they were dependent on Europeans, and the relationship was one of mutual interdependence as long as Europeans did not settle on the coast and trade further inland.

For this reason traders (but not recruiters) were at first welcomed on their visits, but if they tried to settle they were quickly forced to leave by the burning of their houses. Only the Methodist Mission successfully established non-trading settlements staffed by Samoan and Fijian teachers. But when the latter tried to move inland, they too met opposition. Many *ngala* from all districts from Raluana westwards combined in 1878 under a single outstanding leader, the notorious Talili, to drive out all Europeans by murdering four of the resident teachers who had ventured inland. Talili said explicitly that his reason was his fear that trade goods might reach inland otherwise than through his hands (Powell 1884: 123). Combined action by all the local Europeans and their allies of Matupit and Nodup finally defeated Talili and broke his power over parishes other than his own, thus preparing the way for the second phase in this area.

The first phase in the Kokopo area began with settlements by Methodist teachers and visits by Powell and others in the late 1870's, since the earliest traders had avoided this shore. In 1882–83 the first European plantation was established at Ralum, for the *ngala* had been led to accept settlers and even to sell them land, by their experience with missionaries, their desire for gain and the presence of British and German gunboats off the coast. The fact that the *ngala* often did not really own the land, which was the property of their own and other matrilineages, only became clear later (H. 07:153). It is clear that the *ngala* were now acting more arrogantly and independently of their supporters than they had done at the time of first contact. *Ngala* competed among them-

selves for favours from the two missions, Methodist and Catholic
(H. 91:148), which were now established, and for the economic
advantage in having a resident European. On the other hand they
often tried to prevent their subordinates from becoming mission
adherents, and converts were few in number. They also seem to
have been effective in preventing men from signing on for indentured labour. Out of a total of 2,962 labourers who left the Bismarck Archipelago for work in the seven years 1887–94, only 552
were from New Britain—an average of 80 a year.

The *ngala* did not merely become autocratic in their own districts, they promoted inter-district solidarity. Market trading increased under their aegis as it had done in the north (Parkinson
1887:79). Alliances for warfare did likewise, and the attractive
possibility of driving the weak Europeans out and capturing their
wealth led to much discussion among the *ngala*. A conspiracy of
Raluana, Reber and Kinigunan broke up with a scuffle among the
conspirators in the 1880's; another in 1890 attacked Ralum plantation and was barely repelled by the combined Europeans, exclusive of missionaries (H. 90:134). Many Tolai were killed and
their leader, ToRuruk, was captured, tried, and, despite mission
intercession, executed (H. 92:152). Better planning and larger
forces in the next attack (triggered by the arrogant behaviour of
plantation labourers imported from Buka) kept the Europeans on
the defensive from July 1893 until December of that year when a
German cruiser shelled inland hamlets killing 240 Tolai (H. 94:
103). The *ngala* of five districts (including the inland ones of
Tingenavudu and Malagunuan) had combined under a leader who
claimed to possess the secret of a bulletproof ointment. This revolt
caused the German government to replace the *ngala* with appointed
headmen who had jurisdiction over district units. These headmen
were first termed *lualua,* and later *luluai,* and were appointed, so
the official pronouncement said, to get "effective chiefs" and "to
promote district solidarity". These reasons sound anomalous in
view of the effectiveness and solidarity shown by the *ngala,* but
there is no doubt that from the governmental point of view the new
headmen were "responsible chiefs" who facilitated "ease of administration" (N. 94:19). As in the north, the breaking of the power
of the *ngala,* following a period of considerable political consolidation and centralization of authority, marked the end of the southern
first phase.

In both north and south the second phase involved a sudden increase in the number of mission conversions to both Catholicism and Methodism. Both missions hailed this as a turning point in their labours, and noted that young men who joined the church often did so in defiance of their chiefs. The number of men signing on for indentured labour also began to increase, and in 1893 the first men from Matupit began to work on the local plantations in Kokopo (N. 93:24). Kinigunan men began local work for plantations in 1894 (H. 95:132), though Ralum plantation still employed only Buka men as locals were considered "too lazy". But although these are indications of a loss of power by the *ngala,* there was no decline in the inter-district solidarity they had fostered. Three thousand people attended the dances at a clan mortuary ceremony near Ralum in 1894 (Webster 1898:88), while several thousands attended the regular markets there. Interest seems to have switched completely from warfare to peaceful economic gain.

The economic concern was most marked in the change of goods demanded from Europeans. In the north in 1883 guns became less wanted but clothes were avidly sought. Missions began giving a *laplap* to natives after each successive seventeen Sunday attendances (H. 91:23). Tobacco, accepted since its first introduction in the 1870's, became the main item demanded, together with "canned goods, false pearls and rings, etc." (H. 97:117). Guns had not been imported in the south following the Government ban in 1887, so that the change in demand there was from importing axes to buying "tobacco, pipes, pearls, knives, matches, cotton goods and European foods" (N. 94:20). Throughout the switch was from weapons to consumer luxuries.

The earlier exploitation of existing surpluses carried out largely at the behest of the *ngala* did not satisfy the ordinary people, who now began extensive planting of coconut palms—after 1883 in the north and in the 1890's in the south. Total copra production in the Bismarck Archipelago rose from 2,437 tons in 1895 to 8,571 tons in 1911, with native production dropping from an estimated three-quarters of the total to slightly over half (B. 12:xv).

Coconuts were supplemented as a cash crop by vegetable production. Europeans needed food for their employees, whose number rose markedly from the 150 employed at Ralum in 1884 (Parkinson 1887:91). By 1896, 1,744 foreigners were working near Kokopo (N. 96:16, 30), and the number increased to 13,632 in 1911. Individual Tolai began to plant explicitly for this market (N. 96:29), although production was never enough to obviate the need for rice imports. The indigenous market system easily adapted itself with the largest markets being those situated at the buying posts near the labour quarters of each plantation. Where at first contact people had rarely dared to travel more than two miles to market, political consolidation and the encouragement of trade by the *ngala* had enabled people to come in from 6½ miles distant by 1885 (Parkinson 1887:79). By 1894 hundreds of women came to Ralum every third day to sell taro, yams, bread-fruit, bananas and megapod eggs (Webster 1898:77).

The Tolai grew rich with little effort. The native coconut plantings of the twenty years 1883–1903 (as estimated from the copra tonnages cited for 1911) would average out at about one palm per Tolai each year. To grow enough food to feed com-pletely 2,000 foreign workers, in addition to the 20,000 resident Tolais would have meant an increase in garden acreage of about 10 per cent. Nor was Tolai labour used to turn the coconuts into copra, for the nuts were bought whole by the traders and converted to copra by their employees. By 1900 the Tolai were so wealthy that few volunteered for either indentured or local labour. Trade stores sold increasing quantities of umbrellas, eau de cologne and European clothing. Prices asked for vegetables increased yearly, and the Tolai insisted in payment in shell money. Europeans could obtain this only from the Tolai, and after 1899 the latter began to demand a steadily increasing price for it. Three and four marks per fathom were demanded, where previously two marks per fathom had been the recognised exchange rate (H. 02:540). To keep the Tolai working, as they explicitly said, the German gov-ernment decreed that Europeans should now buy only processed copra, and that money and not shell should be the only medium of exchange between Europeans and natives (B. 01:80). Accumula-tion of money, first introduced in 1895 (N. 95:47) but at first little used, now became a main incentive for the Tolai. By 1906 some individuals were earning 750 marks (£37 10s.) a year (Burry 1909:193); by 1909 a few rich men earned 300 marks (£15) a month from copra. Some of the money was used for individual productive investment, with the purchase of large fishing boats built by Chinese shipwrights, and horses and carts. But most of the money was hoarded as silver one mark pieces, some natives having stores of 10,000 marks. Europeans continually complained of a shortage of coin, despite imports of about 150,000 marks annually (B. 10:171). Money was used in competitive giving to missions—many contributions of 500 marks for Catholic church building were noted in 1908; areal contributions to the Methodist mission in 1911 were 41,200 marks. Head taxes, introduced at the rate of 5 marks in 1905, were "paid willingly", and when they were increased to 7 or 10 marks for advanced groups, there was competition to pay the higher rates (B. 11:152). Payment of tax freed the Tolai from their obligation to work on roadbuilding, but enabled the Government to push ahead with an extensive programme of roadbuilding and schools. In this way the Tolai demand for luxury consumption gave an incentive, not merely to individual investments, but also to corporate public investment.[5]

What are the common features of these two histories of a progression from poverty to riches following European contact? In both societies the arrival of European traders and their goods had the effect of providing a windfall surplus to the society, and this surplus enabled a political consolidation to occur. In Siane the surplus was one of time, occasioned by the technological change; in Tolai it was a means of using an existing but incompletely utilized abundance of coconuts. Without changing their habits and without making any great capital investments both societies became rich, groupings became larger and the leaders more powerful. When the new organization had become established and stabilized, both societies increased their consumption of luxury goods. This led to an increase in investment, by both individuals and by groups, and this in its turn allowed the consumption of luxuries to continue expanding.

The parallel sequence does not appear to be fortuitous. One can see how the political consolidation had important consequences in facilitating the later prosperity and investment. In both areas consolidation implied better communications, and this spread the knowledge of and demand for new goods. In the Tolai area the expansion of the market system as inter-district warfare declined enabled people to respond to the needs of the plantations. Elimina-

[5] Rowley (1958) describes the legislative actions during World War I and the subsequent activities of the Expropriation Board which effectively caused Tolai economic activity to stagnate until about 1933. Tolai activities during this period will be discussed by the present author in a subsequent study.

tion of minor skirmishes increased the individual's personal security, encouraging him to accumulate goods, and to be venturesome in private trading. Larger groupings meant larger ceremonials in both societies, and more practice in administrative skills for the men who organized ceremonies. The rise of larger groupings meant a relative decline in the political importance of the lineage heads, although the latter maintained their traditional activities. At first the politicians and warriors increased their importance, and in the second phase of development these were replaced in their turn by economic entrepreneurs. And lastly, the consolidation provided the larger groupings needed to make and maintain the larger corporate investments—larger gardens and coffee plantations in Siane; roads, churches and schools in Tolai. Once personal security, inter-group communications, public services, and the sanctity of private contracts are ensured by an effective local political authority, and once some training in entrepreneurial and organizational skills has occurred, the way is open for an increase in individualism. Paradoxically, an initial increase in the strength and authoritarianism of traditional groupings may be the best guarantee of eventual prosperity and an individualistic economy.

Finally, this sequence of development in two New Guinea societies invites comparison with the "stages of economic growth" of Rostow (1960). Like the societies undergoing industrialization which Rostow discusses, these New Guinea societies undergoing different technological revolutions began with a period of political change. Rostow calls this phase one of "preparation for take-off". But where industrializing societies then began a phase of cumulative capital growth ("take-off into sustained growth"), and only later began to show the signs of "maturity" and affluence ("mass-consumption"), the New Guinea societies first indulged in luxury consumption and only gradually developed the pattern of great net capital investment, appropriate to supporting and expanding such consumption. A further similarity in the processes is the fact that the basic innovation triggering both industrialization and the New Guinea changes, occurred as an unexpected change in the productivity of primary production. Whether the differences in the sequences are due to specific features of New Guinea society, to differences in the political organization evolved in the first phase, or to differences in the technological requirements of industrialization and of other forms of production, the overall similarities outweigh the differences. These similarities suggest the fruitfulness of comparing all cases of social change involving a change of technology. Through such studies it will become possible to discuss more precisely the nature of the political changes required to "prepare for take-off", and to consider the relative importance of such economic features as the nature of demand patterns and the rate of net capital investment.

Periodicals Cited

B. *Jahresberichte Über die deutschen Schutzgebiete in Afrika und der Südsee* (with variant titles). Official Government Annual Reports 1899–1913.

H. *Hiltruper Monatschefte zur Ehre unserer Lieben Frau des Heiligsten Herz Jesu* (with variant titles). 1883 to date. Journal of the Sacred Heart Mission, Hiltrup.

N. *Nachrichten über Kaiser Wilhelmsland und den Bismarck Archipel.* 1885–1898. Organ of the Deutsch Neu Guinea Gesselschaft.

Z. *Deutche Kolonialzeitung.* Deutsche Kolonial Gesselschaft, Berlin.

Bibliography

Aitken, R. T.
   1930   *Ethnology of Tubuai*. Bernice P. Bishop Museum Bulletin 70.
Alkire, William H.
   1959   *Habitat, Economy, and Residence in the Caroline Islands*. Unpublished M.A. Thesis, Department of Anthropology, University of Hawaii.
   1965   *Lamotrek Atoll and Inter-Island Socioeconomic Ties*. Illinois Studies in Anthropology, No. 5. Urbana: University of Illinois Press.
Allan, C. H.
   1951   "Marching Rule: A Nativistic Cult of the British Solomon Islands." *Corona*, 3:93–100.
Andrade, S. Francisco
   1954   "El Océano Pacífico." *Boletín de la Soc. Geogr. de Colombia*, 12:127–48.
Andrews, Ernest C.
   1940   "The Structure of the Pacific Basin." *Sixth Pacific Science Congress, Berkeley and Stanford, 1939, Proc.*, 1:201–4.
Anonymous
   1951   "Community Development Through Rural Progress Societies." *South Pacific*, 5:123–26.
Bacon, Elizabeth E.
   1958   *Obok*. Viking Fund Publications in Anthropology, No. 25. New York: Wenner-Gren Foundation.
Barnes, J. A.
   1962   "African Models in the New Guinea Highlands." *Man*, 62:5–9.
Barnett, H. G.
   1949   *Palauan Society*. Eugene: University of Oregon Press.

Barrau, Jacques

1956   *l'Agriculture vivrière autochtone de la Nouvelle Calédonie.* Nouméa: Commission du Pacifique Sud.

1957   "Les Atolls océaniens, essai d'agronomie." *Études d'Outre-Mer,* 40:253–68.

1958   *Subsistence Agriculture in Melanesia.* Bernice P. Bishop Museum Bulletin 219.

1959   "Fruits et graines du taro, *Colocasia esculenta* (L.) Schott." *Journal d'Agriculture Tropicale et de Botanique Appliquée,* 6:8–9, 436–38.

1960   "Plant Introduction in the Tropical Pacific; Its Role in Economic Development." *Pacific Viewpoint,* 1:1–10.

1962   *Les Plantes alimentaires de l'Océanie, origines, distribution et usages.* Annales du Musée Colonial de Marseille, 7e Série, 3e a 9e volumes (1955–61), 1–275.

Barrett, Charles L.

1950   *The Pacific, Ocean of Islands.* Melbourne: N. H. Seward Pty., Ltd.

Barton, R. F.

1919   *Ifugao Law.* University of California Publications in Archaeology and Ethnology 15, No. 1.

Bascom, W. R.

1965   *Ponape: A Pacific Economy in Transition.* Anthropological Records, Vol. 22. Berkeley: University of California Press.

Bates, Marston

1952   *Where Winter Never Comes; A Study of Man and Nature in the Tropics.* New York: Charles Scribner's Sons.

1963   "Nature's Effect on and Control of Man," in F. R. Fosberg (ed.), *Man's Place in the Island Ecosystem.* Honolulu: Bishop Museum Press.

Beaglehole, Ernest

1937   "Cultural Peaks in Polynesia." *Man,* 37:138–40.

Beaglehole, Ernest and Pearl

1938   *The Ethnology of Pukapuka.* Bernice P. Bishop Museum Bulletin 150.

Beaglehole, J. C. (ed.)

1955   *The Journals of Captain James Cook on his Voyages of Discovery,* Vol. 1, *The Voyage of the Endeavour* 1768–1771. London: Cambridge University Press, for the Hakluyt Society.

Bee, Darlene

1965   "Comparative and Historical Problems in East New Guinea Highland Languages." Linguistic Circle of Canberra Publications, Series A, No. 6:1–37.

Belshaw, C. S.
  1955   *In Search of Wealth.* American Anthropological Association
    Memoir No. 80.
Benedict, R.
  1938   "Religion," in F. Boas (ed.), *General Anthropology.* New
    York: D. C. Heath & Company.
Bentzen, C.
  1949   *Land and Livelihood on Mokil, Part II.* Coordinated Inves-
    tigation of Micronesian Anthropology Report. Washington, D.C.:
    Pacific Science Board (ditto).
Berndt, C. H.
  1953   "Socio-Cultural Change in the Eastern Central Highlands of
    New Guinea." *Southwestern Journal of Anthropology,* 9:112–38.
Berndt, Ronald M.
  1952–53   "A Cargo Movement in the Eastern Central Highlands of
    New Guinea." *Oceania,* 23:40–65, 137–58, 202–34.
  1954   "Reaction to Contact in the Eastern Highlands of New
    Guinea." *Oceania,* 24:190–228, 255–74.
  1954–55   "Kamano, Jate, Usurufa and Fore Kinship of the Eastern
    Highlands of New Guinea: A Preliminary Account." *Oceania,*
    25:23–53, 156–87.
  1955   "Interdependence and Conflict in the Eastern Central High-
    lands of New Guinea." *Man,* 55:105–7.
Betz, Frederick, Jr., and Harry H. Hess
  1942   "The Floor of the North Pacific Ocean." *Geographical Re-
    view,* 32:99–116.
Biggs, Bruce
  1965   "Direct and Indirect Inheritance in Rotuman." *Lingua,* 14:
    383–415.
Birdsell, J. B.
  1949   "The Problem of the Early Peopling of the Americas as
    Viewed from Asia," in W. S. Laughlin and S. L. Washburn (eds.),
    Papers on the Physical Anthropology of the American Indian.
    New York: Viking Fund.
  1950   "The Racial Origin of the Extinct Tasmanians. Results of the
    Harvard-Adelaide Universities Anthropological Expedition, 1938–
    1939." Reprinted from the Records of the Queen Victoria Mu-
    seum, Vol. 2, No. 3 (1949), Launceston, Tasmania. In *Yearbook
    of Physical Anthropology,* G. W. Lasker and J. L. Angel (eds.),
    Vol. 6. New York: Wenner-Gren Foundation.
Blackwood, Beatrice
  1935   *Both Sides of Buka Passage.* London: Clarendon Press.

Blood, N. B.
1946 Extract of Unpublished Report of Patrol by Captain N. B. Blood, A.D.O., from Hagen to Ifitamin. Appendix A. ANGAU (Australian New Guinea Administrative Unit) *Final Report of Activities.*

Blumenstock, David I.
1958 "Distribution and Characteristics of Tropical Climates." *Ninth Pacific Science Congress, Bangkok, 1957, Proc.,* 20:3–24.

Blumenstock, David I. (ed.)
1961 "A Report on Typhoon Effects Upon Jaluit Atoll [Marshall Islands]." *Atoll Research Bulletin,* No. 75:1–105.

Boas, Franz
1940 *Race, Language, and Culture.* New York: The Free Press.

Bondy-Horowitz, E.
1930 Beiträge zur Anthropologie von Nordost-Neu-Guinea. Rudolf Pöchs Nachlass. Serie A: *Physische Anthropologie,* Bd. 2:1–202 (Vienna).

Bowman, R. G.
1951 "Northern Melanesia: New Guinea and the Bismarck Archipelago," in O. W. Freeman (ed.), *Geography of the Pacific.* New York: John Wiley & Sons, Inc.

Boyd, W. C.
1939 "Blood Groups." *Tabulae Biologicae,* 17:113–240.
1952 *Genetics and the Races of Man. An Introduction to Modern Physical Anthropology.* Boston: Little, Brown & Company.

Boykin, J.
1963 "The Voyage of the Ulithians." *Micronesian Reporter,* 11: 18–20.

Braidwood, R. J.
1960 "The Agricultural Revolution." *Scientific American,* 203 (3): 1–10.

Bromley, M.
1960 "A Preliminary Report on Law Among the Grand Valley Dani of Netherlands New Guinea." *Nieuw Guinea Studiën,* 4: 235–59.

Brookfield, H. C.
1964 "The Ecology of Highland Settlement: Some Suggestions." *American Anthropologist,* 66 (4, part 2):20–38.

Brown, Paula
1960 "Chimbu Tribes: Political Organization in the Eastern Highlands of New Guinea." *Southwestern Journal of Anthropology,* 16:22–35.
1963 "From Anarchy to Satrapy." *American Anthropologist,* 65: 1–15.

Brown, P., and H. C. Brookfield
1959 "Chimbu Land and Society." *Oceania*, 30:1–75.
Brues, A. M.
1954 "Selection and Polymorphism in the A-B-O Blood Groups." *American Journal of Physical Anthropology*, N.S. 12:559–97.
Bruyn, J. V. de
1951 "The Mansren Cult of Biak." *South Pacific*, 5:1–11.
Bryan, Edwin H., Jr.
1953 "Check List of Atolls." *Atoll Research Bulletin*, No. 19:1–38.
1963 "Discussion," in F. R. Fosberg (ed.), *Man's Place in the Island Ecosystem*. Honolulu: Bishop Museum Press.
Buck, P. H. [Te Rangi Hiroa]
1930 *Samoan Material Culture*. Bernice P. Bishop Museum Bulletin 75.
1932a *Ethnology of Tongareva*. Bernice P. Bishop Museum Bulletin 92.
1932b *Ethnology of Manihiki and Rakahanga*. Bernice P. Bishop Museum Bulletin 99.
1938a *Ethnology of Mangareva*. Bernice P. Bishop Museum Bulletin 157.
1938b *Vikings of the Sunrise*. New York: Frederick A. Stokes Company.
1939 *Anthropology and Religion*. New Haven: Yale University Press.
1945 *An Introduction to Polynesian Anthropology*. Bernice P. Bishop Museum Bulletin 187.
1950 *The Material Culture of Kapingamarangi*. Bernice P. Bishop Museum Bulletin 200.
1960 *Vikings of the Pacific*. Chicago: The University of Chicago Press.
Bulmer, Ralph
1960–61 "Political Aspects of the Moka Exchange System Among the Kyaka People of the Western Highlands of New Guinea." *Oceania*, 31:1–13.
Burkill, I. H.
1935 *A Dictionary of the Economic Products of the Malay Peninsula*. London: Crown Agents for the Colonies.
1951 "The Rise and Decline of the Greater Yam in the Service of Man." *Advancement of Science*, 7:443–48.
1954 *Dioscoreaceae; Flora Melesiana*. Djakarta: Nordhoff-Kolff.
1960 "The Organography and the Evolution of *Dioscoreaceae*, the Family of Yams." *Journal of the Linnean Society of London*, 56 (367):319–412.

Burridge, K. O. L.
1960 *Mambu: A Melanesian Millennium.* London: Methuen & Company, Ltd.

Burrows, Edwin G.
1936 *Ethnology of Futuna.* Bernice P. Bishop Museum Bulletin 138.
1937 *Ethnology of Uvea.* Bernice P. Bishop Museum Bulletin 145.
1938 "Western Polynesia: A Study in Cultural Differentiation." *Etnologiska Studier,* 7:1–192 (Göteborg).
1939 "Breed and Border in Polynesia." *American Anthropologist,* 41:1–21.

Burrows, Edwin G., and Melford E. Spiro
1953 *An Atoll Culture, Ethnology of Ifaluk in the Central Carolines.* Behavior Science Monographs, Human Relations Area Files (New Haven).

Burry, B. P.
1909 *In a German Colony.* London: Methuen & Company, Ltd.

Byerly, Perry
1953 "Pacific Coast Earthquakes." *The American Scientist,* 41: 572–95.

Capell, A.
1938 "The Word Mana: A Linguistic Study." *Oceania,* 9:89–96.
1940 "Language Study for New Guinea Students." *Oceania,* 11: 40–74.
1962a *A Linguistic Survey of the South-Western Pacific* (New and Revised Edition). South Pacific Commission Technical Paper No. 136. Nouméa: South Pacific Commission.
1962b "Oceanic Linguistics Today." *Current Anthropology,* 3: 371–428.

Catala, R. L. A.
1957 *Report on the Gilbert Islands: Some Aspects of Human Ecology.* Atoll Research Bulletin 59.

Chang, Jen-hu
1962 "Comparative Climatology of the Tropical Western Margins of the Northern Oceans." *Association of American Geographers, Annals,* 52:221–27.

Chown, Bruce, and Marion Lewis
1953 "The ABO, MNSs, P, Rh, Lutheran, Kell, Lewis, Duffy and Kidd Blood Groups and the Secretor Status of the Blackfoot Indians of Alberta, Canada." *American Journal of Physical Anthropology,* 11:369–83.

Clark, Andrew H.
1949 *The Invasion of New Zealand by People, Plants and Ani-*

Clark, Andrew H.
   mals; the South Island. New Brunswick, N.J.: Rutgers University
   Press.
Coe, Michael D.
   1964   "The Chinampas of Mexico." *Scientific American*, 211(1):
   90–98.
Condominas, G., and A. G. Haudricourt
   1952   "Première contribution à l'ethnobotanique indochinoise: essai
   d'ethnobotanique Mnong gar (Proto-indochinois du Viet Nam)."
   *Revue Internationale de Botanique Appliquée et d'Agriculture
   Tropicale*, No. 351–52:19–27, 169–80.
Conklin, Harold C.
   1954   *The Relation of Hanunóo Culture to the Plant World.* Unpublished Ph.D. Dissertation, Department of Anthropology, Yale
   University, New Haven, Connecticut.
   1957   *Hanunóo Agriculture, A Report on an Integral System of
   Shifting Cultivation in the Philippines.* FAO Forestry Development Paper No. 12. Rome: Food and Agriculture Organization
   of the United Nations.
Coon, C. S.
   1950   *The Mountains of Giants.* Peabody Museum Papers, 23, No.
   3. Cambridge, Massachusetts.
   1954   "Climate and Race." *The Smithsonian Report for 1953, Publication 4156.* Washington: The Smithsonian Institution.
   1955   "Some Problems of Human Variability and Natural Selection
   in Climate and Culture." *The American Naturalist*, 89:257–80.
Copeland, E. B.
   1924   *Rice.* London: The Macmillan Company.
Cotton, C. A.
   1958   "The Rim of the Pacific." *Geographical Journal*, 124:223–
   31.
Coulter, J. W.
   1951   "Eastern Melanesia." In O. W. Freeman (ed.), *Geography of
   the Pacific.* New York: John Wiley & Sons, Inc.
Cowan, H. K. J.
   1957a   "Prospects of a 'Papuan' Comparative Linguistics." *Bijdragen tot de Taal-, Land-, en Volkenkunde*, 113:70–91.
   1957b   "Een Tweede Grote Papoea-taalgroepering in Nederlands-
   Nieuw Guinea." *Nieuw Guinea Studiën*, 1:107–17.
   1957–58   "A Large Papuan Language Phylum in West New
   Guinea." *Oceania*, 28:159–66.
   1960   "Nadere gegevens betreffende de verbreiding der West-
   Papoease taalgroep." *Bijdragen tot de Taal-, Land-, en Volkenkunde*, 116:350–64.

Cowan, H. K. J.
 1963 "Le Buna' de Timor: une langue 'Ouest-Papoue.'" *Bijdragen tot de Taal-, Land-, en Volkenkunde,* 119:387–400.
 1965 "The Oirata Language." *Lingua,* 14:360–70.
Crocombe, R. G., and G. R. Hogbin
 1963 *The Erap Mechanical Farming Project.* New Guinea Research Unit Bulletin No. 1 (Canberra and Port Moresby).
Cumberland, Kenneth B.
 1954 *Southwest Pacific.* Wellington: Whitcombe & Tombs, Ltd.
 1956 *Southwest Pacific; a Geography of Australia, New Zealand and Their Pacific Island Neighbourhoods.* London: Methuen & Company, Ltd.
Danielsson, Bengt
 1955 *Work and Life on Raroia.* Stockholm: Saxon and Lindströms.
 1956 *Love in the South Seas.* Translated by F. H. Lyon. London: George Allen & Unwin, Ltd.
Dansereau, P.
 1957 *Biogeography, An Ecological Perspective.* New York: The Ronald Press Co.
Davenport, William
 1962 "Comment on A. Capell, Oceanic Linguistics Today." *Current Anthropology,* 3:400–2.
 1964 "Social Structure of Santa Cruz Island," in W. H. Goodenough (ed.), *Explorations in Cultural Anthropology.* New York: McGraw-Hill Book Co., Inc.
Davis, Charles M.
 1957 *South Sea Islands.* Garden City, New York: Doubleday & Company, Inc.
Deacon, A. Bernard
 1934 *Malekula: A Vanishing People in the New Hebrides,* C. H. Wedgwood (ed.). London: George Routledge & Sons, Ltd.
Dempwolff, Otto
 1937 *Deduktive Anwendung des Urindonesischen auf Austronesische Einzelsprachen.* Zeitschrift für Eingeborenen-Sprachen, Beiheft 17.
Deniker, J.
 1900 *The Races of Man.* New York: Charles Scribner's Sons.
Dening, G. M.
 1962 "The Geographical Knowledge of the Polynesians and the Nature of Inter-Island Contact." *Journal of the Polynesian Society,* 71:102–31 (Suppl. 137).
Department of Island Territories
 1957 "Reports on the Cook, Niue, and Tokelau Islands," in *Ap-*

Department of Island Territories
  *pendix to the Journal of the House of Representatives of New
  Zealand*. Wellington: Government Printer.

Derrick, R. A.
  1957 *The Fiji Islands; A Geographical Handbook*. Suva: Government Printing Office.

De Terra, H.
  1949 "Geology and Climate as Factors of Human Evolution in
  Asia," in W. W. Howells (ed.), *Studies in Physical Anthropology,
  No. 1: Early Man in the Far East*. Philadelphia: Press of the
  Wistar Institute of Anatomy & Biology.

Dietz, Robert S.
  1952 "The Pacific Floor." *Scientific American*, 186 (4):19–23.

Dixon, R. B.
  1923 *The Racial History of Man*. New York: Charles Scribner's
  Sons.
  1928 *The Building of Cultures*. New York: Charles Scribner's
  Sons.

Douglas, R., and J. M. Staveley
  1959 "The Blood Groups of Cook Islanders." *Journal of the Polynesian Society*, 68:14–20.
  1960 "Blood Groups in Maoris." *Journal of the Polynesian Society*,
  69:34–36.

Drapkin, I.
  1934 "Contribution to the Demographic Study of Easter Island."
  Bernice P. Bishop Museum Occasional Papers, Vol. 11, No. 12
  (Honolulu).

Driberg, J. H.
  1936 "The Secular Aspect of Ancestor-Worship in Africa." *Journal
  of the Royal African Society*, 35(138): Supplement (19 pp.).

Drucker, P.
  1955 *Indians of the Northwest Coast*. Anthropological Handbooks
  of The American Museum of Natural History, 10:1–208.

Duff, R.
  1950 *The Moa-Hunter Period of Maori Culture*. Canterbury Museum Bulletin No. 1. Wellington: Government Printer.
  1959 "Neolithic Adzes of Eastern Polynesia," in J. D. Freeman
  and W. R. Geddes (eds.), *Anthropology of the South Seas*. New
  Plymouth, New Zealand: Thomas Avery & Sons, Ltd.

Dyen, Isidore
  1953 "Book Review (of Dahl, *Malgache et Maanjan*)." *Language*,
  29:577–90.
  1960 "Review of *The Position of the Polynesian Languages Within*

Dyen, Isidore

   the Austronesian (Malayo-Polynesian) Language Family" (by
   George W. Grace). *Journal of the Polynesian Society,* 69:180–84.

   1962 "The Lexicostatistical Classification of the Malayopolynesian
   Languages." *Language,* 38:38–46.

   1963 *The Lexicostatistical Classification of the Austronesian Languages.* New Haven.

   1965 *A Lexicostatistical Classification of the Austronesian Languages.* Indiana University Publications in Anthropology and Linguistics. International Journal of American Linguistics Memoir 19.

Edmonson, Munro S.

   1961 "Neolithic Diffusion Rates." *Current Anthropology,* 2:71–
   102.

Elbert, Samuel H.

   1953 "Internal Relationships of Polynesian Languages." *Southwestern Journal of Anthropology,* 9:147–73.

Emery, Kenneth O., J. I. Tracey, and H. S. Ladd

   1954 *Geology of Bikini and Nearby Atolls: Part I. Geology.* U. S.
   Geological Survey, Prof. Paper, No. 2604. Washington, D.C.

Emory, Kenneth P.

   1959 "Origin of the Hawaiians." *Journal of the Polynesian Society,* 68:29–35.

   1963 "East Polynesian Relationships: Settlement Pattern and Time
   Involved as Indicated by Vocabulary Agreements." *Journal of the
   Polynesian Society,* 70:112–36.

   1965 *Kapingamarangi, Social and Religious Life of a Polynesian
   Atoll.* Bernice P. Bishop Museum Bulletin 228.

Emory, Kenneth P., W. J. Bonk, and Y. H. Sinoto

   1959 *Hawaiian Archeology: Fishhooks.* Bernice P. Bishop Museum
   Special Publication No. 47.

Emory, Kenneth P. and Y. H. Sinoto

   1961 *Hawaiian Archeology: Oahu Excavations.* Bernice P. Bishop
   Museum Special Publication No. 49.

Essai, Brian

   1961 *Papua and New Guinea: A Contemporary Survey.* Melbourne: Oxford University Press.

Eyre, S. R.

   1963 *Vegetation and Soils, a World Picture.* London: Edward Ar-
   nold (Publishers) Ltd.

Fenner, F. J.

   1941 "Fossil Human Skull Fragments of Probable Pleistocene Age
   From Aitape, New Guinea." *Records of the Southern Australian
   Museum,* 6(4):335–56 (Adelaide).

Ferdon, E. N.
1961 "The Ceremonial Site of Orongo," in Thor Heyerdahl and Edwin N. Ferdon (eds.), *Reports of the Norwegian Archaeological Expedition to Easter Island*, Vol. I: *Archaeology of Easter Island*. Stockholm: Forum Publishing House.

Finney, Ben R.
1965 "Polynesian Peasants and Proletarians." *Journal of the Polynesian Society*, 74:269–328.

Firth, Raymond
1929 *Primitive Economics of the New Zealand Maori*. London: Routledge & Kegan Paul, Ltd.; New York: E. P. Dutton & Co., Inc.
1936 *We, the Tikopia*. London: George Allen & Unwin, Ltd.
1940 *Work of the Gods in Tikopia*, Vol. 2. London School of Economics Monographs in Social Anthropology No. 2.
1950 *Primitive Polynesian Economy*. New York: Humanities Press, Inc.
1955 "The Theory of 'Cargo' Cults: A Note on Tikopia." *Man*, 55:130–32.
1957 *We, the Tikopia*, 2nd ed. London: George Allen & Unwin, Ltd.

Fischer, John L.
1958 "Folktales, Social Structure, and Environment in Two Polynesian Outliers." *Journal of the Polynesian Society*, 67:11–36.

Fischer, John L. (with the assistance of Ann M. Fischer)
1957 *The Eastern Carolines*. Behavior Science Monographs, Human Relations Area Files and Pacific Science Board (New Haven).

Fisher, Robert L., and Roger Revelle
1955 "The Trenches of the Pacific." *Scientific American*, 193(5): 36–41.

Flint, Richard F.
1957 *Glacial and Pleistocene Geology*. New York: John Wiley & Sons, Inc.

Force, Roland W.
1960 *Leadership and Cultural Change in Palau*. Fieldianna: Anthropology Vol. 50. Chicago: Chicago Natural History Museum.

Fornander, Abraham
1880 *An Account of the Polynesian Race*, Vol. II. London: Trübner.

Fortune, R. F.
1932 *Sorcerers of Dobu, the Social Anthropology of the Dobu Islanders of the Western Pacific*. New York: E. P. Dutton & Co., Inc.

Fosberg, F. R.
  1953 "Vegetation of Central Pacific Atolls, a Brief Summary."
       Atoll Research Bulletin, No. 23:1–23. Washington, D.C.
  1961 "Quantitative Description of the Coral Atoll Ecosystem."
       Atoll Research Bulletin, No. 81:1–11. Washington, D.C.
Frake, C. O.
  1955 *Social Organization and Shifting Cultivation Among the
       Sindangan Subanun.* Unpublished Ph.D. Dissertation, Depart-
       ment of Anthropology, Yale University, New Haven, Connecticut.
  1962 "Cultural Ecology and Ethnography." *American Anthropolo-
       gist,* 64:53–59.
Freeman, J. D.
  1955 *Iban Agriculture.* Colonial Research Studies No. 18. London:
       Her Majesty's Stationery Office.
  1956 "Utrolateral and Utrolocal." *Man,* 56:87–88.
Freeman, Otis W.
  1951a "Geographic Setting of the Pacific," in O. W. Freeman
       (ed.), *Geography of the Pacific.* New York: John Wiley & Sons,
       Inc.
Freeman, Otis W. (ed.)
  1951b *Geography of the Pacific.* New York: John Wiley & Sons,
       Inc.
Fried, Morton H.
  1957 "The Classification of Corporate Unilineal Descent Groups."
       Journal of the Royal Anthropological Institute, 87:1–29.
Fromaget, I., and E. Saurin
  1936 "Note préliminaire sur les formations cénozoïques et plus
       récentes de la Chaîne Annanitique septentrionale et du Haut-
       Laos, etc." *Bulletin Service Géologique de l'Indo-Chine,* 22
       (fasc.3):1–46. (Hanoi).
Furnas, J. C.
  1947 *Anatomy of Paradise: Hawaii and the Islands of the South
       Seas.* New York: William Sloane Associates, Inc.
Garnier, B. J.
  1958 *The Climate of New Zealand; a Geographic Survey.* London:
       Edward Arnold (Publishers) Ltd.
  1961 "Mapping the Humid Tropics: Climatic Criteria." *Geographi-
       cal Review,* 51:339–46.
Gentilli, J.
  1952 "Climatology of the Central Pacific." *Seventh Pacific Science
       Congress, Auckland and Christchurch, 1949, Proc.,* 3:92–100.
Gifford, Edward Winslow
  1929 *Tongan Society.* Bernice P. Bishop Museum Bulletin 61.

Girard, M. B. Françoise
1957 "Quelques Plantes alimentaires et rituelles en usage chez les Buang, district de Morobe, Nouvelle Guinée sous tutelle australienne, suivi de notes complémentaires par J. Barrau." *Journal d'Agriculture Tropicale et de Botanique Appliquée,* 4(5–6): 212–27.

Glass, B.
1956 "On the Evidence of Random Genetic Drift in Human Populations." *American Journal of Physical Anthropology,* 14 (N.S. No. 4):541–55.

Glasse, R. M.
1959 "The Huli Descent System: A Preliminary Account." *Oceania,* 29:171–84.

Goggin, J. M., and W. C. Sturtevant
1964 "The Calusa, a Stratified Nonagricultural Society," in W. H. Goodenough (ed.), *Explorations in Cultural Anthropology.* New York: McGraw-Hill Book Co., Inc.

Goldman, Irving
1955 "Status Rivalry and Cultural Evolution in Polynesia." *American Anthropologist,* 57:680–97.
1957 "Variations in Polynesian Social Organization." *Journal of the Polynesian Society,* 66:374–90.
1960 "The Evolution of Polynesian Societies," in S. Diamond (ed.), *Culture and History.* New York: Columbia University Press.

Goldschmidt, Ernst
1961 "An Interpretation of Polynesian Blood-Group Gene Frequencies." *Abstracts of Symposium Papers, 10th Pacific Science Congress,* Honolulu, p. 99.

Golson, J.
1961 "Polynesian Culture History." *Journal of the Polynesian Society,* 70:498–508.

Goodenough, Ward H.
1951 *Property, Kin, and Community on Truk.* Yale University Publications in Anthropology 46.
1953 *Native Astronomy in the Central Carolines.* Philadelphia: University Museum.
1955 "A Problem in Malayo-Polynesian Social Organization." *American Anthropologist,* 57:71–83.
1957 "Oceania and the Problem of Controls in the Study of Cultural and Human Evolution." *Journal of the Polynesian Society,* 66:146–55.
1961 "Migrations Implied by Relationships of New Britain Dialects

Goodenough, Ward H.
to Central Pacific Languages." *Journal of the Polynesian Society*, 72:78–100.
1962 "Comment on A. Capell, Oceanic Linguistics Today." *Current Anthropology*, 3:406–8.

Gourou, P.
1953 *L'Asie*. Paris: Librairie Hachette.

Grace, George W.
1955 "Subgrouping of Malayo-Polynesian: A Report of Tentative Findings." *American Anthropologist*, 57:337–39.
1959 *The Position of the Polynesian Languages Within the Austronesian (Malayo-Polynesian) Language Family*. Indiana University Publications in Anthropology and Linguistics. IJAL Memoir 16; also Bernice P. Bishop Museum Special Publication 46.
1961 "Austronesian Linguistics and Culture History." *American Anthropologist*, 63:359–68.
1964 "The Linguistic Evidence," in Kwang-chih Chang, George W. Grace, and William G. Solheim II, "Movement of the Malayo-Polynesians." *Current Anthropology*, 5:359–406.

Graydon, J. J.
1952 "Blood Groups and the Polynesians." *Mankind*, 4:329–39.

Graydon, J. J., and R. T. Simmons
1946 "Blood Groups in the Maori." *Medical Journal of Australia*, 1:135–38.

Green, Roger C.
1966 "Linguistic Subgrouping Within Polynesia: the Implications for Prehistoric Settlement." *Journal of the Polynesian Society*, 75:6–38.

Greenberg, Joseph H.
1949–54 "Studies in African Linguistic Classification." *Southwestern Journal of Anthropology*, 5:79–100, 190–98, 309–17; 6:47–63, 143–60, 223–37, 388–98; 10:405–15.
1953 "Historical Linguistics and Unwritten Languages," in A. L. Kroeber (ed.), *Anthropology Today*. Chicago: The University of Chicago Press.
1957 *Essays in Linguistics*. Chicago: The University of Chicago Press.
1958 *Report on the Classification of the Non-Austronesian Languages of the Pacific*. Ms.
1960 *Indo-Pacific Etymologies*. Ms. Mimeographed.

Gregory, Herbert E.
1928 "Types of Pacific Islands." *Third Pan-Pacific Science Conference, Tokyo, 1926, Proc.*, 2:1663–73.

Greiner, Ruth
　1923　*Polynesian Decorative Designs*. Bernice P. Bishop Museum Bulletin 7.
Grimble, Arthur
　1933–34　*The Migrations of a Pandanus People*. Polynesian Society Memoir 12.
Grist, D. H.
　1959　*Rice*, 3rd ed. London: Longmans, Green & Co., Ltd.
Gudgeon, W. E.
　1905　"Mana Tangata." *Journal of the Polynesian Society*, 14: 49–66.
Gudger, E. W.
　1927　*Wooden Hooks Used for Catching Sharks and Ruvettus in the South Seas*. American Museum of Natural History Anthropological Papers 28 (part 3):199–348.
Guiart, J.
　1951　"Forerunners of Melanesian Nationalism." *Oceania*, 22:81–90.
　1952a　"The Co-operative Called 'The Malekula Native Company.'" *South Pacific*, 6:429–32.
　1952b　"The John Frum Movement in Tanna." *Oceania*, 22: 165–77.
Gusinde, M.
　1955　"Pygmies and Pygmoids: Tribes of Tropical Africa." *Anthropological Quarterly*, 28 (N.S. Vol. 3):3–61.
Gutenberg, Beno, and C. F. Richter
　1954　*Seismicity and the Earth and Associated Phenomena*. Princeton, New Jersey: Princeton University Press.
Haddon, A. C.
　1923　"Migrations of Peoples in the South West Pacific." *Proceedings of the Pan-Pacific Scientific Congress*, 1:220–42 (Australia).
　1925　*Races of Man*. New York: The Macmillan Company.
Haden-Guest, Stephen (ed.)
　1956　*A World Geography of Forest Resources*. American Geographical Society Special Publication No. 33.
Hagen, B.
　1898　*Anthropologischer Atlas ostasiatischer und melanesischer Völker*. Wiesbaden: Kreidel.
Hamilton, Edwin L.
　1956　"Sunken Islands of the Mid-Pacific Mountains." Geological Society of America Memoirs, 64:1–97.
Handy, E. S. Craighill
　1923　*The Native Culture in the Marquesas*. Bernice P. Bishop Museum Bulletin 9.

Handy, E. S. Craighill
  1927 *Polynesian Religion.* Bernice P. Bishop Museum Bulletin 34.
  1930 *History and Culture in the Society Islands.* Bernice P. Bishop Museum Bulletin 79.
Hanson, Herbert C.
  1962 *Dictionary of Ecology.* New York: Philosophical Library, Inc.
Harris, Marvin
  1959 "The Economy Has No Surplus?" *American Anthropologist,* 61:185–99.
Haudricourt, A. G.
  1962 "Domestication des animaux, culture des plantes et traitement d'autrui." *L'Homme,* 2:40–50.
  1964 "Nature et culture dans la civilisation de l'igname, l'origine des clones et des clans." *L'Homme,* 4:93–104.
Haudricourt, A. G., and L. Hedin
  1943 *L'Homme et les plantes cultivées.* Paris: Gallimard.
Helbaek, H.
  1959 "How Farming Began in the Old World." *Archeology,* 12: 183–89.
Held, G. J.
  1957 *The Papuans of Waropen.* The Hague: Koninklijk Instituut Voor Taal-, Land-, en Volkenkunde.
Henry, Teuira
  1928 *Ancient Tahiti.* Bernice P. Bishop Museum Bulletin 48.
Hess, Harry H.
  1947 "Drowned Ancient Islands of the Pacific Basin." *International Hydrographical Review,* 24:81–91 (Monaco); also in *American Journal of Science,* 244:772–91 (1946).
  1948 "Major Structural Features of the Western North Pacific, and Interpretation of H.O. 5485, Bathymetric Chart, Korea to New Guinea." *Geological Society of America, Bulletin,* 59:417–45.
Heyerdahl, Thor
  1952 *American Indians in the Pacific.* London: George Allen & Unwin, Ltd.
  1963 "Feasible Ocean Routes to and from the Americas in Pre-Columbian Times." *American Antiquity,* 28:482–88.
Heyerdahl, Thor, and A. Skjölsvold
  1956 *Archeological Evidence for Pre-Spanish Visits to the Galapagos Islands.* The Society for American Archeology Memoir 12, No. 2.
Heyerdahl, Thor, and Carlyle S. Smith
  1961 "Itinerary and Organization," in Thor Heyerdahl and Edwin

Heyerdahl, Thor, and Carlyle S. Smith
    N. Ferdon, Jr. (eds.), *Reports of the Norwegian Archaeological Expedition to Easter Island*, Vol. I: *Archaeology of Easter Island*. Stockholm: Forum Publishing House.
Hill, Albert F.
    1939 "The Nomenclature of the Taro and Its Varieties." *Harvard University Botanical Museum Leaflets*, 7(7):113–24.
Hocart, A. M.
    1922 "Mana Again." *Man*, 22:139–41.
    1929 *Lau Islands, Fiji*. Bernice P. Bishop Museum Bulletin 62.
    1933 *The Progress of Man*. London: Methuen & Company, Ltd.
Hoebel, E. A.
    1954 *The Law of Primitive Man*. Cambridge: Harvard University Press.
Hogbin, H. Ian
    1933–34 "Culture Change in the Solomon Islands: Report of Field Work in Guadalcanal and Malaita." *Oceania*, 4:233–67.
    1934 *Law and Order in Polynesia: A Study of Primitive Legal Institutions*. Introduction by B. Malinowski. New York: Harcourt, Brace & World, Inc.
    1936 "Mana," *Oceania*, 6:241–74.
    1937–38a "The Hill People of North-eastern Guadalcanal." *Oceania*, 8:62–89.
    1937–38b "Social Advancement in Guadalcanal, Solomon Islands." *Oceania*, 8:289–305.
    1939 *Experiments in Civilization*. London: George Routledge & Sons, Ltd.
    1943–44 "Native Councils and Courts in the Solomon Islands." *Oceania*, 14:258–83.
    1951 *Transformation Scene: The Changing Culture of a New Guinea Village*. London: Routledge & Kegan Paul, Ltd.
Hogbin, H. Ian, and Camilla H. Wedgwood
    1952–54 "Local Groupings in Melanesia." *Oceania*, 23:241–76; 24:58–76.
Hooijer, D. A.
    1950 "Excerpts from Man and Other Mammals from Toalian Sites in South-Western Celebes," in G. W. Lasker and J. L. Angel (eds.), *Yearbook of Physical Anthropology, 1950*. New York: Wenner-Gren Foundation.
    1951 "The Geological Age of Pithecanthropus, Meganthropus and Gigantopithecus." *American Journal of Physical Anthropology*, 9(N.S.):265–83.
Howells, W. W.
    1943 "The Racial Elements of Melanesia," in C. S. Coon and J. M.

Howells, W. W.

Andrews (eds.), *Studies in the Anthropology of Oceania and Asia, Papers of the Peabody Museum of American Archaeology and Ethnology*, 20:38–49.

Hubert, Henri, and Marcel Mauss

1904   "Esquisse d'une théorie générale de la magie." *L'Année Sociologique*, 7:1–146.

Inglis, J.

1957   "Cargo Cults: the Problem of Explanation." *Oceania*, 27: 249–63.

International Volcanological Association

1951–63   *Catalogue of the Active Volcanoes of the World, Including Solfatara Fields*. Naples, Italy: International Volcanological Association.

Ivens, W. G.

1927   *Melanesians of the Southeast Solomon Islands*. London: Kegan, Paul Trench, Trubner & Co., Ltd.

Jarvie, I. C.

1964   *The Revolution in Anthropology*. London: Routledge & Kegan Paul, Ltd.

Jenness, D., and A. Ballantyne

1920   *The Northern D'Entrecasteaux*. Oxford: Clarendon Press.

Johnson, C.

n.d.   "Typhoon Effects of Typhoon Ophelia, 1960, on Ulithi Atoll, Caroline Islands." Ms.

Johnston, W. B.

1957   "Human Geography of the Pacific: A Review." *New Zealand Geographer*, 13:67–82.

1959   "The Cook Islands; Land Use in an Island Group of the South-West Pacific." *Journal of Tropical Geography*, 13:38–57.

Kaberry, Phyllis M.

1940–41   "The Abelam Tribe, Sepik District, New Guinea: A Preliminary Report." *Oceania*, 11:233–58, 345–67.

1941–42   "Law and Political Organization in the Abelam Tribe." *Oceania*, 12:79–95, 209–25, 331–63.

Kähler, Hans

1951   "Die Stellung der polynesischen Dialekte innerhalb der austronesischen Sprachen." *Zeitschrift der Deutschen Morgenländischen Gesellschaft*, 25:646–58.

Kano, Tadao, and Kokichi Segawa

1956   *An Illustrated Ethnography of Formosan Aborigines*, Vol. 1, *The Yami*. Tokyo: Maruzen Company, Ltd.

Keane, A. H.
1920 *Man: Past and Present,* Revised Ed. London: Cambridge University Press.
Keesing, Felix
1934 *Modern Samoa.* Stanford: Stanford University Press.
1941 *The South Seas in the Modern World.* New York: The John Day Company.
1945 *Native Peoples of the Pacific World.* New York: The Macmillan Co., Publishers.
1959 *Field Guide to Oceania.* National Research Council Field Guide Series, No. 1 (Washington, D.C.).
1962 *The Ethnohistory of Northern Luzon.* Stanford: Stanford University Press.
Kennedy, R.
1942 *The Ageless Indies.* New York: The John Day Company.
Kidd, K. P., and C. K. Reed
1946 "Typhoons of the Southwest Pacific, 1945." *American Meteorological Society Bulletin,* 27:288–305.
King, C. W.
1956 *Social Movements in the United States.* New York: Random House Inc.
Kirchhoff, Paul
1955 "The Principles of Clanship in Human Society." *Davidson Anthropological Journal,* 1:1–11.
Knauss, John A.
1961 "The Cromwell Current." *Scientific American,* 204 (part 4): 105–16.
Kolb, A.
1953 "The Migrations of the Polynesians and the Cultivation of Taro," in *Abstracts of Papers, Eighth Pacific Science Congress, Manila, 1953,* Quezon City.
Kooptzoff, O., and R. J. Walsh
1955 "Blood Groups of New Caledonian Natives." *Oceania,* 26: 35–41.
1957 "The Blood Groups of Some Native Inhabitants of the Tongan Islands." *Oceania,* 27:214–19.
Kouwenhoven, W. J. H.
n.d. *Nimboran.* The Hague: J. N. Voorhoeve.
Kroeber, A. L.
1925 *Handbook of the Indians of California.* Bureau of American Ethnology Bulletin 78.
1948 *Anthropology.* New York: Harcourt, Brace & World, Inc.

Kuchler, A. W.
1961 "Mapping the Humid Tropics: Vegetation Criteria." *Geographical Review*, 51:346–47.

Laborde, Edward D. (ed.)
1952 *Australia, New Zealand and the Pacific Islands*. London: William Heinemann, Ltd.

Lambert, Bernd
1966 "Ambilineal Descent Groups in the Northern Gilbert Islands." *American Anthropologist*, 68:641–64.

Landtman, Gunnar
1927 *The Kiwai Papuans of British New Guinea*. London: The Macmillan Company.

Lawrence, P.
1955 "The Madang District Cargo Cult." *South Pacific*, 8:6–13.
1964 *Road Belong Cargo*. Manchester: Manchester University Press.

Layard, J.
1942 *Stone Men of Malekula*. London: Chatto & Windus, Ltd.

Laycock, D. C.
1965 *The Ndu Language Family (Sepik District, New Guinea)*. Linguistic Circle of Canberra Publications, Series C, No. 1.

Lea, D. A. M.
1964 *Abelam Land and Sustenance, Swidden Horticulture in an Area of High Population Density, Maprik, New Guinea*. Unpublished Ph.D. Thesis (multilith copies), Department of Geography, Australian National University, Canberra.

Leach, E.
1948 "Some Features of Social Science Research Among Sarawak Pagans." *Man*, 48:91–92.
1950 *Social Science Research in Sarawak*. Colonial Research Studies No. 1. London: Her Majesty's Stationery Office.

LeBar, Frank
1964 *The Material Culture of Truk*. Yale University Publications in Anthropology No. 68.

LeBorgne, Jean P. M.
1957 *Géographie de la Nouvelle-Calédonie et des Îsles Loyauté*. Nouméa, New Caledonia: Ministère de l'éducation, de la jeunesse et des sports.

Leenhardt, M.
1930 "Notes d'ethnologie néo-calédonienne." *Travaux et Mémoires de l'Institut d'Ethnologie de L'Université de Paris*, 7:1–340.
1937 *Gens de la Grande Terre*. Paris: Gallimard.
1946 "Le *Ti*." *Journal de la Société des Océanistes*, 2(2):192–93.

Lehmann, F. R.
1922 *Mana: Der Begriff des ausserordentlich Wirkungsvollen bei Südsee Völkern.* Leipzig: O. Spamer.

Lessa, William A.
1950 *The Ethnography of Ulithi Atoll.* Los Angeles: CIMA Report No. 28.
1950 "Ulithi and the Outer Native World." *American Anthropologist,* 52:27–52.
1955 "Depopulation on Ulithi." *Human Biology,* 27:161–83.
1956 "Myth and Blackmail in the Western Carolines." *Journal of the Polynesian Society,* 65:67–74.
1962 "The Decreasing Power of Myth on Ulithi." *Journal of American Folklore,* 75:153–59.
1966 *Ulithi, a Micronesian Design for Living.* New York: Holt, Rinehart & Winston, Inc.

Lessa, William A., and G. Myer
1962 "Population Dynamics of an Atoll Community." *Population Studies,* 15:244–57.

Levine, P., G. A. Matson, and H. F. Schrader
1935 "Distribution of Blood Groups and Agglutinogen M Among Indian 'Blackfeet' and 'Blood' Tribes." *Proceedings of the Society for Experimental Biology and Medicine,* 33:297–99.

Li, Ching Chun
1955 *Population Genetics.* Chicago: The University of Chicago Press.

Linton, Ralph
1933 *The Tanala.* Field Museum of Natural History, Anthropological Series, Vol. 22.
1939 "Marquesan Culture," in Ralph Linton and Abraham Kardiner, *The Individual and His Society.* New York: Columbia University Press.

Lloyd, Christopher
1946 *Pacific Horizons, the Exploration of the Pacific Before Captain Cook.* London: George Allen & Unwin, Ltd.

Loeb, Edwin M.
1926 *History and Traditions of Niue.* Bernice P. Bishop Museum Bulletin 32.

Lundsgaarde, Henry Peder
1966 *Cultural Adaptation in the Southern Gilbert Islands.* University of Oregon (Mimeographed).

Luomala, Katherine
n.d. *The Maui Hero Cycle in Oceania.* Manuscript in Bernice P. Bishop Museum.

Luomala, Katherine
1940 "Notes on the Development of Polynesian Hero Cycles."
Journal of the Polynesian Society, 49:367–74.
1958 "Review of *Ancient Voyagers in the Pacific*, by Andrew
Sharp." *American Anthropologist*, 60:776–78.

Mabuchi, Toichi
1951 "The Social Organization of the Central Tribes of Formosa."
Journal of East Asiatic Studies, 1:43–69.

Macgregor, G.
1937 *Ethnology of Tokelau Islands*. Bernice P. Bishop Museum
Bulletin 146.

Macintosh, N. W. G.
1952 "The Cohuna Cranium: History and Commentary from November, 1925 to November, 1951." *Mankind*, 4:307–29.
1953 "The Cohuna Cranium: Physiography and Chemical Analysis." *Oceania*, 23:277–96.

Maher, R.
1958 "Tommy Kabu Movement of the Purari Delta." *Oceania*,
29:75–90.
1961 *New Men of Papua*. Madison: The University of Wisconsin
Press.

Malinowski, Bronislaw
1915 "The Natives of Mailu." *Proceedings of the Royal Society
of South Australia*, 39:494–706.
1922 *Argonauts of the Western Pacific*. London: Routledge &
Kegan Paul, Ltd.; New York: E. P. Dutton & Co., Inc.
1926 "Magic, Science and Religion," in J. Needham (ed.), *Science, Religion and Reality*. New York: The Macmillan Company.
1935 *Coral Gardens and Their Magic, A Study of the Methods
of Tilling the Soil and of Agricultural Rites in the Trobriand Islands*, 2 vols. New York: American Book Company.

Malo, David
1903 *Hawaiian Antiquities*. Honolulu: Hawaiian Gazette Co.

Mansuy, H.
1931 *La Préhistoire en Indochine*. Paris: Exposition Coloniale
Internationale.

Mansuy, H., and M. Colani
1925 "Contribution a l'étude de la préhistoire de l'Indo-Chine.
No. 7. Néolithique inférieur (Bacsonien) et Néolithique su-
périeur dans le Haut-Tonkin." *Mémoires du Service géologique
de l'Indo-Chine*, 12:fasc. 3 (Hanoi).

Marett, R. R.
1914 *The Threshold of Religion*, 2nd Ed. London: Methuen &
Company, Ltd.

Margot-Duclos, J., and J. Vernaut
1946 "La Terre et la catégorie du sexe en Mélanésie." *Journal de la Société des Océanistes,* 2(2):5–53.

Mariner, William
1827 *An Account of the Natives of the Tonga Islands,* John Martin, compiler. Edinburgh: Constable & Co.

Marshall, K. H.
1954 "Plants and Vegetation of New Caledonia." *Wellington Botanical Society Bulletin,* 27:19–21.

Mason, Leonard
1959 "Suprafamilial Authority and Economic Process in Micronesian Atolls." *Humanités, Cahiers de l'Institut de Science Economique Appliquée,* Ser. V, No. 1:87–118 (Paris).
1964 "Micronesia. Micronesian Culture [Art]." *Encyclopedia of World Art,* 9:915–18; 918–30. New York: McGraw-Hill Book Co., Inc.

Matson, G. A., and H. F. Schrader
1933 "Blood Grouping Among the 'Blackfeet' and 'Blood' Tribes of American Indians." *Journal of Immunology,* 25:155–63.

Matthiessen, Peter
1962 *Under the Mountain Wall: A Chronicle of Two Seasons in the Stone Age.* New York: The Viking Press, Inc.

Maude, H. E.
1963 *The Evolution of the Gilbertese* Boti, *an Ethnohistorical Interpretation.* Polynesian Society Memoir No. 35.

Maude, H. C. and H. E.
1931 "Adoption in the Gilbert Islands." *Journal of the Polynesian Society,* 40:225–35.

McKaughan, Howard
1964 "A Study of Divergence in Four New Guinea Languages." *American Anthropologist,* 66(4, part 2):98–120.

McKenzie, D. W.
1958 *Man, Map, and Landscape in New Zealand.* 3 vols. Wellington, New Zealand: A. H. and A. W. Reed.

McKern, W. C.
1929 *Archeology of Tonga.* Bernice P. Bishop Museum Bulletin 60.

Mead, Margaret
1928a *Coming of Age in Samoa.* New York: William Morrow & Company, Inc.
1928b "A Lapse of Animism Among a Primitive People." *Psyche,* 9:72–77.
1928c "The Role of the Individual in Samoan Culture." *Journal of the Royal Anthropological Institute,* 58:481–95.

Mead, Margaret

1928d *An Inquiry Into the Question of Cultural Stability in Polynesia.* Columbia University Contributions to Anthropology, Vol. 9. New York: Columbia University Press.

1930 *Social Organization of Manua.* Bernice P. Bishop Museum Bulletin 76.

1934 *Kinship in the Admiralty Islands.* The American Museum of Natural History, Anthropological Papers, 34: part 2.

1937a "The Arapesh of New Guinea," in M. Mead (ed.), *Cooperation and Competition Among Primitive Peoples.* New York and London: McGraw-Hill Book Co., Inc.

1937b "The Manus of the Admiralty Islands," in M. Mead (ed.), *Cooperation and Competition Among Primitive Peoples.* New York and London: McGraw-Hill Book Co., Inc.

1938 *The Mountain Arapesh I. An Importing Culture.* The American Museum of Natural History, Anthropological Papers, 36: 139–349.

1947 *The Mountain Arapesh III. Socio-Economic Life.* The American Museum of Natural History, Anthropological Papers, 40: 159–232.

1956 *New Lives for Old.* New York: William Morrow & Company, Inc.

1964 *Continuities in Cultural Evolution.* New Haven: Yale University Press.

Meggers, Betty J.

1954 "Environmental Limitation on the Development of Culture." American Anthropologist, 56:801–24.

Meggitt, Mervyn

1957 "Enga Political Organization: A Preliminary Description." *Mankind,* 5:133–37.

1957–58 "The Enga of the New Guinea Highlands: Some Preliminary Observations." *Oceania,* 28:253–330.

1964 "Male-Female Relationships in the Highlands of Australian New Guinea." *American Anthropologist,* Special Publication, 66 (4, part 2):204–24.

Menard, H. W.

1961 "The East Pacific Rise." *Science,* 132:1737–46.

Métraux, Alfred

1940 *Ethnology of Easter Island.* Bernice P. Bishop Museum Bulletin 160.

1957 *Easter Island, A Stone-Age Civilization of the Pacific.* Translated by Michael Bullock. London: Andre Deutsch, Limited, Publishers.

Milke, Wilhelm

1958a "Zur inneren Gliederung und geschichtlichen Stellung der ozeanisch-austronesischen Sprachen." *Zeitschrift für Ethnologie,* 83:58–62.

1958b "Ozeanische Verwandtschaftsnamen." *Zeitschrift für Ethnologie,* 83:226–29.

1961 Beiträge zur ozeanischen Linguistik." *Zeitschrift für Ethnologie,* 86:162–82.

1962 "Comment on A. Capell, Oceanic Linguistics Today." *Current Anthropology,* 3:415–16.

1965 "Comparative Notes on the Austronesian Languages of New Guinea." *Lingua,* 14:330–48.

Miller, R. E.

1950 *Blood Groups of the Kapingas, November 1950.* Atoll Research Bulletin 20. Washington, D.C.: The Pacific Science Board.

Montagu, M. F. A.

1951 *An Introduction to Physical Anthropology.* Springfield, Illinois: Charles C. Thomas, Publishers.

Morishima, Hiroko, Kokichi Hinata, and Hiko-ichi Oka

1962 "Floating Ability and Drought Resistance in Wild and Cultivated Species of Rice." *Indian Journal of Genetics and Plant Breeding,* 22(1):1–11.

Morrell, William P.

1960 *Britain in the Pacific Islands.* London: Clarendon Press.

Mourant, A. E.

1954 *The Distribution of the Human Blood Groups.* Oxford: Blackwell Scientific Publications.

Mourant, A. E., A. C. Kopeć, and K. Domaniewska-Sobczak

1958 *The ABO Blood Groups.* Oxford: Blackwell Scientific Publications.

Mulloy, R.

1961 "The Ceremonial Center of Vinapu," in Thor Heyerdahl and Edwin N. Ferdon, Jr. (eds.), *Reports of the Norwegian Expedition to Easter Island,* Vol. I: *Archaeology of Easter Island.* Stockholm: Forum Publishing House.

Murdock, George Peter

1948 "Anthropology in Micronesia." *Transactions of the New York Academy of Sciences.* 2nd Ser., 11:9–16.

1949 *Social Structure.* New York: The Macmillan Co., Publishers.

1959 *Africa.* New York: McGraw-Hill Book Co., Inc.

1963 "Discussion [of Vayda and Rappaport, 1963]," in F. R. Fosberg (ed.), *Man's Place in the Island Ecosystem.* Honolulu: Bishop Museum Press.

Murdock, G. P., C. S. Ford, and J. W. M. Whiting
  1944 *West Caroline Islands.* U. S. Navy Department Civil Affairs Handbooks, No. 7.
Muromçev, A. M.
  1959 *Scheme of General Circulation of the Pacific Ocean Waters* ($T_{323}R$). Ottawa: Canadian Defense Research Board, Director of Scientific Information Service (translated from the Russian by E. R. Hope from Izv. Akad. Nauk SSSR, Geographic Series, 1958, H, 24–32).
Needham, Rodney
  1956 "Discussion of Freeman, 1956, 'Utrolateral and Utrolocal.'" *Man,* 56:148.
Neel, J. V., and W. J. Schull
  1954 *Human Heredity.* Chicago: The University of Chicago Press.
Neuhauss, R.
  1911 *Deutsch Neu-Guinea,* 3 vols. Berlin: D. Reimer.
Nevin, C. M.
  1942 *Principles of Structural Geology.* 3rd Ed. New York: John Wiley & Sons, Inc.
Newman, M. T.
  1953 "The Application of Ecological Rules to the Racial Anthropology of the Aboriginal New World." *American Anthropologist,* 55:311–27.
  1956 "Adaptation of Man to Cold Climates." *Evolution,* 10:101–5.
Nigg, Clara
  1930 "A Study of the Blood Group Distribution Among Polynesians." *Journal of Immunology,* 19:93–98.
Nilles, J.
  1943–44 "Natives of the Bismarck Mountains, New Guinea." *Oceania,* 14:104–24; 15:1–19.
  1950 "The Kuman of the Chimbu Region, Central Highlands, New Guinea." *Oceania,* 21:25–65.
  1953 "The Kuman People: A Study in Cultural Change in a Primitive Society in the Central Highlands of New Guinea." *Oceania,* 24:1–27, 119–31.
Notes and Queries on Anthropology, 5th Ed.
  1929 Edited for the British Association for the Advancement of Science by a Committee of Section H. London: Royal Anthropological Institute.
Odum, Eugene P.
  1953 *Fundamentals of Ecology.* Philadelphia: W. B. Saunders Company.

Officer, Charles B.
1955 "Southwest Pacific Crustal Structure." *American Geophys. Union, Transactions,* 36:449–59.

Oka, Hiko-ichi, and Wen Tsai Chang
1959 "The Impact of Cultivation on Populations of Wild Rice, *Oryza sativa spontanea.*" *Phyton,* 3(2):105–17.

Oliver, Douglas L.
1952 *The Pacific Islands.* Cambridge: Harvard University Press.
1955 *A Solomon Island Society.* Cambridge: Harvard University Press.
1957 "Review of *An Ethnological Sketch of Rennel Island: a Polynesian Outlier in Melanesia,* by Kaj Birket-Smith." *American Anthropologist,* 59:180–81.
1961 *The Pacific Islands,* Revised Ed. Garden City, New York: Doubleday & Company, Inc.

Oliver, W. R. B.
1954 "Changes in the Flora and Fauna of New Zealand." *Forest and Bird,* 113:9–13 (Wellington).

Osborne, Douglas
1966 *The Archeology of the Palau Islands, an Intensive Survey.* Bernice P. Bishop Museum Bulletin 230.

Parkinson, R.
1887 *Im Bismarck Archipel.* Leipzig: Brockhaus.
1907 *Dreissig Jahre in der Südsee.* Stuttgart: Strecker and Schröder.

Pawley, Andrew
1966 "Polynesian Languages: A Subgrouping Based on Shared Innovations in Morphology." *Journal of the Polynesian Society,* 75:39–44.

Pelzer, Karl
1945 *Pioneer Settlement in the Asiatic Tropics.* New York: Institute of Pacific Relations.

Plischke, Hans
1959 "Der Stille Ozean, Entdeckung und Erschliessung. . . ." *Janus-Bücher: Berichte zur Weltgeschichte,* 14:1–94 (München).

Porter, David
1815 *Journal of a Cruise Made to the Pacific Ocean by Captain David Porter, in the United States Frigate Essex, in the Years 1812, 1813, and 1814,* Vol. 2. Philadelphia: Bradford and Inskeep.

Porteres, R.
1960 "La sombre Aroidée cultivée: *Colocasia, antiquorum* Schott ou taro de Polynésie, essai d'étymologie, semantique." *Journal*

Porteres, R.
   d'Agriculture Tropicale et de Botanique Appliquée, 7(4–5):169–92.
Pospisil, Leopold
   1958 *Kapauku Papuans and Their Law.* Yale University Publications in Anthropology 54.
   1958–59 "The Kapauku Papuans and Their Kinship Organization." *Oceania,* 30:188–205.
Powdermaker, Hortense
   1933 *Life in Lesu.* New York: W. W. Norton & Company, Inc., Publishers.
Powell, H. A.
   1960 "Competitive Leadership in Trobriand Political Organization." *Journal of the Royal Anthropological Institute,* 90:118–45.
Powell, W.
   1884 *Wanderings in a Wild Country.* London: Sampson Low.
Prain, Sir David, and I. H. Burkill
   1934 *Dioscoréacées; Flore générale de l'Indochine.* Edited by H. Lecompte, H. Humbert, and F. Gagnepain. Paris: Masson et Cie.
Price, A. Grenfell
   1963 *The Western Invasions of the Pacific and Its Continents; A Study of Moving Frontiers and Changing Landscapes, 1513–1958.* London: Clarendon Press.
Provinse, J. H.
   1937 "Cooperative Ricefield Cultivation Among the Siang Dyaks of Central Borneo." *American Anthropologist,* 39:80–91.
Radin, Paul
   1937 *Primitive Religion: Its Nature and Origin.* New York: The Viking Press, Inc.
Rahm, G.
   1931 "Observaciones sobre los grupos sanguíneos en la Isla de Pascua." *Soc. Biológica de Concepción, Boletín,* 5–6:65 (Chile).
Raitt, Russell W., Robert L. Fisher, and Ronald G. Mason
   1955 "Tonga Trench." *Geological Society of America, Spec. Papers,* 62:237–54.
Ray, Sidney H.
   1926 *A Comparative Study of the Melanesian Island Languages.* London: Cambridge University Press.
Read, K. E.
   1946–47 "Social Organization in the Markham Valley, New Guinea." *Oceania,* 17:93–118.
   1949–50 "The Political System of the Ngara Wapum." *Oceania,* 20:185–223.

Read, K. E.
1951 "The Gahuku-Gama of the Central Highlands." *South Pacific,* 5:154–64.
1952 "The Nama Cult of the Central Highlands, New Guinea." *Oceania,* 23:1–25.
1954 "Cultures of the Central Highlands, New Guinea." *Southwestern Journal of Anthropology,* 10:1–43.
1955 "Morality and the Concept of Person Among the Gahuku-Gama, Eastern Highlands, New Guinea." *Oceania,* 25:233–82.
1958 "A 'Cargo' Situation in the Markham Valley." *Southwestern Journal of Anthropology,* 14:273–94.
1959 "Leadership and Consensus in a New Guinea Society." *American Anthropologist,* 61:425–36.
Reay, Marie
1959a *The Kuma.* Melbourne: Melbourne University Press.
1959b "Two Kinds of Ritual Conflict." *Oceania,* 29:290–96.
1959c "Individual Ownership and Transfer of Land Among the Kuma." *Man,* 59:78–82.
Reichstag, Germany
1908 "Denkschrift über die Entwicklung der Schutzgebeite in Afrika und der Südsee, 1906–1907." *Verhandlung des Reichstags,* XII, Legislaturperiode, I. Session, Vol. 245, Anlagen zu den Stenographischen Berichten No. 622, pp. 4117–26, 4137. Berlin: J. Sittenfield.
Riesenberg, Felix
1940 *The Pacific Ocean.* New York: McGraw-Hill Book Co., Inc.
Rivers, W. H. R.
1914 *The History of Melanesian Society.* 2 vols. London: Cambridge University Press.
1926a *Social Organization.* New York: Alfred A. Knopf.
1926b *Psychology and Ethnology.* London: Kegan, Paul Trench, Trubner & Co., Ltd.
Robbins, R. G.
1961 "The Vegetation of New Guinea." *Australian Territories,* 1:21–32.
Roberts, Helen H.
1926 *Ancient Hawaiian Music.* Bernice P. Bishop Museum Bulletin 29.
Robinson, J. T.
1953 "Meganthropus, Australopithecines, and Hominids." *American Journal of Physical Anthropology,* 11 (N.S.):1–38.
Robinson, Kathleen W.
1960 *Australia, New Zealand and the Southwest Pacific.* London: University of London Press, Ltd.

Rostow, W. W.
   1960   *The Stages of Economic Growth.* Cambridge: Cambridge
   University Press.
Rouse, I.
   1953   "The Strategy of Culture History," in A. L. Kroeber (ed.),
   Anthropology Today. Chicago: The University of Chicago Press.
Rowley, C. D.
   1958   *The Australians in German New Guinea.* Melbourne: Melbourne University Press.
Rumphius, G. E.
   1741–56   *Herbarium amboinense,* J. Burman (ed.), 6 vols. Am-
   sterdam.
Ryan, D'Arcy
   1959   "Clan Formation in the Mendi Valley." *Oceania,* 29:257–81.
   1961   *Gift Exchange in the Mendi Valley.* Unpublished Ph.D.
   Thesis, Department of Anthropology, University of Sydney, Australia.
Ryan, F. I.
   1953   "Evolution Observed." *Scientific American,* 189(4):78–82.
Sahlins, Marshall D.
   1955   "Esoteric Efflorescence in Easter Island." *American Anthropologist,* 57:1045–52.
   1957   "Differentiation by Adaptation in Polynesian Societies." *Journal of the Polynesian Society,* 66:291–300.
   1958   *Social Stratification in Polynesia.* Seattle: University of Washington Press for the American Ethnological Society.
   1961   "The Segmentary Lineage: An Organization of Predatory
   Expansion." *American Anthropologist,* 63:322–45.
Salisbury, R. F.
   1956a   "Asymmetrical Marriage Systems." *American Anthropologist,* 58:639–55.
   1956b   "Unilineal Descent Groups in the New Guinea Highlands."
   Man, 56:2–7.
   1958   "An 'Indigenous' New Guinea Cult." *Kroeber Anthropological Society Papers,* No. 18:67–78.
   1962   *From Stone to Steel.* Cambridge and Melbourne: Cambridge
   and Melbourne University Presses.
Sapir, E.
   1916   *Time Perspective in Aboriginal American Culture.* Memoirs
   of the Canada Department of Mines, Geological Survey, 90:1–87.
Sarasin, Fritz, and Jean Rouz
   1922   *Anthropologie der Neu-Caledonier und Loyalty-Insulaner.*
   Berlin: Kreidel.

Sauer, Carl O.

1952 *Agricultural Origins and Dispersals: Series 2. Bowman Memorial Lectures.* New York: American Geographical Society of New York.

Schilling, Elisabeth

1939 "Die 'schwimmenden Gärten' von Xochimilco." *Schriften des Geographischen Instituts der Universität Kiel,* 9(3).

Schlaginhaufen, O.

1914 *Anthropometrische Untersuchungen an Eingeborenen in Deutsch-Neuguinea.* Museum für Tierkunde und Volkerkunde, Dresden, Abhandlungen und Berichte, 14(5).

Schnee, H. (ed.)

1937 *Das Bush der Deutschen Kolonien.* Leipzig: W. Goldman.

Schneider, David M.

1962 "Double Descent on Yap." *Journal of the Polynesian Society,* 71:1–24.

1963 Discussion [of Vayda and Rappaport 1963] in F. R. Fosberg (ed.), *Man's Place in the Island Ecosystem.* Honolulu: Bishop Museum Press.

Schott, Gerhard

1934 "The Distribution of Rain Over the Pacific Ocean." *Fifth Pacific Science Congress, Victoria and Vancouver, 1933, Proc.,* 3:1987–90 (Toronto).

1935 *Geographie des Indischen und Stillen Ozeans, in Auftrage der Deutschen Seewarte verfasst.* . . . Hamburg: C. Boysen.

1936 "Die Aufteilung der drei Ozeane in natürliche Regionen." *Peterm. Geogr. Mitt.,* 82:165–70, 218–22 (Gotha).

Schwartz, Theodore

1962 *The Paliau Movement in the Admiralty Islands, 1946–54.* The American Museum of Natural History Anthropological Papers, No. 49:part 2.

1963 "Systems of Areal Integration: Some Considerations Based on the Admiralty Islands of Northern Melanesia." *Anthropological Forum,* 1:56–97.

Seelye, C. J.

1952 "Rainfall and its Variability Over the Central and Southwestern Pacific." *New Zealand Journal of Science and Technology,* Sect. B, 32(part 2):11–24.

Sekiguchi, Takeshi

1952 "The Rainfall Distribution in the Pacific Region." *Seventh Pacific Science Congress, Auckland and Christchurch, 1949, Proc.,* 3:101–2 (Wellington).

Seligman, C. G.

1909 "A Classification of the Natives of British New Guinea." *Journal of the Royal Anthropological Institute,* 39:246–75, 314–33.

1910 *The Melanesians of British New Guinea.* London: Cambridge University Press.

Semple, N. M., R. T. Simmons, and J. J. Graydon

1956 "Blood Group Frequencies in Natives of the Central Highlands of New Guinea, and in the Bainings of New Britain." *The Medical Journal of Australia,* 2:365–71.

Service, Elman R.

1962 *Primitive Social Organization: An Evolutionary Perspective.* New York: Random House, Inc.

Shapiro, H. L.

1940 "The Distribution of Blood Groups in Polynesia." *American Journal of Physical Anthropology,* 26:409–16.

Sharp, Andrew

1956 *Ancient Voyagers in the Pacific.* Polynesian Society Memoir No. 32.

1957 *Ancient Voyagers in the Pacific.* Harmondsworth, England: Penguin Books, Ltd.

1960 *The Discovery of the Pacific Islands.* London: Clarendon Press.

1964 *Ancient Voyagers in Polynesia.* Berkeley: University of California Press.

Sheddick, Vernon

1954 *Land Tenure in Basutoland.* Colonial Research Studies No. 13. London: Her Majesty's Stationery Office.

Shepard, F. P., and H. E. Suess

1956 "Rate of Post-Glacial Rise of Sea Level." *Science,* 123: 1082–83.

Shutler, R.

1961 "Application of Palynology to Archeological and Environmental Problems in the Pacific." *Asian Perspectives,* 5:188–92.

Simmons, R. T.

1956 "A Report on Blood Group Genetical Surveys in Eastern Asia, Indonesia, Melanesia, Micronesia, Polynesia, and Australia in the Study of Man." *Anthropos,* 51:500–12.

1962 "Blood Group Genes in Polynesians and Comparisons with Other Pacific Peoples." *Oceania,* 32:198–210.

Simmons, R. T., and J. J. Graydon

1947 "Blood Group Frequencies in Admiralty Islanders: Further Observations on the Fijians and Indonesians and on Rh Gene

Simmons, R. T., and J. J. Graydon
  Frequencies in Some Other Races." *Medical Journal of Australia*, 1:577–81.
  1957 "A Blood Group Genetical Survey in Eastern and Central Polynesians." *American Journal of Physical Anthropology*, 15: 357–66.
Simmons, R. T., J. J. Graydon, and G. Barnes
  1945 "Blood Groups, Sub-Groups, M, N types and the Rh Factor in Fijians." *Medical Journal of Australia*, 1:529–32.
Simmons, R. T., J. J. Graydon, and N. M. Semple
  1953 "A Further Blood Genetical Survey in Micronesia: Palauans, Trukese and Kapingas." *Medical Journal of Australia*, 2:589–96.
Simmons, R. T., J. J. Graydon, N. M. Semple, and E. I. Fry
  1955 "A Blood Group Genetical Survey in Cook Islanders, Polynesia, and Comparisons with American Indians." *American Journal of Physical Anthropology*, 13:667–90.
Simmons, R. T., J. J. Graydon, N. M. Semple, and C. N. D. Taylor
  1951 "Blood, Taste, and Secretion: A Genetical Survey in Maoris." *Medical Journal of Australia*, 1:425–31.
Simmons, R. T., J. J. Graydon, V. Zigas, L. L. Baker, and D. C. Gadjusek
  1961 "Studies on Kuru: V. A Blood Group Genetical Survey of the Kuru Region and Other Parts of Papua-New Guinea." *American Journal of Tropical Medicine and Hygiene*, 10:639–64.
Simpson, G. G.
  1945 *The Principles of Classification and a Classification of Mammals*. Bulletin of The American Museum of Natural History, 85.
  1962 *Evolution and Geography*. Eugene: University of Oregon Press.
Sinclair, A.
  1957 *Field and Clinical Survey Report of the Mental Health of the Indigenes of the Territory of Papua and New Guinea*. Port Moresby: Department of Territories (Mimeographed).
Skinner, H. D.
  1921 "Culture Areas in New Zealand." *Journal of the Polynesian Society*, 30:71–78.
Smith, Bernard W.
  1960 *European Vision and the South Pacific, 1768–1850: A Study in the History of Art and Ideas*. London: Clarendon Press.
Smith, C. S.
  1961 "A Temporal Sequence Derived from Certain Ahu," in Thor Heyerdahl and Edwin N. Ferdon, Jr. (eds.), *Reports of the Norwegian Archaeological Expedition to Easter Island*, Vol. I:

Smith, C. S.
  Archaeology of Easter Island. Stockholm: Forum Publishing House.
Smith, S. Percy
  1902 "Niue Island, and its People." *Journal of the Polynesian Society,* 11:*passim.*
Spencer, J. E., and G. A. Hale
  1961 "The Origin, Nature, and Distribution of Agricultural Terracing." *Pacific Viewpoint,* 2:1–40.
Spier, R. F. G.
  1951 "Some Notes on the Origin of Taro." *Southwestern Journal of Anthropology,* 7:69–76.
Spoehr, Alexander
  1949 *Majuro, a Village in the Marshall Islands.* Fieldiana: Anthropology Vol. 39. Chicago: Natural History Museum.
  1954 *Saipan, the Ethnology of a War-Devastated Island.* Fieldiana: Anthropology Vol. 41. Chicago: Natural History Museum.
  1957 *Marianas Prehistory: Archeological Survey and Excavations on Saipan, Tinian and Rota.* Fieldiana: Anthropology Vol. 48. Chicago: Natural History Museum.
Stanner, W. E. H.
  1953 *The South Seas in Transition.* Sydney: Australasian Publishing Company, Pty., Ltd.
Staveley, J. M., and R. Douglas.
  1958 "Blood Groups in Maoris." *Journal of the Polynesian Society,* 67:239–47.
  1959 "Blood Groups in Tongans (Polynesia)." *Journal of the Polynesian Society,* 68:347–52.
Stephens, Henry Morse, and Herbert E. Bolton (eds.)
  1917 *The Pacific Ocean in History; Papers and Addresses Presented at the Panama-Pacific Historical Congress, Held at San Francisco, Berkeley, and Palo Alto, California, July 19–23, 1915.* New York: The Macmillan Company.
Stirling, M. W.
  1943 *The Native Peoples of New Guinea.* Smithsonian Institution War Background Studies No. 9. Washington, D.C.
Stokes, J. F. G.
  1934 "Japanese Cultural Influences on Hawaii." *Proceedings of 5th Pacific Science Congress, Pacific Science Association.* 4: 2791–2803 (Toronto).
Stone, Earl L., Jr.
  1953 "Summary of Information on Atoll Soils." *Atoll Research Bulletin* No. 22:1–4.

Suggs, R. C.
1960 *The Island Civilizations of Polynesia.* New York: Mentor Books.
1961 *The Archeology of Nuku Hiva, Marquesas Islands, French Polynesia.* The American Museum of Natural History Anthropological Papers No. 49:part I.

Sverdrup, Harold U.
1941 "The Pacific Ocean." *Science,* 94:287–93.

Sverdrup, Harold U., M. W. Johnson and R. H. Fleming
1942 *The Oceans, Their Physics, Chemistry and General Biology.* New York: Prentice-Hall, Inc.

Swadesh, Morris
1950 "Salish Internal Relationships." *International Journal of American Linguistics,* 16:157–67.
1952 "Lexico-Statistic Dating of Prehistoric Ethnic Contacts." *Proceedings of the American Philosophical Society,* 96:452–63.

Tayama, Risaburo
1952 ". . . Coral Reefs in the South Seas . . ." *Japan, Hydrogr. Off. Bull.,* 11:1–292.

Taylor, Walter P.
1934 "Significance of Extreme or Intermittent Conditions in Distribution of Species and Management of Natural Resources, With a Restatement of Liebig's Law of Minimum." *Ecology,* 15: 374–79.

Ter Haar, B.
1948 *Adat Law in Indonesia.* New York: Institute of Pacific Relations.

Thilenius, G. (ed.)
1913–36 *Ergebnisse der Südsee-Expedition 1908–1910, Part I— Allgemeines, Part 2—Ethnographie, B. Micronesien.* Hamburg: De Gruyter.

Thomas, William L., Jr.
1963 "The Variety of Physical Environments Among Pacific Islands," in F. R. Fosberg (ed.), *Man's Place in the Island Ecosystem.* Honolulu: Bishop Museum Press.

Thompson, Laura
1940 *Southern Lau, Fiji.* Bernice P. Bishop Museum Bulletin 162.
1945 *The Native Culture of the Marianas Islands.* Bernice P. Bishop Museum Bulletin 185.

Thomson, Sir Basil
1894 *The Diversions of a Prime Minister.* Edinburgh and London: William Blackwood and Sons.

Tracey, J. I., Jr., P. E. Cloud, Jr., and K. O. Emery
    1955   "Conspicuous Features of Organic Reefs." *Atoll Research Bulletin,* No. 46:1–3.

Trewartha, Glenn T.
    1961   *The Earth's Problem Climates.* Madison: The University of Wisconsin Press.

Tsuchiya, M.
    1961   "An Oceanographic Description of the Equatorial Current System of the Western Pacific." *Oceanog. Mag.,* 13:1–30 (Tokyo).

Umbgrove, J. H. F.
    1945   "Different Types of Island-Arcs in The Pacific." *Geographic Journal,* 106:198–209.

U. S. Weather Bureau
    1956   *U. S. Navy Marine Climatic Atlas of the World. Vol. 2, North Pacific Ocean; Vol. 5, South Pacific Ocean.* Washington: U. S. Government Printing Office.
    1961   "Typhoons of the Western North Pacific, 1960." *Mariners Weather Log,* 5:67–76.

Van Steenis, C. G. G. J.
    1962   "Discussion of Bartlett [H. H.], Possible Separate Origin and Evolution of the Ladang and Sawah Types of Tropical Agriculture." *Proceedings of the Ninth Pacific Science Congress,* 4(Botany):270–73.

Vason, George
    1810   *An Authentic Narrative of Four Years' Residence at Tongataboo, One of the Friendly Islands.* London: Longman, Hurst, Rees and Orme.

Vavilov, N. I.
    1951   *The Origin, Variation, Immunity, and Breeding of Cultivated Plants; Selected Writings of N. I. Vavilov.* Translated by K. Starr Chester. Chronica Botanica, Vol. 13, No. 1/6. New York: The Ronald Press Co.

Vayda, Andrew P.
    1958   "A Voyage by Polynesian Exiles." *Journal of the Polynesian Society,* 67:324–29.
    1959a   "Native Traders in Two Polynesian Atolls." *Humanités, Cahiers de l'Institut de Science Économique Appliquée,* Ser. V, No. 1:119–37.
    1959b   "Polynesian Cultural Distributions in New Perspective." *American Anthropologist,* 61:817–28.
    1966   "Diversity and Uniformity in New Guinea." *Acta Ethnographica,* 15:293–99 (Budapest).

Vayda, Andrew P., A. Leeds, and D. B. Smith
  1961 "The Place of Pigs in Melanesian Subsistence," in *Proceedings of the 1961 Annual Spring Meeting of the American Ethnological Society,* Viola E. Garfield (ed.). Seattle: University of Washington Press.
Vayda, Andrew P., and Roy A. Rappaport
  1963 "Island Cultures," in F. R. Fosberg (ed.), *Man's Place in the Island Ecosystem.* Honolulu: Bishop Museum Press.
Vening Meinesz, F. A.
  1960 "The Difference of the Tectonic Development on the East and the West Side of the Pacific." *Koninkl. Nederl. Akad. van Wetens, Proc.* 63(Ser.B):26–31.
Vicedom, G. V., and H. Tischner
  1943–48 *Die Mbowamb: Die Kultur der Hagenberg-Stämme in östlichen Zentral-Neuguinea.* 3 vols. Hamburg: De Gruyter.
Visher, S. S.
  1925 *Tropical Cyclones of the Pacific.* Bernice P. Bishop Museum Bulletin 20.
Voget, F. W.
  1959 "Toward a Classification of Cult Movements: Some Further Contributions." *Man,* 59:26–28.
Wallace, A. F. C.
  1956 "Revitalization Movements." *American Anthropologist,* 58:264–81.
Walsh, R. K., and O. Kooptzoff
  1954 "Blood Groups of Some Non-Europeans in Fiji." *Oceania,* 25:68–73.
  1955 "The Blood Groups of Some Native Inhabitants of the British Solomon Islands." *Oceania,* 25:188–93.
Washburn, S. L.
  1953 "The Strategy of Physical Anthropology," in A. L. Kroeber (ed.), *Anthropology Today. An Encyclopedic Inventory.* Chicago: The University of Chicago Press.
Wawn, W. T.
  1893 *The South Sea Islanders and the Queensland Labour Trade.* London: Swann, Sonnenschein.
Weaver, J. E., and F. E. Clements
  1938 *Plant Ecology.* New York: McGraw-Hill Book Co., Inc.
Webster, H. C.
  1898 *Through New Guinea and Other Cannibal Countries.* London: Fisher Unwin.
Weckler, J. E.
  1943 *Polynesians—Explorers of the Pacific.* Smithsonian Institution War Background Studies No. 6. Washington, D.C.

Weckler, J. E.

1949 *Land and Livelihood on Mokil, Part I.* Coordinated Investigation of Micronesian Anthropology Report, Pacific Science Board, Washington, D.C.(ditto).

1953 "Adoption on Mokil." *American Anthropologist,* 55:555–68.

Wedgwood, Camilla H.

1933–34 "Report on Research in Manam Island, Mandated Territory of New Guinea." *Oceania,* 4:373–403.

1935–37 "Report on Anthropological Research Work in Nauru Island." *Oceania,* 6:359–91; 7:1–33.

1958–59 "Manam Kinship." *Oceania,* 29:239–56.

Weidenreich, F.

1939 "On the Earliest Representatives of Modern Mankind Recovered on the Soil of East Asia." *Peking Natural History Bulletin,* 13(part 3):161–74.

1943 *The Skull of Sinanthropus Pekinensis: A Comparative Study on a Primitive Hominid Skull.* Paleontological Sinica, Series D (10):1–484.

1945 "The Keilor Skull: A Wadjak Type From Southeast Australia," in S. L. Washburn (ed.), *Anthropological Papers of Franz Weidenreich, 1939–1948.* New York: Viking Fund.

Weiner, J. S.

1957 "Physical Anthropology—an Appraisal." *The American Scientist,* 45(1):79–87.

Wiens, Herold J.

1962a *Atoll Environment and Ecology.* New Haven: Yale University Press.

1962b *Pacific Island Bastions of the United States.* Princeton: D. Van Nostrand Company, Inc.

Wilhelm, O., and L. Sandoval

1956–57 "Blutgruppen und Genealogie der Osterinsel-Bevölkerung." *Acta Genetica et Statistica Medica,* 6:465–70.

Wilkinson, R. J.

1932 *A Malay-English Dictionary.* Mytilene, Greece: Salavopoulos.

Williams, F. E.

1928 *Orokaiva Magic.* London: Oxford University Press, Inc.

1930 *Orokaiva Society.* London: Oxford University Press, Inc.

1934 "The Vailala Madness in Retrospect," in E. E. Evans-Pritchard (ed.), *Essays Presented to C. G. Seligman.* London: Kegan, Paul Trench, Trubner & Co., Ltd.

1940 *Drama of Orokolo.* London: Clarendon Press.

Williams, Bishop H. W.
   1917   *Dictionary of the Maori Language.* Wellington: Government
   Printer.
Williams, W.
   1844   *Dictionary of the New Zealand Language.* Paihia, New Zealand: Church Missionary Society.
Williamson, Robert W.
   1912   *The Mafulu: Mountain People of British New Guinea.* London: The Macmillan Company.
   1924   *The Social and Political Systems of Central Polynesia.* 3 vols.
   London: Cambridge University Press.
   1933   *Religious and Cosmic Beliefs of Central Polynesia.* 2 vols.
   London: Cambridge University Press.
   1937   *Religion and Social Organization in Central Polynesia,*
   R. Piddington (ed.). London: Cambridge University Press.
   1939   *Essays in Polynesian Ethnology,* R. Piddington (ed.). London: Cambridge University Press.
Winkler, Captain
   1901   "On Sea Charts Formerly Used in the Marshall Islands."
   Annual Report of the Smithsonian Institution for 1899, 487–508.
Wissler, C.
   1926   *The Relation of Nature to Man in Aboriginal America.* New
   York and London: Oxford University Press, Inc.
   1938   *The American Indian.* 3rd Ed. New York: Oxford University Press, Inc.
Woensdregt, J.
   1928   "De Landbouw bij de To Bada' in Midden Selebes." *Tijd-
   schrift voor Indische Taal-, Land-, en Volkenkunde,* 68:125–253.
Wollaston, A. F. R.
   1912   *Pygmies and Papuans.* London: Smith, Elder & Co.
Worsley, P.
   1957   *The Trumpet Shall Sound.* London: MacGibbon & Kee.
Wurm, S. A.
   1960–61 "The Changing Linguistic Picture of New Guinea."
   Oceania, 31:121–36.
   1965   "Recent Comparative and Typological Studies in Papuan Languages in Australian New Guinea." *Lingua,* 15:373–99.
Young, Rosemary
   1962   "The Phonemes of Kanite, Kamano, Benabena and Gahuku." *Oceania Linguistic Monographs,* No. 6:90–110.
Zimmerman, E. C.
   1948   *Insects of Hawaii,* Vol. I. Honolulu: University of Hawaii
   Press.

INDEX